SLAVERY
A Worldwide Bibliography, 1900–1982

Joseph C. Miller

KRAUS INTERNATIONAL PUBLICATIONS
Division of Kraus–Thomson Organization Limited
White Plains, New York

First printing 1985

Printed in the United States of America

The paper used in this publication meets the minimum
requirements of American National Standard for
Information Science — Permanence of Papers for
Printed Library Materials, ANSI Z39.48-1984.

Library of Congress Cataloging-in-Publication Data

Miller, Joseph Calder.
 Slavery: a worldwide bibliography, 1900–1982.

 Includes index.
 1. Slavery—Bibliography.   2. Slave Trade—
Bibliography.   I. Title.
Z7164.S6M543 1985   [HT861]   016.306′362   85-16858
ISBN 0-527-63659-2

SLAVERY
A Worldwide Bibliography, 1900–1982

Contents

Acknowledgements

An innocent -- not to say naive -- attempt to introduce undergraduate
students to two or three hundred scattered basic titles in the literature
on slave systems in the Americas more than a decade ago has grown to
become the present comprehensive bibliography intended for both beginning
and experienced users. I would have stopped many times, and indeed tried
several times to do so, publishing a "teaching" bibliography and then
five supplements that each time I optimistically thought were
substantially complete (nos. 275-79), had it not been for the
encouragement, guidance, assistance, and support of many institutions and
individuals.

I have been continually encouraged, and at times outpaced, by the
productivity of hundreds of imaginative scholars writing during the last
fifteen years in the field of slavery and the slave trade. Their
industriousness and their knowledge of specialized literature as
expressed in their footnotes has guided me toward the more complete
coverage of the subject achieved by this consolidated bibliography. I
should mention in particular the nearly forty years of periodic
bibliographies on Caribbean history published by Gabriel Debien and the
Brockmeyer Bibliographie zur antiken Sklaverei (no. 3373), but I cannot

neglect Robert Ross' sharing of his up-to-date knowledge of developments
in the history of slavery in the Cape Colony (South Africa), David
Henige's help with many scattered sources, Rod and Jean Barman's notice
of bibliography concerning Latin America, and several others whose
contributions have received appreciative acknowledgement in preliminary
installments of this bibliography published elsewhere since 1977. I am
also grateful to the Crossroads Press of the African Studies Association
(USA) for permission to publish revised and corrected versions of entries
that appeared in the initial "teaching bibliography", and similarly to
Frank Cass and Co. Ltd. for other entries originally published in <u>Slavery
and Abolition</u>.

A succession of talented graduate students at the University of
Virginia has explored the resources of Alderman Library to verify the
details of references located in these scholars' footnotes and
bibliographies. Alicia Cole, William Hoest, Emilie Inman, Jennifer
James, Brenda Nelms, and John Stephens were among the first. Thomas
Barnett-Robisheaux, Ann Parrella, Kate Murphy, and Robin Good have
contributed much in this way to the precision of the entries listed
here. Daniel H. Borus and, especially, Larissa V. Brown labored well
beyond the research assistant's usual responsibilities, locating and
tracking down new citations, devising search procedures, and generally
contributing as joint compilers of the bibliographical supplements for
1980 and for 1982 and 1983. The bibliography would have reached nothing
like its present size or accuracy without their efforts and enthusiasm.
Lottie McCauley, Ella Wood, Bonnie Rittenhouse Blackwell, and Kathleen
Miller produced much of the indexes, offered their skills in other ways,
and taught me to use the word-processing facilities in the Corcoran
Department of History at the Universty of Virginia, without which no

one -- including me -- would have had the patience to pursue details to the degree attained here. McCauley and Miller produced the pages printed here with efficiency, dispatch, and thorough-going professionalism. To these fine colleagues, I owe a deep debt of gratitude.

None of them would have been associated with the project at all had it not been for the generous financial support of the Department of History of the University of Virginia, the Carter G. Woodson Institute for Afro-American and African Studies at the University of Virginia, and the Research Resources Program of the National Endowment for the Humanities. The support of the National Endowment for the Humanities has been especially important in making possible the extended bibliographical searches conducted in 1982 and 1983, in which more than 2000 of the entries most difficult to locate and verify were turned up and tracked down in most of the major American university libraries east of the Mississippi River. The entire project of consolidating entries scattered through an original bibliography and three supplements and the task of indexing them would not have been undertaken at all without the interest of the Endowment. I am, of course, more than grateful to all these agencies, and particularly the National Endowment for the Humanities, for their substantial contributions to the project.

It should go without saying, although it never does, that none of the above should be assigned any responsibility for the errors that remain in the bibliography. I do not allude to remaining errors out of feigned modesty, as I have utterly no doubt that several lurk undetected, though not unsuspected, in every section, even now that we have verified by direct inspection every entry contained in the bibliography and have rechecked some entries several times to eliminate discrepancies that continue to present themselves. Entries not thus verifiable, or/by consultation of standard bibliographical reference works (The National Union Catalog, Dissertation Abstracts International, etc.), have been marked with an asterisk (*) and left for users to pursue at their own risk and, hopefully, to inform me of the correct details if and when encountered. Indeed, it has been humbling for all who have worked on the project to see the occasional failings of even their very best efforts to attain accuracy and completeness. Verification may have removed most of the mistakes that we detected in the footnotes of others, from which we have developed many entries, but I have learned enough from the careful work of my predecessors to fear for the new errors that I may have introduced myself. The fact is, as any users who have themselves attempted to compile a large bibliography will have anticipated from their own experiences, that scattered errors have turned up even in the last revisions and proofreading of the manuscript. I will not be surprised, therefore, to learn of others that have still eluded detection. On the contrary, I would welcome word of further refinements needing to be made. The continuing series of current bibliographical supplements planned to appear in Slavery and Abolition should afford the opportunity for due rectificaton.

Introduction

This bibliography is designed to guide students and scholars toward modern secondary literature on slavery and the slave trade in fields in which they may have a substantial interest but marginal expertise. It should also provide non-professional readers and researchers with initial access to the vast and rapidly expanding literature on the subject. It represents a belief that comparison among slave systems in different times and places enhances understanding of this particular form of inequality and the slave trades that have supported it in most cases, both in general and with respect to the historical instance of immediate interest.

DEFINITION OF COVERAGE

The bibliography includes secondary scholarly works reflecting directly on slavery or the slave trade anywhere in the world, published in Western European languages, and written from the perspective of any academic discipline. Most works are historical, though ranging within that field from intellectual and legal history through medical and demographic history. Economics, political economy, and sociology are well represented, and anthropology somewhat less so. A few entries arise also from philosophy, linguistics, literary criticism, and other disciplines. The covered publication formats exclude standard, single-page book reviews, unless they are of particular significance, but include all other modes of scholarly discourse: substantial reviews of the literature, conference papers, articles in scholarly periodicals and in serious popular historical magazines, chapters in edited volumes, and books and monographs, including reprints and translations.

Without such formal, if sometimes arbitrary, restrictions, the literature on "slavery" less strictly construed would spread uncontrollably to embrace much of human history. This definition of the subject excludes first-hand recollections of people who lived with or in slavery, thus omitting primary sources from the long years in which slavery figured widely in the human experience. The era of slavery had ended in most parts of the world by the beginning of the twentieth century, and so the concrete implementation of this abstract criterion means that only works published since 1900 are listed.

Also excluded is a modest number of works in Asian and African languages and a much larger body of important scholarship in Slavic tongues (Russian, Polish, Hungarian, etc). For access to this literature, the reader is referred to footnotes in the recent work of Orlando Patterson (nos. 322, 324-25) and the excellent bibliographies to be found in Hellie (nos. 4310-11) and Brockmeyer (no. 3484), as well as to other bibliographies identified as such in the Subject/Keyword Index.[1] Further excluded is a still greater range of works dealing significantly, but only secondarily, with slavery in such other closely related contexts as early Christian theology, Brazilian colonial economic history, race relations in the New World, political institutions in eighteenth-century Africa, forced labor systems of any sort, freed people, the sociology of inequality in general, abolitionism as theory or politics, post-slavery transitions to other labor systems, or the U.S. Civil War. Other examples of important but excluded subjects will, of course, occur to many readers. Finally, writings judged historical fiction, popularized accounts, journalism, or propaganda fall beyond the hazy boundaries of the scholarship included.

If practicality thus imposes a limited definition of the subject, the bibliography still offers access at only a single remove to most excluded categories of literature through the footnotes and reading lists in the works cited. Very few works germane to these larger issues fail to turn up in recent studies by wide-ranging, knowledgeable, and imaginative scholars writing directly on slavery and thus included here. Listed works explicitly setting slavery in the context of these other fields have been indexed as such for the convenience of users interested in them. Primary source materials, while not systematically indexed, also turn up immediately upon consultation of the footnotes in the studies cited.

ORGANIZATION OF THE LISTINGS

The bibliography lists works focused on the issue of slavery or the slave trade and according to primary author or editor. By this definition, a volume of miscellaneous collected essays by a single author does not appear as such, though a single essay on the slave trade from that volume is included. On the other hand, an entire volume of essays by various authors focused specifically on the slave trade receives its own listing under the name(s) of the editor(s), and each of the studies in the volume also receives its own separate listing by author. Serials appear by title only when devoted exclusively to the subject of slavery or the slave trade, but all articles in general serials focused on slavery appear under the names of their respective authors.

Each work, so defined, has been assigned to a single geographical section of the bibliography, starting with general and comparative studies not otherwise classifiable. The geographical sections derive from the structure of the literature as authors have implicitly organized it to date, whether appropriately or not, that is, mostly in terms of the political culture of the master class: Greek, Roman, Muslim, Russian, Spanish, French, British North American, and so on. Where anomalies and ambiguities arise from this strategy, the Subject/Keyword Index provides appropriate cross-references. Alternative strategies of organizing the entries still more implicit than the one adopted or only just emergent in the literature as a whole are similarly accessible through the Subject/Keyword Index; examples of such alternatives include plantation, urban, mining, or family/kinship slavery.

The bibliography presents each entry according to the classification rules of the U.S. Library of Congress cataloguing system and in sufficient detail (according to Modern Language Association formats) that users accustomed to other systems should in each case find some means of access to the work through local rules, or even directly from publishers. Listings should thus be serviceable for requesting needed works through U.S. libraries, the Inter-library loan network, and standard electronic data bases. Entries appear in the language of publication, except in the case of titles in Russian, Polish, or other non-western-European languages published with summaries in French, German, or English, etc., and indicated explicitly as such. Transliterations of names from the Cyrillic, Greek, Arabic, and other non-Roman alphabets may vary from orthographies preferred by some users.

Chapters from edited volumes appearing under their authors' names sometimes utilize a shortened form of reference to the editors' full names and to the complete titles of the main work. Users may locate full bibliographical details of the edited volume by consulting the separate listing for it elsewhere in the bibliography under the editor's name, using the Author Index, if necessary, to ascertain the geographical category where the volume appears.

STRUCTURE OF THE INDEXES

An Author Index and a Subject/Keyword Index follow the main bibliographical listing. They are designed to facilitate access to entries by general subject area, with emphasis on encouraging cross-cultural comparisons within the subject area, by key technical or geographical details mentioned in the title of the work, and by authors and editors. Each listing in the bibliography may thus be accessible by only one index entry (the author only, for a very general essay on "slavery", for example) or by as many as a half dozen or more references (author, geographical sub-section, two or three subject areas involved, and a key technical concept or two). Both indexes refer users to the number of the entry rather than to the page of the bibliography on which it may appear.

The Author Index (pp. 391-423) presents full names for each author or editor writing or editing on the subject of the bibliography. It thus lists editors of volumes focused explicitly on slavery or the slave trade but excludes editors of volumes conceived in terms of more general notions (e.g. Festschriften, collected essays on economic history, and so on). It distinguishes edited contributions with an "ed." prefixing the entry number, and it indicates works of secondary authorship or

editorship by parentheses enclosing the number of the listing.
Alphabetization proceeds without reference to non-English language accent
markings (à, â, and ä are all interfiled with a).

The Subject/Keyword Index (pp. 425-451) makes no attempt to edit or
interpret beyond the intended emphases of the authors listed, as they
defined them in the titles of their works. Within those confines, this
Index is quite complete. All entries are in English, with foreign
language phrases occurring only where they have technical significance or
as cross-references to their English-language equivalents. The entry
numbers do not differentiate among the main geographical/cultural
divisions of the bibliography, so that readers interested in "revolts" or
the "law of slavery", for example, may encounter comparative materials
ranging from the Roman Empire to nineteenth-century Southeast Asia.
Users interested in only a single historical instance may, of course,
confine their attention to entry numbers within the range dealing with
their specific geographical interest, as summarized in the Table of
Contents (pp. v - ix). Reviews and explicit critiques may be found
identified here under the names of the authors discussed.

THE SUBJECT OF THE BIBLIOGRAPHY
Western scholarship turned vigorously toward the study of inequality
after World War II as worldwide humanitarian and egalitarian impulses
produced the United Nations, ended colonial rule throughout much of the
world, stressed civil and human rights, and began to acknowledge the
sufferings of minorities and the poor. Amidst the resulting energetic
study of race relations, plural societies, labor systems, peasantries,
and many other aspects of the profound and persistent disparities in
wealth, power, and status in the world, work on slavery and the slave

trade stood out both in its quantity and in the impact of its
contribution to understanding of the tribulations of the weak in the
course of human experience.

Realization gradually dawned that slavery had been a pervasive
feature of human society since the most remote periods of recorded
history and that it persisted in muted forms even into the present day.
This perception brought a certain element of shock to western scholars
and audiences heir to the proud legacy of nineteenth-century
abolitionists who, in the course of their struggles against what they had
proclaimed an anomalous "peculiar institution", had magnified both the
peculiarity of the New World slaveries of their time and the degree of
"freedom" that their opposition to them had brought forth.[2] The
scholarly quest for understanding the institution of slavery, and the
slave trades that had usually fed it, thus began to range widely over
time and space utilizing concepts adapted from nearly every academic
discipline. This bibliography lists the products of these scholars'
investigations, together with older twentieth-century works taking their
inspirations from other sources and not yet blended into the single
coherent field of studies on slavery and the slave trade that coalesced
in the last quarter century.

Frank Tannenbaum's suggestive essay on North American race relations,
Slave and Citizen, published in 1948 (no. 397) was the key work that
awakened recent scholarly interest in slavery and the slave trade.
Typically of the broad and diffuse concerns that lay behind the genesis
of the field, it muddled issues of race, morality, and slavery that
subsequent work has sought to separate. Tannenbaum compared an
apparently harsh North American legal tradition of slavery with
ostensibly milder laws and customs in South American colonies and

countries of Iberian heritage. He thereby prompted Americanist

successors to explore the sufferings of slaves in the nineteenth-century

United States South (esp. Kenneth Stampp, no. 1456, and Stanley Elkins,

no. 113).[3] These American liberals often reacted against the benign

image of Southern slavery prevailing in the literature, painted by an

earlier generation of Southern apologists (Ulrich B. Phillips, no. 850,

etc.).[4] Discussion gathered momentum through the contributions of many

comparisons and case studies that gradually distinguished more clearly

between slavery and race relations in the Americas, between legal theory

and the actual practices of planters and other masters, between town and

plantation, and among slave systems at different points in their separate

historical developments. In the course of the debate, Tannenbaum's

original assessment of the relative harshness of United States slavery in

ideological terms was considerably modified. In particular, recognition

grew of the fact that the slave population of the U.S. South, uniquely

among slaves in the Americas, had consistently increased its numbers from

the early eighteenth century through Emancipation in 1864.

Emphasis on the demographic aspect of American slavery drew some of

its inspiration from the first modern study of the Atlantic slave trade,

Philip Curtin's 1969 The Atlantic Slave Trade: A Census (no. 4473),

which attempted a systematic count of the numbers of slaves reaching the

New World and reviewed the general demographic history of these new

arrivals and their children. However, the Curtin book had its more

profound impact on studies of the Atlantic slave trade itself, a largely

neglected field before 1969.[5] Post-Census works multiplied during the

1970s in what was referred to as a "numbers game", as scholars searched

archives around the world for new figures that might verify or alter

Curtin's provisional conclusions on volume and direction (for a summary

of the debate, see Paul E. Lovejoy, no. 4564). By the late 1970s, work
in this vein on the slave trade had begun to evolve in the direction of
explaining the specific aspects of it, especially slave mortality
(Herbert S. Klein, no. 4554).[6] A few preliminary studies of the trade
as business and economic history were also beginning to appear. The only
comprehensive survey of the Atlantic trade since Curtin has been that of
James Rawley (no. 4588).

A distinct comparative study of American slave systems had progressed
almost single-handedly in the works of Eugene D. Genovese, partly in
reaction to Stanley Elkins' implicit reduction of United States slaves to
allegedly passive "Sambos"[7] and partly to develop a broad and
systematic Marxist analytical framework that would refine the notion of
the "peculiarity" of slavery in the U.S. South (see author index).
Separate but parallel efforts at restoring initiative and purpose to the
slave's lives focused on rediscovering slave family and community (e.g.
John W. Blassingame, no. 1334, Herbert G. Gutnman, no. 671), on slave
resistance throughout the hemisphere (Herbert Aptheker, no. 447, Michael
Craton, nos. 2386-87), and on other aspects of slave consciousness and
cultures. These efforts, while generally centered in the
densely-populated field of United States history, had important cognates
in work on the Caribbean and South America.

Recently work on American slave systems has expanded to cover, in one
way or another, nearly all known instances of the phenomenon in the New
World (e.g. Hancock, no. 4146). It has begun to merge with broader
questions, drawing not only on the Marxist example set by Genovese but
also on older traditions of scholarship less preoccupied with the issues
of race relations, civil rights, and psychology characteristic of the
liberal stream of North American thought at mid-century (e.g. Eltis, no.

4504) and breaking away from the relatively static and structural tone that the older literature derived from its roots in American social science (e.g. Berlin, no. 463).

At the same time, classical scholars of both liberal and Marxist persuasions revitalized a much older academic interest in slavery in ancient Greece and Rome (Finley, no. 3390). There the historiography had similarly drifted with changing intellectual and ideological preoccupations, just as it had done among scholars working on modern American slavery, but with a much stronger component derived from the Marxist paradigm. European classicists had generally searched for the senses in which ancient Greece and Rome might have approximated Marx's "slave mode of production" and how such a slave mode of production might have been transformed into the "feudal mode of production" believed characteristic of the European middle ages (Padgug no. 318).

For slavery in the European Middle Ages the fundamental research has flowed copiously and virtually sometimes seemingly uniquely for thirty years from the pen of Charles Verlinden (the main monograph, nos. 4158-59, but see also Author Index). Slavery in northern Europe and around the Christian Mediterranean at that time has shared in the recent general revival of interest in the subject (Section IX), with a good deal of the recent work there synthesized in a forthcoming study by William D. Phillips, Jr.[8] Slavery in Russia, hardly known outside of studies in Russian, has now received excellent treatment in English in the work of Richard Hellie (no. 4311).

Contemporaneous uses of slaves by Muslims south and east of the Mediterranean had been subject to studies mostly oriented toward the Muslim law of slavery and modern survivals of the institution since the nineteenth century. Work on Muslim slavery matured apace with developments elsewhere in the field, and it now covers a much wider geographical range (e.g. Cooper, no. 3377) and emphasizes its political and economic aspects (Crone, no. 3233, Pipes, no. 3245).

Studies of slavery in Africa were originally no less influenced by the moralistic orientation deriving from eighteenth- and nineteenth-century abolitionists than work on slavery in the Americas. The question of slavery in Africa initially arose mostly by way of contrasting its supposedly benign character there with the harshness of the comparable institution in the New World. It then moved through an initial period of descriptive study (Miers and Kopytoff, eds., no. 3065, and Meillassoux, ed., no. 3063)[9] and is now being understood analytically, though not without heated debate, as an African method of labour mobilization of considerable antiquity (Inikori, ed., no. 2998, and Lovejoy, no. 3036).

Serious study of slavery and the slave trade in other world regions has only just begun. For Asia, one may consult James L. Watson, ed. (no. 423), but there is no comprehensive work on any of the several American Indian societies holding slaves (see Section X. 6.). Initial work on slave trades other than that of the Atlantic may be found for the trans-Saharan and Red Sea systems in Austin (nos. 5119-21), for the Indian Ocean in Beachey (nos. 5092-93), for the Ottoman empire in Toledano (no. 5137)[10], for southeast Asia in Warren (no. 4367)[11], and for medieval Europe and the Mediterranean in Phillips (see footnote 8).

Broader efforts at understanding slavery in the context of a general theory or history of labor systems, or modes of production, dates from Marx and from the other great sociologists and anthropologists of the late nineteenth century (summarized in Kopytoff, no. 235). The modern field takes its proximate origin largely from H. J. Nieboer's (no. 309) emphasis on the prevalence of slavery in areas adjacent to free land, into which unbound labor would otherwise flee. Scattered article-length general explorations of the phenomenon (Domar, no. 97, Dovring, no. 98, contributions to Reuck and Knight, eds., 353, Finley's famous essay in the International Encyclopedia of the Social Sciences, Verlinden, no. 411, Engerman, no. 125, etc.) have seldom been supplemented by comprehensive monograph-length studies, although one history surveys American slave systems (Rice, no. 355).[12] Orlando Patterson's sociological interpretation (no. 325) achieves by far the most thorough and penetrating modern survey of the general nature and meaning of enslavement. Otherwise, recent attention on slavery in its larger context has focused mostly on its function in the growing differentiation and specialization associated with the development of a "world economy" from the fifteenth through the nineteenth centuries (Wallerstern, no. 1014).[13] There is presently no relatively concise interpretive survey of slavery and the slave trade in world history.

FOOTNOTES

1. See also the historiographical essays identified in the Subject/Keyword Index.

2. For the pecularity of this perception, see Davis (nos. 82-83). The unfreedoms of Emancipation have become a recent center of interest; see the Subject/Keyword Index heading.

3. See also the Subject/Keyword Index listing for Elkins to locate the essential critical response.

4. Historiographical discussion in John David Smith (nos. 932-33).

5. Exceptions, of two very different sorts: Williams (no. 428) and Mannix and Cowley (no. 4567).

6. But cf. Miller (no. 4571) and discussion in Cohn and Jensen (nos. 4466-67).

7. The main critique is collected in Lane, ed. (no. 239).

8. Slavery from Roman Times to the Early Transatlantic Trade (Minneapolis: University of Minnesota Press, 1985).

9. Critiques in Cooper (no. 2920) and Martin A. Klein (no. 3019).

10. Now published, Princeton University Press, 1983.

11. The very insightful introduction and collection of papers edited by Anthony Reid, Slavery, Bondage, and Dependency in Southeast Asia (St. Lucia: University of Queensland Press, 1983), has apppeared since compilation of the bibliography.

12. At a more popular level, Walvin, no. 420.

13. But contra, see Mintz (no. 289, Genovese and Fox-Genovese, no. 163).

SLAVERY
A Worldwide Bibliography, 1900–1982

I. General and Comparative

1. Abbas, Mohammed Galal. "Slavery between Islam and Western Civilization - A Comparative Study of Attitudes," Majallat al-Azhar, 43, 9 (1971), pp. 11-16; 43, 10 (1971), pp. 9-13.

2. Abd al-Wahid, Ali. Contribution à une théorie sociologique de l'esclavage: étude des situations génératrices de l'esclavage avec appendice sur l'esclavage de la femme et bibliographie critique (with preface by Paul Fauconnet). Paris: A. Mechelinck, 1931.

3. Akiwowo, Akinsola. "Racialism and Shifts in the Mental Orientation of Black People in West Africa and the Americas, 1856-1956," Phylon, 31, 3 (1970), pp. 256-64.

4. Alexander, Herbert B. "Brazilian and United States Slavery Compared," Journal of Negro History, 7, 4 (1922), pp. 349-64.

5. Alho, Olli. The Religion of the Slaves. Helsinki, 1976. (FF Communications no. 217)

6. Allen, Theodore W. "Slavery, Racism, and Democracy," Monthly Review, 29, 10 (1978), pp. 57-63.

7. _____. "'...They would have Destroyed Me': Slavery and the Origins of Racism," Radical America, 9, 3 (1975), pp. 41-63. Reprinted separately as "Class Struggle and the Origin of Racial Slavery: The Invention of the White Race" (Hoboken, N.J., 1975).

8. Amia, Amerigo d'. Schiavitù romana e servitù medievale. Milan: U. Hoepli, 1931.

9. Anstey, Roger T. "Capitalism and Slavery - A Critique," in Centre of African Studies, University of Edinburgh, Transatlantic Slave Trade, pp. 13-29. With discussion, pp. 33-43.

10. _____. "Capitalism and Slavery: A Critique," Economic History Review, 21, 2 (1968), pp. 307-20.

11. _____. "Religion and British Slave Emancipation," in Walvin and Eltis, eds., Abolition of the Atlantic Slave Trade, pp. 37–62.

12. _____. "Slavery and the Protestant Ethic," Historical Reflections/Réflexions historiques, 6, 1 (1979), pp. 157–72. Commentaries by Emilia Viotti da Costa (pp. 173–76) and David Brion Davis (pp. 177–82).

13. Ashley Montagu, M. F. "The African Origins of the American Negro and His Ethnic Composition," Scientific Monthly, 58, 1 (1944), pp. 58–65.

14. Aufhauser, R. Keith. "Slavery and Technological Change," Journal of Economic History, 34, 1 (1974), pp. 36–50.

15. Awad, Mohamed. Report on Slavery. New York: United Nations, 1966.

16. Aykroyd, W. R. Sweet Malefactor: Sugar, Slavery, and Human Society. London: Heinemann, 1967.

17. Backhaus, Wilhelm. Marx, Engels und die Sklaverei: zur ökonomischen Problematik der Unfreiheit. Dusseldorf: Pädagogischer Verlag Schwann, 1974.

18. Bailey, Dale S. "Slavery in the Novels of Brazil and the United States: A Comparison" (PhD diss., Indiana University, 1961).

19. Baks, C., J. C. Breman, and A. T. J. Nooij. "Slavery as a System of Production in Tribal Society," Bijdragen tot de Taal-, Land-, en Volkenkunde van Nederlandsche-Indië, 122, 1 (1966), pp. 90–109.

20. Banton, Michael. "1960: A Turning Point in the Study of Race Relations," Daedalus, 103, 2 (1974), pp. 31–44.

21. Barcia, María del Carmen. "Algunas cuestiones teóricas necesarias para el análisis del surgimiento y la crisis de la plantación esclavista," Revista de la Biblioteca Nacional José Martí (Havana), 22, 3 (1980), pp. 53–88.

22. Barker, Anthony. African Link: British Attitudes to the Negro in the Era of the Atlantic Slave Trade, 1550–1807. Totowa, N.J.: Rowman and Littlefield, 1978.

23. Barzel, Yoram. "An Economic Analysis of Slavery," Journal of Law and Economics, 20, 1 (1977), pp. 87–110.

24. Bastide, Roger. Les Amériques noires, les civilisations africaines dans le Nouveau Monde. Paris: Payot, 1967. Translated as African Civilizations in the New World (New York: Harper and Row, 1971).

25. Bean, Richard N., and Robert P. Thomas. "The Adoption of Slave Labor in British America," in Gemery and Hogendorn, eds., Uncommon Market, pp. 377–98.

26. Beeman, Richard R. "Labor Forces and Race Relations: A Comparative View of the Colonization of Brazil and Virginia," _Political Science Quarterly_, 86, 4 (1971), pp. 609-36.

27. Beiguelman, Paula. "The Destruction of Modern Slavery: A Theoretical Issue," _Review_, 2, 1 (1978), pp. 71-80.

28. Beltrán, Gonzalo Aguirre. "African Influences in the Development of Regional Culture in the New World," in Pan American Union, _Seminar on Plantation Systems of the New World_ (Washington, D.C.: Pan American Union, 1959), pp. 64-72. With comment by René Ribeiro. (Social Science Monographs, no. 7) Also Bobbs-Merrill Reprint no. BC-23. In Spanish as "Influencias africanas en el desarrollo de las culturas regionales del Nuevo Mundo," in _Sistemas de plantaciones en el Nuevo Mundo_ (Washington, D.C.: Pan American Union, 1960), pp. 71-81.

29. Berghe, Pierre L. van den. _Race and Racism: A Comparative Perspective_. New York: Wiley, 1967.

30. Bergstrom, T. "Of the Existence and Optimality of Competitive Equilibrium for a Slave Economy," _Review of Economic Studies_, 38, 113 (1971), pp. 23-36.

31. Berlin, Ira. "The Development of Plantation Systems and Slave Societies: A Commentary - II," in Rubin and Tuden, eds., _Comparative Perspectives_, pp. 68-71.

32. Biezunska-Malowist, Iza. "Les recherches sur l'esclavage ancien et le mouvement abolitionniste européen," in J. Burian and L. Vidman, eds., _Antiquitas Graeco-Romana ac Tempora nostra_ (Prague: Academia, 1968), pp. 161-67.

33. _____, and Marian Malowist. "La procréation des esclaves comme source de l'esclavage: quelques observations sur l'esclavage dans l'antiquité au moyen-âge, et au cours des temps modernes," in _Mélanges offerts à Kazimierz Michalowski_ (Warsaw: Panst. Wydawn Naukowe, 1966), pp. 275-80.

34. Blyden, Edward Wilmot. "Noah's Malediction," _Slavery and Abolition_, 1, 1 (1980), pp. 18-24.

35. Boccassina, R., _et al_. "Formes et aspects de l'esclavage," _Annales: économies, sociétés, civilisations_, 22, 6 (1967), pp. 1328-38.

36. Bonilla-Garcia, Luis. _Historia de la esclavitud_. Madrid: Editorial Plus-Ultra, 1961.

37. Booker, George W. (Conrad Oehlrich) _The Slave Business_. Scotch Plains, N.J.: Flanders Hall, 1940.

38. Bowden, Edgar. "Three Stages in the Evolution of Slavery in Pre-civilized Societies," _Behavioral Science Notes_, 8 (1973), pp. 111-21.

39. Bowser, Frederick P. "The Death of Latin-American Slavery: Nineteenth Century Cuba and Brazil," *Journal of Inter-American Studies*, 17, 3 (1975), pp. 350-57.

40. Brady, Terence. *The Fight Against Slavery*. New York: Norton, 1977.

41. Brandfon, Robert. "Specific Purposes and the General Past: Slaves and Slavery (review article: Davis, *Slave Power Conspiracy*; Genovese, *World the Slaveholders Made*, Starobin, *Industrial Slavery in the Old South*)," *Journal of.Interdisciplinary History*, 3, 2 (1972), pp. 351-62.

42. Brathwaite, Edward K. "Commentary (Research Problems)," in Rubin and Tuden, eds., *Comparative Perspectives*, pp. 610-12.

43. Brown, Steven E. "Sexuality and the Slave Community," *Phylon*, 42, 1 (1981), pp. 1-10.

44. Burtt, Joseph. "Slavery in Anno Domini 1913," *Contemporary Review*, 104 (1913), pp. 216-22.

45. Campbell, Mavis C. "The Price of Freedom: On Forms of Manumission. A Note on the Comparative Study of Slavery," *Revista/Review interamericana*, 6, 2 (1976), pp. 239-52.

46. Canarella, Giorgio, and John A. Tomaske. "The Optimal Utilization of Slaves," *Journal of Economic History*, 35, 3 (1975), pp. 621-29.

47. Cardoso, Ciro F. S. *A Afro-americana: a escravidão no novo mundo*. São Paulo: Brasiliense, 1982.

48. _____. "El modo de producción esclavista colonial en América," in Carlos Sempat Assadourian, *et al.*, *Modos de producción en América Latina* (Cordoba, Argentina: Cuadernos de Pasado y Presente, 1973), pp. 193-242. Also published as "O modo de produção escravista colonial na América," in Théo Araujo Santiago, ed., *América colonial: ensaios* (Rio de Janeiro: Pallas, 1975), pp. 89-143. Translated from "La Guyane française," chap. 3.

49. _____. "Propriété de la terre et techniques de production dans les colonies esclavagistes de l'Amérique et des Caraïbes au XVIIIe siècle," *Cahiers des Amériques latines*, 13-14 (1976), pp. 127-51.

50. Cardoso, Geraldo da Silva. "Negro Slavery in the Sugar Plantations of Veracruz and Pernambuco, 1550-1680" (PhD diss., University of Nebraska, Lincoln, 1975).

51. _____. *Negro Slavery in the Sugar Plantations of Veracruz and Pernambuco, 1550-1680: A Comparative Study*. Washington, D.C.: University Press of America, 1983.

52. Chapiseau, Felix. *Au pays de l'esclavage*. Paris: J. Maisonneuve, 1900.

53. Chinweizu. *The West and the Rest of Us: White Predators, Black Slavers and the African Elite*. New York: Random House, 1975.

54. Chrétien, Jean-Pierre. "Esclavage et civilisation," *Esprit*, 40, 1 (1972), pp. 113-22.

55. *Civil War History*, 13, 4 (1967). Special issue devoted to issues raised by Elkins' *Slavery*.

56. Clarke, John Henrik. "African Cultural Continuity and Slave Revolts in the New World," *Black Scholar*, 8, 1 (1976), pp. 41-49; 8, 2 (1976), pp. 2-9.

57. _____. "Black Americans: Immigrants Against their Will," *Présence africaine*, 105-06 (1978), pp. 90-108.

58. _____, and Vincent Harding, eds. *Slave Trade and Slavery*. New York: Holt, Rinehart and Winston, 1970.

59. Cohen, David W., and Jack P. Greene, eds. *Neither Slave nor Free: The Freedman of African Descent in the Slave Societies of the New World*. Baltimore: Johns Hopkins University Press, 1972.

60. Cohen, William B. "Literature and Race: Nineteenth Century French Fiction, Blacks and Africa 1800-1880," *Race and Class*, 16, 2 (1974), pp. 181-205.

61. Corbitt, Duvon C. "Saco's History of Negro Slavery," *Hispanic American Historical Review*, 24 (1944), pp. 452-57.

62. Corrigan, Philip. "Feudal Relics or Capitalist Monuments? Notes on the Sociology of Unfree Labour," *Sociology*, 11, 3 (1977), pp. 435-63.

63. Cortés Alonso, Vicenta. "Algunas ideas sobre la esclavitud y su investigación," *Bulletin de l'Institut historique belge de Rome*, 44 (1974), pp. 127-44. Republished in *Miscellanea offerts à Charles Verlinden* (Ghent, 1975), pp. 127-44.

64. Costa, Emília Viotti da. "Slave Images and Realities," in Rubin and Tuden, eds., *Comparative Perspectives*, pp. 293-310.

65. Craddock, Emmie. "The New World Frontier as a Factor in the Rise and Decline of Modern Slavery" (PhD diss., University of Texas at Austin, 1954).

66. Craton, Michael. *Sinews of Empire: A Short History of British Slavery*. Garden City, N.Y.: Anchor Press, 1974.

67. _____, ed. "Roots and Branches: Current Directions in Slave Studies," *Historical Reflections/Réflexions historiques*, 6, 1 (1979). (Includes "Foreword") Republished as *Roots and Branches: Current Directions in Slave Studies*. New York: Pergamon Press, 1979.

68. _____, James Walvin, and D. Wright, eds., Slavery, Abolition and Emancipation: Black Slaves and the British Empire: A Thematic Documentary. London: Longman, 1976.

69. Cunliffe, Marcus. Chattel Slavery and Wage Slavery: The Anglo-American Context, 1830-1860. Athens: University of Georgia Press, 1979.

70. Curtin, Philip D. "The African Diaspora," Historical Reflections/Réflexions historiques, 6, 1 (1979), pp. 1-18.

71. _____. "The Black Experience of Colonialism and Imperialism," Daedalus, 103, 2 (1974), pp. 17-30.

72. _____. "Black Slavery in Perspective? (review of Rice, Rise and Fall of Black Slavery)," Reviews in American History, 4, 1 (1976), pp. 43-46.

73. _____. "Commentary (Metropolitan Slave Codes and Slave Demography)," in Rubin and Tuden, eds., Comparative Perspectives, pp. 202-04.

74. _____. "Slavery and Empire," in Rubin and Tuden, eds., Comparative Perspectives, pp. 3-11.

75. Daeleman, Jan. "Origine africaine des esclaves noirs du Brésil et du Surinam: critères linguistiques," Likundoli, sér. B, 5, 2 (1977), pp. 93-106.

76. D'Auvergne, Edmond B. Human Livestock. London: Grayson and Grayson, 1933.

77. Davidson, Basil. "Slaves or Captives? Some Notes on Fantasy and Fact," in Huggins, Kilson, and Fox, eds., Key Issues in the Afro-American Experience, vol. 1, pp. 54-73.

78. Davis, David Brion. "A Comparison of British America and Latin America," in Foner and Genovese, eds., Slavery in the Americas, pp. 69-83. (Reprinted from The Problem of Slavery in Western Culture.)

79. _____. "The Continuing Contradiction of Slavery: A Comparison of British America and Latin America," reprinted (from Problem of Slavery in Western Culture, pp. 223-43) in Brown, ed., Slavery in American Society, pp. 78-84.

80. _____. "The Forms of Slavery," The Yale Review, 61, 1 (1971), pp. 117-21.

81. _____. "Of Human Bondage (review of Patterson, Slavery and Social Death)," New York Review of Books, 30, 2 (17 Feb. 1983), pp. 19-22.

82. _____. The Problem of Slavery in the Age of Revolution, 1770-1823. Ithaca: Cornell University Press, 1975.

83. _____. The Problem of Slavery in Western Culture. Ithaca: Cornell University Press, 1966.

84. _____. "Slavery," in C. Vann Woodward, ed., The Comparative Approach to American History (New York: Basic Books, 1968), pp. 121-34. Reprinted as "The Comparative Approach to American History: Slavery," in Foner and Genovese, eds., Slavery in the Americas, pp. 60-68.

85. _____. "Slavery and 'Progress'," in Christine Bolt and Seymour Drescher, eds., Anti-Slavery, Religion and Reform: Essays in Memory of Roger Anstey (Folkestone: William Dawson & Sons, 1980), pp. 351-66.

86. _____. "Slavery and the Post-World War II Historians," Daedalus, 103, 2 (1974), pp. 1-16. Reprinted in Sidney W. Mintz, ed., Slavery, Colonialism, and Racism (New York: Norton, 1974), pp. 1-16.

87. Dean, Warren. "Commentary (Research Tools and Resources)," in Rubin and Tuden, eds., Comparative Perspectives, p. 566.

88. Debbasch, Yvan. Couleur et liberté: le jeu du critère ethnique dans un ordre juridique esclavagiste. Paris: Dalloz, 1967. (Annales de la Faculté de droit et des sciences politiques et économiques de Strasbourg, no. 16)

89. Deerr, Noel. The History of Sugar. 2 vols. London: Chapman and Hall, 1949-50.

90. Degler, Carl N. Neither Black nor White: Slavery and Race Relations in Brazil and the United States. New York: Macmillan, 1971.

91. _____. "Plantation Society: Old and New Perspectives on Hemispheric History," Plantation Society in the Americas, 1, 1 (1979), pp. 9-15.

92. _____. "Slavery in Brazil and the United States: An Essay in Comparative History," American Historical Review, 75, 4 (1970), pp. 1004-28. Reprinted in Haynes, ed., Blacks in White America, pp. 172-200; Weinstein and Gattell, eds., American Negro Slavery (2nd ed.), pp. 342-73.

93. _____. "Slavery in the Atlantic World (review of Rice, Rise and Fall of Black Slavery)," Virginia Quarterly Review, 52, 1 (1976), pp. 133-38.

94. _____. "Why Historians Change Their Minds," Pacific Historical Review, 45, 2 (1976), pp. 167-84.

95. *Diouf, Sylviane. "Résistance et révolte du peuple en Amérique et dans la Caraïbe durant l'esclavage" (Thèse de troisième cycle, Paris VII, 1976).

96. Dirks, Robert. "The Slave Rebellion: Its Political Ecology" (Paper presented to the 73rd Annual Meeting of the American Anthropological Association, Mexico, D.F.)

97. Domar, Evsey D. "The Causes of Slavery or Serfdom: A Hypothesis," Journal of Economic History, 30, 1 (1970), pp. 18-32.

98. Dovring, Folke. "Bondage, Tenure and Progress: Reflections on the Economics of Forced Labour," Comparative Studies in Society and History, 7, 3 (1965), pp. 309-23.

99. Drescher, Seymour. "Capitalism and the Decline of Slavery: The British Case in Comparative Perspective," in Rubin and Tuden, eds., Comparative Perspectives, pp. 132-42.

100. Drimmer, Melvin. "Neither Black nor White: Carl Degler's Study of Slavery in Two Societies," Phylon, 40, 1 (1979), pp. 94-105.

101. _____. "Slaves as People," Caribbean Review, 3, 2 (1971), pp. 5-6.

102. _____. "Thoughts on the Study of Slavery in the Americas and the Writing of Black History," Phylon, 36, 2 (1975), pp. 125-39.

103. Dunn, Richard S. "Quantifying Slavery and the Slave Trade," Journal of Interdisciplinary History, 9, 1 (1978), pp. 147-50.

104. _____. "A Tale of Two Plantations: Slave Life at Mesopotamia in Jamaica and Mount Airy in Virginia, 1799 to 1828," William and Mary Quarterly, 3rd ser., 34, 1 (1977), pp. 32-65.

105. Dupuy, Alex. "Feudalism and Slavery: Processes of Uneven Development in France and Saint-Domingue in the Eighteenth Century" (PhD diss., State University of New York at Binghamton, 1981).

106. Earle, Carville V. "A Staple Interpretation of Slavery and Free Labor," Geographical Review, 68, 1 (1978), pp. 51-65.

107. Eaton, Clement. "Charles Darwin and Catherine Hopley: Victorian Views of Plantation Societies," Plantation Society in the Americas, 1, 1 (1979), pp. 16-30.

108. Eder, Donald Gray. "The Tannenbaum Thesis: A New Black Legend?" (PhD diss., Ohio State University, 1970).

109. _____. "Time Under the Southern Cross: The Tannenbaum Thesis Reappraised," Agricultural History, 50, 4 (1976), pp. 600-14.

110. Edmondson, Locksley. "Trans-Atlantic Slavery and the Internationalization of Race," Caribbean Quarterly, 22, 2-3 (1976), pp. 5-25.

111. Edwards, Paul, and James Walvin. Black Personalities in the Era of the Slave Trade. Baton Rouge: Louisiana State University Press, 1983.

112. Elkins, Stanley M. "The Dynamics of Unopposed Capitalism: Slavery in Capitalist and Non-Capitalist Cultures," reprinted (from Slavery) in Brown, ed., Slavery in American Society, pp. 85-93.

113. _____. Slavery: A Problem in American Institutional and Intellectual Life. Chicago: University of Chicago Press, 1959. 2nd ed., 1968. 3rd ed., 1976.

114. _____. "Slavery and its Aftermath in the Western Hemisphere," in de Reuck and Knight, eds., Caste and Race, pp. 192-203. With discussion, "Attitudes to Slavery in the New World," pp. 204-22.

115. _____. "Slavery and Personality," in Robert J. Brugger, ed., Our Selves/Our Past: Psychological Approaches to American History (Baltimore: Johns Hopkins University Press, 1981), pp. 141-64.

116. _____. "Slavery in Capitalist and Non-Capitalist Cultures," in Foner and Genovese, eds., Slavery in the Americas, pp. 8-26. (Reprinted from Slavery.)

117. Eltis, David. "Nutritional Trends in Africa and the Americas: Heights of Africans 1819-1839," Journal of Interdisciplinary History, 12, 3 (1982), pp. 453-75.

118. Emmer, Pieter C. "Conference on 'Religion, Anti-slavery and Reform' (July 1978, Bellagio, Italy)," Revue française d'histoire d'outre-mer, 66, 3-4 (nos. 244-45)(1979), p. 469.

119. Endresen, Halfden. I slavenes spor. Stavanger: Nomi, 1969.

120. Engerman, Stanley L. "Comments on the Study of Race and Slavery," in Engerman and Genovese, eds., Race and Slavery, pp. 495-530.

121. _____. "The Development of Plantation Systems and Slave Societies: A Commentary - I," in Rubin and Tuden, eds., Comparative Perspectives, pp. 63-67.

122. _____. "Economic Adjustments to Emancipation in the United States and British West Indies," Journal of Interdisciplinary History, 13, 2 (1982), pp. 191-220.

123. _____. "Quantitative and Economic Analysis of West Indian Slave Societies: Research Problems," in Rubin and Tuden, eds., Comparative Perspectives, pp. 597-609.

124. _____. "The Realities of Slavery: A Review of Recent Evidence," International Journal of Comparative Sociology, 20, 1-2 (1979), pp. 46-66.

125. _____. "Some Considerations Relating to Property Rights in Man," Journal of Economic History, 33, 1 (1973), pp. 43-65.

126. _____. "Some Economic and Demographic Comparisons of Slavery in the United States and the British West Indies," Economic History Review, 29, 2 (1976), pp. 258-75.

127. _____, and Eugene D. Genovese, eds. Race and Slavery in the Western Hemisphere: Quantitative Studies. Princeton: Princeton University Press, 1975.

128. "Essays on Slavery," Caribbean Quarterly, 22, 2-3 (1976).

129. Etzel, Eduardo. Escravidão negra e branca: o passado através do presente. São Paulo: Global Editora, 1976.

130. Evans, William McKee. "From the Land of Canaan to the Land of Guinea: The Strange Odyssey of the 'Sons of Ham'," American Historical Review, 85, 1 (1980), pp. 15-43.

131. _____. "Race, Class and Myth in Slaveholding Societies" (Unpublished paper read to Southern Historical Association, Louisville, Kentucky, November 1981).

132. Everett, Susanne. The Slaves. New York: Putnam, 1978.

133. Fahrenfort, J. J. "Over onvrije en vrije arbeid," Mens en maatschappij, 19 (1943), pp. 29-51.

134. Fenoaltea, Stefano. "Slavery and Supervision in Comparative Perspective: A Model" (Unpublished paper, July 1979, revised April 1980).

135. _____. "The Slavery Debate: A Note from the Sidelines," Explorations in Economic History, 18, 3 (1981), pp. 304-08.

136. Findlay, Ronald. "Slavery, Incentives, and Manumission: A Theoretical Model," Journal of Political Economy, 83, 5 (1975), pp. 923-33.

137. Finley, Moses I. "Between Slavery and Freedom," Comparative Studies in Society and History, 6, 3 (1964), pp. 233-49. Translated as "Entre l'esclavage et la liberté," Recherches internationales à la lumière du marxisme, no. 84, 3 (1975), pp. 78-98. Reprinted in idem, Economy and Society in Ancient Greece, pp. 116-32.

138. _____. "The Idea of Slavery (review of Davis, Problem of Slavery in Western Culture)," New York Review of Books, 8, 1 (26 Jan. 1967), pp. 6-10. Reprinted in Foner and Genovese, eds., Slavery in the New World, pp. 256-61; Weinstein and Gatell, eds., American Negro Slavery (2nd ed.), pp. 394-400.

139. _____. "Slavery and the Historians," Histoire
     sociale/Social History, 12, 24 (1979), pp. 247-61.

140. Fogel, Robert W. "Cliometrics and Culture: Some Recent
     Developments in the Historiography of Slavery," Journal of Social
     History, 11, 1 (1977), pp. 34-51.

141. _____. "Past Developments and Future Prospects for
     Ethnic Minority Groups: Three Phases of Cliometric Research on
     Slavery and its Aftermath," American Economic Review (Papers and
     Proceedings), 65, 2 (1975), pp. 37-46.

142. _____, and Stanley L. Engerman. "Recent Findings in the
     Study of Slave Demography and Family Structure," Sociology and
     Social Research, 63, 3 (1979), pp. 566-89.

143. *Foli, Peter K. "Esclavage noir en Amérique et aux Antilles
     pendant la guerre d'indépendance américaine (1778-1783)" (Thèse,
     Université Paris, 1953).

144. Foner, Laura. "The Free People of Color in Louisiana and St.
     Domingue," Journal of Social History, 3, 4 (1970), pp. 406-30.

145. _____, and Eugene D. Genovese, eds. Slavery in the New
     World: A Reader in Comparative History. Englewood Cliffs, N.J.:
     Prentice-Hall, 1969.

146. "Formes et aspects de l'esclavage," Annales: économies, sociétés,
     civilisations, 22, 6 (1967), pp. 1328-38.

147. Franco, José Luciano. La diaspora africana en el nuevo mundo.
     Havana: Editorial de Ciencias Sociales, 1975.

148. _____. La presencia negra en el Nuevo Mundo.
     Havana: Casa de las Americas, 1966. Translated as Présence
     africaine au Nouveau Monde (Dakar: Centre de Hautes Etudes
     Afro-Ibéro-Américaines de l'Université de Dakar, 1967), and as A
     presença negra na América latina by A. Portela Santos (Lisbon:
     Prelo, 1971).

149. _____, ed. Esclavitud, comercio y tráfico negreros.
     Havana: Archivo Nacional, 1972. (Serie Archivo Nacional, no. 9)

150. Franklin, Vincent P. "Slavery, Personality, and Black Culture -
     Some Theoretical Issues," Phylon, 35, 1 (1974), pp. 54-63.

151. Frazier, E. Franklin. "A Comparison of Negro-White Relations in
     Brazil and in the United States," in G. Franklin Edwards, ed., E.
     Franklin Frazier on Race Relations (Chicago: University of Chicago
     Press, 1968), pp. 82-102.

152. _____. Race and Culture Contacts in the Modern
     World. New York: Alfred A. Knopf, 1957.

153. Frucht, Richard, ed. Black Society in the New World. New York: Random House, 1971.

154. Geggus, David. "British Opinion and the Emergence of Haiti, 1791-1805," in Walvin, ed., Slavery and British Society, pp. 123-49.

155. Gemery, Henry A., and Jan S. Hogendorn. "Technological Change, Slavery, and the Slave Trade," in Clive Dewey and A. G. Hopkins, eds., The Imperial Impact: Studies in the Economic History of Africa and India (London: Athlone Press, 1978), pp. 243-58.

156. Genovese, Eugene D. "Concluding Remarks (on Race and Slavery in the Western Hemisphere)," in Engerman and Genovese, eds., Race and Slavery, pp. 531-39.

157. _____. From Rebellion to Revolution. Baton Rouge: Louisiana State University Press, 1979.

158. _____. "Materialism and Idealism in the History of Negro Slavery in the Americas," Journal of Social History, 1, 4 (1968), pp. 371-94. Reprinted in Foner and Genovese, eds., Slavery in the New World, pp. 238-55; Genovese, In Red and Black, pp. 23-52. Also Bobbs-Merrill Reprint no. BC-102.

159. _____. "Rebelliousness and Docility in the Negro Slave: A Critique of the Elkins Thesis," Civil War History, 13, 4 (1967), pp. 293-314. Reprinted in Lane, ed., Debate Over Slavery, pp. 43-74; Haynes, ed., Blacks in White America, pp. 214-35. Also Bobbs-Merrill Reprint no. BC-103.

160. _____. "Slavery: The World's Burden," revised in Fox-Genovese and Genovese, Fruits of Merchant Capital, pp. 391-414.

161. _____. "The Treatment of Slaves in Different Countries: Problems in the Applications of the Comparative Method," in Foner and Genovese, eds., Slavery in the Americas, pp. 202-10. Reprinted in Genovese, In Red and Black, pp. 158-72.

162. _____, ed. The Slave Economies. Volume 1: Historical and Theoretical Perspectives. Volume 2: Slavery in the International Economy. New York: John Wiley and Sons, 1973.

163. _____, and Elizabeth Fox-Genovese. "The Slave Economies in Political Perspective," Journal of American History, 66, 1 (1979), pp. 7-23. Revised in Fox-Genovese and Genovese, Fruits of Merchant Capital, pp. 34-60.

164. Gerbeau, Hubert. Les esclaves noirs: pour une histoire du silence. Paris: A. Balland, 1970.

165. _____. "Un mort-vivant: l'esclavage," Présence africaine, 61 (1967), pp. 180-98.

166. Gerber, David. "The Origins of Black Politics (review of Genovese, From Rebellion to Revolution)," Radical America, 15, 6 (1981), pp. 47-56.

167. Ghersi, Emanuele. La schiavitù e l'evoluzione della politica coloniale. Padua: CEDAM, Casa editrice dott. A. Milani, 1935.

168. Goody, Jack. "Slavery in Time and Space," in Watson, ed., Asian and African Systems of Slavery, pp. 16-43.

169. Goveia, Elsa V. "Comment on 'Anglicanism, Catholicism, and the Negro Slave'," Comparative Studies in Society and History, 8, 3 (1966), pp. 328-30.

170. Graham, Richard. "Slavery and Economic Development: Brazil and the United States South in the Nineteenth Century," Comparative Studies in Society and History, 23, 4 (1981), pp. 620-55.

171. Gratus, Jack. The Great White Lie. New York and London: Monthly Review Press, 1973.

172. Greenberg, Michael. "The New Economic History and the Understanding of Slavery: A Methodological Critique," Dialectical Anthropology, 2 (1977), pp. 131-41.

173. _____. "Slavery and the Protestant Ethic," Louisiana Studies, 15, 3 (1976), pp. 209-39.

174. Greenfield, Sidney M. "Madeira and the Beginning of New World Sugar Cane Cultivation and Plantation Slavery: A Study in Institution Building," in Rubin and Tuden, eds. Comparative Perspectives, pp. 536-52.

175. _____. "Plantations, Sugar Cane and Slavery," Historical Reflections/Réflexions historiques, 6, 1 (1979), pp. 85-120.

176. _____. "Slavery and the Plantation in the New World: The Development and Diffusion of a Social Form," Journal of Inter-American Studies, 11, 1 (1969), pp. 44-57.

177. Greenidge, Charles W. W. Slavery. London: Allen and Unwin, 1958.

178. Günther, Rigobert. "Herausbildung und Systemcharakter der vorkapitalistischen Gesellschaftsformationen," Zeitschrift für Geschichtswissenschaft, 17, 1-2 (1969), pp. 194-208.

179. Guterman, S. S. "Alternative Theories in the Study of Slavery, the Concentration Camp, and Personality," British Journal of Sociology, 26, 2 (1975), pp. 186-202.

180. Haiser, Franz. Die Sklaverei, ihre biologische Begründung und sittliche Rechtfertigung. Munich: J.F. Lehmann, 1923.

181. Hall, Gwendolyn Midlo. "Commentary (Social Institutions and Slave Societies)," in Rubin and Tuden, eds., Comparative Perspectives, pp. 281-83.

182. _____. "Negro Slaves in the Americas," Freedomways, 4, 31(1964), pp. 319-30.

183. _____. Social Control in Slave Plantation Societies: A Comparison of St. Domingue and Cuba. Baltimore: Johns Hopkins University Press, 1972.

184. Hansen, Klaus J. "Review Article: Slaves and Historians," Queens Quarterly, 85, 1 (1978), pp. 109-13.

185. Harris, John Hobbis. "Slavery: A World Review," Contemporary Review, 150 (no. 848)(1936), pp. 164-71. Reprinted, London: The Anti-Slavery and Aborigines' Protection Society, 1936.

186. _____. Slavery or "Sacred Trust"? London: Williams and Norgate, 1926. Reprinted New York: Negro Universities Press, 1969.

187. Harris, Marvin. "The Origin of the Descent Rule," in Foner and Genovese, eds., Slavery in the Americas, pp. 48-59. (Reprinted from Patterns of Race in the Americas.) Also adapted in Brown, ed., Slavery in American Society, pp. 65-71.

188. _____. Patterns of Race in the Americas. New York: Walker, 1964.

189. Heinen, Heinz. "Slavery," in Marxism, Communism and Western Society: A Comparative Encyclopedia, vol. 7 (1973), pp. 336-41.

190. Hellie, Richard. "Muscovite Slavery in Comparative Perspective," Russian History/Histoire russe, 6, 2 (1979), pp. 133-209.

191. Herskovits, Melville J. "The Ahistorical Approach to Afroamerican Studies: A Critique," American Anthropologist, 62, 4 (1960), pp. 559-68.

192. _____. The Myth of the Negro Past. New York: Harper, 1941.

193. _____. "On the Provenience of New World Negroes," Social Forces, 12, 2 (1933), pp. 247-62. Also Bobbs-Merrill Reprint no. BC-132.

194. _____, ed. The New World Negro: Selected Papers in Afroamerican Studies. Bloomington: Indiana University Press, 1966.

195. Higman, Barry W. "Methodological Problems in the Study of the Slave Family," in Rubin and Tuden, eds., Comparative Perspectives, pp. 591-96

196. _____. "Slavery and the Development of Demographic Theory in the Age of the Industrial Revolution," in Walvin, ed., Slavery and British Society, pp. 164-94.

197. Hine, William L. "American Slavery and Russian Serfdom: A Preliminary Comparison," Phylon, 36 (1975), pp. 378-84.

198. Hodson, John D. "Mill, Paternalism, and Slavery," Analysis, 41, 1 (1981), pp. 60-62.

199. Hoetink, Harry. "The Cultural Links," in Margaret E. Crahan and Franklin W. Knight, eds., Africa and the Caribbean: The Legacies of a Link (Baltimore: Johns Hopkins University Press, 1979), pp. 20-40.

200. _____. "Diferencias en relaciones raciales entre Curazao y Surinam," Revista de ciencias sociales, 5, 4 (1961), pp. 499-514. Translated as "Race Relations in Curaçao and Surinam," in Foner and Genovese, eds., Slavery in the New World, pp. 178-88.

201. _____. "Slavery and Race," Historical Reflections/Réflexions historiques, 6, 1 (1979), pp. 255-68. Commentary by Arnold Sio (pp. 269-74).

202. _____. Slavery and Race Relations in the Americas: Comparative Notes on their Nature and Nexus. New York: Harper and Row, 1973.

203. _____. The Two Variants in Caribbean Race Relations: A Contribution to the Sociology of Segmented Societies. Translated from the Dutch by Eva M. Hooykaas. London: Oxford University Press, 1967.

204. Hogg, Peter. Slavery: The Afro-American Experience. London: British Library Reference Division, 1979.

205. Horowitz, Donald L. "Color Differentiation in the American Systems of Slavery," Journal of Interdisciplinary History, 3, 3 (1973), pp. 509-41.

206. Hunting, Claudine. "The Philosophes and Black Slavery: 1748-1765," Journal of the History of Ideas, 39, 3 (1978), pp. 405-18.

207. Irwin, Graham W., ed. Africans Abroad: A Documentary History of the Black Diaspora in Asia, Latin America, and the Caribbean during the Age of Slavery. New York: Columbia University Press, 1977.

208. Isaac, Ephraim. "Genesis, Judaism, and the 'Sons of Ham'," Slavery and Abolition, 1, 1 (1980), pp. 3-17.

209. James, C. L. R. "The Atlantic Slave Trade and Slavery: Some Interpretations of their Significance in the Development of the United States and the Western World," in Amistad (New York: Random House, 1970), vol. 1, pp. 119-64.

210. Johnson, Harry G. "Negro Slavery," Encounter, 44, 1 (1975), pp. 56-59.

211. Johnston, Harry H. The Negro in the New World. New York: Macmillan, 1910.

212. Jones, Archer, and Robert J. Carlsson. "Slavery and Slaving," American Journal of Economics and Sociology, 30, 2 (1971), pp. 171-77.

213. Jones, Rhett S. "Slavery in the Colonial Americas," Black World, 24, 4 (1975), pp. 28-39.

214. Jordan, Winthrop D. "American Chiaroscuro: The Status and Definition of Mulattoes in the British Colonies," William and Mary Quarterly, 3rd series, 19, 2 (1962), pp. 183-200. Reprinted in Foner and Genovese, eds., Slavery in the New World, pp. 189-201. Also Bobbs-Merrill Reprint no. BC-158.

215. _____. "Planter and Slave Identity Formation: Some Problems in the Comparative Approach," in Rubin and Tuden, eds., Comparative Perspectives, pp. 35-40.

216. Journal of Social History, 3, 4 (1970). Special issue on slavery.

217. Kautsky, Karl. "Sklaverei und Kapitalismus," Die Neue Zeit, 29, Bd. 2, Nr. 47 (1910-11), pp. 713-25.

218. Kilian, Martin A., and E. Lynn Tatom. "Marx, Hegel, and the Marxian of the Master Class: Eugene D. Genovese on Slavery," Journal of Negro History, 66, 3 (1981), pp. 189-208.

219. Kilson, Martin L., and Robert I. Rotberg, eds. The African Diaspora: Interpretive Essays. Cambridge, Mass.: Harvard University Press, 1976.

220. Kiple, Kenneth F. "La dimensión epidemiológica de la esclavitud de las Antillas, Florida, y Luisiana" (Paper read to the Second Conference of the Florida-Spanish Alliance, 1981).

221. _____. "Historical Dimensions of Disease in the Plantation Economies" (Paper read to Seminar on Health, Welfare, and Development in Latin America and the Caribbean, Ontario Cooperative Program in Latin Caribbean Studies, 1980).

222. _____. "Twentieth Century Views of Slavery in the Americas," in Lysle E. Meyer, ed., Historical Papers: Selected Proceedings of the Sixth Northern Great Plains History Conference (Moorehead, Minn.: 1972), pp. 175-202.

223. _____, and Virginia Kiple. "The African Connection: Slavery, Disease, and Racism," Phylon, 41, 3 (1980), pp. 211-22.

224. _____, and Virginia Himmelsteib King. Another Dimension to the Black Diaspora. New York: Cambridge University Press, 1981.

225. Klein, Herbert S. "Anglicanism, Catholicism, and the Negro Slave," Comparative Studies in Society and History, 8, 3 (1966), pp. 295-327. Reprinted in Foner and Genovese, eds., Slavery in the New World, pp. 138-67 (with comment by Elsa V. Goveia, pp. 167-69); Lane, ed., Debate Over Slavery, pp. 137-90. Also Bobbs-Merrill Reprint no. BC-170.

226. _____. "Patterns of Settlement of the Afro-American Population in the New World," in Huggins, Kilson, and Fox, eds., Key Issues in the Afro-American Experience, vol. 1, pp. 99-115.

227. _____. Slavery in the Americas: A Comparative Study of Virginia and Cuba. Chicago: University of Chicago Press, 1967.

228. _____. "Sociedades esclavistas en las Américas - un estudio comparativo," Desarrollo económico (Buenos Aires: Instituto de Desarrollo Económico), 6, 22-23 (1966), pp. 227-45.

229. _____, and Stanley L. Engerman. "Fertility Differentials between Slaves in the United States and the British West Indies: A Note on Lactation Practices and their Possible Implications," William and Mary Quarterly, 3rd ser., 35, 2 (1978), pp. 357-74.

230. Kloosterboer, Willemina. Onvrije arbeid na de afschaffing van de slavernij. Leiden: E. J. Brill, 1960. Translated as Involuntary Labour Since the Abolition of Slavery: A Survey of Compulsory Labour Throughout the World. Leiden, 1960.

231. Knight, Franklin W. "The Caribbean Sugar Industry and Slavery (review of Hagelberg, Caribbean Sugar Industries, Kiple, Blacks in Colonial Cuba, and Moreno Fraginals, El ingenio)," Latin American Research Review, 18, 2 (1983), pp. 219-29.

232. _____, and Margaret E. Crahan. "The African Migration and the Origins of an Afro-American Society and Culture," in Margaret E. Crahan and Franklin W. Knight, eds., Africa and the Caribbean: The Legacies of a Link (Baltimore: Johns Hopkins University Press, 1979), pp. 1-19.

233. *Kolchin, Peter. "In Defense of Servitude: A Comparison of American Pro-Slave and Russian Proserfdom Arguments, 1750-1860" (Paper presented to American Historical Association, San Francisco, 1978).

234. _____. "The Process of Confrontation: Patterns of Resistance to Bondage in Nineteenth-Century Russia and the United States," Journal of Social History, 11, 4 (1978), pp. 457-90.

235. Kopytoff, Igor. "Slavery," Annual Review of Anthropology, 11 (1982), pp. 207-30.

236. Korostovtsev, Michail A. "Was ist ein Sklave?" Altorientalische Forschungen, 5 (1977), pp. 5-16.

237. Krieger, Leonard. "Reassessing Slavery," Partisan Review, 46, 1 (1979), pp. 152-58.

238. Kuitenbrower, M. "De nederlandse afschaffing van de slavernij in vergelijkend perspectief," Bijdragen en Mededelingen betreffende de Geschiedenis der Nederlanden, 93, 1 (1978), pp. 69-100.

239. Lane, Ann J., ed. The Debate Over Slavery: Stanley Elkins and his Critics. Urbana, Ill.: University of Illinois Press, 1971.

240. Lara, Oruno D. "De l'Atlantique à l'aire Caraïbe: nègres cimarrons et révoltes d'esclaves" (Paris, 1971, 4 vols, typed).

241. _____. "Negro Resistance to Slavery and the Atlantic Slave Trade from Africa to Black America," in UNESCO, African Slave Trade, pp. 101-18.

242. _____. "Resistance to Slavery: From Africa to Black America," in Rubin and Tuden, eds., Comparative Perspectives, pp. 464-80.

243. _____. "Témoignages afro-américains sur l'esclavage," Présence africaine, 109 (1979), pp. 144-51.

244. Lawler, Peter Augustine. "Tocqueville on Slavery, Ancient and Modern," South Atlantic Quarterly, 80, 4 (1981), pp. 466-77.

245. Leach, Edmund. "Caste, Class and Slavery: The Taxonomic Problem," in de Reuck and Knight, eds., Caste and Race, pp. 5-16. (With discussion, pp. 17-27)

246. League of Nations 1925-1936. Evidence and Reports of the Temporary Slavery Commission, 1924-1925; The Committee of Experts on Slavery, 1931-1932; The Advisory Committee of Experts on Slavery, 1934-1936.

247. Lengellé, Maurice. L'esclavage. Paris: Presses Universitaires de France, 1955.

248. Levine, Robert M. Race and Ethnic Relations in Latin America and the Caribbean (An Historical Dictionary and Bibliography). Metuchen, N.J.: Scarecrow Press, 1980.

249. Lévy-Bruhl, Henri. "Esquisse d'une théorie de l'esclavage," Revue générale du droit, de la législation et de la jurisprudence, 55 (1931), pp. 1-17. Reprinted as "Théorie de l'esclavage," in Quelques problèmes du très ancien droit romain (Paris: Domat-Montchrestien, 1934), pp. 15-33, and in Finley, ed., Slavery in Classical Antiquity, pp. 151-69.

250. Lewis, Gordon K. Slavery: Imperialism and Freedom: Studies in English Radical Thought. New York: Monthly Review Press, 1978.

251. Lewis, Mary Agnes. "Slavery and Personality: A Further Comment," American Quarterly, 19, 1 (1967), pp. 114-21. Reprinted in Lane, ed., Debate Over Slavery, pp. 75-86.

252. Liedel, Donald E. "Slavery and Abolition: Stanley Elkins and His Critics (review article)," Journal of Popular Culture, 5, 3 (1971), pp. 616-19.

253. Littlefield, Daniel C. "Plantations, Paternalism, and Profitability: Factors Affecting African Demography in the Old British Empire," Journal of Southern History, 47, 2 (1981), pp. 167-82.

254. Llavador Mira, J. "Modificación y límites de la esclavitud," in Atti del XL Congresso Internazionale degli Americanisti (Roma-Genova, 1972) (Genoa: Tilgher, 1975), vol. 3, pp. 445-51.

255. Logan, Paul E. "Tales of the Customs and Fates of Negro Slaves: Johann Ernst Kolb," Negro History Bulletin, 44, 4 (1981), pp. 78-81.

256. Lombardi, John V. "Comparative Slave Systems in the Americas: A Critical Review," in Richard Graham and Peter H. Smith, eds., New Approaches to Latin American History (Austin: University of Texas Press, 1974), pp. 156-74.

257. Losada, Juan, and Jorge Mayor. "Esclavitud y psicología: una investigación interdisciplinaria," Revista de la Biblioteca Nacional José Martí, 22, 3 (1980), pp. 133-44.

258. Lumenga-Neso, Kiobe. "La révolution américaine et la question de l'esclavage au 18e siècle," Zaire-Afrique, 16 (1976), pp. 327-36.

259. Luraghi, Raimondo. "Wage Labor in the 'Rice Belt' of Northern Italy and Slave Labor in the American South - A First Approach," Southern Studies, 16, 2 (1977), pp. 109-27.

260. McDonald, Roderick Alexander. "'Goods and Chattels': The Economy of Slaves on Sugar Plantations in Jamaica and Louisiana" (PhD diss., University of Kansas, 1981).

261. MacInnes, Charles M. England and Slavery. Bristol: Arrowsmith, 1934.

262. McKitrick, Eric, and Stanley M. Elkins. "Institutions and the Law of Slavery: The Dynamics of Unopposed Capitalism," American Quarterly, 9, 1 (1957), pp. 3-21; 9, 2 (1957), pp. 159-79.

263. MacMunn, George. Slavery Through the Ages. London: Nicholson and Watson, 1938.

264. *Mactoux, M. M. "Pour une approche nouvelle du champ lexical de l'esclavage," Revue de l'Université de Varsovie, (1977), pp. .

265. Malowist, Marian. "Les débuts du système de plantations dans la période des grandes découvertes," Africana Bulletin, 10 (1969), pp. 9-30.

266. Mandle, Jay R. "The Plantation Economy: An Essay in Definition," Science and Society, 36, 1 (1972), pp. 49-62.

267. Markoe, William M. "The Catholic Church and Slavery," America, 28, 18 (1923), pp. 415-17.

268. Marsh, Henry (Saklatvala, Beram). Slavery and Race. Newton Abbot: David and Charles, 1974.

269. Maxwell, John Francis. Slavery and the Catholic Church: The History of the Catholic Teaching Concerning the Moral Legitimacy of the Institution of Slavery. Chichester: Rose, for the Anti-Slavery Society for the Protection of Human Rights, 1975.

270. Meillassoux, Claude. "Correspondence on Slavery," Economy and Society, 7, 3 (1978), pp. 321-31.

271. *_____. "Les enfants du néant (essai sur l'esclavagisme)," Economy and Society, forthcoming.

272. *_____. "Modalités historiques de l'exploitation et de la surexploitation du travail" (Unpublished manuscript).

273. Meltzer, Milton. Slavery from the Rise of Western Civilization to the Renaissance. New York: Cowles, 1971.

274. *Miers, Suzanne. "Britain and the Suppression of Slavery 1919-39" (Seminar paper, University of London, 1981).

275. Miller, Joseph C. Slavery: A Comparative Teaching Bibliography. Waltham, Mass.: Crossroads Press, 1977.

276. _____. "Slavery: A Further Supplementary Bibliography," Slavery and Abolition, 1, 2 (1980), pp. 199-258.

277. _____. "Slavery: Annual Bibliographical Supplement (1981)," Slavery and Abolition, 2, 2 (1981), pp. 146-205.

278. _____, and Daniel H. Borus. "Slavery: A Supplementary Teaching Bibliography," Slavery and Abolition, 1, 1 (1980), pp. 63-108.

279. _____, and Larissa V. Brown. "Slavery: Annual Bibliographical Supplement (1982): Part I," Slavery and Abolition, 3, 2 (1982), pp. 163-208; Part II, forthcoming 3, 3 (1982).

280. Minchinton, Walter. "The Economic Relations between Metropolitan Countries and the Caribbean: Some Problems," in Rubin and Tuden, eds., Comparative Perspectives, pp. 567-80.

281. Mintz, Sidney W. "History and Anthropology: A Brief Reprise," in Engerman and Genovese, eds., Race and Slavery, pp. 477-94.

282. _____. "Labor and Sugar in Puerto Rico and in Jamaica, 1800-1850," Comparative Studies in Society and History, 1, 3 (1959), pp. 273-80. Reprinted in Foner and Genovese, eds., Slavery in the New World, pp. 170-77. Also Bobbs-Merrill Reprint no. BC-207.

283. _____. "(Review of Elkins, Slavery)," American Anthropologist, 63, 3 (1961), pp. 579-87. Reprinted as "Slavery and Emergent Capitalisms," in Foner and Genovese, eds., Slavery in the New World, pp. 27-37. Also Bobbs-Merrill Reprint no. A-81.

284. _____. "Le rouge et le noir," Les Temps Modernes, 27 (nos. 299-300)(1971), pp. 2354-61.

285. _____. "Slavery and the Afro-American World," in John F. Szwed, ed., Black America (New York: Basic Books, 1970), pp. 29-44. Revised and reprinted in idem, Caribbean Transformations (Chicago: Aldine, 1974), pp. 59-81.

286. _____. "Slavery and the Rise of Peasantries," Historical Reflections/Réflexions historiques, 6, 1 (1979), pp. 213-42. Commentaries by Woodville K. Marshall (pp. 243-57), Mary Karasch (pp. 248-51), and Richard Frucht (pp. 252-54).

287. _____. "Slavery and the Slaves (review of Patterson, Sociology of Slavery)," Caribbean Studies, 8, 4 (1969), pp. 65-70.

288. _____. "Slavery, Forced Labor and the Plantation System," in idem, Caribbean Transformations (Chicago: Aldine, 1974), pp. 43-58.

289. _____. "The So-Called World System: Local Initiative and Local Response," Dialectical Anthropology, 2 (1977), pp. 253-70.

290. _____. "Toward an Afro-American History," Cahiers d'histoire mondiale/Journal of World History, 13, 2 (1971), pp. 317-32. Reprinted in Herbert G. Gutman and Gregory S. Kealey, eds., Many Pasts: Readings in American Social History (Englewood Cliffs, N.J.: Prentice-Hall, 1973), vol. 1, pp. 115-30.

291. _____. "Was the Plantation Slave a Proletarian?" Review, 2, 1 (1978), pp. 81-100.

292. Miramón, Alberto. "Los negros del Caribe," Boletin de historia e antigüedades (Bogotá), 31 (nos. 351-52)(1944), pp. 168-87.

293. Miscellanea offerts à Charles Verlinden, "Histoire de l'esclavage et de la traite," pp. xlv-xlvii.

294. Moraes Farias, Paulo Fernando de. "Models of the World and Categorical Models: The 'Enslavable Barbarian' as a Mobile Classificatory Label," Slavery and Abolition, 1, 2 (1980), pp. 115-31.

295. *Morgan, Philip. "The Development of Slave Culture in Eighteenth-Century Plantation America" (PhD diss., University College, London, 1977).

296. _____. "Whither the Comparative History of New World Slavery (review essay)," Journal of Ethnic Studies, 8, 1 (1980), pp. 94-109.

297. Mörner, Magnus. Buy or Breed? The Alternative Sources of Slave Supply in the Plantation Societies of the New World. Stockholm: Institute of Latin American Studies, Research Paper Series, no. 23, 1980. Translated as "'Comprar ou criar': fuentes alternativas de suministro de esclavos en las sociedades plantacionistas del Nuevo Mundo," Revista de historia de América, no. 91 (1981), pp. 37-81; also in Rapports du XVe Congrès international des sciences historiques (Bucharest, 1980), vol. 2, pp. 463-78.

298. _____. "Det jämforande studiet av negerslaveriet i Angloamerika och i Latinamerika i aktuell forskningsdebatt," Historiallinen Arkisto (Helsinfors), 62 (1967), pp. 253-65.

299. _____. "Discussão sôbre raças e classes na América Latina durante o período nacional," Revista de história (São Paulo), 36 (no. 74)(1968), pp. 349-76.

300. _____. "Los jesuitas y la esclavitud de los negros," Revista chilena de historia y geografía, 135 (1967), pp. 92-109.

301. _____. "Slavery and Race in the Evolution of Latin American Societies: Some Recent Contributions to the Debate," Journal of Latin American Studies, 8, 1 (1976), pp. 127-35.

302. _____. "Die vergleichende Studium der Negersklaverei in Anglo- und Lateinamerika," Jahrbuch für Geschichte von Staat, Wirtschaft, und Gesellschaft Lateinamerikas, 5 (1968), pp. 405-21.

303. _____, ed. Race and Class in Latin America. New York: Columbia University Press, 1970.

304. Mufassir, Sulayman Shahid. "Solutions to the Problem of Slavery (Then and Now)," Black World, 19, 9 (1970), pp. 12-18.

305. Murapa, R. "Maroons: Mau Mau Predecessors," Black World, 19, 9 (1970), pp. 33-38.

306. Murtaugh, Frank M. "La 'nuova' storia economica, vent'anni di dibattiti sulla schiavitù," Economia e storia, 24, 3 (1977), pp. 325-39.

307. Nevins, Allan. "Slavery in a World Setting," in idem, The Emergence of Lincoln (New York: Scribner, 1950), vol. 2, pp. 132-70.

308. New York Academy of Sciences. Annals, vol. 292 (1977): "Comparative Perspectives on Slavery in New World Plantation Societies". Eds. Vera Rubin and Arthur Tuden.

309. Nieboer, H. J. Slavery as an Industrial System: Ethnological Researches. The Hague: M. Nijhoff, 1900. 2nd rev. ed.: The Hague: Nijhoff, 1910.

310. Nisbet, Robert. "The Unfree (review of Patterson, Slavery and Social Death)," Commentary, 75, 4 (1983), pp. 74-76.

311. Noel, Donald L. "Slavery and the Rise of Racism," in idem, ed., Origins of American Slavery and Racism, pp. 153-74.

312. Ofusu-Appiah, L. H. Slavery: A Brief Survey. Accra: Waterville, 1969.

313. *Olivier, Geneviève. "Le noir américain dans l'idéologie créole entre 1770 et 1825" (Thèse de troisième cycle, Paris, 1975).

314. Onwood, Maurice. "'Impulse and Honor': The Place of Slave and Master in the Ideology of Planterdom," Plantation Society in the Americas, 1, 1 (1979), pp. 31-57.

315. Oppenheim, Leonard. "The Law of Slaves: A Comparative Study of the Roman and Louisiana Systems," Tulane Law Review, 14 (1940), pp. 384-406.

316. Opstall, Margaretha E. van. "Archival Sources in the Netherlands," in Rubin and Tuden, eds., Comparative Perspectives, pp. 501-09.

317. Padgug, Robert A. "Commentary (Research Problems)," in Rubin and Tuden, eds., Comparative Perspectives, pp. 613-18.

318. _____. "Problems in the Theory of Slavery and Slave Society," Science and Society, 40, 1 (1976), pp. 3-27.

319. Palmer, Colin. "Slavery, Abolition, and Emancipation in the New World (review of Murray, Odious Commerce, Sharp, Slavery on the Spanish Frontier, and Levy, Emancipation, Sugar and Federalism)," Latin American Research Review, 17, 3 (1982), pp. 276-83.

320. Pan American Union. Seminar on Plantation Systems of the New World (San Juan, Puerto Rico, 1957). Washington, D.C.: Pan American Union Division of Social Science Development, 1959. (Social Science Monograph no. 7)

321. Patri, Aimé. "Dialectique du maître et de l'esclave," Le contrat social, 5, 4 (1961), pp. 231-35.

322. Patterson, Orlando. "On Slavery and Slave Formations," New Left Review, 117 (1979), pp. 31-67.

323. _____. "Recent Studies on Caribbean Slavery and the Atlantic Slave Trade (review of Craton, Searching for the Invisible Man, Higman, Slave Population and Economy in Jamaica, Klein, The Middle Passage, and others)," Latin American Research Review, 17, 3 (1982), pp. 251-75.

324. _____. "Slavery," Annual Review of Sociology, 3 (1977), pp. 407-49.

325. _____. Slavery and Social Death: A Comparative Study. Cambridge, Mass.: Harvard University Press, 1982.

326. _____. "The Socialization and Personality Structure of the Slave," in Comitas and Lowenthal, eds., Slaves, Free Men, Citizens, pp. 21-45. (Reprinted from Sociology of Slavery)

327. _____. "The Structural Origins of Slavery: A Critique of the Nieboer-Domar Hypothesis from a Comparative Perspective," in Rubin and Tuden, eds., Comparative Perspectives, pp. 12-34.

328. Pecirka, Jan. "Die sowjetischen Diskussionen über die asiatische Produktionsweise und über die Sklavenhalterformation," Eirene: Studia graeca et latina, 3 (1964), pp. 147-69.

329. Pescatello, Ann M. "The Afro-American in Historical Perspective," in idem, ed., Old Roots in New Lands, pp. 3-35.

330. _____, ed. The African in Latin America. New York: Knopf, 1975.

331. _____, ed. Old Roots in New Lands: Historical and Anthropological Perspectives on Black Experiences in the Americas. Westport, Conn.: Greenwood Press, 1977.

332. Pfaff-Giesberg, Robert. Geschichte der Sklaverei. Meisenheim: A. Hein, 1955.

333. _____. Die Sklaverei: ein wirtschaftliches, soziales und kulturelles Problem. Stuttgart: Strecker und Schröder, 1935.

334. *Pfister, Anne Marie. "Essai sur le code noir et la condition juridique des esclaves dans l'ancien droit française" (Thèse droit, Bordeaux, 1945).

335. *_____. "Le 'cimarrón' dans le Nouveau Monde" (Mémoire de maîtrise, Paris III, 1975).

336. Pipes, Daniel. "The Strategic Rationale for Military Slavery," Journal of Strategic Studies, 2, 1 (1979), pp. 34-46.

337. Piras, Giorgio. "Studi recenti sul problema storico della schiavitù," Storia contemporanea, 4, 2 (1973), pp. 345-59.

338. Plantation Society in the Americas: An Interdisciplinary Journal of Tropical and Subtropical History and Culture. Vol. 1, no. 1 (February, 1979).

339. Plimmer, Charlotte, and Denis Plimmer. Slavery: The Anglo-American Involvement. New York: Barnes and Noble, 1973.

340. Plumb, J. H. "Plantation Power," in In the Light of History (London: Penguin, 1972), pp. 114-22.

341. _____. "Slavery, Race, and the Poor," in idem, In the Light of History (London: Penguin, 1972), pp. 102-13.

342. Pollard, Leslie J. "Aging and Slavery: A Gerontological Perspective," Journal of Negro History, 66, 3 (1981), pp. 228-34.

343. Pollaud-Dulien, Marcel. Aujourd'hui l'esclavage: servitude et esclavage contemporains. Paris: Editions économie et humanisme, Les éditions ouvrières, 1967.

344. Postma, Johannes. "Research Tools and Resources," in Rubin and Tuden, eds., Comparative Perspectives, pp. 564-65.

345. Price, Richard. "Commentary (Slave Revolts)," in Rubin and Tuden, eds., Comparative Perspectives, pp. 495-500.

346. _____, ed. Maroon Societies: Rebel Slave Communities in the Americas. New York: Anchor Press, 1973. 2nd edition with a new afterword (Baltimore: Johns Hopkins University Press, 1979).

347. Pryor, Frederick L. "A Comparative Study of Slave Societies," Journal of Comparative Economics, 1, 1 (1977), pp. 25-49.

348. Puckrein, Gary. "Climate, Health, and Black Labor in the English Americas," Journal of American Studies, 13, 2 (1979), pp. 179-93.

349. Quéneuil, Henry. De la traite des noirs et de l'esclavage. La conférence de Bruxelles et ses résultats. Paris: L. Larose & L. Tenin, 1907.

350. Quinney, Valerie. "Decisions on Slavery, the Slave Trade, and Civil Rights for Negroes in the Early French Revolution," Journal of Negro History, 55, 2 (1970), pp. 117-30.

351. *Ravin, Anne Marie. "Le 'cimarron' dans le Nouveau Monde" (Thèse de maîtrise, Paris III, 1975).

352. Reed, Harry A. "Slavery in Ashanti and Colonial South Carolina," Black World, 20, 4 (1971), pp. 37-40.

353. Reuck, Anthony de, and Julie Knight, eds. Caste and Race:
     Comparative Approaches. London: Ciba Foundation, 1967.

354. Rice, C. Duncan. "Critique of the Eric Williams Thesis. The
     Anti-Slavery Interest and the Sugar Duties, 1841-1853," in Centre
     of African Studies, University of Edinburgh, Transatlantic Slave
     Trade, pp. 44-60.

355. _____. The Rise and Fall of Black Slavery. New York.
     Harper and Row, 1975.

356. Richardson, Patrick. Empire and Slavery. New York. Harper and Row,
     1968.

357. Riddell, William Renwick. "When Human Beings were Real Estate,"
     Canadian Magazine, 57 (1921), pp. 147-49.

358. Rodney, Walter. "Slavery and Underdevelopment," Historical
     Reflections/Réflexions historiques, 6, 1 (1979), pp. 275-86.
     Commentary by Orlando Patterson (pp. 287-92).

359. _____. "Upper Guinea and the Significance of the Origins
     of Africans Enslaved in the New World," Journal of Negro History,
     54, 4 (1969), pp. 327-45.

360. Romero, Patricia. "The Slave Traders' Images of Slaves," in Rubin
     and Tuden, eds., Comparative Perspectives, pp. 286-92.

361. Rubin, Vera, and Arthur Tuden, eds. Comparative Perspectives on
     Slavery in New World Plantation Societies (Annals of the New York
     Academy of Sciences, vol. 292). New York. New York Academy of
     Sciences, 1977.

362. Russell-Wood, A. J. R. "The Black Family in the Americas,"
     Societas, 8, 1 (1978), pp. 1-38.

363. Saco, José Antonio. Historia de la esclavitud de la raza africana
     en el Nuevo Mundo. Havana. Cultural S.A., 1938.

364. _____. Historia de la esclavitud de los Indios en el
     Nuevo Mundo. Havana. Cultural S.A., 1938.

365. _____. Historia de la esclavitud desde los tiempos
     más remotos hasta nuestros dias. Paris. Tipografía Lahure,
     1875-77. 2nd ed. 4 vols. Havana, 1936-45.

366. Salomon, Robert. L'esclavage en droit comparé juif et romain.
     Paris. Librairie E. Leroux, 1931.

367. Sanders, Ronald. Lost Tribes and Promised Lands. Boston. Little
     Brown, 1978.

368. Schapiro, Herbert. "Eugene Genovese, Marxism, and the Study of
     Slavery," Journal of Ethnic Studies, 9, 4 (1982), pp. 87-100.

369. Schmidt, Gerhard. "Slavery," Sociologia (São Paulo), 28, 2-3 (1966), pp. 173-92.

370. Schmitz, Mark D., and Donald F. Schaefer. "Slavery, Freedom, and the Elasticity of Substitution," Explorations in Economic History, 15, 3 (1978), pp. 327-37.

371. Schoelcher, Victor. Esclavage et colonisation. Paris: Presses Universitaires de France, 1948.

372. Schooler, Carmi. "Serfdom's Legacy: An Ethnic Continuum," American Journal of Sociology, 81, 6 (1976), pp. 1265-86.

373. Schuler, Monica. "Afro-American Slave Culture," Historical Reflections/ Réflexions historiques, 6, 1 (1979), pp. 121-37. Commentaries by Mary Karasch (pp. 138-40), Richard Price (pp. 141-49), Edward Kamau Brathwaite (pp. 150-56).

374. _____. "Commentary (Slave Images and Identities)," in Rubin and Tuden, eds., Comparative Perspectives, pp. 376-78.

375. Sewell, Richard H. "Slavery in the Americas: An Essay Review," Wisconsin Magazine of History, 51, 3 (1968), pp. 238-43.

376. Sheridan, Richard B. "'Sweet Malefactor': The Social Costs of Slavery and Sugar in Jamaica and Cuba, 1807-54," Economic History Review, 2nd ser., 29, 2 (1976), pp. 236-57.

377. Sherrard, Owen Aubrey. Freedom from Fear: The Slave and His Emancipation. London: The Bodley Head, 1959.

378. Shtaerman, Elena M. "Die ideologische Vorbereitung des Zusammenbruchs der Produktionsweise der Sklavereigesellschaft," Klio, 60, 2 (1978), pp. 225-34.

379. Siegel, Bernard J. "Some Methodological Considerations for a Comparative History of Slavery," American Anthropologist, 47, 3 (1945), pp. 357-92.

380. Simon, Kathleen. Slavery. London: Hodder and Stoughton, 1929.

381. Sio, Arnold. "Commentary (Social Institutions and Slave Societies)," in Rubin and Tuden, eds., Comparative Perspectives, pp. 284-85.

382. _____. "Interpretations of Slavery: The Slave Status in the Americas," Comparative Studies in Society and History, 7, 3 (1965), pp. 289-308. Reprinted in Foner and Genovese, eds., Slavery in the New World, pp. 96-112; Weinstein and Gatell, eds., American Negro Slavery (1st ed.), pp. 310-32. Also Bobbs-Merrill Reprint no. BC-274.

383. _____. "Society, Slavery and the Slaves (review article)," Social and Economic Studies, 16, 3 (1967), pp. 330-44.

384. Skidmore, Thomas E. "O Negro no Brasil e nos Estados Unidos," Argumento (Rio de Janeiro), 1, 1 (1973), pp. 25-45.

385. Slicher van Bath, B. H. "De historische demografie van Latijns Amerika. problemen en resultaten van onderzoek," Tijdschrift voor geschiedenis (Leiden), 92, 4 (1979), pp. 527-56.

386. Smith, G. W. "Slavery, Contentment, and Social Freedom," Philosophical Quarterly, 27 (no. 108)(1977), pp. 236-48.

387. Smith, John David. Black Slavery in the Americas. An Interdisciplinary Bibliography, 1865-1980. Westport, Conn.. Greenwood Press, 1982.

388. Smith, Michael G. "Slavery and Emancipation in Two Societies," Social and Economic Studies, 3, 3-4 (1954), pp. 239-90. Reprinted in idem, ed., The Plural Society in the British West Indies (Berkeley. University of California Press, 1965), pp. 116-61.

389. Smith, Roland M. "The Comparative Approach to the Study of Slavery," Black Lives, 2 (1972), pp. 39-46.

390. Steckel, Richard H. "Slave Marriage and the Family," Journal of Family History, 5, 4 (1980), pp. 406-21.

391. Steger, Hanns-Albert. "Revolutionäre Hintergründe des kreolischen Synkretismus," Internationales Jahrbuch für Religions-Soziologie, 6 (1970), pp. 99-141.

392. Stevens, William. The Slave in History. London, 1904.

393. Symposium on Caste and Race. Comparative Approaches (London, 1966). Anthony de Reuck and Julie Knight, eds. London. Ciba Foundation, 1967.

394. Sypher, Wylie. Guinea's Captive Kings. British Antislavery Literature of the Eighteenth Century. New York. Octagon Books, 1969.

395. Szabó, I. "Serfdom - Peasantry - Concept, Terminology, Social Structure," Ethnografia, 76, 1 (1965), pp. 10-31. (In Hungarian with Russian and English summaries)

396. Tannenbaum, Frank. "A Note on the Economic Interpretation of History," Political Science Quarterly, 61, 2 (1946), pp. 247-53.

397. _____. Slave and Citizen. The Negro in the Americas. New York. Knopf, 1947.

398. Taylor, Sally. "Marx and Greeley on Slavery and Labor," Journalism History, 6, 4 (1979-80), pp. 103-06.

399. Temperley, Howard. "Capitalism, Slavery, and Ideology," Past and Present, 75 (1977), pp. 94-118.

400. _____. "The Ideology of Antislavery," in Walvin and Eltis, eds., Abolition of the Atlantic Slave Trade, pp. 21-36.

401. Thomas, John I. "Historical Antecedents and Impact of Blacks on the Indigenous White Population of Brazil and the American South, 1500-1800," Ethnohistory, 19, 2 (1972), pp. 147-69.

402. Thompson, Edgar. "The Plantation" (PhD diss., University of Chicago, 1932).

403. *Thompson, Vincent. The African Diaspora. 2 vols. London. Longmans, forthcoming.

404. Thorpe, Earle E. "Chattel Slavery and Concentration Camps," Negro History Bulletin, 25, 8 (1962), pp. 171-76. Reprinted in Lane, ed., Debate Over Slavery, pp. 23-42, Bracey, Meier, and Rudwick, eds., American Negro Slavery, pp. 86-98.

405. Thurnwald, R. "Sklave," in Max Ebert, ed., Reallexikon der Vorgeschichte (Berlin. W. de Grueyter, 1924-32), vol. 12, pp. 209-28.

406. Tomich, Dale. "Original Accumulation, Colonial Slavery, and the Transition from Feudalism to Capitalism" (Unpublished paper, Binghamton, New York, 1981).

407. Töpfer, Bernhard. "Zur Problematik der vorkapitalistischen Klassengesellschaften," Jahrbuch für Wirtschaftsgeschichte (1967), pt. 4, pp. 259-86.

408. Toplin, R. Brent, ed. Slavery and Race Relations in Latin America. Westport, Conn.. Greenwood Press, 1974.

409. Turbet-Delof, Guy. "Un texte antiesclavagiste publié en 1689," Les cahiers de Tunisie, 16 (1968), pp. 111-18.

410. Turner, Lorenzo D. "African Survivals in the New World with Special Emphasis on the Arts," in John A. Davis, ed., Africa Seen by American Negroes (Paris. Présence Africaine, 1958), pp. 101-16. Reprinted in Haynes, ed., Blacks in White America, pp. 63-76.

411. Verlinden, Charles. "Esclavitud medieval en Europa y esclavitud colonial en América," Revista de la Universidad Nacional de Córdoba. Homenaje a Monseñor P. Cabrera (1958), vol. 1, pp. 177-91. Translated as "Esclavage médiéval en Europe et esclavage colonial en Amérique," Cahiers de l'Institut des hautes études de l'Amérique latine, 6 (1964), pp. 27-45. Also as "Medieval Slavery in Europe and Colonial Slavery in America," in idem, The Beginnings of Modern Colonization (trans. Yvonne Freccero) (Ithaca. Cornell University Press, 1970), pp. 33-51.

412. _____. "Les origines coloniales de la civilisation atlantique. antécédents et types de structure," Cahiers d'histoire mondiale/Journal of World History, 1, 2 (1953), pp. 378-98.

413. _____. "Précédents et parallèles européens de l'esclavage colonial," O Instituto. Revista científica e literária (Coimbra), 113 (1949), pp. 113-53.

414. _____. "Le problème de la continuité en histoire coloniale. de la colonisation médiévale à la colonisation moderne," Revista de Indias, 11 (nos. 43-44)(1951), pp. 219-36.

415. Vignols, Léon. "Etudes négrières de 1774 à 1928," Revue d'histoire économique et sociale, 16, 1 (1928), pp. 5-11.

416. Vila Vilar, Enriqueta. "Conferencias sobre la esclavitud en conmemoración de la Independencia de los Estados Unidos, Nueva York, 24-27 de mayo de 1976," Historiografía y bibliografía americanistas, 19-20 (1975-76), pp. 171-75.

417. Wagley, Charles. "Plantation-America. A Culture Sphere," in Vera Rubin, ed., Caribbean Studies. A Symposium (Seattle, 1960)(Seattle. University of Washington Press, 1960), pp. 3-13. Also Bobbs-Merrill Reprint no. BC-306.

418. Walvin, James. "The Impact of Slavery on British Radical Politics. 1787-1838," in Rubin and Tuden, eds., Comparative Perspectives, pp. 343-55.

419. _____. "The Public Campaign in England against Slavery, 1787-1834," in Walvin and Eltis, eds., Abolition of the Atlantic Slave Trade, pp. 63-82.

420. _____. Slavery and the Slave Trade. A Short Illustrated History. Jackson. University Press of Mississippi, 1983.

421. _____, ed. Slavery and British Society, 1780-1846. London. Macmillan, 1981.

422. Watson, James L. "Slavery as an Institution, Open and Closed Systems," in Watson, ed., Asian and African Systems of Slavery, pp. 1-15.

423. _____, ed. Asian and African Systems of Slavery. Berkeley and Los Angeles. University of California Press, 1980.

424. Wax, Darold D. "Whither the Comparative History of Slavery?" Virginia Magazine of History and Biography, 80, 1 (1972), pp. 85-93.

425. Wendel, Hugo C. M. "The Attitude of the Church Toward Slavery," Lutheran Church Review, 30, 2 (1911), pp. 352-64.

426. Werner, Ernst. "De l'esclavage à la féodalité. la périodisation de l'histoire mondiale," Annales. économies, sociétés, civilisations, 17, 5 (1962), pp. 930-39.

427. Whitman, Daniel. "Slavery and the Rights of Frenchmen: View of Montesquieu, Rousseau, and Raynal," French Colonial Studies, 1 (1977), pp. 17-33.

428. Williams, Eric. Capitalism and Slavery. Chapel Hill, N.C.: University of North Carolina Press, 1944.

429. _____. "The Origin of Negro Slavery," in Frucht, eds., Black Society in the New World, pp. 3-25. (Reprinted from Capitalism and Slavery)

430. Williams, Eric Eustace. "The Blackest Thing in Slavery Was Not The Black Man," Revista/Review Interamericana, 3, 1 (1973), pp. 1-23.

431. Williams, Mary M. "The Treatment of Negro Slaves in the Brazilian Empire: A Comparison with the United States of America," Journal of Negro History, 15, 2 (1930), pp. 315-36.

432. Wilson, William J. "Slavery, Paternalism and White Hegemony," American Journal of Sociology, 81, 5 (1976), pp. 1190-98.

433. Wimmer, Wolfgang. Die Sklaven: Herr und Knecht - Eine Sozialgeschichte mit Gegenwart. Hamburg: Rowohlt, 1979.

434. Winks, Robin W., ed. Slavery: A Comparative Perspective: Readings on Slavery from Ancient Times to the Present. New York: New York University Press, 1972.

435. Woodward, C. Vann. "Protestant Slavery in a Catholic World," in American Counterpoint, pp. 47-77.

436. Work, Monroe Nathan. A Bibliography of the Negro in Africa and America. New York: H. W. Wilson, 1928.

437. Wright, David. Slavery, Abolition and Emancipation: Black Slaves and the British Empire: A Thematic Documentary. New York, 1976.

438. Wyatt-Brown, Bertram. "Stanley Elkins' Slavery: The Antislavery Interpretation Reexamined," American Quarterly, 25, 2 (1973), pp. 154-76.

439. Yeo, Cedric A. "The Economics of Roman and American Slavery," Finanz-archiv, 13, 3 (1951-52), pp. 445-85.

440. Zavala, Silvio Arturo. Servidumbre natural y libertad cristiana, según los tratadistas españoles de los siglos XVI y XVII. Buenos Aires, 1944. (Publicaciones del Instituto de investigaciones historicas, no. 87)

II. North America

1. General and comparative

441. "Absentee Ownership of Slaves in the United States in 1830," Journal of Negro History, 9, 2 (1924), pp. 196-231.

442. Aitken, Hugh G. J., ed. Did Slavery Pay? Readings in the Economics of Black Slavery in the United States. Boston: Houghton-Mifflin, 1971.

443. Allen, Cuthbert Edward. "The Slavery Question in Catholic Newspapers, 1850-1865," Historical Records and Studies: U.S. Catholic Historical Society, 26 (1936), pp. 99-169.

444. Anderson, James D. "Aunt Jemima in Dialectics: Genovese on Slave Culture (review essay on Roll, Jordan, Roll)," Journal of Negro History, 61, 1 (1976), pp. 99-114.

445. _____. "Political and Scholarly Interests in the 'Negro Personality': A Review of The Slave Community," in Gilmore, ed., Revisiting Blassingame's The Slave Community, pp. 123-34.

446. Aptheker, Herbert. "Additional Data on American Maroons," Journal of Negro History, 32, 4 (1947), pp. 452-60.

447. _____. American Negro Slave Revolts. New York: Columbia University Press, 1943.

448. _____. "Commentary (Slave Revolts)," in Rubin and Tuden, eds., Comparative Perspectives, pp. 491-94.

449. _____. "Maroons within the Present Limits of the United States," Journal of Negro History, 24, 2 (1939), pp. 167-84.

450. Asch, Michael I. "Social Context and the Musical Analysis of Slavery Drum Dance Songs," Ethnomusicology, 19, 2 (1975), pp. 245-57.

451. Aufhauser, R. Keith. "Slavery and Scientific Management," Journal of Economic History, 33, 4 (1973), pp. 811-24.

452. Auping, J. "The Relative Efficiency of Evangelical Non-Violence: The Influence of a Revival of Religion on the Abolition of Slavery in North America, 1740-1865" (Soc. D., Pontificia Universitas Gregoriana, Rome, 1977).

453. Bailey, David Thomas. "A Divided Prism: Two Sources of Black Testimony on Slavery," Journal of Southern History, 46, 3 (1980), pp. 381-404.

454. Balme, Joshua Rhodes. American States, Churches and Slavery. New York: Negro Universities Press, 1969.

455. Bartlett, Irving H., and Richard L. Schoenwald. "The Psychodynamics of Slavery (review of Thorpe, The Old South: A Psychohistory)," Journal of Interdisciplinary History, 4, 4 (1974), pp. 627-33.

456. Bassett, Victor H. "Plantation Medicine," Journal of the Medical Association of Georgia, 29, 3 (1940), pp. 112-22.

457. Bateman, Fred, and Thomas Weiss. A Deplorable Scarcity: The Failure of Industrialization in the Slave Economy. Chapel Hill: University of North Carolina Press, 1981.

458. Bauer, Raymond A., and Alice H. Bauer. "Day to Day Resistance to Slavery," Journal of Negro History, 27, 4 (1942), pp. 388-419. Reprinted in Herbert Gutman and Gregory Kealey, eds., Many Pasts: Readings in American Social History (Englewood Cliffs, N.J.: Prentice-Hall, 1973), vol. 1, pp. 319-41; in Bracey, Meier, and Rudwick, eds., American Slavery, pp. 37-60; in Rose, ed., Americans from Africa, vol. 2, pp. 5-29; in Haynes, ed., Blacks in White America Before 1865, pp. 235-59. Also Bobbs-Merrill Reprint no. BC-19.

459. Bean, Richard N., and Robert P. Thomas. "The Adoption of Slave Labor in British America," in Gemery and Hogendorn, eds., Uncommon Market, pp. 377-98.

460. Bean, William G. "An Aspect of Know Nothingism - The Immigrant and Slavery," South Atlantic Quarterly, 23, 4 (1929), pp. 319-34.

461. Belin, H. E. "A Southern View of Slavery," American Journal of Sociology, 13, 4 (1908), pp. 513-22.

462. Berlin, Ira. "The Revolution in Black Life," in Alfred F. Young, ed., The American Revolution: Explorations in the History of American Radicalism (Dekalb, Ill.: Northern Illinois University Press, 1976), pp. 349-82.

463. _____. "Time, Space, and the Evolution of Afro-American Society on British Mainland North America," American Historical Review, 85, 1 (1980), pp. 44-78.

464. _____, and Ronald Hoffman, eds. Slavery and Freedom in the Age of the American Revolution. Charlottesville: University of Virginia Press, 1983.

465. Berquist, Harold E., Jr. "Henry Middleton and the Arbitrament of the Anglo-American Slave Controversy by Tsar Alexander I," South Carolina Historical Magazine, 82, 1 (1981), pp. 20-31.

466. Berry, Mary Frances. "The Slave Community: A Review of Reviews," in Gilmore, ed., Revisiting Blassingame's The Slave Community, pp. 3-16.

467. _____, and John W. Blassingame. "African Slavery and the Roots of Contemporary Black Culture," Massachusetts Review, 18, 3 (1977), pp. 501-16.

468. Berwanger, Eugene H. The Frontier Against Slavery: Western Anti-Negro Prejudice and the Slavery Expansion Controversy. Urbana: University of Illinois Press, 1967.

469. _____, ed. As They Saw Slavery. Minneapolis: Winston Press, 1973.

470. Billings, Warren M. "The Legal Treatment of Slavery in Early America (review of Higginbotham, In the Matter of Color)," Plantation Society in the Americas, 1, 2 (1979), pp. 265-71.

471. Blassingame, John W. "Redefining The Slave Community: A Response to the Critics," in Gilmore, ed., Revisiting Blassingame's The Slave Community, pp. 135-68.

472. _____. "(Review of Genovese, Roll, Jordan, Roll)," Journal of Social History, 9, 3 (1976), pp. 403-09.

473. _____. "Sambos and Rebels: The Character of the Southern Slave," in Lorraine A. Williams, ed., Africa and the Afro-American Experience (Washington, D.C.: Howard University Press, 1981), pp. 149-66.

474. _____. "Using the Testimony of Ex-Slaves: Approaches and Problems," Journal of Southern History, 41, 4 (1975), pp. 473-92. Reprinted as an appendix in Gilmore, ed., Revisiting Blassingame's The Slave Community, pp. 169-94.

475. _____, ed. Slave Testimony: Two Centuries of Letters, Interviews, and Autobiographies. Baton Rouge: Louisiana State University Press, 1977.

476. Boller, Paul F., Jr. "Washington, the Quakers, and Slavery," Journal of Negro History, 46, 2 (1961), pp. 83-88.

477. Bonacich, Edna. "Abolition, the Extension of Slavery, and the Position of Free Blacks: A Study of Split Labor Markets in the United States, 1830-1863," American Journal of Sociology, 81, 3 (1975), pp. 601-28.

478. Boney, F. Nash. "Assessments of Some Recent Works in Black History: The Continuing Slavery Debate: An Essay Review (of Fogel and Engerman, Time on the Cross)," Georgia Historical Quarterly, 58, 4 (1974), pp. 409-13.

479. _____. "The South's Peculiar Institution," Louisiana Studies, 12, 4 (1973), pp. 565-77.

480. Bontemps, Arna W. Great Slave Narratives. Boston: Beacon Press, 1969.

481. Boritt, G. S. "The Voyage to the Colony of Linconia: The Sixteenth President, Black Colonization, and the Defense Mechanism of Avoidance," Historian, 37, 4 (1975), pp. 619-32.

482. Botkin, B. A., ed. Lay My Burden Down: A Folk History of Slavery. Chicago: University of Chicago Press, 1945.

483. Bracey, John H., Jr., August Meier, and Elliott Rudwick, eds. American Slavery: The Question of Resistance. Belmont, Cal.: Wadsworth, 1971.

484. Brand, Norman E. "Power in the Blood: The Polemics of the Fugitive Slave Narrative" (PhD diss., Arizona State University, 1972).

485. Breeden, James O., ed. Advice Among Masters: The Ideal in Slave Management in the Old South. Westport, Conn.: Greenwood Press, 1980.

486. Brown, Richard D., ed. Slavery in American Society. New York: Heath, 1969. (Problems in American Civilization Series)

487. Bruce, Dickson D., Jr. "Racial Fear and the Proslavery Argument: A Rhetorical Approach," Mississippi Quarterly, 33, 4 (1980), pp. 461-78.

488. Bryce-Laporte, Roy Simon. "The American Slave Plantation and our Heritage of Communal Deprivation," American Behavioral Scientist, 12, 4 (1969), pp. 2-8. Reprinted in Norman R. Yetman and C. Hoy Steele, eds., Majority and Minority: The Dynamics of Race and Ethnic Relations (Boston: Allyn and Bacon, 1975), pp. 184-91.

489. _____. "The Slave Plantation: Background to Present Conditions of Urban Blacks," in Peter Orleans and William Russell Ellis, Jr., eds., Race, Change, and Urban Society (Urban Affairs Annual Review), 5 (1971), pp. 257-84. *Reprinted in Edgar G. Epps, ed., Race Relations: Current Perspectives (Cambridge, Mass.: Winthrop Publishers, forthcoming. Excerpted in Robert K. Yin, ed., Race, Creed, Color, or National Origin (Washington, D.C.: F. E. Peacock, 1973), pp. 148-54.

490. Bullock, Henry Allen. "A Hidden Passage in the Slave Regime," in Curtis and Gould, eds., Black Experience, pp. 3-32.

491. Burnham, Dorothy. "The Life of the Afro-American Woman in Slavery," International Journal of Women's Studies, 1, 4 (1978), pp. 363-77.

492. Cade, John B. "Out of the Mouths of Ex-Slaves," Journal of Negro History, 20, 3 (1935), pp. 294-337.

493. Calhoun, Daniel. "Call to Quarters: A Review Essay (of Genovese, Roll, Jordan, Roll)," Agricultural History, 49, 2 (1975), pp. 448-54.

494. Campbell, Penelope. Maryland in Africa: The Maryland State Colonization Society, 1831-1857. Urbana: University of Illinois Press, 1971.

495. Cardell, Nicholas Scott, and Mark Myron Hopkins. "The Effect of Milk Intolerance on the Consumption of Milk by Slaves in 1860," Journal of Interdisciplinary History, 8, 3 (1978), pp. 507-13.

496. Carper, N. Gordon. "Slavery Re-visited: Peonage in the South," Phylon, 37, 1 (1976), pp. 85-99.

497. Carroll, Joseph C. Slave Insurrections in the United States, 1800-1865. Boston: Chapman and Grimes, 1938.

498. Carstensen, Fred V., and S. E. Goodman. "Trouble on the Auction Block: Interregional Slave Sales and the Reliability of a Linear Equation," Journal of Interdisciplinary History, 8, 2 (1977), pp. 315-18.

499. Carter, Ralph D. "Slavery and the Climate of Opinion," in Gilmore, ed., Revisiting Blassingame's The Slave Community, pp. 70-95.

500. Cassity, Michael J. "Slaves, Families, and 'Living Space': A Note on Evidence and Historical Context," Southern Studies, 17, 2 (1978), pp. 209-15.

501. Catterall, Helen T., ed. Judicial Cases Concerning American Slavery and the Negro. 5 vols. Washington, D.C.: Carnegie Institute of Washington, 1926-37. (Papers of the Division of Historical Research, no. 374)

502. Caulfield, Mina Davis. "Slavery and the Origins of Black Culture: Elkins Revisited," in Rose, ed., Americans from Africa, vol. 1, pp. 171-93.

503. Chambers, William. American Slavery and Colour. New York: Negro Universities Press, 1968.

504. Chapman, Abraham, comp. Steal Away: Stories of the Runaway Slaves. New York: Praeger, 1971.

505. Cheek, William F., ed. Black Resistance Before the Civil War. Beverly Hills, Cal.: Glencoe Press, 1970.

506. Cimbala, Paul A. "Fortunate Bondsmen: Black 'Musicianers' and Their Role as an Antebellum Southern Plantation Slave Elite," Southern Studies, 18, 3 (1979), pp. 291-303.

507. Clinton, Catherine. "The Plantation Mistress: Another Side of Southern Slavery, 1780-1835" (PhD diss., Princeton University, 1980).

508. Cocke, Margaret Ritchie Harrison. "Sir Joseph de Courcy Laffan's Views on Slavery," William and Mary Quarterly, 2nd ser., 19, 1 (1939), pp. 42-48.

509. Collins, Bruce. "American Slavery and its Consequences," Historical Journal, 22, 4 (1979), pp. 997-1015.

510. "A Colloquium on Herbert Gutman's The Black Family in Slavery and Freedom, 1750-1925," Social Science History, 3, 3-4 (1979), pp. 45-85.

511. Colp, Ralph, Jr. "Charles Darwin: Slavery and the American Civil War," Harvard Library Bulletin, 26, 4 (1978), pp. 471-89.

512. Conway, Alan. "Slavery in the United States," Historical News (Christchurch, New Zealand), 35 (1977), pp. 1-6.

513. Cooper, William J. The South and the Politics of Slavery. Baton Rouge: Louisiana State University Press, 1978.

514. Cottrol, Robert J. "Comparative Slave Studies: Urban Slavery as a Model, Travelers' Accounts as a Source - Bibliographical Essay," Journal of Black Studies, 8, 1 (1977), pp. 3-12.

515. _____, and Raymond T. Diamond. "(Review of Higginbotham, In the Matter of Color)", Tulane Law Review, 56, 3 (1982), pp. 1107-23.

516. Cowdrey, Albert E. "Slave into Soldier," History Today, 20, 10 (1970), pp. 704-15.

517. Crane, Verner W. "Benjamin Franklin on Slavery and American Liberties," Pennsylvania Magazine of History and Biography, 62, 1 (1938), pp. 1-11.

518. Crawford, Stephen Cooban. "Quantified Memory: A Study of the WPA and Fisk University Slave Narrative Collections" (PhD diss., University of Chicago, 1980).

519. Crowe, Charles. "Historians and 'Benign Neglect': Conservative Trends in Southern History and Black Studies," Reviews in American History, 2, 2 (1974), pp. 163-72.

520. _____. "Slavery, Ideology, and 'Cliometrics'," Technology and Culture, 17, 2 (1976), pp. 271-85.

521. _____. "Time on the Cross: The Historical Monograph as a Pop Event," History Teacher, 9, 4 (1976), pp. 588-630.

522. Curtis, James C., and Lewis L. Gould, eds. The Black Experience in America: Selected Essays. Austin: University of Texas Press, 1970.

523. Daniel, Pete. "The Metamorphosis of Slavery, 1865-1900," Journal of American History, 66, 1 (1979), pp. 88-99.

524. Daniel, W. Harrison. "Southern Presbyterians and the Negro in the Early National Period," Journal of Negro History, 58, 3 (1973), pp. 291-312.

525. Daniels, Winthrop More. "The Slave Plantation in Retrospect," Atlantic Monthly, 107 (1911), pp. 363-69.

526. *David, Paul A. "Child Care in the Slave Quarters: Critical Notes on Some Uses of Demography in Time on the Cross" (Research memorandum, Stanford Center for Research in Economic Growth, 1975, unpublished).

527. _____, Herbert G. Gutman, Richard Sutch, Peter Temin, and Gavin Wright, with an introduction by Kenneth Stampp. Reckoning with Slavery: A Critical Study in the Quantitative History of American Negro Slavery. New York: Oxford University Press, 1976.

528. _____, and Peter Temin. "Capitalist Masters, Bourgeois Slaves," in David, et al., Reckoning with Slavery, pp. 33-54.

529. _____. "The Relative Efficiency of Slave Agriculture: Comment," American Economic Review, 69, 1 (1979), pp. 213-18.

530. _____. "Slavery: The Progressive Institution?" Journal of Economic History, 34, 3 (1974), pp. 739-83. Reprinted in David, et al., Reckoning with Slavery, pp. 165-230.

531. _____. "Time on the Cross: Two Views, Capitalist Masters, Bourgeois Slaves," Journal of Interdisiplinary History, 5, 3 (1975), pp. 445-57.

532. David, Paul A., et al. "Time on the Cross and the Burden of Quantitative History," in idem, Reckoning with Slavery, pp. 339-57.

533. Davies, Charles Huntington. From Slavery to Freedom. Aurora, Ill.: Press of C. B. Phillips (published by the author), 1900.

534. Davis, Angela. "Reflections on the Black Woman's Role in the Community of Slaves," Black Scholar, 3, 9 (1971), pp. 2-15.

535. Davis, David Brion. "American Slavery and the American Revolution," in Berlin and Hoffman, eds., Slavery and Freedom in the Age of the American Revolution, pp. 262-80.

536. _____. "Slavery and the American Mind," in Owens, ed., _Perspectives and Irony_, pp. 51-69.

537. Davis, Thomas J. "Slave Testimony: A Review Essay and a Bibliography," _Afro-Americans in New York Life and History_, 3, 1 (1979), pp. 73-85.

538. "Un débat historiographique: l'esclavage aux Etats-Unis," _Bulletin de la Société de l'histoire moderne_, 18 (1977), pp. 8-17.

539. Degler, Carl N. "Discussions of New Books: Freedom After Slavery (review of Litwack, _Been in the Storm So Long_)," _Virginia Quarterly Review_, 56, 2 (1980), pp. 344-56.

540. _____. "The Irony of American Negro Slavery," in Owens, ed., _Perspectives and Irony_, pp. 3-35.

541. _____. "Slavery and the Genesis of American Race Prejudice," _Comparative Studies in Society and History_, 2, 1 (1959), pp. 49-66. Reprinted in Noel, ed., _Origins of American Slavery and Racism_, pp. 59-80; in Martin, ed., _Interpreting Colonial America_, pp. 141-58; in Meier and Rudwick, eds., _Making of Black America_, pp. 91-108. Also Bobbs-Merill Reprint no. H-355.

542. _____. "Starr on Slavery," _Journal of Economic History_, 19, 2 (1959), pp. 271-77.

543. DeJong, Gerald Francis. "The Dutch Reformed Church and Negro Slavery in Colonial America," _Church History_, 40, 4 (1971), pp. 423-36.

544. Dew, Charles B. "The Sambo and Nat Turner in Everyslave: A Review of _Roll, Jordan, Roll_," _Civil War History_, 21, 3 (1975), pp. 261-68.

545. Dickson, Bruce D., Jr. "The 'John and Old Master Stories' and the World of Slavery: A Study in Folktales and History," _Phylon_, 35, 4 (1974), pp. 418-29.

546. Dinkins, James. "Negroes as Slaves," _Southern Historical Society Papers_, 35 (1907), pp. 60-68.

547. Dorman, James H. "Time on the Cross While Jordan Rolled: America's Peculiar Institution and its Recent Historians," _Revue de Louisiane/Louisiana Review_, 4, 1 (1975), pp. 59-77.

548. _____, and Robert R. Jones. _The Afro-American Experience: A Cultural History Through Emancipation_. New York: Wiley, 1974.

549. Dover, Cedric. "The Manual Arts," in Newton and Lewis, eds., _The Other Slaves_, pp. 221-25.

550. Dubois, W. E. B. "The African Artisan," in Newton and Lewis, eds., _The Other Slaves_, pp. 171-74.

551. _____. "The Ante-Bellum Negro Artisan," in Newton and Lewis, eds., The Other Slaves, pp. 175-82.

552. Duff, John B., and Larry A. Greene, eds. Slavery, Its Origin and Legacy. New York: Crowell, 1975.

553. Early, Gerald Lyn. "'A Servant of Servants Shall He Be . . . ': Paternalism and Millennialism in American Slavery Literature, 1850-59" (PhD diss., Cornell University, 1982).

554. Eblen, Jack E. "Growth of the Black Population in Ante Bellum America, 1820-1860," Population Studies, 26, 2 (1972), pp. 273-89.

555. _____. "New Estimates of the Vital Rates of the United States Black Population During the Nineteenth Century," Demography, 11, 2 (1974), pp. 301-20. Reprinted in Maris A. Vinovskis, ed., Studies in American Historical Demography (New York: Academic Press, 1979), pp. 339-57.

556. "The Econometrics of Slavery: A Symposium (reviews of Fogel and Engerman, Time on the Cross by Bertram Wyatt-Brown, pp. 457-65; William N. Parker, pp. 466-74; Stephen DeCanio, pp. 474-87)," Reviews in American History, 2, 4 (1974), pp. 457-87.

557. Egnal, Marc. "American Slavery: The Newer Exegesis (review of Fogel and Engerman, Time on the Cross and Genovese, Roll, Jordan, Roll)," Canadian Review of American Studies, 6, 1 (1975), pp. 110-17.

558. Ehrlich, Walter. They Have No Rights: Dred Scott's Struggle for Freedom. Westport, Conn.: Greenwood Press, 1979.

559. Elbert, Sarah. "Good Times on the Cross: A Marxian Review," Review of Radical Political Economics, 7, 3 (1975), pp. 55-66.

560. Elkins, Stanley M. "Slavery," in Haynes, ed., Blacks in White America Before 1865, pp. 203-13. (From Slavery: A Problem in American Institutional and Intellectual Life)

561. _____. "Slavery and Negro Personality," in Rose, ed., Americans from Africa, vol. 1, pp. 131-54.

562. _____. "The Slavery Debate," Commentary, 60, 6 (1975), pp. 40-54.

563. _____. "The Social Consequences of Slavery," in Huggins and Kilson, eds., Key Issues in the Afro-American Experience, vol. 1, pp. 138-53.

564. Emmer, P. C. "Proletariaat of kleine bourgeoisie? Nieuwe literatuur over de slavernij in de V.S.," Tijdschrift voor Geschiedenis, 91, 2 (1978), pp. 263-69.

565. Engelder, Conrad James. "The Churches and Slavery: A Study of the Attitudes Toward Slavery of the Major Protestant Denominations" (PhD diss., University of Michigan, 1964).

566. Engerman, Stanley L. "The Effects of Slavery Upon the Southern Economy: A Review of the Recent Debate," Explorations in Entrepreneurial History, 2nd ser., 4, 2 (1967), pp. 71–97.

567. _____. "The Heights of Slaves in the United States," Local Population Studies, 16 (1976), pp. 45–49.

568. _____. "Introduction (to the Special Issue on Colonial Slavery)," Southern Studies, 16, 4 (1977), pp. 347–54.

569. _____. "Marxist Economic Studies of the Slave South," Marxist Perspectives, 1, 1 (1978), pp. 148–64.

570. _____. "Reconsidering The Slave Community," in Gilmore, ed., Revisiting Blassingame's The Slave Community, pp. 96–110.

571. _____. "Slavery as an Obstacle to Economic Growth in the United States: A Panel Discussion," Journal of Economic History, 27, 4 (1967), pp. 518–60. (Panel members: Alfred H. Conrad, Douglas Dowd, Stanley Engerman, Eli Ginzberg, Charles Kelso, John R. Meyer, Harry N. Scheiber, Richard Sutch)

572. _____. "The Southern Slave Economy," in Owens, ed., Perspectives and Irony, pp. 71–101.

573. _____, and Robert W. Fogel. "The Relative Efficiency of Slavery: A Comparison of Northern and Southern Agriculture in 1860," Explorations in Economic History, 8, 3 (1971), pp. 353–67.

574. Eppes, Susan Bradford. The Negro of the Old South: A Bit of Period History. Chicago: Joseph G. Branch, 1925.

575. Escott, Paul D. "Jefferson Davis and Slavery in the Territories," Journal of Mississippi History, 39, 2 (1977), pp. 97–116.

576. _____. "Reflections on Slavery Remembered," North Carolina Historical Review, 57, 2 (1980), pp. 178–85.

577. _____. Slavery Remembered: A Record of Twentieth-Century Slave Narratives. Chapel Hill: University of North Carolina Press, 1979.

578. Essig, James D. "Connecticut Ministers and Slavery, 1790–1795," Journal of American Studies, 15, 1 (1981), pp. 27–44.

579. Evans, Robert, Jr. "The Economics of American Negro Slavery," in National Bureau of Economic Research, Aspects of Labor Economics (Princeton: Princeton University Press, 1962), pp. 185–256.

580. Fairbanks, Charles H. "Spaniards, Planters, Ships and Slaves: Historical Archaeology in Florida and Georgia," Archaeology, 29, 3 (1976), pp. 164-72.

581. Farley, Ena L. "The Fugitive Slave Law of 1850 Revisited," Western Journal of Black Studies, 3, 2 (1979), pp. 110-15.

582. Farley, Reynolds. "The Demographic Rates and Social Institutions of the Nineteenth-Century Negro Population: A Stable Population Analysis," Demography, 2 (1965), pp. 386-98.

583. Fehrenbacher, Don E. Slavery, Law, and Politics: The Dred Scott Case in Historical Perspective. New York: Oxford University Press, 1981.

584. Feldstein, Stanley. Once a Slave: The Slave's View of Slavery. New York: W. Morrow, 1971.

585. _____. "The Slave's View of Slavery" (PhD diss., New York University, 1969).

586. Filler, Louis. Slavery in the United States of America. New York: Van Nostrand, 1972.

587. Finkelman, Paul. An Imperfect Union: Slavery, Federalism, and Comity. Chapel Hill: University of North Carolina Press, 1981.

588. _____. "The Peculiar Laws of the Peculiar Institution (review-essay of Tushnet, American Law of Slavery)," Reviews in American History, 10, 3 (1982), pp. 358-65.

589. _____. "Prigg v. Pennsylvania and Northern Courts: Anti-Slavery Use of a Pro-Slavery Decision," Civil War History, 25, 1 (1979), pp. 5-35.

590. Fishel, Leslie H., Jr., and Benjamin Quarles. The Black American: A Documentary History. Glenview, Ill.: Scott, Foresman, 1976.

591. Fisher, Walter. "Physicians and Slavery in the Antebellum Southern Medical Journal," Journal of the History of Medicine and Allied Sciences, 23, 1 (1968), pp. 36-49. Reprinted in Meier and Rudwick, eds., Making of Black America, pp. 153-64.

592. Flanigan, Daniel J. "The Criminal Law of Slavery and Freedom, 1800-1868" (PhD diss., Rice University, 1973).

593. _____. "Criminal Procedure in Slave Trials in the Antebellum South," Journal of Southern History, 40, 4 (1974), pp. 537-64.

594. Fleissig, Heywood. "Slavery, the Supply of Agricultural Labor and the Industrialization of the South," Journal of Economic History, 36, 3 (1976), pp. 572-97.

595. Fleming, John E. "Slavery, Civil War and Reconstruction: Black Women in Microcosm," Negro History Bulletin, 38, 6 (1975), pp. 430–33.

596. Flusche, Michael. "Joel Chandler Harris and the Folklore of Slavery," Journal of American Studies, 9, 3 (1975), pp. 347–63.

597. Fogel, Robert W., and Stanley L. Engerman. "The Economics of Slavery," in Fogel and Engerman, eds., Reinterpretation, pp. 311–41.

598. _____. "Philanthropy at Bargain Prices: Notes on the Economics of Gradual Emancipation," Journal of Legal Studies, 3, 2 (1974), pp. 377–401.

599. _____. Time on the Cross: The Economics of American Negro Slavery. 2 vols. Boston: Little, Brown, 1974.

600. _____, eds. The Reinterpretation of American Economic History. New York: Harper and Row, 1971.

601. Fohlen, Claude. "L'esclavage aux Etats–Unis: divergences et convergences," Revue historique, 257, 2 (1977), pp. 345–60.

602. _____. Les noirs aux Etats–Unis. Paris: Presses Universitaires de France, 1972.

603. Foner, Eric. "Redefining the Past (review essay on Fogel and Engerman, Time on the Cross)," Labor History, 16, 1 (1975), pp. 127–38.

604. _____. "Symposium on Roll, Jordan, Roll: Introductory Note," Radical History Review, 3, 4 (1976), pp. 26–28.

605. Foner, Philip. History of Black Americans From Africa to the Emergence of the Cotton Kingdom. Westport, Conn.: Greenwood Press, 1975.

606. Fordham, Monroe. "Nineteenth–Century Black Thought in the United States: Some Influences of the Santo Domingo Revolution," Journal of Black Studies, 6, 2 (1975), pp. 115–26.

607. Forness, Norman O. "The Master, the Slave, and the Patent Laws: A Vignette of the 1850s," Prologue, 12, 1 (1980), pp. 23–27.

608. Foster, Frances S. "Slave Narratives: Text and Social Context" (PhD diss., University of California, San Diego, 1976).

609. _____. Witnessing Slavery: The Development of Ante-bellum Slave Narratives. Westport, Conn.: Greenwood Press, 1979.

610. "Four Essays on Abolition and Slavery," special issue of
     Conservative Historians' Forum (ed. Robert J. Loewenberg), 6
     (1982).

611. Fox-Genovese, Elizabeth. "Poor Richard at Work in the Cotton
     Fields: A Critique of the Psychological and Ideological
     Presuppositions of Time on the Cross," Review of Radical Political
     Economics, 7, 3 (1975), pp. 67-83. Revised as "Poor Richard at
     Work in the Cotton Fields; The Psychological and Ideological
     Presuppositions of Time on the Cross and Other Studies of
     Slavery," in Fox-Genovese and Genovese, Fruits of Merchant
     Capital, pp. 90-135.

612. Franklin, Benjamin V. "Theodore Dwight's 'African Distress': An
     Early Anti-Slavery Poem," Yale University Library Gazette, 54, 1
     (1979), pp. 26-36.

613. Franklin, John Hope. From Slavery to Freedom: A History of
     American Negroes. New York: Knopf, 1947.

614. _____. "Slavery and the Martial South," Journal of
     Negro History, 37, 1 (1952), pp. 36-53. Also Bobbs-Merrill Reprint
     no. H-265.

615. Frazier, E. Franklin. The Negro Family in the United States.
     Chicago: University of Chicago Press, 1939.

616. _____. "The Negro Slave Family," Journal of Negro
     History, 15, 1 (1930), pp. 198-259. Also Bobbs-Merrill Reprint no.
     BC-95.

617. Frederickson, George M. "The Gutman Report," New York Review of
     Books, 23, 15 (30 Sept. 1976), pp. 18-27. Reprinted as "On Herbert
     G. Gutman's 'The Black Family in Slavery and Freedom, 1750-1925',"
     in Weinstein, Gatell, and Sarasohn, eds., American Negro Slavery
     (3rd ed.), pp. 273-86.

618. _____. "Slavery and Race: The Southern Dilemma,"
     in Weinstein, Gatell, and Sarasohn, eds., American Negro Slavery
     (3rd ed.), pp. 34-58. Reprinted from Frederickson, The Black Image
     in the White Mind (New York: Harper and Row, 1971), pp. 43-70.

619. _____. "White Images of Black Slaves in the
     Southern United States," in Rubin and Tuden, eds., Comparative
     Perspectives, pp. 368-75.

620. _____, and Christopher Lasch. "Resistance to
     Slavery," Civil War History, 13, 4 (1967), pp. 315-29. Reprinted
     in Lane, ed., Debate over Slavery, pp. 223-44; in Bracey, Meier,
     and Rudwick, eds., American Slavery, pp. 179-82; in Weinstein and
     Gatell, eds., American Negro Slavery (2nd ed.), pp. 118-33.

621. Freehling, William W. "The Founding Fathers and Slavery," American Historical Review, 77, 1 (1972), pp. 81–93. Reprinted in Weinstein and Gatell, eds., American Negro Slavery (2nd ed.), pp. 207–23; in Weinstein, Gatell, and Sarasohn, eds., American Negro Slavery (3rd ed.), pp. 3–19.

622. Freidel, Frank. "Francis Lieber, Charles Sumner, and Slavery," Journal of Southern History, 9, 1 (1943), pp. 75–93.

623. Fuller, John D. P. "Slavery Propaganda During the Mexican War," Southwestern Historical Quarterly, 38, 4 (1935), pp. 235–45.

624. Furet, F., and Robert W. Fogel. "An Interview on the Historiographic and Political Implications of Time on the Cross" (mimeographed, Department of Economics, University of Rochester, 1974).

625. Furman, Marva Janett. "The Slave Narrative: Prototype of the Early Afro-American Novel" (PhD diss., Florida State University, 1979).

626. Galenson, David W. "White Servitude and the Growth of Black Slavery in Colonial America," Journal of Economic History, 41, 1 (1981), pp. 39–49. With commentary by Lorna S. Walsh.

627. _____. White Servitude in Colonial America: An Economic Analysis. New York: Cambridge University Press, 1981.

628. Gallerano, Nicola. "Schiavitù e famiglia nera America: un dibattito sulla Radical History Review," Movimento operaio e socialista, 1, 4 (1978), pp. 426–37.

629. Gallman, Robert E. "Slavery and Southern Economic Growth," Southern Economic Journal, 45, 4 (1979), pp. 1007–22.

630. _____, and Ralph V. Anderson. "Slaves as Fixed Capital: Slave Labor and Southern Economic Development," Journal of American History, 64, 1 (1977), pp. 24–46.

631. Gara, Larry. The Liberty Line: The Legend of the Underground Railroad. Lexington: University of Kentucky Press, 1961.

632. Garner, Reuben. "Responses of Colonial Inspectors to Slavery and the Slave Trade, 1815–1849," Negro History Bulletin, 35, 7 (1972), pp. 155–58.

633. Gatewood, Willard B., Jr. "Frederick Douglass and the Building of a 'Wall of Anti-Slavery Fire,' 1845–1846: An Essay Review," Florida Historical Quarterly, 59, 3 (1981), pp. 340–44.

634. Genovese, Eugene D. "American Slaves and Their History," New York Review of Books, 15, 10 (3 Dec. 1970), pp. 34–43. Reprinted in Lane, ed., Debate over Slavery, pp. 293–321; in Weinstein and Gatell, eds., American Negro Slavery (2nd ed.), pp. 183–204.

635. _____. "Black Plantation Preachers in the Slave South," Louisiana Studies, 11, 3 (1972), pp. 188-214.

636. _____. "Capitalist and Pseudo-Capitalist Features of the Slave Economy," reprinted (from Political Economy of Slavery, pp. 19-23, 28-36) in Brown, ed., Slavery in American Society, pp. 93-98.

637. _____. "The Debate over Time on the Cross: A Critique of Bourgeois Criticism," in Fox-Genovese and Genovese, Fruits of Merchant Capital, pp. 136-71.

638. _____. "Getting to Know the Slaves (review of Yetman, ed., Life Under the 'Peculiar Institution', Myers, Children of Pride, Rawick, The American Slave: A Composite Autobiography)," New York Review of Books, 19, 4 (21 Sept. 1972), pp. 16-19.

639. _____. In Red and Black: Marxian Explorations in Southern and Afro-American History. New York: Pantheon, 1971.

640. _____. "In the Name of Humanity and the Cause of Reform (excerpt from Roll, Jordan, Roll)," in Review of Radical Political Economics, 7, 3 (1975), pp. 84-99.

641. _____. "The Legacy of Slavery and the Roots of Black Nationalism," Studies on the Left, 6, 6 (1966), pp. 2-26. Reprinted in Rose, ed., Americans from Africa, vol. 2, pp. 31-51. Revised in Genovese, In Red and Black, pp. 129-57.

642. _____. "Marxian Interpretations of the Slave South," in Barton J. Bernstein, ed., Towards a New Past: Dissenting Essays in American History (New York: Pantheon Books, 1968), pp. 90-125.

643. _____. "The Medical and Insurance Costs of Slaveholding in the Cotton Belt," Journal of Negro History, 45, 3 (1960), pp. 141-55.

644. _____. "The Negro Laborer in Africa and the Slave South," Phylon, 21, 4 (1960), pp. 343-50. Reprinted in Rose, ed., Americans from Africa, vol. 1, pp. 71-82; also in Genovese, Political Economy of Slavery, pp. 70-84.

645. _____. The Political Economy of Slavery: Studies in the Economy and Society of the Slave South. New York: Pantheon, 1965.

646. _____. "A Reply to Criticism," Radical History Review, 4, 1 (1977), pp. 94-110.

647. _____. "(Review of Gutman, Black Family in Slavery and Freedom)," incorporated in "The Debate over Time on the Cross: A Critique of Bourgeois Criticism," in Fox-Genovese and Genovese, Fruits of Merchant Capital, pp. 136-71.

648. _____. Roll, Jordan, Roll: The World the Slaves Made. New York: Pantheon, 1974.

649. _____. "Significance of the Slave Plantation for Southern Economic Development," Journal of Southern History, 28, 4 (1962), pp. 422-37.

650. _____. "The Slave South: An Interpretation," Science and Society, 25, 4 (1961), pp. 320-37. Reprinted in Weinstein and Gatell, eds., American Negro Slavery (2nd ed.), pp. 262-78.

651. _____. "The Slave States of North America," in Cohen and Greene, eds., Neither Slave nor Free, pp. 258-77.

652. _____. "Slavery - The World's Burden," in Owens, ed., Perspectives and Irony, pp. 27-50.

653. _____. "Solidarity and Servitude (review of Gutman, Black Family in Slavery and Freedom)," Times Literary Supplement, 76 (no. 3911)(25 Feb. 1977), pp. 198-99.

654. _____. "Toward a Psychology of Slavery: An Assessment of the Contribution of The Slave Community," in Gilmore, ed., Revisiting Blassingame's The Slave Community, pp. 27-42.

655. _____. The World the Slaveholders Made: Two Essays in Interpretation. New York: Pantheon, 1969.

656. _____. "Yeoman Farmers in a Slaveholders' Democracy," Agricultural History, 49, 2 (1975), pp. 331-42.

657. _____, ed. The Slave Economy of the Old South: Selected Essays in Economic and Social History. Baton Rouge: Louisiana State University Press, 1968. (Essays by U. B. Phillips)

658. George, James Zachariah. The Political History of Slavery in the United States. New York: Neale Publishing Company, 1915.

659. Gilmore, Al-Tony, ed. Revisiting Blassingame's The Slave Community: The Scholars Respond. Westport, Conn.: Greenwood Press, 1978.

660. Goldin, Claudia D. "American Slavery: De Jure and De Facto," Journal of Interdisciplinary History, 10, 1 (1979), pp. 129-36.

661. _____. "A Model to Explain the Relative Decline of Urban Slavery: Empirical Results," in Engerman and Genovese, eds., Race and Slavery, pp. 427-50. (With comment by Harold D. Woodman, pp. 451-54.)

662. _____. Urban Slavery in the American South, 1820-1860: A Quantitative History. Chicago: University of Chicago Press, 1976.

663. _____. "Urbanization and Slavery: The Issue of Compatibility," in Leo F. Schnore, ed., The New Urban History: Quantitative Explorations by American Historians (Princeton: Princeton University Press, 1975), pp. 231-46.

664. Goodson, Martia Graham. "An Introductory Essay and Subject Index to Selected Interviews from the Slave Narrative Collecction" (PhD diss., Union Graduate School, 1977).

665. _____. "The Slave Narrative Collection: A Tool for Reconstructing Afro-American Women's History," Western Journal of Black Studies, 3, 2 (1979), pp. 116-22.

666. Green, Mitchell A. "Impact of Slavery on the Black Family: Social, Political, and Economic," Journal of Afro-American Studies, 3, 3-4 (1975), pp. 343-56.

667. Greenberg, Michael. "The New Economic History and the Understanding of Slavery: A Methodological Critique," Dialectical Anthropology, 2 (1977), pp. 131-42.

668. Greenberg, Michael. "Roll, Jordan, Roll: The World the Slaves Made, by Eugene Genovese: A Review Essay," Radical History Review, 3, 4 (1976), pp. 29-40.

669. Gudeman, Stephen. "An Anthropologist's View of Herbert Gutman's The Black Family in Slavery and Freedom, 1750-1925," Social Science History, 3, 3-4 (1979), pp. 56-65.

670. Gujer, B. "Free Trade and Slavery: Calhoun's Defense of Southern Interests Against British Interference, 1811-1848" (Diss., Universität Zürich, 1971).

671. Gutman, Herbert G. The Black Family in Slavery and Freedom, 1750-1925. New York: Pantheon, 1976.

672. _____. "Slave Family and its Legacies," Historical Reflections/Réflexions historiques, 6, 1 (1979), pp. 183-99. Commentaries by Barry Higman (pp. 200-03), Stanley L. Engerman (pp. 204-12).

673. _____. Slavery and the Numbers Game: A Critique of Time on the Cross. Urbana: University of Illinois Press, 1975.

674. _____. "The World Two Cliometricians Made (review of Fogel and Engerman, Time on the Cross)," Journal of Negro History, 60, 1 (1975), pp. 53-227. Republished as Slavery and the Numbers Game: A Critique of Time on the Cross (Urbana: University of Illinois Press, 1975).

675. _____, and Richard Sutch. "Sambo Makes Good, or Were Slaves Imbued with the Protestant Work Ethic," in David, et al., Reckoning with Slavery, pp. 55-93.

676. _____. "The Slave Family: Protected
Agent of Capitalist Masters or Victim of the Slave Trade?" in
David, et al., Reckoning with Slavery, pp. 94-133.

677. _____. "Victorians All? The Sexual
Mores and Conduct of Slaves and their Masters," in David, et al.,
Reckoning with Slavery, pp. 134-62.

678. Hall, Mark. "The Proslavery Thought of J.D.B. De Bow: A Practical
Man's Guide to Economics," Southern Studies, 21, 1 (1982), pp.
97-104.

679. Halliburton, R., Jr. "Free Black Owners of Slaves: A Reappraisal
of the (Carter G.) Woodson Thesis," South Carolina Historical
Magazine, 76, 3 (1975), pp. 129-42.

680. Handlin, Oscar. "The Capacity of Quantitative History,"
Perspectives in American History, 9 (1975), pp. 7-26. With a
reply: Robert W. Fogel, "Reply to Oscar Handlin," pp. 29-32.

681. *Harlan, Louis, Arthur P. Middleton, and B. Marie Perinbaum.
Commentaries on Slave Biographies. Washington, D. C.: American
Historical Association, 1971. (AHA Pamphlet   )

682. Harris, Marvin. "The Myth of the Friendly Master," in Foner and
Genovese, eds., Slavery in the Americas, pp. 38-47. (Reprinted
from Patterns of Race in the Americas.)

683. Harris, Robert L., Jr. "The Heart of the Slave: Attitudes Toward
Bondage in America," Black Lives, 2, 4 (1972), pp. 28-38.

684. Harvard Law Review. "Higginbotham: In the Matter of Color (review
essay)," Plantation Society in the Americas, 1, 2 (1979), pp.
262-64.

685. Haskell, Thomas L. "The True and Tragical History of 'Time on the
Cross'," New York Review of Books, 22, 15 (2 Oct. 1975), pp. 33-39.

686. _____. "Were Slaves More Efficient? Some Doubts about
'Time on the Cross'," New York Review of Books, 21, 14 (19 Sept.
1975), pp. 38-42.

687. Haynes, Robert V., ed. Blacks in White America Before 1865: Issues
and Interpretations. New York: D. McKay, 1972.

688. Hedin, Raymond. "Muffled Voices: The American Slave Narrative,"
Clio, 10, 2 (1981), pp. 129-42.

689. Higginbotham, A. Leon, Jr. In the Matter of Color: Race and the
American Legal Process: The Colonial Period. New York: Oxford
University Press, 1978.

690. Higginbotham, Don, and William S. Price, Jr. "Was it Murder for a White Man to Kill a Slave? Chief Justice Martin Howard Condemns the Peculiar Institution in North Carolina," William and Mary Quarterly, 3rd ser., 36, 4 (1979), pp. 593-601.

691. Hine, Darlene C. "Female Slave Resistance: The Economics of Sex," Western Journal of Black Studies, 3, 2 (1979), pp. 123-27.

692. Hill, James D. "Some Economic Aspects of Slavery, 1850-1860," South Atlantic Quarterly, 26, 2 (1927), pp. 161-77.

693. Hoffert, Sylvia. "This 'One Great Evil'," American History Illustrated, 12 (1977), pp. 37-41.

694. Hoffmann, Elliot W. "Black Hessians: American Blacks as German Soldiers," Negro History Bulletin, 44, 4 (1981), pp. 81-82, 91.

695. Hollander, Barnett. Slavery in America. New York: Barnes and Noble, 1963.

696. Holt, Thomas. "On the Cross: The Role of Quantitative Methods in the Reconstruction of the African-American Experience," Journal of Negro History, 61, 2 (1976), pp. 158-72.

697. Hood, R. E. "From a Headstart to a Deadstart: The Historical Basis for Black Indifference Toward the Episcopal Church 1800-1860," Historical Magazine of the Protestant Episcopal Church, 51, 3 (1982), pp. 269-96.

698. Hopkins, James F. "Slavery in the Hemp Industry," in Newton and Lewis, eds., The Other Slaves, pp. 145-56.

699. Horris, Allan. "Did You Know There Were Indentured Africans Too?" New Vision, 1, 1 (1974), pp. 16-20.

700. Howard, Warren S. American Slaves and the Federal Law, 1837-1862. Berkeley: University of California Press, 1963.

701. Hudson, Gossie Harold. "Black Americans vs. Citizenship: The Dred Scott Decision," Negro History Bulletin, 46, 1 (1983), pp. 26-28.

702. Huffman, Wallace E. "Black-White Human Capital Differences: Impact on Agricultural Productivity in the U.S. South," American Economic Review, 71, 1 (1981), pp. 94-107.

703. Huggins, Nathan Irvin. Black Odyssey: The Afro-American Ordeal in Slavery. New York: Pantheon, 1977.

704. _____, Martin Kilson, and Daniel M. Fox, eds. Key Issues in the Afro-American Experience. New York: Harcourt, Brace, Jovanovich, 1971.

705. Ianni, O. "Notes on Slavery and History" (unpublished paper presented at MSSB Conference on Time on the Cross, Rochester, New York, 1974).

706. Isaac, Rhys. "Idleness Ethic and the Liberty of Anglo-Americans (review of Morgan, American Slavery-American Freedom)," Reviews in American History, 4, 1 (1976), pp. 47-52.

707. Issel, William. "History, Social Science, and Ideology: Elkins and Blassingame on Ante-Bellum American Slavery," History Teacher, 9, 1 (1975), pp. 56-72.

708. Jackson, Bruce, ed. The Negro and His Folklore in Nineteenth Century Periodicals. Austin: University of Texas Press, 1967.

709. Jacobs, Donald M. "Twentieth-Century Slave Narratives as Source Materials: Slave Labor as Agricultural Labor," Agricultural History, 57, 2 (1983), pp. 223-27.

710. Jaffa, Harry V. "Wills's Inventing America, and the Pathology of Ideological Scholarship," Conservative Historians' Forum, 6 (1982), pp. 2-5.

711. Jenkins, William Sumner. Pro-Slavery Thought in the Old South. Chapel Hill: University of North Carolina Press, 1935.

712. Jentz, John. "A Note on Genovese's Account of the Slaves' Religion," Civil War History, 23, 2 (1977), pp. 161-69.

713. Jernegan, Marcus W. "Slavery and Conversion in the American Colonies," American Historical Review, 21, 3 (1916), pp. 504-27.

714. _____. "Slavery and the Beginning of Industrialization in the American Colonies," in Newton and Lewis, eds., The Other Slaves, pp. 3-20.

715. Johnson, Michael P. "Smothered Slave Infants: Were Slave Mothers at Fault?" Journal of Southern History, 47, 4 (1981), pp. 493-520.

716. Johnston, James H. "Race Relations in Virginia and Miscegenation in the South, 1776-1860" (PhD diss., University of Chicago, 1937).

717. _____. Race Relations in Virginia and Miscegenation in the South, 1776-1860. Amherst: University of Massachusetts Press, 1970. Foreword by Winthrop Jordan.

718. Jordan, Weymouth T. "Plantation Medicine in the Old South," Alabama Review, 3, 2 (1950), pp. 83-107.

719. Jordan, Winthrop D. "Modern Tensions and the Origins of American Slavery," Journal of Social History, 28, 1 (1962), pp. 18-30. Reprinted in Weinstein and Gatell, eds., American Negro Slavery (1st ed.), pp. 13-24 (with omissions); in Noel, ed., Origins of American Slavery and Racism, pp. 81-94; in Rose, ed., Americans from Africa, vol. 1, pp. 103-15; in Haynes, ed., Blacks in White America Before 1865, pp. 104-16. Also Bobbs-Merrill Reprint no. BC-159.

720. _____. "Unthinking Decision: Enslavement of Negroes in America to 1700," reprinted (from White Over Black, pp. 44-98) in Brown, ed., Slavery in American Society, pp. 1-22.

721. _____. White Over Black: American Attitudes Toward the Negro, 1550-1812. Chapel Hill: University of North Carolina Press, 1968.

722. Joyner, Charles W. "Soul Food and the Sambo Stereotype: Foodlore from the Slave Narrative Collection," Keystone Folklore Quarterly, 16, 4 (1971), pp. 171-78.

723. Karcher, Carolyn L. Shadow Over the Promised Land: Slavery, Race, and Violence in Melville's America. Baton Rouge: Louisiana State University Press, 1980.

724. Kates, Don B., Jr. "Abolition, Deportation, Integration: Attitudes Toward Slavery in the Early Republic," Journal of Negro History, 53, 1 (1968), pp. 33-47.

725. Kaufman, Martin. "Medicine and Slavery (Savitt): An Essay Review," Georgia Historical Quarterly, 64, 3 (1979), pp. 380-90.

726. Keller, Frances Richardson. "The Perspective of a Black American on Slavery and the French Revolution: Anna Julia Cooper," Proceedings of the Third Annual Meeting of the Western Society for French History (Denver, 1975) (n.p.: Western Society for French History, 1976), pp. 165-76.

727. Kett, Joseph F. "The Black Family under Slavery (review of Gutman, Black Family in Slavery and Freedom)," History of Education Quarterly, 17, 4 (1977), pp. 455-60.

728. Kilson, Marion D. de B. "Afro-American Social Structure, 1790-1970," in Kilson and Rotberg, eds., African Diaspora, pp. 414-58.

729. _____. "Towards Freedom: An Analysis of Slave Revolts in the United States," Phylon, 25, 2 (1964), pp. 175-87. Reprinted in Meier and Rudwick, eds., Making of Black America, vol. 1, pp. 165-78.

730. King, Richard H. "Marxism and the Slave South," American Quarterly, 29, 1 (1977), pp. 117-31. Reprinted as "On Eugene D. Genovese's 'Roll, Jordan, Roll: The World the Slaves Made,' and Other Works," in Weinstein, Gatell, and Sarasohn, eds., American Negro Slavery (3rd ed.), pp. 257-72.

731. Kiple, Kenneth F., and Virginia H. Kiple. "Black Tongue and Black Men: Pellagra and Slavery in the Antebellum South," Journal of Southern History, 43, 3 (1977), pp. 411-28.

732. _____. "Black Yellow Fever Immunities, Innate and Acquired, as Revealed in the American South," Social Science History, 1, 4 (1977), pp. 419-36.

733. _____. "Slave Child Mortality:
Some Nutritional Answers to a Perennial Puzzle," Journal of Social
History, 10, 3 (1977), pp. 284-309. Reprinted in Patricia Branca,
ed., The Medicine Show: Patients, Physicians, and the Perplexities
of the Health Revolution in Modern Society (New York: Science
History Publications, 1977), pp. 21-46.

734. Klotter, James C. "Slaves and Race: A Family Perspective,"
Southern Studies, 17, 4 (1978), pp. 375-97.

735. Kneebone, John T. "Sambo and the Slave Narratives: A Note on
Sources," Essays in History, 19 (1975), pp. 7-23.

736. Knight, Franklin W. "The American Revolution and the Caribbean,"
in Berlin and Hoffman, eds., Slavery and Freedom in the Age of the
American Revolution, pp. 237-61.

737. Kolchin, Peter. "Comparing American History," Reviews in American
History, 10, 4 (1982), pp. 64-81.

738. _____. "Toward a Reinterpretation of Slavery (review of
Fogel and Engerman, Time on the Cross)," Journal of Social
History, 9, 1 (1975), pp. 99-113.

739. Kugler, R. F. "U. B. Phillips' Use of Sources," Journal of Negro
History, 47, 3 (1962), pp. 153-68.

740. Kulikoff, Allan. "Uprooted Peoples: Black Migrants in the Age of
the American Revolution, 1790-1820," in Berlin and Hoffman, eds.,
Slavery and Freedom in the Age of the American Revolution, pp.
143-71.

741. Landes, Ruth. "Negro Slavery and Female Status," in Les
Afro-Américains (Amsterdam, 1953), pp. 265-68. (Mémoires de
l'Institut Française d'Afrique Noire, no. 27)

742. Lantz, Herman R. "Family and Kin as Revealed in the Narratives of
Ex-Slaves," Social Science Quarterly, 60, 4 (1980), pp. 667-75.

743. Laprade, William T. "Some Problems in Writing the History of
American Slavery," South Atlantic Quarterly, 10, 2 (1911), pp.
134-41.

744. Leaming, Hugo Prosper. "Hidden Americans: Maroons of Virginia and
the Carolinas" (PhD diss., University of Illinois, Chicago Circle,
1979).

745. Levine, Lawrence W. Black Culture and Black Consciousness:
Afro-American Folk Thought from Slavery to Freedom. New York:
Oxford University Press, 1977.

746. _____. "Slave Songs and Slave Consciousness: An
     Exploration in Neglected Sources," in Tamara K. Hareven, ed.,
     Anonymous Americans: Explorations in Nineteenth-Century Social
     History (Englewood Cliffs, N.J.: Prentice-Hall, 1971), pp. 99-130.
     Reprinted in Weinstein, Gatell, and Sarasohn, eds., American Negro
     Slavery (3rd ed.), pp. 143-72.

747. Levy, David W. "Racial Stereotypes in Antislavery Fiction,"
     Phylon, 31, 3 (1970), pp. 265-79.

748. Lewis, Ronald L. "The 'American Dream' and the Rationalization of
     Slavery," Crisis, 83, 7 (1976), pp. 253-54.

749. Lindsay, Arnett G. "Diplomatic Relations Between the United States
     and Great Britain Bearing on the Return of Negro Slaves,
     1783-1828," Journal of Negro History, 5, 4 (1920), pp. 391-419.

750. Liston, R. A. Slavery in America, The Heritage of Slavery. New
     York: McGraw Hill, 1972.

751. Lloyd, Arthur Young. The Slavery Controversy, 1831-1860. Chapel
     Hill: University of North Carolina Press, 1939.

752. Locke, Alain. "The Negro as Artist," in Newton and Lewis, eds.,
     The Other Slaves, pp. 205-07.

753. Loewenberg, Robert J. "The Proslavery Roots of Socialist Thought,"
     Conservative Historians' Forum, 6 (1982), pp. 14-21.

754. _____, ed. "Four Essays on Abolition and Slavery,"
     special issue of Conservative Historians' Forum, 6 (1982).

755. Logue, Cal M. "Transcending Coercion: The Communicative Strategies
     of Black Slaves on Antebellum Plantations," Quarterly Journal of
     Speech, 67, 1 (1981), pp. 31-46.

756. Lord, Donald C. "Slave Ads as Historical Evidence," History
     Teacher, 5, 4 (1972), pp. 10-16.

757. Lynd, Staughton. Class Conflict, Slavery, and the United States
     Constitution: Ten Essays. Indianapolis: Bobbs-Merrill, 1968.

758. _____. "On Turner, Beard and Slavery," Journal of Negro
     History, 48, 4 (1963), pp. 235-50. Reprinted in Lynd, Class
     Conflict, pp. 135-52.

759. *McCants, E. C. "The Beginning of Slavery," Southern Magazine, 2
     (1939), pp. 7-42.

760. McDonald, Forrest, and Grady McWhiney. "The South from
     Self-Sufficiency to Peonage: An Interpretation," American
     Historical Review, 85, 5 (1980), pp. 1095-1118.

761. McFaul, John M. "Expediency vs. Morality: Jacksonian Politics and
     Slavery," Journal of American History, 62, 1 (1975), pp. 24-39.

762. McGinty, Brian. "A Heap O' Trouble (Dred Scott's Fight for Freedom)," American History Illustrated, 16, 2 (1981), pp. 34-49.

763. McKenzie, Edna Chappell. "Self-Hire Among Slaves, 1820-1860: Institutional Variation or Aberration?" (PhD diss., University of Pittsburgh, 1973).

764. McKivigan, John R. "The Gospel Will Burst the Bonds of the Slave: The Abolitionists (sic) Bibles for Slaves Campaign," Negro History Bulletin, 45, 3 (1982), pp. 62-64, 77.

765. _____. "Prisoner of Conscience: George Gordon and the Fugitive Slave Law," Journal of Presbyterian History, 60, 4 (1982), pp. 336-54.

766. Maclear, J. F. "The Evangelical Alliance and the Antislavery Crusade," Huntington Library Quarterly, 42, 4 (1979), pp. 141-64.

767. MacLeod, Duncan J. "Measuring Slavery (review of Fogel and Engerman, Time on the Cross)," Historical Journal, 18, 1 (1975), pp. 202-05.

768. _____. Slavery, Race, and the American Revolution. New York: Cambridge University Press, 1974.

769. _____. "Toward Caste," in Berlin and Hoffman, eds., Slavery and Freedom in the Age of the American Revolution, pp. 217-36.

770. McManus, Edgar J. "The Negro Under Slavery," in Haynes ed., Blacks in White America Before 1865, pp. 134-47. (From A History of Negro Slavery in New York)

771. Marable, Manning. "The Meaning of Faith in the Black Mind in Slavery," Rocky Mountain Review of Language and Literature, 30, 4 (1976), pp. 248-64.

772. Margo, Robert A., and Richard H. Steckel. "The Heights of American Slaves: New Evidence on Slave Nutrition and Health," Social Science History, 6, 4 (1982), pp. 516-38.

773. Marketti, Jim. "Black Equity in the Slave Industry," Review of Black Political Economy, 2, 2 (1972), pp. 43-66.

774. Marshall, Mary Louise. "Plantation Medicine," Bulletin of the Medical Library Association, 26, 3 (1937-38), pp. 115-28.

775. _____. "Plantation Medicine," Bulletin of the Tulane University Medical Faculty, 1, 3 (1942), pp. 45-58.

776. Martin, James Kirby, ed. Interpreting Colonial America: Selected Readings. New York: Harper and Row, 1973.

777. Matlock, Gene D. "When Negroes Owned Slaves," Negro Digest, 12, 5 (1963), pp. 72-82.

778. Matthews, Donald G. "Religion and Slavery - the Case of the American South," in Christine Bolt and Seymour Drescher, eds., Anti-Slavery, Religion and Reform: Essays in Memory of Roger Anstey (Folkestone: William Dawson & Sons, 1980), pp. 207-32.

779. _____. Slavery and Methodism: A Chapter in American Morality, 1780-1845. Princeton: Princeton University Press, 1965.

780. Matthewson, Timothy M. "Slavery and Diplomacy: The United States and Saint Dominique, 1791-1793" (PhD diss., University of California, Santa Barbara, 1976).

781. Maxwell, John F. "The Anti-Slavery Society and the Campaign Against Slavery," The Clergy Review (London), 59, 7 (1974), pp. 451-67.

782. _____. "The Charismatic Origins of the Christian Anti-Slavery Movement in North America," The Clergy Review (London), 60, 4 (1975), pp. 208-17. Also in Quaker History, 63, 2 (1974), pp. 108-16.

783. _____. Slavery and the Catholic Church. Little London: Barry Rose, 1975.

784. May, Robert E. "John A. Quitman and His Slaves: Reconciling Slave Resistance with the Pro-Slavery Defense," Journal of Southern History, 46, 4 (1980), pp. 551-70.

785. Meier, August. "Benjamin Quarles and the Historiography of Black America," Civil War History, 26, 2 (1980), pp. 101-16.

786. _____. "Old Wine in New Bottles: A Review of Time on the Cross," Civil War History, 20, 3 (1974), pp. 251-60.

787. _____. "Slavery: A Different View of the 'Cross' (review of Genovese, Roll, Jordan, Roll)," Reviews in American History, 3, 2 (1975), pp. 206-12.

788. _____, and Elliott Rudwick, eds. The Making of Black America: Essays in Negro Life and History. New York: Atheneum, 1969.

789. Mellon, Matthew T. Early American Views on Negro Slavery. Boston: Meador, 1934.

790. Metzer, Jacob. "The Records of U. S. Colored Troops as a Historical Source: An Exploratory Examination," Historical Methods, 14, 3 (1981), pp. 123-31.

791. Miller, Elinor, and Eugene D. Genovese, eds. Plantation, Town and County - Essays on the Local History of American Slave Society. Urbana: University of Illinois Press, 1974.

792. Miller, M. Sammy. "The Law and Bondage in Early America," Crisis, 83, 7 (1976), pp. 255-56.

793. Miller, Randall M. "Black Catholics in the Slave South: Some Needs and Opportunities for Study," Records of the American Catholic Historical Society of Philadelphia, 86 (1975), pp. 93-106.

794. _____. 'Dear Master': Letters of a Slave Family. Ithaca: Cornell University Press, 1978.

795. _____, ed. "'It is Good to be Religious': A Loyal Slave on God, Masters, and the Civil War," North Carolina Historical Review, 54, 1 (1957), pp. 66-71.

796. Miller, Richard Roscoe. Slavery and Catholicism. Durham: North State Publishers, 1977.

797. Miller, William L. "J. E. Cairnes on the Economics of American Negro Slavery," Southern Economic Journal, 30, 4 (1963-64), pp. 333-41.

798. Mills, Gary B., and Elizabeth Shown. "Roots and the New 'Faction': A Legitimate Tool for Clio?" Virginia Magazine of History and Biography, 89, 1 (1981), pp. 3-26.

799. Modell, John. "Demographic Perspectives on Herbert Gutman's Black Family in Slavery and Freedom, 1750-1925," Social Science History, 3, 3-4 (1979), pp. 45-55.

800. Mohr, Clarence L. "Southern Blacks in the Civil War: A Century of Historiography," Journal of Negro History, 59, 2 (1974), pp. 177-95.

801. Mooney, Chase C. "The Literature of Slavery: A Re-Evaluation," Indiana Magazine of History, 47, 3 (1951), pp. 251-60.

802. Moore, Wilbert E. American Negro Slavery and its Abolition. New York: Third Press, 1971.

803. _____. "Slave Law and the Social Structure," Journal of Negro History, 26, 2 (1941), pp. 171-202.

804. Morgan, Edmund S. "Slavery and Freedom: The American Paradox," Journal of American History, 59, 1 (1972), pp. 5-29.

805. Morgan, James Calvin. "Negro Culture in the United States: A Study of Four Models for Interpreting Slavery in the United States" (PhD diss., New York University, 1982).

806. Morgan, Kathryn L. "The Ex-Slave Narrative as a Source for Folk History" (PhD diss., University of Pennsylvania, 1970).

807. Morris, Richard B. "The Measure of Bondage in the Slave States," Mississippi Valley Historical Review, 41, 2 (1954), pp. 219-40.

808. Morrison, Larry R. "'Nearer to the Brute Creation': The Scientific Defense of American Slavery Before 1830," Southern Studies, 19, 3 (1980), pp. 228-42.

809. Mugleston, William F. "Southern Literature as History: Slavery in the Antebellum Novel," History Teacher, 8, 1 (1974), pp. 17-30.

810. Mullin, Gerald W. "Rethinking American Negro Slavery from the Vantage Point of the Colonial Era," Louisiana Studies, 12, 2 (1973), pp. 398-422.

811. _____. "(Review of Fogel and Engerman, Time on the Cross)," William and Mary Quarterly, 3rd ser., 32, 3 (1975), pp. 496-500.

812. Mullin, Michael, ed. American Negro Slavery: A Documentary History. Columbia: University of South Carolina Press, 1976.

813. Mullin, Robert Bruce. "Biblical Critics and the Battle Over Slavery," Journal of Presbyterian History, 61, 2 (1983), pp. 210-26.

814. Murphy, Jeanette R. "The Survival of African Music in America," in Jackson, ed., The Negro and his Folklore, pp. 327-39. Also Bobbs-Merrill Reprint no. BC-148.

815. Naison, Mark. "Course Syllabus: Afro-American History, 1512-1865," Radical History Review, 3, 1-2 (1975), pp. 92-95.

816. Nash, Gary B. "Afro-American History in the Revolutionary Era," Journal of Ethnic Studies, 9, 1 (1981), pp. 89-95.

817. _____. "Red, White, and Black: The Origins of Racism in Colonial America," in Gary B. Nash and Richard Weiss, eds., The Great Fear: Race in the Mind of America (New York: Holt, Rinehart and Winston, 1970), pp. 1-26. Reprinted in Noel, ed., Origins of American Slavery and Racism, pp. 131-52.

818. _____. Red, White, and Black: The Peoples of Early America. Englewood Cliffs, N.J.: Prentice-Hall, 1974. 2nd ed., 1982.

819. Nash, Howard P., Jr. "General Butler's Fugitive Slave Law," Negro Digest, 13, 6 (1964), pp. 19-23.

820. Nelson, William Stuart. "The Christian Church and Slavery in America," Howard Review, 2, 1 (1925), pp. 41-77.

821. Newton, James E. "Slave Artisans and Craftsmen: The Roots of Afro-American Art," Black Scholar, 9, 3 (1977), pp. 35-42. Reprinted in Newton and Lewis, eds., The Other Slaves, pp. 233-41.

822. _____, and Ronald L. Lewis, eds. The Other Slaves: Mechanics, Artisans, and Craftsmen. Boston: G. K. Hall, 1978.

823. New York Times Magazine (August, 1926). "Negro's Art Lives in his Wrought Iron," in Newton and Lewis, eds., The Other Slaves, pp. 14-15.

824. Nichols, Charles H., comp. Black Men in Chains: Narratives of Escaped Slaves. New York: L. Hill, 1972.

825. _____. Many Thousand Gone: The Ex-Slaves' Account of Their Bondage and Freedom. Leiden: Brill, 1963.

826. _____, comp. Black Men in Chains: Narratives by Escaped Slaves. New York: Hill, 1972.

827. Nichols, William W. "Slave Narratives: Dismissed Evidence in the Writing of Southern History," Phylon, 32, 4 (1971), pp. 403-09.

828. Noel, Donald L., ed. The Origins of American Slavery and Racism. Columbus: Merrill, 1972.

829. Noonan, John T., Jr. The Antelope: The Ordeal of Recaptured Africans in the Administrations of James Monroe and John Quincy Adams. Berkeley: University of California Press, 1977.

830. Norton, Mary Beth, Herbert G. Gutman, and Ira Berlin. "The Afro-American Family in the Age of Revolution," in Berlin and Hoffman, eds., Slavery and Freedom in the Age of the American Revolution, pp. 175-91.

831. *Ofcansky, Thomas P. "North American Slavery in the Eighteenth Century," East Central/American Society for Eighteenth Century Studies Newsletter,   (Fall, 1979), pp.   .

832. Ohline, Howard A. "Slavery, Economics, and Congressional Politics, 1790," Journal of Southern History, 46, 3 (1980), pp. 335-60.

833. Okoye, F. Nwabueze. "Chattel Slavery as the Nightmare of the American Revolutionaries," William and Mary Quarterly, 3rd ser., 37, 1 (1980), pp. 3-28.

834. Oneal, James. "The Philosophy of the Slave Regime," Modern Quarterly, 3 (1925), pp. 38-50.

835. Onstott, Kyle. "The Truth About Slavery in America," Negro Digest, 10, 8 (1961), pp. 55-68.

836. Ortù, Leopoldo. "La schiavitù, 'istituzione peculiare' degli Stati Uniti d'America, del 1787 a 1860," Annali della Facoltà di Lettere Filosofia e Magistero dell'Università di Cagliari, 35 (1972), pp. 329-82.

837. Osofsky, Gilbert, ed. Puttin' on Ole Massa: The Slave Narratives of Henry Bibb, William Wells Brown, and Solomon Northrup. New York: Harper and Row, 1969.

838. Owens, Harry P., ed. Perspectives and Irony in American Slavery. Jackson: University Press of Mississippi, 1976.

839. Owens, Leslie H. "Blacks in The Slave Community," in Gilmore, ed., Revisiting Blassingame's The Slave Community, pp. 61-70.

840. _____. "This Species of Property: Slave Personality and Behavior in the Old South, 1776-1861" (PhD diss., University of California, Riverside, 1972).

841. _____. This Species of Property: Slave Life and Culture in the Old South. New York: Oxford University Press, 1976.

842. Palmer, Jaclyn C. "Images of Slavery: Black and White Writers," Negro History Bulletin, 41, 5 (1978), pp. 888-89.

843. Parker, William N. "The Slave Plantation in American Agriculture," Contributions to the (First) International Conference of Economic History (Stockholm, 1960) (Paris: Mouton, 1960), pp. 321-31.

844. _____. "Slavery and Economic Development: An Hypothesis and Some Evidence," Agricultural History, 44, 1 (1970), pp. 115-25.

845. Parkhurst, Jessie W. "The Role of the Black Mammy in the Plantation Household," Journal of Negro History, 23, 3 (1938), pp. 349-69.

846. Passell, Peter, and Gavin Wright. "The Effects of Pre-Civil War Territorial Expansion on the Price of Slaves," Journal of Political Economy, 80, 6 (1972), pp. 1188-1202.

847. Patterson, David L. "The Constitution: An Exslave Interpretation" (PhD diss., University of California, Berkeley, 1978).

848. Perkins, Eric. "Roll, Jordan, Roll: A 'Marx' for the Master Class," Radical History Review, 3, 4 (1976), pp. 41-59.

849. Perotin, C. "Le courant abolitionniste dans la littérature américaine de 1808 à 1861" (Diss., Université de Paris IV, 1973).

850. Phillips, Ulrich B. American Negro Slavery: A Survey of the Supply, Employment and Control of Negro Labor as Determined by the Plantation Regime. New York: Appleton, 1918.

851. _____. Life and Labor in the Old South. Boston: Little, Brown, 1929.

852. _____. "Slavery in the Old South," in Rose, ed., Americans from Africa, vol. 1, pp. 117-30.

853. Piersen, William D. "White Cannibals, Black Martyrs: Fear, Depression, and Religious Faith as Causes of Suicide Among New Slaves," Journal of Negro History, 62, 2 (1977), pp. 147-59.

854. Pitman, Frank Wesley. "Fetishism, Witchcraft and Christianity among the Slaves," Journal of Negro History, 11, 4 (1926), pp. 650-68.

855. Placucci, A. "Cristianismo e schiavitù negra negli Stati Uniti d'America (1619-1865)" (Diss., Pontificia Universitas Urbaniana, V, 1972).

856. Polsky, Milton. "American Slave Narrative: Dramatic Resource Material for the Classroom," Journal of Negro Education, 45 (1976), pp. 166-78. Also in Negro Educational Review, 26 (1975), pp. 22-36.

857. Pontoppidan, Morten Oxenboll. Kampen mod Negerslaveriet i de Forenede Stater: en historisk skildring. Copenhagen: G. E. C. Gad, 1925.

858. Porter, James A. "Negro Craftsmen and Artists of Pre-Civil War Days," in Newton and Lewis, eds., The Other Slaves, pp. 209-20.

859. Posey, William Brownlow. "Influence of Slavery upon the Methodist Church in the Early South and Southwest," Mississippi Valley Historical Review, 17, 4 (1931), pp. 530-42.

860. Pressly, Thomas J., and Harvey H. Chamberlin. "Slavery and Scholarship: Some Problems of Evidence (review of Fogel and Engerman, Time on the Cross, and Blassingame, Slave Community)," Pacific Northwest Quarterly, 66, 2 (1975), pp. 79-84.

861. Puckett, N. N. "Names of American Negro Slaves," in George Peter Murdock, ed., Studies in the Science of Society Presented to Albert Galloway Keller (New Haven: Yale University Press, 1937), pp. 471-94.

862. Pugh, Evelyn L. "Women and Slavery: Julia Gardiner Tyler and the Duchess of Sutherland," Virginia Magazine of History and Biography, 88, 2 (1980), pp. 186-202.

863. Putnam, Mary Burnham. The Baptists and Slavery, 1840-1845. Ann Arbor, Mich.: G. Wahr, 1913.

864. Pybus, Cassandra. "Eugene D. Genovese: The Neo-Marxist Interpretation of the Slave South," Flinders Journal of History and Politics, 3 (1973), pp. 32-44.

865. Quarles, Benjamin. "Antebellum Free Blacks and the 'Spirit of '76'," Journal of Negro History, 61, 3 (1976), pp. 229-42.

866. _____. "Black History Unbound," Daedalus, 103, 2 (1974), pp. 163-78.

867. _____. "The Revolutionary War as a Black Declaration of Independence," in Berlin and Hoffman, eds., Slavery and Freedom in the Age of the American Revolution, pp. 283-301.

868. Raboteau, Albert J. "The Slave Church in the Era of the American Revolution," in Berlin and Hoffman, eds., Slavery and Freedom in the Age of the American Revolution, pp. 193-213.

869. Ransom, Roger L. "Was It Really All That Great to Be a Slave?: A Review Essay," Agricultural History, 48, 4 (1974), pp. 578-85.

870. Ratcliffe, Donald. "The Das Kapital of American Negro Slavery? Time on the Cross after Two Years (review article)," Durham University Journal, 69, 1 (1976), pp. 103-30.

871. Rawick, George P. From Sundown to Sunup: The Making of the Black Community. Westport, Conn.: Greenwood Press, 1972.

872. _____. "Some Notes on a Social Analysis of Slavery: A Critique and Assessment of The Slave Community," in Gilmore, ed., Revisiting Blassingame's The Slave Community, pp. 17-26.

873. _____, ed. The American Slave: A Composite Autobiography. 19 vols. Westport, Conn.: Greenwood Press, 1972.

874. _____, ed. The American Slave: A Composite Autobiography, Supplement, Series II. Westport, Conn.: Greenwood Press, 1979.

875. _____, and Evelyn Brooks Barnett, eds. "A Symposium on Herbert Gutman's The Black Family in Slavery and Freedom," Radical History Review, 4, 2-3 (1977), pp. 76-108.

876. Reed, Harry. "The Slave as Abolitionist: Henry Highland Garnet's Address to the Slaves of the United States of America," Centennial Review, 20, 4 (1976), pp. 385-94.

877. Rice, C. Duncan. "The Indestructible Institution (review essay on Gutman, The Black Family in Slavery and Freedom, 1750-1925)," Journal of Interdisciplinary History, 8, 2 (1977), pp. 343-52.

878. Rice, Madeline Hooke. American Catholic Opinion in the Slavery Controversy. New York: Columbia University Press, 1944.

879. Rinchon, Dieudonné. L'esclavage aux Etats-Unis; aperçu historique et bibliographie. Paris: Vanelsche, 1952.

880. Roark, James L. "Mastering Slavery (review essay on Rose, Slavery and Freedom)," Reviews in American History, 11, 1 (1983), pp. 72-76.

881. Robert, John Clarke. "Slavery in Tobacco Factories," in Newton and Lewis, eds., The Other Slaves, pp. 135-44.

882. Roberts, Wesley A. "The Black Experience and the American Revolution," Fides et Historia, 8, 2 (1976), pp. 50-62.

883. Robinson, Donald L. "Slavery and Sectionalism in the Founding of the United States, 1787-1808" (PhD diss., Cornell University, 1966).

884. _____. Slavery in the Structure of American Politics, 1765-1820. New York: Harcourt, Brace, Jovanovich, 1971.

885. Robinson, Jean Wealmont. "Black Healers during the Colonial Period and Early 19th Century America" (PhD diss., Southern Illinois University at Carbondale, 1979).

886. Roediger, David R. "And Die in Dixie: Funerals, Death and Heaven in the Slave Community, 1700-1865," Massachusetts Review, 22, 1 (1981), pp. 163-83.

887. Roediger, David. "The Meaning of Africa for the American Slave," Journal of Ethnic Studies, 4, 4 (1977), pp. 1-15.

888. Rose, Peter I., ed. Americans from Africa. 2 vols. New York: Atherton, 1970.

889. Rose, Willie Lee. "An American Family (review of Haley, Roots)," New York Review of Books, 23, 18 (11 Nov. 1976), pp. 3-6. Reprinted in Rose (Freehling ed.), Slavery and Freedom, pp. 115-23.

890. _____. "Off the Plantation (review essay)," New York Review of Books, 22, 14 (18 Sept. 1975), pp. 46-49. Reprinted in Rose (Freehling ed.), Slavery and Freedom, pp. 137-49.

891. _____. Slavery and Freedom. Ed. William W. Freehling. New York: Oxford University Press, 1982.

892. _____. "What We Didn't Know about Slavery (review essay)," New York Review of Books, 21, 16 (17 Oct. 1974), pp. 29-33. Reprinted in Rose (Freehling ed.), Slavery and Freedom, pp. 150-63.

893. _____, ed. A Documentary History of Slavery in North America. New York: Oxford University Press, 1976.

894. Rubin, Ernest. "Les esclaves aux Etats-Unis de 1790 à 1860: données sur leur nombre et leurs caracteristiques démographiques," Population, 14, 1 (1959), pp. 33-46.

895. Russell, Marion J. "American Slave Discontent in Records of the High Courts," Journal of Negro History, 31, 4 (1946), pp. 411-34.

896. Russell, Robert R. "The Economic History of Negro Slavery in the United States," Agricultural History, 11, 4 (1937), pp. 308-21. Also Bobbs-Merrill Reprint no. BC-258.

897. _____. "The General Effects of Slavery upon Southern Economic Progress," Journal of Southern History, 6, 1 (1938), pp. 34-54.

898. *Salwen, Bert, and Geoffrey M. Gyrisco. "Archeology of Black American Culture: An Annotated Bibliography" (U. S. Department of Interior, National Park Service, n.d.(1978)).

899. Sanderson, Warren C. "A Cliometric Reconsideration of Herbert Gutman's Black Family in Slavery and Freedom, 1750-1925," Social Science History, 3, 3-4 (1979), pp. 66-85.

900. Sandin, Bengt. "Sklaven som medelklassamerikan: Fogel och Engerman och debatten om slaveriet i USA," Historisk tidskrift (Stockholm), 97, 1 (1977), pp. 39-70. With English summary.

901. Savitt, Todd L. Medicine and Slavery. Champaign: University of Illinois Press, 1979.

902. Scarborough, William K. The Overseer: Plantation Management in the Old South. Baton Rouge: Louisiana State University Press, 1966.

903. _____. "Slavery - The White Man's Burden," in Owens, ed., Perspectives and Irony, pp. 103-35.

904. Schaefer, Donald F., and Mark D. Schmitz. "The Relative Efficiency of Slave Agriculture: A Comment," American Economic Review, 69, 1 (1979), pp. 208-12.

905. *Scheiber, Harry N. "Black is Computable," American Soldier, 44 (1975), pp. 656-73.

906. Scherer, Lester B. "A New Look at Personal Slavery Established," William and Mary Quarterly, 3rd ser., 30, 4 (1973), pp. 645-52.

907. _____. Slavery and the Churches in Early America, 1619-1819. Grand Rapids: Eerdmans, 1975.

908. Schlüter, Herman. Lincoln, Labor and Slavery: A Chapter from the Social History of America. New York: Socialist Literature, 1913; reprinted, New York: Russell and Russell, 1965.

909. Schmitz, Mark, and Donald Schaefer. "Paradox Lost: Westward Expansion and Slave Prices Before the Civil War," Journal of Economic History, 41, 2 (1981), pp. 402-07.

910. Scott, John Anthony. Hard Trials on My Way: Slavery and the Struggle Against It, 1800-1860. New York: Knopf, 1974.

911. Scruggs, Otey M. "Studies in American Negro Slavery: A Review Essay," Agricultural History, 53, 2 (1979), pp. 506-12.

912. Sellers, Charles G., Jr. "The Travail of Slavery," in Sellers, ed., The Southerner as American (Chapel Hill: University of North Carolina Press, 1960), pp. 40-71. Reprinted in Weinstein and Gatell, eds., American Negro Slavery (1st ed.), pp. 172-98.

913. Sellin, Johan Thorsten. Slavery and the Penal System. New York: Elsevier, 1976.

914. Sernett, Milton C. Black Religion and American Evangelicalism: White Protestants, Plantation Missions, and the Flowering of Negro Christianity, 1787-1865. Metuchen, N.J.: Scarecrow Press, 1975.

915. _____. "Black Religion and American Evangelicanism (sic): White Protestants, Plantation Missions, and the Independent Negro Church, 1788-1865" (PhD diss., University of Delaware, 1972).

916. Settle, E. Ophelia. "Social Attitudes During the Slave Regime: Household Servants versus Field Hands," in Racial Contacts and Social Research (American Sociological Society), 28 (1933), pp. 95-98. Reprinted in Meier and Rudwick, eds., Making of Black America, vol. 1, pp. 148-52.

917. Sherrard, Owen Aubrey. Freedom from Fear: The Slave and his Emancipation. New York: St. Martin's Press, 1961.

918. Short, Kenneth R. M. "English Baptists and American Slavery," Baptist Quarterly, 20, 6 (1964), pp. 243-62.

919. Sides, Sudie Duncan. "Slave Weddings and Religion," History Today, 24, 2 (1974), pp. 77-87.

920. _____. "Southern Women and Slavery, Part One: Before the Civil War," History Today, 20, 1 (1970), pp. 54-60.

921. _____. "Southern Women and Slavery, Part Two," History Today, 20, 2 (1970), pp. 124-30.

922. _____. "Women and Slaves: An Interpretation Based on the Writings of Southern Women" (PhD diss., University of North Carolina at Chapel Hill, 1969).

923. Siegel, Fred. "Parameters for Paternalism," Radical History Review, 3, 4 (1976), pp. 60-67.

924. Sikes, Lewright. "Medical Care for Slaves: A Preview of the Welfare State," Georgia Historical Quarterly, 62, 4 (1968), pp. 405-13.

925. Silverman, Jason H. "Kentucky, Canada, and Extradition: The Jesse Happy Case (fugitive slaves)," Filson Club History Quarterly, 54, 1 (1980), pp. 50-60.

926. Smith, Burton M. "A Study of American Historians and Their Interpretation of Negro Slavery in the United States" (PhD diss., Washington State University, 1970).

927. Smith, Daniel Blake. Inside the Great House: Planter Family Life in Eighteenth-Century Chesapeake Society. Ithaca, New York: Cornell University Press, 1980.

928. Smith, Dwight L. Afro-American History: A Bibliography. Santa Barbara: Clio Press, 1974.

929. Smith, Earl. "William Cooper Nell on the Fugitive Slave Act of 1850," Journal of Negro History, 66, 1 (1981), pp. 37-40.

930. Smith, Elbert B. The Death of Slavery: The United States, 1837-1865. Chicago: University of Chicago Press, 1967.

931. Smith, John David. "A Different View of Slavery: Black Historians Attack the Proslavery Argument, 1890-1920," Journal of Negro History, 65, 4 (1980), pp. 298-311.

932. _____. "The Formative Period of American Slave Historiography" (PhD diss., University of Kentucky, 1977).

933. _____. "Historical or Personal Criticism? Frederic Bancroft vs. Ulrich B. Phillips," Washington State University Research Studies, 49, 2 (1981), pp. 73-86.

934. _____. "More than Slaves, Less than Freedmen: The 'Share Wages' Labor System," Civil War History, 26, 3 (1980), pp. 256-66.

935. _____. "An Old Creed for the New South: Southern Historians and the Revival of the Proslavery Argument, 1890-1920," Southern Studies, 18, 1 (1979), pp. 75-87.

936. Smith, T. V. "Slavery and the American Doctrine of Equality," Southwestern Political and Social Science Quarterly, 7, 4 (1927), pp. 333-52.

937. Smith, Timothy L. "Slavery and Theology: The Emergence of Black Christian Consciousness in Nineteenth-Century America," Church History, 41, 4 (1972), pp. 497-512.

938. Smith, William Henry. A Political History of Slavery: Being an Account of the Slavery Controversy from the Earliest Agitation in the Eighteenth Century to the Close of the Reconstruction Period in America. New York: G. P. Putnam's Sons, 1903.

939. Sobel, Mechal. Trabelin' On: The Slave Journey to an Afro-Baptist Faith. Westport, Conn.: Greenwood Press, 1979.

940. "Some Usages of Long-Ago," Americana, 17, 4 (1923), pp. 399-426.

941. Sonnino, Paul, and Rick Sturdevant. "Marxism for Mystics (discussion of Luraghi, 'Wage Labor ...')," Plantation Society in the Americas, 1, 2 (1979), pp. 281-86.

942. Soule, Joshua. "The Methodist Church and Slavery," Methodist Quarterly Review, 57, 4 (1908), pp. 637-50.

943. Southern Studies, 16, 4 (1977). Special issue on Colonial Slavery (British North America).

944. Spero, Sterling D., and Abram L. Harris. "The Slave Regime: Competition Between Negro and White Labor," in Newton and Lewis, eds., The Other Slaves, pp. 41-50.

945. Stampp, Kenneth M. "The Historian and Southern Negro Slavery," American Historical Review, 57, 3 (1952), pp. 613-24. Reprinted in Weinstein and Gatell, eds., American Negro Slavery (1st ed.), pp. 221-33. Also Bobbs-Merrill Reprint no. H-204.

946. _____. "Introduction," in David et al., Reckoning with Slavery, pp. 1-30.

947. _____. "Rebels and Sambos: The Search for the Negro's Personality in Slavery," Journal of Southern History, 37, 3 (1971), pp. 367-92. Reprinted as "Rebels and Sambos," in Weinstein, Gatell, and Sarasohn, eds., American Negro Slavery (3rd ed.), pp. 228-54.

948. _____. "Slavery - The Historian's Burden," in Owens, ed., Perspectives and Irony, pp. 153-70.

949. Stange, Douglas C. "'A Compassionate Mother to Her Poor Negro Slaves': The Lutheran Church and Negro Slavery in Early America," Phylon, 29, 3 (1968), pp. 272-81.

950. _____. "From Treason to Antislavery Patriotism, Unitarian Conservatives and the Fugitive Slave Law," Harvard Library Bulletin, 25, 4 (1977), pp. 466-88.

951. _____. Patterns of Anti-Slavery Among American Unitarians, 1831-1860. Rutherford, N.J.: Fairleigh Dickinson University Press, 1977.

952. Starling, Marion. "The Slave Narrative: Its Place in American Literary History" (PhD diss., New York University, 1946).

953. _____. The Slave Narrative: Its Place in American History. Boston: G. K. Hall, 1981.

954. Starkey, Marion L. Striving to Make it my Home: The Story of Americans from Africa. New York: Norton, 1964.

955. Starobin, Robert S., ed. Blacks in Bondage: Letters of American Slaves. New York: New Viewpoints, 1974.

956. _____, ed. Slavery as it Was: The Testimony of the Slaves Themselves While in Bondage. Chicago, 1971.

957. Starr, Raymond. "Historians and the Origins of British North American Slavery," Historian, 36, 1 (1973), pp. 1-18.

958. Stavisky, Leonard. "Negro Craftsmanship in Early America," in Newton and Lewis, eds., The Other Slaves, pp. 193-203.

959. _____. "The Origins of Negro Craftsmen in Colonial America," in Newton and Lewis, eds., The Other Slaves, pp. 183-91.

960. Steckel, Richard H. "The Economics of U. S. Slave and Southern White Fertility" (PhD diss., University of Chicago, 1977).

961. _____. "Miscegenation and the American Slave Schedules," Journal of Interdisciplinary History, 11, 2 (1980), pp. 251-63.

962. _____. "Slave Height Profiles from Coastwise
     Manifests," Explorations in Economic History, 16, 4 (1979), pp.
     363-80.

963. _____. "Slave Mortality: Analysis of Evidence from
     Plantation Records," Social Science History, 3, 3-4 (1979), pp.
     86-114.

964. Stephens, Lester D. "'Forget Their Color': J. Peter Lesley on
     Slavery and the South," New England Quarterly, 53, 2 (1980), pp.
     212-21.

965. Sterne, Richards, and Jean Loftin Rothseiden. "Master-Slave
     Clashes as Forerunners of Patterns in Modern American Urban
     Eruptions," Phylon, 30, 3 (1969), pp. 251-60.

966. Stitt, Edward Rhodes. "Our Disease Inheritance from Slavery,"
     United States Naval Medical Bulletin, 26, 4 (1928), pp. 801-17.

967. Storing, Herbert. "Slavery and the Moral Foundations of the
     American Republic," in Robert H. Horwitz, ed., The Moral
     Foundations of the American Republic (Charlottesville, Va.:
     University Press of Virginia, 1977), pp. 214-33.

968. Stuckey, Sterling. "Through the Prism of Folklore: The Black Ethos
     in Slavery," Massachusetts Review, 9, 3 (1968), pp. 417-37.
     Reprinted in Haynes, ed., Blacks in White America, pp. 259-68; in
     Weinstein and Gatell, eds., American Negro Slavery (2nd ed.), pp.
     134-52; in Lane, ed., Debate Over Slavery, pp. 245-68.

969. Sutch, Richard. "The Care and Feeding of Slaves," in David et al.,
     Reckoning with Slavery, pp. 231-301.

970. _____. "The Profitability of Ante Bellum Slavery -
     Revisited," Southern Economic Journal, 31, 4 (1965), pp. 365-77.
     Reprinted in Aitken, ed., Did Slavery Pay?, pp. 221-41.

971. _____. "The Treatment Received by American Slaves: A
     Critical Review of the Evidence Presented in Time on the Cross,"
     Explorations in Economic History, 12, 4 (1975), pp. 335-438.

972. Sutherland, Daniel E. "A Special Kind of Problem: The Response of
     Household Slaves and their Masters to Freedom," Southern Studies,
     20, 2 (1981), pp. 151-66.

973. Suttles, William C., Jr. "African Religious Survivals as Factors
     in American Slave Revolts," Journal of Negro History, 56, 2
     (1971), pp. 97-104.

974. _____. "A Trace of Soul: The Religion of Negro
     Slaves on the Plantations of North America" (PhD diss., University
     of Michigan, 1979).

975. Swaney, Charles Baumer. Episcopal Methodism and Slavery: With Sidelights on Ecclesiastical Politics. Boston: Richard Gorham Press, 1926.

976. Sweig, Donald M. "Reassessing the Human Dimension of the Interstate Slave Trade," Prologue, 12, 1 (1980), pp. 5-19.

977. Takaki, Ronald T. Iron Cages: Race and Culture in Nineteenth-Century America. New York: Alfred A. Knopf, 1979.

978. Tannenbaum, Frank. "Slave and Citizen," in Haynes, ed., Blacks in White America Before 1865, pp. 150-72. (From Slave and Citizen, pp. 42-82) "Slave and Citizen" also reprinted (from Slave and Citizen, pp. 42-107) in Brown, ed., Slavery in American Society, pp. 55-65.

979. _____. "Slavery, the Negro, and Racial Prejudice," in Foner and Genovese, eds., Slavery in the Americas, pp. 3-7. (Reprinted from "Toward an Appreciation of Latin America," in Herbert L. Matthews, ed., The United States and Latin America (2nd ed.)(New York: The American Assembly, Columbia University, 1963), pp. 23ff.)

980. Taylor, Olive. "Before the Civil War: History of Commitment," Negro History Bulletin, 44, 1 (1981), pp. 9-10.

981. _____. "The Final Arbiter: A History of the Decisions Rendered by the Supreme Court of the United States Relative to the Negro Prior to the Civil War," Negro History Bulletin, 43, 1 (1980), pp. 8-10.

982. Taylor, Rosser H. "Feeding Slaves," Journal of Negro History, 9, 2 (1924), pp. 139-43.

983. Terry, Eugene. "The Shadow of Slavery in Charles Chesnutt's The Conjure Woman," Ethnic Groups, 4, 1-2 (1982), pp. 103-25.

984. Thompson, Edgar T. Plantation Societies, Race Relations, and the South: The Regimentation of Populations. Selected Papers of Edgar T. Thompson. Durham, N.C.: Duke University Press, 1975.

985. Thorpe, Earle E. "Chattel Slavery and Concentration Camps," Negro History Bulletin, 25, 8 (1962), pp. 171-76. Reprinted in Rose, ed., Americans from Africa, vol. 1, pp. 155-69.

986. _____. "The Slave Community: Studies of Slavery Need Freud and Marx," in Gilmore, ed., Revisiting Blassingame's The Slave Community, pp. 42-60.

987. Tilley, John Shipley. The Coming of the Glory. New York: Stratford House, 1949.

988. Tipton, Frank B., Jr., and Clarence E. Walker. "(Review of Fogel and Engerman, Time on the Cross, and Wood, Black Majority)," History and Theory, 14, 1 (1975), pp. 91-120.

989. Tise, Larry Edward. "Proslavery Ideology: A Social and Intellectual History of the Defence of Slavery in America, 1790-1840" (PhD diss., University of North Carolina at Chapel Hill, 1975).

990. Toll, William. "Were We 'The Last Best Hope'? Slavery in the Social Order (essay review of Genovese, Roll, Jordan, Roll)," Pacific Northwest Quarterly, 67, 1 (1976), pp. 29-32.

991. "Travelers' Impressions of Slavery in America from 1750-1800," Journal of Negro History, 1, 4 (1916), pp. 399-435.

992. Trussel, James, and Richard Steckel. "The Age of Slaves at Menarche and their First Birth," Journal of Interdisciplinary History, 8, 3 (1978), pp. 477-506.

993. Tushnet, Mark V. The American Law of Slavery, 1810-1860: Considerations of Humanity and Interest. Princeton: Princeton University Press, 1981.

994. _____. "Approaches to the Study of the Law of Slavery," Civil War History, 25, 4 (1979), pp. 329-38.

995. Unger, Irwin, and David Reimers, eds. The Slavery Experience in the United States. New York: Holt, Rinehart and Winston, 1970.

996. Uya, Okon Edet. "The Culture of Slavery: Black Experience Through a White Filter," Afro-American Studies, 1, 3 (1971), pp. 203-09.

997. _____. "Life in the Slave Community," Afro-American Studies, 1, 4 (1971), pp. 281-90.

998. Van Deburg, William L. "Elite Slave Behaviour during the Civil War: Black Drivers and Foremen in Historiographical Perspective," Southern Studies, 16, 4 (1977), pp. 253-70.

999. _____. The Slave Drivers: Black Agricultural Labor Supervisors in the Antebellum South. Westport, Conn.: Greenwood Press, 1979.

1000. _____. "Slave Drivers and Slave Narratives: A New Look at the 'Dehumanized Elite'," Historian, 39, 4 (1977). pp. 717-32.

1001. _____. "Who Were the Slave Drivers," Negro History Bulletin, 41, 2 (1978), pp. 808-11.

1002. Van Horne, John C. "Impediments to the Christianization and Education of Blacks in Colonial America: The Case of the Associates of Dr. Bray," Historical Magazine of the Protestant Episcopal Church, 50, 3 (1981), pp. 243-69.

1003. Vassar, Rena. "William Knox's Defense of Slavery," Proceedings of the American Philosophical Society, 111, 4 (1970), pp. 310-26.

1004. Vedder, Richard K. "The Slave Exploitation (Expropriation) Rate," Explorations in Economic History, 12, 4 (1975), pp. 453-57.

1005. _____, and David C. Stockdale. "The Profitability of Slavery Revisited: A Different Approach," Agricultural History, 49, 2 (1975), pp. 392-404.

1006. Vinovskis, Maris A. "The Demography of the Slave Population in Antebellum America," Journal of Interdisciplinary History, 5, 3 (1975), pp. 459-67.

1007. Wagstaff, Tom. "Political Economy of Slavery (review of Genovese, The Political Economy of Slavery)," Studies on the Left, 6, 4 (1966), pp. 58-70.

1008. Walker, Clarence E. "Massa's New Clothes: A Critique of Eugene D. Genovese on Southern Society, Master-Slave Relations, and Slave Behavior," Umoja: A Scholarly Journal of Black Studies, 4, 2 (1980), pp. 114-30.

1009. Walker, James W. St. G. "Blacks as American Loyalists: The Slaves' War for Independence," Historical Reflections/Réflexions historiques, 2, 1 (1975), pp. 51-67.

1010. Wall, Bennett H. "African Slavery," in Arthur S. Link and Rembert W. Patrick, eds., Writing Southern History (Baton Rouge: Louisiana State University Press, 1965), pp. 175-97.

1011. _____. "An Epitaph for Slavery," Louisiana History, 16, 3 (1975), pp. 229-56.

1012. _____."The Myth of the Planter Past (discussion of Luraghi, 'Wage Labor . . .')," Plantation Society in the Americas, 1, 2 (1979), pp. 273-80.

1013. Wall, Cary. "The Boomerang of Slavery: The Child, the Aristocrat, and Hidden White Identity in Huck Finn," Southern Studies, 21, 2 (1982), pp. 208-21.

1014. Wallerstein, Immanuel. "American Slavery and the Capitalist World Economy (review of Fogel and Engerman, Time on the Cross)," American Journal of Sociology, 81, 5 (1976), pp. 1199-1212. Reprinted in idem, The Capitalist World-Economy (Cambridge: Cambridge University Press, 1979), pp. 202-21.

1015. Wallin, Jeffrey D. "History, or Interpretation? David Brion Davis on American Slavery," Conservative Historians' Forum, 6 (1982), pp. 22-25.

1016. Walters, Ronald G. "The Erotic South: Civilization and Sexuality in American Abolitionism," American Quarterly, 25, 2 (1973), pp. 177-201.

1017. Walton, Gary M., ed. "Symposium on Time on the Cross," Explorations in Economic History, 12, 4 (1975), pp. 333-457.

1018. Wares, Lydia Jean. "Dress of the African American Woman in Slavery and Freedom" (PhD diss., Purdue University, 1981).

1019. Wax, Darold D. "Preferences for Slaves in Colonial America," Journal of Negro History, 58, 4 (1973), pp. 371-401.

1020. Weatherford, Willis Duke. American Churches and the Negro. Boston: Christopher Publishing House, 1957.

1021. Weiher, Kenneth. "Slavery and Southern Urbanization: A Reformulation of the Argument," in James H. Soltow, ed., Essays in Economic and Business History: Selected Papers from the Economic and Business Historical Society, 1976, 1977, 1978 (East Lansing: Michigan State University, Graduate School of Business Administration, 1979), pp. 259-67.

1022. Weinstein, Allen, and Frank Otto Gatell, eds. American Negro Slavery: A Modern Reader. New York: Oxford University Press, 1968. 2nd revised edition, 1973.

1023. _____, and David Sarasohn, eds. American Negro Slavery. 3rd revised edition. New York: Oxford University Press, 1979.

1024. Wenzel, Peter. "Pre-Modern Concepts of Society and Economy in American Pro-Slavery Thought: On the Intellectual Foundations of the Social Philosophy of George Fitzhugh," Amerikastudien/American Studies (Munich), 27, 2 (1982), pp. 157-75.

1025. Wesley, Charles H. "Slavery and Industrialism," in Newton and Lewis, eds., The Other Slaves, pp. 21-40.

1026. Weyl, Nathaniel, and William Marina. American Statesmen on Slavery and the Negro. New Rochelle, N.Y.: Arlington House, 1971.

1027. White, John. "Whatever Happened to the Slave Family in the Old South? (review article)," Journal of American Studies, 8, 3 (1974), pp. 383-90.

1028. Whitten, David O. "Medical Care of Slaves: Louisiana Sugar Region and South Carolina Rice District," Southern Studies, 16, 4 (1977), pp. 153-80.

1029. Wiecek, William M. "Slavery and Abolition Before the United States Supreme Court, 1820-1860," Journal of American History, 65, 1 (1978), pp. 34-59.

1030. _____. "The Statutory Law of Slavery and Race in the Thirteen Mainland Colonies of British America," William and Mary Quarterly, 3rd ser., 34, 2 (1977), pp. 258-80.

1031. Wiggins, David Kenneth. "Sport and Popular Pastimes in the Plantation Community: The Slave Experience" (PhD diss., University of Maryland, 1979).

1032. Wilson, G. R. "The Religion of the American Negro Slave: His Attitude toward Life and Death," Journal of Negro History, 8, 1 (1923), pp. 41-71.

1033. Wiltshire, Susan Ford. "Jefferson, Calhoun, and the Slavery Debate: The Classics and the Two Minds of the South," Southern Humanities Review, Special Issue (1977), pp. 33-40.

1034. Windley, Lathan A. "A Profile of Runaway Slaves in Virginia and South Carolina from 1730 through 1787" (PhD diss., University of Iowa, 1974).

1035. Winkler, Allan M. "Ulrich Bonnell Phillips, a Reappraisal," South Atlantic Quarterly, 71, 2 (1972), pp. 234-45.

1036. Winston, Michael R. "Selected Documents Illustrative of Some Aspects of the Life of Blacks between 1774 and 1841," Journal of Negro History, 61, 1 (1976), pp. 88-97.

1037. Wish, Harvey. "American Slave Insurrections Before 1861," Journal of Negro History, 22, 3 (1937), pp. 299-320. Reprinted in Bracey, Meier, and Rudwick, eds., American Slavery, pp. 21-36. Also Bobbs-Merrill Reprint no. BC-324.

1038. Wood, Peter H. "'I Did the Best I Could for My Day': The Study of Early Black History During the Second Reconstruction, 1960-1976," William and Mary Quarterly, 3rd ser., 35, 2 (1978), pp. 185-225.

1039. _____. "Phillips Upside Down: Dialectic or Equivocation (review of Genovese, Roll, Jordan, Roll, and Miller and Genovese, eds., Plantation, Town, and Country)," Journal of Interdisciplinary History, 6, 2 (1975), pp. 289-97.

1040. Woodman, Harold D. "Economic History and Economic Theory: The New Economic History in America," Journal of Interdisciplinary History, 3, 2 (1972), pp. 323-50.

1041. _____. "The Profitability of Slavery: A Historical Perennial," Journal of Southern History, 29, 3 (1963), pp. 303-25. Reprinted in Weinstein and Gatell, eds., American Negro Slavery (1st ed.), pp. 259-81 (2nd ed., pp. 294-316); in Genovese, ed., Slave Economies, vol. 2, pp. 231-56. Also Bobbs-Merrill Reprint no. BC-259.

1042. _____, ed. Slavery and the Southern Economy, Sources and Readings. New York: Harcourt, Brace and World, 1966.

1043. Woodward, C. Vann. American Counterpoint: Slavery and Racism in the North-South Dialogue. Boston: Little, Brown, 1971.

1044. _____. "History from Slave Sources (review of Rawick, ed., The American Slave)," American Historical Review, 79, 2 (1974), pp. 470-81.

1045. _____. "The Jolly Institution (review of Fogel and Engerman, Time on the Cross)," New York Review of Books, 31, 7 (2 May 1974), pp. 3-6.

1046. _____. "Southern Slaves in the World of Thomas Malthus," in idem, American Counterpoint, pp. 78-106.

1047. Woolfolk, George R. "Planter Capitalism and Slavery: The Labor Thesis," Journal of Negro History, 41, 2 (1956), pp. 103-16. Also Bobbs-Merrill Reprint no. BC-327.

1048. Wright, Gavin. "The Efficiency of Slavery: Another Interpretation," American Economic Review, 69, 1 (1979), pp. 219-26.

1049. _____. "New and Old Views on the Economics of Slavery (review article on Aitken, ed., Did Slavery Pay?, and Butlin, Ante-Bellum Slavery)," Journal of Economic History, 33, 2 (1973), pp. 452-66.

1050. _____. "Prosperity, Progress, and American Slavery," in David, et al., Reckoning with Slavery, pp. 302-36.

1051. *Yasuba, Yasukichi. "The Profitability and Viability of Plantation Slavery in the United States," Economic Studies Quarterly, 12 (1961), pp. 60-67. Reprinted in Fogel and Engerman, eds., Reinterpretation, pp. 362-68.

1052. Yetman, Norman R. "The Background of the Slave Narrative Collection," American Quarterly, 19, 3 (1967), pp. 534-53.

1053. _____. "The Rise and Fall of Time on the Cross," Reviews in American History, 4, 2 (1976), pp. 195-202.

1054. _____. "The Slave Personality: A Test of the 'Sambo' Hypothesis" (PhD diss., University of Pennsylvania, 1969).

1055. _____, ed. Life Under the "Peculiar Institution": Selections from the Slave Narrative Collection. New York: Holt, Rinehart and Winston, 1970.

1056. _____, comp. Voices from Slavery. New York: Holt, Rinehart and Winston, 1970.

1057. Zelnik, Melvin. "Fertility of the American Negro in 1830 and 1850," Population Studies, 20, 1 (1966), pp. 77-83.

1058. Zepp, Thomas M. "On Returns to Scale and Input Substitutability in Slave Agriculture," Explorations in Economic History, 13, 2 (1976), pp. 165-78.

2. New England and the Middle Colonies

1059. Bartlett, Irving H. "Abolitionists, Fugitives, and Imposters in Boston, 1846–1847," New England Quarterly, 55, 1 (1982), pp. 97–110.

1060. *Belknap, Jeremy. "Queries Respecting the Slavery and Emancipation of Negroes in Massachusetts," Collections of the Massachusetts Historical Society, 1st ser., 4 (1935), pp. 191–211.

1061. Brouwer, Merle G. "Marriage and Family Life among Blacks in Colonial Pennsylvania," Pennsylvania Magazine of History and Biography, 99, 3 (1975), pp. 368–72.

1062. _____. "The Negro as a Slave and as a Free Black in Colonial Pennsylvania" (PhD diss., Wayne State University, 1973).

1063. Calligaro, Lee. "The Negro's Legal Status in Pre–Civil War New Jersey," New Jersey History, 85, 3–4 (1967), pp. 167–80.

1064. Clarke, T. Wood. "The Negro Plot of 1741," New York History, 25, 2 (1944), pp. 167–81.

1065. Cottrol, Robert J. The Afro-Yankees: Providence's Black Community in the Antebellum Era. Westport, Conn.: Greenwood Press, 1982.

1066. Crew, Spencer. "Black New Jersey Before the Civil War: Two Case Studies," New Jersey History, 99, 1–2 (1981), pp. 67–86.

1067. Davis, Thomas J. "The New York Slave Conspiracy of 1791 as Black Protest," Journal of Negro History, 56, 1 (1971), pp. 17–30.

1068. _____. "New York's Long Black Line: A Note on the Growing Slave Population, 1626–1790," Afro-Americans in New York Life and History, 2, 1 (1978), pp. 41–60.

1069. _____. "Northern Slaves – Neglected People in the Historiography of American Negro Slavery," Journal of Ethnic Studies, 8, 1 (1979), pp. 1–14.

1070. _____. "Slavery in Colonial New York City" (PhD diss., Columbia University, 1974).

1071. _____, ed. The New York Conspiracy (by Daniel Horsmanden). New York: Negro Universities Press, 1969.

1072. Dean, John Gary. "The Free Negro in Delaware" (MA thesis, University of Delaware, 1970).

1073. Drake, Thomas E. Quakers and Slavery in America. New Haven: Yale University Press, 1950.

1074. Galpin, W. Freeman. "The Jerry Rescue," New York History, 26, 1 (1945), pp. 19–34.

1075. Goodfriend, Joyce D. "Burghers and Blacks: The Evolution of a Slave Society at New Amsterdam," New York History, 59, 2 (1978), pp. 125-44.

1076. Greene, Lorenzo Johnston. The Negro in Colonial New England, 1620-1776. New York: Columbia University Press, 1942.

1077. _____. "The New England Negro as Seen in Advertisements for Runaway Slaves," Journal of Negro History, 29, 2 (1944), pp. 125-46.

1078. Hammond, Isaac W. "Slavery in New Hampshire," Granite State Magazine, 4, 5 (1907), pp. 199-203.

1079. Hershberg, Theodore. "Free Blacks in Antebellum Philadelphia," Journal of Social History, 5, 2 (1971-72), pp. 183-209. Reprinted in Miller and Genovese, eds., Plantation, Town, and County, pp. 415-40.

1080. _____. "Free-Born and Slave-Born Blacks in Ante-bellum Philadelphia," in Engerman and Genovese, eds., Race and Slavery, pp. 395-426.

1081. Hill, Charles L. "Slavery and its Aftermath in Beverly, Massachusetts: Juno Larcom and her Family," Essex Institute Historical Collections, 116, 2 (1980), pp. 111-30.

1082. Jordan, Winthrop D. "The Influence of the West Indies on the Origins of New England Slavery," William and Mary Quarterly, 3rd ser., 18, 2 (1961), pp. 243-50.

1083. Katz, Jonathan. Resistance at Christiana: The Fugitive Slave Rebellion, Christiana, Pennsylvania, September 11, 1851: A Documentary Report. New York: Crowell, 1974.

1084. Klingberg, Frank J. "The African Immigrant to Colonial Pennsylvania and Delaware," Historical Magazine of the Protestant Episcopal Church, 11, 2 (1942), pp. 126-53.

1085. Kull, Irving Stoddard. "Slavery in New Jersey," Americana, 24, 4 (1930), pp. 443-72.

1086. Launtiz-Schurer, Leopold S., Jr. "Slave Resistance in Colonial New York: An Interpretation of Daniel Horsmanden's New York Conspiracy," Phylon, 41, 2 (1980), pp. 137-52.

1087. McManus, Edgar J. Black Bondage in the North. Syracuse: Syracuse University Press, 1973.

1088. _____. A History of Negro Slavery in New York. Syracuse: Syracuse University Press, 1966.

1089. Miller, M. Sammy. "Slavery in an Urban Area - District of Columbia," Negro History Bulletin, 37, 5 (1974), pp. 293-95.

1090. Moss, Simeon F. "The Persistence of Slavery and Involuntary Servitude in a Free State 1685-1865," Journal of Negro History, 35, 3 (1950), pp. 289-314.

1091. Munroe, John A. "The Negro in Delaware," South Atlantic Quarterly, 56, 4 (1957), pp. 428-44.

1092. Nash, Gary B. "Forging Freedom: The Emancipation Experience in the Northern Seaport Cities, 1775-1820," in Berlin and Hoffman, eds., Slavery and Freedom in the Age of the American Revolution, pp. 3-48.

1093. _____. "Slaves and Slaveowners in Colonial Philadelphia," William and Mary Quarterly, 3rd ser., 30, 2 (1973), pp. 223-56.

1094. Newman, Debra. "Black Women in the Era of the American Revolution in Pennsylvania," Journal of Negro History, 61, 3 (1976), pp. 276-89.

1095. Nordstrom, Carl. "The New York Slave Code," Afro-Americans in New York Life and History, 4, 1 (1980), pp. 7-25.

1096. _____. "Slavery in a New York County: Rockland County 1686-1827," Afro-Americans in New York Life and History, 1, 2 (1977), pp. 145-66.

1097. Northrup, A. Judd. Slavery in New York: A Historical Sketch. Albany: New York State Library, 1900. (History Bulletin no. 4)

1098. Olson, Edwin. "The Slave Code in Colonial New York," Journal of Negro History, 29, 2 (1944), pp. 147-65.

1099. Piersen, William D. "Afro-American Culture in Eighteenth-Century New England: A Comparative Examination" (PhD diss., Indiana University, 1975).

1100. Pingeon, Frances D. "Slavery in New Jersey on the Eve of the Revolution," in William C. Wright, ed., New Jersey in the American Revolution (rev. ed.)(Trenton: New Jersey Historical Commission, 1974), pp. 48-64. (1st Annual New Jersey History Symposium, 1969)

1101. Reidy, Joseph P. "'Negro Election Day' and Black Community Life in New England, 1750-1860," Marxist Perspectives, 1, 3 (1978), pp. 102-17.

1102. Riddell, William Renwick. "The Slave in Early New York," Journal of Negro History, 13, 1 (1928), pp. 53-86.

1103. Rosenberg, Leonard B. "William Patterson and Attitudes in New Jersey on Slavery," New Jersey History, 95, 4 (1977), pp. 197-206.

1104. Schwartz, Karen Jean. "Negro Slavery in Colonial New York City, 1664-1765" (MA thesis, University of Virginia, 1980).

1105. Scott, Kenneth. "The Slave Insurrection in New York in 1712," New York Historical Society Quarterly, 45, 1 (1961), pp. 43-74. Also Bobbs-Merrill Reprint no. BC-265.

1106. Soderland, Jean R. "Black Women in Colonial Pennsylvania," Pennsylvania Magazine of History and Biography, 107, 1 (1983), pp. 49-68.

1107. _____. "Conscience, Interest and Power: The Development of Quaker Opposition to Slavery in the Delaware Valley, 1688-1780" (PhD diss., Temple University, 1982).

1108. Sokolow, Jayme A. "The Jerry McHenry Rescue and the Growth of Northern Antislavery Sentiment during the 1850s," Journal of American Studies, 16, 3 (1982), pp. 427-45.

1109. Stewart, Helen B. "The Negro in Delaware to 1829" (MA thesis, University of Delaware, 1940).

1110. Stuart, William. "Negro Slavery in New Jersey and New York," Americana, 16, 4 (1922), pp. 347-67.

1111. Szasz, Ferenc M. "The New York Slave Revolt of 1741: A Re-Examination," New York History, 48, 3 (1967), pp. 215-30.

1112. Tully, Alan. "Patterns of Slaveholding in Colonial Pennsylvania: Chester and Lancaster Counties, 1729-1758," Journal of Social History, 6, 3 (1973), pp. 284-305.

1113. Turner, Edward R. The Negro in Pennsylvania, Slavery-Servitude-Freedom, 1639-1861. Washington, D.C.: American Historical Association, 1911.

1114. _____. "Slavery in Colonial Pennsylvania," Pennsylvania Magazine of History and Biography, 35, 2 (no. 138)(1911), pp. 141-51.

1115. Twombley, Robert C. "Black Resistance to Slavery in Massachusetts," in William L. O'Neill, ed., Insights and Parallels (Minneapolis: Burgess Publishing Co., 1973), pp. 11-56.

1116. _____, and Robert H. Moore. "Black Puritan: The Negro in Seventeenth Century Massachusetts," William and Mary Quarterly, 3rd ser., 24, 2 (1967), pp. 224-42. Reprinted in Haynes, ed., Blacks in White America, pp. 117-33; in Meier and Rudwick, eds., Making of Black America, pp. 109-24. Also Bobbs-Merrill Reprint no. BC-303.

1117. Wacker, Peter O. "Patterns and Problems in the Historical Geography of the Afro-American Population of New Jersey, 1726-1860," in Ralph E. Ehrenberg, ed., Pattern and Process: Research in Historical Geography (Washington, D.C.: Howard University Press, 1975), pp. 25-72. (Conference on the National Archives and Research in Historical Geography, 1971)

1118. Wagman, Morton. "Corporate Slavery in New Netherland," Journal of Negro History, 65, 1 (1980), pp. 34-42.

1119. Wax, Darold D. "The Demand for Slave Labor in Colonial Pennsylvania," Pennsylvania History, 34, 4 (1967), pp. 331-45.

1120. _____. "Negro Imports into Pennsylvania, 1720-1766," Pennsylvania History, 32, 3 (1965), pp. 254-87.

1121. Williams, Oscar R., Jr. "Blacks and Colonial Legislation in the Middle Colonies" (PhD diss., Ohio State University, 1969).

1122. Wood, Jerome H., Jr. "The Negro in Early Pennsylvania: The Lancaster Experience, 1730-90," in Miller and Genovese, eds., Plantation, Town, and County, pp. 441-52.

1123. Wright, Marion Thompson. "New Jersey Laws and the Negro," Journal of Negro History, 28, 2 (1943), pp. 156-99.

1124. Zilversmit, Arthur. The First Emancipation: The Abolition of Slavery in the North. Chicago, 1967.

3. Chesapeake

1125. Agonito, Joseph. "St. Inigoes Manor: A Nineteenth Century Jesuit Plantation," Maryland Historical Magazine, 72, 1 (1977), pp. 83-98.

1126. Albert, Peter Joseph. "The Protean Institution: The Geography, Economy, and Ideology of Slavery in Post-Revolutionary Virginia" (PhD diss., University of Maryland, 1976).

1127. Angel, J. L., and J. O. Kelley. "Health Status of Colonial Iron-Worker Slaves" (Paper given to 52nd Annual Meeting of the American Association of Physical Anthropologists, Indianapolis, Indiana, April 1983). Abstract in American Journal of Physical Anthropology, 60, 2 (1983), pp. 170-71.

1128. Aptheker, Herbert. Nat Turner's Slave Rebellion. New York: Humanities Press, 1966.

1129. Ballagh, James C. A History of Slavery in Virginia. Baltimore: Johns Hopkins University Press, 1902.

1130. Billings, Warren M. "The Case of Fernando and Elizabeth Key: A Note on the Status of Blacks in Seventeenth-Century Virginia," William and Mary Quarterly, 3rd ser., 30, 3 (1973), pp. 467-74.

1131. Bogger, Tommy Lee. "The Slave and Free Black Communities in Norfolk, 1775-1865" (PhD diss., University of Virginia, 1976).

1132. _____. "Slave Resistance in Virginia During the Haitian Revolution, 1791-1804," Journal of Ethnic Studies, 5, 1 (1978), pp. 86-100.

1133. *Bonekemper, Edward H. "Negroes' Freedom of Contract in Ante-bellum Virginia, 1620-1860" (MA thesis, Old Dominion University, 1971).

1134. Boney, F. N. "The Blue Lizard: Another View of Nat Turner's Country on the Eve of Rebellion," Phylon, 31, 4 (1970), pp. 351-58.

1135. Boskin, Joseph. Into Slavery: Racial Decisions in the Virginia Colony. Philadelphia: Lippincott, 1976.

1136. _____. "The Origins of American Slavery: Education as an Index of Early Differentiation," Journal of Negro Education, 35, 2 (1966), pp. 125-33.

1137. _____. "Race Relations in Seventeenth-Century America: The Problem of the Origin of Negro Slavery," Sociology and Social Research, 49, 4 (1965), pp. 446-55. Reprinted in Noel, ed., Origins of American Slavery and Racism, pp. 95-105.

1138. Bradford, S. Sydney. "The Negro Iron-worker in Ante Bellum Virginia," Journal of Southern History, 25, 2 (1959), pp. 194-206. Reprinted in Meier and Rudwick, eds., Making of Black America, pp. 137-47. Also Bobbs-Merrill Reprint no. BC-35.

1139. Bradley, Michael R. "The Role of the Black Church in the Colonial Slave Society," Louisiana Studies, 14, 4 (1975), pp. 413-21.

1140. Bratton, Mary J. "Fields's Observations: The Slave Narrative of a Nineteenth-Century Virginian," Virginia Magazine of History and Biography, 88, 1 (1980), pp. 75-93.

1141. Breen, Timothy H. "A Changing Labor Force and Race Relations in Virginia 1660-1710," Journal of Social History, 7, 1 (1973), pp. 3-25.

1142. _____, and Stephen Innes. "Myne Owne Ground": Race and Freedom on Virginia's Eastern Shore, 1640-1676. New York: Oxford University Press, 1980.

1143. Brewer, James H. "Negro Property Owners in Seventeenth-Century Virginia," William and Mary Quarterly, 3rd ser., 12, 4 (1955), pp. 575-80. Reprinted in Meier and Rudwick, eds., Making of Black America, pp. 201-05. Also Bobbs-Merrill Reprint no. BC-36.

1144. Bromberg, Alan Bruce. "Slavery in the Virginia Tobacco Factories, 1800-1860" (MA thesis, University of Virginia, 1968).

1145. *Brooks, Albert. "Education of Negroes in Virginia Prior to 1861" (MA thesis, Howard University, 1938).

1146. Bruce, Kathleen. "Slave Labor in the Virginian Iron Industry," William and Mary Quarterly, 2nd ser., 6, 4 (1926), pp. 289-302; 7, 1 (1927), pp. 21-31.

1147. _____. Virginia Iron Manufacture in the Slave Era. New York: Century, 1930.

1148. *Buehler, Richard D. "Virginia's Attitude Toward Slavery, 1776-1800" (MA thesis, Columbia University, 1964).

1149. Carroll, Kenneth L. "Maryland Quakers and Slavery," Quaker History, 72, 1 (1983), pp. 27-42.

1150. _____. "Religious Influences on the Manumission of Slaves in Caroline, Dorchester, and Talbot Counties," Maryland Historical Magazine, 56, 2 (1961), pp. 176-97.

1151. Cassell, Frank A. "Slaves of the Chesapeake Bay Area and the War of 1812," Journal of Negro History, 57, 2 (1972), pp. 144-55.

1152. Cassimere, Raphael, Jr. "The Origins and Early Development of Slavery in Maryland, 1633 to 1715" (PhD diss., Lehigh University, 1971).

1153. Clarke, John Henrik, ed. William Styron's Nat Turner: Ten Black Writers Respond. Boston: Beacon, 1968.

1154. Cope, Robert S. Carry Me Back: Slavery and Servitude in Seventeenth Century Virginia. Pikeville, Ky.: Pikeville College Press of the Appalachian Studies Center, 1973.

1155. _____. "Slavery and Servitude in the Colony of Virginia in the Seventeenth Century" (PhD diss., Ohio State University, 1951).

1156. Craven, Wesley Frank. "Twenty Negroes to Jamestown in 1619?" Virginia Quarterly Review, 47, 3 (1971), pp. 416-20.

1157. *Curran, R. Emmet. "'Splendid Paupers': Jesuit Slaveholding in Maryland, 1805-38" (Paper read to the Annual Meeting of the American Historical Association, Los Angeles, 1981).

1158. Dabney, Virginius. "Gabriel's Insurrection," American History Illustrated, 11, 4 (1976), pp. 24-32.

1159. Daniel, W. Harrison. "Virginia Baptists and the Negro in the Antebellum Era," Journal of Negro History, 56, 1 (1971), pp. 1-16.

1160. Deal, Joseph Douglas III. "Race and Class in Colonial Virginia: Indians, Englishmen and Africans on the Eastern Shore during the Seventeenth Century" (PhD diss., University of Rochester, 1981).

1161. Dew, Charles B. "David Ross and the Oxford Iron Works: A Study of Industrial Slavery in the Early Nineteenth-Century South," William and Mary Quarterly, 3rd ser., 31, 2 (1974), pp. 189-224.

1162. Drewry, William Sidney. "Slave Insurrections in Virginia (1830-1865)" (PhD diss., Johns Hopkins University, 1900).

1163. Duff, John B., and Peter M. Mitchell, eds. The Nat Turner Rebellion: The Historical Event and the Modern Controversy. New York: Harper and Row, 1971.

1164. Dunn, Richard S. "Black Society in the Chesapeake, 1776-1810," in Berlin and Hoffman, eds., Slavery and Freedom in the Age of the American Revolution, pp. 49-82.

1165. Dunne, Gerald T. "Bushrod Washington and the Mount Vernon Slaves," Yearbook - Supreme Court Historical Society, 5 (1980), pp. 25-29.

1166. Ernst, William J. "Changes in the Slave Population of the Virginia Tidewater and Piedmont, 1830-1860: A Stable Population Analysis," Essays in History, 19 (1975), pp. 75-88.

1167. _____. "Gabriel's Revolt: Black Freedom, White Fear" (MA thesis, University of Virginia, 1968).

1168. Essig, James David. "A Very Wintry Season: Virginia Baptists and Slavery, 1785-1797," Virginia Magazine of History and Biography, 88, 2 (1980), pp. 170-85.

1169. Farley, M. Foster. "The Fear of Negro Slave Revolts in South Carolina, 1690-1865," Afro-American Studies, 3, 3 (1972), pp. 199-208.

1170. _____. "The South Carolina Negro During the American Revolution, 1775-1783," Afro-American Studies, 3, 3 (1972), pp. 209-16.

1171. Fields, Barbara. "The Maryland Way from Slavery to Freedom" (PhD diss., Yale University, 1978).

1172. *Fleetwood, George Barham. "Southside Virginia in the Middle Period, with Specific Reference to the Relation between Local Government and Slavery" (MA thesis, Wake Forest University, 1940).

1173. Foner, Eric, ed. Nat Turner. Englewood Cliffs, N.J.: Prentice-Hall, 1971.

1174. Forster, Robert, and Edward C. Papenfuse. "Les grands planteurs du Maryland au XVIIIe siècle: une élite politique et économique," Annales: économies, sociétés, civilisations, 37, 3 (1982), pp. 552-73.

1175. Green, Rodney Dale. "Urban Industry, Black Resistance, and Racial Restriction in the Antebellum South: A General Model and a Case Study in Urban Virginia" (PhD diss., American University, 1980).

1176. _____. "Urban Industry, Black Resistance, and Racial Restriction in the Antebellum South: A General Model and a Case Study in Urban Virginia," Journal of Economic History, 41, 4 (1981), pp. 189-91.

1177. Handlin, Oscar, and Mary Handlin. "Origins of the Southern Labor System," William and Mary Quarterly, 3rd ser., 7, 2 (1950), pp. 199-222. Reprinted in Noel, ed., Origins of American Slavery and Racism, pp. 21-44; as "Origins of Negro Slavery" in Handlin, Race and Nationality in American Life (New York, 1957), pp. 3-28.

1178. Hast, Adele. "The Legal Status of the Negro in Virginia, 1705-1765," Journal of Negro History, 54, 3 (1969), pp. 217-39.

1179. Herndon, G. Melvin. "Slavery in Antebellum Virginia: William Galt Jr., 1839-1851: A Case Study," Southern Studies, 16, 4 (1977), pp. 309-20.

1180. Holland, C. G. "The Slave Population on the Plantation of John C. Cohoon, Jr., Nansemond County, Virginia, 1811-1863: Selected Demographic Characteristics," Virginia Magazine of History and Biography, 80, 3 (1972), pp. 333-40.

1181. Hook, Francis Moore. "The Negro in Colonial Virginia, 1619-1765" (MA thesis, College of William and Mary, 1952).

1182. Hope, Corrie S. "The Social Psychological Determinants of Minority Uprising: A Comparison of the Nat Turner Slave Rebellion (1831) and the Newark Riot (1967)" (PhD diss., University of Massachusetts, 1975).

1183. Hughes, Sarah S. "Slaves for Hire: The Allocation of Black Labor in Elizabeth City County, Virginia, 1782 to 1810," William and Mary Quarterly, 3rd ser., 35, 2 (1978), pp. 260-86.

1184. Jackson, Luther P. "Religious Development of the Negro in Virginia from 1760-1860," Journal of Negro History, 16, 1 (1931), pp. 168-239. Also Bobbs-Merrill Reprint no. BC-149.

1185. *Jennings, Stephen. "The Origins of Racial Caste in Seventeenth-Century Virginia" (MA thesis, Case-Western Reserve University, 1968).

1186. Johnson, Frank Roy. The Nat Turner Slave Insurrection. Murfreesboro, N.C.: Johnson Publishing Co., 1966.

1187. Johnson, James Hugo. "The Participation of White Men in Virginia Negro Insurrections," Journal of Negro History, 16, 1 (1931), pp. 158-67.

1188. Johnson, Whittington B. "The Origin and Nature of African Slavery in Seventeenth-Century Maryland," Maryland Historical Magazine, 73, 3 (1978), pp. 236-45.

1189. Kimmel, Ross M. "Free Blacks in Seventeenth-Century Maryland," Maryland Historical Magazine, 71, 1 (1976), pp. 19-25.

1190. Klein, Herbert S. "The Negro and the Church of England in Virginia," reprinted (from Slavery in the Americas, pp. 113-16, 119-25) in Brown, ed., Slavery in American Society, pp. 32-37.

1191. Kulikoff, Allan. "The Beginnings of the Afro-American Family in Maryland," in Aubrey C. Land, Lois Green Carr, and Edward C. Papenfuse, eds., Law, Society and Politics in Early Maryland: Essays in Honor of Morris Leon Radloff (Baltimore: Johns Hopkins University Press, 1976), pp. 171-96. (Proceedings of the First Conference on Maryland History, June 14-15, 1974)

1192. _____. "Black Society and the Economics of Slavery," Maryland Historical Magazine, 70, 2 (1975), pp. 203-10.

1193. _____. "The Origins of Afro-American Society in Tidewater Maryland and Virginia, 1700 to 1790," William and Mary Quarterly, 3rd ser., 35, 2 (1978), pp. 226-59.

1194. _____. "A 'Prolifick' People: Black Population Growth in the Chesapeake Colonies, 1700-1790," Southern Studies, 16, 4 (1977), pp. 396-428.

1195. _____. "Tobacco and Slaves: Population, Economy, and Society in Eighteenth-Century Prince George's County, Maryland" (PhD diss., Brandeis University, 1976).

1196. Laprade, William T. "The Domestic Slave Trade in the District of Columbia," Journal of Negro History, 11, 1 (1926), pp. 17-34.

1197. Lewis, Ronald L. "Black Labor in Eastern Virginia Coal Fields, 1765-1865," in Newton and Lewis, eds., The Other Slaves, pp. 87-108.

1198. _____. Coal, Iron, and Slaves: Industrial Slavery in Maryland and Virginia 1715-1865. Westport, Conn.: Greenwood Press, 1979.

1199. _____. "'The Darkest Abode of Man': Black Miners in the First Southern Coal Fields, 1780-1865," Virginia Magazine of History and Biography, 87, 2 (1979), pp. 190-202.

1200. _____. "Slave Families at Early Chesapeake Ironworks," Virginia Magazine of History and Biography, 86, 2 (1978), pp. 169-79.

1201. _____. "Slavery in the Chesapeake Iron Industry, 1716-1865" (PhD diss., University of Akron, 1974).

1202. _____. "Slavery on Chesapeake Iron Plantations Before the American Revolution," Journal of Negro History, 59, 3 (1974), pp. 242-54.

1203. _____. "The Use and Extent of Slave Labor in the Chesapeake Iron Industry: The Colonial Era," Labor History, 17, 3 (1976), pp. 388-405.

1204. _____. "The Use and Extent of Slave Labor in the Virginia Iron Industry: The Ante-Bellum Era," West Virginia History, 38, 2 (1977), pp. 141-56.

1205. *Logan, Josephine M. "Some Views of Slavery from the Writings of Virginia Authors, 1824-1865" (MA thesis, University of Richmond, 1956).

1206. McColley, Robert McNair. "Gentlemen and Slavery in Jefferson's Virginia" (PhD diss., University of California, Berkeley, 1961).

1207. _____. Slavery and Jeffersonian Virginia. Urbana: University of Illinois Press, 1964. 2nd revised edition, 1973.

1208. Marks, Bayly Ellen. "Economics and Society in a Staple Plantation System: St. Marys County, Maryland, 1790-1840" (PhD diss., University of Maryland, 1979).

1209. Menard, Russell R. "From Servants to Slaves: The Transformation of the Chesapeake Labor System," Southern Studies, 16, 4 (1977), pp. 355-90.

1210. _____. "The Maryland Slave Population, 1658 to 1730: A Demographic Profile of Blacks in Four Counties," William and Mary Quarterly, 3rd ser., 32, 1 (1975), pp. 29-54. Reprinted in Maris A. Vinovskis, ed., Studies in American Historical Demography (New York: Academic Press, 1979), pp. 313-38.

1211. Miller, John Chester. The Wolf by the Ears: Thomas Jefferson and Slavery. New York: Free Press, 1977.

1212. Mitchell, James N. "Nat Turner: Slave, Preacher, Prophet, and Messiah, 1800-1931 (sic): A Study of the Call of a Black Slave to Prophethood and to the Messiahship of the Second Coming of Christ" (D. Min. diss., Vanderbilt University Divinity School, 1975).

1213. Morgan, Edmund S. American Slavery - American Freedom: The Ordeal of Colonial Virginia. New York: Norton, 1975.

1214. _____. "The First American Boom: Virginia 1618 to 1630," William and Mary Quarterly, 3rd ser., 28, 2 (1971), pp. 169-98.

1215. _____. "The Labor Problem at Jamestown, 1607-1618," American Historical Review, 76, 3 (1971), pp. 595-611. Reprinted in Martin, ed., Interpreting Colonial America, pp. 20-36.

1216. Mullin, Gerald W. Flight and Rebellion: Slave Resistance in Eighteenth Century Virginia. New York: Oxford University Press, 1972.

1217. _____. "Gabriel's Insurrection," in Rose, ed., Americans from Africa, vol. 2, pp. 53-73.

1218. _____. "Patterns of Slave Behavior in Eighteenth Century Virginia" (PhD diss., University of California, Berkeley, 1968).

1219. _____. "Religion, Acculturation and American Negro
Slave Rebellions: Gabriel's Insurrection," reprinted in Bracey,
Meier, and Rudwick, eds., American Slavery, pp. 160-78; in Herbert
G. Gutman and Gregory S. Kealey, eds., Many Pasts: Readings in
American Social History (Englewood Cliffs, N.J.: Prentice-Hall,
1973), vol. 1, pp. 209-29.

1220. *Musser, Carl W. "Economic and Social Aspects of Negro Slavery in
Wythe County, Virginia, 1790-1861" (MA thesis, George Washington
University, 1958).

1221. Nash, Gary B. "From Freedom to Bondage in Seventeenth Century
Virginia (review essay on Breen and Innes, "Myne Owne Ground"),"
Reviews in American History, 10, 1 (1982), pp. 33-37.

1222. Oates, Stephen B. The Fires of Jubilee: Nat Turner's Fierce
Rebellion. New York: Harper and Row, 1975.

1223. Palmer, Paul C. "Servant into Slave: The Evolution of the Legal
Status of the Negro Laborer in Colonial Virginia," South Atlantic
Quarterly, 65, 3 (1966), pp. 355-70.

1224. Parent, Anthony S., Jr. "'Either a Fool or a Fury': The Emergence
of Paternalism in Colonial Virginia Slave Society" (PhD diss.,
University of California, Los Angeles, 1982).

1225. Perdue, Charles L., Jr., Thomas E. Barden, and Robert K. Phillips,
eds. and comps. Weevils in the Wheat: Interviews with Virginia
Ex-Slaves. Charlottesville: University Press of Virginia, 1976.

1226. Provine, Dorothy. "The Economic Position of Free Blacks in the
District of Columbia, 1800-1860," Journal of Negro History, 58, 1
(1973), pp. 61-72.

1227. *Pulley, Richard Demone. "The Role of the Virginia Slave in Iron
and Tobacco Manufacturing" (MA thesis, University of Richmond,
1962).

1228. Riches, William. "Race, Slavery, and Servitude: Virginia
1607-1705" (MA thesis, University of Tennessee, 1969).

1229. Robson, David W. "'An Important Question Answered': William
Graham's Defense of Slavery in Post-Revolutionary Virginia,"
William and Mary Quarterly, 3rd series, 37, 4 (1980), pp. 642-52.

1230. Russell, John H. The Free Negro in Virginia, 1619-1865. Baltimore:
Johns Hopkins University Press, 1913.

1231. Savitt, Todd L. "Smothering and Overlaying of Virginia Slave
Children: A Suggested Explanation," Bulletin of the History of
Medicine, 49, 3 (1975), pp. 400-04.

1232. _____. "Sound Minds and Sound Bodies: The Diseases and
Health Care of Blacks in Ante-Bellum Virginia" (PhD diss.,
University of Virginia, 1975).

1233. Schlotterbeck, John Thomas. "Plantation and Farm: Social and Economic Change in Orange and Greene Counties, Virginia, 1716-1860" (PhD diss., Johns Hopkins University, 1980).

1234. Schwarz, Philip J. "Gabriel's Challenge: Slaves and Crime in Late Eighteenth-Century Virginia," Virginia Magazine of History and Biography, 90, 3 (1982), pp. 283-309.

1235. Seip, Terry L. "Slaves and Free Negroes in Alexandria, 1850-1860," Louisiana History, 10, 2 (1969), pp. 147-65. Reprinted in Miller and Genovese, eds., Plantation, Town, and County, pp. 397-414.

1236. Starke, Barbara M. "A Mini View of the Microenvironment of Slaves and Freed Blacks Living in the Virginia and Maryland Areas from the 17th through the 19th Century," Negro History Bulletin, 41, 5 (1978), pp. 878-80.

1237. Stegmaier, Mark J. "Maryland's Fear of Insurrection at the Time of Braddock's Defeat," Maryland Historical Magazine, 71, 4 (1976), pp. 467-83.

1238. *Strachan, Dorothy M. "The Southampton Insurrection of 1831" (MA thesis, St. John's University, 1950).

1239. Styron, William. The Confessions of Nat Turner. New York: Random House, 1967.

1240. Tate, Thaddeus W. "The Eighteenth Century: The Growth of Slavery, Colonial Black Codes," reprinted (from Negro in Eighteenth-Century Williamsburg, pp. 23-42) in Brown, ed., Slavery in American Society, pp. 23-32.

1241. _____. The Negro in Eighteenth-Century Williamsburg. Williamsburg, Va.: University Press of Virginia, 1965.

1242. Thelwell, Michael. "Arguments: The Turner Thesis (review essay on Styron, Confessions of Nat Turner)," Partisan Review, 35, 3 (1968), pp. 403-14. Reprinted as "The White Nat Turner," in Rose, ed., Americans from Africa, vol. 2, pp. 103-15.

1243. _____. "Back with the Wind: Mr. Styron and the Reverend Turner," in Clark, ed., William Styron's Nat Turner, pp. 79-91. Reprinted in Haynes, ed., Blacks in White America, pp. 276-85.

1244. Thomas, Arthur Dicken, Jr. "The Second Great Awakening in Virginia and Slavery Reform, 1785-1837" (PhD diss., Union Theological Seminary in Virginia, 1981).

1245. Tragle, Henry I. "The Southampton Slave Revolt" (PhD diss., University of Massachusetts, 1971).

1246. _____, ed. The Southampton Slave Revolt of 1831: A Compilation of Source Material. Amherst: University of Massachusetts Press, 1971.

1247. Vaughan, Alden T. "Blacks in Virginia: A Note on the First Decade," William and Mary Quarterly, 3rd ser., 29, 3 (1972), pp. 469-78.

1248. Virginia Writers' Program. The Negro in Virginia. New York, 1940.

1249. Wax, Darold D. "Black Immigrants: The Slave Trade in Colonial Maryland," Maryland Historical Magazine, 73, 1 (1978), pp. 30-45.

1250. Wayland, Francis F. "Slavebreeding in America: The Stevenson-O'Connell Imbroglio of 1838," Virginia Magazine of History and Biography, 50, 1 (1942), pp. 47-54.

1251. Werner, Randolph. "An Inquiry into Some Aspects of Nat Turner's Rebellion" (MA thesis, College of William and Mary, 1971).

1252. White, John. "The Novelist as Historian: William Styron and American Negro Slavery," Journal of American Studies, 4, 2 (1971), pp. 233-45.

1253. Winkler, K. T. "Von der Sklaverei in den Kolonien: eine Untersuchung des Zusammenhanges zwischen der Entfaltung überseeisches Territorien und der Sklaverei an Hand von Virginia im 18. Jahrhundert" (Dr. Phil., Universität München, 1976).

1254. Wright, James M. The Free Negro in Maryland, 1634-1860. New York: Columbia University Press, 1921.

4. Colonial South

1255. *Blake, Russell L. "Slave Runaways in Colonial South Carolina" (Unpublished paper, University of Michigan, 1972).

1256. Blassingame, John W. "Black Majority: Essay Review," Georgia Historical Quarterly, 59, 1 (1975), pp. 67-71.

1257. Butler, Alfloyd. The Africanization of American Christianity. New York: Carlton Press, 1980.

1258. Byrne, William Andrew. "The Burden and Heat of the Day: Slavery and Servitude in Savannah, 1733-1865" (PhD diss., Florida State University, 1979).

1259. Candler, Mark Allen. "The Beginnings of Slavery in Georgia," Magazine of History (New York), 14 (1911), pp. 342-51.

1260. Childs, St. Julien Ravenel. "Kitchen Physick: Medical and Surgical Care of Slaves on an Eighteenth Century Rice Plantation," Mississippi Valley Historical Review, 20, 4 (1934), pp. 549-54.

1261. Clifton, Denzil T. "Anglicanism and Negro Slavery in Colonial America," Historical Magazine of the Protestant Episcopal Church, 39, 1 (1970), pp. 27-70.

1262. Clifton, James M. "The Rice Driver: His Role in Slave Management," South Carolina Historical Magazine, 82, 4 (1981), pp. 331-53.

1263. Cobb, Herschel P. "Old Slave Laws of Georgia," Case and Comment, 23, 1 (1916), pp. 7-10.

1264. Cody, Cheryll Ann. "A Note on Changing Patterns of Slave Fertility in the South Carolina Rice District, 1735-1845," Southern Studies, 16, 4 (1977), pp. 457-63.

1265. * _____. "Slave Demography and Family Formation: A Community Study of the Ball Family Plantations, 1720 - 1896" (PhD diss., University of Minnesota, 1982).

1266. Cohen, Hennig. "Slave Names in Colonial South Carolina," American Speech, 28, 1 (1952), pp. 102-07.

1267. Crow, Jeffrey J. "Slave Rebelliousness and Social Conflict in North Carolina, 1775 to 1802," William and Mary Quarterly, 3rd ser., 37, 1 (1980), pp. 79-102.

1268. Drago, Edmund, and Ralph Melnick. "The Old Slave Mart Museum, Charleston, South Carolina: Rediscovering the Past," Civil War History, 27, 2 (1981), pp. 138-54.

1269. Duncan, John D. "Servitude and Slavery in Colonial South Carolina, 1670-1776" (PhD diss., Emory University, 1972).

1270. _____. "Slave Emancipation in Colonial South Carolina," American Chronicle, 1, 1 (1972), pp. 64-66.

1271. Farley, M. Foster. "A History of Negro Slave Revolts in South Carolina," Afro-American Studies, 3, 2 (1972), pp. 97-102.

1272. Fitchett, E. Horace. "The Origin and Growth of the Free Negro Population of Charleston, South Carolina," Journal of Negro History, 26, 4 (1941), pp. 421-37. Also Bobbs-Merrill Reprint no. BC-81.

1273. Fleming, John E. "Stono River Rebellion: South Carolina Slave Code," Negro History Bulletin, 42, 3 (1979), pp. 66-68.

1274. Gehrke, William Herman. "Negro Slavery Among the Germans in North Carolina," North Carolina Historical Magazine, 14, 4 (1937), pp. 307-24.

1275. Gray, Ralph, and Betty Wood. "The Transition from Indentured Servant to Involuntary Servitude in Colonial Georgia," Explorations in Economic History, 13, 4 (1976), pp. 353-70.

1276. Greene, Jack P. "'Slavery or Independence': Some Reflections on the Relationship Among Liberty, Black Bondage, and Equality in Revolutionary South Carolina," South Carolina Historical Magazine, 80, 3 (1979), pp. 193-214.

1277. Gutman, Herbert G. "Family and Kinship Groupings among the Enslaved Afro-Americans on the South Carolina Good Hope Plantation: 1760-1860," in Rubin and Tuden, eds., Comparative Perspectives, pp. 242-58.

1278. Haywood, C. Robert. "Mercantilism and Colonial Slave Labor, 1700-1763," Journal of Southern History, 23, 4 (1957), pp. 454-64. Also Bobbs-Merrill Reprint no. BC-131.

1279. Henry, H. M. "The Police Control of the Slave in South Carolina" (PhD diss., Vanderbilt University, 1914).

1280. Hertzler, James R. "Slavery in the Yearly Sermons Before the Georgia Trustees," Georgia Historical Quarterly, 59, supplement, (1975), pp. 118-26.

1281. Higgins, W. Robert. "Charleston: Terminus and Entrepôt of the Colonial Slave Trade," in Kilson and Rotberg, eds., African Diaspora, pp. 114-31.

1282. _____. "The Geographical Origins of Negro Slaves in Colonial South Carolina," South Atlantic Quarterly, 70, 1 (1971), pp. 34-47.

1283. *_____. "The South Carolina Negro Duty Law, 1703-1775" (MA thesis, University of South Carolina, 1967).

1284. Kay, Marvin L. Michael, and Lorin Lee Cary. "'The Planters Suffer Little or Nothing': North Carolina Compensations for Executed Slaves, 1748-1772," Science and Society, 40, 3 (1976), pp. 288-306.

1285. Killens, John O., ed. The Trial Record of Denmark Vesey. Boston: Beacon Press, 1970.

1286. Klein, Rachel. "The Rise of the Planters in the South Carolina Backcountry, 1767-1808" (PhD diss., Yale University, 1979).

1287. Klingberg, Frank J. An Appraisal of the Negro in Colonial South Carolina: A Study in Americanization. Washington, D.C.: Associated Publishers, 1941.

1288. Littlefield, Daniel C. "Planter Preferences: A Study of Slavery and the Slave Trade in Colonial South Carolina" (PhD diss., Johns Hopkins University, 1977).

1289. _____. Rice and Slaves: Ethnicity and the Slave Trade in Colonial South Carolina. Baton Rouge: Louisiana State University Press, 1981.

1290. Lofton, John M., Jr. "White, Indian, and Negro Contacts in Colonial South Carolina," Southern Indian Studies, 1, 1 (1949), pp. 3-12.

1291. Meaders, Daniel E. "South Carolina Fugitives as Viewed through Local Colonial Newspapers with Emphasis on Runaway Notices," Journal of Negro History, 60, 2 (1975), pp. 288-319.

1292. Morgan, Philip D. "Black Society in the Lowcountry, 1760-1810," in Berlin and Hoffman, eds., Slavery and Freedom in the Age of the American Revolution, pp. 83-141.

1293. *_____. "The Development of Slave Culture in Eighteenth-Century Plantation America" (PhD diss., University College, London, 1981).

1294. _____. "En Caroline du Sud: marronnage et culture civile," Annales: économies, sociétés, civilisations, 37, 3 (1982), pp. 574-90.

1295. _____. "Work and Culture: The Task System and the World of Lowcountry Blacks, 1700 to 1880," William and Mary Quarterly, 3rd ser., 39, 4 (1982), pp. 563-99.

1296. _____, and George D. Terry. "Slavery in Microcosm: A Conspiracy Scare in Colonial South Carolina," Southern Studies, 21, 2 (1982), pp. 121-45.

1297. Padgett, James A. "The Status of Slaves in Colonial North Carolina," Journal of Negro History, 14, 3 (1929), pp. 300-27.

1298. Phillips, Ulrich B. "The Slave Labor Problem in the Charleston District," Political Science Quarterly, 22, 3 (1907), pp. 416-39. Reprinted in Miller and Genovese, eds., Plantation, Town, and County, pp. 7-28.

1299. Porter, Kenneth W. "Negroes on the Southern Frontier, 1670-1763," Journal of Negro History, 33, 1 (1948), pp. 53-78.

1300. Singleton, Theresa Ann. "The Archaeology of Afro-American Slavery in Coastal Georgia: A Regional Perception of Slave Household and Community Patterns" (PhD diss., University of Florida, 1980).

1301. Sirmans, M. Eugene. "The Legal Status of the Slave in South Carolina, 1670-1740," Journal of Southern History, 28, 4 (1962), pp. 462-73.

1302. Stoddard, Albert H. "Origin, Dialect, Beliefs, and Characteristics of the Negroes of the South Carolina and Georgia Coasts," Georgia Historical Quarterly, 28, 3 (1944), pp. 186-95.

1303. Stone, James Herbert. "Black Leadership in the Old South: The Slave Drivers of the Rice Kingdom" (PhD diss., Florida State University, 1976).

1304. Wall, Bennett H. "The Founding of the Pettigrew Plantations," North Carolina Historical Review, 27, 4 (1950), pp. 395-418. Reprinted in Miller and Genovese, eds., Plantation, Town, and County, pp. 163-85.

1305. Watson, Alan D. "Impulse Toward Independence: Resistance and Rebellion Among North Carolina Slaves, 1750-1775," Journal of Negro History, 63, 4 (1978), pp. 317-28.

1306. _____. "North Carolina Slave Courts, 1715-1785," North Carolina Historical Review, 60, 1 (1983), pp. 24-36.

1307. Watson, Larry Darnell. "The Quest for Order: Enforcing Slave Codes in Revolutionary South Carolina, 1760-1800" (PhD diss., University of South Carolina, 1980).

1308. Wax, Darold D. "Georgia and the Negro Before the American Revolution," Georgia Historical Quarterly, 51, 1 (1967), pp. 63-77.

1309. _____. "'The Great Risque We Run': The Aftermath of Slave Rebellion at Stono, South Carolina, 1739-1745," Journal of Negro History, 67, 2 (1982), pp. 136-47.

1310. Willis, William S., Jr. "Anthropology and Negroes on the Southern Colonial Frontier," in Curtis and Gould, eds., Black Experience, pp. 33-50.

1311. _____. "Divide and Rule: Red, White, and Black in the Southeast," Journal of Negro History, 48, 3 (1963), pp. 157-76.

1312. Wood, Betty C. "The One Thing Needful: The Slavery Debate in Georgia, 1732-1750" (PhD diss., University of Pennsylvania, 1975).

1313. _____. Slavery in Colonial Georgia, 1730-1775. Athens: University of Georgia Press, 1984.

1314. _____. "Thomas Stephens and the Introduction of Black Slavery in Georgia," Georgia Historical Quarterly, 58, 1 (1974), pp. 24-40.

1315. Wood, Peter H. Black Majority: Negroes in Colonial South Carolina from 1670 through the Stono Rebellion. New York: Knopf, 1974.

1316. _____. "'It was a Negro Taught Them': A New Look at African Labor in Early South Carolina," in Roger D. Abrahams and John F. Szwed, eds., Discovering Afro-America (Leiden: E. J. Brill, 1975), pp. 26-45.

1317. _____. "'More Like a Negro Country': Demographic Patterns in Colonial South Carolina, 1700-1740," in Engerman and Genovese, eds., Race and Slavery, pp. 131-72.

5. Ante-Bellum South

1318. Adefila, Johnson Ajibade. "Slave Religion in the Antebellum South: A Study of the Role of Africanisms in the Black Response to Christianity" (PhD diss., Brandeis University, 1975).

1319. Africa, Philip. "Slaveholding in the Salem Community, 1771-1851," North Carolina Historical Review, 54, 3 (1977), pp. 271-307.

1320. Albanese, Anthony. "The Plantation as a School: The Sea-Islands of Georgia and South Carolina, A Test Case, 1800-1860" (PhD diss., Rutgers University, 1970).

1321. _____. The Plantation School. New York: Vantage Press, 1976.

1322. Alho, Olli. The Religion of the Slaves: A Study of the Religious Tradition and Behaviour of Plantation Slaves in the United States, 1835-1860. Helsinki: Finnish Academy of Science and Letters, 1976. (FF Communications, no. 217)

1323. Allen, Jeffrey Brooke. "The Racial Thought of White North Carolina Opponents of Slavery, 1789-1876," North Carolina Historical Review, 59, 1 (1982), pp. 49-66.

1324. Allison, Rebecca P. "The Force of Argument: George Fitzhugh's Defense of Slavery," Conservative Historians' Forum, 6 (1982), pp. 5-13.

1325. Anderson, Ralph V. "Labor Utilization and Productivity: Diversification and Self Sufficiency, Southern Plantations, 1800-1840" (PhD diss., University of North Carolina at Chapel Hill, 1974).

1326. Aptheker, Herbert. "Notes on Slave Conspiracies in Confederate Mississippi," Journal of Negro History, 29, 1 (1944), pp. 75-79.

1327. Ascher, Robert, and Charles H. Fairbanks. "Excavation of a Slave Cabin: Georgia, U.S.A.," Historical Archaeology, 5 (1971), pp. 3-17.

1328. "Autobiography of Omar ibn Said, Slave in North Carolina, 1831," American Historical Review, 30, 4 (1925), pp. 787-95.

1329. Bailey, Kenneth K. "Protestantism and Afro-Americans in the Old South: Another Look," Journal of Southern History, 41, 4 (1975), pp. 451-72.

1330. Banes, Ruth A. "Antebellum Slave Narratives as Social History: Self and Community in the Struggle Against Slavery," Journal of American Culture, 5, 2 (1982), pp. 62-70.

1331. Beasley, J. "Blacks - Slave and Free - Vicksburg, 1850-1860," Journal of Mississippi History, 38, 1 (1976), pp. 1-32.

1332. Bellamy, Donnie D. "Slavery in Microcosm: Onslow County, North Carolina," Journal of Negro History, 62, 4 (1977), pp. 339-50.

1333. Berlin, Ira. Slaves Without Masters: The Free Negro in the Antebellum South. New York: Pantheon, 1974.

1334. Blassingame, John W. The Slave Community: Plantation Life in the Antebellum South. New York: Oxford University Press, 1972. Revised edition, 1979.

1335. _____. "Status and Social Structure in the Slave Community: Evidence from New Sources," in Owens, ed., Perspectives and Irony, pp. 137-51.

1336. Bonner, James C. "Profile of a Late Antebellum Community," American Historical Review, 49, 4 (1944), pp. 663-80. Reprinted in Miller and Genovese, eds., Plantation Town, and County, pp. 29-49.

1337. Bryce-Laporte, Roy S. "The Conceptualization of the American Slave Plantation as a Total Institution" (PhD diss., University of California, Los Angeles, 1968).

1338. *Burrows, Edward F. "The Literary Education of Negroes in Ante-bellum Virginia, North Carolina, South Carolina, and Georgia, with Special Reference to Regulatory and Prohibitive Laws" (MA thesis, Duke University, 1941).

1339. Butlin, Noel G. Ante-bellum Slavery – A Critique of a Debate. Canberra: Australian National University, 1971.

1340. Butts, Donald Cleveland. "A Challenge to Planter Rule: The Controversy Over the Ad Valorem Taxation of Slaves in North Carolina, 1858-1862" (PhD diss., Duke University, 1978).

1341. _____. "The 'Irrepressible Conflict': Slave Taxation and North Carolina's Gubernatorial Election of 1860," North Carolina Historical Review, 58, 1 (1981), pp. 44-66.

1342. Chester, S. H. "African Slavery as I Knew It in Southern Arkansas," Tennessee Historical Magazine, 9, 3 (1925), pp. 178-84.

1343. Clark, Ernest J., Jr. "Aspects of the North Carolina Slave Code, 1715-1860," North Carolina Historical Review, 39, 2 (1962), pp. 148-64.

1344. Clarke, T. Erskine. "An Experiment in Paternalism: Presbyterians and Slaves in Charleston, South Carolina," Journal of Presbyterian History, 53, 3 (1975), pp. 223-38.

1345. Collins, Winfield H. The Domestic Slave Trade of the Southern States. Port Washington, N.Y.: Broadway Publishing Co., 1904.

1346. Conrad, Alfred H., and John R. Meyer. "The Economics of Slavery in the Ante Bellum South," Journal of Political Economy, 66, 2 (1958), pp. 95-130. Reprinted in Conrad and Meyer, eds., The Economics of Slavery and Other Studies in Econometric History (Chicago: Aldine, 1964), pp. 43-84.

1347. _____, Douglas Dowd, Stanley Engerman, Eli Ginzberg, Charles Kelso, John R. Meyer, Harry N. Scheiber, and Richard Sutch. "Slavery as an Obstacle to Economic Growth in the United States: A Panel Discussion," Journal of Economic History, 27, 4 (1967), pp. 518-60. Also Bobbs-Merrill Reprint no. BC-48.

1348. Cornelius, Janet Duitsman. "God's Schoolmasters: Southern Evangelists to the Slaves, 1830-1860" (PhD diss., University of Illinois, 1977).

1349. _____. "Slave Marriages in a Georgia Congregation," in Orville Vernon Burton and Robert C. McMath, Jr., eds., Class, Conflict, and Consensus: Antebellum Southern Community Studies (Westport, Conn.: Greenwood Press, 1982), pp. 128-45.

1350. Coulter, E. Merton. "Slavery and Freedom in Athens, Georgia, 1860-66," Georgia Historical Quarterly, 49, 3 (1965), pp. 264-93. Reprinted in Miller and Genovese, eds., Plantation, Town, and County, pp. 337-64.

1351. Coyner, Martin Boyd, Jr. "John Hartwell Cocke of Bremo: Agriculture and Slavery in the Ante-Bellum South" (PhD diss., University of Virginia, 1961).

1352. Creel, Margaret Washington. "Antebellum Religion among the Gullahs: A Study of Slave Conversion and Religious Culture in the South Carolina Sea Islands" (PhD diss., University of California, Davis, 1980).

1353. _____, and Dennis C. Smith. "Challenging Perspectives on Slave Life in the Ante-Bellum South," New Scholar, 5, 2 (1975), pp. 335-50.

1354. Cresto, Kathleen M. "Negro Contributions to the Confederacy," Negro History Bulletin, 44, 2 (1981), pp. 30-43.

1355. _____. "Sherman and Slavery," Civil War Times Illustrated, 17, 7 (1978), pp. 12-21.

1356. Currier, James T. "From Slavery to Freedom in Mississippi's Legal System," Journal of Negro History, 65, 2 (1980), pp. 112-25.

1357. Davis, Edwin Adams, and William Ransom Hogan. The Barber of Natchez. Baton Rouge: Louisiana State University Press, 1954.

1358. Dew, Charles B. "Disciplining Slave Ironworkers in the Antebellum South: Coercion, Conciliation, and Accommodation," American Historical Review, 79, 2 (1974), pp. 393-418. Reprinted in Newton and Lewis, eds., The Other Slaves, pp. 63-85.

1359. Durden, Robert F. The Gray and the Black: The Confederate Debate on Emancipation. Baton Rouge: Louisiana State University Press, 1972.

1360. Edwards, John C. "Slave Justice in Four Middle Georgia Counties," Georgia Historical Quarterly, 57, 2 (1973), pp. 256-73.

1361. Escott, Paul D. "The Context of Freedom: Georgia's Slaves During the Civil War," Georgia Historical Quarterly, 58, 1 (1974), pp. 79-104.

1362. Faust, Drew Gilpin. "Culture, Conflict and Community: The Meaning of Power on an Ante-Bellum Plantation," Journal of Social History, 14, 1 (1980), pp. 83-97.

1363. _____, ed. The Ideology of Slavery: Proslavery Thought in the Antebellum South, 1830-1860. Baton Rouge: Louisiana State University Press, 1981.

1364. Flanders, Ralph B. "Two Plantations and a County of Antebellum Georgia," Georgia Historical Quarterly, 12, 1 (1928), pp. 1-37. Reprinted in Miller and Genovese, eds., Plantation, Town, and County, pp. 225-43.

1365. Fogel, Robert W., and Stanley L. Engerman. "A Comparison of the Relative Efficiency of Slave and Free Agriculture in the United States during 1860," Papers of the 5th International Congress of Economic History (Leningrad, 1970) (Moscow, 1976), vol. 7, pp. 141-46.

1366. _____. "Explaining the Relative Efficiency of Slave Agriculture in the Antebellum South," American Economic Review, 67, 3 (1977), pp. 275-96.

1367. _____. "Explaining the Relative Efficiency of Slave Agriculture in the Antebellum South: Reply," American Economic Review, 70, 4 (1980), pp. 672-90.

1368. Foust, James D., and Dale E. Swan. "Productivity and Profitability of Antebellum Slave Labor: A Micro-Approach," Agricultural History, 44, 1 (1970), pp. 39-62.

1369. Franklin, John Hope. "The Enslavement of Free Negroes in North Carolina," Journal of Negro History, 29, 4 (1944), pp. 401-28.

1370. _____. "The Free Negro in the Economic Life of Ante-Bellum North Carolina," North Carolina Historical Review, 19, 3 (1942), pp. 239-59; 19, 4 (1942), pp. 359-75. Also Bobbs-Merrill Reprint no. BC-89.

1371. _____. "Slaves Virtually Free in Ante-Bellum North Carolina," Journal of Negro History, 28, 3 (1943), pp. 284-310. Also Bobbs-Merrill Reprint no. BC-88.

1372. Genovese, Eugene D. "Cotton, Slavery and Soil Exhaustion in the Old South," Cotton History Review, 2, 1 (1961), pp. 3-17.

1373. _____. "Livestock in the Slave Economy of the Old South - A Revised View," Agricultural History, 36, 3 (1962), pp. 143-49.

1374. _____. "The Origins of Slavery Expansionism," reprinted (from Political Economy of Slavery, pp. 243-51, 256-70) in Brown, ed., Slavery in American Society, pp. 98-106.

1375. _____. "Yeoman Farmers in a Slaveholders' Democracy," revised (from Political Economy of Slavery) in Fox-Genovese and Genovese, Fruits of Merchant Capital, pp. 249-64.

1376. Govan, Thomas P. "Was Plantation Slavery Profitable?" Journal of Southern History, 8, 4 (1942), pp. 513-35. Also Bobbs-Merrill Reprint no. BC-110.

1377. Halasz, Nicholas. The Rattling Chains: Slave Unrest and Revolt in the Antebellum South. New York: D. McKay Co., 1966.

1378. Harding, Vincent. "Religion and Resistance among Antebellum Negroes, 1800-1860," in Meier and Rudwick, eds., Making of Black America, pp. 179-97.

1379. Harper, C. W. "House Servants and Field Hands: Fragmentation in the Ante-Bellum Slave Community," North Carolina Historical Review, 55, 1 (1978), pp. 42-59.

1380. Haskell, Thomas L. "Explaining the Relative Efficiency of Slave Agriculture in the Ante-Bellum South: A Reply to Fogel-Engerman," American Economic Review, 69, 1 (1979), pp. 206-07.

1381. Hawes, Ruth B. "Slavery in Mississippi," Sewanee Review, 21, 2 (1913), pp. 223-34.

1382. Hayden, J. Carleton. "Conversion and Control: Dilemma of Episcopalians in Providing for the Religious Instruction of Slaves, Charleston, South Carolina, 1845-1860," Historical Magazine of the Protestant Episcopal Church, 40, 2 (1971), pp. 143-71.

1383. Henderson, William C. "The Slave Court System in Spartanburg County," Proceedings of the South Carolina Historical Association (1976), pp. 24-38.

1384. _____. "Spartan Slaves: A Documentary Account of Blacks on Trial in Spartanburg, South Carolina, 1830 to 1865" (PhD diss., Northwestern University, 1978).

1385. Henry, Howell M. The Police Control of the Slave in South Carolina. Emory, Virginia, 1914.

1386. Hewett, David Gerald. "Slavery in the Old South: The British Travelers' Image, 1825-1860" (PhD diss., Florida State University, 1968).

1387. Hindus, Michael S. "Black Justice Under White Law: Criminal Prosecutions of Blacks in Antebellum South Carolina," Journal of American History, 63, 3 (1976), pp. 575-99.

1388. Hunter, Frances L. "Slave Society on the Southern Plantation," Journal of Negro History, 7, 1 (1922), pp. 1-10.

1389. Jackson, Harvey H. "American Slavery, American Freedom, and the Revolution in the Lower South: The Case of Lachlan McIntosh," Southern Studies, 19, 1 (1980), pp. 81-93.

1390. Jackson, James Conroy. "The Religious Education of the Negro in South Carolina Prior to 1850," Historical Magazine of the Protestant Episcopal Church, 36, 1 (1967), pp. 35-61.

1391. Jackson, Shirley M. "Black Slave Drivers in the Southern United States" (PhD diss., Bowling Green State University, 1977).

1392. January, Alan F. "The South Carolina Association: An Agency for Race Control in Antebellum Charleston," South Carolina Historical Magazine, 78, 3 (1977), pp. 191-201.

1393. Jervey, Edward D., and C. Harold Huber. "The Creole Affair," Journal of Negro History, 65, 3 (1980), pp. 195-211.

1394. Johnson, Kenneth R. "Slavery and Racism in Florence, Alabama, 1841-1862," Civil War History, 27, 2 (1981), pp. 155-71.

1395. Johnson, Michael P. "Planters and Patriarchy: Charleston, 1800-1860," Journal of Southern History, 46, 1 (1980), pp. 45-72.

1396. _____. "Runaway Slaves and the Slave Communities in South Carolina, 1799 to 1830," William and Mary Quarterly, 3rd series, 38, 3 (1981), pp. 418-41.

1397. Johnson, Whittington B. "Free Blacks in Antebellum Savannah: An Economic Profile," Georgia Historical Quarterly, 64, 4 (1980), pp. 418-31.

1398. Jones, Archer, and Robert J. Carlsson. "Slavery and Saving," American Journal of Economics and Sociology, 30, 2 (1971), pp. 171-77.

1399. Jones, Bobby Frank. "A Cultural Middle Passage: Slave Marriage and Family in the Ante-Bellum South" (PhD diss., University of North Carolina at Chapel Hill, 1965).

1400. Jones, Howard. "The Peculiar Institution and National Honor: The Case of the Creole Slave Revolt," Civil War History, 21, 1 (1975), pp. 28-50.

1401. Jones, Norrece Thomas. "Control Mechanisms in South Carolina Slave Society, 1800-1865" (PhD diss., Northwestern University, 1981).

1402. Joyner, Charles W. "The Creolization of Slave Folklife: All Saints Parish, South Carolina, as a Test Case," Historical Reflections/Réflexions historiques, 6, 2 (1979), pp. 435-53.

1403. _____. "Slave Folklore on the Waccaman Neck: Antebellum Black Culture in the South Carolina Low Country" (PhD diss., University of Pennsylvania, 1977).

1404. Kerr, Norwood Alan. "The Mississippi Colonization Society (1831-1860)," Journal of Mississippi History, 43, 1 (1981), pp. 1-30.

1405. Kleinman, Max L. "The Denmark Vesey Conspiracy," Negro History Bulletin, 37, 2 (1974), pp. 225-29.

1406. Kotlikoff, Laurence J., and Sebastian Pinera. "The Old South's Stake in the Inter-Regional Movement of Slaves, 1850-1860," Journal of Economic History, 37, 2 (1977), pp. 434-50.

1407. Labinjoh, Justin. "The Sexual Life of the Oppressed: An Examination of the Family Life of Ante-Bellum Slaves," Phylon, 35, 4 (1974), pp. 375-97.

1408. Lale, Max S., and Randolph B. Campbell, eds. "The Plantation Journal of John B. Webster, February 17, 1858 - November 5, 1859," Southwestern Historical Quarterly, 84, 1 (1980), pp. 49-79.

1409. Lander, Ernest M., Jr. "Slave Labor in the South Carolina Cotton Mills," Journal of Negro History, 38, 2 (1953), pp. 161-73.

1410. Lee, Anne S., and Everett S. Lee. "The Health of Slaves and the Health of Freedmen: A Savannah Study," Phylon, 38, 2 (1977), pp. 170-80.

1411. Littlefield, Daniel F., Jr., and Mary Littlefield. "The Beams Family: Free Blacks in Indian Territory," Journal of Negro History, 61, 1 (1976), pp. 17-35.

1412. Lofton, John M., Jr. Insurrection in South Carolina: The Turbulent World of Denmark Vesey. Yellow Springs, Ohio: Antioch Press, 1964.

1413. Luraghi, Raimondo. The Rise and Fall of the Plantation South. New York: New Viewpoints, 1978.

1414. Maddex, Jack P., Jr. "Proslavery Millenialism: Social Eschatology in Antebellum Southern Calvinism," American Quarterly, 31, 1 (1979), pp. 46-62.

1415. Meeker, Edward. "Mortality Trends of Southern Blacks, 1850-1910: Some Preliminary Findings," Explorations in Economic History, 13, 1 (1976), pp. 13-42.

1416. Mercer, P. M. "Tapping the Slave Narrative Collection for the Responses of Black South Carolinians to Emancipation and Reconstruction," Australian Journal of Politics and History, 25, 3 (1979), pp. 358-74.

1417. Metzer, Jacob. "Institutional Change and Economic Analysis: Some Issues Related to American Slavery," Louisiana Studies, 15, 4 (1976), pp. 321-43.

1418. _____. "Rational Management, Modern Business Practices, and Economies of Scale in the Ante-Bellum Southern Plantations," Explorations in Economic History, 2, 2 (1975), pp. 123-50.

1419. Miller, Randall M. "The Fabric of Control: Slavery in Antebellum Southern Textile Mills," Business History Review, 55, 4 (1981), pp. 471-90.

1420. Miller, William L. "A Note on the Importance of the Interstate Slave Trade of the Antebellum South," Journal of Political Economy, 73, 2 (1965), pp. 181-87.

1421. Mills, Gary B. "Miscegenation and the Free Negro in Antebellum 'Anglo' Alabama: A Reexamination of Southern Race Relations," Journal of American History, 68, 1 (1981), pp. 16-34.

1422. Moes, John E. "The Absorption of Capital in Slave Labor in the Ante-Bellum South and Economic Growth," American Journal of Economics and Sociology, 20, 5 (1960), pp. 535-41.

1423. Mohr, Clarence L. "Slavery in Oglethorpe County, Georgia, 1773-1865," Phylon, 33, 1 (1972), pp. 4-21.

1424. Myers, Robert Manson. The Children of Pride: A True Story of Georgia and the Civil War. New Haven: Yale University Press, 1972.

1425. Nash, A. E. Keir. "Fairness and Formalism in the Trials of Blacks in the State Supreme Courts of the Old South," Virginia Law Review, 56, 1 (1970), pp. 64-100.

1426. _____. "A More Equitable Past? Southern Supreme Courts and the Protection of the American Negro," North Carolina Law Review, 48 (1969-70), pp. 197-242.

1427. _____. "Negro Rights, Unionism, and Greatness on the South Carolina Court of Appeals: The Extraordinary Chief Justice John Belton O'Neall," South Carolina Law Review, 21, 1 (1969), pp. 141-90.

1428. _____. "Reason of Slavery: Understanding the Judicial Role in the Peculiar Institution," Vanderbilt Law Review, 32, 1 (1979), pp. 7-218. Comment by Robert B. Jones on Part One, pp. 219-23.

1429. Niemi, Albert W., Jr. "Inequality in the Distribution of Slave Wealth: The Cotton South and Other Southern Agricultural Regions," Journal of Economic History, 37, 3 (1977), pp. 747-54.

1430. Olson, John F. "Some Empirical Evidence on the Men Between: Slave Drivers on Antebellum Plantations" (Unpublished paper presented to Indiana University Economic History Workshop, 1982).

1431. Opper, Peter Kent. "North Carolina Quakers: Reluctant Slaveholders," North Carolina Historical Review, 52, 1 (1975), pp. 37-58.

1432. * _____. "'Old James Seems to Be a Coming Too': A History of Migration, Emigration and Colonization of the North Carolina Negro, 1816-1836" (MA thesis, University of North Carolina, Chapel Hill, 1969).

1433. Otto, John Solomon. "Artifacts and Status Differences: A Comparison of Ceramics from Planter, Overseer, and Slave Sites on an Antebellum Plantation," in Stanley South, ed., Research Strategies in Historical Archeology (New York: Academic Press, 1977), pp. 91-118.

1434. _____. "Slavery in a Coastal Community - Glynn County (1790-1860)," Georgia Historical Quarterly, 64, 4 (1979), pp. 461-68.

1435. _____. "Status Differences and the Archeological Record - A Comparison of Planter, Overseer, and Slave Sites from Cannon's Point Plantation (1794-1861), St. Simon's Island, Georgia" (PhD diss., University of Florida, 1975).

1436. Phifer, Edward W. "Slavery in Microcosm: Burke County, North Carolina," Journal of Southern History, 28, 2 (1962), pp. 137-65. Reprinted in Weinstein and Gatell, eds., American Negro Slavery (1st ed.), pp. 74-97; in Miller and Genovese, eds., Plantation, Town, and County, pp. 71-95. Also Bobbs-Merrill Reprint no. BC-211.

1437. Postell, William Dosite. The Health of Slaves on Southern Plantations. Baton Rouge: Louisiana State University Press, 1951.

1438. _____. "A Review of Slave Care on Southern Plantations," Virginia Medical Monthly, 79, 2 (1952), pp. 101-05.

1439. Preyer, Norris W. "The Historian, the Slave, and the Ante-Bellum Textile Industry," Journal of Negro History, 46, 2 (1961), pp. 67-82.

1440. Raboteau, Albert J. Slave Religion: The 'Invisible Institution' in the Antebellum South. New York: Oxford University Press, 1978.

1441. Rachleff, Marshall. "Big Joe, Little Joe, Bill and Jack: An Example of Slave-Resistance in Alabama," Alabama Review, 32, 2 (1979), pp. 141-46.

1442. Reidy, Joseph Patrick. "Masters and Slaves, Planters and Freedmen: The Transition from Slavery to Freedom in Central Georgia, 1820-1880" (PhD diss., Northern Illinois University, 1982).

1443. Ricards, Sherman L., and George M. Blackburn. "A Demographic History of Slavery: Georgetown County, South Carolina, 1850," South Carolina Historical Magazine, 76, 4 (1975), pp. 215-24.

1444. Robinson, Armstead L. "In the Shadow of Old John Brown: Insurrection Anxiety and Confederate Mobilization," Journal of Negro History, 65, 4 (1980), pp. 279-97.

1445. Rothstein, Morton. "The Changing Social Networks and Investment Behavior of a Slaveholding Elite in the Ante Bellum South: Some Natchez 'Nabobs' 1800-1860," in Sidney M. Greenfield et al., eds., Entrepreneurs in Cultural Context (Albuquerque: University of New Mexico Press, 1979), pp. 65-88.

1446. Russell, Robert R. "The Effects of Slavery Upon Nonslaveholders in the Ante Bellum South," Agricultural History, 15, 2 (1941), pp. 112-26.

1447. Saraydar, Edward. "A Note on the Profitability of Ante Bellum Slavery," Southern Economic Journal, 30, 4 (1964), pp. 325-32.

1448. Savannah Unit, Georgia Writers Project, Work Projects Administration. "Drakies Plantation," Georgia Historical Quarterly, 24, 3 (1940), pp. 207-35. Reprinted in Miller and Genovese, eds., Plantation, Town, and County, pp. 186-208.

1449. Schneider, Tracy Whittaker. "The Institution of Slavery in North Carolina, 1860-1865" (PhD diss., Duke University, 1979).

1450. Sellers, James B. Slavery in Alabama. University: University of Alabama Press, 1950.

1451. Shingleton, Royce G. "Rural Life in the Old South: The British Travelers' Image, 1820-1860" (PhD diss., Florida State University, 1971).

1452. _____. "The Trial and Punishment of Slaves in Baldwin County, Georgia, 1812-1826," Southern Humanities Review, 8, 1 (1974), pp. 67-73.

1453. Shore, Laurence. "Making Mississippi Safe for Slavery: The Insurrectionary Panic of 1835," in Orville Vernon Burton and Robert C. McMath, Jr., eds., Class, Conflict, and Consensus: Antebellum Southern Community Studies (Westport, Conn.: Greenwood Press, 1982), pp. 96-127.

1454. Stampp, Kenneth M. "Chattels Personal," reprinted (from Peculiar Institution, pp. 192-235) in Brown, ed., Slavery in American Society, pp. 44-54.

1455. _____. "The Daily Life of the Southern Slave," in Kilson and Huggins, eds., Key Issues in the Afro-American Experience, vol. 1, pp. 116-37.

1456. _____. The Peculiar Institution: Slavery in the Ante-Bellum South. New York: Knopf, 1956.

1457. Starobin, Robert S. "Denmark Vesey's Slave Conspiracy of 1822: A Study in Rebellion and Repression," in Bracey, Meier, and Rudwick, eds., American Slavery, pp. 142-57.

1458. _____. "Disciplining Industrial Slaves in the Old South," Journal of Negro History, 53, 1 (1968), pp. 111-28. Also Bobbs-Merrill Reprint no. BC-283.

1459. _____. "The Economics of Industrial Slavery in the Old South," Business History Review, 44, 2 (1970), pp. 131-74.

1460. _____. Industrial Slavery in the Old South. New York: Oxford University Press, 1970.

1461. _____. "Privileged Bondsmen and the Process of Accommodation: The Role of Houseservants and Drivers as Seen in Their Own Letters," Journal of Social History, 5, 1 (1971), pp. 46-70.

1462. _____. "Race Relations in Old South Industries," in Weinstein and Gatell, eds., American Negro Slavery (2nd ed.), pp. 317-27. Also as "Race Relations in the Old South Industries," in Newton and Lewis, eds., The Other Slaves, pp. 51-60.

1463. _____, ed. Denmark Vesey: The Slave Conspiracy of 1822. Englewood Cliffs, N.J.: Prentice-Hall, 1970.

1464. Strickland, John Scott. "The Great Revival and Insurrectionary Fears in North Carolina: An Examination of Antebellum Southern Society and Slave Revolt Panics," in Orville Vernon Burton and Robert C. McMath, Jr., eds., Class, Conflict, and Consensus: Antebellum Southern Community Studies (Westport, Conn.: Greenwood Press, 1982), pp. 57-95.

1465. Stuckey, Sterling. "Remembering Denmark Vesey," Negro Digest, 15, 4 (1966), pp. 28-41.

1466. Sutch, Richard. "The Breeding of Slaves for Sale and the Westward Expansion of Slavery, 1850-1860," in Engerman and Genovese, eds., Race and Slavery, pp. 173-210.

1467. Swados, Felice. "Negro Health on the Ante Bellum Plantations," Bulletin of the History of Medicine, 10, 3 (1941), pp. 460-72.

1468. Sydnor, Charles S. "Life Span of Mississippi Slaves," American Historical Review, 35, 3 (1930), pp. 566-74.

1469. _____. Slavery in Mississippi. New York: Appleton-Century, 1933.

1470. Tadman, Michael. "Slave Trading in the Ante-Bellum South: An Estimate of the Extent of the Inter-Regional Slave Trade," Journal of American Studies, 13, 2 (1979), pp. 195-220.

1471. Taylor, Rosser H. "Humanizing the Slave Code in North Carolina," North Carolina Historical Review, 2, 3 (1925), pp. 323-31.

1472. _____. Slave Holding in North Carolina: An Economic View. Chapel Hill: University of North Carolina Press, 1926.

1473. Toplin, Robert Brent. "Between Black and White: Attitudes Toward Southern Mulattoes, 1830-1861," in idem, Freedom and Prejudice: The Legacy of Slavery in the United States and Brazil (Westport, Conn.: Greenwood Press, 1981), pp. 21-40. (Contributions in Afro-American and African Studies, no. 56)

1474. _____. "Proslavery, Anti-Black: The Hardening of Racial Attitudes in the Antebellum South," in idem, Freedom and Prejudice: The Legacy of Slavery in the United States and Brazil (Westport, Conn.: Greenwood Press, 1981), pp. 3-20.

1475. Touchstone, Donald Blake. "Planters and Slave Religion in the Deep South" (PhD diss., Tulane University, 1973).

1476. Wade, Richard C. Slavery in the Cities: The South, 1820-1860. New York: Oxford University Press, 1964.

1477. _____. "The Vesey Plot: A Reconsideration," Journal of Southern History, 30, 2 (1964), pp. 143-61. Reprinted in Bracey, Meier, and Rudwick, eds., American Slavery, pp. 127-41.

1478. Webber, Thomas L. Deep Like the Rivers: Education in the Slave Quarter Community, 1831-1865. New York: Norton, 1978.

1479. _____. "The Education of the Slave Quarter Community: White Teaching and Black Learning on the Antebellum Plantation" (PhD diss., Columbia University, 1976).

1480. Wesley, Charles. "Manifests of Slave Shipments Along the Waterways, 1808-1864," Journal of Negro History, 37, 2 (1942), pp. 155-74.

1481. Westwood, Howard C. "Captive Black Union Soldiers in Charleston - What to Do?" Civil War History, 28, 1 (1982), pp. 28-44.

1482. Wetherell, Charles. "Slave Kinship: A Case Study of the South Carolina Good Hope Plantation, 1835-1856," Journal of Family History, 6, 3 (1981), pp. 294-308.

1483. White, Deborah G. "Ain't I a Woman? Female Slaves in the Antebellum South" (PhD diss., University of Illinois, Chicago Circle, 1979).

1484. Wiggins, D. "Good Times on the Old Plantation: Popular Recreations of the Black Slave in Ante Bellum South, 1810-1860," _Journal of Sport History_, 4, 3 (1977), pp. 260-84.

1485. Wikramanayake, Marina. _A World in Shadow: The Free Black in Antebellum South Carolina_. Columbia: University of South Carolina Press, 1973.

1486. Wiley, Bell Irvin. _Southern Negroes, 1861-1865_. Baton Rouge: Louisiana State University Press, 1974. (First published New Haven: Yale University Press, 1938, 1965.)

1487. Wilkie, Jane Riblett. "The Black Urban Population of the Pre-Civil War South," _Phylon_, 37, 3 (1976), pp. 250-62.

1488. Williams, Walter L. "Again in Chains: Black Soldiers Suffering in Captivity," _Civil War Times Illustrated_, 20, 2 (1981), pp. 36-46.

1489. Windley, Lathan Algerna. "A Profile of Runaway Slaves in Virginia and South Carolina from 1730 through 1787" (PhD diss., University of Iowa, 1974).

1490. Wish, Harvey, ed. _Slavery in the South: First-Hand Accounts of the Ante-Bellum American Southland from Northern and Southern Whites, Negroes, and Foreign Observers_. New York: Farrar, Straus, 1964.

1491. Wright, Gavin. _The Political Economy of the Cotton South, Households, Markets, and Wealth in the Nineteenth Century_. New York: Norton, 1978.

1492. _____. "Slavery and the Cotton Boom," _Explorations in Economic History_, 12, 4 (1975), pp. 439-51.

1493. Yankovic, Donald J. "A Micro Study of the Cotton Plantation Economy of Dallas County, Alabama, Based on the Manuscript Census Returns of 1860" (PhD diss., University of Pittsburgh, 1972).

1494. Zepp, Thomas M. "Agricultural Labor in the American South, 1860-1870: An Analysis of Elasticity of Substitution and Change in Functional Shares" (PhD diss., University of Florida, 1971).

6. Ante-Bellum Upper South

1495. Bellamy, Donnie D. "The Education of Blacks in Missouri Prior to 1861," _Journal of Negro History_, 59 (1974), pp. 143-57.

1496. _____. "Free Blacks in Antebellum Missouri, 1820-1860," _Missouri Historical Review_, 67, 2 (1973), pp. 198-226.

1497. _____. "Slavery, Emancipation, and Racism in Missouri, 1850-1865" (PhD diss., University of Missouri, 1971).

1498. Berlin, Ira. "Slaves Who were Free: The Free Negro in the Upper South, 1776-1861" (PhD diss., University of Wisconsin, Madison, 1970).

1499. Calderhead, William. "How Extensive Was the Border State Slave Trade? A New Look," Civil War History, 18, 1 (1972), pp. 42-55.

1500. Cimprich, John. "Slave Behavior during the Federal Occupation of Tennessee, 1862-1865," Historian, 44, 3 (1982), pp. 335-46.

1501. _____. "Slavery Amidst Civil War in Tennessee: The Death of an Institution" (PhD diss., Ohio State University, 1977).

1502. Coleman, J. Winston, Jr. Slavery Times in Kentucky. Chapel Hill: University of North Carolina Press, 1940.

1503. Corlew, Robert E. "Some Aspects of Slavery in Dickson County," Tennessee Historical Quarterly, 10, 3 (1951), pp. 224-48; 10, 4 (1951), pp. 344-65. Reprinted in Miller and Genovese, eds., Plantation, Town, and County, pp. 96-145.

1504. Dew, Charles B. "Black Ironworkers and the Slave Insurrection Panic of 1856," Journal of Southern History, 41, 3 (1975), pp. 321-38.

1505. Dorsett, Lyle Wesley. "Slaveholding in Jackson County, Missouri," Missouri Historical Society Bulletin, 20, 1 (1963), pp. 25-37. Reprinted in Miller and Genovese, eds., Plantation, Town, and County, pp. 146-60.

1506. Duffner, Robert W. "Slavery in Missouri River Counties, 1820-1865" (PhD diss., University of Missouri, 1974).

1507. Eaton, Clement. "Slave-Hiring in the Upper South: A Step Toward Freedom," Mississippi Valley Historical Review, 46, 4 (1960), pp. 663-78.

1508. England, J. Merton. "The Free Negro in Ante-Bellum Tennessee," Journal of Southern History, 9, 1 (1943), pp. 37-58. Also Bobbs-Merrill Reprint no. BC-73.

1509. Goodstein, Anita S. "Black History on the Nashville Frontier, 1780-1810," Tennessee Historical Quarterly, 38, 4 (1979), pp. 401-20.

1510. Green, Barbara L. "Slave Labor at the Maramec Iron Works, 1828-1850," Missouri Historical Review, 73, 2 (1979), pp. 150-64.

1511. _____. "The Slavery Debate in Missouri, 1831-1855" (PhD diss., University of Missouri, 1980).

1512. Harrison, Lowell H. "Recollections of Some Tennessee Slaves," Tennessee Historical Quarterly, 33, 2 (1974), pp. 175-90.

1513. Hedrick, Charles Embury. "Social and Economic Aspects of Slavery in the Transmontane Prior to 1850" (PhD diss., George Peabody College for Teachers, 1927).

1514. Henry, Howell M. "The Slave Laws of Tennessee," _Tennessee Historical Magazine_, 2, 3 (1916), pp. 175-203.

1515. Hickey, Donald R., ed. "Slavery and the Republican Experiment: A View from Western Virginia in 1806," _West Virginia History_, 39, 2-3 (1978), pp. 236-40.

1516. Howard, Victor B. "The Civil War in Kentucky: The Slave Claims his Freedom," _Journal of Negro History_, 67, 3 (1982), pp. 245-56.

1517. _____. "Lincoln Slave Policy in Kentucky: A Study of Pragmatic Strategy," _Register of the Kentucky Historical Society_, 80, 3 (1982), pp. 281-308.

1518. _____. "Robert J. Breckinridge and the Slavery Controversy in Kentucky in 1849," _Filson Club History Quarterly_, 53, 4 (1979), pp. 328-43.

1519. Howington, Arthur F. "'Not in the Condition of a Horse or an Ox': Ford v. Ford, the Law of Testamentary Manumission, and the Tennessee Courts' Recognition of Slave Humanity," _Tennessee Historical Quarterly_, 34, 3 (1975), pp. 249-63.

1520. _____. "The Treatment of Slaves and Free Blacks in the State and Local Courts of Tennessee" (PhD diss., Vanderbilt University, 1982).

1521. Hunter, Lloyd A. "Slavery in St. Louis 1804-1860," _Bulletin of the Missouri Historical Society_, 30, 4 (1974), pp. 233-65.

1522. Lack, Paul D. "An Urban Slave Community: Little Rock, 1831-1862," _Arkansas Historical Quarterly_, 41, 3 (1982), pp. 258-87.

1523. Lovett, Bobby L. "The Negro's Civil War in Tennessee," _Journal of Negro History_, 61, 1 (1976), pp. 36-50.

1524. McDougle, Ivan Eugene. _Slavery in Kentucky, 1792-1865_. Lancaster, Pa.: New Era Printing Co., 1918.

1525. McGettigan, James William, Jr. "Boone County Slaves: Sales, Estate Divisions and Families, 1820-1865," _Missouri Historical Review_, 72, 2 (1978), pp. 176-97; 72, 3 (1978), pp. 271-95.

1526. Magnaghi, Russell M. "The Role of Indian Slavery in Colonial St. Louis," _Bulletin of the Missouri Historical Society_, 31, 4 (1975), pp. 264-72.

1527. Mooney, Chase C. _Slavery in Tennessee_. Bloomington: Indiana University Press, 1957.

1528. Murphy, James B. "Slavery and Freedom in Appalachia: Kentucky as a Demographic Case Study," Register of the Kentucky Historical Society, 80, 2 (1982), pp. 151-69.

1529. Otto, John Solomon. "The Case for Folk History: Slavery in the Highlands South," Southern Studies, 20, 2 (1981), pp. 167-73.

1530. _____. "Slaveholding General Farmers in a 'Cotton County'," Agricultural History, 55, 2 (1981), pp. 167-78.

1531. _____. "Slavery in the Mountains: Yell County Arkansas, 1840-1860," Arkansas Historical Quarterly, 39, 1 (1980), pp. 35-52.

1532. Poole, Stafford, and Douglas Slawson. "'Necessity Knows no Law': Vicentian Slaveholding in Perry County, Missouri, 1818-60" (Paper read to the Annual Meeting of the American Historical Association, Los Angeles, 1981).

1533. Robinson, Armstead Louis. "Days of Jublio: Civil War and the Demise of Slavery in the Mississippi Valley, 1861-1865" (PhD diss., University of Rochester, 1977).

1534. Sheldon, Randall G. "From Slave to Caste Society: Penal Changes in Tennessee, 1830-1915," Tennessee Historical Quarterly, 38, 4 (1979), pp. 462-78.

1535. Sobel, Mechal. "'They Can Never Both Prosper Together': Black and White Baptists in Antebellum Nashville, Tennessee," Tennessee Historical Quarterly, 38, 3 (1979), pp. 296-307.

1536. Stealey, John Edmund III. "Slavery and the Western Virginia Salt Industry," Journal of Negro History, 59, 2 (1974), pp. 105-31. Reprinted in Newton and Lewis, eds., The Other Slaves, pp. 109-33.

1537. Steel, Edward M., Jr. "Black Monongalians: A Judicial View of Slavery and the Negro in Monongalia County 1776-1865," West Virginia History, 34, 4 (1973), pp. 331-59.

1538. Taylor, Orville W. "Baptists and Slavery in Arkansas: Relationships and Attitudes," Arkansas Historical Quarterly, 38, 3 (1979), pp. 199-226.

1539. _____. Negro Slavery in Arkansas. Durham: Duke University Press, 1958.

1540. Trexler, Harrison Anthony. Slavery in Missouri, 1804-1865. Baltimore: Johns Hopkins University Press, 1914.

1541. Van Deburg, William L. "The Slave Drivers of Arkansas: A New View from the Narratives," Arkansas Historical Quarterly, 35, 3 (1976), pp. 231-45.

7. Louisiana

1542. Allain, Mathé. "Slave Policies in French Louisiana," Louisiana History, 21, 2 (1980), pp. 127-37.

1543. Baade, Anne A. "Slave Indemnities: A German Coast Response, 1795," Louisiana History, 20, 1 (1979), pp. 102-09.

1544. Brasseaux, Carl A. "The Administration of Slave Regulations in French Louisiana, 1724-1766," Louisiana History, 21, 2 (1980), pp. 139-58.

1545. Cook, Charles Orson, and James M. Poteet, eds. "'Dem was Black Times, Sure 'Nough': The Slave Narratives of Lydia Jefferson and Stephen Williams," Louisiana History, 20, 3 (1979), pp. 281-92.

1546. "Destrehan's Slave Roll," Louisiana Historical Quarterly, 7, 2 (1924), pp. 302-03.

1547. Dormon, James H. "The Persistent Specter: Slave Rebellion in Territorial Louisiana," Louisiana History, 18, 4 (1977), pp. 389-405.

1548. Fiehrer, Thomas Marc. "The African Presence in Colonial Louisiana: An Essay on the Continuity of Caribbean Culture," in Robert L. MacDonald, John R. Kemp, and Edward F. Haas, eds., Louisiana's Black Heritage (New Orleans: Louisiana State Museum, 1979), pp. 32-62.

1549. Fischer, Roger A. "Racial Segregation in Ante-Bellum New Orleans," American Historical Review, 74, 3 (1969), pp. 926-37.

1550. Hackett, D. L. A. "Slavery, Ethnicity, and Sugar: An Analysis of Voting Behavior in Louisiana, 1828-1844," Louisiana Studies, 13, 2 (1974), pp. 73-118.

1551. Holmes, Jack D. L. "The Abortive Slave Revolt at Point Coupée, Louisiana: 1795," Louisiana History, 11, 4 (1970), pp. 341-62.

1552. Kotlikoff, Laurence J. "The Structure of Slave Prices in New Orleans, 1804 to 1862," Economic Inquiry, 17, 4 (1979), pp. 496-518.

1553. _____, and Anton J. Rupert. "The Manumission of Slaves in New Orleans, 1827-46," Southern Studies, 19, 2 (1980), pp. 172-81.

1554. McGowan, James T. "Creation of a Slave Society: Louisiana Plantations in the Eighteenth Century" (PhD diss., University of Rochester, 1976).

1555. _____. "Planters Without Slaves: Origins of a New World Labor System," Southern Studies, 16, 4 (1977), pp. 5-26.

1556. Menn, Joseph K. The Large Slaveholders of Louisiana, 1860. New Orleans: Pelican, 1964.

1557. Messner, William F. "Black Violence and White Response: Louisiana, 1862," Journal of Southern History, 41, 1 (1975), pp. 19-38.

1558. Miceli, Mary Veronica. "The Influence of the Roman Catholic Church on Slavery in Colonial Louisiana under French Domination, 1718-1763" (PhD diss., Tulane University, 1979).

1559. Moody, V. Alton. "Slavery on Louisiana Sugar Plantations," Louisiana Historical Quarterly, 7, 2 (1924), pp. 191-301.

1560. Price, John M. "Slavery in Winn Parish," Louisiana History, 8, 2 (1967), pp. 137-48. Reprinted in Miller and Genovese, eds., Plantation, Town, and County, pp. 60-70.

1561. Pritchard, Walter. "Routine on a Louisiana Sugar Plantation under the Slavery Regime," Mississippi Valley Historical Review, 14, 2 (1927), pp. 168-78.

1562. Rankin, David C. "The Tannenbaum Thesis Reconsidered: Slavery and Race Relations in Antebellum Louisiana," Southern Studies, 18, 1 (1979), pp. 5-31.

1563. Reilly, Timothy F. "Slavery and the Southwestern Evangelist in New Orleans (1860-1861)," Journal of Mississippi History, 41, 4 (1979), pp. 301-17.

1564. Reinders, Robert C. "Slavery in New Orleans in the Decade before the Civil War," Mid-America: An Historical Review, 44, 4 (1962), pp. 211-21. Reprinted in Miller and Genovese, eds., Plantation, Town, and County, pp. 365-76.

1565. Richter, William L. "Slavery in Baton Rouge, 1820-60," Louisiana History, 10, 2 (1969), pp. 125-45. Reprinted in Miller and Genovese, eds., Plantation, Town, and Country, pp. 377-96.

1566. Ripley, C. Peter. "Black, Blue and Grey: Slaves and Freedmen in Civil War Louisiana" (PhD diss., Florida State University, 1973).

1567. _____. "The Black Family in Transition: Louisiana, 1860-1865," Journal of Southern History, 41, 3 (1975), pp. 369-80.

1568. _____. Slaves and Freedmen in Civil War Louisiana. Baton Rouge: Louisiana State University Press, 1976.

1569. Schafer, Judith Kelleher. "The Immediate Impact of Nat Turner's Insurrection on New Orleans," Louisiana History, 21, 4 (1980), pp. 361-76.

1570. _____. "New Orleans Slavery in 1850 as Seen in Advertisements," Journal of Southern History, 47, 1 (1981), pp. 33-56.

1571. Schmitz, Mark D. "Economies of Scale and Farm Size in the Antebellum Sugar Sector," Journal of Economic History, 37, 4 (1977), pp. 959–80.

1572. Schweninger, Loren. "A Negro Sojourner in Antebellum New Orleans," Louisiana History, 20, 3 (1979), pp. 305–16.

1573. Tansey, Richard. "Bernard Kendig and the New Orleans Slave Trade," Louisiana History, 23, 2 (1982), pp. 159–78.

1574. _____. "Out-of-State Free Blacks in Late Antebellum New Orleans," Louisiana History, 22, 4 (1981), pp. 369–86.

1575. Taylor, Joe. Negro Slavery in Louisiana. Baton Rouge: Louisiana Historical Association, 1963.

1576. Unser, Daniel H., Jr. "From Captivity to American Slavery: The Introduction of Black Laborers to Colonial Louisiana," Louisiana History, 20, 1 (1979), pp. 25–48.

1577. Vandal, Gilles. "Violence et relations raciales à la Nouvelle-Orléans pendant la guerre civile: un prélude à l'émeute du 30 juillet 1866," Canadian Review of American Studies, 13, 1 (1982), pp. 15–38.

1578. Whitten, David O. "Sugar Slavery: A Profitability Model for Slave Investments in the Antebellum Louisiana Sugar Industry," Louisiana Studies, 12, 2 (1973), pp. 423–42.

1579. Young, Tommy R., II. "The United States Army and the Institution of Slavery in Louisiana, 1803–1815," Louisiana Studies, 13, 3 (1974), pp. 201–22.

8. Texas

1580. Addington, Wendell G. "Slave Insurrections in Texas," Journal of Negro History, 35, 4 (1950), pp. 408–34.

1581. Bailey, David Thomas. "Slavery and the Churches: The Old Southwest" (PhD diss., University of California, Berkeley, 1979).

1582. Barker, Eugene C. "The African Slave Trade in Texas," Texas Historical Association Quarterly, 6, 2 (1903), pp. 145–58.

1583. Barr, Alwyn. Black Texans: A History of Negroes in Texas, 1528–1971. Austin: Jenkins, 1973.

1584. Campbell, Randolph B. "Human Property: The Negro Slave in Harrison County, 1850–1860," Southwestern Historical Quarterly, 76, 4 (1973), pp. 384–96.

1585. _____. "Local Archives as a Source of Slave Prices: Harrison County, Texas as a Test Case," Historian, 36, 4 (1974), pp. 660–69.

1586. _____. "The Productivity of Slave Labor in East Texas: A Research Note," Louisiana Studies, 13, 2 (1974), pp. 154-72.

1587. _____, and Donald K. Pickens. "'My Dear Husband': A Texas Slave's Love Letter, 1862," Journal of Negro History, 65, 4 (1980), pp. 361-64.

1588. Coles, Harry L., Jr. "Some Notes on Slaveownership and Landownership in Louisiana, 1850-1860," Journal of Southern History, 9, 3 (1943), pp. 381-94.

1589. Curlee, Abigail. "The History of a Texas Slave Plantation, 1831-1863," Southwestern Historical Quarterly, 26, 2 (1922), pp. 79-127. Reprinted in Miller and Genovese, eds., Plantation, Town, and County, pp. 303-34.

1590. _____. "A Study of Texas Slave Plantations, 1822 to 1865" (PhD diss., University of Texas, 1932).

1591. Durham, Philip, and Everett L. Jones. The Negro Cowboys. New York: Dodd, Mead, 1965.

1592. Lack, Paul D. "Slavery and Vigilantism in Austin, Texas, 1840-1860," Southwestern Historical Quarterly, 85, 1 (1981), pp. 1-20.

1593. _____. "Urban Slavery in the Southwest" (PhD diss., Texas Tech University, 1973).

1594. Ledbetter, Billy D. "White Over Black in Texas: Racial Attitudes in the Antebellum Period," Phylon, 34, 4 (1973), pp. 406-18.

1595. Lowe, Richard, and Randolph Campbell. "Slave Property and the Distribution of Wealth in Texas, 1860," Journal of American History, 63, 2 (1976), pp. 316-24.

1596. Sunseri, Alvin R. "Slavery and the Black Man in New Mexico, 1846-1861," Negro History Bulletin, 38, 7 (1975), pp. 457-59.

1597. White, William W. "The Texas Slave Insurrection of 1860," Southwestern Historical Quarterly, 52, 3 (1949), pp. 259-85.

9. Florida

1598. Dibble, Ernest F. "Slave Rentals to the Military: Pensacola and the Gulf Coast," Civil War History, 23 (1977), pp. 101-13.

1599. Fairbanks, Charles H. "The Kingsley Slave Cabins in Duval County, Florida, 1968," Conference on Historic Site Archaeology Papers (Institute of Archaeology and Anthropology, University of South Carolina, Columbia), vol. 7 (1972), pp. 62-93.

1600. Granade, Ray. "Slave Unrest in Florida," Florida Historical Quarterly, 55, 1 (1976), pp. 18–36.

1601. Hering, Julia. "Plantation Economy in Leon County, 1830–40," Florida Historical Quarterly, 33, 1 (1954), pp. 32–47. Reprinted in Miller and Genovese, eds., Plantation, Town, and County, pp. 50–59.

1602. Klingman, Peter D. "A Florida Slave Sale," Florida Historical Quarterly, 52, 1 (1973), pp. 62–66.

1603. McFarlane, Suzanne B. "The Ethnoarchaeology of a Slave Community: The Couper Plantation Site" (MA thesis, University of Florida, 1975).

1604. Milligan, John D. "Slave Rebelliousness and the Florida Maroon," Prologue, 6, 1 (1974), pp. 4–18.

1605. Ordoñez, Margaret T. "Plantation Self-Sufficiency in Leon County, Florida: 1824–1860," Florida Historical Quarterly, 60, 4 (1982), pp. 428–39.

1606. Porter, Kenneth W. "Florida Slaves and Free Negroes in the Seminole War, 1835–1842," Journal of Negro History, 28, 4 (1943), pp. 390–421. Also Bobbs-Merrill Reprint no. BC-222.

1607. Rea, Robert R. "Planters and Plantations in British West Florida," Alabama Review, 29, 3 (1976), pp. 220–35.

1608. Rivers, Larry E. "'Dignity and Importance': Slavery in Jefferson County, Florida – 1827 to 1860," Florida Historical Quarterly, 61, 4 (1983), pp. 404–30.

1609. _____. "Slavery in Microcosm: Leon County, Florida, 1824 to 1860," Journal of Negro History, 66, 3 (1981), pp. 235–45.

1610. Smith, Julia Floyd. Slavery and Plantation Growth in Antebellum Florida, 1821–1860. Gainesville: University of Florida Press, 1973.

1611. _____. "Slavetrading in Antebellum Florida," Florida Historical Quarterly, 50, 3 (1972), pp. 252–61.

1612. Wright, J. Leitch, Jr. "Blacks in British East Florida," Florida Historical Quarterly, 54, 4 (1976), pp. 425–42.

10. Other

1613. Aldrich, Orlando. "Slavery or Involuntary Servitude in Illinois Prior to and After its Admission as a State," Transactions of the Illinois State Historical Society, 22 (1916), pp. 89–99. Also as "Slavery or Involuntary Servitude in Illinois Prior to and After its Admission as a State," Journal of the Illinois State Historical Society, 9, 2 (1916), pp. 119–32.

Other

1614. Alilunas, Leo. "Fugitive Slave Cases in Ohio prior to 1850," Ohio Archaeological and Historical Quarterly, 49 (1940), pp. 160-84.

1615. Bailey, David Thomas. "Slavery and the Churches: The Old Southwest" (PhD diss., University of California, Berkeley, 1979).

1616. Beauregard, Erving E. "Slavery, Higher Education and Academic Freedom in Ohio," Journal of Presbyterian History, 60, 2 (1982), pp. 210-26.

1617. Beller, Jack. "Negro Slaves in Utah," Utah Historical Quarterly, 2, 1 (1929), pp. 122-26.

1618. Billington, Monroe. "Black Slavery in Indian Territory: The Ex-Slave Narratives," Chronicles of Oklahoma, 60, 1 (1982), pp. 56-65.

1619. Bridges, Roger D., ed. "John Mason Peck on Illinois Slavery," Journal of the Illinois State Historical Society, 75, 3 (1982), pp. 179-217.

1620. Bringhurst, Newell G. "The 'Descendants of Ham' in Zion: Discrimination Against Blacks Along the Shifting Mormon Frontier, 1830-1920," Nevada Historical Society Quarterly, 24, 4 (1981), pp. 298-318.

1621. _____. "The Mormons and Slavery - A Closer Look," Pacific Historical Review, 50, 3 (1981), pp. 329-38.

1622. _____. Saints, Slaves, and Blacks: The Changing Place of Black People Within Mormonism. Westport, Conn.: Greenwood Press, 1981.

1623. Christensen, James B. "Negro Slavery in the Utah Territory," Phylon, 18, 3 (1957), pp. 298-305.

1624. Coleman, Ronald Gerald. "A History of Blacks in Utah, 1825-1910" (PhD diss., University of Utah, 1980).

1625. Davenport, T. W. "Slavery Question in Oregon - II," Oregon Historical Society Quarterly, 9, 4 (1908), pp. 309-73.

1626. Forbes, Gerald. "The Part Played by the Enslavement of the Indian in the Removal of the Tribes to Oklahoma," Chronicles of Oklahoma, 16, 2 (1938), pp. 163-70.

1627. Harris, Newton D. "Negro Servitude in Illinois," Transactions of the Illinois State Historical Society, 11 (1906), pp. 49-56.

1628. Harris, Norman Dwight. The History of Negro Servitude in Illinois, and of the Slavery Agitation in that State, 1719-1864. Chicago: A. C. McClurg, 1904.

1629. Haynes, N. S. "The Disciples of Christ in Illinois and their Attitude toward Slavery," Transactions of the Illinois State Historical Society, 19 (1913), pp. 52-59.

1630. Lyons, John F. "The Attitude of Presbyterians in Ohio, Indiana and Illinois toward Slavery, 1825-1861," Journal of the Presbyterian History Society, 11, 2 (1921), pp. 69-82.

1631. Lythgoe, Dennis L. "Negro Slavery and Mormon Doctrine," Western Humanities Review, 21, 4 (1967), pp. 327-38.

1632. _____. "Negro Slavery in Utah," Utah Historical Quarterly, 39, 1 (1971), pp. 40-54.

1633. Pelzer, Louis. "The Negro and Slavery in Early Iowa," Iowa Journal of History and Politics, 2, 4 (1904), pp. 471-84.

1634. Posey, William Brownlow. "The Slavery Question in the Presbyterian Church in the Old Southwest," Journal of Southern History, 15, 3 (1949), pp. 311-24.

1635. Prince, Benjamin F. "The Rescue Case of 1857," Ohio Archaeological and Historical Publications, 16 (1907), pp. 292-309.

1636. Reat, James L. "Slavery in Douglas County, Illinois," Journal of the Illinois State Historical Society, 11, 2 (1918-19), pp. 177-79.

1637. Savage, William Sherman. Blacks in the West. Westport, Conn.: Greenwood Press, 1976.

1638. Schoonover, Thomas. "Misconstrued Mission: Expansionism and Black Colonization in Mexico and Central America during the Civil War," Pacific Historical Review, 49, 4 (1980), pp. 607-20.

1639. Schwartz, Rosalie. Across the Rio to Freedom: U.S. Negroes in Mexico. El Paso: Texas Western Press, University of Texas at El Paso, 1975.

1640. Sharpe, Esther E. "Slavery in the Territories under the Compromise of 1850," Historical Outlook, 18, 3 (1927), pp. 107-09.

1641. Zucker, Charles N. "The Free Negro Question: Race Relations in Ante-Bellum Illinois, 1801-1860" (PhD diss., Northwestern University, 1972).

11. Biographies

1642. Alford, Terry. Prince Among Slaves. New York: Harcourt, Brace, Jovanovich, 1977.

1643. Bogin, Ruth. "'Liberty Further Extended': A 1776 Antislavery Manuscript by Lemuel Haynes," William and Mary Quarterly, 3rd ser., 40, 1 (1983), pp. 85-105.

Biographies

1644. Boles, John B. "Tension in a Slave Society: The Trial of the Reverend Jacob Gruber," _Southern Studies_, 18, 2 (1979), pp. 179–97.

1645. Boney, F. N. "Doctor Thomas Hamilton: Two Views of a Gentleman of the Old South," _Phylon_, 28, 3 (1967), pp. 288–92.

1646. Bulkley, Robert D., Jr. "A Democrat and Slavery: Robert Rantoul, Jr.," _Essex Institute Historical Collections_, 110 (1974), pp. 261–38.

1647. Calderhead, William. "The Professional Slave Trader in a Slavery Economy: Austin Woolfolk, A Case Study," _Civil War History_, 23, 3 (1977), pp. 195–211.

1648. Faust, Drew Gilpin. "A Slaveowner in a Free Society: James Henry Hammond on the Grand Tour, 1836–1837," _South Carolina Historical Magazine_, 81, 3 (1980), pp. 189–206.

1649. Gatewood, Willard B., Jr., ed. _Slave and Freeman: The Autobiography of George L. Knox_. Lexington: University Press of Kentucky, 1979.

1650. Gillespie, J. David, and Judi F. Gillespie. "Struggle for Identity: The Life of Jordan Chambers (A _Phylon_ document)," _Phylon_, 40, 2 (1979), pp. 107–18.

1651. Howell, Isabel. "John Armfield, Slave-Trader," _Tennessee Historical Quarterly_, 2, 1 (1943), pp. 3–29.

1652. Logan, Paul E. "Tales of the Customs and Fate of Negro Slaves: Johann Ernst Kolb," _Negro History Bulletin_, 44, 4 (1981), pp. 78–80.

1653. Moore, John Hebron. "Simon Gray, Riverman: A Slave Who Was Almost Free," _Mississippi Valley Historical Review_, 49, 3 (1962), pp. 472–84. Reprinted in Newton and Lewis, eds., _The Other Slaves_, pp. 157–67. Also Bobbs-Merrill Reprint no. BC-208.

1654. Northrup, Solomon. _Twelve Years a Slave_. Eds. Sue Eakin and Joseph Logsdon. Baton Rouge: Louisiana State University Press, 1968.

1655. Schweninger, Loren. "John Rapier, Sr.: A Slave and Freedman in the Ante-Bellum South," _Civil War History_, 20, 1 (1974), pp. 23–34.

1656. _____. "A Negro Sojourner in Antebellum New Orleans," _Louisiana History_, 20, 3 (1979), pp. 305–14.

1657. _____. "A Slave Family in the Ante-Bellum South," _Journal of Negro History_, 60, 1 (1975), pp. 29–44.

1658. Stanley, Linda. "Notes and Documents: James Carter's Account of His Sufferings in Slavery," _Pennsylvania Magazine of History and Biography_, 105, 3 (1981), pp. 335–39.

1659. Stephenson, Wendell Holmes. Isaac Franklin: Slave Trader and Planter in the Old South, with Plantation Records. University, La.: Louisiana State University Press, 1938.

1660. Tyner, Wayne C. "Charles Colcock Jones: Mission to Slaves," Journal of Presbyterian History, 55, 4 (1977), pp. 363-80.

1661. Vacheenas, Jean, and Betty Volk. "Born in Bondage: History of a Slave Family," Negro History Bulletin, 36, 5 (1973), pp. 101-06.

1662. Walker, Juliet E. K. "'Free' Frank and New Philadelphia: Slave and Freedman, Frontiersman and Town Founder" (PhD diss., University of Chicago, 1976).

1663. Williamson, Hugh P. "The Case of Celia the Slave," Negro Digest, 13, 7 (1964), pp. 78-87.

1664. Willis, John Ralph (JRW). "New Light on the Life of Ignatius Sancho: Some Unpublished Letters," Slavery and Abolition, 1, 3 (1980), pp. 345-58.

1665. Wynes, Charles E. "Dr. James Durham, Mysterious Eighteenth-Century Black Physician: Man or Myth?" Pennsylvania Magazine of History and Biography, 103, 3 (1979), pp. 325-33.

12. Canada

1666. Grant, John N. Black Nova Scotians. Halifax, Nova Scotia: Nova Scotia Museum, 1980.

1667. Lapalice, O. M. H. "Les esclaves noirs à Montréal sous l'ancien régime," Canadian Antiquarian and Numismatic Journal, 3rd ser., 12, 3 (1915), pp. 136-58.

1668. Macaulay, A. J., and D. A. Boag. "Waterfowl Harvest by Slave Indians in Northern Alberta," Arctic, 27, 1 (1974), pp. 15-26.

1669. Massicote, E. Z. "L'esclavage au Canada sous le régime anglais," Bulletin des recherches historiques, 24, 11 (1918), pp. 344-47.

1670. Riddell, William Renwick. "The Baptism of Slaves in Prince Edward Island," Journal of Negro History, 6, 3 (1921), pp. 307-09.

1671. _____. "Further Notes on Slavery in Canada," Journal of Negro History, 9, 1 (1924), pp. 26-33.

1672. _____. "An International Complication between Illinois and Canada Arising out of Slavery," Illinois State Historical Society Journal, 25, 1 (1932), pp. 123-26.

1673. _____. "Notes on Slavery in Canada," Journal of Negro History, 4, 4 (1919), pp. 396-411.

1674. _____. "Notes on the Slave in Nouvelle-France," Journal of Negro History, 8, 3 (1923), pp. 316-30.

1675. _____. "The Slave in Canada," Journal of Negro History, 5, 3 (1920), pp. 261-377. Reprinted as The Slave in Canada (Washington, D.C.: Association for the Study of Negro Life and History, 1920).

1676. _____. "The Slave in Upper Canada," Journal of Negro History, 4, 4 (1919), pp. 372-95.

1677. _____. "The Slave in Upper Canada," Canadian Magazine, 54 (1920), pp. 377-81.

1678. _____. "The Slave in Upper Canada," Journal of the American Institute of Criminal Law and Criminology, 14 (1923), pp. 249-78.

1679. Scott, Nolvert P., Jr. "The Black Peoples of Canada," in Donald G. Baker, ed., Politics of Race: Comparative Studies (Farnborough, England: Saxon, 1975), pp. 143-62.

1680. Silverman, Jason H. "The American Fugitive Slave in Canada: Myths and Realities," Southern Studies, 19, 3 (1980), pp. 215-27.

1681. _____. "Unwelcome Guests: American Fugitive Slaves in Canada, 1830-1860" (PhD diss., University of Kentucky, 1981).

1682. Trudel, Marcel. L'esclavage au Canada français: histoire et conditions de l'esclavage. Québec: Presses Universitaires Laval, 1960.

1683. Winks, Robin W. The Blacks in Canada: A History. New Haven: Yale University Press, 1971.

1684. _____. "The Canadian Negro: A Historical Assessment," Journal of Negro History, 53, 4 (1968), pp. 283-300; 54, 1 (1969), pp. 1-18.

III. Spanish Mainland

1. General and comparative

1685. Acosta Saignes, Miguel. "Introducción al estudio de los repositorios documentales sobre los africanos y sus descendientes en América," América indígena, 29, 3 (1969), pp. 727-86.

1686. Aimes, Hubert H. S. "Coartación: A Spanish Institution for the Advancement of Slaves into Freedmen," Yale Review, 17, 4 (1909), pp. 412-31.

1687. Alberro, Solange B. de. "Juan de Morga and Gertrudis de Escobar: Rebellious Slaves," in David G. Sweet and Gary B. Nash, eds., Struggle and Survival in Colonial America (Berkeley and Los Angeles: University of California Press, 1981), pp. 165-88.

1688. * _____. "Negroes y mulatos en los documentos inquisitoriales: rechazo e integración," in Frost, et al., Trabajo y trabajadores, pp. 132-61.

1689. Alcalá y Henke, Agustín. La esclavitud de los negros en la América española. Madrid: J. Pueyo, 1919.

1690. Arenal, Celestino del. "La teoría de la servidumbre natural en el pensamiento español de los siglos XVI y XVII," Historiografia e bibliografia americanistas, 19-20 (1975-76), pp. 67-126.

1691. Armas Medina, Fernando de. "El santo de los esclavos," Estudios americanos, 9 (nos. 40-41)(1955), pp. 55-61.

1692. Bastide, Roger. "The Present Status of Afro-American Research in Latin America," Daedalus, 103, 2 (1974), pp. 111-24.

1693. Bowser, Frederick P. "The African in Colonial Spanish America: Reflections on Research Achievements and Priorities," Latin American Research Review, 7, 1 (1972), pp. 77-94.

1694. _____. "Africans in Colonial Spanish American Colonial Society," in Leslie Bethell, ed., The Cambridge History of Latin America (Cambridge: Cambridge University Press, 1984), vol. 2, pp. 357-79.

1695. _____. "Colonial Spanish America," in Cohen and Greene, eds., Neither Slave nor Free, pp. 19-58.

1696. _____. "The Free Person of Color in Mexico City and Lima: Manumission and Opportunity, 1580-1650," in Engerman and Genovese, eds., Race and Slavery, pp. 331-68.

1697. Brady, Robert L. "The Role of Las Casas in the Emergence of Negro Slavery in the New World," Revista de historia de América, 61-62 (1966), pp. 43-55.

1698. Browning, James. Negro Companions of the Spanish Explorers in the New World. Cambridge, Mass., 1938. (Harvard University Studies in History, no. 11)

1699. Carrancá y Trujillo, Raúl. "El estatuto jurídico de los esclavos en las postrimerías de la colonización española," Revista de historia de América, 3 (1938), pp. 20-59.

1700. Carrera Damas, Germán. "La supuesta empresa antiesclavista del Conde de Tovar," Anuario del Instituto de antropología e historia (Caracas), 2 (1965), pp. 67-84.

1701. Chandler, David L. "Slave Over Master in Colonial Colombia and Ecuador," Americas, 38, 3 (1982), pp. 315-26.

1702. Clementi, Hebe. La abolición de la esclavitud en America Latina. Buenos Aires: Editorial La Pléyade, 1974.

1703. Cobb, M. K. "Africans in Latin America," Black World, 21, 10 (1972), pp. 4-19.

1704. Comas, Juan. "Fray Bartoleme, la esclavitud y el racismo," Historiografia y bibliografia americanistas, 19-20 (1975-76), pp. 1-10.

1705. Cortés Alonso, Vicenta. "Los esclavos domésticos en América," Anuario de estudios americanos, 24 (1967), pp. 955-83.

1706. Dolinger, J. "Slavery in South America," Sepia, 18 (1969), pp. 34-37.

1707. Duncan, Kenneth, and Ian Rutledge, eds. Land and Labour in Latin America: Essays on the Development of Agrarian Capitalism in the Nineteenth and Twentieth Centuries. Cambridge: Cambridge University Press, 1977.

1708. Gräbener, Jürgen, ed. Klassengesellschaft und Rassismus: Zur Marginalisierung der Afroamerikaner in Lateinamerika. Dusseldorf: Bertlesmann Universitätsverlag, 1971. (Interdiziplinäre Studien, Bd. 4)

1709. Granda Gutierrez, Germán de. "Cimarronismo, palenques y hablas 'criollas' en Hispano-America," Thesaurus (Bogotá), 25, 3 (1970), pp. 448-69.

1710. _____. "Papiamento en Hispanoamérica (siglos XVII-XIX)," Thesaurus (Bogotá), 28, 1 (1973), pp. 1-13.

1711. Guillot, Carlos Federico. Negros rebeldes y negros cimarrones. perfil afroamericano en la historia del Nuevo Mundo durante el siglo XVI. Buenos Aires. "El Ateneo", 1961.

1712. Hall, Gwendolyn Midlo. "The Myth of Benevolent Spanish Slave Law," Negro Digest, 19, 4 (1970), pp. 31-38.

1713. Harth-Terré, Emilio. "Indios del común proprietarios de esclavos. un estamento de la sociedad virreinal no historiado," in Jornadas americanistas (Simposio conmemorativo del V centenario del padre Las Casas. "Estudios sobre politica indigenista española en America")(Valladolid, 1974)(Valladolid, 1977), vol. 3, pp. 183-200. (Serie Americanista, no. 7)

1714. Kamen, Henry. "El negro en Hispanoamérica (1500-1700)," Anuario de estudios americanos, 28 (1971), pp. 121-37.

1715. King, James F. "The Case of José Ponciano de Ayarza. A Document on Gracias al Sacar," Hispanic American Historical Review, 33, 4 (1951), pp. 640-47.

1716. _____. "Descriptive Data on Negro Slaves in Spanish Importation Records and Bills of Sale," Journal of Negro History, 28, 2 (1943), pp. 204-30.

1717. _____. "Negro History in Continental Spanish America," Journal of Negro History, 29, 1 (1944), pp. 7-23.

1718. _____. "The Negro in Continental Spanish-America. A Select Bibliography," Hispanic American Historical Review, 24, 3 (1944), pp. 547-59.

1719. Konetzke, Richard. "La esclavitud de los indios como elemento en la estructuración social de Hispanoamérica," Estudios de historia social de España, 1 (1949), pp. 441-79.

1720. _____. "Die Sklavenfamilie im kolonialen Hispanoamerika," Bulletin de l'Institut historique belge de Rome, 44 (1974), pp. 321-34. Republished in Miscellanea offerts à Charles Verlinden (Ghent, 1975), pp. 321-34.

1721. Lafaye, Jacques. "L'église et l'esclavage des Indiens de 1537 à 1708," Bulletin de la Faculté des Lettres de Strasbourg, 43, 7 (1965), pp. 691-703. (Travaux de l'Institut d'études latino-américaines, no. 5)

1722. Llavador Mira, José. "Modificación y límites de la esclavitud," in Atti del XL Congresso Internazionale degli Americanisti (Rome-Genoa, 1972)(Genoa: Tilgher, 1975), vol. 3, pp. 445-50.

1723. McCaa, Robert. "Modeling Social Interaction: Marital Miscegenation in Colonial Spanish America," Historical Methods, 15, 2 (1982), pp. 45-66.

1724. Mellafe, Rolando. Breve historia de la esclavitud en America latina. Mexico, 1974.

1725. _____. La esclavitud en Hispanoamérica. Buenos Aires: Editorial Universitaria de Buenos Aires, 1964. Translated (J. W. S. Judge) as Negro Slavery in Latin America (Berkeley: University of California Press, 1975).

1726. Mörner, Magnus. "Los esfuerzos realizados por la Corona para separar negros e indios en Hispanoamérica durante el siglo XVI," in Homenaje: estudios de filología e historia literaria lusohispanas e iberoamericanas publicados para celebrar el tercer lustro del Instituto de estudios hispánicos, portugueses e iberoamericanos de la Universidad Estatal de Utrecht (The Hague: Van Goor Zonen, 1966), pp. 331-44.

1727. _____. "The History of Race Relations in Latin America: Some Comments on the State of Research," Latin American Research Review, 1, 3 (1966), pp. 17-44.

1728. _____. "Investigaciones recientes sobre la esclavitud negra y la abolición en América Latina," Revista de historia (Heredia), 2 (no.3)(1976), pp. 9-42. Translated as "Recent Research on Negro Slavery and Abolition in Latin America," Latin American Research Review, 13, 2 (1978), pp. 265-89.

1729. _____. "Los jesuitas y la esclavitud de los negros: algunas sugestiones para la investigación histórica," Revista chilena de historia y geografía, 135 (1967), pp. 92-109.

1730. _____. Race Mixture in the History of Latin America. Boston: Little, Brown, 1967.

1731. _____. "Slavery and Race in the Evolution of Latin American Societies: Some Recent Contributions to the Debate," Journal of Latin American Studies, 8, 1 (1976), pp. 127-35.

1732. _____. "The Theory and Practice of Racial Segregation in Colonial Spanish America," Proceedings of the 32nd International Congress of Americanists (Copenhagen, 1956), pp. 708-14.

1733. Nodal, Roberto. "Estebanillo: pionero negro en la conquista de América," Revista de história de América, 89 (1980), pp. 49-55.

1734. Ots y Capdequi, J. M. "Sobre la esclavitud de indios y negros en la América española en el período colonial," Revista javeriana (Bogotá), 18 (no. 86)(1942), pp. 22-25.

1735. Pacheco, Francisco. Facetas del esclavo africano en América latina. Havana: Academia de Ciencias de Cuba, Instituto de historia, 1970.

1736. Pattee, Richard. "The Efforts Made in Latin America to Document the History of the Negro," Journal of Negro History, 24, 1 (1939), pp. 57-64.

1737. Picón-Salas, Mariano. Pedro Claver, el santo de los esclavos. Mexico: Fondo de Cultura Economica, 1950.

1738. Pollack-Eltz, Angelina. "Donde provêm os Negros da América do Sul," Afro-Asia (Revista do Centro de estudos afro-orientais da Bahia), 10-11 (1970), pp. 99-107.

1739. Porras Troconis, Gabriel. Vida de San Pedro Claver, esclavo de los esclavos. Bogotá: Santafé, 1954.

1740. *Quiroz, Juan B. "El continido laboral en los códigos negro americanos," Revista mexicana de sociología, 5, 4 (1943), pp. 473-510.

1741. Quintero, Rodolfo. "La cultura de conquista engendra la esclavitud," Anuario del Instituto de antropología e historia (Caracas), 1 (1964), pp. 99-110.

1742. Rippy, J. Fred. "The Negro and the Spanish Pioneer in the New World," Journal of Negro History, 6, 2 (1921), pp. 183-99.

1743. Rodriguez, Frederick Marshall. "Cimarron Revolts and Pacification in New Spain, the Isthmus of Panama and Colonial Colombia, 1503-1800" (PhD diss., Loyola University of Chicago, 1979).

1744. Romero, Fernando. "El negro en tierra firme durante el siglo XVI," Actas y memorias del XXVII Congreso Internacional de Americanistas (Sesión de Lima)(1939), vol. 2, pp. 441-61. Reprinted in Boletín de la Academia Panameña de la Historia, segunda época, 1 (1943), pp. 3-34.

1745. _____. "The Slave Trade and the Negro in South America," Hispanic American Historical Review, 24, 3 (1944), pp. 368-86. *Translated as "La trata y el negro en Sud América," Revista peruana de cultura, 3 (1945), pp.

1746. Rout, Leslie B. The African Experience in Spanish America: 1502 to the Present Day. New York: Cambridge University Press, 1976.

1747. Saco, José. Historia de la esclavitud de la raza africana en el nuevo mundo y en especial en los países américo-hispanos. 4 vols. Havana. Cultural, 1938. (Vols. 4 and 5 of Historia de la esclavitud desde los tiempos más remotas hasta nuestros dias (Barcelona. Imprenta de J. Jepús, 1879).) With prologue by Fernando Ortiz (Havana. Cultural, 1938)

1748. _____. Historia de la esclavitud de los indios en el nuevo mundo, seguida de la historia de los repartimientos y encomiendas. Havana. Cultural, 1932. Introduction by Fernando Ortiz.

1749. Sales de Bohigas, Nuria. "Esclavos y reclutas en Sudamérica," Revista de historia de América, 70 (1970), pp. 279-337.

1750. _____. Sobre esclavos, reclutas, y mercaderes de quintas. Barcelona. Editorial Ariel, 1974.

1751. Sampaio Garcia, Rozendo. "Contribuição ao estudo do approvisionamento de escravos negros na América Espanhola (1580-1640)," Anais do Museu Paulista, 16 (1962), pp. 1-195.

1752. Sweet, David G. "Black Robes and 'Black Destiny'. Jesuit Views of African Slavery in 17th-Century Latin America," Revista de historia de América, 86 (1978), pp. 87-133.

1753. Toplin, Robert B., ed. Slavery and Race Relations in Latin America. Westport, Conn.. Greenwood Press, 1974.

1754. Torre Revello, José. "Origen y aplicación del Código Negrero en la América Española (1788-1794)," Boletín del Instituto de investigaciones históricas (Buenos Aires), 15 (año 11)(no. 53)(1932), pp. 42-50.

1755. Vigil, Ralph H. "Negro Slaves and Rebels in the Spanish Possessions, 1503-1558," Historian, 33, 4 (1971), pp. 637-55.

1756. Vila Vilar, Enriqueta. "La esclavitud americana en la política española del siglo XIX," Anuario de estudios americanos, 34 (1977), pp. 563-88.

1757. Wright, Richard. "Negro Companions of the Spanish Explorers," American Anthropologist, 4, 2 (1902), pp. 217-28.

1758. Zavala, Silvio. "Relaciones históricas entre indios y negros en Ibero-América," Revista de Indias, 28 (1946), pp. 53-65.

1759. Zelinsky, Wilbur. "The Historical Geography of the Negro Population of Latin America," Journal of Negro History, 34, 2 (1949), pp. 153-221.

2. Mexico

1760. Acosta Saignes, Miguel. "La etnohistoria y el estudio del negro en Mexico," in Sol Tax, ed., Acculturation in the Americas (Chicago, 1952), part 2, pp. 161-68. (29th International Congress of Americanists, 1949)

1761. _____. "Vida de negros e indios en las minas de Cocorote, durante el siglo XVII," in Estudios antropológicos publicados en homenaje al Dr. Manuel Gamio (Mexico. Dirección General de Publicaciones, 1956), pp. 555-72.

1762. Aguirre Beltrán, Gonzalo. "Comercio de esclavos en México por 1542," Afroamérica, 1, 1-2 (1945), pp. 25-40.

1763. _____. Cujila. esbozo etnográfico de un pueblo negro. Mexico. Fondo de Cultura Económica, 1958.

1764. _____. La población negra de México, 1519-1810. estudo etnohistórico. Mexico. Ediciones Fuente Cultura, 1946. 2nd edition, enlarged and corrected. La población negra de México. estudio etnohistórico (México. Fondo de Cultura Económica, 1972)

1765. _____. "Races in 17th Century Mexico," Phylon, 6, 3 (1945), pp. 212-18.

1766. _____. "The Slave Trade in Mexico," Hispanic American Historical Review, 24, 3 (1944), pp. 412-31.

1767. _____. "El trabajo del Indio comparado con el del negro en Nueva España," México agrario, 4, 3 (1942), pp. 203-07.

1768. _____. "The Tribal Origins of Slaves in Mexico," Journal of Negro History, 31, 3 (1946), pp. 269-352.

1769. Alberro, Solange B. de. "Noirs et mulâtres dans la société coloniale mexicaine, d'après les archives de l'inquisition (XVIe-XVIIe siècles)," Cahiers des Amériques latines, no. 17 (1978), pp. 57-87.

1770. Barker, Nancy. "The 'Factor of Race' in the French Experience in Mexico, 1821-1861," Hispanic American Historical Review, 59, 1 (1979), pp. 64-80.

1771. Berthe, Jean-Pierre. "Aspects de l'esclavage des Indiens en Nouvelle-Espagne pendant la première moitié du XVIe siècle," Journal de la Société des américanistes, 54, 2 (1965), pp. 189-209.

1772. Blanchard, R. "Les tableaux et métissage au Mexique," Journal de la Société des Américanistes, 5 (1908), pp. 59-66, 7 (1910), pp. 37-60.

1773. Borah, Woodrow. "Race and Class in Mexico," Pacific Historical Review, 23, 4 (1954), pp. 331-42.

1774. Boyd-Bowman, Peter. "Negro Slaves in Early Colonial Mexico," Americas, 26, 2 (1969), pp. 134-51.

1775. Brady, Robert L. "The Domestic Slave Trade in Sixteenth-Century Mexico," Americas, 24, 3 (1968), pp. 281-89.

1776. _____. "The Emergence of a Negro Class in Mexico, 1542-1640" (PhD diss., University of Iowa, 1965).

1777. Cantú Corro, José. La esclavitud en el mundo y en Mejico. Mexico. Escuela Tipográfica Salesiana, 1926.

1778. Carroll, Patrick J. "Mandinga. The Evolution of a Mexican Runaway Slave Community, 1735-1827," Comparative Studies in Society and History, 19, 4 (1977), pp. 488-505.

1779. Clemence, Stella Risley. "Deed of Emancipation of a Negro Woman Slave, Dated Mexico, September 14, 1585," Hispanic American Historical Review, 10, 1 (1930), pp. 51-57.

1780. Davidson, David M. "Negro Slave Control and Resistance in Colonial Mexico, 1519-1650," Hispanic American Historical Review, 46, 3 (1966), pp. 235-53.

1781. _____. "Negroes in Colonial Mexico, 1519-1650" (MA thesis, University of Wisconsin, 1965).

1782. Duke, Cathy. "The Family in Eighteenth-Century Plantation Society in Mexico," in Rubin and Tuden, eds., Comparative Perspectives, pp. 226-41.

1783. Heath, Jim F., and Frederick M. Nunn. "Negroes and Discrimination in Colonial New Mexico. Don Pedro Bautista Pino's Startling Statements of 1812 in Perspective," Phylon, 31, 4 (1970), pp. 372-78.

1784. Katz, Friedrich. "Plantagenwirtschaft und Sklaverei. Die Sisalbau auf der Halbinsel Yucatan bis 1910," Zeitschrift für Geschichtswissenschaft, 7, 5 (1959), pp. 1002-27.

1785. Logan, Rayford W. "Estevanico, Negro Discoverer of the Southwest. A Critical Reexamination," Phylon, 1, 4 (1940), pp. 305-14.

1786. Love, Edgar F. "Legal Restrictions on Afro-Indian Relations in Colonial Mexico," Journal of Negro History, 55, 2 (1970), pp. 131-39.

1787. _____. "Marriage Patterns of Persons of African Descent in a Colonial Mexico City Parish," Hispanic American Historical Review, 51, 1 (1971), pp. 79-91.

1788. _____. "Negro Resistance to Spanish Rule in Colonial Mexico," Journal of Negro History, 52, 2 (1967), pp. 89-103.

Mexico

1789. Martin, Norman F. "Antecedentes y prática de la esclavitud negra en la Nueva España del siglo XVI," in Bernardo García Martínez, et al., eds., Historia y sociedad en el mundo de habla española: homenaje a José Miranda (Mexico: El Colegio de México, 1970), pp. 49-68.

1790. Martínez Montiel, Luz María. "Integration Patterns and the Assimilation Process of Negro Slaves in Mexico," in Rubin and Tuden, eds., Comparative Perspectives, pp. 446-54.

1791. Mayer, Vincent Villanueva, Jr. "The Black Slave on New Spain's Northern Frontier: San José de Parral, 1632-1676" (PhD diss., University of Utah, 1975).

1792. Palmer, Colin A. "Negro Slavery in Mexico, 1570-1650" (PhD diss., University of Wisconsin, Madison, 1970).

1793. _____. "Religion and Magic in Mexican Slave Society, 1570-1650," in Engerman and Genovese, eds., Race and Slavery, pp. 311-28.

1794. _____. Slaves of the White God: Blacks in Mexico, 1570-1650. Cambridge, Mass.: Harvard University Press, 1976.

1795. Pi-Sunyer, Oriol. "Historical Background to the Negro in Mexico," Journal of Negro History, 42, 4 (1957), pp. 237-46.

1796. *Querol y Roso, Luis. "Negros y mulatos de Nueva España: historia de su alzamiento de 1612," Anales de la Universidad de Valencia, año 12, cuaderno 90 (1935), pp. 121-62.

1797. Radiles, Ignacio Marques. "The Slave Trade with America, Negroes in Mexico, Part I," Freedomways, 1, 3 (1961), pp. 296-307.

1798. _____. "The Slave Trade with America, Negroes in Mexico, Part II," Freedomways, 2, 1 (1962), pp. 39-52.

1799. Riley, G. Michael. "Labor in Cortesian Enterprise: The Cuernavaca Area, 1522-1549," Americas, 28, 3 (1972), pp. 271-87.

1800. Rodrigues de Mello, Astrogildo. O trabalho forçado de indígenas nas lavouras de Nova-Espanha. São Paulo: Universidade de São Paulo, Faculdade de filosofia, ciências e letras, 1946. (Boletim no. 69, História de civilisação americana)

1801. Roncal, Joaquím. "The Negro Race in Mexico," Hispanic American Historical Review, 24, 3 (1944), pp. 530-40.

1802. Ruz Menéndez, Rodolfo. "La emancipación de los esclavos en Yucatán," Revista de la Universidad de Yucatán (Mérida), 12 (no. 67)(1970), pp. 19-39.

1803. _____. La emancipación de los esclavos en Yucatán. Mérida: Ediciones de la Universidad de Yucatán, 1970.

1804. Saraiba Viejo, Maria Justidna. "La esclavitud indígena en la gobernación de Pánuco," in Atti del XL Congresso Internazionale degli Americanisti (Roma-Genova, 1972)(Genoa: Tilgher, 1975), vol. 3, pp. 423-28.

1805. Simpson, Leslie B. "The Emancipation of the Indian Slaves and the Resettlement of the Freedmen, 1548-1553," in Studies in the Administration of the Indians of New Spain, IV (Berkeley: University of California Press, 1940). (Ibero-Americana: 16)

1806. Taylor, William B. "The Foundation of Nuestra Señora de Guadalupe de los Morenos de Amapa," Americas, 26, 4 (1970), pp. 439-46.

1807. *Tutino, John. "Slavery and Assimilation in a Peasant Society: Afro-Mexico" (forthcoming).

1808. Tyler, Ronnie C. "Fugitive Slaves in Mexico," Journal of Negro History, 57, 1 (1972), pp. 1-12.

1809. Winfield Capitaine, Fernando. "Comercio de esclavos en Xalapa durante el siglo XVIII," in Actas del XLI Congreso internacional de americanistas (Mexico, 2-7 September 1974) (Mexico City, 1976), vol. 2, pp. 489-95.

1810. Zavala, Silvio. Los esclavos indios de Nueva España. Mexico, 1967.

1811. _____. "Nuño de Guzmán y la esclavitud de los indios," Historia mexicana, 1, 3 (no. 3)(1952), pp. 411-28.

3. Central America

1812. Aguilar Bulgarelli, Oscar R. "La esclavitud en Costa Rica durante el período colonial (hipótesis de trabajo)," Estudios sociales centroamericanos (San José), 22 (1973), pp. 187-99.

1813. Barrantes Ferrero, Mario. Un caso de esclavitud en Costa Rica. San José: Instituto geográfico nacional, 1968.

1814. Cruz, Pedro Tobar. "La esclavitud del negro en Guatemala," Antropología e historia de Guatemala, 17, 1 (1965), pp. 3-14.

1815. Diez-Castillo, Luis A. Los cimarones y la esclavitud en Panamá. Panama: Editorial Litográfica, 1968.

1816. "La esclavitud en Centroamérica," special section in Revista del pensamiento centroamericano, 31 (no. 152)(1976), pp. 61-116. See Sherman, Huper Argüello, Riismandel, and Levitt.

1817. Fiehrer, Thomas. "Hacia una definición de la esclavitud en la Guatemala colonial," Revista del pensamiento centroamericano, 31, (no. 153)(1976), pp. 41-55.

1818. _____. "Slaves and Freedmen in Colonial Central America: Rediscovering a Forgotten Black Past," Journal of Negro History, 64, 1 (1979), pp. 39-47.

1819. Fortune, Armando. "Estudio sobre la insurreción de los negros esclavos: los cimarrones de Panamá," Lotería (Panamá), 1, 5 (1956), pp. 61-68; 1, 6 (1956), pp. 46-51; 1, 9 (1956), pp. 44-67.

1820. Guardia, Roberto de la. "El fenómeno de la esclavitud en la civilización panameña," Hombre y cultura, 2, 3 (1972), pp. 27-73.

1821. *Gudmundson, Lowell. "Mechanisms of Social Mobility for the Population of African Descent in Colonial Costa Rica" (Heredia: IDELA, Universidad Nacional, n.d. - mimeo). Translated as Lowell Gudmundson Kristjanson, "Mecanismos de movilidad social para la población de procedencia africana en Costa Rica colonial: manumisión y mestizaje," in idem, Estratificación socio-racial y económica de Costa Rica: 1700-1850 (San José: Editorial Universidad Estatal a Distancia, 1978), pp. 19-78.

1822. Hüper Argüello, William. "Rasgos de la esclavitud en Nicaragua," Revista del pensamiento centroamericano, 31 (no. 152)(1976), pp. 76-99.

1823. Kunst, J. "Notes on Negroes in Guatemala during the Seventeenth Century," Journal of Negro History, 1, 4 (1916), pp. 392-98.

1824. "La libertad de los esclavos," Boletín del Archivo General del Gobierno (Guatemala), 3, 2 (1938), pp. 277-95.

1825. Meléndez Chaverri, Carlos. "Los orígenes de los esclavos africanos en Costa Rica," in XXXVI Congresso Internacional de Americanistas: Actas y memorias (Seville, 1966)(Buenos Aires, 1968), vol. 4, pp. 387-91.

1826. _____, and Quince Duncan. El negro en Costa Rica: antología. San José: Editorial Costa Rica, 1972.

1827. Olien, Michael D. "Black and Part-Black Populations in Colonial Costa Rica: Ethnohistorical Resources and Problems," Ethnohistory, 27, 1 (1980), pp. 13-29.

1828. _____. "The Negro in Costa Rica: The Ethnohistory of an Ethnic Minority in a Complex Society" (PhD diss., University of Oregon, 1967).

1829. Radell, David R. "The Indian Slave Trade and Population of Nicaragua during the Sixteenth Century," in William Denevan, ed., The Native Population of the Americas in 1492 (Madison: University of Wisconsin Press, 1976), pp. 67-76.

1830. Riismandel, John N., and James H. Levitt. "Algunos aspectos cuantitativos de la esclavitud en Costa Rica en tiempos de la colonia," Revista del pensamiento centroamericano, 31 (no. 152)(1976), pp. 101-16.

1831. _____. "Costa Rican Slavery: A
Computerized Approach" (forthcoming).

1832. Robert Luján, Enrique. "La abolición de la esclavitud en Costa
Rica," Anales de la Academia de geografía y historia de Costa Rica
(1962-63), pp. 68-74.

1833. Romero, Fernando. "El 'Rey Bayano' y los negros panameños en los
mediados del siglo XVI," Hombre y cultura, 3, 1 (1975), p. 39.

1834. Sherman, William L. Forced Native Labor in Sixteenth-Century
Central America. Lincoln: University of Nebraska Press, 1979.

1835. _____. "Indian Slavery and the Cerrato Reforms,"
Hispanic American Historical Review, 51, 1 (1971), pp. 25-50.
Translated as "La esclavitud indígena y las reformas de Cerrato,"
Revista del pensamiento centroamericano, 31 (no. 152)(1976), pp.
62-75.

1836. *_____. "Indian Slavery in Guatemala 1524-1550" (MA
thesis, University of New Mexico, 1966).

1837. Zavala, Silvio. "Los esclavos indios en Guatemala," Historia
mexicana, 19, 4 (no. 76)(1970), pp. 459-65.

4. New Granada and Gran Colombia

1838. Bierck, Harold C., Jr. "The Struggle for Abolition in Gran
Colombia," Hispanic American Historical Review, 33, 3 (1953), pp.
365-86.

1839. Chandler, David L. "Health and Slavery: A Study of Health
Conditions among Negro Slaves in the Viceroyalty of New Granada
and its Associated Slave Trade, 1600-1810" (PhD diss., Tulane
University, 1972).

1840. _____. Health and Slavery in Colonial Colombia. New
York: Arno, 1981.

1841. Gomez, Tomaz. "Un aspect de l'exploitation du travail indigène en
Nouvelle Grenade au XVIe siècle: le portage," Journal de la
Société des Américanistes, 64 (1977), pp. 89-106.

1842. Granda Gutierrez, Germán de. "Datos antroponímicos sobre negros
esclavos musulmanos en Nueva Granada," Thesaurus, 27, 1 (1972),
pp. 89-103.

1843. _____. "Testimonios documentales sobre la
preservación del sistema antroponímico TWI entre los esclavos
negros de la Nueva Granada," Revista española de lingüística, 1, 2
(1971), pp. 265-74.

1844. Hudson, Randall O. "The Status of the Negro in Northern South America, 1820-1860," Journal of Negro History, 49, 4 (1964), pp. 225-39.

1845. Jaramillo Uribe, Jaime. "La controversia jurídica y filosófica librada en la Nueva Granada en torno a la liberación de los esclavos y la importancia económica-social de la esclavitud en el siglo XIX," Anuario colombiano de historia social y de la cultura, 4 (1969), pp. 63-86.

1846. King, James F. "Negro Slavery in New Granada," in Adele Ogden and Engel Sluiter, eds., Greater America: Essays in Honor of H. E. Bolton (Berkeley: University of California Press, 1945), pp. 295-318.

1847. _____. "Negro Slavery in the Viceroyalty of New Granada" (PhD diss., University of California, Berkeley, 1940).

1848. Kitchens, John W., and J. León Helguera. "Los vecinos de Popayán y la esclavitud en la Nueva Granada," Boletín de historia y antigüedades (Bogotá), 63, 2 (no. 713)(1976), pp. 219-39.

1849. Kuethe, Allan J. "The Status of the Free Pardo in the Disciplined Militia of New Granada," Journal of Negro History, 56, 2 (1971), pp. 105-17.

1850. León Helguera, J., and Alberto Lee López, eds. "La exportación de esclavos en la Nueva Granada," Archivos (Academia Colombiana de Historia, Bogotá), 1, 3 (1967), pp. 447-59.

1851. Meiklejohn, Norman A. "The Implementation of Slave Legislation in Eighteenth-Century New Granada," in Toplin, ed., Slavery and Race Relations in Latin America, pp. 176-203.

1852. _____. "The Observance of Negro Slave Legislation in Colonial Nueva Granada" (PhD diss., Columbia University, 1968).

1853. Noyes, Antonio José Galvis. "La abolición de la esclavitud en la Nueva Granada, 1820-1832," Boletín de historia y antigüedades (Bogotá), 67, 3 (no. 730)(1980), pp. 469-572.

5. Colombia

1854. *Arboleda, José Rafael. "The Ethnohistory of the Colombian Negroes" (MA thesis, Northwestern University, 1950).

1855. Borrego Plá, Maria del Carmen. "Palenques de negros cimarrones en Cartagena de Indias," in Atti del XL Congresso Internazionale degli Americanisti (Roma-Genova, 1972)(Genoa: Tilgher, 1975), vol. 3, pp. 429-32.

1856. _____. Palenques de negros en Cartagena de Indias a fines del siglo XVII. Seville: Escuela de Estudios Hispano-Americanos de Sevilla, 1973.

1857. Castellanos, Jorge. La abolición de la esclavitud en Popayán, 1832-1852. Cali, Colombia: Departamento de Publicaciones, Universidad del Valle, 1980.

1858. Chandler, David L. "Family Bonds and Bondsmen: The Slave Family in Colonial Colombia," Latin American Research Review, 16, 2 (1981), pp. 107-31.

1859. Eguren, Juan A. "Sandoval frente a la raza esclavizada," Revista de la Academia colombiana de historia eclesiastica, 29-30 (1973), pp. 57-86.

1860. _____. "Sandoval frente a los esclavos negros (1607-1652)," Montalbán, 1 (1972), pp. 405-32.

1861. Escalante, Aquiles. El negro en Colombia. Bogotá: Universidad Nacional de Colombia, 1964.

1862. Fernándes Esquivel, Franco. "Procedencia de los esclavos negros, analizada através del complejo de distribución, desarrollado desde Cartagena," Revista de historia (Heredia), 2 (no. 3)(1976), pp. 43-80.

1863. García, Julio César. "El movimiento antiesclavista en Colombia," Boletín de historia y antigüedades (Bogotá), 41 (nos. 473-74)(1954), pp. 130-43.

1864. González, Margarita. "El proceso de manumisión en Colombia," Cuadernos colombianos (Bogotá), 2 (1974), pp. 147-240.

1865. Granda Gutierrez, Germán de. "Onomástica y procedencia africana de esclavos negros en las minas del sur de la gobernación de Popayán (siglo XVIII)," Revista española de antropologia americana, 6 (1971), pp. 381-442.

1866. Hernandez de Alba, Gregorio. Libertad de los esclavos en Colombia. Bogotá: Editorial ABD, 1950.

1867. Jaramillo Uribe, Jaime. "Esclavos y señores en la sociedad colombiana del siglo XVIII," Anuario colombiano de historia social y de la cultura, 1, 1 (1963), pp. 3-62.

1868. Meisel, Adolfo. "Rural Slavery and Racial Mixture in the Province of Cartagena" (Paper read to the Annual Meeting of the American Historical Association, Los Angeles, 1981).

1869. Meisel Roca, Adolfo. "Esclavitud, mestizaje y haciendas en la Provincia de Cartagena: 1533-1851," Desarrollo y sociedad, 4 (1980), pp. 229-77.

1870. Mina, Mateo. Esclavitud y libertad en el Valle del Rio Cauca. Bogotá: Fundación Rosca de Investigación y Acción Social, 1975.

1871. *Navarrete Pelaes, Maria Cristina. "Los negros en Colombia, 1600-1725" (Diss., Universidad Complutense de Madrid, 1971).

1872. *Palacios Preciado, Jorge. "Cartagena de Indias, gran factoría de mano de obra esclava" (Unpublished?, 1975).

1873. Posada, Eduardo. "La esclavitud en Colombia," Boletín de historia y antigüedades (Bogotá), 16 (no. 187)(1927), pp. 398-403; (no. 189), pp. 526-44; (no. 190), pp. 614-28.

1874. _____. La esclavitud en Colombia. Bogotá: Imprenta Nacional, 1933. Bound with Carlos Restrepo Canal, Leyes de manumisión.

1875. Restrepo Canal, Carlos. "Documentos sobre esclavos," Boletín de historia y antigüedades (Bogotá), 24 (no. 274)(1937), pp. 486-92.

1876. _____. La libertad de los esclavos en Colombia; o leyes de manumisión. II. Bogotá: Imprenta nacional, 1938.

1877. Rojas Gómez, Roberto. "La esclavitud en Colombia," Boletín de historia y antigüedades (Bogotá), 14 (no. 158)(1922), pp. 83-108.

1878. Sharp, William F. "Forsaken but for Gold: An Economic Study of Slavery and Mining in the Colombian Chocó, 1680-1810" (PhD diss., University of North Carolina, 1970).

1879. _____. "Manumission, Libres, and Black Resistance: The Colombian Chocó, 1680-1810," in Toplin, ed., Slavery and Race Relations in Latin America, pp. 89-111.

1880. _____. "El negro en Colombia: manumisión y posición social," Razón y fábula (Bogotá), 8 (1968), pp. 91-107.

1881. *_____. "The Negro in Colombia's Choco 1528-1830" (MA thesis, University of North Carolina, 1966).

1882. _____. "The Profitability of Slavery in the Colombian Chocó, 1680-1810," Hispanic American Historical Review, 55, 3 (1975), pp. 468-95. Translated as "La rentabilidad de la esclavitud en el Chocó, 1680-1810," Anuario colombiano de historia social y de la cultura, 8 (1976), pp. 19-45.

1883. _____. Slavery on the Spanish Frontier: The Colombian Choco, 1680-1810. Norman, Okla.: University of Oklahoma Press, 1976.

1884. Taussig, Michael. "Black Religion and Resistance in Colombia: Three Centuries of Social Struggle in the Cauca Valley," Marxist Perspectives, 2, 2 (1979), pp. 84-116.

1885. _____. "The Evolution of Rural Wage Labour in the Cauca Valley of Colombia, 1700-1970," in Kenneth Duncan and Ian Rutledge, eds., Land and Labour in Latin America (New York: Cambridge University Press, 1977), pp. 397-434.

1886. Torres Giraldo, Ignacio. Los inconformes: historia de la rebeldía de las masas en Colombia. 3 vols. Bogotá, 1972.

1887. Zulueta, Eduardo. "Movimiento antiesclavista en Antioquia,"
Boletín de historia y antigüedades (Bogotá), 10 (no. 109)(1915),
pp. 32-37.

6. Venezuela

1888. Acosta Saignes, Miguel. "Gentilicios africanos en Venezuela,"
Archivos venezolanos de folklore, ano IV-V, tomo 3, no. 4
(1955-56), pp. 9-30.

1889. _____. "Los negros cimarrones de Venezuela," in
El movimiento emancipador de Hispanoamérica: Actas y ponencias
(Caracas: Academia nacional de la historia, 1961), vol. 3, pp.
351-98.

1890. _____. Vida de los esclavos negros en Venezuela.
Caracas: Hespérides, 1967.

1891. Arcaya, Pedro M. Insurrección de los negros de la Serranía de
Coro. Caracas: Instituto panamericano de geografia e historia,
1949.

1892. Arcila Farías, Eduardo. "La abolición de la esclavitud en
Venezuela," La Torre, 21, 81-82 (1973), pp. 257-66.

1893. Brito Figueroa, Federico. "El comercio de esclavos negros y la
mano de obra esclava en la economia colonial venezolana," Economia
y ciencias sociales (Caracas), 6, 3 (1964), pp. 5-46.

1894. _____. Las insurrecciones de los esclavos
negros en la sociedad colonial venezolana. Caracas: Editorial
Cantaclare, 1961.

1895. _____. El problema tierra y esclavos en la
historia de Venezuela. Caracas: Ediciones Teoría y Praxis, 1973.

1896. Castillo, Aureo Yépez. "Los esclavos negros en Venezuela en la
segunda década del siglo XIX: fundamentos legales y actuación,"
Boletín de la Academia nacional de la historia (Caracas), 63, 3
(no. 249)(1980), pp. 113-41.

1897. Ferry, Robert J. "Encomienda, African Slavery, and Agriculture in
Seventeenth Century Caracas," Hispanic American Historical Review,
61, 4 (1981), pp. 609-35.

1898. Friede, Juan. "Orígenes de la esclavitud indígena en Venezuela,"
Boletín de la Academia nacional de la historia (Caracas), 44, 173
(1961), pp. 61-75.

1899. Herrero, Rafael. The Colonial Slave Plantation as a Form of
Hacienda: A Preliminary Outline of the Case of Venezuela. Glasgow:
Institute of Latin American Studies, University of Glasgow, 1978.
(Occasional Papers, no. 25)

1900. Liscano, Juan. "Lugar de origen de los tambords redondos barloventeños de Venezuela," Folklore americano (Lima), 17/18 (no. 16)(1969-70), pp. 134-39.

1901. Lombardi, John V. "The Abolition of Slavery in Venezuela: A Nonevent," in Toplin, ed., Slavery and Race Relations in Latin America, pp. 228-52.

1902. _____. "The Decline and Abolition of Negro Slavery in Venezuela (1820-1854)" (PhD diss., Columbia University, 1968).

1903. _____. The Decline and Abolition of Negro Slavery in Venezuela, 1820-1854. Westport, Conn.: Greenwood Publishing Co., 1971. Translated as Decadencia y abolición de la esclavitud en Venezuela (Caracas: Ediciones de la Biblioteca Universidad Central de Venezuela, 1974)

1904. _____. "Los esclavos en la legislación republicana de Venezuela," Fundación John Boulton: Boletín histórico, 5 (no. 13)(1967), pp. 43-67.

1905. _____. "Manumission, manumisos, and aprendizaje in Republican Venezuela," Hispanic American Historical Review, 49, 4 (1969), pp. 656-78.

1906. Muñoz, Pedro José. "Breves anotaciones acerca de la esclavitud y de la liberación de los esclavos en Venezuela," Boletín de la Academia nacional de la historia (Caracas), 57, 2 (no. 225)(1974), pp. 41-56.

1907. Nuñez Ponte, José Manuel. Estudio histórico acerca de la esclavitud y de su abolición en Venezuela. Caracas: Tip. Emp. El Cojo, 1911.

1908. Pollack-Eltz, Angelina. "Slave Revolts in Venezuela," in Rubin and Tuden, eds., Comparative Perspectives, pp. 439-45.

1909. Troconis de Veracoechea, Ermila. "Esclavos blancos en la Venezuela colonial," Boletín del Archivo General de la Nación (Venezuela), 62 (no. 222)(1972), pp. 64-67.

1910. _____. "Notas sobre los esclavos y la guerra de independencia de Venezuela," Cuadernos afro-americanos, 1, 1 (1975), pp. 159-70.

1911. _____. "Tres cofradías de negros en la iglesia de 'San Mauricio' en Caracas," Montalbán, 5 (1976), pp. 339-76.

1912. _____, ed. Documentos para el estudio de los esclavos negros en Venezuela. Caracas: Academia Nacional de la Historia, 1969.

7. Ecuador

1913. Alcina Franch, José. "El problema de las poblaciones negroides de Esmeraldas, Ecuador," Anuario de estudios americanos, 31 (1974), pp. 33-46.

1914. Estupinián Tello, Julio. El negro en Esmeraldas: apuntes para su estudio. Quito, 1967.

1915. Phelan, John L. "The Road to Esmeraldas: The Failure of a Spanish Conquest in the Seventeenth Century," in Henry Bluhm, ed., Essays in History and Literature Presented by the Fellows of the Newberry Library to Stanley Pargellis (Chicago: The Newberry Library, 1965), pp. 91-107.

8. Peru

1916. Bowser, Frederick P. The African Slave in Colonial Peru, 1524-1650. Stanford: Stanford University Press, 1974.

1917. Cushner, Nicholas P. "Slave Mortality and Reproduction on Jesuit Haciendas in Colonial Peru," Hispanic American Historical Review, 55, 2 (1975), pp. 177-99.

1918. Harth-Terré, Emilio. "El esclavo negro en la sociedad indoperuana," Journal of Inter-American Studies, 3, 3 (1961), pp. 297-340.

1919. _____. Informe sobre el descubrimiento de documentos que revelan la trata y comercio de esclavos negros por los indios del común durante el gobierno virreinal en el Perú. Lima: Editorial Tierra y Arte, 1961. Translated by Jean Fitch Costa as Report on the Discovery of Documents which Reveal the Negro Slave Trade among the Lower-Class Indians during the Viceregal Government in Peru.

1920. _____. Negros e indios: un estamento social ignorado de Perú colonial. Lima: Editorial Juan Mejia Baca, 1973.

1921. Helmer, Marie. "Note sur les esclaves indiens au Pérou (XVIe siècle)," Bulletin de la Faculté des Lettres de Strasbourg, 43, 7 (1965), pp. 683-90. (Travaux de l'Institut d'études latino-américaines, no. 5)

1922. Kapsoli E., Wilfredo. Sublevaciones de esclavos en el Perú, s. XVIII. Lima: Universidad Ricardo Palma, 1975.

1923. Millones, Luis. "Gente negra en el Perú: esclavos y conquistadores," América indígena, 31, 3 (1971), pp. 593-624.

1924. Peralta Rivera, E. G. "Informe preliminar al estudio de la tributación de negros libres mulatos y zambahigos en el siglo XVIII perunao," in Atti del XL Congresso Internazionale degli Americanisti (Roma-Genova, 1972)(Genoa: Tilgher, 1975), vol. 3, pp. 433-38.

9. Bolivia

1925. Crespo R., Alberto. Esclavos negros en Bolivia. La Paz: Academia Nacional de Ciencias de Bolivia, 1977.

1926. Portugal Ortiz, Max. "Anotaciones para el estudio de la venta de esclavos negros en la ciudad de La Paz," Illimani, 1 (1972), pp. 66-75.

1927. _____. La esclavitud negra en las épocas colonial y nacional de Bolivia. La Paz: Instituto boliviano de cultura, 1977.

1928. Wolff, Inge. "Negersklaverei und Negerhandel in Hochperu 1545-1640," Jahrbuch für Geschichte von Staat, Wirtschaft und Gesellschaft Lateinamerikas, 1 (1964), pp. 157-86.

10. Chile

1929. Feliú Cruz, Guillermo. La abolición de la esclavitud en Chile: estudio histórico y social. Santiago: Universidad de Chile, 1942.

1930. Jara, Alvaro. "Los asientos de trabajo y la provisión del mano de obra para los no-encomenderos en la ciudad de Santiago 1586-1600," Revista chilena de historia y geografía, 125 (1957), pp. 21-95.

1931. _____. "Importación de trabajadores indígenas en el siglo XVII," in Miscellanea Paulo Revet (Mexico: Universidad Autónoma, 1958), vol. 2, pp. 733-63. Republished in Revista chilena de historia y geografía, 124 (1958), pp. 177-212.

1932. Mellafe, Rolando. La introducción de la esclavitud negra en Chile: tráfico y rutas. Santiago: Universidad de Chile, 1959.

1933. Sater, William F. "The Black Experience in Chile," in Toplin, ed., Slavery and Race Relations in Latin America, pp. 13-50.

1934. Segall, Marcelo. "Esclavitud y tráfico culíes en Chile," Journal of Inter-American Studies, 10, 1 (1968), pp. 117-33.

1935. Vial Correa, Gonzalo. El africano en el reino de Chile: ensayo histórico-jurídico. Santiago: Universidad Católica de Chile, 1957.

11. Argentina

1936. Andrews, George Reid. The Afro-Argentines of Buenos Aires, 1800-1900. Madison: University of Wisconsin Press, 1980.

1937. Chace, Russell Edward, Jr. "The African Impact on Colonial Argentina" (PhD diss., University of California, Santa Barbara, 1969).

1938. Diggs, Irene. "The Negro in the Viceroyalty of the Rio de la Plata," Journal of Negro History, 36, 3 (1951), pp. 281-301.

1939. Flichman, Marta B. Goldberg de, and Laura Beatriz Jany. "Algunos problemas referentes a la situación del esclavo en el Río de la Plata," IV Congreso Internacional de Historia de América (Buenos Aires, 1966), vol. 6, pp. 61-75.

1940. Garcia, Emanuel Soares da Veiga. "Sôbre os serviços portuários de Buenos Aires na primeira metade do século XVIII," Anais do VI Simpósio nacional dos professores universitários de história (Goiâna, 1971)(São Paulo, 1973), vol. 1, pp. 373-84.

1941. Garzón Maceda, Ceferino, and José Walter Dorflinger. "Esclavos y mulatos en un dominio rural del siglo XVIII en Córdoba: contribución a la demografía histórica," Revista de la Universidad Nacional de Córdoba, 2nd ser., 2 (1961), pp. 627-40.

1942. Goldberg, Marta B. "La población negra y mulata de la ciudad de Buenos Aires, 1810-1840," Desarrollo económico, 16 (no. 61)(1976), pp. 75-99.

1943. González Arzac, Alberto Ricardo. La esclavitud en la Argentina. Buenos Aires: Editorial Polémica, 1974.

1944. Johnson, Lyman L. "La manumisión de esclavos en Buenos Aires durante el Virreinato," Desarrollo económico, 16 (no. 63)(1976), pp. 333-48.

1945. _____. "La manumisión en el Buenos Aires colonial: un análisis ampliado," Desarrollo económico, 17 (no. 68)(1978), pp. 637-46.

1946. _____. "Manumission in Colonial Buenos Aires, 1776-1810," Hispanic American Historical Review, 59, 2 (1979), pp. 258-79.

1947. Lopez, Nelly Beatriz. "La esclavitud en Córdoba, 1790-1853" (Thesis, Universidad Nacional de Córdoba, 1972).

1948. Masini Calderón, José Luís. "La esclavitud negra en la República Argentina Epoca independiente," Revista de la Junta de estudios historicos de Mendoza (Argentina), ser. 2, 1, 1 (1961), pp. 135-61.

1949. _____. La esclavitud negra en Mendoza: época independiente. Mendoza: D'Accurzio, 1962.

1950. Massini Ezcurra, José M. "Redhibitoria y esclavos en el Río de la Plata," Archivo Iberoamericano de historia de la medicina y antropología médica (Madrid), 13 (1961), pp. 213-26.

1951. *Rodríguez Molas, Ricardo. "El negro en el Río de la Plata,"
Polémica, 2 (1970), pp. 38-56.

1952. _____. "Algunos aspectos del negro en la
sociedad rioplatense del siglo XVIII," Anuario del Instituto de
investigaciones históricas (Rosario), 3 (1958), pp. 81-106.

1953. _____. "Esclavos indios y africanos en los
primeros momentos de la conquista y colonización del Río de la
Plata," Ibero-Amerikanisches Archiv, 7, 4 (1981), pp. 325-66.

1954. Torres, Felix A. "El comercio de esclavos en Córdoba, 1700-1731"
(Thesis, Universidad Nacional de Córdoba, 1972).

1955. Zavala, Silvio. "Esclavitud indígena en los comienzos de la
colonización del Rio de la Plata," Bulletin de l'Institut
historique belge de Rome, 44 (1974), pp. 651-62. Republished in
Miscellanea offerts à Charles Verlinden (Ghent, 1975), pp. 651-62.

1956. Zavalía Matienzo, Roberto. "La esclavitud en Tucumán después de la
asamblea de 1813," Investigaciones y ensayos (Buenos Aires), 14
(1973), pp. 295-323.

1957. Zuluaga, Rosa Mercedes. "La trata de negros en la región cuyana
durante el siglo XVII," Revista de la Junta de estudios históricos
de Mendoza, ser. 2, 6, 1 (1970), pp. 39-66.

12. Uruguay

1958. Carvalho-Neto, Paulo de. El negro uruguayo; hasta la abolición.
Quito: Editorial Universitaria, 1965.

1959. Isola, Ema. La esclavitud en el Uruguay desde sus comienzos hasta
su extinción, 1743-1852. Montevideo, 1975.

1960. Martinez Montero, Homero. "La esclavitud en el Uruguay:
contribución a su estudio historico-social," Revista nacional:
Literatura, arte, ciencia (Montevideo), 3, 32 (1940), pp. 261-73.

1961. O'Gorman, Edmundo, ed. "Un matrimonio de esclavos," Boletin del
Archivo General de la Nación (Uruguay), 6 (1935), pp. 541-56.

1962. Pereda Valdés, Ildefonso. El negro en la epopeya artiguista.
Montevideo: Barreiro y Ramos, 1964.

1963. _____. El negro en el Uruguay, pasado y
presente. Montevideo, 1965. Also as Revista del Instituto
histórico y geográfico del Uruguay, vol. 25.

1964. _____. El negro rioplatense, y otros ensayos.
Montevideo: C. García, 1937.

1965. _____. "Negros esclavos, pardos libres y negros
      libres en Uruguay," Estudios afrocubanos, 4, 1-4 (1940), pp.
      121-27.

1966. _____. Negros esclavos y negros libres: esquema
      de una sociedad esclavista y aporte del negro en nuestra formación
      nacional. Montevideo: Imprenta "Gaceta Comercial", 1941.

1967. Petit Muñoz, Eugenio, Edmundo M. Narancio, and José M. Traibel
      Nelcis. La condición jurídica, social, económica y política de los
      negros durante el coloniaje en la Banda Oriental. Montevideo:
      Tall. Gráf."33", 1947.

1968. Rama, Carlos M. Los afro-uruguayos. Montevideo: El Siglo
      Ilustrado, 1967.

13. Paraguay

1969. Carvalho Neto, Paulo de. "Antología del negro paraguayo," Anales
      de la Universidad Central del Ecuador, 91 (no. 346)(1962), pp.
      37-66.

1970. Cooney, Jerry W. "Abolition in the Republic of Paraguay,
      1840-1870," Jahrbuch für Geschichte von Staat, Wirtschaft, und
      Gesellschaft Lateinamerikas, 11 (1974), pp. 149-66.

1971. Plá, Josefina. "La esclavitud en el Paraguay: el rescate del
      esclavo," Revista paraguaya de sociología, 11 (no. 31)(1974), pp.
      29-49.

1972. _____. Hermano negro: la esclavitud en el Paraguay.
      Madrid: Paraninfo, 1972.

1973. Williams, John Hoyt. "Black Labor and State Ranches: The Tabapí
      Experience in Paraguay," Journal of Negro History, 62, 4 (1977),
      pp. 378-89.

1974. _____. "Esclavos y pobladores: observaciones sobre
      la historia parda del Paraguay en el siglo XIX," Revista paraguaya
      de la sociología, 11 (no. 31)(1974), pp. 7-27.

1975. _____. "Paraguay's Nineteenth Century Estancias de
      la Republica," Agricultural History, 47, 3 (1973), pp. 206-15.

1976. _____. "Tevegó on the Paraguayan Frontier: A Chapter
      in the Black History of the Americas," Journal of Negro History,
      56, 4 (1971), pp. 272-83.

IV. Brazil

1. General and comparative

1977. Abranches, Dunshee de. O captiveiro: memórias. Rio de Janeiro: Jornal do Comércio, 1941.

1978. Alves, Henrique L. Bibliografia afro-brasileira: estudos sobre o negro. São Paulo: Edições H., 1976.

1979. Alves, João Luis. "A questão do elemento servil: a extinção do tráfico e a lei de represão de 1850: liberdade dos nascituros," Revista do Instituto histórico e geográfico brasileiro (tomo especial: 1º Congresso de História Nacional, Rio de Janeiro, 1914), parte 4, pp. 187-257.

1980. Alves, Valter. "Síntese histórica da escravidão no Brasil," Revista do Instituto geográfico e histórico da Bahia, 73 (1946), pp. 247-55.

1981. Amaral, Braz de. "Os grandes mercados de escravos africanos - As tribus importadas - Sua distribuição regional," Annaes do 1 Congresso International de História da America (Rio de Janeiro, 1922) (Rio de Janeiro: Imprensa Nacional, 1925-30), vol. 5, pp. 435-96. Also in idem, Fatos da Vida do Brazil (Bahia: Tip. Naval, 1941), pp. 89-167.

1982. Andrada e Silva, Paulo de. "O libelo de José Bonifácio contra a escravatura e o trabalho servil," Anais do VI Simpósio nacional dos professores universitários de história (Goiâna, 1971) (São Paulo, 1973), vol. 1, pp. 490-516.

1983. Andrade, Nair de. "Musicalidade do escravo negro no Brasil," in Freyre et al., Novos estudos afro-brasileiros, pp. 194-202.

1984. Araújo, Carlos da Silva. "Como o Doutor Chernoviz viu a escravidão no Brasil (1840-1841)," Revista de história e arte, 3-4 (1963), pp. 80-83.

1985. Ascoli, Haroldo Renato. "A escravidão e sua abolição no Brasil," Revista do Instituto histórico e geográfico de São Paulo, 34, (1938), pp. 109-43.

1986. Bandecchi, Brasil. "Legislação básica sôbre a escravidão africana no Brasil," Revista de história, 23 (no. 89)(1972), pp. 207-14.

1987. Bandeira de Mello, Afonso Toledo. "A escravidão – da supressão do tráfico à Lei Aurea," Annaes do 1 Congresso Internacional de História da America (Rio de Janeiro, 1922) (Rio de Janeiro: Imprensa Nacional, 1925-30), vol. 3, pp. 379-406.

1988. _____. O trabalho servil no Brasil. Rio de Janeiro: Departamento de Estatística e Publicidade, 1936.

1989. Barros, Jacy Rego. Senzala e mocumba. Rio de Janeiro: Rodrigues e Cia., 1939.

1990. Beiguelman, Paula. "The Destruction of Modern Slavery: The Brazilian Case," Review, 6, 3 (1983), pp. 305-20.

1991. _____. "O encaminhamento político do problema da escravidão no Império," in Sérgio Buarque de Holanda, ed., História geral da civilização brasileira (São Paulo: DIFEL, 1969), tomo II, vol. 3, pp. 189-219.

1992. Benci, S. I., Jorge. Economia cristã dos senhores no governo dos escravos (livro brasileiro de 1700). Porto: Livraria Apostolado de Imprensa, 1954.

1993. Blair, Thomas. "Mouvements afro-brésiliens de libération depuis la période esclavagiste jusqu'à nos jours," Présence africaine, 53 (1965), pp. 96-101.

1994. Boxer, Charles R. "Negro Slavery in Brazil: A Portuguese Pamphlet (1764)," Race, 5, 3 (1964), pp. 38-47.

1995. _____. Race Relations in the Portuguese Colonial Empire, 1415-1825. Oxford: Clarendon Press, 1963.

1996. Braga, Julio Santana. "Anciens esclaves brésiliens au Dahomey," Etudes dahoméennes, 17 (1970), pp. 91-98.

1997. Brandão, Guilherme Euclides. "The Colonial Slave Mode of Production in Brazil" (PhD diss., American University, 1979).

1998. Brandão, Júlio de Freitas. "O escravo e o direito (breve abordagem histórico-jurídico)," in Anais do VI Simpósio nacional dos professores universitários de história (Goiâna, 1971) (São Paulo, 1973), vol. 1, pp. 255-84.

1999. Buescu, Mircea. "Notas sôbre o custo da mão-de-obra escrava," Verbum, 31, 3 (1975), pp. 33-44.

2000. _____. "Notas sôbre o volume da importação de escravos," in História econômica do Brasil: pesquisas e análises (Rio de Janeiro: APEC, 1970), pp. 201-08.

2001. _____. "Novas notas sôbre a importação de escravos," Estudos históricos (Marília), 7 (1968), pp. 79-86. Reprinted in idem, História econômica do Brasil: pesquisas e análises (Rio de Janeiro: APEC, 1970), pp. 209-18.

2002. _____. "Preço de escravos no século XIX," in História econômica do Brasil: pesquisas e análises (Rio de Janeiro: APEC, 1970), pp. 244-49.

2003. _____. "Sôbre o volume da importação de escravos," in Exercícios de história econômica do Brasil (Rio de Janeiro: APEC, 1969), pp. 101-17.

2004. Calmon, Pedro. "A abolição," Revista do Arquivo municipal (São Paulo), 47 (1938), pp. 127-46.

2005. Cardozo, Manoel. "Slavery in Brazil as Described by Americans," Americas, 17, 3 (1961), pp. 241-60.

2006. Carneiro, Edison. Ladinos e crioulos: estudos sôbre o negro no Brasil. Rio de Janeiro: Civilização Brasileira, 1964.

2007. Carvalho, Rodrigues de. "Aspectos da influencia africana na formação social do Brasil," in Freyre et al., Novos estudos afro-brasileiros, pp. 17-76.

2008. Carvalho de Mello, Pedro, and Robert W. Slenes. "Análise econômica da escravidão no Brasil," in Paulo Neuhaus, coord., Economia brasileira: uma visão histórica (Rio de Janeiro: Campus, 1980), pp. 89-122.

2009. Carvalho-Neto, Paulo de. "Notícia sobre uma coleção inédita de documentos afro-brasileiros," Revista de história (São Paulo), 50 (1974), pp. 705-09.

2010. Castro, Antônio Barros de. "A autonomia do sistema escravista," Cadernos de debate: história do Brasil, no. 1 (1976), pp. 71-73.

2011. _____. "Escravos e senhores nos engenhos do Brasil: um estudo sôbre os trabalhos do açúcar e a política econômica dos senhores," Estudos econômicos, 7, 1 (1977), pp. 177-220.

2012. Castro, Hélio Oliveira Portocarrero de. "Viabilidade econômica da escravidão no Brasil, 1880-1888," Revista brasileira de economia, 27, 1 (1973), pp. 43-67.

2013. Castro, Jeanne Berrance de. "O negro na Guarda Nacional brasileira," Anais do Museu Paulista, 23 (1969), pp. 149-72.

2014. Chaia, Josephina, and Luis Lisanti. "O escravo na legislação brasileira (1808-1889)," Revista de história, 49 (no. 99)(1974), pp. 241-48.

2015. Chiavenatto, Julio José. O negro no Brasil da senzala à Guerra do Paraguai. São Paulo: Brasiliense, 1980.

2016. Claudio, Affonso. "As tribus negras importadas: estudo etnográfico, sua distribuição regional no Brasil," Revista do Instituto histórico e geográfico brasileiro (tomo especial: 1º Congresso de Historia Nacional, Rio de Janeiro, 1914), parte 2, pp. 595-657.

2017. Coelho de Senna, Nelson. Africanos no Brasil. Belo Horizonte: Queiroz Breyner, 1938.

2018. 1º Congresso Afro-brasileiro do Recife (1934). Trabalhos, 2 vols. See Estudos afro-brasileiros (vol. 1) and Novos estudos afro-brasileiros (vol. 2), Freyre et al.

2019. Conrad, Robert. "The Brazilian Slave," in Lewis Hanke, ed., History of Latin American Civilization: Sources and Interpretations (Boston: Little, Brown, 1967), vol. 2, pp. 206-13.

2020. _____. Brazilian Slavery: An Annotated Research Bibliography. Boston: G. K. Hall, 1977.

2021. _____. The Destruction of Brazilian Slavery, 1850-1888. Berkeley: University of California Press, 1972.

2022. _____. "Neither Slave nor Free: The Emancipados of Brazil, 1818-1868," Hispanic American Historical Review, 53, 1 (1973), pp. 50-70.

2023. _____. "Nineteenth-Century Brazilian Slavery," in Toplin, ed., Slavery and Race Relations in Latin America, pp. 146-75.

2024. Costa, Emilia Viotti da. "Da escravidão ao trabalho livre," in idem, Da monarquia à República: Momentos decisivos (São Paulo: Grijalbo, 1977), pp. 209-26.

2025. _____. Da senzala à colonia. São Paulo: Difusão Européia do Livro, 1966.

2026. _____. "O escravo na grande lavoura," in Sérgio Buarque de Holanda, ed., História geral da civilização brasileira (São Paulo: DIFEL, 1969), tomo II, vol. 3, pp. 135-88.

2027. Couceiro, Solange Martins. Bibliografia sôbre o negro brasileiro. São Paulo: Universidade de São Paulo, 1971.

2028. Coutinho, Ruy. "Alimentação e estado nutricional do escravo no Brasil," in Estudos afro-brasileiros (1º Congresso Afro-Brasileiro, Recife, 1934) (Rio de Janeiro, 1935), pp. 199-213.

2029. Cunha, Ciro Vieira da. No tempo de Patrocínio. São Paulo: Saraiva, 1960.

2030. Daglione, Vivaldo W. F. "A libertação dos escravos no Brasil através de alguns documentos," Anais de história, 1 (1968-69), pp. 131-34.

2031. Dornas, João. A escravidão no Brasil. Rio de Janeiro: Civilização, 1939.

2032. Duque-Estrada, Osório. A abolição (esboço histórico) 1831-1888. Rio de Janeiro: Leite Ribeiro e Maurillo, 1918.

2033. Eads, J. K. "The Negro in Brazil," Journal of Negro History, 21, 4 (1936), pp. 365-75.

2034. Egas, Eugênio. "Libertação dos escravos (1871-1888 - síntese)," in Anais do 3 Congresso Sul-Riograndense de História e Geografia (Porto Alegre, 1940), vol. 4, pp. 2017-29. Reprinted in Revista do Instituto arqueológico, histórico e geográfico pernambucano, 40 (1945), pp. 226-40.

2035. Einaar, J. F. E. "Abschaffing van de Slavernij in Brazilie," West-Indische Gids, 34 (1953), pp. 56-58. With English summary.

2036. Eisenberg, Peter L. "Escravo e proletário na história do Brasil," Estudos econômicos, 13, 1 (1983), pp. 55-69.

2037. Elias, Maria José. "Os debates sôbre o trabalho dos chins e o problema da mão-de-obra no Brasil durante o século XIX," Anais do VI Simpósio nacional dos professores universitários de história (Goiâna, 1971) (São Paulo, 1973), vol. 1, pp. 697-716.

2038. Ellis, Myriam. "Escravos e assalariados na antiga pesca da baleia (Um capítulo esquecido da história do trabalho no Brasil colonial)," Anais do VI Simpósio nacional dos professores universitários de história (Goiâna, 1971) (São Paulo, 1973), vol. 1, pp. 307-52.

2039. Falcon, Francisco C., and Fernando A. Novais. "A extinção da escravatura africana em Portugal no quadro da política econômica pombalina," Anais do VI Simpósio nacional dos professores universitários de história (Goiâna, 1971) (São Paulo, 1973), vol. 1, pp. 405-32.

2040. Fenelon, Dea Ribeiro. "Levantamento e sistematização da legislação relativa aos escravos no Brasil," Anais do VI Simpósio nacional dos professores universitários de história (Goiâna, 1971) (São Paulo, 1973), vol. 2, pp. 199-307.

2041. Fernandes, Florestan. "Slaveholding Society in Brazil," in Rubin and Tuden, eds., Comparative Perspectives, pp. 311-42.

2042. _____. "The Weight of the Past," Daedalus, 96 (1967), pp. 560-79.

2043. Flory, Thomas. "Fugitive Slaves and Free Society: The Case of Brazil," Journal of Negro History, 64, 2 (1979), pp. 116-30.

2044. _____. "Race and Social Control in Independent Brazil," Journal of Latin American Studies, 9, 2 (1977), pp. 199-224.

2045. Fonseca, Célia Freire d'Aquino. "O Brasil oitocentista e a abolição (Estrutura, população e abolição)," Anais do VI Simpósio nacional dos professores universitários de história (Goiâna, 1971) (São Paulo, 1973), vol. 1, pp. 739-60.

2046. _____. "Comentários sôbre o projeto de libertação dos escravos, elaborado por José Bonifácio em 1823," Anais do VI Simpósio nacional dos professores universitários de história (Goiâna, 1971) (São Paulo, 1973), vol. 1, pp. 517-20.

2047. Freitas, Décio. Escravidão de índios e negros no Brasil. Porto Alegre: Escola Superior de Teologia São Lourenço de Brindes/Editora Vozes, 1980.

2048. _____. O escravismo brasileiro. Porto Alegre: Escola Superior de Teologia São Lourenço de Brindes/Editora Vozes, 1980.

2049. _____. Escravos e senhores-de-escravos. Porto Alegre: Caxias do Sul, 1977.

2050. _____. Insurreições escravas. Porto Alegre: Movimento, 1976.

2051. Freitas, Octavio de. Doenças africanas no Brasil. São Paulo: Editora Nacional, 1935.

2052. Freyre, Gilberto. "Deformações de corpo dos negros fugidos," in Freyre et al., Novos estudos afro-brasileiros, pp. 245-50.

2053. _____. O escravo nos anúncios de jornais brasileiros do século XIX. Recife: Imprênsa Universitária, 1963.

2054. _____. Casa-grande e senzala. Rio de Janeiro: Olympio, 1933. Translated by Samuel Putnam as The Masters and the Slaves: A Study in the Development of Brazilian Civilization (New York: Knopf, 1946).

2055. _____, et al. Novos estudos afro-brasileiros (Trabalhos apresentados ao 1º Congresso Afro-brasileiro do Recife, vol. 2). Rio de Janeiro: Editora Civilização Brasileira, 1937.

2056. Gerson, Brasil. A escravidão no Império. Rio de Janeiro: Pallas, 1975.

2057. _____. "O problema da escravidão no Brasil," Studia, 37 (1973), pp. 217-24.

2058. Gomes, Alfredo. "Achegas para a história do tráfico africano no Brasil - aspectos numéricos," Anais do 4 Congresso de História Nacional (Rio de Janeiro, 1949) (Rio de Janeiro. Imprensa Nacional, 1950), vol. 5, pp. 25-78.

2059. Gorender, Jacob. O escravismo colonial. São Paulo. Editora Atica, 1978.

2060. Goulart, José Alpício. Da fuga ao suicídio (Aspectos da rebeldia do escravo no Brasil). Rio de Janeiro. Editora Conquista, 1972.

2061. _____. Da palmatória ao patíbulo. castigos de escravos no Brasil. Rio de Janeiro. Editora Conquista, 1971.

2062. Goulart, Maurício. Escravidão africana no Brasil (das origens à extinção do tráfico). São Paulo. Editora Alfa-Omega, 1949.

2063. _____. "O problema da mão-de-obra. o escravo africano," in Sérgio Buarque de Holanda, ed., História geral da civilização brasileira (São Paulo. DIFEL, 1968), tomo I, vol. 2, pp. 183-91.

2064. Gouveia, Maurilio de. História da escravidão. Rio de Janeiro, 1955.

2065. Graham, Richard. "Causes for the Abolition of Negro Slavery in Brazil. An Interpretive Essay," Hispanic American Historical Review, 46, 2 (1966), pp. 123-37.

2066. _____. "Slave Families of a Rural Estate in Colonial Brazil," Journal of Social History, 9, 3 (1976), pp. 382-402.

2067. Hanke, Lewis, ed. "Negro Slavery in Brazil," in History of Latin American Civilization. Sources and Interpretations (Boston. Little, Brown, 1967), vol. 2, pp. 155-213.

2068. Hell, Jürgen. "Der brasilianische Plantagen-Komplex (1532-1808). Ein Beitrag zur Charakteristik der Sklaverei in Amerika," Asien-Afrika-Latein-Amerika, 6 (1978), pp. 117-38.

2069. Hemming, John. Red Gold. The Conquest of the Brazilian Indians, 1500-1760. Cambridge, Mass.. Harvard University Press, 1978.

2070. Höner, Urs. Die Versklavung der brasilianischen Indianer: Der Arbeitsmarkt im portugiesisch Amerika im XVI. Jahrhundert. Zürich: Atlantis, 1980.

2071. Ianni, Octavio. "Escravidão e história," Debate e Crítica (Revista quadrimestral de ciências sociais), 6 (1975), pp. 131-44.

2072. _____. Escravidão e racismo. São Paulo. Editora HUCITEC, 1978.

2073. _____. "Escravismo e racismo," Anais de história, 7 (1975), pp. 66-94.

2074. _____. Raças e classes sociais no Brasil. Rio de Janeiro: Civilização Brasileira, 1966. 2nd revised edition, 1972.

2075. Jurema, Aderbal. Insurreições negras no Brasil. Recife: Edições da Casa Mozart, 1935.

2076. Klein, Herbert S. "The Colored Freedmen in Brazilian Slave Society," Journal of Social History, 3, 1 (1969), pp. 30-52.

2077. _____. "Nineteenth-Century Brazil," in Cohen and Greene, eds., Neither Slave nor Free, pp. 309-34.

2078. Koval, B. I. "Colonial Plantation Slavery and Primary Capital Accumulation in Western Europe," in Russell H. Bartley, ed. and trans., Soviet Historians on Latin America: Recent Scholarly Contributions (Madison: University of Wisconsin Press, 1978), pp. 89-108.

2079. Leff, Nathaniel H. "Long-Term Viability of Slavery in a Backward Closed Economy," Journal of Interdisciplinary History, 5, 1 (1974), pp. 103-08.

2080. _____, and Herbert S. Klein. "O crescimento da população não européia antes do início do desenvolvimento: O Brasil do século XIX," Anais de história, 6 (1974), pp. 51-70.

2081. Leme, Luiz António Padovani. "As origens da escravidão negra na América: uma necessidade interna," Cadernos de pesquisa: tudo é história, no. 3 (1978), pp. 53-57.

2082. Lisanti, Luis. "Autoconsumo e economia de mercado: o papel de livres e escravos - indagações," Anais de história, 3 (1971), pp. 159-62.

2083. Lopes, Edmundo Correia. A escravatura: subsídios para a sua história. Lisbon: Agência Geral das Colónias, 1944.

2084. Luna, Francisco Vidal, and Iraci del Nero da Costa. "A presença do elemento forro no conjunto de proprietários de escravos," Ciência e cultura, 32, 7 (1980), pp. 836-41.

2085. Luna, Luiz. O negro na luta contra a escravidão. Rio de Janeiro: Editora Leitura, 1968.

2086. Macedo, Sérgio D. Teixeira de. Crónica do negro no Brasil. Rio de Janeiro: Distribuidora Record, 1974.

2087. Machado (Filho), Aires da Mata. "A procedência dos negros brasileiros e os arquivos eclesiasticos," Afroamérica, 1, 1-2 (1945), pp. 67-70.

2088. Marchant, Alexander. From Barter to Slavery: The Economic Relations of Portuguese and Indians in the Settlement of Brazil, 1500-1800. Baltimore: Johns Hopkins University Press, 1942.

2089. Marcílio, Maria Luiza, Rubens Murillo Marques, and José Carlos Barreiro. "Considerações sobre o preço do escravo no período imperial, " Anais de história, 5 (1973), pp. 179-94.

2090. Martin, Percy Alvin. "A escravatura e a sua abolição no Brasil," Anais do 3 Congresso Sul-Riograndense de História e Geografia (Porto Alegre, 1940), vol. 3, pp. 1203-38.

2091. _____. "Slavery and Abolition in Brazil," Hispanic American Historical Review, 13, 2 (1933), pp. 151-96.

2092. Mattoso, Kátia M. de Queirós. "A carta de alforria como fonte complementar para o estudo da rentabilidade de mão-de-obra escrava urbana (1819-1888)," in Carlos Manuel Peláez and Mircea Buescu, eds., Moderna história econômica (Rio de Janeiro: APEC, 1976), pp. 149-63.

2093. _____. Etre esclave au Brésil: XVIe-XIXe. Paris: Hachette, 1979.

2094. Mello, Evaldo Cabral de. "El norte, el sur y la prohibición del tráfico interprovincial de esclavos," Revista de cultura brasileña, 49 (1979), pp. 27-52.

2095. Mello, Pedro Carvalho de. "The Economics of Labor in Brazilian Coffee Plantations, 1850-1888" (PhD diss., University of Chicago, 1977).

2096. Mendes, M. Maia. "Escravatura no Brasil (1500-1700)," Congresso do Mundo Português (Lisbon, 1940), tomo 2, 2ª secção, 1ª parte, vol. 10, pp. 31-55.

2097. Moraes, Evaristo de. A escravidão africana no Brasil (das origens à extincção). São Paulo: Companhia Editora Nacional, 1933.

2098. Mott, Luiz R. B. "A escravatura: o propósito de uma representação a El-Rei sobre a escravatura no Brasil," Revista do Instituto de estudos brasileiros, 14 (1973), pp. 127-36.

2099. Moura, Clovis. O negro, de bom escravo a mau cidadão. Rio de Janeiro: Conquista, 1977.

2100. _____. Rebeliões da senzala: Quilombos, insurreições, guerrilhas. São Paulo: Edições Zumbí, 1959.

2101. Mulvey, Patricia Ann. "Black Brothers and Sisters: Membership in the Black Lay Brotherhoods of Colonial Brazil," Luso-Brazilian Review, 19, 2 (1980), pp. 253-79.

2102. _____. "The Black Lay Brotherhoods of Colonial Brazil: A History" (PhD diss., City University of New York, 1976).

2103. _____. "Slave Confraternities in Brazil: Their Role in Colonial Society," Americas, 39, 1 (1982), pp. 39-68.

2104. Nabuco, Carolina. "O elemento servil - a abolição," Anais do 3 Congresso de História Nacional (Rio de Janeiro, 1938) (Rio de Janeiro: Instituto histórico e geográfico brasileiro, 1941), vol. 3, pp. 239-56.

2105. Nabuco, Joaquim. "A escravidão," Revista do Instituto histórico e geográfico brasileiro, 204 (1949), pp. 5-106.

2106. Nelson, Margaret V. "The Negro in Brazil as Seen through the Chronicles of Travelers, 1800-1868," Journal of Negro History, 30, 2 (1945), pp. 203-18.

2107. *Nequete, Lenine. O escravo na jurisprudência brasileira, forthcoming.

2108. _____. "As relações entre senhor e escravo no século XIX: o caso da escrava Honorata," Revista brasileira de estudos políticos, no. 53 (1981), pp. 223-48.

2109. Nina Rodrigues, Raymundo. Os africanos no Brasil. 3rd edition. São Paulo: Companhia Editora Nacional, 1945.

2110. Novais, Fernando. "Escravidão: uma façanha do capital mercantil," Cadernos de debate: história do Brasil, no. 1 (1976), pp. 74-75.

2111. Novinsky, Anita. "Impedimento ao trabalho livre no período inquisitorial e as respostas da realidade brasileira," Anais do VI Simpósio nacional dos professores universitários de história (Goiâna, 1971) (São Paulo, 1973), vol. 1, pp. 231-54.

2112. Odalia, Nilo. "A abolição da escravatura," Anais do Museu Paulista, 18 (1964), pp. 121-45.

2113. Oliveira, Arcebispo Dom Oscar de. "O que fez a Igreja no Brasil pelo escravo africano," Revista do Instituto histórico e geográfico brasileiro, 326 (1980), pp. 311-26.

2114. *Palha, Américo. Os precursores da abolição. Rio de Janeiro: Distribuidore Record, 1965.

2115. Pang, Eul-Soo. "Modernization and Slavocracy in Nineteenth Century Brazil," Journal of Interdisciplinary History, 9, 4 (1979), pp. 667-88.

2116. _____. "Tecnologia e escravocracia no Brasil durante o século XIX: legislação e evidências," Anais do Museu Paulista, 30 (1980-81), pp. 55-135.

2117. Pedreira, Pedro Tomás. Os quilombos brasileiros. Salvador, Bahia: Prefeitura Municipal, 1973.

2118. Perdigão Malheiros, Agostinho Marques. A escravidão no Brasil: ensaio histórico-jurídico-social. 2 vols. Rio de Janeiro, 1866-67. Reprinted São Paulo: Edições Cultura, 1944.

2119. Pescatello, Ann M. "Prêto Power, Brazilian Style: Modes of Reactions to Slavery in the Nineteenth Century," in Pescatello, ed., Old Roots in New Lands, pp. 77-106.

2120. Porter, Dorothy B. "The Negro in the Brazilian Abolition Movement," Journal of Negro History, 37, 1 (1952), pp. 54-80.

2121. Queiroz, Suely Robles Reis de. "Brandura da escravidão brasileira: mito ou realidade?" Revista de história, 52 (no. 103, tomo II) (1975), pp. 443-82.

2122. _____. "El orígen de los negros brasileños," Revista de la Universidad de México, 25, 2 (1970), pp. 18-24.

2123. Querino, Manuel Raymundo. A raça africana e os seus costumes. Salvador, Bahia: Livraria Progresso Editora, 1955.

2124. Ramos, Artur. A aculturação negra no Brasil. São Paulo: Editora Nacional, 1942.

2125. _____. "Castigos de escravos," Revista do Arquivo municipal (São Paulo), 47 (1938), pp. 79-103.

2126. _____. O negro na civilização brasileira. Rio de Janeiro: Livraria Editôra da Casa do Estudante do Brasil, 1971. Translated by Richard Pattee as The Negro in Brazil (New York: Associated Publishers, 1939).

2127. *Ramos, Donald. "The Black Family in Brazil, 1760-1840" (Unpublished, 1978).

2128. Ramos, Luis A. de Oliveira. "Pombal e o esclavagismo," Revista da Faculdade de Letras da Universidade do Porto (Série de história), 2 (1971), pp. 169-78.

2129. Reis, Jaime. "Brazil: The Peculiar Abolition (review of Conrad, Destruction of Brazilian Slavery, and Toplin, Abolition of Slavery in Brazil)," Ibero-Amerikanisches Archiv, 3, 3 (1977), pp. 281-94.

2130. Renault, Delso. "Atos cruéis e humanos - extremos da escravidão brasileira," Revista brasileira de cultura, 6 (no. 20)(1974), pp. 71-80.

2131. Ribeiro, João. O elemento negro: história, folclore, linguística. Rio de Janeiro: Record, 193?.

2132. Ribeiro, René. "Relations of the Negro with Christianity in Portuguese America: The Negro and the New Social Slavery Structure," Americas, 14, 4 (1958), pp. 454-84.

2133. Ribeiro, Sílvia Lara. "Do mouro cativo ao escravo negro: continuidade ou ruptura?" Anais do Museu Paulista, 30 (1980-81), pp. 375-400.

2134. Rios, José Artur. "A fazenda de café: da escravidão ao trabalho livre," in Ensaios sobre café e desenvolvimento econômico (Rio de Janeiro: Instituto brasileiro do café, 1973), pp. 3-27. Translated by Magnolia Maciel Peláez as "Coffee and Agricultural Labor," in Carlos Manoel Peláez, ed., Essays on Coffee and Economic Development (Rio de Janeiro: Instituto brasileiro do café, 1973), pp. 3-26.

2135. Rodrigues, José Honório. Brasil e Africa: outro horizonte. Rio de Janeiro: Editora Civilização, 1961. 2nd revised edition, 1964. Translated by Richard A. Mazzara and Sam Hileman as Brazil and Africa (Berkeley: University of California Press, 1965).

2136. _____. "A rebeldia negra e a abolição," in História e historiografia (Petrópolis: Vozes, 1970), pp. 65-88.

2137. Rosário, Adalgisa Maria Vieira do. "Relação de documentos do Arquivo Histórico da Câmara Federal relativos à escravatura no Brasil," Anais do VI Simpósio nacional dos professores universitários de história (Goiâna, 1971) (São Paulo, 1973), vol. 2, pp. 309-23.

2138. Rout, Leslie B. "The African in Colonial Brazil," in Kilson and Rotberg, eds., African Diaspora, pp. 132-72.

2139. _____. "Race and Slavery in Brazil," Wilson Quarterly, 1, 1 (1976), pp. 73-89.

2140. Russell-Wood, A. J. R. "Black and Mulatto Brotherhoods in Colonial Brazil: A Study in Collective Behavior," Hispanic American Historical Review, 54, 4 (1974), pp. 567-602. Revised as "Collective Behaviour: The Brotherhoods," in idem, Black Man in Slavery and Freedom, pp. 128-60.

2141. _____. "The Black Family in the Americas," revised as "Domestic Behaviour: Family and Kinship," in idem, Black Man in Slavery and Freedom, pp. 161-97.

2142. _____. The Black Man in Slavery and Freedom in Colonial Brazil. New York: St. Martin's Press, 1982.

2143. _____. "Colonial Brazil," in Cohen and Greene, eds., Neither Slave nor Free, pp. 84-133. Pp. 98-108 revised as "Free Blacks and Free Mulattoes in the Economy of Portuguese America," in idem, Black Man in Slavery and Freedom, pp. 50-66; pp. 109-17 revised as "Free Blacks and Free Mulattos in the Society of Portuguese America," in idem, Black Man in Slavery and Freedom, pp. 67-82.

2144. _____. "Iberian Expansion and the Issue of Black Slavery: Changing Portuguese Attitudes, 1440-1770," American Historical Review, 83, 1 (1978), pp. 16-42.

2145. Santos, Juana E. dos. "O negro e a abolição," Vozes (Revista católica de cultura) (Petrópolis), 73, 3 (1979), pp. 5-12.

2146. Saraiva, Antônio José. "Le père Antonio Vieira, S.J., et la question de l'esclavage des noirs au XVIIe siècle," Annales: économies, sociétés, civilisations, 22, 6 (1967), pp. 1289-1309.

2147. Saunders, J. V. D. "The Brazilian Negro," Americas, 15, 3 (1959), pp. 271-90.

2148. Schwartz, Stuart B. "Colonial Brazil: The Role of the State in a Slave Social Formation," in Karen Spalding, ed., Essays in the Political, Economic and Social History of Colonial Latin America (Newark, Del.: University of Delaware Latin American Studies Program, 1982), pp. 1-23. (Occasional Papers and Monographs, no. 3)

2149. _____. "Patterns of Slaveholding in the Americas: New Evidence from Brazil," American Historical Review, 87, 1 (1982), pp. 55-86.

2150. _____. "Resistance and Accommodation in Eighteenth-Century Brazil: The Slaves' View of Slavery," Hispanic American Historical Review, 57, 1 (1977), pp. 69-81.

2151. Simpósio nacional dos professores universitários de história, 6th. (Goiâna, 1971). Anais (3 vols.). São Paulo, 1973. "Trabalho livre e trabalho escravo".

2152. Siqueira, Sônia Aparecida. "A escravidão negra no pensamento do bispo Azeredo Coutinho: contribuição ao estudo da mentalidade do último inquisidor geral," in Actas V Colóquio internacional de estudos luso-brasileiros (Coimbra, 1963) (Coimbra: n.p., 1966), vol. 3, pp. 147-212.

2153. _____. "Trabalho compulsório: a pena inquisitorial das galés," Anais do VI Simpósio nacional dos professores universitários de história (Goiâna, 1971) (São Paulo, 1973), vol. 1, pp. 353-72.

2154. Skidmore, Thomas E. "The Death of Brazilian Slavery, 1866-88," in Frederick B. Pike, ed., Latin American History: Select Problems (New York: Harcourt, Brace, and World, 1969), pp. 133-71.

2155. Slenes, Robert W. "The Demography and Economics of Brazilian Slavery: 1850-1888" (PhD diss., Stanford University, 1976).

2156. Soares, Ubaldo. A escravatura na misericórdia: subsídios. Rio de Janeiro: n.p., 1958.

2157. Sodré, Alcindo. "O elemento servil - a abolição," Anais do 3 Congresso de História Nacional (Rio de Janeiro, 1938) (Rio de Janeiro: Instituto histórico e geográfico brasileiro, 1941), vol. 4, pp. 51-146.

2158. Souza, José Antônio Soares de. "Os escravos e a pena de morte no Império," Revista do Instituto histórico e geográfico brasileiro, 313 (1976), pp. 5-19.

2159. Spinazzola, Vittorio. "Islam e schiavitù in Brasile," Oriente moderno, 47, 4 (1967), pp. 269-85.

2160. Stein, Stanley J. "Freyre's Brazil Revisited: A Review of New World in the Tropics," Hispanic American Historical Review, 41, 1 (1961), pp. 111-13.

2161. Sweet, David. "Francisca: Indian Slave," in David G. Sweet and Gary B. Nash, eds., Struggle and Survival in Colonial America (Berkeley and Los Angeles: University of California, 1981), pp. 274-91.

2162. *Tavares, Luis Henrique Dias. O desembarque da pontinha. Salvador, 1971.

2163. Toplin, Robert Brent. "Abolition in Brazil: The Collapse of Slavery," in idem, Freedom and Prejudice: The Legacy of Slavery in the United States and Brazil (Westport, Conn.: Greenwood, 1981), pp. 55-76.

2164. _____. The Abolition of Slavery in Brazil. New York: Atheneum, 1972.

2165. _____. "From Slavery to Fettered Freedom: Attitudes Toward the Negro in Brazil," Luso-Brazilian Review, 7, 1 (1970), pp. 3-12. Reprinted in idem, Freedom and Prejudice: The Legacy of Slavery in the United States and Brazil (Westport, Conn.: Greenwood, 1981), pp. 41-52.

2166. Trabalho livre e trabalho escravo. (Org. Prof. Eurípedes Simões de Paula.) (Anais do VI Simpósio nacional dos professores universitários de história, Goiâna, 1971). São Paulo, 1973. 3 vols.

2167. Vianna, Hélio. "A abolição da escravidão no Brasil," Revista de história de America, 60 (1965), pp. 69-90.

2168. Vianna Filho, Luis. "O trabalho do engenho e a reacção do índio - estabelecimento da escravatura africana," Congresso do Mundo Português (Lisbon, 1940), tomo 2, 2ª secção, 1ª parte, vol. 10, pp. 11-29.

2169. Willeke, Venantius. "Kirche und Negersklaven in Brasilien, 1550-1888," Neue Zeitschrift für Missionswissenschaft, 32 (1976), pp. 15-26.

2170. _____. "Klostersklaven in Brasilien," Archivum franciscanum historicum, 69, 3-4 (1976), pp. 423-43.

2. Northern

2171. MacLachlan, Colin M. "African Slave Trade and Economic Development in Amazonia, 1700-1800," in Toplin, ed., Slavery and Race Relations in Latin America, pp. 112-45.

2172. _____. "Slavery, Ideology and Institutional Change: The Impact of the Enlightenment on Slavery in Late Eighteenth-Century Maranhão," Journal of Latin American Studies, 11, 1 (1979), pp. 1-17.

2173. Mott, Luiz R. B. "Cautelas de alforria de duas escravas na província do Pará (1829-1846)," Revista de história, 47 (no. 95)(1973), pp. 263-68.

2174. Pereira, Nunes. "O negro na Ilha Grande de Marajó," in Abdias do Nascimento, ed., O negro revoltado (Congresso do Negro Brasileiro, Rio de Janeiro, 1950) (Rio de Janeiro: Edições GRD, 1968), pp. 99-146.

2175. Salles, Vicente. O negro no Pará sob o regime da escravidão. Rio de Janeiro: Fundação Getúlio Vargas, 1971.

3. Northeast

2176. *Alves Filho, Ivan. "Le 'Quilombo de Palmares' dans le processus historique du Brésil" (Thèse de maîtrise, EHESS, 1978).

2177. Andrade, Maria José de Souza. "A mão de obra escrava em Salvador de 1811 a 1860: Um estudo de história quantitativa" (Tese de licenciatura, Universidade Federal da Bahia, 1975).

2178. Brandão, Alfredo. "Os negros na história de Alagôas," in Estudos afro-brasileiros (1º Congresso Afro-Brasileiro, Recife, 1934) (Rio de Janeiro, 1935), vol. 1, pp. 55-91.

2179. Caldas Britto, Eduardo A. "Levantes de pretos na Bahia," Revista do Instituto geográfico e histórico da Bahia, 29 (1903), pp. 69-94. Reprinted from Jornal do Comércio (Rio de Janeiro), 26 May 1903.

2180. Cardoso, José Fábio Barreto P. "Modalidade de mão-de-obra escrava na cidade do Salvador," Vozes (Revista católica de cultura) (Petrópolis), 79, 3 (1979), pp. 13-15.

2181. Carneiro, Edison. O quilombo dos Palmares. México: Fondo de Cultura Economica, 1946.

2182. Delgado, Luiz. Escravos em Olinda sob a Lei Rio Branco. Recife: Ministério da Educação e Cultura, 1967.

2183. *Denslow, David. "The High Importation to Stock Ratio for Slaves in Northeastern Brazil: An Interpretation" (Paper delivered at Southwestern Social Sciences Conference, San Antonio, Texas, 1975).

2184. Eisenberg, Peter L. "Abolishing Slavery: The Process on Pernambuco's Sugar Plantations," Hispanic American Historical Review, 52, 4 (1972), pp. 580-97.

2185. _____. "The Consequences of Modernization for Brazil's Sugar Plantations in the Nineteenth Century," in Kenneth Duncan and Ian Rutledge, eds., Land and Labour in Latin America (New York: Cambridge University Press, 1977), pp. 345-67.

2186. Ennes, Ernesto, ed. As guerras nos Palmares (subsídios para a sua história). São Paulo: Companhia Editora Nacional, 1938. Vol. 1, Domingos Jorge Velho e a "Tróia Negra" 1687-1700.

2187. Etienne, (l'Abbé) Ignace. "La secte musulmane des Malès du Brésil et leur révolte en 1835," Anthropos, 4 (1909), pp. 99-105, 405-15.

2188. Ferraz, Aydano do Couto. "O escravo negro na revolução da independência da Baia," Revista do Arquivo municipal (São Paulo), 56 (1939), pp. 195-202.

2189. Ferreira, José Carlos. "As insurreições dos africanos na Bahia," Revista do Instituto geográfico e histórico da Bahia, 29 (1903), pp. 95-119.

2190. Freitas, Décio. Palmares: a guerra dos escravos. 1st ed. Porto Alegre: Editôra Movimento, 1973.

2191. Freitas, Mario Martins de. Reino negro de Palmares. Vol. 1. Rio de Janeiro: Companhia Editora Americana, 1954.

2192. Galloway, J. H. "The Last Years of Slavery on the Sugar Plantations of Northeastern Brazil," Hispanic American Historical Review, 51, 4 (1971), pp. 586-605.

2193. Girão, Raimundo. A abolição no Ceará. Fortaleza: Editora A. Batista Fentenele, 1956.

2194. Huggins, Martha Diane Knisely. "From Slave to Free Labor in the Brazilian Sugar Industry: The Political Economy of Social Control and Crime in Pernambuco, 1850-1922" (PhD diss., University of New Hampshire, 1981).

2195. Ignace, Pe Etienne. "A revolta dos Malês," Afro-Asia (Revista do Centro de estudos afro-orientais da Bahia), nos. 10-11 (1970), pp. 121-35.

2196. Kent, Raymond K. "African Revolt in Bahia: 24-25 January 1835," Journal of Social History, 3, 4 (1970), pp. 334-56.

2197. _____. "Palmares: An African State in Brazil," Journal of African History, 6, 2 (1965), pp. 161-75. Also Bobbs-Merrill Reprint no. BC-166.

2198. Knox, Miridan Britto. "A questão servil na fala dos presidentes da Província do Piauí," Anais do VI Simpósio nacional dos professores universitários de história (Goiâna, 1971) (São Paulo, 1973), vol. 2, pp. 335-70.

2199. Macedo, Sérgio D. Teixeira de. Palmares: a tróia negra. Rio de Janeiro: Distribuidora Record, 1963.

2200. Marcílio, Maria Luiza. "The Price of Slaves in XIXth Century Brazil: A Quantitative Analysis of the Registration of Slave Sales in Bahia," in Studi in memoria di Federigo Melis (Napoli: Giannini Editore, 1978), vol. 5, pp. 83-97.

2201. Mattoso, Kátia M. de Queirós. "A propósito de cartas de alforria – Bahia 1779-1850" Anais de história, 4 (1972), pp. 23-52.

2202. _____. "Les esclaves de Bahia au début du XIXᵉ siècle (étude d'un groupe social)," Cahiers des Amériques Latines, 9-10 (1974), pp. 105-29. Also published as "Os escravos na Bahia no alvorecer do século XIX (estudo de um grupo social)," Revista de historia, 48 (no. 97)(1974), pp. 109-35.

2203. _____. Testaments d'esclaves libérés à Bahia au XIXe siècle: Une source pour l'étude de mentalités d'un groupe social. Forthcoming.

2204. Mello, Mário. "A Republica dos Palmares," in Estudos afro-brasileiros (1º Congresso Afro-Brasileiro, Recife, 1934) (Rio de Janeiro, 1935), pp. 181-86. Also as "A Republica dos Palmares," Revista do Instituto arqueológico, histórico e geográfico pernambucano, 32 (1932), pp. 189-92.

2205. Mello Neto, J. A. Gonçalves de. "A situação do negro sob o domínio hollandez," in Freyre et al., Novos estudos afro-brasileiros, pp. 201-21.

2206. Mott, Luiz R. B. "Brancos, pardos, pretos e índios em Sergipe: 1825-1830," Anais de história, 6 (1974), pp. 139-84.

2207. _____. "Pardos e pretos em Sergipe, 1774-1851," Revista do Instituto de estudos brasileiros, 18 (1976), pp. 7-37.

2208. Nascimento, Beatriz. "O quilombo do Jabaquara," Vozes (Revista católica de cultura) (Petrópolis), 73, 3 (1979), pp. 16-18.

2209. Nina Rodrigues, Raymundo. "A troia negra (erros e lacunas da história de Palmares)," Revista do Instituto histórico e geográfico brasileiro, 75, 1 (1912), pp. 231-58.

2210. Ott, Carlos B. "O negro bahiano," in Les Afro-américains (Paris, 1953), pp. 141-51. (Mémoires de l'Institut Français de l'Afrique Noire, no. 27)

2211. Pierson, Donald. "The Negro in Bahia, Brazil," American Sociological Review, 4, 4 (1939), pp. 524-33.

2212. _____. Negroes in Brazil: A Study of Race Contact at Bahia. Chicago: University of Chicago Press, 1942.

2213. Pontes, Carlos. "Uma escrava original," in Freyre et al., Novos estudos afro-brasileiros, pp. 132-40.

2214. Prince, Howard M. "Slave Rebellion in Bahia, 1807-35" (PhD diss., Columbia University, 1972).

2215. Reis, Jaime. "Abolition and the Economics of Slaveholding in North East Brazil" (Occasional Paper no 11, Institute of Latin American Studies, University of Glasgow, 1974). Also in Boletín de estudios latinoamericanos y del Caribe (Amsterdam), 17 (1974), pp. 3-20.

2216. _____. "From banguê to usina: Social Aspects of Growth and Modernization in the Sugar Industry of Pernambuco, Brazil, 1850-1920," in Kenneth Duncan and Ian Rutledge, eds., Land and Labour in Latin America (New York: Cambridge University Press, 1977), pp. 369-96.

2217. _____. "The Impact of Abolitionism in Northeast Brazil: A Quantitative Approach," in Rubin and Tuden, eds., Comparative Perspectives, pp. 107-22.

2218. Reis, João José. "Slave Revolt in Bahia 1790-1835: Economy, Society, Demography" (MA thesis, University of Minnesota, 1977).

2219. Ribeiro, René. "O negro em Pernambuco," Revista do Instituto arqueológico, histórico e geográfico pernambucano, 42 (1948-49), pp. 7-25.

2220. Schwartz, Stuart B. "Buraco de Tatú: The Destruction of a Bahian Quilombo," in Verhandlungen der XXXVIII Internationalen Amerikanistenkongresses (Stuttgart-Munich, 1968) (München: K. Renner, 1969), vol. 3, pp. 429-38.

2221. _____. "Free Labor in a Slave Economy: The Lavradores de cana of Colonial Bahia," in Dauril Alden, ed., Colonial Roots of Modern Brazil (Berkeley: University of California Press, 1973), pp. 147-97.

2222. _____. "Indian Labor and New World Plantations: European Demands and Indian Responses in Northeastern Brazil," American Historical Review, 83, 1 (1978), pp. 43-79.

2223. _____. "The Manumission of Slaves in Colonial Brazil: Bahia, 1684-1745," Hispanic American Historical Review, 54, 4 (1974), pp. 603-35. Also as "A manumissão dos escravos no Brasil colonial: Bahia, 1684-1745," Anais de história, 6 (1974), pp. 71-114.

2224. _____. "The Mocambo: Slave Resistance in Colonial Bahia," Journal of Social History, 3, 4 (1970), pp. 313-33.

2225. Taylor, Kit Sims. "The Economics of Sugar and Slavery in Northeastern Brazil," Agricultural History, 44, 3 (1970), pp. 267-80.

2226. Titton, Gentil Avelino. "O sínodo da Bahia (1707) e a escravatura," in Anais do VI Simpósio nacional dos professores universitários de história (Goiâna, 1971) (São Paulo, 1973), vol. 1, pp. 285-306.

2227. Viana, Luiz. O negro na Bahia. Rio de Janeiro: J. Olympio, 1946.

2228. Vidal, Adhemar. "Tres séculos de escravidão na Parahyba," Estudos afro-brasileiros (1º Congresso Afro-Brasileiro, Recife, 1934) (Rio de Janeiro, 1935), pp. 105-32.

4. Center-South

2229. *Assis, B. F. Eugenio de. Levante dos escravos no Distrito de S. José do Queimado, municipio da Serra. Espirito Santo: Estado do Espirito Santo, 1948.

2230. Barbosa, Waldemar de Almeida. Negros e quilombos em Minas Gerais. Belo Horizonte, 1972.

2231. Bergstresser, Rebecca Baird. "The Movement for the Abolition of Slavery in Rio de Janeiro, Brazil, 1880-1889" (PhD diss., Stanford University, 1973).

2232. Carvalho de Mello, Pedro. "Aspectos econômicos da organização do trabalho da economia cafeeira do Rio de Janeiro, 1850-88," Revista brasileira de economia, 32, 1 (1978), pp. 19-67.

2233. Coelho, Lucinda Coutinho de Mello. "Mão-de-obra escrava na mineração e tráfico negreiro no Rio de Janeiro (Levantamento de fontes)," Anais do VI Simpósio nacional dos professores universitários de história (Goiâna, 1971) (São Paulo, 1973), vol. 1, pp. 449-82.

2234. Costa, Iraci del Nero da. "Análise da morbidade nas Gerais (Villa Rica, 1799-1801)," Revista de história, 54 (no. 107)(1976), pp. 241-62.

2235. Donald, Cleveland, Jr. "Slave Resistance and Abolitionism in Brazil: The Campista Case, 1879-1888," Luso-Brazilian Review, 13, 2 (1976), pp. 182-93.

2236. _____. "Slavery and Abolition in Campos, Brazil, 1830-1888" (PhD diss., Cornell University, 1973).

2237. Golgher, Isaías. "O negro e a mineração em Minas Gerais," Revista brasileira de estudos políticos, 18 (1965), pp. 133-50.

2238. Graham, Richard. "Brazilian Slavery Re-examined: A Review Article," Journal of Social History, 3, 4 (1970), pp. 431-53.

2239. Karasch, Mary C. "The African Heritage of Rio de Janeiro," in Pescatello, ed. Old Roots in New Lands, pp. 36-76.

2240. _____. "From Porterage to Proprietorship: African Occupations in Rio de Janeiro, 1808-1850," in Engerman and Genovese, eds., Race and Slavery, pp. 369-93.

2241. _____. "Manumission in the City of Rio de Janeiro, 1807-1851" (Paper presented at the American Historical Association, San Francisco, 1973).

2242. _____. "Slave Life in Rio de Janeiro, 1808-1850" (PhD diss., University of Wisconsin - Madison, 1972).

2243. Kiernan, James Patrick. "Baptism and Manumission in Brazil: Paraty, 1789-1822," Social Science History, 3, 1 (1978), pp. 56-71.

2244. _____. "The Manumission of Slaves in Colonial Brazil: Paraty, 1789-1822" (PhD diss., New York University, 1977).

2245. Levy, Barbara. "Participação da população livre e escrava numa codificação sócio-profissional do Rio de Janeiro (1850-1870): alguns aspectos," Anais do VI Simpósio nacional dos professores universitários de história (Goiâna, 1971) (São Paulo, 1973), vol. 1, pp. 639-58.

2246. *Libby, Douglas C. "O trabalho escravo na Mina de Morro Velho" (Thesis, Universidade federal de Minas Gerais, 1979).

2247. *Lima, Lana Lage da Gama. "A rebeldia negra em Campos na última decada da escravidão" (MA diss., Universidade Federal Fluminense, Niterói, 1977).

2248. Lopes, José da Paz. "A presença de escravos negros em uma corporação religiosa mineira durante os séculos XVIII e XIX," Anais do VI Simpósio nacional dos professores universitários de história (Goiâna, 1971) (São Paulo, 1973), vol. 2, pp. 325-27.

2249. *Luna, Francisco Vidal. "Minas Gerais: escravos e senhores - analise de estrutura populacional e econômica de alguns centros mineratorios" (PhD diss., Universidade de São Paulo, 1980).

2250. _____, and Iraci del Nero da Costa. "Algumas características do contingente de cativos em Minas Gerais," Anais do Museu Paulista, 29 (1979), pp. 79-97.

2251. _____. "Estrutura da massa escrava de algumas localidades mineiras (1804)," Revista do Instituto de estudos brasileiros, 23 (1981), pp. 137-42.

2252. _____. "Vila Rica: Nota sobre casamentos de escravos (1727-1826)," Africa (São Paulo), 4 (1981), pp. 105-09.

2253. Machado (Filho), Aires da Mata. O negro e o garimpo em Minas Gerais. Rio de Janeiro: José Olimpio, 1943.

2254. Martins, Roberto Borges. "Growing in Silence: The Slave Economy of Nineteenth-Century Minas Gerais, Brazil" (PhD diss., Vanderbilt University, 1980).

2255. _____. "Growing in Silence: The Slave Economy of Nineteenth-Century Minas Gerais, Brazil," Journal of Economic History, 42, 1 (1982), pp. 222-23.

2256. Martins Filho, Amilcar, and Roberto B. Martins. "Slavery and Economy in Nineteenth-Century Minas Gerais, Brazil: A Revisionist View" (Paper read to the Annual Meeting of the American Historical Association, Los Angeles, 1981).

2257. Nielson, Lawrence J. "Of Gentry, Peasants, and Slaves: Rural Society in Sabará and its Hinterland, 1780-1930" (PhD diss., University of California - Davis, 1975).

2258. Novaes, Maria Stella de. A escravidão e a abolição no Espírito Santo, história e folclore. Vitória: Departamento de Imprensa Oficial, 1963.

2259. Pinto, Luiz de Aguiar Costa. O negro no Rio de Janeiro, relações de raças numa sociedade em mudança. São Paulo: Companhia Editora Nacional, c. 1953.

2260. Renault, Delso. Industria, escravidão, sociedade: uma pesquisa historiográfica do Rio de Janeiro do século XIX. Rio de Janeiro: Civilização Brasileira, 1976.

2261. Russell-Wood, A. J. R. "Technology and Society: The Impact of Gold Mining on the Institution of Slavery in Portuguese America," Journal of Economic History, 37, 1 (1977), pp. 59-86. Reprinted as "The Other Slavery: Gold Mining and the 'Peculiar Institution'," in idem, Black Man in Slavery and Freedom, pp. 104-27.

2262. Santos, Corcino Medeiros dos. "O trabalho escravo numa grande propriedade rural: a Fazenda da Santa Cruz," Estudos históricos (Marília), 16 (1977), pp. 51-69.

2263. Scarano, Julita. Devoção e escravidão: Irmandade de Nossa Senhora do Rosário dos Pretos no Distrito Diamantino no século XVIII. São Paulo, 1976.

2264. Sousa, José Antônio Soares de. "O efêmero quilombo do Pati do Alferes em 1838," Revista do Instituto histórico e geográfico brasileiro, 295 (1972), pp. 33-69.

2265. Stein, Stanley J. Vassouras: A Brazilian Coffee County, 1850-1900. Cambridge, Mass.: Harvard University Press, 1957.

5. South

2266. Andrada, Antônio Manoel Bueno de. "A abolição em São Paulo," Revista do Arquivo municipal (São Paulo), 77 (1941), pp. 261-72.

2267. Bandecchi, Brasil. "Legislação da Província de São Paulo sobre escravos," Revista de história, 49 (no. 99)(1974), pp. 235-40.

2268. Boccia, Ana Maria Mathias, and Eneida Maria Malerbi. "O contrabando de escravos para São Paulo," Revista de história, 56 (no. 112)(1977), pp. 321-79.

2269. Canabrava, A. P. "Um desembarque clandestino de escravos em Canaéia," Revista de história, 1 (no. 4)(1950), pp. 559-62.

2270. Cardoso, Fernando Henrique. Capitalismo e escravidão no Brasil meridional: o negro na sociedade escravocrata do Rio Grande do Sul. São Paulo: Difusão Européia do Livro, 1962.

2271. Cardoso, Jayme Antônio, Sérgio Odilan Nadalin, and Carlos Roberto A. dos Santos. "Nota prévia sôbre o 'arrolamento de fontes para a história da escravidão' na correspondência dos presidentes da provincia do Paraná," Anais do VI Simpósio nacional dos professores universitários de história (Goiâna, 1971) (São Paulo, 1973), vol. 2, pp. 371-407.

2272. Castro, Jeanne Berrance de, and Júlia Maria Leonor Scarano. "A mão-de-obra escrava e estrangeira numa região de economia cafeeira (Uma experiência de pesquisa quantitativa na história rioclarense - 1875-1930)," Anais do VI Simpósio nacional dos professores universitários de história (Goiâna, 1971) (São Paulo, 1973), vol. 1, pp. 717-38.

2273. Cerqueira, Beatriz Westin de. "Um estudo da escravidão em Ubatuba," Estudos históricos (Marília), 5 (1966), pp. 7-58; 6 (1967), pp. 9-66.

2274. Dean, Warren. "The Planter as Entrepreneur: The Case of São Paulo," Hispanic American Historical Review, 46, 2 (1966), pp. 138-52.

2275. _____. Rio Claro: A Brazilian Plantation System. Stanford: Stanford University Press, 1976.

2276. _____. "A Slave Autograph, São Paulo, 1876," Luso-Brazilian Review, 7, 1 (1970), pp. 81-83.

2277. * _____. "Slavery on Coffee Plantations: Rio Claro, Brazil, 1820-1880" (Communication, II Symposium on Latin American Social and Economic History, 1972).

2278. El Murr, Victoria Namestnikov, and Joubran Jamil El Murr. "Fontes primárias do Município de Porto Belo (SC) (Escrituras referentes à compra e venda de escravos)," Anais do VI Simpósio nacional dos professores universitários de história (Goiâna, 1971) (São Paulo, 1973), vol. 2, pp. 429-32.

2279. Ellis Junior, Alfredo. "O negro no bandeirismo," Anais do 3 Congresso Sul-Riograndense de História e Geografia (Porto Alegre, 1940), vol. 3, pp. 1571-94.

2280. Ericksen, Nestor. O Negro no Rio Grande do Sul (Subsidios para a história da escravidão no Brasil). Porto Alegre: Of. Graf. da Libraria do Globo, 1941.

2281. _____. O negro no Rio Grande no sesquicentenário da imprensa rio-grandense. Porto Alegre: Sulina, 1977.

2282. Ferrarini, Sebastião. A escravidão negra na Província do Paraná. Curitiba: Editôra Lítero-Técnica, 1971.

2283. Franco, Maria Sylvia de Carvalho. Homens livres na ordem escravocrata. São Paulo: Instituto de estudos brasileiros, 1969.

2284. Gandía, Enrique de. Los misiones jesuíticas y los bandeirantes paulistas. Buenos Aires: Editorial "La Facultad", 1936.

2285. Gebara, Ademir. "O fazendeiro de escravos na cidade que cresce," Anais de história, 9 (1977), pp. 127-39.

2286. Holloway, Thomas H. "Immigration and Abolition: The Transition from Slave to Free Labor in the São Paulo Coffee Zone," in Dauril Alden and Warren Dean, eds., Essays Concerning the Socioeconomic History of Brazil and Portuguese India (Gainesville: University Presses of Florida, 1977), pp. 160-77.

2287. Ianni, Octavio. As metamorfoses do escravo: apogeu e crise da escravatura no Brasil meridional. São Paulo: Difusão Européia do Livro, 1962.

2288. *Laytano, Dante de. Alguns aspectos da história do negro no Rio Grande do Sul. Porto Alegre: Kosmos, 1942. (Rio Grande do Sul, Imagem da Terra Gaucha)

2289. _____. "O negro e o espírito guerreiro nas origens do Rio Grande do Sul," Revista do Instituto histórico e geográfico do Rio Grande do Sul, 17, 1 (no. 65), pp. 95-117.

2290. Leitman, Spencer L. "The Black Ragamuffins: Racial Hypocrisy in Nineteenth Century Southern Brazil," Americas, 33, 3 (1977), pp. 504-18.

2291. _____. "Slave Cowboys in the Cattle Lands of Southern Brazil, 1800-1850," Revista de história, 51 (no. 101)(1975), pp. 167-77.

2292. _____. "Slavery and Racial Democracy in Southern Brazil: A Look Back to the 19th Century," Présence africaine, 89 (1974), pp. 227-33.

2293. Lowrie, Samuel Harman. "O elemento negro na população de São Paulo," Revista do Arquivo municipal (São Paulo), 48 (1938), pp. 5-56.

2294. Maestri Filho, Mário José. "A origem do escravo gaúcho e a capitania do Rio Grande de São Pedro do Sul," Revista do Departamento de biblioteconomia e história (Fundação Universidade do Rio Grande), 1, 1 (1978), pp. 13-54.

2295. _____. Quilombos e quilombolas em terras gaúchas. Porto Alegre: Escola Superior de Teologia São Lourenço de Brindes, Caxias do Sul: Universidade de Caxias, 1979.

2296. _____. "A redução do cidadão José Martins, uruguaio, à escravidão: um documento," Revista do Departamento de biblioteconomia e história (Fundação Universidade do Rio Grande do Sul), 1, 2 (1979), pp. 37-44.

2297. Morse, Richard M. "The Negro in São Paulo, Brazil," Journal of Negro History, 38, 3 (1953), pp. 290-306.

2298. Morton, G. Nash. "Fazenda de Ibicada," Revista do Instituto histórico e geográfico de São Paulo, 23 (1925), pp. 255-78.

2299. Moura, Clovis. "Revoltas de escravos em São Paulo," Revista do Arquivo municipal (São Paulo), 181 (1970), pp. 101-11.

2300. Pádua, Ciro T. de. "O negro em São Paulo," Revista do Arquivo municipal (São Paulo), 77 (1941), pp. 201-20.

2301. _____. "O negro no planalto (do século XVI ao século XIX)," Revista do Instituto histórico e geográfico de São Paulo, 41 (1942), pp. 127-264.

2302. Piazza, Walter. O escravo numa economia minifundiária. São Paulo: Editora Resenha Universitária, 1975.

2303. Piccolo, Helga I. L. "Considerações em tôrno da interpretação de leis abolicionistas numa província fronteiriça: Rio Grande do Sul," Anais do VI Simpósio nacional dos professores universitários de história (Goiâna, 1971) (São Paulo, 1973), vol. 1, pp. 533-64.

2304. Queiroz, Suely Robles Reis de. Escravidão negra em São Paulo. Rio de Janeiro: Livraria José Olympio Editora, 1977.

2305. _____. "Uma insurreição de escravos em Campinas," Revista de história, 49 (no. 99)(1974), pp. 193-234.

2306. Ricardo, Cassiano. "O negro no bandeirismo paulista," Revista do Arquivo municipal (São Paulo), 47 (1938), pp. 5-46.

2307. *Santos, Carlos Roberto Antunes dos. "Economie de l'esclavage au Paraná, 1860-1887" (Thèse de 3ème cycle, Paris X, 1976).

2308. _____. "L'économie et la société esclavagistes au Paraná (Brésil) de 1854 à 1887," Cahiers des Amériques latines, 19 (1979), pp. 101-11.

2309. _____. "Nota prévia sôbre preços e
profissões de escravos na Província do Paraná," in Anais do VI
Simpósio nacional dos professores universitários de história
(Goiâna, 1971) (São Paulo, 1973), vol. 2, pp. 409-27.

2310. Santos, Ronaldo Marcos dos. O término do escravismo na província
de São Paulo (1885-1888). São Paulo, 1972.

2311. Silva, Maria Beatriz Nizza da. "Casamentos de escravos na
capitania de São Paulo," Ciência e cultura, 32, 7 (1980), pp.
816-21.

2312. Spalding, Walter. "A escravatura em Porto-Alegre," Anais do 3
Congresso Sul-Riograndense de História e Geografia (Porto Alegre,
1970), vol. 2, pp. 203-09.

2313. Toplin, Robert Brent. "Upheaval, Violence, and the Abolition of
Slavery in Brazil: The Case of São Paulo," Hispanic American
Historical Review, 49, 4 (1969), pp. 639-55. Also Bobbs-Merrill
Reprint no. BC-296.

2314. Westphalen, Cecília Maria. "A introdução de escravos novos no
litoral paranaense," Revista de história, 44 (no. 89)(1972), pp.
139-54.

6. West

2315. Moraes, Maria Augusta de Santana. "O abolicionismo em Goiás,"
Anais do VI Simpósio nacional dos professores universitários de
história (Goiâna, 1971) (São Paulo, 1973), vol. 1, pp. 659-96.

2316. Moreyra, Sérgio Paulo, Dulce Helená Alvares Pessoa Ramos, and
Katia Abud. "Arrolamento de fontes: livros de receita de siza de
escravos ladinos da Capitania de Goiás (1810-1822)," Anais do VI
Simpósio nacional dos professores universitários de história
(Goiâna, 1971) (São Paulo, 1973), vol. 2, pp. 433-86.

2317. Palacín, Luis. "Trabalho escravo: produção e produtividade nas
minas de Goias," Anais do VI Simpósio nacional dos professores
universitários de história (Goiâna, 1971) (São Paulo, 1973), vol.
1, pp. 433-48.

2318. Salles, Gilka Vasconcelos Ferreira de. "O trabalhador escravo em
Goiás nos séculos XVIII e XIX," Anais do VI Simpósio nacional dos
professores universitários de história (Goiâna, 1971) (São Paulo,
1973), vol. 1, pp. 599-638.

V. Caribbean

1. General and comparative

2319. Alden, John. "The Struggle Against Slavery: The Caribbean Collections of the Boston Public Library," Caribbean Archives/Archives antillaises/Archivos del Caribe, 2 (1974), pp. 7-12.

2320. *Alexandre, Mireille. "Le problème des races aux Antilles françaises et anglaises de 1800 à 1914 d'après les voyageurs" (Mémoire de maîtrise, Nanterre, 1970).

2321. Bangou, Henri. "L'abolition de l'esclavage dans la Caribe du point de vue de ses lois économiques et des initiatives humains," in Le passage de la société esclavagiste à la société post-esclavagiste au 19e siècle (Colloque d'histoire antillaise, Point-à-Pitre, 1971) (Point-à-Pitre, GURIC, Centre d'Enseignement Supérieur Littéraire, 1969-71), vol. 1, pp. 4-22.

2322. *Cardoso, Ciro Flamarion S. "Les économies esclavagistes dans l'aire des Caraïbes aux XVIIe et XVIIIe siècles: études comparées" (Thèse, Université de Paris X, 1976).

2323. *_____. "Método comparativo y técnicas de producción: el caso de las colonias esclavistas (siglo XVIII)" (Unpublished paper, III Simposio de historia económica de América latina, XLI International Congress of Americanists, Mexico, 1972).

2324. Clarke, John Henrik. "Slave Revolt in the Caribbean," Black World, 22, 4 (1973), pp. 12-25.

2325. _____. "Slave Revolts in the Caribbean Islands," Présence africaine, 84 (1972), pp. 117-30.

2326. Colloque d'histoire antillaise (1969). Le passage de la société esclavagiste à la société post-esclavagiste aux Antilles au XIXe siècle. 2 vols. Pointe-à-Pitre, 1971.

2327. Dirks, Robert. "Resource Fluctuations and Competitive Transformation in West Indian Slave Societies," in Charles D. Laughlin, Jr., and Ivan A. Brady, eds., Extinction and Survival in Human Populations (New York, 1978), pp. 122-80.

2328. _____. "Slaves Holiday," Natural History, 84, 10 (1975), pp. 82-91. Reprinted in David Rosen, ed., Readings in Anthropology 77/78 (Gilford: Dushkin Publishing, 1977); also in idem, Readings in Anthropology 80/81 (Gilford: Dushkin Publishing, 1979).

2329. Gaspar, D. Barry. "A Dangerous Spirit of Liberty: Slave Rebellion in the West Indies during the 1730s," Cimarrons, 1 (1981), pp. 79-91.

2330. Goveia, Elsa V. "Influence of Religion in the West Indies," Americas, 14, 4 (1958), pp. 510-16. Reprinted in History of Religion in the New World (Conference on the History of Religion in the New World During Colonial Times, Washington, 1958), pp. 174-80.

2331. _____. "The West Indian Slave Laws of the Eighteenth Century," Revista de ciencias sociales, 4, 1 (1960), pp. 75-106. Reprinted in Foner and Genovese, eds., Slavery in the New World, pp. 113-37.

2332. Green, William A. "Caribbean Historiography, 1600-1900: The Recent Tide," Journal of Interdisciplinary History, 7, 3 (1976-77), pp. 509-30.

2333. Groot, Silvia W. de. "The Boni Maroon War 1765-1793, Surinam and French Guyana," Boletín de estudios latinoamericanos y del Caribe (Amsterdam), 18 (1975), pp. 30-48.

2334. Hancock, Ian F. "The Fate of Gypsy Slaves in the West Indies" (Mimeographed, Trinidad, 1979).

2335. Handler, Jerome. "The Amerindian Slave Population of Barbados in the Seventeenth and Early Eighteenth Centuries," Journal of the Barbados Museum and Historical Society, 33, 3 (1970), pp. 111-36.

2336. Higman, Barry W. "Economics of Circum-Caribbean Slavery," in Rubin and Tuden, eds., Comparative Perspectives, pp. 143-44.

2337. _____. "Growth in Afro-Caribbean Slave Populations," American Journal of Physical Anthropology, 50, 3 (1979), pp. 373-85.

2338. Hoetink, Harmannus. "Master-Slave Relations and Race Relations, Negro and Coloured," reprinted (from Two Variants in Caribbean Race Relations) in Brown, ed., Slavery in American Society, pp. 72-77.

2339. Katz, Wallace. "Slavery and Caste: Plantation Society in the British and French Caribbean in the Eighteenth Century," King's Crown Essays, 6, 1 (1958-59), pp. 13-44.

2340. Kiple, Kenneth F., and Virginia H. Kiple. "Deficiency Diseases in the Caribbean," Journal of Interdisciplinary History, 11, 2 (1980), pp. 197-216.

2341. Lowenthal, David. "The Range and Variation of Caribbean Societies," in Social and Cultural Pluralism in the Caribbean (New York, 1960), pp. 786-95. (Annals of the New York Academy of Sciences, vol. 83, no. 5) Also Bobbs-Merrill Reprint no. BC-187.

2342. Mintz, Sidney W. "Caribbean Nationhood in Anthropological Perspective," in S. Lewis and T. G. Mathews, eds., Caribbean Integration: Papers on Social, Political and Economic Integration (3rd Caribbean Scholars Conference, Georgetown, Guyana, 1966) (Rio Piedras: Puerto Rican Institute of Caribbean Studies, University of Puerto Rico, 1967), pp. 141-54.

2343. _____. "The Caribbean Region," Daedalus, 103, 2 (1974), pp. 45-72.

2344. _____. Caribbean Transformations. Chicago: Aldine, 1974.

2345. _____. "Movements in Slave Populations of the Caribbean during the Period of Slave Registration," in Rubin and Tuden, eds., Comparative Perspectives, pp. 145-60.

2346. *Moore, R. Bobbie. "Lecture on the Socio-economic Background of the Caribbean" (Paper presented at the First Pan-Caribbean Consultation on Youth Work in the Provinces of the West Indies, University of Guyana, Georgetown, 1970).

2347. Schuler, Monica. "Ethnic Slave Rebellions in the Caribbean and the Guianas," Journal of Social History, 3, 4 (1970), pp. 374-85.

2348. Smith, M. G. "The African Heritage in the Caribbean," in Rubin, ed., Caribbean Studies, pp. 34-46.

2. English

2349. Abrahams, Roger D. After Africa: Extracts from British Travel Accounts and Journals of the Seventeenth, Eighteenth, and Nineteenth Centuries Concerning the Slaves, their Manners, and Customs in the British West Indies. New Haven: Yale University Press, 1983.

2350. Aufhauser, R. Keith. "Profitability of Slavery in the British Caribbean," Journal of Interdisciplinary History, 5, 1 (1974), pp. 45-67.

2351. Bean, Richard N. "Food Imports into the British West Indies: 1680-1845," in Rubin and Tuden, eds., Comparative Perspectives, pp. 581-90.

2352. Bennett, J. Harry, Jr. Bondsmen and Bishops: Slavery and Apprenticeship on the Codrington Plantations of Barbadoes, 1710-1838. Berkeley: University of California Press, 1958.

2353. _____. "The Problem of Slave Labor Supply at the Codrington Plantations," Journal of Negro History, 35, 4 (1951), pp. 406-41.

2354. Blouet, Olwyn M. "To Make Society Safe for Freedom, Slave Education in Barbados, 1823-1833," Journal of Negro History, 65, 2 (1980), pp. 126-34.

2355. Brathwaite, Edward K. "Caliban, Ariel, and the Unprospero in the Conflict of Creolization: A Study of the Slave Revolt in Jamaica in 1831-32," in Rubin and Tuden, eds., Comparative Perspectives, pp. 41-62.

2356. *_____. "Controlling Slaves in Jamaica" (Unpublished paper, 3rd Annual Conference of Caribbean Historians, University of Guyana, Georgetown, 1971).

2357. _____. The Development of Creole Society in Jamaica, 1770-1820. Oxford: Clarendon Press, 1971.

2358. _____. Folk Culture of the Slaves in Jamaica. London: New Beacon Press, 1970.

2359. _____. "Jamaican Slave Society, A Review," Race, 9, 3 (1968), pp. 331-42.

2360. *_____. White Power in Jamaica: The Interdynamics of Slave Control. Mona: ISER, forthcoming.

2361. Buckley, Roger Norman. "'Black Man': The Mutiny of the 8th (British) West India Regiment: A Microcosm of War and Slavery in the Caribbean," Jamaican Historical Review, 12 (1980), pp. 52-74.

2362. _____. Slaves in Red Coats: The British West India Regiments, 1795-1815. New Haven: Yale University Press, 1979.

2363. Buhler, Richard O. "Slavery in Belize," National Studies (Belize City), 1, 2 (1973), pp. 2-4; 1, 3 (1973), pp. 9-11; 1, 4 (1973), pp. 12-14.

2364. Buisseret, David J. "Slaves Arriving in Jamaica, 1684-1692," Revue française d'histoire d'outre-mer, 64, 1 (no. 234)(1977), pp. 85-88.

2365. Bush, Barbara. "White 'Ladies', Coloured 'Favorites' and Black 'Wenches': Some Considerations on Sex, Race and Class Factors in Social Relations in White Creole Society in the British Caribbean," Slavery and Abolition, 2, 3 (1981), pp. 245-62.

2366. Campbell, Mavis C. The Dynamics of Change in a Slave Society: A Sociopolitical History of the Free Coloreds of Jamaica, 1800-1865. Rutherford, N.J.: Fairleigh Dickinson University Press, 1976.

2367. _____. "The Maroons of Jamaica: Imperium in Imperio," Pan-African Journal, 6, 1 (1975), pp. 45-55.

2368. _____. "Marronage in Jamaica: Its Origin in the Seventeenth Century," in Rubin and Tuden, eds., Comparative Perspectives, pp. 389-419.

2369. Carroll, William Edward. "The End of Slavery: Imperial Policy and Colonial Reaction in British Guiana" (PhD diss., University of Michigan, 1970).

2370. Cary, Beverley. "The Windward Maroons after the Peace Treaty," Jamaica Journal, 4, 4 (1970), pp. 19-22.

2371. Cave, Roderick. "Four Slave Songs from St. Bartholomew," Caribbean Quarterly, 25, 1-2 (1979), pp. 85-90.

2372. Chamberlin, David. Smith of Demerara (Martyr-Teacher of the Slaves). London: Simpkin, Marshall, Hamilton, Kent & Co., 1923.

2373. Chancellor, V. E. "Slave-Owner and Anti-Slaver: Henry Richard Vassall Fox, 3rd Lord Holland, 1800-1840," Slavery and Abolition, 1, 3 (1980), pp. 263-75.

2374. *Clarke, John Henrik. Testing the Chains: Slave Rebellions in the British West Indies. Ithaca, N.Y.: Cornell University Press, forthcoming.

2375. Comitas, Lambros, and David Lowenthal, eds. Slaves, Free Men, Citizens: West Indian Perspectives. Garden City: Anchor Books, 1973.

2376. Cousins, Winifred M. "Slave Family Life in the British Colonies: 1800-1834," Sociological Review, 27, 1 (1935), pp. 35-55.

2377. Cox, Edward Locksley. "Fedon's Rebellion 1795-96: Causes and Consequences," Journal of Negro History, 67, 1 (1982), pp. 7-19.

2378. _____. "The Shadow of Freedom: Freemen in the Slave Societies of Granada and St. Kitts, 1763-1833" (PhD diss., Johns Hopkins University, 1977).

2379. Craton, Michael M. "Changing Patterns of Slave Family in the British West Indies," Journal of Interdisciplinary History, 10, 1 (1979), pp. 1-37.

2380. _____. "Christianity and Slavery in the British West Indies 1750-1865," Historical Reflections/Réflexions historiques, 5, 2 (1978), pp. 141-60.

2381. _____. "A Cresting Wave? Recent Trends in the Historiography of Slavery, with Special Reference to the British Caribbean," Historical Reflections/Réflexions historiques, 9, 3 (1982), pp. 403-19.

2382. _____. "Death, Disease and Medicine on Jamaican Slave Plantations: The Example of Worthy Park, 1767-1838," Histoire sociale/Social History, 9 (no. 18)(1976), pp. 237-55.

2383. _____. "Hobbesian or Panglossian? The Two Extremes of Slave Conditions in the British Caribbean, 1783 to 1834," William and Mary Quarterly, 3rd ser., 35, 2 (1978), pp. 324-56.

2384. _____. "Jamaican Slave Mortality: Fresh Light from Worthy Park, Longville, and the Tharp Estates," Journal of Caribbean History, 3 (1971), pp. 1-27.

2385. _____. "Jamaican Slavery," in Engerman and Genovese, eds., Race and Slavery, pp. 249-84.

2386. _____. "The Passion to Exist: Slave Rebellions in the British West Indies, 1650-1822," Journal of Caribbean History, 13 (1980), pp. 1-20.

2387. _____. "Proto-Peasant Revolts? The Late Slave Rebellions in the British West Indies 1816-1832," Past and Present, 85 (1979), pp. 99-125.

2388. _____. "Searching for the Invisible Man: Problems of Writing on Slave Society in the British West Indies," Historical Reflections/Réflexions historiques, 1, 1 (1974), pp. 37-57.

2389. _____. Searching for the Invisible Man: Slaves and Plantation Life in Jamaica. Cambridge, Mass.: Harvard University Press, 1977.

2390. _____. "Slave Culture, Resistance and the Achievement of Emancipation in the British West Indies, 1783-1838," in Walvin, ed., Slavery and British Society, pp. 100-22.

2391. *_____, and Susan Chackco. "Perceptions of Slavery: A Preliminary Excursion into the Possibilities of Oral History in Rural Jamaica" (Paper presented to the 6th Annual Conference of Caribbean Historians, University of Puerto Rico, 1974).

2392. _____, and James Walvin. A Jamaican Plantation: The History of Worthy Park, 1670-1970. Toronto: University of Toronto Press, 1970.

2393. Davis, David Brion. "British Emancipation as a New Moral Dispensation," Rice University Studies, 67, 1 (1981), pp. 43-55. (Martin J. Wiener, ed., "'Humanitarianism or Control?' A Symposium on Aspects of Nineteenth Century Social Reform in Britain and America")

2394. *Dirks, Robert. Black Saturnalia: An Ethnohistory of the British West Indian Slave Culture. Forthcoming.

2395. Drescher, Seymour. Econocide: British Slavery in the Era of Abolition. Pittsburgh: University of Pittsburgh Press, 1977.

2396. Dunn, Richard S. Sugar and Slaves: The Rise of the Planter Class in the English West Indies, 1624-1713. Chapel Hill: University of North Carolina Press, 1972.

2397. Eyre, L. Alan. "The Maroon Wars in Jamaica – a Geographical Appraisal," Jamaican Historical Review, 12 (1980), pp. 5-19.

2398. Farley, Rawle. "The Shadow and the Substance: A Study of Aspects of the Economic and Social Structure and the Change in Economic and Social Relations Between Whites and Coloured Free in Slave Society in British Guiana," Caribbean Quarterly, 4, 2 (1955), pp. 132-53.

2399. *Friedman, Gerald. "The Demography of Trinidad Slavery" (Unpublished Paper, Harvard University, n.d.).

2400. _____. "The Heights of Slaves in Trinidad," Social Science History, 6, 4 (1982), pp. 482-515.

2401. Frucht, Richard. "Emancipation and Revolt in the West Indies: St. Kitts, 1834," Science and Society, 39, 2 (1975), pp. 199-214.

2402. _____. "From Slavery to Unfreedom in the Plantation Society of St. Kitts," in Rubin and Tuden, eds., Comparative Perspectives, pp. 379-88.

2403. Furley, Oliver W. "Moravian Missionaries and Slaves in the West Indies," Caribbean Studies, 5, 2 (1965), pp. 3-16.

2404. Furness, A. E. "The Maroon War of 1795," Jamaican Historical Review, 5 (1965), pp. 30-49.

2405. Gaspar, D. Barry. "The Antigua Slave Conspiracy of 1736: A Case Study of the Origins of Collective Resistance," William and Mary Quarterly, 3rd ser., 35, 2 (1978), pp. 308-23.

2406. _____. "Runaways in Seventeenth-Century Antigua, West Indies," Boletín de estudios latinoamericanos y del Caribe (Amsterdam), 26 (1979), pp. 3-13.

2407. _____. "Slave Resistance and Social Control in Antigua, 1700-1763" (PhD diss. Johns Hopkins University, 1974).

2408. Geggus, David P. "Jamaica and the Saint Domingue Slave Revolt, 1791-1793," Americas, 38, 2 (1981), pp. 219-33.

2409. Gemery, Henry A., and Jan S. Hogendorn. "Elasticity of Slave Labor Supply and the Development of Slave Economies in the British Caribbean: The Seventeenth Century Experience," in Rubin and Tuden, eds., Comparative Perspectives, pp. 72-83.

2410. Goveia, Elsa V. Slave Society in the British Leeward Islands at the End of the 18th Century. New Haven: Yale University Press, 1965.

2411. Green, William A. British Slave Emancipation: The Sugar Colonies and the Great Experiment, 1830-1865. Oxford: Clarendon Press, 1976.

2412. Greene, Jack P. "Society and Economy in the British Caribbean during the Seventeenth and Eighteenth Centuries (review article)," American Historical Review, 79, 5 (1974), pp. 1499-1517.

2413. Gross, Izhak. "The Abolition of Negro Slavery and British Parliamentary Politics, 1832-1833," Historical Journal, 23, 1 (1980), pp. 63-85.

2414. Hadel, Richard E. "Slave Trials in Belize," National Studies (Belize City), 3, 2 (1975), pp. 1-7.

2415. Hall, Douglas. "Absentee-Proprietorship in the British West Indies, to About 1850," Jamaican Historical Review, 4 (1964), pp. 15-34. Reprinted in Comitas and Lowenthal, eds., Slaves, Free Men, Citizens, pp. 107-35.

2416. _____. "The Apprenticeship Period in Jamaica, 1834-1838," Caribbean Quarterly, 3, 3 (1953), pp. 142-66.

2417. _____. "Jamaica," in Cohen and Greene, eds., Neither Slave nor Free, pp. 193-213.

2418. _____. "Slaves and Slavery in the British West Indies," Social and Economic Studies, 11, 4 (1962), pp. 305-18.

2419. _____. "The Social and Economic Background to Sugar in Slave Days (with Special Reference to Jamaica)," Caribbean Historical Review, 3-4 (1954), pp. 149-69.

2420. Hall, Neville. "The Judicial System of a Plantation Society – Barbados on the Eve of Emancipation," in Le passage de la société esclavagiste à la société post-esclavagiste au 19e siècle (Colloque d'histoire antillaise, Point-à-Pitre, Guadeloupe, 1971) (Point-à-Pitre, GURIC, Centre d'Enseignement Supérieur Littéraire, 1969-71), vol. 1, pp. 38-70.

2421. Handler, Jerome S. "The Amerindian Slave Population of Barbados in the Seventeenth and Early Eighteenth Centuries," Caribbean Studies, 8, 4 (1969), pp. 38-64.

2422. _____. "An Archaeological Investigation of the Domestic Life of Plantation Slaves in Barbados," Journal of the Barbados Museum and Historical Society, 34, 2 (1972), pp. 64-72.

2423. _____. The Unappropriated People: Freedmen in the Slave Society of Barbados. Baltimore: Johns Hopkins University Press, 1974.

2424. _____, and Robert S. Corruccini. "Plantation Life in Barbados: A Physical Anthropological Analysis," Journal of Interdisciplinary History, 14, 1 (1983), pp. 65-90.

2425. _____, and Charlotte J. Frisbie. "Aspects of Slave Life in Barbados: Music and its Cultural Context," Caribbean Studies, 11, 4 (1972), pp. 5-46.

2526. _____, and Frederick W. Lange (with the assistance of Robert V. Riordan). Plantation Slavery in Barbados: An Archeological and Historical Investigation. Cambridge, Mass.: Harvard University Press, 1978.

2427. _____, and Arnold A. Sio. "Barbados," in Cohen and Greene, eds., Neither Slave nor Free, pp. 214-57.

2428. Hart, Richard. "Cudjoe and the First Maroon War," Caribbean Historical Review, 1 (1950), pp. 46-79.

2429. _____. Out of the House of Bondage: A Brief Account of Some of the Principal Events in the Struggle Against Slavery in Jamaica. Georgetown, Guyana, 1965.

2430. _____. Slaves Who Abolished Slavery. Mona, Jamaica: Institute of Social and Economic Research, University of the West Indies, 1980.

2431. Heuman, Gad J. Between Black and White: Race, Politics, and the Free Coloreds in Jamaica, 1792-1865. Westport, Conn.: Greenwood Press, 1981.

2432. Higham, C. S. S. "The Negro Policy of Christopher Codrington," Journal of Negro History, 10, 1 (1925), pp. 150-53.

2433. Higman, Barry W. "African and Creole Slave Family Patterns in Trinidad," Journal of Family History, 3, 2 (1978), pp. 163-80. Also in Margaret E. Crahan and Franklin W. Knight, eds., Africa and the Caribbean: The Legacies of a Link (Baltimore: Johns Hopkins University Press, 1979), pp. 41-64.

2434. *_____. "The Demography of Slavery in Jamaica, 1817-34" (Paper presented to the 3rd Annual Conference of Caribbean Historians, University of Guyana, Georgetown, 1971).

2435. _____. "Household Structure and Fertility on Jamaican Slave Plantations: A Nineteenth-century Example," Population Studies, 27, 3 (1973), pp. 527-50.

2436. _____. "The Slave Family and Household in the British West Indies, 1800-1834," Journal of Interdisciplinary History, 6, 2 (1975), pp. 261-87.

2437. _____. Slave Population and Economy in Jamaica, 1807-1834. Cambridge: Cambridge University Press, 1976.

2438. _____. "The Slave Populations of the British Caribbean: Some Nineteenth-Century Variations," in Samuel Proctor, ed., Eighteenth-Century Florida and the Caribbean (Gainesville: University Presses of Florida, 1976), pp. 60-70.

2439. _____. "Slavery Remembered: The Celebration of Emancipation in Jamaica," Journal of Caribbean History, 12 (1979), pp. 55-74.

2440. Hurwitz, Samuel J., and Edith F. Hurwitz. "A Token of Freedom: Private Bill Legislation for Free Negroes in Eighteenth-Century Jamaica," William and Mary Quarterly, 3rd ser., 24, 3 (1967), pp. 423-31.

2441. *Jesse, Rev. Charles. "Sketch for a Picture of Slavery in St.-Lucia in the 18th and 19th Centuries" (Typescript, n.p., n.d.).

2442. Keith, Nelson, and Novella Keith. "The Evolution of Social Classes in Jamaica," Plantation Society in the Americas, 1, 1 (1979), pp. 81-108.

2443. *Kerns, Virginia. "Feast and Famine: Slave Hunger and Theft in the British West Indies" (unpublished paper, n.d.).

2444. Kopytoff, Barbara Klamon. "Colonial Treaty as Sacred Charter of the Jamaican Maroons," Ethnohistory, 26, 1 (1979), pp. 45-64.

2445. _____. "The Development of Jamaican Maroon Ethnicity," Caribbean Quarterly, 22, 2-3 (1976), pp. 33-50.

2446. _____. "The Early Political Development of Jamaican Maroon Societies," William and Mary Quarterly, 3rd ser., 35, 2 (1978), pp. 287-307.

2447. _____. "Guerrilla Warfare in Eighteenth Century Jamaica," Expedition, 19, 2 (1977), pp. 20-26.

2448. _____. "Jamaican Maroon Political Organization: The Effects of the Treaties," Social and Economic Studies, 25, 2 (1976), pp. 87-105.

2449. _____. "Maroon Jerk Pork and Other Jamaican Cooking," in Jessica Kuper, ed., The Anthropologists' Cookbook (London: Routledge and Kegan Paul, 1977), pp. 141-46.

2450. _____. "The Maroons of Jamaica: An Ethnohistorical Study of Incomplete Polities" (PhD diss., University of Pennsylvania, 1973).

2451. Lane, Carl A. "Concerning Jamaica's 1760 Slave Rebellions," Jamaica Journal, 7, 4 (1973), pp. 2-4.

2452. Lange, Frederick W. "Slave Mortuary Practices, Barbados, West Indies," in Actas del XLI Congresso Internacional de Americanistas (México, 1974) (Mexico, 1976), vol. 2, pp. 477-83.

2453. Latimer, James. "The Apprenticeship System in the British West Indies during the Period Just Before Emancipation to Prepare the Slaves for Freedom," Journal of Negro Education, 33, 1 (1964), pp. 52-57.

2454. Laurence, K. O. "The Settlement of Free Negroes in Trinidad before Emancipation," Caribbean Quarterly, 9, 1-2 (1963), pp. 26-52.

2455. Levy, Claude. "Barbados: The Last Years of Slavery 1823-1833," Journal of Negro History, 44, 4 (1959), pp. 308-45.

2456. _____. "Slavery and the Emancipation Movement in Barbados, 1650-1833," Journal of Negro History, 55, 1 (1970), pp. 1-14.

2457. Lindo, Locksley. "Francis Williams - A Free Negro in a Slave World," Savacou, 1, 1 (1970), pp. 75-80.

2458. Low, W. Augustus, ed., "A Record from an Eighteenth Century Jamaican Estate," Journal of Negro History, 59, 2 (1974), pp. 168-69.

2459. Lowenthal, David, and Colin G. Clarke. "Slave-Breeding in Barbuda: The Past of a Negro Myth," in Rubin and Tuden, eds., Comparative Perspectives, pp. 510-35.

2460. "The Maroons in the 18th Century: A Note on Indirect Rule in Jamaica," Caribbean Quarterly, 8, 1 (1962), pp. 25-27.

2461. Marshall, Bernard A. "The Black Caribs: Native Resistance to British Penetration into the Windward Side of St. Vincent, 1763-1773," Pan-African Journal, 8, 2 (1975), pp. 139-52.

2462. * _____. "The Free Coloureds in the Slave Society of the Ceded Islands of the Eastern Caribbean up to the Decade Before Emancipation" (Paper presented to the 6th Annual Conference of Caribbean Historians, University of Puerto Rico, 1974).

2463. _____. "Maronage in Slave Plantation Societies: A Case Study of Dominica, 1785-1815," Caribbean Quarterly, 22, 2-3 (1976), pp. 26-32.

2464. * _____. "Slavery and the Plantation System in the British Windward Islands up to the First Quarter of the 19th Century" (Paper presented to the 3rd Annual Conference of Caribbean Historians, University of Guyana, Georgetown, 1971).

2465. Mathieson, William L. British Slavery and Its Abolition, 1823-1838. London: Longmans Green, 1926.

2466. Mathurin, Lucille. The Rebel Woman in the British West Indies During Slavery. Kingston: Institute of Jamaica for the African-Caribbean Institute of Jamaica, 1975.

2467. Mintz, Sidney W. "Slavery and the Slaves (review essay on Patterson, Sociology of Slavery)," Caribbean Studies, 8, 4 (1969), pp. 65-70.

2468. Molen, Patricia A. "Population and Social Patterns in Barbados in the Early Eighteenth Century," William and Mary Quarterly, 3rd ser., 28, 2 (1971), pp. 287-300.

2469. Moohr, Michael. "The Economic Impact of Slave Emancipation in British Guiana, 1832-1852," Economic History Review, 25, 4 (1972), pp. 588-607.

2470. Moore, Robert J. "La abolición de la esclavitud en el Caribe británico: supuestos y respuestas," La Torre, 21, 81-82 (1973), pp. 267-82.

2471. * _____. "Slave Rebellions in Guyana," in Papers Presented at the 3rd Annual Conference of Caribbean Historians (University of Guyana, Georgetown, 1971), pp. 62-74.

2472. *Mullin, Michael. "Maroon Women" (Paper presented at the 12th Conference of Caribbean Historians, Trinidad, 1980).

2473. _____. "Slave Obeahmen and Slaveowning Patriarchs in an Era of War and Revolution (1776-1807)," in Rubin and Tuden, eds., Comparative Perspectives, pp. 481-90.

2474. Newman, Peter. "Persistent Plantations," _Caribbean Studies_, 14, 3 (1974), pp. 121-26.

2475. Ottley, Carlton Robert. _Slavery Days in Trinidad: A Social History of the Island from 1797-1838_. Trinidad, 1974.

2476. Packwood, Cyril Outerbridge. _Chained on the Rock: Slavery in Bermuda_. New York: Eliseo Torres & Sons, 1975.

2477. Pares, Richard. _Merchants and Planters_. Cambridge: Cambridge University Press, 1960.

2478. Patterson, Orlando. "From Endo-deme to Matri-deme: An Interpretation of the Development of Kinship and Social Organization among the Slaves of Jamaica, 1655-1830," in Samuel Proctor, ed., _Eighteenth-Century Florida and the Caribbean_ (Gainesville: University Presses of Florida, 1976), pp. 50-59.

2479. _____. "The General Causes of Jamaican Slave Revolts," in Foner and Genovese, eds., _Slavery in the Americas_, pp. 211-18. (Reprinted from _The Sociology of Slavery_.)

2480. _____. "Slavery, Acculturation and Social Change: The Jamaican Case," _British Journal of Sociology_, 17, 2 (1966), pp. 151-64.

2481. _____. "Slavery and Slave Revolts: A Socio-Historical Analysis of the First Maroon War, 1655-1740," _Social and Economic Studies_, 19, 3 (1970), pp. 289-325.

2482. _____. _The Sociology of Slavery: An Analysis of the Origins, Development and Structure of Negro Slave Society in Jamaica_. London: MacGibbon and Kee, 1967.

2483. Phillips, Ulrich B. "An Antigua Plantation, 1769-1818," _North Carolina Historical Review_, 3, 3 (1926), pp. 439-45.

2484. _____. "A Jamaica Slave Plantation," _American Historical Review_, 19, 3 (1914), pp. 543-58.

2485. Pierre, C. E. "The Work of the Society for the Propagation of the Gospel in Foreign Parts among Negroes in the Colonies," _Journal of Negro History_, 1, 4 (1916), pp. 349-60.

2486. Pitman, Frank Wesley. "Slavery on the British West India Plantations in the Eighteenth Century," _Journal of Negro History_, 11, 4 (1926), pp. 584-668.

2487. Ragatz, Lowell J. _The Fall of the Planter Class in the British Caribbean 1763-1833: A Study in Social and Economic History_. New York: Century, 1928.

2488. Reckord, Mary. "The Jamaican Slave Rebellion of 1831," _Past and Present_, 40 (1968), pp. 108-25. Reprinted in Frucht, ed., _Black Society in the New World_, pp. 50-66.

2489. _____. "Missions in Jamaica before Emancipation: A Comment on 'Moravian Missionaries and Slaves in the West Indies' (by O. W. Furley)," Caribbean Studies, 8, 1 (1968), pp. 69-74. Also "A Reply" by Furley, p. 74.

2490. Reynolds, C. Roy. "Tacky and the Great Slave Rebellion of 1760," Jamaica Journal, 6, 2 (1972), pp. 5-8.

2491. Rice, C. Duncan. "Enlightenment, Evangelism, and Economics: An Interpretation of the Drive towards Emancipation in British West India," in Rubin and Tuden, eds., Comparative Perspectives, pp. 123-31.

2492. Roberts, G. W. "A Life Table for a West Indian Slave Population," Population Studies, 5, 3 (1952), pp. 238-43.

2493. Robinson, Carey. The Fighting Maroons of Jamaica. London: Collins and Sangster, 1969.

2494. Rodney, Walter, and Earl Augustus. "The Negro Slave," Caribbean Quarterly, 10, 2 (1964), pp. 40-47.

2495. Rooke, Patricia T. "The 'New Mechanic' in Slave Society: Socio-Psychological Motivations and Evangelical Missionaries in the British West Indies," Journal of Religious History, 11, 1 (1980), pp. 77-94.

2496. Rouse-Jones, Margaret Deanne. "St. Kitts, 1713-1763: A Study of the Development of a Plantation Colony" (PhD diss., Johns Hopkins University, 1978).

2497. Rubin, Vera, ed. Caribbean Studies: A Symposium. Seattle: University of Washington Press, 1960. (American Association for the Advancement of Science, Papers for Annual Meeting, 1956)

2498. Schafer, Daniel L. "The Maroons of Jamaica: African Slave Rebels in the Caribbean" (PhD diss., University of Minnesota, 1973).

2499. Schuler, Monica. "Akan Slave Rebellions in the British Caribbean," Savacou, 1, 1 (1970), pp. 8-31.

2500. _____. "Ethnic Slave Rebellions in the Caribbean and the Guianas," Journal of Social History, 3, 4 (1970), pp. 374-85.

2501. Senior, Carl H. "Robert Kerr Emigrants of 1840: Irish 'Slaves' for Jamaica," Jamaica Journal, 12 (no. 42)(1978), pp. 104-16.

2502. Sheppard, Jill. "The Slave Conspiracy That Never Was," Journal of the Barbados Museum and Historical Society, 34, 4 (1974), pp. 190-97.

2503. Sheridan, Richard B. "The Crisis of Slave Subsistence in the British West Indies During and After the American Revolution," William and Mary Quarterly, 3rd ser., 33, 4 (1976), pp. 615-41.

2504. _____. "The Jamaican Slave Insurrection Scare of 1776 and the American Revolution," Journal of Negro History, 61, 3 (1976), pp. 290-309.

2505. _____. "Mortality and the Medical Treatment of Slaves in the British West Indies," in Engerman and Genovese, eds., Race and Slavery, pp. 285-310.

2506. _____. "The Role of the Scots in the Economy and Society of the West Indies," in Rubin and Tuden, eds., Comparative Perspectives, pp. 94-106.

2507. * _____. "Slave Demography in the British West Indies and the Abolition of the Slave Trade" (forthcoming).

2508. _____. Sugar and Slavery: An Economic History of the British West Indies, 1623-1775. Baltimore: Johns Hopkins University Press, 1974.

2509. _____. "The West India Sugar Crisis and British Slave Emancipation, 1830-1833," Journal of Economic History, 21, 4 (1961), pp. 539-51.

2510. Short, K. R. M. "Jamaican Christian Missions and the Great Slave Rebellion of 1831-32," Journal of Ecclesiastical History, 27, 1 (1976), pp. 57-72.

2511. Sio, Arnold. "Race, Color and Miscegenation: The Free Coloured of Jamaica and Barbados," Caribbean Studies, 16, 1 (1976), pp. 5-21.

2512. Smith, Robert Worthington. "The Legal Status of Jamaican Slaves before the Anti-Slavery Movement," Journal of Negro History, 30, 3 (1945), pp. 293-303.

2513. *Synnott, Anthony. "Slave Revolts in Guyana and Trinidad: A History and Comparative Analysis" (Unpublished manuscript, Sir George Williams University, 1971).

2514. Taylor, S. A. G. "The Genesis of the Leeward Maroons," Bulletin of the Jamaica Historical Society, 4, 16 (1968), pp. 301-04.

2515. Teulon, Alan E. "The Windward Maroons," Bulletin of the Jamaica Historical Society, 4, 16 (1968), pp. 304-09.

2516. *Thompson, Alvin. "Some Problems of Slave Desertion in Guyana, c. 1750-1814" (Unpublished paper, University of the West Indies, 1976).

2517. Thoms, D. W. "Slavery in the Leeward Islands in the Mid-Eighteenth Century: A Reappraisal," Bulletin of the Institute of Historical Research, 42 (no. 105)(1969), pp. 76-85.

2518. Turner, Mary. "The Bishop of Jamaica and Slave Instruction," Journal of Ecclesiastical History, 26, 4 (1975), pp. 363-78.

2519. <u>West Indian Slavery: Selected Pamphlets</u>. Westport, Conn.: Negro Universities Press, 1970.

2520. White, Elain. "The Maroon Warriors of Jamaica and their Successful Resistance to Enslavement," <u>Pan-African Journal</u>, 6, 3 (1973), pp. 297-312.

3. Spanish

2521. "Acta del Ayuntamiento de la Habana: sobre manumisión de esclavos (Archivos Cubanos)," <u>Revista bimestre cubana</u>, 7 (1912), pp. 474-78.

2522. Aimes, Hubert H. S. <u>A History of Slavery in Cuba, 1511 to 1868</u>. New York: G. P. Putnam's Sons, 1907.

2523. *Aizy, Christian. "La condition socio-politique du noir à Hispaniola aux XVIe et XVIIe siècles" (Thèse d'état, Université de Paris X, n.d.).

2524. Alegría, Ricardo E. "El Rey Miguel: Heroe puertorriqueño de la lucha por la libertad de los esclavos," <u>Revista de historia de América</u>, 85 (1976), pp. 9-26.

2525. _____. "Los orígenes de la esclavitud negra en Puerto Rico, <u>Revista del Instituto de cultura puertorriqueña</u>, 16 (no. 61)(1973), pp. 3-7.

2526. Alvarez Nazario, Manuel. "Nuevos datos sobre las procedencias de los antiguos esclavos de Puerto Rico," <u>La Torre</u>, 21, 81-82 (1973), pp. 23-37.

2527. Andreu Ocariz, Juan José. "La rebelión de los esclavos de Boca Nigua," <u>Anuario de estudios americanos</u>, 27 (1970), pp. 551-81.

2528. *_____. "Un proyecto para la limitación de la esclavitud negra en Santo Domingo en 1795," in <u>Miscelánea ofrecida al Ilmo. José María Lacarra y de Miguel</u> (Zaragoza: Universidad de Zaragoza, 1968), vol. 1, pp. 103-45.

2529. Baralt, Guillermo Antonio. "Slave Conspiracies and Uprisings in Puerto Rico, 1796-1848" (PhD diss., University of Chicago, 1977). Translated as <u>Esclavos rebeldes: conspiraciones y sublevaciones de esclavos en Puerto Rico (1795-1873)</u>. Río Piedras: Ediciones Huracán, 1982.

2530. Barnet, Miguel. "Biografía de un cimarrón," <u>Etnología y folklore</u> (Havana), 1 (1966), pp. 65-83.

2531. Bernaldo de Quiros, Constancio. "Penalidad en el Código Negro de la Isla Española," <u>Boletín del Archivo General de la Nación</u> (Santo Domingo), 5 (no. 23)(1942), pp. 271-81.

2532. Cantos, Angel López. "Notas para el estudio de la esclavitud en Puerto Rico," <u>Revista del Instituto de cultura puertorriqueña</u>, 16 (no. 61)(1973), pp. 20-26.

2533. Cardoso, Onelio Jorge. "La conversación de un hombre de 106 años," *Bohemia*, 58, 37 (1966), p. 33.

2534. Caro Costas, Cirda R. "La real cédula de 1788 y dos reglamentos antillanos sobre la educación, trato y ocupación de los esclavos," *La Torre*, 21, 81-82 (1973), pp. 103-30.

2535. Carpentier, Alejo. "Busca e indagación del tiempo ido," *Bohemia*, 58, 37 (1966), p. 33.

2536. "Centenario de la abolición de la esclavitud," special issue of the *Revista de la Biblioteca Nacional José Martí*, 22, 3 (1980).

2537. Cepero Bonilla, Raúl. *Obras históricas*. Havana: Instituto de historia, 1963.

2538. Corwin, Arthur F. *Spain and the Abolition of Slavery in Cuba, 1817-1886*. Austin: University of Texas Press, 1967.

2539. Cortés Alonso, Vicenta. "La liberación del esclavo," *Anuario de estudios americanos*, 22 (1965), pp. 533-68.

2540. Cosculluela, Juan Antonio. "Cuatro años en la Ciénaga de Zapata: epoca de esclavitud," *Revista de arqueología y etnología* (Havana), año 6, epoca 2 (no. 12)(1951), pp. 82-86.

2541. Cuchi-Coll, Isabel. *Historia de la esclavitud en Puerto Rico*. San Juan: Sociedad de Autores Puertorriqueños, 1969.

2542. Curet, José. "From Slave to *Liberto*: A Study on Slavery and its Abolition in Puerto Rico, 1840-1880" (PhD diss., Columbia University, 1980).

2543. Dalton, Margarita. "Los depósitos de cimarrones en el siglo XIX," *Etnología y folklore* (Havana), 3 (1967), pp. 5-29.

2544. Davila, Arturo V. "Aspectos de una pastoral de esclavitud en Puerto Rico durante el siglo diecinueve: 1803-1873," *La Torre*, 21, 81-82 (1973), pp. 39-102.

2545. _____. "Don Jerónimo Mariano Usera y Alarcón, Dean de Puerto Rico - 1853-1863 - en la crisis del sistema esclavista," *La Torre*, 21, 81-82 (1973), pp. 131-73.

2546. Deive, Carlos Esteban. *La esclavitud del negro en Santo Domingo (1492-1844)*. Santo Domingo: Museo del Hombre Dominicano, 1980. 2 vols.

2547. Deschamps Chapeaux, Pedro. "Cimarrones urbanos," *Revista de la Biblioteca Nacional José Martí*, 11, 2 (1969), pp. 145-64. Reprinted in Juan Pérez de la Riva and idem, *Contribución a la historia de la gente sin historia* (Havana: Editorial de Ciencias Sociales, 1974), pp. 29-53.

2548. _____. *El negro en la economía habanera del siglo XIX*. Havana: Union de Escritores y Artistas de Cuba, 1971.

2549. "Diálogo con Miguel Barnet, autor de 'Biografía de un cimarrón'," Bohemia, 58, 37 (1966), p. 34.

2550. Díaz Soler, Luis M. "The Abolition of Slavery in Puerto Rico, 1868-1873," Caribbean Historical Review, 2 (1951), pp. 1-25.

2551. _____. "La experiencia abolicionista de Puerto Rico," La Torre, 21, 81-82 (1973), pp. 293-305.

2552. _____. Historia de la esclavitud negra en Puerto Rico. Madrid: Revista de Occidente, 1953. Revised edition, Río Piedras: Editorial Universitaria, 1965.

2553. Dumont, Henry. "Antropología e patología comparada de los negros esclavos: memoria inédita referente a Cuba," Revista bimestre cubana, 10 (1915), pp. 161-71, 263-74, 344-53, 407-20; 11 (1916), pp. 15-30, 78-90.

2554. Durán, Vetilio Alfau. "Ordenanzas para el gobierno de los negros de la Isla Española," Anales de la Universidad de Santo Domingo, 16 (nos. 57-60)(1951), pp. 251-91.

2555. Eblen, Jack E. "On the Natural Increase of Slave Populations: The Example of the Cuban Black Population, 1775-1900," in Engerman and Genovese, eds., Race and Slavery, pp. 211-47.

2556. Fick, Carolyn Elaine. "Black Masses in the San Domingo Revolution, 1791-1803" (PhD diss., Concordia University, 1980).

2557. Flinter, Jorge. "La esclavitud negra en Puerto Rico hacia 1830," Revista del Instituto de cultura puertorriqueña, 16 (no. 61)(1973), pp. 8-17.

2558. Fontana, Josep. "El problema de los 'emancipados' cubanos ante el consejo de estado español (1828)," Revista de la Biblioteca Nacional José Martí, 17, 2 (1975), pp. 89-98.

2559. Franco, José Luciano. "Los cimarrones en el Caribe," Revista de la Biblioteca Nacional José Martí, 22, 3 (1980), pp. 7-20.

2560. _____. "Los cobreros y los palenques de negros cimarrones," Revista de la Biblioteca Nacional José Martí, 15, 1 (1973), pp. 37-46.

2561. _____. "La conjura de los negreros," in idem, Ensayos históricos (Havana: Editorial de Ciencias Sociales, 1974), pp. 191-200.

2562. _____. La conspiración de Aponte. Havana: Archivo Nacional, 1963.

2563. _____. "Cuatro siglos de lucha por la libertad: los palenques," Revista de la Biblioteca Nacional José Martí, 9, 1 (1967), pp. 5-44.

2564. _____. Ensayos históricos. Havana: Editorial de Ciencias Sociales, 1974.

2565. _____. Ensayos sobre el caribe. Havana: Información Científica y Técnica, Universidad de la Habana, 1975.

2566. _____. Las minas de Santiago del Prado y la rebelión de los cobreros, 1530-1800. Havana: Editorial de Ciencias Sociales, 1975.

2567. _____. Los palenques de los negros cimarrones. Havana: Departamento de Orientación Revolucionaria del Comité Central del Partido Comunista de Cuba, 1973.

2568. _____. Rebeldías negras en los siglos XVIII y XIX. Havana: CICT, Universidad de la Habana, 1975.

2569. García Agüero, Salvador. "El negro en nuestra cultura," Revista de la Biblioteca Nacional José Martí, 22, 3 (1980), pp. 173-78.

2570. García-Gallo, Concepción. "Sobre el ordenamiento jurídico de la esclavitud en las Indias españolas," Anuario de historia del derecho español, 50 (1980), pp. 1005-38.

2571. Gárciga García, Orestes. "Una obra inédita de José Antonio Saco?" Revista de la Biblioteca José Martí, 22, 3 (1980), pp. 145-54.

2572. Gonzelez del Valle, Francisco. "Luz, Saco, y Del Monte ante la esclavitud negra: cinco cartas inéditas de Félix Tancoy Bosmeniel a Domingo del Monte, relativas a la propaganda abolicionista inglesa," Revista bimestre cubana, 47 (1941), pp. 190-96.

2573. Gunst, Laurie Barbara. "Bartolomé de las Casas and the Question of Negro Slavery in the Early Spanish Indies" (PhD diss., Harvard University, 1982).

2574. Hell, Jürgen. "Essay über die Entwicklung der Plantagenwirtschaft auf der Insel Kuba (1800 bis 1898)," Jahrbüch für Wirtschaftsgeschichte, 1 (1971), pp. 273-89.

2575. Hernández y Sánchez-Barbara, Mario. "David Turnbull y el problema de la esclavitud en Cuba," Anuario de estudios americanos, 14 (1957), pp. 241-99.

2576. Holmes, Jack D. L. "The Role of Blacks in Spanish Alabama: The Mobile District, 1780-1813," Alabama Historical Quarterly, 37, 1 (1975), pp. 5-18.

2577. Iglésias, Fe. "Características de la población cubana en 1862," Revista de la Biblioteca Nacional José Martí, 22, 3 (1980), pp. 89-110.

2578. La institución de la esclavitud y su crisis: 1823-1873. (Vol. 1 of El proceso abolicionista en Puerto Rico: Documentos para su estudio). San Juan de Puerto Rico: Centro de Investigaciones Históricas, 1974.

2579. Kiple, Kenneth F. Blacks in Colonial Cuba, 1774-1899. Gainesville. University Presses of Florida, 1976.

2580. _____. "Summary, Overview and Questions. Excerpt from Blacks in Colonial Cuba, 1774-1899," Caribbean Quarterly, 22, 2-3 (1976), pp. 59-61.

2581. Klein, Herbert S. "Consideraciones sobre de la viabilidad de la esclavitud y las causas de la abolición en la Cuba del siglo diecinueve," La Torre, 21, 81-82 (1973), pp. 307-18.

2582. Knight, Franklin W. "Cuba," in Cohen and Greene, eds., Neither Slave nor Free, pp. 278-308.

2583. _____. Slave Society in Cuba during the Nineteenth Century. Madison. University of Wisconsin Press, 1970.

2584. _____. "Slavery, Race, and Social Structure in Cuba During the Nineteenth Century," in Toplin, ed., Slavery and Race Relations in Latin America, pp. 204-27.

2585. _____. "The Social Structure of Cuban Slave Society in the Nineteenth Century," in Rubin and Tuden, eds., Comparative Perspectives, pp. 259-66.

2586. Lachatañere, Rómulo. "Notas sobre la formación de la población afro-cubana," Actas del folklore (Havana), 1, 4 (1961), pp. 3-11.

2587. _____. "Tipos étnicos africanos que concurrieron en la amalgama cubana," Actas del folklore (Havana), 1, 3 (1961), pp. 5-12.

2588. Lainer, Clemente. "Cuba et la conspiration d'Aponte en 1812," Revue de la Société haïtienne d'histoire, de géographie et de géologie, 23 (no. 86)(1952), pp. 19-30.

2589. Lamore, Jean. "Cecilia Valdés. realidades económicas y comportamientos sociales en la Cuba esclavista de 1830," Casa de las Américas, 19, 110 (1978), pp. 41-53.

2590. Langley, Lester D. "Slavery, Reform, and American Policy in Cuba, 1823-1878," Revista de historia de América, 65-66 (1968), pp. 71-84.

2591. Larrazábel Blanco, Carlos. Los negros y la esclavitud en Santo Domingo (Colección Pensamiento Dominicano). Santo Domingo. Julio de Postigo, 1967.

2592. Leante, César. "Cecilia Valdés, espejo de la esclavitud," Casa de las Américas, 15, 89 (1975), pp. 19-25.

2593. Levine, Edwin A. "The Seed of Slavery in the New World. An Examination of the Factors Leading to the Impressment of Indian Labor in Hispaniola," Revista de historia de América, 60 (1965), pp. 1-68.

2594. López Valdés, Rafael. "Problemas del estudio de los componentes africanos en la historia étnica de Cuba," Revista de la Biblioteca Nacional José Martí, 22, 3 (1980), pp. 155-72.

2595. Malagón, Javier. "Un documento del siglo XVIII para la historia de la esclavitud en las Antillas," in Miscelánea de estudios dedicados a Fernando Ortiz (Havana: Sociedad Económica de Amigos del Pais, 1955), vol. 2, pp. 951-68. Also in Imago Mundi (Buenos Aires), 9 (1955), pp. 38-56.

2596. Maluquer de Motes, Jordi. "La burguesía catalana y la esclavitud en Cuba: política y producción," Revista de la Biblioteca Nacional José Martí, 18, 2 (año 67)(1976), pp. 11-81.

2597. Maluquer de Motes Bernet, J. "El problema de la esclavitud y la revolución de 1868," Hispania, 31 (no. 117)(1971), pp. 55-75.

2598. Manzano, Juan Francisco. Autobiografía, cartas y versos. Havana: Municipio de la Habana, 1937. (Cuadernos de historia habanera, no. 8.) With an introduction by José L. Franco.

2599. Martínez-Alier, Verena. Marriage, Class and Colour in Nineteenth-Century Cuba: A Study of Racial Attitudes and Sexual Values in a Slave Society. New York: Cambridge University Press, 1974.

2600. Méndez, Eugenio Fernández. "Las encomiendas y esclavitud de los Indios en Puerto Rico, 1508-1550," Anuario de estudios americanos, 23 (1966), pp. 337-443.

2601. Minguet, Charles. "Liberalismo y conservadorismo en Cuba en la primera mitad del siglo XIX: contradicción entre 'lo específico e lo general'," Historiografía y bibliografía americanistas, 16 (1972), pp. 59-67.

2602. _____. "Les 'lumières', l'esclavage et les problèmes de l'indépendance dans les Antilles (1810-1820)," in Mélanges à la mémoire de Jean Sarrailh (Paris: Centre de Recherches de l'Institut d'etudes hispaniques, 1966), vol. 2, pp. 177-92.

2603. Mintz, Sidney W. "Cuba: terre et esclaves," Etudes rurales, 48 (1972), pp. 135-47.

2604. _____. "The Role of Forced Labor in Nineteenth-Century Puerto Rico," Caribbean Historical Review, 2 (1951), pp. 134-41. Revised as "Slavery and Forced Labor in Puerto Rico," in idem, Caribbean Transformations (Chicago: Aldine, 1974), pp. 82-94.

2605. Montejo, Esteban. Biografía de un cimarrón. (Miguel Barnet, ed.) Havana: Academia de Ciencias de Cuba, 1966. Translated by Jocasta Innes as The Autobiography of a Slave (New York: Pantheon, 1968).

2606. Moreno Fraginals, Manuel. "Africa in Cuba: A Quantitative Analysis of the African Population in the Island of Cuba," in Rubin and Tuden, eds., Comparative Perspectives, pp. 187-201.

2607. _____. The Sugarmill: The Socioeconomic Complex of Sugar in Cuba. New York: Monthly Review Press, 1976.

2608. Moya Pons, Frank. "Notas sobre la primera abolición de la esclavitud en Santo Domingo," La Torre, 21, 81-82 (1973), pp. 229-55.

2609. _____. "La primera abolición de la esclavitud en Santo Domingo," Eme eme: estudios dominicanos, 3, no. 13 (1974), pp. 3-25.

2610. Mullen, Edward J., ed. The Life and Poems of a Cuban Slave: Juan Francisco Manzano, 1797 to 1854. Hamden, Conn.: Shoe String Press, 1981.

2611. Nistal-Moret, Benjamín. "El pueblo de Nuestra Señora de la Candelaria y del Apostal San Matías de Manatí, 1800-1880: Its Ruling Classes and the Institution of Black Slavery" (PhD diss., State University of New York at Stony Brook, 1977).

2612. Ortiz Fernández, Fernando. "Los cabildos afro-cubanos," Revista bimestre cubana, 16 (1921), pp. 5-39.

2613. _____. "La fiesta afro-cubana del 'Día de Reyes'," Revista bimestre cubana, 15 (1920), pp. 5-26.

2614. _____. Hampa afro-cubana: los negros esclavos: estudio sociológico y de derecho publico. Havana: Revista bimestre cubana, 1916.

2615. Otero, Lisandro. "Algo para recordar," Bohemia, 58, 37 (1966), p. 34.

2616. Padrón, Francisco Morales. "La vida cotidiana en una hacienda de esclavos," Revista del Instituto de cultura puertorriqueña, 4 (no. 10)(1961), pp. 23-33.

2617. Pedraja, T. René Andres de la. "Politics and the Economy in the Hispanic Antilles, 1789-1820" (PhD diss., University of Chicago, 1977).

2618. Peraza, Norma. "'Esclavos' gallegos en Cuba," Revista de la Biblioteca Nacional José Martí, 22, 3 (1980), pp. 111-32.

2619. Perez Bento, Manuel. "La condición social de los negros en la Habana durante el siglo XVI," Revista bimestre cubana, 17 (1922), pp. 266-94.

2620. _____. "Procedencia dos negros de Cuba," Revista bimestre cubana, 5 (1910), pp. 161-63.

2621. Perez de la Riva, Francisco. "El negro y la tierra: el canuco y el palenque," Revista bimestre cubana, 48 (1946), pp. 97-139.

2622. Pérez de la Riva, Juan. "Antiguos esclavos cubanos que regresan a Lagos," in idem, and Pedro Deschamps-Chapeaux, Contribución a la historia de la gente sin historia (Havana: Editorial de Ciencias Sociales, 1974), pp. 163-90.

2623. _____. "Documentos para la historia de las gentes sin historia," Revista de la Biblioteca Nacional José Martí, 6, 1 (1964), pp. 27-52.

2624. _____. "Historia de las gentes sin historia," Bohemia, 58, 37 (1966), p. 33.

2625. Pichardo, Hortensia. "Las ordenanzas antiguas para los indios (Las Leyes de Burgos, 1512)," Revista de la Biblioteca Nacional José Martí, 22, 3 (1980), pp. 21-32.

2626. Quintero Rivera, A. G. "Background to the Emergence of Imperialist Capitalism in Puerto Rico," Caribbean Studies, 13, 3 (1973), pp. 31-63.

2627. "Representación a S. M. en 19 de Enero de 1790 sobre el régimen de los esclavos (Archivos cubanos)," Revista bimestre cubana, 8 (1913), pp. 57-75.

2628. Riverend, Julio Le. "El esclavismo en Cuba (perspectivas del tema)," Revista de la Biblioteca Nacional José Martí, 22, 3 (1980), pp. 33-52.

2629. Roig de Leuchsenring, Emilio. "La introducción de los esclavos africanos - Trato que se daba a los negros y horros - Vida, costumbres y actividades de unos y otros - Disposiciones del Cabildo," in Actas capitulares del Ayuntamiento de la Habana (Havana: Municipio de la Habana, 1937), vol. 1, pp. 113-19.

2630. Roller, Arnold. "El marfil negro y el oro blanco en Cuba," Revista bimestre cubana, 25 (1930), pp. 281-86.

2631. Romero, Fernando. "Los 'estudios afrocubanos' y el negro en la Patria de Martí," Revista bimestre cubana, 47 (1941), pp. 395-401.

2632. Ruiz Belvis, Segundo, José Jilián Acosta, and Francisco Mariano Quiñones. Proyecto para la abolición de la esclavitud en Puerto Rico. San Juan: Instituto de cultura puertorriqueña, 1969.

2633. Scarano, Francisco. "Slavery and Free Labor in the Puerto Rican Sugar Economy: 1815-1873," in Rubin and Tuden, eds., Comparative Perspectives, pp. 553-63.

2634. _____. "Sugar and Slavery in Puerto Rico: The Municipality of Ponce, 1815-1849" (PhD diss., Columbia University, 1979).

2635. Schulman, Ivan A. "The Portrait of the Slave: Ideology and Aesthetics in the Cuban Antislavery Novel," in Rubin and Tuden, eds., Comparative Perspectives, pp. 356-67.

2636. *Scott, Rebecca J. "Explaining Abolition: Contradiction, Adaptation and Challenge in Cuban Slave Society, 1860-1886," Comparative Studies in Society and History (forthcoming).

2637. *_____. "Gradual Abolition and the Dynamics of Slave Emancipation in Cuba, 1868-1886," Hispanic American Historical Review (forthcoming August 1983).

2638. _____. "Slave Emancipation and the Transition to Free Labor in Cuba, 1868-1895" (PhD diss., Princeton University, 1982).

2639. Silié, Rubén. Economia, esclavitud y población: ensayos de interpretación histórica del Santo Domingo español en el siglo XVIII. Santo Domingo: Edit. Universidad Autonoma, 1976.

2640. _____. "Los esclavos de la parte francesa y sus efectos sobre la esclavitud de la parte española de Santo Domingo," in idem, Economía, esclavitud y población, pp. 77-99.

2641. _____. "Los negros jornaleros," in idem, Economía, esclavitud y población, pp. 101-21.

2642. Sosa, Enrique. "La esclavitud en la novelistica cubana del XIX," Revista de la Biblioteca Nacional José Martí, 18, 3 (1976), pp. 53-92.

2643. Szászdi, Adám. "Apuntes sobre la esclavitud en Puerto Rico, 1800-1811," Anuario de estudios americanos, 24 (1967), pp. 1433-77.

2644. Tolentino Dipp, Hugo. Raza e historia en Santo Domingo: los orígines del prejuicio racial en América. Vol. 1. Santo Domingo: Edit. Universidad Autónoma, 1974.

2645. * _____. "La trata de negros en Santo Domingo," Revista ciencia, 1, 3 (1973), pp.

2646. _____, and Ruben Silié. "Research on African Influence in the Dominican Republic," in UNESCO, African Slave Trade, pp. 306-10.

2647. Torre Revello, José. "Esclavas blancas en las Indias Occidentales," Boletín del Instituto de investigaciones históricas (Buenos Aires), 6 (no. 34)(1927), pp. 263-71.

2648. Utera, Fray Cipriano de. "La condición social del negro en la época colonial," Eme eme: estudios dominicanos, 3, no. 17 (1975), pp. 43-59.

2649. Wessman, James W. "The Demographic Structure of Slavery in Puerto Rico: Some Aspects of Agrarian Capitalism in the Late Nineteenth Century," Journal of Latin American Studies, 12, 2 (1980), pp. 271-89.

2650. West, Dennis. "Slavery and Cinema in Cuba: The Case of Gutiérrez Alea's 'The Last Supper'," Western Journal of Black Studies, 3, 2 (1979), pp. 128-33.

2651. *Yacou, Alain. "Esclavage et conscience revolutionnaire à Cuba dans la première moitié du XIXe siècle," Revista de la Biblioteca Nacional José Martí, 18, 3 (1976), pp. 142-87.

2652. Yero Pérez, Luis. "El tema de la esclavitud en la narrativa cubana," Islas, 49 (1974), pp. 65-94.

4. French

2653. Adelaide, Jacques. "La colonisation française aux Antilles à la fin du 17e siècle d'après les 'Voyages aux Isles d'Amérique' de Père Labat. Troisième partie: les esclaves," Bulletin de la Société d'histoire de la Guadeloupe, 8 (1967), pp. 26-41.

2654. _____. "Demography and Names of Slaves of Le Moule, 1845 to May 1848," Bulletin de la Société d'histoire de la Guadeloupe, 22, 2 (1974), pp. 65-71.

2655. "Aux origines de l'abolition de l'esclavage: proclamations de Polverel et de Sonthonax 1793-1794," Revue d'histoire des colonies, 36, 3-4 (nos. 127-128)(1949), pp. 348-423.

2656. Bangou, Henri. La Guadeloupe, 1492-1848; ou l'histoire de la colonisation de l'île liée à l'esclavage noir de ses débuts à sa disparition. Aurillac, France: Editions du Centre, 1962.

2657. Bastide, Roger. "Nègres marrons et nègres libres," Annales: économies, sociétés, civilisations, 20, 1 (1965), pp. 169-74.

2658. Benoist, Jean. "Anthropologie physique de la population de l'île de la Tortue (Haïti): contribution à l'étude de l'origine des noirs des Antilles françaises," Bulletin de la Société d'anthropologie de Paris, 11th ser., 3 (1962), pp. 315-35.

2659. *Blaise, Jeanine. "Les esclaves de Haïti y el triofo de la libertad en les Americas (sic)" (Mémoire de maîtrise, Ecole normale supérieure de Haïti, 1950-77).

2660. Brace, Joan. "From Chattel To Person: Martinique, 1635-1848," Plantation Society in the Americas, 2, 1 (1983), pp. 63-80.

2661. Brace, Richard, and Joan Brace. "Code noir: Intention and Practice, 1685-1794 (Abstract)," in Proceedings of the Second Meeting of the Western Society for French History (San Francisco, 21-23 November 1974) (Austin, Tex.: Western Society for French History, 1975), pp. 41-43. With commentary by John C. Kendall.

2662. Breathett, George. "Catholic Missionary Activity and the Negro Slave in Haiti," Phylon, 23, 3 (1962), pp. 278-85.

2663. *Cabrera, Christian. "La Martinique sous la révolution (1789-1791): la question des hommes de couleur libres et des mulâtres" (Mémoire de maîtrise, Paris VII, 1976).

2664. *Cardoso, Ciro Flamarion S. "La Guyane française (1715-1817): aspects économiques et sociaux. Contribution à l'étude des sociétés esclavagistes d'Amérique" (Diss., Institut des hautes études de l'Amérique Latine, Université de Paris X, 1971).

2665. Charles, Jean-Claude. "Le corps de l'esclave, Saint-Domingue, 1764: le travail idéologique de l'information," Les temps modernes, 33 (no. 383)(1978), pp. 1972-2020.

2666. Chatillon, Marcel. "Un philanthrope anglais à la Guadeloupe à la fin du XVIIIe siècle ou le bonheur dans l'esclavage," Revue française d'histoire d'outre-mer, 67, 1-2 (nos. 246-47)(1980), pp. 55-72.

2667. *Chauleau, Félix. "Essai sur la condition servile à la Martinique, 1635-1848: contribution à l'étude de l'inefficacité juridique" (Thèse de droit, Paris, 1964).

2668. Cornevin, Robert. "Note au sujet des origines des esclaves des Antilles," Bulletin de l'Institut française d'Afrique noire, sér. B, 27, 1-2 (1965), pp. 370-71.

2669. Crouchett, Lawrence. "Toussaint L'Ouverture: Black Liberator," Negro Digest, 19, 4 (1970), pp. 16-20.

2670. Dauvergne, R. "La Guadeloupe à l'époque de l'abolition de l'esclavage," Bulletin de la Société d'histoire moderne, ser. 11, 53 (nos. 11-12)(1954), pp. 2-5.

2671. Debbasch, Yvan. "Les associations serviles à la Martinique au XIXe siècle: contribution à l'histoire de l'esclavage colonial," in Etudes de droit privé offertes à Pierre Petot (Paris: Librairie générale de droit et de jurisprudence, 1959), pp. 121-30.

2672. _____. "Le marronnage: essai sur la désertion de l'esclave antillais," L'année sociologique, 3rd sér. (1961), pp. 3-161; (1962), pp. 117-95.

2673. _____. "Opinion et droit: le crime d'empoisonnement aux Iles pendant la période esclavagiste," Revue française d'histoire d'outre-mer, 50, 2 (no. 179)(1963), pp. 137-88.

2674. _____. "Le rapport au travail dans les projets d'affranchissement: l'exemple français (XVIIIe-XIXe siècles)," in Actes du XLIIe Congrès international des américanistes (Paris, 2-8 septembre 1976) (Paris, 1977), vol. 1, pp. 209-22.

2675. Debien, Gabriel. "Les affranchissements aux Antilles françaises aux XVIIe et XVIIIe siècles," Anuario de estudios americanos, 24 (1967), pp. 1177-1203.

2676. _____. "Assemblées nocturnes d'esclaves à Saint Domingue (La Marmelade, 1786)," Annales historiques de la révolution française, 44 (no. 208)(1972), pp. 273-84. (Notes d'histoire coloniale, no. 147)

2677. _____. "Au sujet des origines ethniques de quelques esclaves des Antilles," Notes africaines, no. 106 (1965), p. 58.

2678. _____. "Les cases des esclaves de plantation," Conjonction (Port-au-Prince), 101 (1961), pp. 19-32. (Notes d'histoire coloniale, no. 98)

2679. _____. "La christianisation des esclaves aux Antilles françaises aux XVIIe et XVIIIe siècles," Revue d'histoire de l'Amérique française, 20, 4 (1967), pp. 525-55; 21, 1 (1967), pp. 99-111. (Notes d'histoire coloniale, no. 105)

2680. _____. "Les colons des Antilles et leur main-d'oeuvre à la fin du XVIIIe siècle," Annales historiques de la révolution française, 27 (1955), pp. 259-83. *Reprinted as "Sur les grandes plantations de Saint-Domingue aux dernières années du XVIIIe siècle," Annales des Antilles, 1-2 (1956), pp. 9-32.

2681. _____. "Comptes, profits, esclaves et travaux de deux sucreries de Saint-Domingue (1774-1798)," Revue de la Société haïtienne d'histoire et de géographie et de géologie, 15 (no. 55)(1944), pp. 1-60; 16 (no. 56)(1945), pp. 1-51. (Notes d'histoire coloniale, no. 6)

2682. _____. "La crainte des assemblées d'esclaves à Port-au-Prince au lendemain des tremblements de terre de 1770," Conjonction (Port-au-Prince), 144 (1979), pp. 52-60. (Notes d'histoire coloniale, no. 199)

2683. _____. "Destinées d'esclaves à la Martinique," Bulletin de l'Institut française d'Afrique noire, sér. B, 22, 1-2 (1960), pp. 1-91.

2684. _____. "Les esclaves des plantations Mauger à Saint-Domingue (1763-1802)," Bulletin de la Société d'histoire de la Guadeloupe, 43-44 (1980), pp. 31-164. (Notes d'histoire coloniale, no. 201)

2685. _____. Etudes antillaises; XVIIIe siècle. Paris: Armand Colin, 1956.

2686. _____. "Le marronage aux Antilles françaises au XVIIIe siècle," Caribbean Studies, 6, 3 (1966), pp. 3-42. (Notes d'histoire coloniale, no. 105)

2687. _____. "Les marrons à Saint-Domingue en 1766," Jamican Historical Review, 6 (1966), pp. 9-20. (Notes d'histoire coloniale, no. 124)

2688. _____. "Un nantais à la chasse aux marrons en Guyane (octobre-décembre 1808)," Enquêtes et documents (Nantes: Centre de Recherches sur l'Histoire de la France Atlantique), vol. 1 (1971), pp. 163-72.

2689. _____. "Notes bibliographiques sur le soulèvement des esclaves," Revue de la Société d'histoire et de géographie d'Haïti, 17 (no. 62)(1946), pp. 41-57.

2690. _____. "La nourriture des esclaves sur les plantations des Antilles Françaises aux XVIIe et XVIIIe siècles," Caribbean Studies, 4, 2 (1964), pp. 3-27. (Notes d'histoire coloniale, no. 82)

2691. _____. "Les origines des esclaves des Antilles," Bulletin de l'Institut français d'Afrique noire, sér. B, 23, 3-4 (1961), pp. 363-87. (Notes d'histoire coloniale, no. 69)

2692. _____. "Les origines des esclaves des Antilles (suite)," Bulletin de l'Institut français d'Afrique noire, sér. B, 27, 3-4 (1965), pp. 755-99. (Notes d'histoire coloniale, no. 94)

2693. _____. "Les origines des esclaves aux Antilles (conclusion)," Bulletin de l'Institut fondamental d'Afrique noire, sér. B, 29, 3-4 (1967), pp. 536-58. (Notes d'histoire coloniale, no. 110)

2694. _____. Plantations et esclaves à Saint-Domingue: La sucrerie Cottineau (1750-1777), La sucrerie Foäche à Jean-Rabel et ses esclaves (1770-1803). Dakar: Université de Dakar, 1962. (Publications de la Section d'histoire, no. 3) (Notes d'histoire coloniale, nos. 66, 68)

2695. _____. "La question des vivres pour les esclaves aux Antilles françaises aux XVIIe et XVIIIe siècles," Anuario del Instituto de antropología e historia del Estado Carabobo (Caracas), 7-8 (1970-71), pp. 131-73. (Notes d'histoire coloniale, no. 146)

2696. _____. "Religion des esclaves et réaction des colons à la Martinique en 1802: le curé Robert, Ponce Champroux, prêtre manceau," La province du Maine, ser. 3, 10 (no. 38)(1970), pp. 233-43. (Notes d'histoire coloniale, no. 127)

2697. _____. "Sources de l'histoire de l'esclavage aux Antilles," Revue de la Société haïtienne d'histoire et de géographie et de géologie, 34 (no. 111)(1967), pp. 12-48. (Notes d'histoire coloniale, no. 107)

2698. _____. "Sur les plantations Mauger à l'Artibonite (Saint-Domingue 1763-1803)," Enquêtes et documents (Nantes: Centre de recherches sur l'histoire de la France atlantique), vol. 6 (1981), pp. 219-314.

2699. _____, et al. Les esclaves aux Antilles françaises (XVIIe-XVIIIe siècles). Basse-Terre: Société d'histoire de la Guadeloupe, 1974.

2700. _____, and Johanna Felhoen Kraal. "Esclaves et plantations de Surinam vus par Malouet, 1777," West-Indische Gids, 36, 1 (1955), pp. 53-60. (Notes d'histoire coloniale, no. 38)

2701. _____, and J. Fouchard. "Aspects de l'esclavage aux Antilles françaises: le petit marronage à Saint-Domingue autour du Cap (1790-1791)," Cahiers des Amériques latines, Série Sciences de l'Homme, no. 3 (1969), pp. 31-67. (Notes d'histoire coloniale, no. 125)

2702. _____, and Marie Antoinette Ménier. "Toussaint Louverture avant 1789: légendes et réalités," Conjonction (Port-au-Prince), 134 (1977), pp. 65-80. (Notes d'histoire coloniale, no. 177)

2703. _____, and Jacques Houdaille. "Les origines des esclaves aux Antilles (suite)," Bulletin de l'Institut français d'Afrique noire, sér. B, 26, 1-2 (1964), pp. 166-211. (Notes d'histoire coloniale, no. 78)

2704. _____. "Les origines africaines des esclaves des Antilles françaises," Caribbean Studies, 10, 2 (1970), pp. 5-29.

2705. _____, and R. Richard. "Les origines des esclaves des Antilles (suite)," Bulletin de l'Institut français d'Afrique noire, sér. B, 25, 1-2 (1963), pp. 1-38. (Notes d'histoire coloniale, no. 71)

2706. Delafosse, M., and Gabriel Debien. "Les origines des esclaves aux Antilles (suite)," Bulletin de l'Institut français d'Afrique noire, sér. B, 1-2 (1965), pp. 319-69. (Notes d'histoire coloniale, no. 88)

2707. *Duval, Christiane. "La condition juridique des hommes de couleur libres à la Martinique au temps de l'esclavage" (Thèse de 3ème cycle, Paris I, 1975).

2708. Elisabeth, Léo. "The French Antilles," in Cohen and Greene, eds., Neither Slave nor Free, pp. 134-71.

2709. Fallope, J. "Les affranchissements d'esclaves à la Guadeloupe entre 1815 et 1848," Annales de l'Université d'Abidjan (Histoire, série I), 6 (1978), pp. 5-32.

2710. *Fick, Carolyn. "Black Masses in the San Domingo Revolution, 1791-1803" (PhD diss., Université Concordia de Montréal, 1979).

2711. Foubert, Bernard. "Colons et esclaves du sud de Saint-Domingue au début de la Révolution," Revue française d'histoire d'outre-mer, 61, 2 (no. 223)(1974), pp. 199-217.

2712. Fouchard, Jean. Les marrons de la liberté. Paris: Editions de l'Ecole, 1972.

2713. _____. Les marrons du syllabaire: quelques aspects du problème de l'instruction et de l'éducation des esclaves et affranchis de Saint-Domingue. Port-au-Prince: Editions Henri Duchamps, 1953.

2714. Geggus, David P. "The British Government and the Saint Domingue Slave Revolt, 1791-1793," English Historical Review, 96 (no. 379)(1981), pp. 285-305.

2715. _____. "The British Occupation of Saint Domingue, 1793-98" (D. Phil., University of York, 1979).

2716. *_____. "From His Most Catholic Majesty to the Godless Republic: The 'Volte-face' of Toussaint Louverture and the Ending of Slavery in Saint Domingue," Revue française d'histoire d'outre-mer, 65, 4 (no. 241)(1978), pp. 481-99. (Notes d'histoire coloniale, no. 202)

2717. _____. "Slave, Soldier, Rebel: The Strange Career of Jean Kina," Jamaican Historical Review, 12 (1980), pp. 33-51. (Notes d'histoire coloniale, no. 205)

2718. _____. Slavery, War and Revolution: The British Occupation of Saint Domingue, 1793-1798. New York: Oxford University Press, 1981.

2719. _____. "The Slaves of British-Occupied Saint-Domingue: An Analysis of the Workforces of 197 Absentee Plantations, 1796-1797," Caribbean Studies, 18, 1-2 (1978), pp. 5-41.

2720. _____. "Unexploited Sources for the History of the Haitian Revolution," Latin American Research Review, 18, 1 (1983), pp. 95-103.

2721. Gisler, Antoine. L'esclavage aux Antilles françaises (17e-19e siècle): contribution au problème de l'esclavage. Fribourg: Editions Universitaires, 1965. Reprinted as L'esclavage aux Antilles françaises (XVIIe - XIXe siècle). Paris: Karthala, 1981.

2722. *Goveia, Elsa. "Gabriel Debien's Contribution to the History of French West Indian Slavery" (Paper presented to the 3rd Annual Conference of Caribbean Historians, University of Guyana, Georgetown, 1971).

2723. Hall, Gwendolyn Midlo. "What Toussaint L'Ouverture can Teach Us," Black World, 21, 4 (1972), pp. 46-48.

2724. _____. "Saint Domingue," in Cohen and Greene, eds., Neither Slave nor Free, pp. 172-92.

2725. Hayot, Emile. "Les gens de couleur libres du Fort-Royal, 1679-1823," Revue française d'histoire d'outre-mer, 56, 1 (no. 202)(1969), pp. 1-98; 56, 2 (no. 203)(1969), pp. 99-163.

2726. Houdaille, Jacques. "Les esclaves dans la zone d'occupation anglaise de Saint-Domingue en 1796," Population, 26, 1 (1971), pp. 152-57.

2727. _____. "Origines des esclaves des Antilles (suite): 6 pyramides d'âges," Bulletin de l'Institut français d'Afrique noire, sér. B, 26, 3-4 (1964), pp. 601-75. (Notes d'histoire coloniale, no. 84)

2728. _____. "Trois paroisses de Saint-Domingue au XVIIIe siècle: étude démographique," Population, 18, 1 (1963), pp. 93-110.

2729. _____, R. Massio, and G. Debien. "Les origines des esclaves des Antilles (suite)," Bulletin de l'Institut français d'Afrique noire, sér. B, 25, 3-4 (1963), pp. 215-65. (Notes d'histoire coloniale, no. 75)

2730. Hurault, Jean. "A propos de la recension par A. Trouwborst du livre de J. Hurault sur 'Les noirs réfugiés Boni de la Guyane française'," Anthropologica (Ottawa), 6, 2 (1964), pp. 235-37.

2731. _____. "Comment on review of 'Les noirs réfugiés Boni de la Guyane française'," Caribbean Studies, 7, 4 (1968), pp. 65-67. With a reply by A. J. F. Kobben, pp. 67-68.

2732. _____. Français et indiens en Guyane, 1604-1972. Paris: Union Générale d'Editions, 1972.

2733. _____. "Histoire des noirs réfugiés Boni de la Guyane française," Revue française d'histoire d'outre-mer, 47, 1 (no. 166)(1960), pp. 76-137.

2734. _____. Les noirs réfugiés Boni de la Guyane française. Dakar: Institut français d'Afrique noire, 1961. (Mémoires de l'IFAN, no. 63)

2735. *Jabbour, Micheline. "La crise de 1848 en Martinique: les conséquences de l'acte d'émancipation sur la vie économique de la Martinique" (Mémoire de maîtrise, Paris I, n.d.).

2736. James, C. L. R. The Black Jacobins: Toussaint l'Ouverture and the San Domingo Revolution. 2nd revised edition. New York: Vintage Books, 1963.

2737. _____. "The Free Colored in a Slave Society," in Comitas and Lowenthal, eds., Slaves, Free Men, Citizens, pp. 95-103. (From Black Jacobins)

2738. _____. "The Slaves," in Comitas and Lowenthal, eds., Slaves, Free Men, Citizens, pp. 4-19. (From Black Jacobins)

2739. Jenkins, H. J. K. "Guadeloupe, Savagery and Emancipation: British Comment of 1794-1796," Revue française d'histoire d'outre-mer, 65, 3 (no. 240)(1978), pp. 325-31.

2740. Jesse, C. "Religion among the Early Slaves in the French Antilles," Journal of the Barbados Museum and Historical Society, 28, 1 (1960), pp. 4-10.

2741. *Joseph, L. C. "Rapports esclavigistes et rapports capitalistes à la Guadeloupe et à la Martinique (1625-1727)" (Mémoire, Université de Grenoble II, U.E.R. des sciences économiques et sociales, n.d.).

2742. Kobben, A. J. F. "(Review of Hurault, Les noirs réfugiés Boni de la Guyane française)," Caribbean Studies, 5, 3 (1965), pp. 63-65.

2743. *Lafare, Georges. "Revoltes d'esclaves à la Martinique (1815-1831)" (Mémoire pour diplôme d'études supérieures, Paris, 1961).

2744. Laguerre, Michel S. "The Failure of Christianity among the Slaves of Haiti," Freeing the Spirit, 2, 4 (1973), pp. 10-23.

2745. Lamberterie, R. de. "Notes sur les Boni de la Guyane française," Journal de la Société des américanistes, 2e sér., 35 (1947), pp. 123-47.

2746. Lara, Oruno D. "Le procès de résistance des nègres de Guadeloupe: guérilla et conspiration des nègres cimarrons, 1736-1738 (1ère partie)," Cimarrons, 1 (1981), pp. 13-78.

2747. *_____. "Le processus de résistance des nègres de Guadeloupe: guérilla et conspiration des nègres cimarrons, 1736-1738 (2ème partie)," Cimarrons, 2 (forthcoming).

2748. *Lasacade, Pierre. Esclavage et immigration: la question de la main d'oeuvre aux Antilles. Paris, 1907.

2749. Le Gardeur, René J., Jr. "Un empoisonnement aux Antilles," Conjonction (Port-au-Prince), 106 (1968), pp. 27-40. Reprinted as "Note d'histoire sociale coloniale: un empoisonnement aux Antilles," Comptes rendus de l'Athénée Louisianais (1964-67), pp. 54-68.

2750. Lokke, Carl Ludwig. "Malouet and the St. Domingue Mulatto Question in 1793," Journal of Negro History, 24, 4 (1939), pp. 381-89.

2751. Ly, Abdoulaye. "La formation de l'économie sucrière et le développement du marché d'esclaves africaines dans les îles françaises d'Amérique au XVIIe siècle," Présence africaine, 13 (1957), pp. 7-22; 16 (1957), pp. 112-34.

2752. Manigat, Leslie F. "La experiencia histórica de la abolición de la esclavitud en Haiti," La Torre, 21, 81-82 (1973), pp. 203-28.

2753. _____. "The Relationship between Marronage and Slave Revolts and Revolution in St. Domingue-Haiti," in Ruben and Tuden, eds., Comparative Perspectives, pp. 420-38.

2754. McCloy, Shelby. The Negro in the French West Indies. Lexington, Ky.: University of Kentucky Press, 1966.

2755. Marchand-Thébault, M. "L'esclavage en Guyane française sous l'ancien régime," Revue française d'histoire d'outre-mer, 47, 1 (no. 166)(1960), pp. 5-75.

2756. Martin, Gaston. Histoire de l'esclavage dans les colonies françaises. Paris: Presses Universitaires de France, 1948.

2757. Massio, Roger. "Les gens de couleur en Bigorre au XVIIIe siécle," Revue d'histoire de l'Amérique française, 10, 2 (1956), pp. 245-46.

2758. Mirot, S. "Un document inédit sur le marronnage à la Guyane française au XVIIIe siècle," Revue d'histoire des colonies, 41, 2 (no. 143)(1954), pp. 245-56.

2759. Nicholls, David. "Race, couleur et indépendance en Haïti (1804-1825)," Revue d'histoire moderne et contemporaine, 25, 2 (1978), pp. 177-212.

2760. Peytraud, Lucien P. L'esclavage aux Antilles françaises avant 1789, d'après des documents inédits des archives coloniales. Paris: Hachette, 1897.

2761. Philip, Clyde. "Is James' Hero Toussaint or Dessalines?" Savacou, 11-12 (1975), pp. 68-71.

2762. Pluchon, Pierre. Toussaint Louverture: de l'esclavage au pouvoir. Paris: Editions de l'Ecole, 1979.

2763. Poupart-Lafargue. "La revendication d'une esclave à Saint-Domingue en 1776," Bulletin de l'Académie des sciences, belles-lettres et arts d'Angers, sér. 8, 5, 4 (1961), pp. I-II.

2764. Price-Mars, Jean. "Puissance de la foi religieuse chez les nègres de Saint-Domingue dans l'insurrection générale des esclaves de 1791 à 1803," Revue française d'histoire d'outre-mer, 41, 1 (no. 142)(1954), pp. 5-13.

2765. Proesmans, Father R. "Notes on the Slaves of the French," in Aspects of Dominican History (Roseau, Dominica: Government Printing Division, 1972), pp. 163-72.

2766. Quris, Bernard. "Etre esclave aux Antilles françaises," Historia, no. 415 (1981), pp. 114-26.

2767. Reible, Marcel. "Les esclaves et leurs travaux sur la sucrerie Lugé à Saint-Domingue (1788-1791)," Mémoires de la Société archéologique et historique de la Charente (1973-74), pp. 105-70. (Notes d'histoire coloniale, no. 174)

2768. Rigaud, Odette Mennesson. "Le rôle du Vaudou dans l'indépendance d'Haïti," Présence africaine, nos. 17-18 (1958), pp. 43-67.

2769. *Romens, Wilhelm. "Vocabulaire schématique et chronologique pour l'étude de la société coloniale esclavigiste de Saint-Domingue (1625-1803)" (Mémoire de maîtrise, Ecole normale supérieure d'Haïti, 1950-77).

2770. *Sainville, Léonard. "La condition des noirs à Haïti et dans les Antilles françaises de 1600 à 1850" (Doctorat d'état, Paris IV, 1970, 4 vols.).

2771. *Salvin, Edouard. "De l'esclavage au travail forcé: la société antillaise de 1845 à 1856" (Thèse de maîtrise, Paris VII, 1974).

2772. Schnakenbourg, Christian. Histoire de l'industrie sucrière en Guadeloupe aux XIXe et XXe siècles: vol. 1, La crise du système esclavagiste, 1835-1847. Paris: l'Harmattan, 1980.

2773. Siguret, Roseline. "Deux ateliers d'esclaves au quartier de l'Artibonite, 1783-1787," Revue de la Faculté d'ethnologie de l'Université de Haïti (Port-au-Prince), 13 (1968), pp. 42-50.

2774. _____. "Esclaves d'indigoteries et de caféières au quartier de Jacmel (1757-1791)," Revue française d'histoire d'outre-mer, 55, 2 (no. 199)(1968), pp. 190-230. (Notes d'histoire coloniale, no. 116)

2775. Simpson, George E. "The Belief System of Haitian Vodun," American Anthropologist, 47, 1 (1945), pp. 35-59. Also Bobbs-Merrill Reprint no. BC-272.

2776. _____. "The Vodun Service in Northern Haiti," American Anthropologist, 42, 2 (part 1) (1940), pp. 236-54. Also Bobbs-Merrill Reprint no. BC-272.

2777. Singham, Archie. "C. L. R. James on the Black Revolution in San Domingo," Savacou, 1, 1 (1970), pp. 82-96.

2778. Stein, Robert. "The Free Men of Colour and the Revolution in Saint Domingue, 1789-1792," Histoire sociale/Social History, 14 (no. 27)(1981), pp. 7-28.

2779. _____. "The Revolution of 1789 and the Abolition of Slavery," Canadian Journal of History, 17, 3 (1982), pp. 447-67.

2780. Szajkowski, Zosa. "Bordeaux et l'abolition de l'esclavage dans les colonies en 1848," Revue historique de Bordeaux et du Département de la Gironde, new ser., 3, 2 (1954), pp. 113-41.

2781. Teychenié, Henri. "Les esclaves de l'indigoterie Belin à Saint-Domingue (1762-1793)," Revista de ciencias sociales (Puerto Rico), 4, 1 (1960), pp. 237-66.

2782. Thesée, Françoise. "Sur deux sucreries de Jacquezy (nord de Saint-Domingue) 1778-1802," in Actes du 92e Congrès national des sociétés savantes (Strasbourg et Colmar, 1967) (Paris. Bibliothèque Nationale, 1970), vol. 2, pp. 217-95.

2783. Tomich, Dale W. "Prelude to Emancipation. Sugar and Slavery in Martinique, 1830-1848" (PhD diss., University of Wisconsin - Madison, 1976).

2784. Trouillot, Hénock. "La condition des nègres domestiques à Saint-Domingue," Revue de la Société haïtienne d'histoire, 28 (no. 99)(1955), pp. 4-34.

2785. _____. "La condition des travailleurs à Saint-Domingue," Revue de la Société haïtienne d'histoire, 34 (no. 114)(1967), pp. 1-144.

2786. _____. "L'enfance de l'esclave à Saint-Domingue," Optique, no. 14 (1955), pp. 27-34; no. 17 (1955), pp. 19-33.

2787. _____. "Motion in the System: Coffee, Color, and Slavery in Eighteenth-Century Saint-Domingue," Review, 5, 3 (1982), pp. 331-88.

2788. _____. "Les sans-travail, les pacotilleurs et les marchands à Saint-Domingue," Revue de la Société haïtienne d'histoire, 29 (no. 100)(1956), pp. 47-66.

2789. Vaissière, Pierre de. Saint-Domingue. la société et la vie créoles sous l'Ancien Régime, 1629-1789. Paris. Perrin, 1909.

2790. *Vassoigne, Yolène. "Les diverses formes de la résistance des esclaves pendant la période de l'esclavage à la Martinique et à la Guadeloupe" (Mémoire de maîtrise, Université de Paris I, n.d.).

2791. Vaulx, Bernard. "Mère Javouhey, libératrice des noirs à Mana," Missions catholiques, 21-22 (1953), pp. 147-50.

2792. Vérin, Pierre. "Les caraibes de Saint-Lucie depuis les contacts coloniaux," Nieuwe West-Indische Gids, 41, 2 (1961), pp. 66-82.

2793. Vignols, Léon. "Les esclaves coloniaux en France aux XVIIe et XVIIIe siècles et leur retour aux Antilles," in Mélanges bretons et celtiques offerts à M. J. Loth (Rennes. Plihon, 1927), pp. 211-21.

2794. _____. "L'institution des engagés, 1624-1774," Revue d'histoire économique et sociale, 16, 1 (1928), pp. 12-45.

2795. _____. "Une question mal posée. le travail manuel des blancs et des esclaves aux Antilles (XVIIe-XVIIIe siècles)," Revue historique, 175, 2 (1937), pp. 308-15.

5. Dutch

2796. Abbenhuis, fr. M. F. "De requesten van Pater Stoppel en Prefect Wennekers in 1817 en 1819," West-Indische Gids, 34 (1953), pp. 38-50. (With English summary)

2797. Boogaart, Ernst van den, and Pieter C. Emmer. "Plantation Slavery in Surinam in the Last Decade before Emancipation. The Case of Catharina Sophia," in Rubin and Tuden, eds., Comparative Perspectives, pp. 205-25.

2798. Cappelle, H. van. "Van slavenstaat naar Boschneger-maatschappij," Tropisch Nederland: Tijdschrift ter verbreiding van kennis omtrent Nederlandsch Oost- en West-Indië (Amsterdam), 3 (1931), pp. 373-77; 387-93; 405-12.

2799. Corwin, Charles E. "Efforts of the Dutch Colonial Pastors for the Conversion of the Negroes," Journal of the Presbyterian Historical Society, 12, 7 (1927), pp. 425-35.

2800. Dantzig, A. van. "Slavernij," in C. F. A. Bruijning, J. Voorhoeve, and W. Gordijn, eds., Encyclopedie van Suriname (Amsterdam. Elsevier, 1977), pp. 561-66.

2801. De Goeje, C. H. "Suriname outdekt," Tijdschrift van het Koninklijk Nederlands Aardrijkskundig Genootschap (Leiden), 2e ser., 51, 1 (1934), pp. 51-89.

2802. Deursen, A. Th. van. "De Surinaamse negerslaaf in de negentiende eeuw," Tijdschrift voor Geschiedenis, 88, 2 (1975), pp. 210-23.

2803. Douglas, Charles. Een blik in het verleden van Suriname, beknopt verhaal omtrent gebeurtenissen met de slaven en toestanden in Suriname gedurende de jaren 1630-1863. Paramaribo. J. H. Oliveira, 1930.

2804. Felhoen Kraal, Johanna. "Slaven-brandmerken," West-Indische Gids, 32 (1951), pp. 103-05.

2805. Gaay Fortman, B. de. "Namen van vrijgelaten slaven in Curaçao," West-Indische Gids, 27 (1946), pp. 159-60.

2806. _____. "Slavernij in West-Indië," West-Indische Gids, 28 (1947), pp. 89-90.

2807. Getrouw, C. F. G. "De stemming van de bevolking vóór, tijdens en na de Emancipatie van de slaven in Suriname," West-Indische Gids, 34 (1953), pp. 3-12. With English summary.

2808. Goslinga, Cornelis Christiaan. Emancipatie en emancipator: de geschiedenis van de slavernij op de Benedenwindse eilanden en van het werk de bevrijding. Assen: Van Gorcum, 1956.

2809. *Groenhuis, G. "De zonen van Cham: gereformeerde predikanten over de slavernij, van Udemans Coopmansschip (1640) tot Capiteins Godgeleerd Ondersoekschrift (1742)," Kleio (The Hague), 21, 7 (1980), pp. 221-25.

2810. Groot, Silvia W. de. "The Boni Maroon War 1765-1793, Surinam and French Guyana," Boletín informativo sobre estudios Latino-Americanos en Europa, 18 (1975), pp. 30-48.

2811. _____. "Maroons of Surinam: Dependence and Independence," in Rubin and Tuden, eds., Comparative Perspectives, pp. 455-63.

2812. _____. "Rebellie der zwarte jagers," De Gids (Amsterdam), 133 (no. 9)(1970), pp. 291-304.

2813. Herskovits, Melville J., and Frances S. Herskovits. Rebel Destiny: Among the Bush Negroes of Dutch Guiana. New York: McGraw Hill, 1934.

2814. _____. Suriname Folk-Lore. New York: Columbia University Press, 1936.

2815. Hoetink, Harmannus. "La abolición de la esclavitud en las Antillas Holandesas," La Torre, 21, 81-82 (1973), pp. 283-91.

2816. _____. "Surinam and Curaçao," in Cohen and Greene, eds., Neither Slave nor Free, pp. 59-83.

2817. Jong, Gerald Francis de. "The Dutch Reformed Church and Negro Slavery in Colonial America," Church History, 40, 4 (1971), pp. 423-36.

2818. Kahn, Morton Charles. Djuka: The Bush Negroes of Dutch Guiana. New York: Viking, 1931.

2819. Keller, Saskia. "Researching Slave Culture at the General State Archives," Itinerario (Leiden), 4, 2 (1980), pp. 64-70.

2820. Kesler, C. K. "Na 100 jaar: branden in Paramaribo," West-Indische Gids, 14 (1932-33), pp. 164-74.

2821. _____. "Slavenopstanden in de West," West-Indische Gids, 22 (1940), pp. 257-79, 289-302.

2822. Kom, Anton de. Wij slaven van Suriname. Amsterdam: Contact N. V., 1934.

2823. Koulen, P. R. S. "Manumissie," in C. F. A. Bruijning, J. Voorhoeve, and W. Gordijn, eds., Encyclopedie van Suriname (Amsterdam: Elsevier, 1977), pp. 392-93.

2824. Lamur, Humphrey E. "Demographic Performance of Two Slave Populations of the Dutch Speaking Caribbean," Boletín de estudios latinoamericanos y del Caribe (Amsterdam), 30 (1980), pp. 87-102.

2825. _____. "Demography of Surinam Plantation Slaves in the Last Decade Before Emancipation. The Case of Catharina Sophia," in Rubin and Tuden, eds., Comparative Perspectives, pp. 161-73.

2826. *_____. Slave Fertility and Plantation Labor in Surinam. Forthcoming.

2827. Lenoir, John D. "Surinam National Development and Maroon Cultural Autonomy," Social and Economic Studies, 24, 3 (1975), pp. 308-19.

2828. Lier, R. van. "Negro Slavery in Surinam," Caribbean Historical Review, 3-4 (1954), pp. 108-48.

2829. Linde, Jan Marinus van der. "De emancipatie der negerslaven in Suriname en de zendingsarbeid der Moravische Broeders," West-Indische Gids, 34 (1953), pp. 23-37. With English summary.

2830. _____. Heren-slaven-broeders, momenten uit de geschiedenis der slavernij. Nijkerk, the Netherlands. G. F. Callenbach, 1963.

2831. Menkman, W. R. "Nederlandsche en vreemde slavenvaart," West-Indische Gids, 26 (1944-45), pp. 97-110.

2832. _____. "Slavernij - Slavenhandel - Emancipatie," West-Indische Gids, 34 (1953), pp. 103-12. With English summary.

2833. Müller, M. "Tien jaren Surinaamse guerilla en slavenopstanden, 1750-1759," Tijdschrift voor Geschiedenis, 86, 1 (1973), pp. 21-50.

2834. Nagelkerke, Gerard A. Netherlands Antilles. A Bibliography, 17th Century - 1980. The Hague. Smits Drukkers-Uitgevers, 1982.

2835. Oudschans Dentz, Fred. "De afzetting van het Groot-Opperhoofd der Saramaccaners Koffy in 1835 en de politieke contracten met de Boschnegers in Suriname," Bijdragen tot de Taal-, Land- en Volkenkunde van Nederlandsch Indië, 104 (1948), pp. 33-43.

2836. Paula, A. F. From Objective to Subjective Social Barriers. A Historico-Philosophical Analysis of Certain Negative Attitudes Among the Negroid Population of Curaçao. Foreword by H. Hoetink. Curaçao. Paula, 1967.

2837. *_____. "1795, the Slave Insurrection on the Island of Curaçao. Possible Connection Between the Curaçao and Venezuelan Revolts in 1795," Cimarrons, 2 (forthcoming).

2838. "Politieke contracten met de Boschnegers in Suriname," Bijdragen tot de Taal-, Land- en Volkenkunde van Nederlandsch Indië, 71 (1916), pp. 371-411.

2839. Price, Richard. The Guiana Maroons. A Historical and Bibliographical Introduction. Baltimore. Johns Hopkins University Press, 1976.

2840. _____. Saramaka Social Structure. Analysis of a Maroon Society in Surinam. Rio Piedras. Institute of Caribbean Studies, University of Puerto Rico, 1975.

2841. Reinsma, R. Een merkwaardige episode uit de geschiedenis van de slaven-emancipatie, 1863-1963. The Hague. Van Goor Zonen, 1963.

2842. Renkema, W. E. "De export van Curaçaose slaven, 1819-1847," in P. Boomgaard a. o., ed., Exercities in ons verleden. twaalf opstellen over de ekonomische en sociale geschiedenis van Nederland en Kolonien, 1800-1950 (Assen. Van Gorcum, 1981), pp. 188-208.

2843. Samson, Ph. A. "De status van piekie-njan," West-Indische Gids, 34 (1953), pp. 51-55. With English summary.

2844. Siwpersad, J. P. De nederlandse regering en de afschaffing van de Surinaamse slavernij (1833-1863). Groningen. Bouma's Boekhuis, 1979. With English summary.

2845. "Slavernij," in H. D. Benjamins and Joh. F. Snelleman, eds., Encyclopaedie van Nederlandsch West Indië (The Hague: Nijhoff, 1914-17), pp. 637-40.

2846. Waaldijk, Eugenius Theodorus. Die Rolle der niederländischen Publizistik bei der Meinungsbildung hinsichtlich der Aufhebung der Sklaverei in den westindischen Kolonien. Münster, 1959.

2847. Winter, Johanna Maria van. "Lijst van bronnen betreffende de afschaffing van de slavernij in Nederlands West-Indië," West-Indische Gids, 34 (1953), pp. 91-102.

2848. Wong, L. "Hoofdenverkiezing, stamverdeeling en stamverspreiding der Boschnegers van Suriname in de 18e en 19e eeuw," Bijdragen tot de Taal-, Land- en Volkenkunde van Nederlandsch Indië, 97 (1938), pp. 295-362.

6. Other

2849. Brown, Soi-Daniel W. "From the Tongues of Africa. A Partial Translation of Oldendorp's Interviews," Plantation Society in the Americas, 2, 1 (1983), pp. 37-61.

2850. Green-Pedersen, Svend. "Slave Demography in the Danish West Indies and the Abolition of the Danish Slave Trade," in Walvin and Eltis, eds., Abolition of the Atlantic Slave Trade, pp. 231-58.

2851. Hall, Neville. "Slave Laws of the Danish Virgin Islands in the Later Eighteenth Century," in Rubin and Tuden, eds., Comparative Perspectives, pp. 174-86.

2852. _____. "Slaves Use (sic) of their 'Free' Time in the Danish Virgin Islands in the late Eighteenth and Early Nineteenth Century," Journal of Caribbean History, 13 (1980), pp. 21-43.

2853. Johansen, Hans Christian. "Slave Demography of the Danish West Indian Islands," Scandinavian Economic History Review, 29, 1 (1981), pp. 1-20.

2854. *Olweg, K. F. "Slavery and Social Reproduction on St. John, The Danish West Indies" (Paper presented at the Annual Conference, Society for Caribbean Studies, York, 1977).

2855. Pope, Pauline Holman. "Cruzan Slavery: An Ethnohistorical Study of Differential Responses to Slavery in the Danish West Indies" (PhD diss., University of California, Davis, 1969).

2856. Spingarn, Lawrence P. "Slavery in the Danish West Indies," American Scandinavian Review, 45, 1 (1957), pp. 35-43.

2857. Trier, C. A. "Det dansk-vestindiske negerindforselsforbud af 1792," Historisk Tidsskrift (Copenhagen), 7th ser., 5 (1904-05), pp. 405-508.

2858. Westergaard, Waldemar. "Account of the Negro Rebellion on St. Croix, Danish West Indies, 1759," Journal of Negro History, 11, 1 (1926), pp. 50-61.

VI. Africa

2859. Abraham, Arthur. "The Institution of 'Slavery' in Sierra Leone," Genève-Afrique, 14, 2 (1975), pp. 46-57.

2860. "Abyssinia, the Home of Slavery," Living Age, 312 (no. 4052)(1922), pp. 508-11.

2861. Adamu, Mahdi. "The Delivery of Slaves from the Central Sudan to the Bight of Benin in the Eighteenth and Nineteenth Centuries," in Gemery and Hogendorn, eds., Uncommon Market, pp. 163-80.

2862. Afigbo, A. E. "The Eclipse of the Aro Slaving Oligarchy of Southeastern Nigeria, 1901-1927," Journal of the Historical Society of Nigeria, 6, 1 (1971), pp. 3-24.

2863. African Economic History, 5 (1977), pp. 37-61. Multiple reviews of Miers and Kopytoff, eds., Slavery in Africa; Meillassoux, ed., L'esclavage en Afrique précoloniale; Engerman and Genovese, eds., Race and Slavery in the Western Hemisphere; Cooper, Plantation Slavery on the East Coast of Africa.

2864. Agiri, Babatunde. "Slavery in Yoruba Society in the 19th Century," in Lovejoy, ed., Ideology of Slavery in Africa, pp. 123-48.

2865. Aguessy, Honorat. "Le Dan-Home du XIXe siècle était-il une société esclavagiste?" Revue française d'études politiques africaines, 50 (1970), pp. 71-91.

2866. Ajayi, J. F. Ade, and E. J. Alagoa. "Black Africa: the Historian's Perspective," Daedalus, 103, 4 (1974), pp. 125-34.

2867. Almeida, Pedro Ramos de. Portugal e a escravatura em Africa. Lisbon: Editorial Estampa, 1978.

2868. *Alpers, Edward A. "The Role of the Yao in the Development of Trade in East Central Africa, 1698-1750" (PhD diss., University of London, 1966).

2869. _____. "The Story of Swema: Female Vulnerability in Nineteenth-Century East Africa," in Robertson and Klein, eds., Women and Slavery in Africa, pp. 185-99.

2870. _____. "Trade, State, and Society among the Yao in the Nineteenth Century," Journal of African History, 10, 3 (1969), pp. 405-20.

2871. Amenumey, D. E. K. "Geraldo de Lima: A Reappraisal," Transactions of the Historical Society of Ghana, 9 (1968), pp. 65-78.

2872. Appel, A. "Die Gekleurdes van die Westelike Klein-Karoo gedurende die 19de eeu: 'n sosiaal ekonomiese voorstudie," Kronos, 6 (1983), pp. 37-58.

2873. Armstrong, James C. "The Slaves, 1652-1795," in Richard Elphick and Hermann Giliomee, eds., The Shaping of South African Society, 1652-1820 (London: Longmans, 1979), pp. 75-115.

2874. Arnaud, Robert. "Les formes anciennes de l'esclavage dans le boucle méridionale du Niger," Etudes de sociologie et d'ethnologie juridiques, 12 (1932), pp. 23-64.

2875. Asiegbu, J. U. J. "British Slave Emancipation and 'Free' Labour Recruitment from West Africa, 1841-1861," Sierra Leone Studies, 26 (1970), pp. 37-47.

2876. Augé, Marc. "Les faiseurs d'ombre: servitude et structure lignagère dans la société alladian," in Meillassoux, ed., L'esclavage en Afrique précoloniale, pp. 455-75.

2877. Austen, Ralph R. "Slavery among Coastal Middlemen: The Duala of Cameroon," in Miers and Kopytoff, eds., Slavery in Africa, pp. 305-33.

2878. Azevedo, Mario. "Power and Slavery in Central Africa: Chad (1890-1925)," Journal of Negro History, 67, 3 (1982), pp. 198-211.

2879. Baldus, Bernd. "Responses to Dependence in a Servile Group: The Machube of Northern Benin," in Miers and Kopytoff, eds., Slavery in Africa, pp. 435-58.

2880. Baravelli, Giulio Cesare. The Last Stronghold of Slavery: What Abyssinia Is. Roma: Società Editrio di Novissima, 1935.

2881. Bay, Edna G. "Servitude and Worldly Success in the Palace of Dahomey," in Robertson and Klein, eds., Women and Slavery in Africa, pp. 340-67.

2882. *Baye-Gueye. "L'esclavage au Sénégal de la fin du XVIIe au début du XXe siècle" (Thèse de troisième cycle, Nantes, 1969).

2883. Bazin, Jean. "War and Servitude in Segou," Economy and Society, 3, 2 (1974), pp. 107-44. Translated from "Guerre et servitude à Ségou," in Meillassoux, ed., L'esclavage en Afrique précoloniale, pp. 135-81.

2884. Beachey, R. W. "The East African Ivory Trade in the Nineteenth Century," Journal of African History, 8, 2 (1967), pp. 269-90.

2885. Becker, Charles. "La Sénégambie à l'époque de la traite des esclaves. à propos d'un ouvrage récent de Philip D. Curtin, Economic Change in Senegambia in the Era of the Slave Trade," Revue française d'histoire d'outre-mer, 64, 2 (no. 235)(1977), pp. 203-24.

2886. _____, and Victor Martin. "Kayor and Baol. Senegalese Kingdoms and the Slave Trade in the Eighteenth Century," in Inikori, ed., Forced Migration, pp. 100-25. Translation of "Kayor et Baol. royaumes sénégalais et traite des esclaves au XVIIIᵉ siècle".

2887. Bloch, Maurice. "Modes of Production and Slavery in Madagascar. Two Case Studies," in Watson, ed., Asian and African Systems of Slavery, pp. 100-34.

2888. _____. "Social Implications of Freedom for Merina and Zafimaniry Slaves," in Raymond K. Kent, ed., Madagascar in History. Essays from the 1970's (Albany, Cal.. Foundation for Malagasy Studies, 1979), pp. 269-97.

2889. Blommaert, W. "Het Invoeren van de Slavernij aan de Kaap," Archives Yearbook for South African History, 1, 1 (1938), pp. 1-29.

2890. Boccassino, R. "Les diverses formes de l'esclavage en usage chez les acholi de l'Ouganda et la condition sociale de l'esclavage," VII-me Congrès international des sciences anthropologiques et ethnologiques (Moscow, 1964), vol. 9, pp. 193-95. Also as "Le varie forme della schiavitù in uso tra gli Acioli dell'Uganda e la condizione dello schiavo," Genus, 20, 1-4 (1964), pp. 1-22.

2891. _____. "Le varie forme della schiavitù in uso tra le popolazioni nilotiche e nilo-camitiche del già Sudan Anglo-Egiziano e dell'Uganda," Annali lateranensi, 29 (1965), pp. 325-95.

2892. Böeseken, A. J. Slaves and Free Blacks at the Cape 1658-1700. Cape Town: Tafelberg, 1977.

2893. _____. "Wie was die vader van Lijsbeth van die Kaap," Kronos, 5 (1982), pp. 61-67.

2894. Bonnafé, Pierre. "Les formes d'asservissement chez les Kukuya d'Afrique centrale," in Meillassoux, ed., L'esclavage en Afrique précoloniale, pp. 529-55.

2895. Botha, C. Graham. "Slavery at the Cape," South African Law Journal, 50, 1 (1933), pp. 4-12.

2896. Bouche, Denise. Les villages de liberté en Afrique Noire Française, 1887-1910. La Haye. Mouton, 1968.

2897. Bourgeot, André. "Rapports esclavagistes et conditions d'affranchissement chez les Imuhag (Twaog kel Ahaggar)," in Meillassoux, ed., L'esclavage en Afrique précoloniale, pp. 77-97.

2898. Boutillier, J.-L. "Les captifs en A.O.F. (1903-1905)," Bulletin de l'Institut fondamental d'Afrique noire, sér. B, 30, 2 (1968), pp. 513-35.

2899. _____. "Les trois esclaves de Bouina," in Meillassoux, ed., L'esclavage en Afrique précoloniale, pp. 253-80.

2900. Broadhead, Susan Herlin. "Slave Wives, Free Sisters: Bakongo Women and Slavery c. 1700-1850," in Robertson and Klein, eds., Women and Slavery in Africa, pp. 160-81.

2901. Brooks, George E. "A Nhara of the Guinea-Bissau Region: Mãe Aurélia Correia," in Robertson and Klein, eds., Women and Slavery in Africa, pp. 295-319.

2902. Buxton, Travers. "Is Slavery Dead in Africa?" Missionary Review of the World, 44, 11 (1921), pp. 853-55.

2903. Cadbury, William A. Labour in Portuguese West Africa. London: E. Routledge and Sons, 1910.

2904. _____. "Portuguese Slavery," Spectator, 110 (no. 4425)(1913), pp. 651-52.

2905. Cairns, Margaret. "Slave Transfers, 1658-1795: A Preliminary Survey," Kronos, 6 (1983), pp. 21-32.

2906. Caldwell, John C., Joseph E. Inikori, and Patrick Manning. "Two Comments on Manning, 'The Enslavement of Africans: A Demographic Model,' CJAS/RCEA, 15 (1981), and a Response," Canadian Journal of African Studies/Revue canadienne des études africaines, 16, 1 (1982), pp. 127-39.

2907. Campbell, Gwyn. "Labour and the Transport Problem in Imperial Madagascar," Journal of African History, 21, 3 (1980), pp. 341-56.

2908. Carreira, António. Cabo Verde: Formação de uma sociedade escravocrata - 1460-1878. Porto: Imprensa Portuguesa, 1972.

2909. *Cassanelli, Lee V. "Social Constructs on the Somali Frontier: Bantu Ex-Slave Communities in Nineteenth-Century Somaliland," in Igor Kopytoff, ed., The Internal African Frontier (Philadelphia: Institute for the Study of Human Issues, forthcoming).

2910. Cave, Basil S. "The End of Slavery in Zanzibar and British East Africa," Journal of the African Society, 9 (1909), pp. 20-33.

2911. *Cerulli, E. "Ordinamento fondiario e servitù della gelba nell'Etiopia antica," VII-me Congrès International des Sciences Anthropologiques et Ethnologiques (Moscow, 1964), vol. 9, pp. 203-

2912. Chauleur, Pierre. "L'Afrique des enchaînés," Etudes, 12 (1968), pp. 635-52.

2913. Clarence-Smith, W. G. "Slavery in Coastal Southern Angola, 1875-1913," Journal of Southern African Studies, 2 (1976), pp. 214-23.

2914. _____. "Slaves, Commoners, and Landlords in Bulozi," Journal of African History, 20, 2 (1979), pp. 219-34.

2915. Cohen, Ronald. "Introduction (to 'Slavery in Africa')," Trans-Action, 4, 3 (1967), pp. 44-46.

2916. _____. "Slavery Among the Kanuri," Trans-Action, 4, 3 (1967), pp. 48-50.

2917. _____, ed. "Slavery in Africa," special supplement in Trans-Action, 4, 3 (1967), pp. 44-56.

2918. Conrad, David C. "Slavery in Bambara Society: Segou 1712-1861," Slavery and Abolition, 2, 1 (1981), pp. 69-80.

2919. Cookey, S. J. S. "An Igbo Slave Story of the late Nineteenth Century and its Implications," Ikenga, 1, 2 (1979), pp. 1-9.

2920. Cooper, Frederick. "The Problem of Slavery in African Studies," Journal of African History, 20, 1 (1979), pp. 103-24.

2921. Cordell, Dennis Dale. "Dal al-Kuti: A History of the Slave Trade and State Formation on the Islamic Frontier in Northern Equatorial Africa (Central African Republic and Chad), in the Nineteenth and Early Twentieth Centuries" (PhD diss., University of Wisconsin, Madison, 1977).

2922. Cuthbertson, G. C. "The Impact of the Emancipation of Slaves on St. Andrew's Scottish Church, Cape Town, 1838-1878," in Christopher Saunders and Howard Phillips, eds., Studies in the History of Cape Town, 3 (1980), pp. 49-63.

2923. Daget, Serge. "Role et contribution des états-cotiers dans l'évolution des rapports entre Africains et Européens du XVe au XIXe siècles," Annales de l'Université d'Abidjan (série D, Lettres), 13 (1980), pp. 313-36.

2924. Dantzig, Albert van. "Les Hollandais sur la Côte des Esclaves: parties gagnées et parties perdues," in Etudes africaines offertes à Henri Brunschwig (Paris: Editions de l'Ecole des hautes études en sciences sociales, 1982), pp. 79-89.

2925. Darley, Henry Algernon Cholmley. Slaves and Ivory in Abyssinia: A Record of Adventure and Exploration Among the Ethiopian Slave-Raiders. London: H. F. & G. Witherby, 1926.

2926. Dehérain, Henri. "L'esclavage au Cap de Bonne-Espérance aux XVIIe et XVIIIe siècles," Journal des savants (Paris), 5, 9 (Sept. 1907), pp. 488-503.

2927. de Jonghe, E., and Julien Vanhove. "Les formes d'asservissement dans les sociétés indigènes du Congo belge," Mémoires de l'Académie royale des sciences d'outre-mer, 19, 1 (1948), pp. 483-95.

2928. del Gaudio, Giovanni. Il problema della schiavitù: con particolare riferimento alle popolazione del Sudan occidentale e della Guinea settentrionale. Napoli: Morano, 1972.

2929. Delius, Peter, and Stanley Trapido. "Inboekselings and Oorlans: The Creation and Transformation of a Servile Class," Journal of Southern African Studies, 8, 2 (1982), pp. 214-42.

2930. Den, Deniele Surùr Pharim. "Le pene dei negri schiavi in Africa (ed. R. Boccassino)," Euntes docete, 17 (1964), pp. 51-93.

2931. Derrick, Jonathan. Africa's Slaves Today. London: Allen and Unwin, 1975.

2932. Dieng, Amady Aly. Classes sociales et mode de production esclavagiste en Afrique de l'ouest. Paris: Centre d'études et de recherches marxistes, 1974.

2933. Diogo Júnior, Alfredo. Angola perante a escravatura. Luanda: Editora Quissanje, n.d. (c. 1966-68).

2934. Duffy, James. A Question of Slavery. Cambridge, Mass.: Harvard University Press, 1967.

2935. Dumett, Raymond E. "Pressure Groups, Bureaucracy, and the Decision-Making Process: The Case of the Slavery Abolition and Colonial Expansion in the Gold Coast, 1874," Journal of Imperial and Commonwealth History, 9, 2 (1981), pp. 193-215.

2936. Edwards, Isobel. Towards Emancipation: A Study in South African Slavery. Cardiff: Llandyssul, 1942.

2937. Edwards, Jon R. "Slavery, the Slave Trade and the Economic Reorganization of Ethiopia, 1916-1934," African Economic History, 11 (1982), pp. 3-14.

2938. Ekejiuba, F. I. "The Aro Trade System in the Nineteenth Century," Ikenga, 1, 1 (1972), pp. 11-26; 1, 2 (1972), pp. 10-21.

2939. Elphick, Richard, and Robert Shell. "Intergroup Relations: Khoikhoi, Settlers, Slaves and Free Blacks, 1652-1795," in Richard Elphick and Hermann Giliomee, eds., The Shaping of South African Society (London: Longmans, 1979), pp. 116-69.

2940. Elwert, Georg. Wirtschaft und Herrschaft von 'Däxome' (Dahomey) im 18. Jahrhundert: Ökonomie des Sklavenraubs und Gesellschaftsstruktur 1724 bis 1818; verbunden mit Untersuchungen über Verwendung und Bestimmung der Begriffe Klasse, Macht und Religion in diesem Kontext. Munich: Rennes, 1973.

2941. *Etienne, Mona. "Women and Slaves: Stratification in an African Society (The Baule, Ivory Coast)" (Paper delivered to American Anthropological Association, Washington, D.C., 1976).

2942. Fage, John D. "The Effect of the Export Slave Trade on African Populations," in R. P. Moss and R. J. A. R. Rathbone, eds., The Population Factor in African Studies (London: University of London Press, 1975), pp. 15-23.

2943. _____. "Slavery and the Slave Trade in the Context of West African History," Journal of African History, 10, 3 (1969), pp. 393-404. Reprinted in Haynes, ed., Blacks in White America Before 1865, pp. 50-62. Also in Inikori, ed., Forced Migration, pp. 154-66. Excerpted in Martin A. Klein and G. Wesley Johnson, eds., Perspectives on the African Past (Boston: Little, Brown, 1972), pp. 140-52.

2944. _____. "Slaves and Society in Western Africa, c. 1445 - c. 1700," Journal of African History, 21, 3 (1980), pp. 289-310.

2945. _____. "States and Subjects in Sub-Saharan African History" (Tenth Raymond Dart Lecture, 5 February 1973). Johannesburg: Witwatersrand University Press, 1974.

2946. Farrant, Leda. Tippu Tip and the East African Slave Trade. London: Hamilton, 1975.

2947. Feeley-Harnick, Gillian. "The King's Men in Madagascar: Slavery, Citizenship and Sakalava Monarchy," Africa, 52, 2 (1982), pp. 31-50.

2948. Fleming, C. J. W. "The Peculiar Institution Among the Early Tumbuka," Society of Malawi Journal, 25, 1 (1972), pp. 5-10.

2949. Franken, J. L. M. "Die taal van die slawekinders en fornikasie met slavinne," Tydskrif vir Wetenskap en Kuns (Bloemfontein), 6, 1 (1927), pp. 20-39.

2950. Fyle, Magbaily. "The Idea of Slavery in Nineteenth Century Sierra Leone: The Career of Bilali," Journal of the Historical Society of Sierra Leone, 2, 2 (1978), pp. 57-61.

2951. Gann, Lewis. "The End of the Slave Trade in British Central Africa: 1889-1912," Rhodes-Livingstone Journal, 16 (1954), pp. 27-51. Excerpted in Martin A. Klein and G. Wesley Johnson, eds., Perspectives on the African Past (Boston: Little, Brown, 1972), pp. 181-205.

2952. Gemery, Henry A., and Jan S. Hogendorn. "The Economic Costs of West African Participation in the Atlantic Slave Trade: A Preliminary Sampling for the Eighteenth Century," in Gemery and Hogendorn, eds., Uncommon Market, pp. 143-61.

2953. Gibson, A. E. M. "Slavery in Western Africa," Journal of the African Society, 3 (1903-04), pp. 17-52.

2954. Gleave, M. B., and R. M. Prothero. "Population Density and 'Slave Raiding': A Comment," Journal of African History, 12, 2 (1971), pp. 319-27. With reply by Michael Mason.

2955. Godée-Molsbergen, E. G. "Hottentotten, Slaven en Blanken in Compagniestijd in Zuid-Afrika," Handelingen en Mededeelingen van de Maatschappij der Nederlandsche Letterkunde te Leiden (1912-13), pp. 102-18.

2956. Grace, John. Domestic Slavery in West Africa: With Particular References to the Sierra Leone Protectorate, 1896-1927. London: F. Muller, 1975.

2957. _____. "Slavery and Emancipation among the Mende in Sierra Leone, 1896-1928," in Miers and Kopytoff, eds., Slavery in Africa, pp. 415-431.

2958. Graham, James D. "The Slave Trade, Depopulation, and Human Sacrifice in Benin History," Cahiers d'études africaines, 5, 2 (no. 18)(1965), pp. 317-34. Translated as "O tráfico de escravos, despovoamento e sacrifícios humanos na história de Benim," Afro-Asia, nos. 4-5 (1967), pp. 35-52.

2959. Grant, Douglas. The Fortunate Slave: An Illustration of African Slavery in the Early Eighteenth Century. London: Oxford University Press, 1968.

2960. Green-Pedersen, Svend E. "Negro Slavery and Christianity (on Erik Pontoppidan's preface to L. F. Roemer, Tilforladelig Efterretning om Kysten Guinea)," Transactions of the Historical Society of Ghana, 15 (1974), pp. 85-102.

2961. Greenstein, Lewis J. "Slave and Citizen: The South African Case," Race, 15, 1 (1973), pp. 25-46.

2962. Guéye, M'Baye. "L'affaire Chautemps (avril 1904) et la suppression de l'esclavage de case au Sénégal," Bulletin de l'Institut français d'Afrique noire, sér. B, 27, 3-4 (1965), pp. 543-59.

2963. _____. "La fin de l'esclavage à Saint-Louis et à Gorée en 1848," Bulletin de l'Institut fondamental d'Afrique noire, sér. B, 28, 3-4 (1966), pp. 637-56. (Notes d'histoire coloniale, no. 102)

2964. _____. "The Slave Trade Within the African Continent," UNESCO, African Slave Trade, pp. 150-63.

2965. Haile, Getatchew. "From the Markets of Damot to that of Bärara: A Note on Slavery in Medieval Ethiopia," Paideuma, 27 (1981), pp. 173-80.

2966. Hair, P. E. H. "The Enslavement of Koelle's Informants," Journal of African History, 6, 2 (1965), pp. 193-203.

2967. Harms, Robert W. "Sustaining the System: Trading Towns along the Middle Zaire," in Robertson and Klein, eds., Women and Slavery in Africa, pp. 95-110.

2968. _____. River of Wealth, River of Sorrow: The Central Zaire Basin in the Era of the Slave and Ivory Trade, 1500-1891. New Haven: Yale University Press, 1981.

2969. _____ . "Slavery Systems in Africa," History in Africa, 5 (1978), pp. 327-35.

2970. Harries, Patrick. "Slavery amongst the Gaza Nguni: Its Changing Shape and Function and its Relationship to Other Forms of Exploitation," in J. B. Peires, ed., Before and After Shaka: Papers in Nguni History (Grahamstown: Rhodes University, Institute of Social and Economic Research, 1981), pp. 210-29.

2971. _____ . "Slavery, Social Incorporation, and Surplus Extraction: The Nature of Free and Unfree Labor in South-East Africa," Journal of African History, 22, 3 (1981), pp. 309-30.

2972. Harris, J. S. "Some Aspects of Slavery in Southeastern Nigeria," Journal of Negro History, 27, 1 (1942), pp. 37-54.

2973. Harris, John Hobbis. Africa: Slave or Free? London: Student Christian Movement, 1919.

2974. _____ . Domestic Slavery in Southern Nigeria (report to the Committee of the Anti-Slavery and Aborigines Protection Society). London: Anti-Slavery and Aborigines Protection Society, 1911.

2975. _____ . "Liberian Slavery: The Essentials," Contemporary Review, 139, 1 (1931), pp. 303-09.

2976. _____ . Portuguese Slavery: Britain's Dilemma. London: Methuen, 1931.

2977. _____ . "Slavery in Africa - Curious Portuguese Attitude," Spectator, 129 (no. 4917)(1922), pp. 398-99.

2978. _____ . Slavery or "Sacred Trust"?. London: Williams and Norgate, 1926.

2979. Harris, Rosemary. "The History of Trade at Ikom, Eastern Nigeria," Africa, 42, 2 (1972), pp. 122-39.

2980. Hartwig, Gerald W. "Changing Forms of Servitude among the Kerebe of Tanzania," in Miers and Kopytoff, eds., Slavery in Africa, pp. 261-85.

2981. Hattingh, J. L. "Beleid en praktyk: die doop van slawenkinders en die sluit van gemengde verhoudings aan die Kaap voor 1720," Kronos, 5 (1982), pp. 25-42.

2982. _____ . "Naamgewing aan Slawe: Vryswartes en ander Gekleurdes," Kronos, 6 (1983), pp. 5-20.

2983. * _____ . "Slawe en Vryswartes in die Stellenbosse Distrik, 1679-1795" (Unpublished paper, presented to the Conference on the History of Stellenbosch, 1979).

2984. _____ . "Slawevrystellings aan die Kaap tussen 1700 en 1720," Kronos, 4 (1981), pp. 24-37.

2985. Heese, H. F. "Slawegesinne in die Wes-Kaap, 1665-1795," Kronos, 4 (1981), pp. 38-48.

2986. *Hengherr, E. C. W. "Emancipation - and After: A Study of Cape Slavery and Issues Arising from it, 1830-1843" (MA thesis, University of Cape Town, 1953).

2987. Henige, David P., and Marion Johnson. "Agaja and the Slave Trade: Another Look at the Evidence," History in Africa, 3 (1976), pp. 57-67.

2988. Héritier, Françoise. "Des cauris et des hommes: production d'esclaves et accumulation de cauris chez les Samo (Haute-Volta)," in Meillassoux, ed., L'esclavage en Afrique précoloniale, pp. 477-507.

2989. Herskovits, Melville J. Dahomey: An Ancient West African Kingdom. 2 vols. New York: J. J. Augustin, 1938.

2990. _____. "The Significance of West Africa for Negro Research," Journal of Negro History, 21, 1 (1936), pp. 15-30. Also Bobbs-Merrill Reprint no. BC-133.

2991. Hogendorn, Jan S., and Henry A. Gemery. "Abolition and its Impact on Monies Imported to West Africa," in Walvin and Eltis, eds., Abolition of the Atlantic Slave Trade, pp. 99-116.

2992. Holsoe, Svend E. "Slavery and Economic Response among the Vai (Liberia and Sierra Leone)," in Miers and Kopytoff, eds., Slavery in Africa, pp. 287-303.

2993. Horton, W. R. G. "The Ohu System of Slavery in a Northern Ibo Village-Group," Africa, 24, 4 (1954), pp. 311-36.

2994. Igbafe, Philip A. "Slavery and Emancipation in Benin, 1897-1945," Journal of African History, 16, 3 (1975), pp. 409-29.

2995. Ijagbemi, Adeleye. "Gumbu Smart: Slave Turned Abolitionist," Journal of the Historical Society of Sierra Leone, 4, 1-2 (1980), pp. 45-60.

2996. Inikori, J. E. "Introduction," in idem, ed., Forced Migration, pp. 13-60.

2997. _____. "Slave Trade: A Retardative Factor in West African Economic Development, 1451-1870," in Mahdi Adamu, ed., Economic History of the Central Savanna of West Africa (forthcoming).

2998. _____, ed. Forced Migration: The Impact of the Export Slave Trade on African Societies. London: Hutchinson, 1981.

2999. Isaacman, Barbara, and Allen Isaacman. "Slavery and Social Stratification among the Sena of Mozambique: A Study of the Kaporo System," in Miers and Kopytoff, eds., Slavery in Africa, pp. 105-20.

3000. Izard, Michel. "Les captifs royaux dans l'ancien Yatenga," in Meillassoux, ed., L'esclavage en Afrique précoloniale, pp. 281-96.

3001. Jeffreys, M. D. W. "The Gold Miners of Monomotapa," NADA (Salisbury, Southern Rhodesia), 9, 5 (1968), pp. 42-46.

3002. Jennings, Lawrence Charles. "Réflexions d'un observateur sur l'émancipation des esclaves brittaniques à l'Ile Maurice," Revue d'histoire moderne et contemporaine, 29, 3 (1982), pp. 462-70.

3003. Jewsiewicki, Bogumil, and Mumbanza mwa Bawele. "The Social Context of Slavery in Equatorial Africa during the Nineteenth and Twentieth Centuries," in Lovejoy, ed., Ideology of Slavery in Africa, pp. 73-98.

3004. Johnson, Marion. "Polanyi, Peukert, and the Political Economy of Dahomey (review essay on Peukert, Der atlantische Sklavenhandel von Dahomey, 1750-1797)," Journal of African History, 21, 3 (1980), pp. 395-98.

3005. *Joubert, D. C. "Die Slave-oppstand van 1808 in die Koe-Tijgerberg en Swartland distrikte" (MA these, UNISA, 1946).

3006. Keim, Curtis A. "Women in Slavery among the Mangbetu c. 1800-1910," in Robertson and Klein, eds., Women and Slavery in Africa, pp. 144-59.

3007. Keith, Henry H. "Masters and Slaves in Portuguese Africa in the Nineteenth Century: First Soundings," Studia, 33 (1971), pp. 235-48.

3008. Kersaint-Gilly, Félix de. "Essai sur l'évolution de l'esclavage en Afrique occidentale française: son dernier stade au Soudan français," Bulletin du Comité d'études historiques et scientifiques de l'Afrique Occidentale Française, 9 (1924), pp. 469-78.

3009. *Kika-Mavunda, Michel. "L'esclavage traditionel chez les Basuku," Présence universitaire, 33 (1970), pp. 37-42.

3010. Kilkenny, Roberta Walker. "The Slave Mode of Production: Precolonial Dahomey," in Donald Crummey and Charles C. Stewart, eds., Modes of Production in Africa: The Precolonial Era (Beverly Hills, Calif.: Sage Publications, 1981), pp. 157-73.

3011. Kilson, Marion. "West African Society and the Atlantic Slave Trade, 1441-1865," in Huggins, Kilson, and Fox, eds., Key Issues in the Afro-American Experience, vol. 1, pp. 39-53.

3012. King, M. "Slavery in South Africa," The Mentor (Natal Teachers' Society, Durban), 34, 9 (1952), pp. 3-4.

3013. KiZerbo, Joseph. "L'économie de traite en Afrique Noire ou le pillage organisé (XVe-XXe siècles)," Présence africaine, 11 (1956-57), pp. 7-31.

3014. Klein, A. Norman. "Inequality in Asante: A Study of the Forms and Meanings of Slavery and Social Servitude in Pre- and Early Colonial Akan-Asante Society and Culture" (2 vols.)(PhD diss., University of Michigan, 1980).

3015. _____. "Karl Polanyi's Dahomey: To Be or Not to be a State: A Review Article," Canadian Journal of African Studies/Revue canadienne d'études africaines, 2, 2 (1968), pp. 210-23.

3016. _____. "The Two Asantes: Competing Interpretations of 'Slavery' in Akan-Asante Culture and Society," in Lovejoy, ed., Ideology of Slavery in Africa, pp. 149-68. Reprinted in part in Research Review (Legon, Ghana), 12, 1 (1980), pp. 37-51.

3017. _____. "West African Unfree Labor Before and After the Rise of the Atlantic Slave Trade," in Foner and Genovese, eds., Slavery in the New World, pp. 87-95.

3018. Klein, Martin A. "Slavery, the Slave Trade, and Legitimate Commerce in Late Nineteenth Century Africa," Etudes d'histoire africaine, 2 (1971), pp. 5-28.

3019. _____. "The Study of Slavery in Africa (review of Miers and Kopytoff, eds., Slavery in Africa, and of Meillassoux, ed., L'esclavage en Afrique précoloniale)," Journal of African History, 19, 4 (1978), pp. 599-609.

3020. _____. "Women in Slavery in the Western Sudan," in Robertson and Klein, eds., Women and Slavery in Africa, pp. 67-92.

3021. _____, and Paul E. Lovejoy. "Slavery in West Africa," in Gemery and Hogendorn, eds., Uncommon Market, pp. 181-212.

3022. Kock, Victor de. Those in Bondage: An Account of the Life of the Slave at the Cape in the Days of the Dutch East India Company. London: B. Allen, 1950.

3023. Kodjo, Niamkey Georges. "Contribution à l'étude des tribus dites serviles du Songai," Bulletin de l'Institut fondamental d'Afrique noire, sér. B, 38, 4 (1976), pp. 790-812.

3024. Kopytoff, Igor, and Suzanne Miers. "Introduction: African 'Slavery' as an Institution of Marginality," in Miers and Kopytoff, eds., Slavery in Africa, pp. 3-81.

3025. Labouret, H. "Le servage étape entre l'esclavage et la liberté en Afrique occidentale," in Johannes Lukas, ed., Afrikanistiche Studien (Berlin: Akademie Verlag, 1955), pp. 147-53.

3026. Lamba, I. C. "British Commerce as an Anti-Slavery Device in Malawi in the 1870s and 1880s: A Study in Miscalculated Strategy," Rhodesian History, 9 (1978), pp. 13-21.

3027. Lauffer (Missionar). "Sklaverei und Sklavenhandel in Kamerun," Afrika (Evangelische Afrika-Verein zu Berlin für die sittliche und soziale Entwicklung der deutschen Schutzgebiet), 8 (1901), pp. 132-26.

3028. Launay, Robert. "Joking Slavery," Africa, 47, 4 (1977), pp. 413-22.

3029. Law, Robin. "Royal Monopoly and Private Enterprise in the Atlantic Trade. The Case of Dahomey," Journal of African History, 18, 4 (1977), pp. 555-77.

3030. _____. "Slavery, Trade and Taxes. The Material Basis of Political Power in Pre-Colonial West Africa," Research in Economic Anthropology. An Annual Compilation of Research (series editor, George Dalton)(Greenwood, Conn.. JAI Press, 1978), pp. 37-52.

3031. Leith-Ross, S. "Notes on the Osu System among the Ibo of Owerri Province, Nigeria," Africa, 10, 2 (1937), pp. 206-20.

3032. Levine, Nancy E. "Opposition and Interdependence. Demographic and Economic Perspectives on Nyinba Slavery," in Watson, ed., Asian and African Systems of Slavery, pp. 195-222.

3033. *Liebenberg, B. J. "Die Vrystelling van die Slawe in die Kaapkolonie en die Implikasies Daarvan" (MA thesis, University of the Orange Free State, 1959).

3034. Lovejoy, Paul E. "Indigenous African Slavery," Historical Reflections/Réflexions historiques, 6, 1 (1979), pp. 19-61. Commentaries by Igor Kopytoff (pp. 62-76) and Frederick Cooper (pp. 77-84).

3035. _____. "Slavery in the Context of Ideology," in idem, ed., Ideology of Slavery in Africa, p. 11-38.

3036. _____. Transformations in Slavery. A History of Slavery in Africa. Cambridge. Cambridge University Press, 1983.

3037. _____, and Jan S. Hogendorn. "Slave Marketing in West Africa," in Gemery and Hogendorn, eds., Uncommon Market, pp. 213-35.

3038. _____, ed. The Ideology of Slavery in Africa. Beverly Hills. Sage, 1981.

3039. Lugard, Lord. "Slavery in all its Forms," Africa, 6, 1 (1933), pp. 1-14.

3040. McCall, David. "Slavery in Ashanti (Ghana)," Trans-Action, 4, 3 (1967), pp. 55-56.

3041. MacCormack, Carol P. "Slaves, Slave Owners, and Slave Dealers. Sherbro Coast and Hinterland," in Robertson and Klein, eds., Women and Slavery in Africa, pp. 271-94.

3042. _____. "Wono. Institutionalized Dependency in Sherbro Descent Groups (Sierra Leone)," in Miers and Kopytoff, eds., Slavery in Africa, pp. 181-203.

3043. MacGaffey, Wyatt. "Economic and Social Dimensions of Kongo Slavery (Zaïre)," in Miers and Kopytoff, eds., Slavery in Africa, pp. 235-57.

3044. McSheffrey, G. M. "Slavery, Indentured Servitude, Legitimate Trade and the Impact of Abolition in the Gold Coast, 1874-1901," _Journal of African History_, 24, 3 (1983), pp. 349-68.

3045. Maianga, José. "A luta dos escravos em S. Tomé no século XVI," _Africa: literatura, arte, cultura_ (Lisbon), 2, 9 (1980), pp. 437-43.

3046. Malowist, Marian. "Le commerce d'or et d'esclaves au Soudan occidental," _Africana Bulletin_, 4 (1966), pp. 49-72.

3047. Manning, Patrick. "A Demographic Model of African Slavery," in _African Historical Demography: Volume II_ (Edinburgh: Centre of African Studies, University of Edinburgh, 1981), pp. 371-84.

3048. _____. "Un document sur la fin de l'esclavage au Dahomey," _Notes africaines_ (IFAN, Dakar), no. 147 (1975), pp. 88-92.

3049. _____. "The Enslavement of Africans: A Demographic Model," _Canadian Journal of African Studies_, 15, 2 (1981), pp. 499-526.

3050. _____. "The Political Economy of African Slavery" (Unpublished paper, Johns Hopkins University, 1981).

3051. _____. _Slavery, Colonialism and Economic Growth in Dahomey, 1640-1960_. Cambridge: Cambridge University Press, 1982.

3052. _____. "Slaves, Palm Oil and Political Power on the West African Coast," _African Historical Studies_, 2, 2 (1969), pp. 279-88.

3053. Mantero, Francisco. _A mão d'obra em São Tomé e Principe_. Lisbon, 1910. Translated as _Manual Labour in S. Thomé and Principe_. Lisbon, 1910.

3054. Mason, Michael. "Population Density and 'Slave Raiding' - The Case of the Middle Belt of Nigeria," _Journal of African History_, 10, 4 (1969), pp. 551-64.

3055. Mauny, Raymond. "Révoltes d'esclaves à Gorée au milieu du XVIIIe siècle d'après Pruneau de Pommegorge," _Notes africaines_, 141 (1974), pp. 11-13.

3056. Mbotela, James Juma. _The Freeing of the Slaves in East Africa_. London: Evans Bros., 1956.

3057. Mboukou, Alexander. "Reflections on the Slave Trade among the Laris: A Linguistic Study," in Sulayman S. Nyang, ed., _Seminar Papers on African Studies_ (Washington: African Studies and Research Program, Howard University, 1974), pp. 53-63.

3058. Meillassoux, Claude. "Le commerce pré-colonial et le développment de l'esclavage à Gubu du Sahel (Mali)," in idem, _The Development of Indigenous Trade and Markets in West Africa_ (London: Oxford University Press, 1971), pp. 182-95. (Studies presented and discussed at the Tenth International African Seminar at Fourah Bay College, Freetown, Sierra Leone, 1969)

3059. _____. "Etat et conditions des esclaves à Gumbu (Mali) au XIXe siècle," Journal of African History, 14, 3 (1973), pp. 429-52. Reprinted in Meillassoux, ed., L'esclavage en Afrique pré-coloniale, pp. 221-51.

3060. _____. "Female Slavery," in Robertson and Klein, eds., Women and Slavery in Africa, pp. 49-68.

3061. _____. "Introduction," in idem, The Development of Indigenous Trade and Markets in West Africa (London: Oxford University Press, 1971), pp. 3-48; English translation, pp. 49-86. (Studies presented and discussed at the Tenth International African Seminar at Fourah Bay College, Freetown, Sierra Leone, 1969)

3062. _____. "Rôle de l'esclavage dans l'histoire de l'Afrique occidentale," Anthropologie et sociétés, 2, 1 (1978), pp. 117-48. Translated as "The Role of Slavery in the Economic and Social History of Sahelo-Sudanic Africa," in Inikori, ed., Forced Migration, pp. 74-99.

3063. _____, ed. L'esclavage en Afrique précoloniale. Paris: Maspero, 1975.

3064. Mertens, J. "L'esclavage chez les Ba Dzing de la Kamtsha," Congo, 1, 5 (1936), pp. 641-76.

3065. Miers, Suzanne, and Igor Kopytoff, eds. Slavery in Africa: Historical and Anthropological Perspectives. Madison: University of Wisconsin Press, 1977.

3066. _____, and Neal Sobania. "Slaving and Raiding on the Borderlands of Southwestern Ethiopia 1919-29: A Preliminary Inquiry" (Seminar Paper, University of London, 1980).

3067. Miller, Joseph C. "Cokwe Trade and Conquest," in Richard Gray and David Birmingham, eds., Pre-Colonial African Trade (London: Oxford University Press, 1970), pp. 175-201.

3068. _____. "Imbangala Lineage Slavery," in Miers and Kopytoff, eds., Slavery in Africa, pp. 205-33.

3069. _____. "Lineages, Ideology, and the History of Slavery in Western Central Africa," in Lovejoy, ed., Ideology of Slavery in Africa, pp. 41-72.

3070. _____. "Slaves, Slavers, and Social Change in Nineteenth Century Kasanje," in Franz-Wilhelm Heimer, ed., Social Change in Angola (Munich: Weltforum Verlag, 1973), pp. 9-29.

3071. Molet, L. "Le vocabulaire concernant l'esclavage dans l'ancien Madagascar," in Pespectives nouvelles sur le passé de l'Afrique Noire et de Madagascar: Mélanges offerts à Hubert Deschamps (Paris: Publications de la Sorbonne, 1974), pp. 45-65.

3072. Morton, Rodger Frederic. "Slaves, Fugitives, and Freedmen on the Kenya Coast, 1873-1907" (PhD diss., Syracuse University, 1976).

3073. Morton-Williams, Peter. "The Oyo Yoruba and the Atlantic Trade, 1670-1830," Journal of the Historical Society of Nigeria, 3, 1 (1964), pp. 24-45. Reprinted in Inikori, ed., Forced Migration, pp. 167-86.

3074. Müller, A. L. "The Economy of Slavery at the Cape of Good Hope," South African Journal of Economics, 49, 1 (1981), pp. 46-58.

3075. _____. "The Impact of Slavery on the Economic Development of South Africa," Kronos, 5 (1982), pp. 1-24.

3076. _____. "Slavery and the Development of South Africa," South African Journal of Economics, 49, 2 (1981), pp. 153-65.

3077. Naber, S. P. L'Honoré. "Nota van Pieter Moorthamer over het gewest Angola (met een bijlage)," Bijdragen en mededelingen van het Historisch Genootschap, 54 (1933), pp. 1-42.

3078. Nevinson, Henry W. A Modern Slavery. London and New York: Harper and Bros., 1906.

3079. Newbury, C. W. "An Early Inquiry into Slavery and Captivity in Dahomey," Zaire, 14 (1960), pp. 53-67.

3080. Newman, E. W. Polson. "Slavery in Abyssinia," Contemporary Review, 148 (no. 840) (1935), pp. 650-57.

3081. Nöel, Karl. "La condition matérielle des esclaves à l'Ile de France, période française (1715-1810)," Revue française d'histoire d'outre-mer, 41, 3-4 (nos. 144-45), pp. 303-13.

3082. Nooteboom, C. "Slavenhandel, levensbron van een oud koninkrijk: economische analyse van de geschiedenis van het oude Dahomey," Afrika (Mededelingen van het Afrika Instituut [Rotterdam]), 4 (1967), pp. 100-03.

3083. Northrup, David. "The Compatibility of the Slave and Palm Oil Trades in the Bight of Benin," Journal of African History, 17, 3 (1976), pp. 353-64.

3084. _____. "The Growth of Trade among the Igbo before 1800," Journal of African History, 13, 2 (1972), pp. 217-36.

3085. _____. "The Ideological Context of Slavery in Southeastern Nigeria in the 19th Century," in Lovejoy, ed., Ideology of Slavery in Africa, pp. 101-22.

3086. _____. "Nineteenth Century Patterns of Slavery and Economic Growth in Southeastern Nigeria," International Journal of African Historical Studies, 12, 1 (1979), pp. 1-16.

3087. *_____. "The Slave Trade to Calabar, 1800-1850," Calabar Historical Journal, forthcoming.

3088. Nukunya, G. K. "A Note on Anlo (Ewe) Slavery and the History of a Slave," in Robertson and Klein, eds., Women and Slavery in Africa, pp. 243-45.

3089. Nwachukwu-Ogedengbe, K. "Gods and Slaves: An Ideological Interpretation of Cult Slavery among the Igbo" (Unpublished paper presented to Conference on The Ideology of Slavery in Africa, York University, Toronto, 1980).

3090. _____. "Slavery in Nineteenth-Century Aboh (Nigeria)," in Miers and Kopytoff, eds., Slavery in Africa, pp. 133-54.

3091. Nwulia, Moses D. E. Britain and Slavery in East Africa. Washington, D.C.: Three Continents Press, 1975.

3092. Obichere, Boniface I. "Women and Slavery in the Kingdom of Dahomey," Revue française d'histoire d'outre-mer, 65, 1-2 (nos. 237-38)(1978), pp. 5-20.

3093. Olivier de Sardan, Jean-Pierre. "Esclavage d'échange et captivité familiale chez les Songhay-Zerma," Journal de la Société des Africanistes, 43, 1 (1973), pp. 151-67.

3094. _____. Quand nos pères étaient captifs: récits paysans du Niger. Paris, 1976.

3095. _____. "The Songhay-Zarma Female Slave: Relations of Production and Ideological Status," in Robertson and Klein, eds., Women and Slavery in Africa, pp. 130-43.

3096. Oloruntimehin, B. Olatunji. "The Impact of the Abolition Movement on the Social and Political Development of West Africa in the Nineteenth and Twentieth Centuries," African Notes, 7, 1 (1971), pp. 33-58.

3097. Oriji, J. N. "A Re-Assessment of the Organization and Benefits of the Slave and Palm Produce Trade Amongst the Ngwa-Igbo," Canadian Journal of African Studies, 16, 3 (1982), pp. 523-48.

3098. Orlova, A. S. "Institution de l'esclavage dans l'état du Congo au Moyen Age (XVIe-XVIIe siècles)," in VIIe Congrès international des sciences anthropologiques et ethnologiques (Moscow, 3-10 August 1964) (Moscow, 1970), vol. 9, pp. 196-202.

3099. Oroge, E. Adeniyi. "The Fugitive Slave Question in Anglo-Egba Relations, 1861-1886," Journal of the Historical Society of Nigeria, 8, 1 (1975), pp. 61-80.

3100. _____. "The Fugitive Slave Crisis of 1859: A Factor in the Growth of Anti-British Feelings Among the Yoruba," Odu, no. 12 (1975), pp. 40-54.

3101. _____. "The Institution of Slavery in Yorubaland with Particular Reference to the Nineteenth Century" (PhD diss., University of Birmingham, 1971).

3102. Ortoli, Henri. "Le gage des personnes au Soudan français," Bulletin de l'Institut français d'Afrique noire, 1, 1 (1939), pp. 313-24.

3103. O'Sullivan, John Michael. "Developments in the Social Stratification of Northwest Ivory Coast During the Eighteenth and Nineteenth Centuries: From a Malinke Frontier Society to the Liberation of Slaves by the French - 1907" (PhD diss., University of California, Los Angeles, 1976).

3104. _____. "Slavery in the Malinke Kingdom of Kabadougou (Ivory Coast)," International Journal of African Historical Studies, 13, 4 (1980), pp. 633-50.

3105. Page, Melvin E. "The Manyema Hordes of Tippu Tip: A Case Study in Social Stratification and the Slave Trade in Eastern Africa," International Journal of African Historical Studies, 7, 1 (1974), pp. 69-84.

3106. _____. "Tippu Tip and the Arab 'Defense' of the East African Slave Trade," Etudes d'histoire africaine, 6 (1974), pp. 105-17.

3107. Pankhurst, Richard. "Ethiopian Slave Reminiscences of the Nineteenth Century," Transafrican Journal of History, 5, 1 (1976), pp. 98-110.

3108. _____. "Mahbuda, the 'Beloved': The Life and Romance of an Ethiopian Slave-Girl in Early Nineteenth-Century Europe," Journal of African Studies, 6, 12 (1979), pp. 47-55.

3109. Pasquier, Roger. "A propos de l'emancipation des esclaves au Sénégal en 1848," Revue française d'histoire d'outre-mer, 54, 1 (nos. 194-97)(1967), pp. 188-208.

3110. Perrot, Claude. "Les captifs dans le royaume anyi du Ndényé," in Meillassoux, ed., L'esclavage en Afrique précoloniale, pp. 351-88.

3111. Perrot, Claude-Hélène. "Hommes libres et captifs dans le royaume agni de l'Indénié," Cahiers d'études africaines, 9, 3 (no. 35)(1969), pp. 482-501.

3112. Peukert, Werner. Der Atlantische Sklavenhandel von Dahomey, 1740-1797. Wiesbaden: Franz Steiner, 1978.

3113. Piault, Marc Henri. "Captifs du pouvoir et pouvoir des captifs," in Meillassoux, ed., L'esclavage en Afrique précoloniale, pp. 321-50.

3114. Poku, K. "Traditional Roles and People of Slave Origin in Modern Ashanti - A Few Impressions," Ghana Journal of Sociology, 5, 1 (1969), pp. 34-38.

3115. Polanyi, Karl. Dahomey and the Slave Trade: An Analysis of an Archaic Economy. Seattle: University of Washington Press, 1966.

3116. Pretorius, Celestine. "Die verhaal van Anna Marais en die slaaf claas van Bengalen," Historia (Pretoria), 24, 1 (1979), pp. 42-49.

3117. Prins, Pierre. "Servitude et liberté dans les sultanats du Haut-Oubangui," Revue indigène, 2 (no. 12)(1907), pp. 126-36.

3118. Ratsimamanga, Rafaralahy. De la condition de l'esclave à Madagascar comparée avec le droit des autres sociétés. Montpellier: Imprimerie Mari-Lavit, 1933.

3119. Rayner, Mary. "Slaves, Slave Owners and the British State: The Cape Colony 1806-1834" (Unpublished seminar paper, The Societies of Southern Africa in the Nineteenth and Twentieth Centuries, Institute of Commonwealth Studies, University of London, January 1981).

3120. Renault, François. L'abolition de l'esclavage au Sénégal: l'attitude de l'administration française, 1848-1905. Paris: Société française d'histoire d'outre-mer, 1972.

3121. _____. Lavigerie, l'esclavage africaine et l'Europe. 2 vols. Paris: De Boccard, 1971.

3122. _____. Libération d'esclaves et nouvelle servitude: les rachats de captifs africains pour le compte des colonies françaises après l'abolition de l'esclavage. Abidjan: Nouvelles Editions Africaines, 1976.

3123. Rey, Pierre-Philippe. "Articulation des modes de dépendence et des modes de reproduction dans deux sociétés lignagères (Punu et Kunyi du Congo-Brazzaville)," Cahiers d'études africaines, 9, 3 (no. 35)(1969), pp. 415-40.

3124. _____. "L'esclavage lignager chez les tsangui, les punu et les kuni du Congo-Brazzaville: sa place dans le système d'ensemble des rapports de production," in Meillassoux, ed., L'esclavage en Afrique précoloniale, pp. 509-28.

3125. Rey-Hulman, Diana. "Les dépendants des maîtres tyokossi pendant la période précoloniale," in Meillassoux, ed., L'esclavage en Afrique précoloniale, pp. 297-320.

3126. Reynolds, Edward. "Abolition and Economic Change on the Gold Coast," in Walvin and Eltis, eds., Abolition of the Atlantic Slave Trade, pp. 141-54.

3127. _____. "Agricultural Adjustments on the Gold Coast after the End of the Slave Trade, 1807-1874," Agricultural History, 47, 4 (1973), pp. 308-18.

3128. Rinchon, Dieudonné. "Notes sur le marché des esclaves au Congo du XVe au XIXe siècle," Congo (Brussels), 6, tome II (no. 3)(1925), pp. 388-409.

3129. Roberts, Richard. "Ideology, Slavery and Social Formation: The Evolution of Maraka Slavery in the Middle Niger Valley," in Lovejoy, ed., Ideology of Slavery in Africa, pp. 171-200.

3130. _____, and Martin A. Klein. "The Banamba Slave Exodus of 1905 and the Decline of Slavery in the Western Sudan," Journal of African History, 21, 3 (1980), pp. 375-94.

3131. Robertson, Claire C. "Post-Proclamation Slavery in Accra: A Female Affair?" in Robertson and Klein, eds., Women and Slavery in Africa, pp. 220-45.

3132. _____, and Martin A. Klein. "Women's Importance in African Slave Systems," in Robertson and Klein, eds., Women and Slavery in Africa, pp. 3-25.

3133. _____, eds. Women and Slavery in Africa. Madison: University of Wisconsin Press, 1983.

3134. Rodney, Walter. "African Slavery and Other Forms of Social Oppression on the Upper Guinea Coast in the Context of the Atlantic Slave-Trade," Journal of African History, 7, 3 (1966), pp. 431-43. Reprinted in Inikori, ed., Forced Migration, pp. 61-73. Excerpted in Martin A. Klein and G. Wesley Johnson, eds., Perspectives on the African Past (Boston: Little, Brown, 1972), pp. 152-66.

3135. _____. "Upper Guinea and the Significance of the Origins of Africans Enslaved in the New World," Journal of Negro History, 54, 4 (1969), pp. 327-45.

3136. Ronen, Dov. "On the African Role in the Trans-Atlantic Slave Trade in Dahomey," Cahiers d'études africaines, 11, 1 (no. 41)(1971), pp. 5-13.

3137. Ross, Robert. Cape of Torments: Slavery and Resistance in South Africa. London: Routledge and Kegan Paul, 1982.

3138. _____. "The Occupations of Slaves in Eighteenth Century Cape Town," in Christopher Saunders and Howard Phillips, eds., Studies in the History of Cape Town, 2 (1980), pp. 1-14.

3139. _____. "The Rule of Law at the Cape of Good Hope in the Eighteenth Century," Journal of Imperial and Commonwealth History, 9, 1 (1980), pp. 5-16.

3140. _____. "Sexuality and Slavery at the Cape in the Eighteenth Century," Collected Seminar Papers on the Societies of Southern Africa in the Nineteenth and Twentieth Centuries (Institute of Commonwealth Studies, London), 8 (1978), pp. 21-30. Revised as "Oppression, Sexuality, and Slavery at the Cape of Good Hope," in Historical Reflections/Refléxions historiques, 6, 2 (1979), pp. 421-33.

3141. Russell, Margo. "Slaves or Workers? Relations between Bushmen, Tswana, and Boers in the Kalahari," Journal of Southern African Studies, 2, 2 (1976), pp. 178-97.

3142. *Saunders, Christopher. "Prize Negroes at the Cape of Good Hope" (forthcoming).

3143. *Shell, R. C.-H. "The Impact of the Cape Slave Trade and its Abolition on the Demography, Regional Distribution and Ethnic Composition of the Cape Slave Population 1652-1825" (Unpublished seminar paper, Yale University, 1979).

3144. Sousberghe, Léon de. "Deux palabres d'esclaves chez les Pende (Province de Léopoldville, 1956)," Mémoires de l'Académie royale des sciences d'outre-mer, 25, 5 (1961).

3145. Stockenström, Eric. Vrystelling van die Slawe. Cape Town: S. A. Bybelvereniging, 1934.

3146. Strickland, D. A. "Kingship and Slavery in African Thought: A Conceptual Analysis," Comparative Studies in Society and History, 18, 3 (1976), pp. 371-94.

3147. Sundiata, I. K. "A Note on an Abortive Slave Trade: Fernando Po, 1778-1781," Bulletin de l'Institut fondamental d'Afrique noire, sér. B, 35, 4 (1973), pp. 793-804.

3148. Suret-Canale, Jean. "Contexte et conséquences sociales de la traite africaine," Présence africaine, 50 (1964), pp. 127-50. Reprinted in idem, Essais d'histoire africaine: de la traite des Noirs au néo-colonialisme (Paris: Editions Sociales, 1980), pp. 73-96.

3149. _____. "Les origines ethniques des anciens captifs au Fouta-Djalon," Notes africaines, 123 (1969), pp. 91-92.

3150. Swan, Charles A. The Slavery of Today: or, The Present Position of the Open Sore of Africa. New York: D. T. Bass, 1909.

3151. Swann, Alfred James. Fighting the Slave-hunters in Central Africa: A Record of Twenty-Six Years of Travel and Adventure Round the Great Lakes and of the Overthrow of Tip-Pu-Tib, Rumaliza and Other Great Slave-Traders. Philadelphia: J. B. Lippincott, 1910; reprint ed., London: Frank Cass, 1969.

3152. *Swartenbroeckx, P. "L'esclavage chez les Yansí," Bulletin de la Société royale belge d'anthropologie et de préhistoire de Bruxelles, 77 (1966), pp. 145-204.

3153. Swindell, Kenneth. "Domestic Production, Labour Mobility and Population Change in West Africa, 1900-1980," African Historical Demography - II (Edinburgh: University of Edinburgh, Centre of African Studies, 1981), pp. 655-90.

3154. Teixeira, Maria Geralda. "Notas sôbre o Reino do Congo no século XVI," Afro-Asia, nos. 4-5 (1967), pp. 77-88.

3155. Terray, Emmanuel. "La captivité dans le royaume abron du Gyaman," in Meillassoux, ed., L'esclavage en Afrique précoloniale, pp. 389-453.

3156. Thornton, John K. "Sexual Demography: The Impact of the Slave Trade on Family Structure," in Robertson and Klein, eds., Women and Slavery in Africa, pp. 39-48.

3157. _____. "The Slave Trade in Eighteenth Century Angola. Effects on Demographic Structures," Canadian Journal of African Studies/Revue canadienne d'études africaines, 14, 3 (1980), pp. 417-27.

3158. Tisserant, Charles. Ce que j'ai connu de l'esclavage en Oubangui-Chari. Paris. Société Antiesclavagiste de France, 1955.

3159. Tlou, Thomas. "Servility and Political Control. Botlhanka among the BaTawana of Northwestern Botswana, ca. 1750-1906," in Miers and Kopytoff, eds., Slavery in Africa, pp. 367-90.

3160. Trapido, Stanley. "Aspects in the Transition from Slavery to Serfdom. The South African Republic, 1842-1902," Collected Seminar Papers on the Societies of Southern Africa in the Nineteenth and Twentieth Centuries (Institute of Commonwealth Studies, London), 6 (1976), pp. 24-31.

3161. Tuden, Arthur. "Ila Slavery," Rhodes-Livingstone Journal, 24 (1958), pp. 68-78.

3162. _____. "Ila Slavery (Zambia)," Trans-Action, 4, 3 (1967), pp. 51-52.

3163. _____. "Slavery and Stratification among the Ila of Central Africa," in A. Tuden and L. Plotnicov, eds., Social Stratification in Africa (New York. Free Press, 1970), pp. 47-58.

3164. Turner, J. Michael. "Escravos brasileiros no Daomé," Afro-Asia (Revista do Centro de Estudos Afro-Orientais da Bahia), nos. 10-11 (1970), pp. 5-24.

3165. (Turner, Jerry M.) "Les Brésiliens. The Impact of Former Brazilian Slaves upon Dahomey" (PhD diss., Boston University, 1975).

3166. Uchendu, Victor. "Slavery in Southeast Nigeria," Trans-Action, 4, 3 (1967), pp. 53-54.

3167. _____. "Slaves and Slavery in Igboland, Nigeria," in Miers and Kopytoff, eds., Slavery in Africa, pp. 121-32.

3168. Uzoigwe, G. N. "The Slave Trade and African Societies," Transactions of the Historical Society of Ghana, 14, 2 (1973), pp. 187-212.

3169. Vaughan, James H. "Mafakur. A Limbic Institution of the Margi (Nigeria)," in Miers and Kopytoff, eds., Slavery in Africa, pp. 85-102.

3170. Vogelsanger, C. M. R. "Pietismus und afrikanische Kultur an der Goldküste. Die Einstellung der Basler Mission zur Haussklaverei" (Diss., Universitat Zürich, 1977).

3171. Wege, Arthur. "Die rechtlichen Bestimmungen über die Sklaverei in den deutschen afrikanischen Schutzgebieten," Mitteilungen des Seminars für Orientalische Sprachen. Afrikanische Studien, 18 (1915), pp. 1-41.

3172. Weidner, Fritz. Die Haussklaverei in Ostafrika. Jena: G. Fischer, 1915. (Veröffentlichungen des Reichskolonialamtes, Nr. 7)

3173. Weiskel, Timothy C. "Labor in the Emergent Periphery: From Slavery to Migrant Labor among the Baule Peoples, 1880-1925," in Walter L. Goldfrank, ed., The World System of Capitalism: Past and Present (Beverly Hills: Sage Publications, 1979), pp. 207-33.

3174. White, C. M. N. "Clan, Chieftainship, and Slavery in Luvale Political Organization," Africa, 27, 1 (1957), pp. 59-75.

3175. Wiley, Bell I., ed. Slaves No More: Letters from Liberia 1833-1869. Lexington, Ky.: University Press of Kentucky, 1980.

3176. Wirz, Albert. Vom Sklavenhandel zum kolonialen Handel: Wirtschaftsräume und Wirtschaftsformen in Kamerun vor 1914. Freiburg: Atlantis Verlag, 1972.

3177. Woortman, Klass. "O colonialismo português em Angola," Debate e crítica, 3 (1974), pp. 27-60.

3178. Worden, Nigel. "The Distribution of Slaves in the Western Cape during the Eighteenth Century," in K. Gottschalk and C. Saunders, eds., Africa Seminar: Collected Papers (Cape Town: Centre for African Studies, University of Cape Town, 1981), vol. 2, pp. 1-23. *Republished in South African Historical Journal, 10 (1982), pp.

3179. _____. "Rural Slave Ownership in the Stellenbosch and Drakenstein Districts of the Cape Colony during the Eighteenth Century" (Unpublished paper, 1980).

3180. _____. "Rural Slavery in the Western Districts of Cape Colony during the Eighteenth century" (PhD diss., Cambridge University, 1982). Forthcoming, Cambridge University Press.

3181. _____. "Violence, Crime and Slavery on Cape Farmsteads in the Eighteenth Century," Kronos, 5 (1982), pp. 43-60.

3182. Wright, Marcia. "Bwanikwa: Consciousness and Protest Among Slave Women in Central Africa, 1886-1911," in Robertson and Klein, eds., Women and Slavery in Africa, pp. 246-67.

3183. _____. "Women in Peril: A Commentary on the Life Stories of Captives in Nineteenth Century East Central Africa," African Social Research, 20 (1975), pp. 800-19.

3184. Wrigley, Christopher C. "Historicism in Africa: Slavery and State Formation," African Affairs, 70 (no. 279)(1971), pp. 113-24.

3185. Wylie, Kenneth C. "The Slave Trade in Nineteenth Century Temneland and the British Sphere of Influence," African Studies Review, 16, 2 (1973), pp. 203-17.

3186. Zimmermann, Matilde. "The French Slave Trade at Moçambique, 1770-1794" (MA thesis, University of Wisconsin - Madison, 1967).

3187. Zyl, D. J. van. "Die Slaaf in die Ekonomiese Lewe van die Westelike Distrikte van die Kaapkolonie, 1795-1834," South African Historical Journal, 10 (1978), pp. 3-25.

VII. Muslim

1. General and comparative

3188. Ahmad, Shafiq. L'esclavage au point de vue musulman. Cairo: Imprimerie Nationale, 1891.

3189. Arafat, W. "The Attitude of Islam to Slavery," Islamic Quarterly, 10, 1-2 (1966), pp. 12-18.

3190. *Barbour, Bernard, and Michelle Jacobs. "The Miraj: A Legal Treatise on Slavery by Ahmad Baba," in Willis, ed., Islam and the Ideology of Enslavement, forthcoming.

3191. Bashir Ahmad, Mirza. Islam and Slavery. Qadian, Punjab: Book Depot Talifo-Isha'at, 1935.

3192. *Bousquet, G. H. "Des droits de l'esclave: fragment extrait de l'Ih'ya de Ghazali," Annales de l'Institute d'études occitanes, 10 (1952), pp. 420-27.

3193. Brunschvig, R. "Abd," in The Encyclopaedia of Islam (2nd ed.)(Leiden: E. J. Brill, 1960), vol. 1, pp. 24-40.

3194. Burton-Page, J. "Habshi," Encyclopedia of Islam (new ed.)(Leiden and London, 1971), vol. 3, pp. 14-16.

3195. El Wahid Wafi, Ali Abd. "Human Rights in Islam," Islamic Quarterly, 11, 1-2 (1967), pp. 64-75.

3196. Fisher, Allan G. B., and Humphrey J. Fisher. Slavery and Muslim Society in Africa: The Institution in Saharan and Sudanic Africa, and the Trans-Saharan Trade. London: C. Hurst, 1970.

3197. Forand, Paul G. "The Relation of the Slave and the Client to the Master or Patron in Medieval Islam," International Journal of Middle East Studies, 2, 1 (1971), pp. 59-66.

3198. Ghoraba, Hammouda. "Islam and Slavery," Islamic Quarterly, 2, 3 (1955), pp. 153-59.

3199. Goldstein, Ferdinand. "Die Sklaverei in Nordafrika und im Sudan," Zeitschrift für Socialwissenschaft, 11 (1908), pp. 352-69.

3200. Greenidge, C. W. W. "Slavery in the Middle East," Middle Eastern Affairs, 7, 12 (1956), pp. 435-40.

3201. Haas, Samuel S. "The Contribution of Slaves to and Their Influence upon the Culture of Early Islam" (PhD diss., Princeton University, 1942).

3202. *Hambly, Gavin R. G. "Islamic Slavery: An Overview" (Unpublished paper, 1972).

3203. Hunwick, J. O. "Black Africans in the Islamic World: An Understudied Dimension of the Black Diaspora," Tarikh, 5 (1978), pp. 20-40.

3204. Leckie, J. D. "Slavery in Mohammedan Countries," Chambers's Journal, 7th ser., 15 (1925), pp. 276-77.

3205. *Levtzion, Nehemia. "Slavery and Islamization in Africa," in Willis, ed., Islam and the Ideology of Enslavement, forthcoming.

3206. Lewis, Bernard. "The African Diaspora and the Civilization of Islam," in Kilson and Rotberg, eds., African Diaspora, pp. 37-56.

3207. _____. Race and Color in Islam. New York: Harper and Row, 1971.

3208. *Moraes Farias, Paulo Fernando de. "Models of the World and Categorical Models: The 'Enslavable Barbarian' as a Mobile Classificatory Label," in Willis, ed., Islam and the Ideology of Enslavement, forthcoming.

3209. *Muhammad, Akbar. "The Image of Africans in Arabic Literature: Some Unpublished Manuscripts," in Willis, ed., Islam and the Ideology of Enslavement, forthcoming.

3210. Müller, Hans. "Sklaven," in B. Spuler, ed., Handbuch der Orientalistik, Abt. 1: Der Nahe und der Mittlere Osten (Leiden, 1977), Bd. 6, Abt. 6, pp. 53-83.

3211. Nars, Helmi Mohamed Ibrahim. "A escrabatura (sic) no Corão," Anais do VI Simpósio nacional dos professores universitários de história (Goiâna, 1971)(São Paulo, 1973), vol. 1, pp. 215-24.

3212. Oded, Aryeh. "Slaves and Oil: The Arab Image in Black Africa," Wiener Library Bulletin, 27 (no. 32)(1974), pp. 34-47.

3213. Odoom, Kobina Osan. "Slavery and the Concept of Man in the Qur'an" (MA thesis, McGill University, 1964-65).

3214. Roberts, Robert. Das Familien-, Sklaven-, und Erbrecht im Qorân. Leipzig, 1908. (Leipziger Semitistische Studien, Bd. 2, Heft 6) Translated as The Social Laws of the Qorân . . . (London: Williams and Norgate, 1925).

3215. Rotter, Gerhard. "Die Stellung des Negers in der islamisch-arabischen Gesellschaft bis zum XVI Jahrhundert" (PhD diss., Rheinische Friedrich-Wilhelms-Universität, Bonn, 1967).

3216. *Serson, William John. "Stereotypes and Attitudes towards Slaves in Arabic Proverbs," in Willis, ed., Islam and the Ideology of Enslavement, forthcoming.

3217. Sundiata, I. K. "Beyond Race and Color in Islam," Journal of Ethnic Studies, 6, 1 (1978), pp. 1-24.

3218. Vesely, Rudolf. "De la situation des esclaves dans l'institution du wakf," Archiv Orientální, 32, 3 (1964), pp. 345-53.

3219. Weckwarth, Kurt E. Der Sklave im muhammedanischen Recht. Berlin, 1909.

3220. Wesselski, Albert. "Die gelehrten Sklavninnen des Islams und ihre byzantinischen Vorbilder," Archiv Orientální, 9, 3 (1937), pp. 353-78.

3221. *Willis, John Ralph. "Introduction," in Willis, ed., Islam and the Ideology of Enslavement, forthcoming.

3222. *_____. "Introduction," in Willis, ed., Servile Estate, forthcoming.

3223. _____. "Islamic Africa: Reflections on the Servile Estate," Studia Islamica, 52 (1980), pp. 183-97.

3224. *_____. "Jihad and the Ideology of Enslavement," in Willis, ed., Islam and the Ideology of Enslavement, forthcoming.

3225. *_____, ed. Islam and the Ideology of Enslavement. London: Cass, forthcoming. (Vol. 1 of Slaves and Slavery in Muslim Africa)

3226. *_____, ed. The Servile Estate. London: Cass, forthcoming. (Vol. 2 of Slaves and Slavery in Muslim Africa)

3227. _____, ed. Slaves and Slavery in Muslim Africa. London: Cass, forthcoming. Vol. 1: Islam and the Ideology of Enslavement; Vol. 2: The Servile Estate.

3228. *Zeys, Ernest. "Esclavage et guerre sainte: consultation adressée aux gens du Touat par un érudit nègre de Timcoubtou au XVIIe siècle," Bulletin de la Réunion d'études algériennes (Paris) (1900), pp.   .

2. Caliphate and Arabia

3229. Abdul Jabbar Beg, Muhammad. "The 'Serfs' of Islamic Society under the Abbasid Regime," Islamic Culture, 49, 2 (1975), pp. 107-18.

3230. Bacharach, Jere L. "African Military Slaves in the Medieval Middle East: The Cases of Iraq (869-955) and Egypt (868-1171)," International Journal of Middle East Studies, 13, 4 (1981), pp. 471-95.

3231. Bosworth, C. E. "Ghaznevid Military Organization," Der Islam, 36, 1-2 (1960), pp.. 37-77.

3232. Chejne, Anwar G. "The Boon-Companion in Early Abbasid Times," Journal of the American Oriental Society, 85 (1965), pp. 327-35.

3233. Crone, Patricia. Slaves on Horses: The Evolution of the Islamic Polity. New York: Cambridge University Press, 1980.

3234. DeJong, Garrett E. "Slavery in Arabia," Moslem World, 24, 2 (1934), pp. 126-44.

3235. Forand, Paul Glidden. "The Development of Military Slavery under the Abbasid Caliphs of the Ninth Century A.D. (Third Century A.H.), With Special Reference to the Reigns of Mu'Tasim and Mu'Tadid" (PhD diss., Princeton University, 1962).

3236. Harrison, Paul W. "Slavery in Arabia," Moslem World, 29, 2 (1939), pp. 207-09.

3237. Hrbek, Ivan. "Die Slawen in Dienste der Fatimiden," Archiv Orientální, 21, 4 (1953), pp. 543-81.

3238. Kreissig, Heinz. "Versuch über den Status der Lohnarbeiter im hellenistischen Orient (Seleukidenreich),"in Schiavitù, manomissione e classi dipendenti, pp. 105-13. With intervention from I. Biezunska-Malowist and response by Kreissig.

3239. Lara, Oruno D. "Esclavage et révoltes négro-africaines dans l'Empire musulman du Haut Moyen Age," Présence africaine, 2 (1976), pp. 50-103.

3240. Little, Donald P. "Six Fourteenth Century Purchase Deeds for Slaves from Al-Haram As-Sarif," Zeitschrift der Deutschen morgenländischen Gesellschaft, 131, 2 (1981), pp. 297-337.

3241. _____. "Two Fourteenth-Century Court Records from Jerusalem Concerning the Disposition of Slaves by Minors," Arabica: revue d'études arabes, 29, 1 (1982), pp. 16-49.

3242. Nadiradze, L. I. "Vopros o rabstve v ghalifate VII-VIIIvv," Narodni Azii i Afriki, 5 (1968), pp. 75-85. (In Russian with English summary: "The Problem of Slavery in the Caliphate (7th-8th Centuries)")

3243. Petrushevsky, I. P. "K istorii rabstva v khalifate VII-X vekov," Narodni Azii i Afriki, 3 (1971), pp. 60-71. (In Russian with English summary: "On the History of Slavery in the Khalifate from the Seventh to the Tenth Century")

3244. Pipes, Daniel. "Mawlas: Freed Slaves and Converts in Early Islam," Slavery and Abolition, 1, 2 (1980), pp. 132-77. *Also in Willis, ed., Islam and the Ideology of Enslavement, forthcoming.

3245. _____. Slave Soldiers and Islam: The Genesis of a Military System. New Haven: Yale University Press, 1981.

3246. Popovic, Alexandre. "Ali b. Muhammed et la révolte des esclaves à Basra" (PhD diss., Université de Paris, 1965).

3247. _____. "Quelques renseignements inédits concernant 'le Maître des Zang', Ali b. Muhammad," Arabica, 12, 2 (1965), pp. 175-87.

3248. _____. La révolte des esclaves en Iraq au IIIe/IXe siècles. Paris: Geuthner, 1976.

3249. Serjeant, R. B. "South Arabia and Ethiopia - African Elements in the South Arabian Population," Proceedings of the Third International Conference of Ethiopian Studies (Addis Ababa: Institute of Ethiopian Studies, Haile Selassie I University, 1966), vol. 1, pp. 25-33.

3. Ottoman Empire - Muslim Turkey

3250. Barkan, Ömer Lutfi. "Le servage existait-il en Turquie?" Annales: économies, sociétés, civilisations, 11, 1 (1956), pp. 54-60. In Turkish: "Türkiyede 'servaj' var mi ich?" Belleten, 20 (1956), pp. 237-46.

3251. Cahen, Claude. "Note sur l'esclavage musulman et le devshirme ottoman, à propos de travaux récents," Journal of the Economic and Social History of the Orient, 13, 2 (1970), pp. 211-18.

3252. *Fisher, Alan W. "Chattel Slave Procurement in the Ottoman Empire" (Paper presented to 12th Annual Meeting of the Middle East Studies Association, Ann Arbor, 1978).

3253. _____. "Chattel Slavery in the Ottoman Empire," Slavery and Abolition, 1, 1 (1980), pp. 25-45.

3254. _____. "The Sale of Slaves in the Ottoman Empire: Markets and State Taxes on Slave Sales, Some Preliminary Considerations," Bogaziçi Universitesi Dergisi, 6 (1978), pp. 149-71.

3255. _____. "Studies in Ottoman Slavery and Slave Trade, II: Manumission," Journal of Turkish Studies, 4 (1980), pp. 49-56.

3256. Gurlitt, Cornelius. "Die Sklaverei bei den Türken im 16. Jahrhundert, nach europäischen Berichten," Beiträge zur Kenntnis des Orients, 10 (1913), pp. 84-102.

3257. Inalcik, Halil. "Servile Labor in the Ottoman Empire," in Abraham Ascher, Tibor Halasi-Kun and Béla K. Király, eds., The Mutual Effects of the Islamic and Judeo-Christian Worlds: The East European Pattern (Brooklyn: Brooklyn College Press, 1979), pp. 25-52.

3258. Jahn, Karl. "Zum Loskauf christlicher und türkischer Gefangener und Sklaven im 18. Jahrhundert," Zeitschrift der Deutschen morgenländischen Gesellschaft, 111, 1 (1961), pp. 63-85.

3259. Millant, Richard. L'esclavage en Turquie. Paris, 1912.

3260. Penzer, Norman Mosley. The Harem: An Account of the Institution as it Existed in the Palace of the Turkish Sultans, with a History of the Grand Seraglio from its Foundation to the Present Time. London: G. G. Harrap, 1936.

3261. Prager, Carolyn. "'Turkish' and Turkish Slavery: English Renaissance Perceptions of Levantine Bondage," Centerpoint, 2, 1 (1976), pp. 57-64.

3262. Sacca, V. "Mercato di schiavi turchi," Archivio storico messinese, 6, 1-2 (1906), pp. 151-53.

4. Muslim Egypt

3263. Abd-ar-Raziq, Ahmed. "Un document concernant le mariage des esclaves au temps des Mamluks," Journal of the Economic and Social History of the Orient, 13 (1970), pp. 309-14.

3264. Ayalon, David. Gunpowder and Firearms in the Mamluk Kingdom: A Challenge to Medieval Society. London: Vallentine, Mitchell, 1956.

3265. _____. L'esclavage du Mamelouk. Jerusalem: Israel Oriental Society, 1951.

3266. _____. "Studies on the Structure of the Mamluk Army," Bulletin of the School of Oriental and African Studies, 15, 1 (1953), pp. 203-28; 15, 2 (1953), pp. 448-76; 16, 1 (1954), pp. 57-90.

3267. Baer, Gabriel. "Slavery and its Abolition," in idem, Studies in the Social History of Modern Egypt (Chicago and London, 1969), pp. 161-89.

3268. _____. "Slavery in Nineteenth Century Egypt," Journal of African History, 8, 3 (1967), pp. 417-41.

3269. Fredriksen, B. "Slavery and its Abolition in Nineteenth Century Egypt" (Hovedfag thesis, University of Bergen, 1977).

3270. Goitein, S. D. "Slaves and Slave Girls in the Cairo Geniza Records," Arabica, 9 (1962), pp. 1-20.

3271. Neustadt, David. "The Plague and its Effects upon the Mamluk Army," Journal of the Royal Asiatic Society, 3rd ser., 1-2 (1946), pp. 67-73.

3272. Swiderek, Anna. "Gli Egiziani di Al Fayyum," in Storia sociale ed economica, pp. 165-87.

3273. Toledano, Ehud R. "Slave Dealers, Women, Pregnancy, and Abortion: The Story of a Circassian Slave-Girl in Mid-Nineteenth Century Cairo," Slavery and Abolition, 2, 1 (1981), pp. 53-68.

3274. Verlinden, Charles. "Mamelouks et traitants: économies et sociétés médiévales," in Economies et sociétés au Moyen Age: mélanges offerts à Edouard Perroy (Paris: Publications de la Sorbonne, 1973), pp. 737-47. (Série Etudes, no. 5)

3275. *Walz, Terence. "Black Slavery in Egypt during the Nineteenth Century as Reflected in the Mahkama Archives of Cairo," in Willis, ed., Servile Estate, forthcoming.

5. North Africa and the Sahara

3276. Baier, Stephen, and Paul E. Lovejoy. "The Tuareg of the Central Sudan: Gradations in Servility at the Desert Edge (Niger and Nigeria)," in Miers and Kopytoff, eds., Slavery in Africa, pp. 391-411.

3277. *Batran, Aziz Abdalla. "The Ulama of Fas, Mulay Ismail, and the Issue of the Haratin of Fas," in Willis, ed., Servile Estate, forthcoming.

3278. Bennett, Norman R. "Christian and Negro Slavery in Eighteenth-Century North Africa," Journal of African History, 1, 1 (1960), pp. 65-82.

3279. Bernus, Edmond, and Suzanne Bernus. "L'évolution de la condition servile chez les Touareg sahéliens," in Meillassoux, ed., L'esclavage en Afrique pré-coloniale, pp. 27-47.

3280. Bonte, Pierre. "Esclavage et relations de dépendance chez les Touregs Kel Gress," in Meillassoux, ed., L'esclavage en Afrique pré-coloniale, pp. 49-76.

3281. Clissold, Stephen. The Barbary Slaves. Totowa, N.J.: Rowman and Littlefield, 1977.

3282. Derrick, Jonathan. "Slavery and Mauritanian Society," West Africa, 3287 (1980), pp. 1329-30.

3283. Friedman, Ellen G. "Christian Captives at 'Hard Labor' in Algiers, 16th-18th Centuries," International Journal of African Historical Studies, 13, 4 (1980), pp. 616-32.

3284. Hunkanrin, Louis. "L'esclavage en Mauritanie," Etudes dahoméennes, 3 (1964), pp. 31-50.

3285. Larquié, Claude. "Le rachat des chrétiens en terre d'Islam au XVIIe siècle (1660-1665)," Revue d'histoire diplomatique, 94 (no. 4)(1980), pp. 297-351.

3286. McDonough, Craig. "Slavery in Production and Trade: The Case of the Modern Tuareg," Peasant Studies, 8, 3 (1979), pp. 45-58.

3287. Meyers, Allan Richard. "The Abid 'l-Buhari: Slave Soldiers and Statecraft in Morocco, 1671-1790" (PhD diss., Georgia Institute of Technology, 1974).

3288. _____. "Slave Soldiers and State Politics in Early 'Alawi Morocco, 1668-1727," International Journal of African Historical Studies, 16, 1 (1983), pp. 39-48.

3289. Michaux-Bellaire, E. "L'esclavage au Maroc," Revue du monde musulman, 11 (1910), pp. 422-27.

3290. *Nicolaisen, Johannes N. "L'esclavage entre les peuples pastoraux Touareg en Ahaggar en Air" (1er Congrès international des Africanistes, Accra, 1962).

3291. _____. "Slaveri hos Tuaregerne i Sahara," Kuml (1957), pp. 91-113. (In Danish, with English summary: "Slavery among the Tuareg in the Sahara: A Preliminary Analysis of its Structure")

3292. Pignon, Jean. "L'esclavage en Tunisie de 1590 à 1620," Revue tunisienne (1930), pp. 18-37; (1932), pp. 345-77. Reprinted in Cahiers de Tunisie, 24, 1-2 (nos. 93-94)(1976), pp. 143-65.

3293. Riggio, Achille. "Un censimento di schiavi in Tunisia ottocentesca," Archivio storico per la Calabria e la Lucania, 8, 3-4 (1938), pp. 333-52.

3294. Serfass, Charles. Les esclaves chrétiens au Maroc du XVIe au XVIIe siècle. Paris, 1930.

3295. Starrett, Priscilla Ellen. "Tuareg Slavery and Slave Trade," Slavery and Abolition, 2, 2 (1981), pp. 83-113.

3296. Talbi, Mohamed. "Law and Economy in Ifriqiya (Tunisia) in the Third Islamic Century: Agriculture and the Role of Slaves in the Country's Economy," in A. L. Udovitch, ed., The Islamic Middle East, 700-1900: Studies in Economic and Social History (Princeton: Darwin Press, 1981), pp. 209-50.

3297. Valensi, Lucette. "Esclaves chrétiens et esclaves noirs à Tunis au XVIIIe siècle," Annales: économies, sociétés, civilisations, 22, 6 (1967), pp. 1267-88.

3298. *Verlinden, Charles. "Un belge esclave à Alger au XVIIIe siècle: Emanuel d'Aranda," Les Beaux-Arts, (1936), pp. 22-24.

6. Nilotic Sudan

3299. Ali, Abbas Ibrahim Muhammad. The British, the Slave Trade, and Slavery in the Sudan, 1820-1881. Khartoum: Khartoum University Press, 1972.

3300. *Hilliard, Constance. "Zuhur al-Basatin and Ta'rikh al-Turubbe: Some Legal and Ethical Aspects of Slavery in the Sudan as seen in the Works of Shaykh Musa Kamara," in Willis, ed., Islam and the Ideology of Enslavement, forthcoming.

3301. Kapteijns, Lidwien. "The Use of Slaves in Precolonial Western Dar Fur: The Case of Dar Masalit, 1870-1915" (Unpublished paper, Conference on the Political Economy of Northeast Africa, Michigan State University, April 1983).

3302. McLoughlin, Peter F. M. "Economic Development and the Heritage of Slavery in the Sudan Republic," Africa, 32, 4 (1962), pp. 355-91.

3303. *O'Fahey, R. S. "Slavery and Society in Dar Fur," in Willis, ed., Servile Estate, forthcoming.

3304. Shaked, Haim. "Charles George Gordon and the Problem of Slavery in the Sudan," Slavery and Abolition, 1, 3 (1980), pp. 276-91.

3305. Shukry, M. R. The Khedive Ismail and Slavery in the Sudan, 1863-79. Cairo: Librairie la Renaissance d'Egypte, 1937.

3306. Spaulding, Jay. "Slavery, Land Tenure and Social Class in the Northern Turkish Sudan," International Journal of African Historical Studies, 15, 1 (1982), pp. 1-20.

3307. Warburg, Gabriel R. "Ideological and Practical Considerations Regarding Slavery in the Mahdist State and the Anglo-Egyptian Sudan, 1881-1918," in Lovejoy, ed., Ideology of Slavery in Africa, pp. 245-70.

3308. _____. "Slavery and Labour in the Anglo-Egyptian Sudan," Asian and African Studies, 12, 2 (1978), pp. 221-45. *Also in Willis, ed., Servile Estate, forthcoming.

7. Muslim West Africa

3309. Armstrong, R. "The Nightwatchmen of Kano," Middle Eastern Studies, 3, 3 (1967), pp. 269-82.

3310. Ayandele, E. A. "Observations on Some Social and Economic Aspects of Slavery in Pre-Colonial Northern Nigeria," Nigerian Journal of Economic and Social Studies, 9, 3 (1967), pp. 329-38. Reprinted in idem, Nigerian Historical Studies (London: Frank Cass, 1979), pp. 65-78.

3311. Baldé, Mamadou Saliou. "L'esclavage et la guerre sainte au Fuuta-Jalon (Maccujaaku e jihaadi Fuuta-Jaloo)," in Meillassoux, ed., L'esclavage en Afrique pré-coloniale, pp. 183-220.

3312. Burnham, Philip. "Raiders and Traders in Adamawa: Slavery as a Regional System," in Watson, ed., Asian and African Systems of Slavery, pp. 43-72.

3313. Büttner, Thea. "On the Social-Economic Structure of Adamawa in the Nineteenth Century: Slavery or Serfdom?" in Walter Markov, ed., African Studies (Leipzig: Karl Marx Universität, 1967), pp., 43-61.

3314. Dunbar, Roberta Ann. "Slavery and the Evolution of Nineteenth-Century Damagaram (Zinder, Niger)," in Miers and Kopytoff, eds., Slavery in Africa, pp. 155-77.

3315. Hill, Polly. "From Slavery to Freedom: The Case of Farm-Slavery in Nigerian Hausaland," Comparative Studies in Society and History, 18, 3 (1976), pp. 395-426.

3316. *Hiskett, Mervyn. "The Image of Slaves in Hausa Literature," in Willis, ed., Islam and the Ideology of Enslavement, forthcoming.

3317. Hogendorn, Jan S. "The Economics of Slave Use on Two 'Plantations' in the Zaria Emirate of the Sokoto Caliphate," International Journal of African Historical Studies, 10, 3 (1977), pp. 369-83.

3318. _____. "Slave Acquisition and Delivery in Precolonial Hausaland," in Raymond E. Dumett and Ben K. Swartz, eds., West African Culture Dynamics: Archeological and Historical Perspectives (The Hague: Mouton, 1980), pp. 477-93.

3319. *Hunwick, J. O. "Notes on Slavery in the Songhay Empire," in Willis, ed., Servile Estate, forthcoming.

3320. Klein, Martin A. "Servitude among the Wolof and Sereer of Senegambia," in Miers and Kopytoff, eds., Slavery in Africa, pp. 335-63.

3321. Knops, P. "L'esclavage chez les soudanais d'Afrique occidentale," Bulletin de la Société royale belge d'anthropologie et de préhistoire, 78 (1967), pp. 71-80.

3322. Lovejoy, Paul E. "Slavery in the Sokoto Caliphate," in idem, ed., Ideology of Slavery in Africa, pp. 201-44.

3323. Mason, Michael. "Captive and Client Labour and the Economy of the Bida Emirate: 1857-1901," Journal of African History, 14, 3 (1973), pp. 453-71.

3324. Maugham, Robin. The Slaves of Timbuktu. New York: Harper, 1961.

3325. Meyers, Allan. "Slavery in the Hausa-Fulani Emirates," in Daniel F. McCall and Norman R. Bennett, eds., Aspects of West African Islam (Boston: African Studies Center, Boston University, 1971), pp. 173-84.

3326. Olusanya, G. O. "The Freed Slaves' Homes - An Unknown Aspect of Northern Nigerian Social History," Journal of the Historical Society of Nigeria, 3, 3 (1966), pp. 523-38.

3327. Patton, Adell, Jr. "Ningi Raids and Slavery in Nineteenth Century Sokoto Caliphate," Slavery and Abolition, 2, 2 (1981), pp. 114-45.

3328. Poussibet, Félix. "Réflexions sur l'esclavage au Sahara et au Sahel maliens," Notes africaines (IFAN, Dakar), no. 162 (1979), pp. 36-42.

3329. Sanneh, L. O. "Slavery, Islam, and the Jakhanke People of West Africa," Africa, 46, 1 (1976), pp. 80-97.

3330. Sellnow, Irmgard. "Die Stellung der Sklaven in der Hausa-Gesellschaft," Mitteilungen des Instituts für Orientforschung, 10 (1964), pp. 85-102.

3331. Tambo, David C. "The Sokoto Caliphate Slave Trade in the Nineteenth Century," International Journal of African Historical Studies, 9, 2 (1976), pp. 187-217.

8. Muslim East Africa

3332. Akinola, G. A. "Slavery and Slave Revolts in the Sultanate of Zanzibar in the Nineteenth Century," Journal of the Historical Society of Nigeria, 6, 2 (1972), pp. 215-28.

3333. Beech, Mervyn W. H. "Slavery on the East Coast of Africa," Journal of the African Society, 15 (1915-16), pp. 145-49.

3334. Benedict, Burton. "Slavery and Indenture in Mauritius and Seychelles," in Watson, ed., Asian and African Systems of Slavery, pp. 135-68.

3335. Blais, P. J. "Les anciens esclaves à Zanzibar," Anthropos, 10-11 (1915-16), pp. 504-11.

3336. Cooper, Frederick. From Slaves to Squatters: Plantation Labor and Agriculture in Zanzibar and Coastal Kenya, 1890-1925. New Haven: Yale University Press, 1980.

3337. _____. "Islam and Cultural Hegemony: The Ideology of Slaveowners on the East African Coast," in Lovejoy, ed., Ideology of Slavery in Africa, pp. 271-308.

3338. _____. "Plantation Slavery on the East Coast of Africa in the Nineteenth Century" (PhD diss., Yale University, 1974).

3339. _____. Plantation Slavery on the East Coast of Africa. New Haven: Yale University Press, 1977.

3340. _____. "The Treatment of Slaves on the Kenya Coast in the 19th Century," Kenya Historical Review, 1, 2 (1973), pp. 87-107.

3341. Le Roy, Paul E. "Slavery in the Horn of Africa," Horn of Africa, 2, 3 (1979), pp. 10-19.

3342. Lodhi, Abdulaziz Y. The Institution of Slavery in Zanzibar and Pemba. Uppsala: Scandinavian Institute of African Studies, 1973.

3343. Martin, Jean. "L'affranchissement des esclaves de Mayotte, décembre 1846 - juillet 1847," Cahiers d'études africaines, 16, 1-2 (nos. 61-62)(1976), pp. 207-33.

3344. _____. "Les débuts du protectorat et la révolte servile de 1891 dans l'île d'Anjouan," Revue française d'histoire d'outre-mer, 60, 1 (no. 218)(1973), pp. 45-85.

3345. Mazrui, Muhammad Kasim. Historia ya Utumwa Katika Uislamu na Dini Nyengine. Nairobi: Islamic Foundation, 1970.

3346. Middleton, John. "Slavery in Zanzibar," Trans-Action, 4, 3 (1967), pp. 46-48.

3347. Nwulia, Moses D. E. "The Role of Missionaries in the Emancipation of Slaves in Zanzibar," Journal of Negro History, 60, 2 (1975), pp. 268-87.

3348. Romero, Patricia. "An Examination of Material Life among Slave Families in Lamu, Kenya 1900-1963" (Unpublished paper read to the Annual Meeting of the African Studies Association, Bloomington, Indiana, October 1981).

3349. Sakarai, Lawrence J. "Indian Merchants in East Africa, Part II: Transformation of the Slave Economy," Slavery and Abolition, 2, 1 (1981), pp. 2-30.

3350. *Sheriff, A. M. H. "The Slave Mode of Production Along the East African Coast," in Willis, ed., Servile Estate, forthcoming.

3351. Strobel, Margaret. "Slave and Free in Mombasa," Kenya Historical Review, 6, 1-2 (1978), pp. 53-62. Also as following entry.

3352. _____. "Slavery and Reproductive Labor in Mombasa," in Robertson and Klein, eds., Women and Slavery in Africa, pp. 111-29.

9. Muslim India

3353. Hambly, Gavin. "A Note on the Trade in Eunuchs in Mughul Bengal," Journal of the American Oriental Society, 94, 1 (1974), pp. 125-31.

3354. _____. "Who were the Chihilgani, the Forty Slaves of Sultan Shams al-din Iltutmish of Delhi?" Iran, 10 (1972), pp. 57-62.

3355. Pal, Dharam. "The Influence of Slaves in the Muslim Administration of India," Islamic Culture, 18 (1944), pp. 409-17.

3356. Pankhurst, Richard. "The Habshi of India," Introduction to the Economic History of Ethiopia from Early Times to 1800 (London: Lalibela House, 1961), pp. 409-22.

10. Other

3357. Djajadiningrat, R. A. Dr. Hoesein. "Toepassing van het Mohammedaansche slavenrecht in de Lampoengs," Feestbundel uitgegeven door het Koninklijk Bataviaasch Genootschap van Kunsten en Wetenschappen (Lembaga Kebudajaan, Indonesia) (Weltevreden: G. Kolff, 1929), vol. 1, pp. 87-92.

VIII. Ancient

1. General and comparative

3358. Acta antiqua philippopolitana (6ème Conférence internationale d'études classiques des pays socialistes. Plovdiv, Bulgaria, 1962.) Sendicae: Typographicis Academiae Scientiarum Bulgaricae, 1963. Vol. 1: Studia archaeologica; Vol. 2: Studia historica et philologica.

3359. Actes du colloque sur l'esclavage. Annales Littéraires de l'Université de Besançon (Paris). Centre de recherches d'histoire ancienne, vol. 6 (Colloque 1971), 1972; vol. 11 (Colloque 1972), 1974; vol. 18 (Colloque 1973), 1976.

3360. Annequin, Jacques. "M. I. Finley et l'esclavage antique: décrire et expliquer une forme d'exploitation du travail," Dialogues d'histoire ancienne, 7 (1981), pp. 437-49.

3361. _____, M. Clavel-Lévêque, and F. Favory. "Présentation: Formes d'exploitation du travail et rapports sociaux dans l'Antiquité classique," Recherches internationales à la lumière du marxisme, no. 84, 3 (1975), pp. 3-44.

3362. Ashley, Winston Norman. "The Theory of Natural Slavery According to Aristotle and St. Thomas" (PhD diss., University of Notre Dame, 1941).

3363. Backhaus, Wilhelm. "John Elliott Cairnes und die Erforschung der antiken Sklaverei," Historische Zeitschrift, no. 220, 3 (1975), pp. 543-67.

3364. _____, and N. Brockmeyer. Antike Quellen zur Sklaverei. Bochum, forthcoming.

3365. Badian, E. "The Bitter History of Slave History (review of Finley, Ancient Slavery and Modern Ideology, and Wiedemann, Greek and Roman Slavery)," New York Review of Books, 28, 16 (22 Oct. 1981), pp. 49-53.

3366. _____. "Marx in the Agora (review of de Ste. Croix, Class Struggle in the Ancient Greek World)," New York Review of Books, 29, 19 (2 Dec. 1982), pp. 47-51.

3367. Beardsley, Grace Maynard Hadley. The Negro in Greek and Roman Civilization: A Study of the Ethiopian Type. Baltimore: Johns Hopkins Press, 1929. (Johns Hopkins University Studies in Archaeology, no. 4)

3368. Biezunska-Malowist, Iza. "Ancient Slavery Reconsidered (review-essay of Finley, Ancient Slavery and Modern Ideology)," Review, 6, 1 (1982), pp. 111-26.

3369. * _____. "Quelques formes non typiques de l'esclavage dans le monde ancien," in Academy of the Arts and Sciences, USSR, Antekhnoe Obschestvo (Moscow: Nauka, 1976), pp. 91-95.

3370. _____, ed. Storia sociale ed economica dell'età classica negli studi polacchi contemporanei. Milan: Cisalpino-Goliardica, 1975.

3371. Bloch, Marc. "Comment et pourquoi finit l'esclavage antique," Annales: économies, sociétés, civilisations, 2, 1 (1947), pp. 30-44; 2, 2 (1947), pp. 161-70. Reprinted in Finley, ed., Slavery in Classical Antiquity, pp. 204-28; in Bloch, Mélanges historiques (Paris: S.E.V.P.E.N., 1963), vol. 1, pp. 261-85; trans. in Bloch, Slavery and Serfdom, pp. 1-31.

3372. Brockmeyer, Norbert. Antike Sklaverei. Darmstadt: Wissenschaftliche Buchgesellschaft, 1979. (Erträge der Forschung, Bd. 116)

3373. _____. Bibliographie zur antiken Sklaverei (ed. J. Vogt). Bochum: Buchhandlung Brockmeyer, 1971.

3374. Capozza, Maria, et al. Schiavitù, manomissione e classi dipendenti del mondo antico. Roma: L'Erma di Bretschneider, 1979. (Pubblicazioni dell'Istituto di Storia Antica, Università degli Studi di Padova, vol. 13)

3375. Casson, Lionel. "Galley Slaves," Transactions and Proceedings of the American Philological Association, 97 (1966), pp. 35-44.

3376. Centre de recherches d'histoire ancienne, Université de Besançon. See Actes du colloque sur l'esclavage.

3377. Ceska, Josef. "Über die Vernichtung von Arbeitsgeräten durch die antiken Sklaven," Bibliotheca Classica Orientalis, 2 (1957), pp. 201-02. (In Slovak, summarized in German)

3378. Ciccotti, Ettore. Il tramonto della schiavitù nel mondo antico. Revised edition. Udine: Istituto delle Edizioni Accademiche, 1940. Original edition (Torino, 1899) translated by Oda Olberg as Der Untergang der Sklaverei im Altertum (Berlin, 1910).

3379. Cohen, Boaz. "Civil Bondage in Jewish and Roman Law," Louis Ginzberg Jubilee Volume (English Section) (New York: American Academy for Jewish Research, 1945), pp. 113-32.

3380. Croiset, Alfred. "L'affranchissement des esclaves pour faits de guerre," in Mélanges Henri Weil (Paris: A. Fontemoing, 1898), pp. 67-72.

3381. Debord, Pierre. "L'esclavage sacré: état de la question," Actes du colloque sur l'esclavage (1971), pp. 135-50.

3382. Deininger, Jürgen. "Neue Forschungen zur antiken Sklaverei," Historische Zeitschrift, 222, 2 (1976), pp. 359-74.

3383. de Ste. Croix, Geoffrey E. M. "(Review of Westermann, Slave Systems)," Classical Review, n.s. 7, 1 (1957), pp. 54-59.

3384. Diakonoff, I. M. "Slaves, Helots and Serfs in Early Antiquity," Vestnik Drevnei Istorii, 126 (1973), pp. 3-29. (In Russian with English summary) Translated as "Slaves, Helots and Serfs in Early Antiquity," Acta antiqua (Academiae Scientiarum Hungaricae), 22 (1974), pp. 45-78.

3385. Diesner, Hans-Joachim. "Römische und vandalische Sklaven," Acta antiqua philippopolitana, vol. 1, pp. 53-57.

3386. Dobschütz. "Sklaverei und Christentum," in Johann Jakob Herzog, ed., Realencyklopädie für Protestantische Theologie und Kirch (Leipzig: J. C. Hinrichs, 1896-1913), vol. 18, pp. 423-33.

3387. Erles, Adalbert. Ältere Ansätze zur Überwindung der Sklaverei. Wiesbaden: Steiner, 1978.

3388. "Etat et classes dans l'Antiquité esclavagiste," Recherches internationales à la lumière du marxisme, cahier no. 2 (1957).

3389. Finley, Moses I. The Ancient Economy. Berkeley: University of California Press, 1973.

3390. _____. Ancient Slavery and Modern Ideology. New York: Viking Press, 1980.

3391. _____. "Masters and Slaves," in idem, The Ancient Economy, pp. 62-94.

3392. _____. "The Significance of Ancient Slavery (A Brief Reply)," Acta antiqua (Academiae Scientiarum Hungaricae), 9, 3-4 (1961), pp. 285-86.

3393. _____, ed. Slavery in Classical Antiquity: Views and Controversies. Cambridge: Cambridge University Press, 1960.

3394. Fiore, Lanfranco. La condizione dello schiavo nell'antichità classica. Teramo: CETI, 1968.

3395. Flory, Marleen Boudreau. "Family in Familia: Kinship and Community in Slavery," American Journal of Ancient History, 3, 1 (1978), pp. 79-95.

3396. Forbes, Clarence A. "The Education and Training of Slaves in Antiquity," Transactions and Proceedings of the American Philological Association, 86 (1955), pp. 321-60.

3397. "Formes d'exploitation du travail et rapports sociaux dans l'antiquité classique," Recherches internationales à la lumière du marxisme, no. 84, 3 (1975).

3398. Gaudemet, J. "Esclavage et dépendance dans l'antiquité: bilan et perspectives," Tijdschrift voor Rechtsgeschiedenis, 50, 2 (1982), pp. 119-56.

3399. Grace, E. "The Legal Position of Slaves in Homicide Cases," Vestnik Drevnei Istorii, 128 (1974), pp. 34-56. (In Russian with English summary)

3400. Green, Peter. "Downtreading the demos (review of de Ste. Croix, Class Struggle in the Ancient Greek World, and of Lintott, Violence, Civil Strife and Revolution in the Classical City)," Times Literary Supplement, no. 4167 (11 February 1983), pp. 125-26.

3401. Groupe Internationale de Recherches sur l'Esclavage Ancien (GIREA). See Schiavitù, manomissione e classi dipendenti.

3402. Günther, Rigobert. "Einige Bermerkungen zur historischen Gesetzmässigkeit in der Sklavenhalterordnung," in E.-Ch. Welskopf, ed., Neue Beiträge zur Geschichte der alten Welt (Berlin: Akademie Verlag, 1964), vol. 1, pp. 41-47.

3403. _____. "Die Epoche der sozialen und politischen Revolution beim Übergang von der antiken Sklavereigesellschaft zum Feudalismus," Klio, 60, 2 (1978), pp. 235-46.

3404. _____. "Die Klasse der Sklaven und ihr Klassenkampf," Zeitschrift für Geschichtswissenschaft, 8, 1 (1960), pp. 104-12.

3405. _____, and Gerhard Schrot. "Bemerkungen zur Gesetzmässigkeit in der auf Sklaverei berühenden Gesellschaftsordnung," Wissenschaftliche Zeitschrift der Karl-Marx Universität (Leipzig), 12 (1963), pp. 229-40.

3406. _____. "Einige Probleme zur
Theorie der an Sklaverei berührenden Gesellschaftsordung,"
Zeitschrift für Geschichtswissenschaft, 4, 5 (1956), pp. 990–1008.
Translated as "Problèmes théoriques de la société esclavagiste,"
in Etat et classes dans l'antiquité esclavagiste: structure,
evolution (Paris: Editions de la Nouvelle Critique, 1957), pp.
7–29. (Recherches internationales à la lumière du marxisme, no. 2)

3407. Guyot, Peter. Eunuchen als Sklaven und Freigelassene in der
griechisch-römischen Antike. Stuttgart: Klett-Cotta, 1980.

3408. *Gyürki Kis, P. A. "Gedanken des hl. Augustinus über die Sklaverei
mit Rückblick auf den antiken Zeitgeist" (Diss., Wien, 1941).

3409. Hahn, István. "Freie Arbeit und Sklavenarbeit in der spätantiken
Stadt," Annales Universitatis Scientiarum Budapestinensis, 3
(1961), pp. 23–39.

3410. _____. "Sklaven und Sklavenfrage im politischen Denken der
Spätantike," Klio, 58 (1976), pp. 459–70.

3411. Haufe, Christoph. "Die antike Beurteilung der Sklaven,"
Wissenschaftliche Zeitschrift (Leipzig), 9 (1959–60), pp. 603–16.

3412. Heinen, Heinz. "Neue sowjetische Veröffentlichungen zur antiken
Sklaverei," Historia, 28, 1 (1979), pp. 125–28.

3413. _____. "Neuere sowjetische Veröffentlichungen zur antiken
Sklaverei," Historia, 25, 4 (1976), pp. 501–05.

3414. Hopkins, Keith. "Slavery in Classical Antiquity," in de Reuck and
Knight, eds., Caste and Race, pp. 166–77. With discussion,
"Classical and American Slavery Compared," pp. 178–91.

3415. Jerovsek, A. Die antik-heidnische Sklaverei und das Christentum.
Marburg: Kralík, 1903.

3416. Jones, A. H. M. "Slavery in the Ancient World," Economic History
Review, 9, 2 (1956), pp. 185–99.

3417. Joukovsky, F. "L'esclavage antique et les humanistes," in Actes du
IXe Congrès de l'Association Guillaume Budé (Rome, 13–28 April
1973) (Paris: Société d'Edition "Les Belles Lettres", 1975), vol.
2, pp. 678–704.

3418. Kahane, Henry, and Renée Kahane. "Notes on the Linguistic History
of Sclavus," in Studi in onore di Ettore Lo Gatto e Giovanni Maver
(Florence: Sansoni, 1962), pp. 345–60.

3419. Kaser, M. "Zur Kriminalgerichtsbarkeit gegen Sklaven," Studia et
documenta historiae et iuris, 6 (1940), pp. 357–68.

3420. Kehnscherper, Gerhard. Die Stellung der Bibel und der alten christlichen Kirche zur Sklaverei: eine biblische und kirchengeschichtliche Untersuchung von den alttestamentlichen Propheten bis zum Ende des Römischen Reiches. Halle: M. Niemeyer, 1957.

3421. Kolendo, Jerzy. "Elements pour une enquête sur l'iconographie des esclaves dans l'art hellénistique et romain," in Schiavitù, manomissione e classi dipendenti, pp. 161-74 (and photos following).

3422. Kotsevalov, Andrei Stepanovich. Soviet Studies of Ancient Slavery and Slave Uprisings. Munich: Institute for the Study of the USSR, 1956. (In Russian with English summary)

3423. Kreissig, Heinz. "Um einige offene Probleme in der historischen Rolle der Slavereigesellschaft," Altertum, 27, 2 (1981), pp. 69-76.

3424. _____. "Weitere Literatur zur antiken Sklaverei und anderen Abhängigkeitsformen im griechischen und hellenistischen Raum (review essay)," Klio, 64, 2 (1982), pp. 571-75.

3425. _____, and Hagen Fischer. "Aufgaben und Probleme der Wirtschaftsgeschichte des Altertums in der DDR," Jahrbuch für Wirtschaftsgeschichte (1967), pt. 1, pp. 270-84.

3426. Kuzishchin, V. I. "The Concept 'Socio-Economic Formation' and the Periodisation of Ancient Slave Society," Vestnik Drevnei Istorii, 129 (listed as 127)(1974), pp. 69-87.

3427. Lauffer, Siegfried. "Bermerkungen zum Sklavenproblem," Acta antiqua (Academiae Scientiarum Hungaricae), 12 (1964), pp. 359-63.

3428. _____. "Die Sklaverei in der griechisch-römischen Welt," in Rapports du XIe Congrès international des sciences historiques (Stockholm, 1960)(Uppsala, 1960), vol. 3, pp. 71-97. Also in Gymnasium, 68 (1961), pp. 370-95.

3429. Lefebvre des Noëttes, Commandant. "L'esclavage antique devant l'histoire," Mercure de France, 241 (no. 831)(1933), pp. 567-78.

3430. Levi, Mario Attilio. "En marge du Congrès sur l'Esclavage dans l'Antiquité (Besançon, 1971)," Actes du colloque sur l'esclavage (1972), pp. 5-14.

3431. _____. Né liberi, né schiavi; gruppi sociali e rapporti di lavoro nel mondo ellenistico-romano. Milan: Cisalpino-Goliardica, 1976.

3432. Lévy-Bruhl, Henri. "Esclavage," Revue de synthèse (Section Synthèse historique) (1931), pp. 204-08.

3433. _____. "Une nouvelle théorie sur l'esclavage," Revue des études latines, 8, 1 (1930), pp. 151-52.

3434. Lotze, Detlef. Metaxy eleutheron kai doulon. Berlin: Akademie Verlag, 1959. (Deutsche Akademie der Wissenschaften zu Berlin, Schriften der Sektion für Altertumswissenschaft, 17)

3435. Louis, Paul. "L'esclavage dans l'industrie antique," Revue politique et littéraire; Revue bleue, 49, 2 (1911), pp. 585-89.

3436. McCartney, Eugene S. "The Removal of Bonds from Prisoners and Slaves in Times of Stress," Classical Philology, 26, 2 (1931), pp. 166-71.

3437. Maroti, E. "Bewusstheit und ideologische Faktoren in den Sklavenbewegungen," Acta antiqua (Academiae Scientiarum Hungaricae), 15 (1967), pp. 319-26.

3438. Mazza, Mario. "Tra diritto e storia: 'Il tramonto della schiavitù nel mondo antico' di Ettore Ciccotti," Klio, 61, 1 (1979), pp. 57-83.

3439. Mehl, Andreas. "Die antike Sklavenhaltergesellschaft und der Begriff der Volksmassen in neuerer marxistischen Literatur zur alten Geschichte," Gymnasium, 84, 5 (1977), pp. 444-66.

3440. Meyer, Eduard. "Die Sklaverei in Altertum," in Kleine Schriften (Halle: Verlag von Mat Niemeyer, 1924), Bd. 1, pp. 169-212.

3441. Mitteis, L. "Über die Freilassung durch den Teileigentümer eines Sklaven," Archiv für Papyrusforschung und verwandte Gebiete, 3 (1906), pp. 252-56.

3442. Modrzejewski, J. "Aut nascuntur, aut fiunt: les schémas des sources de l'esclavage dans la théorie grecque et dans le droit romain," Actes du colloque sur l'esclavage (1973), pp. 351-84.

3443. Muñoz Valle, Isidoro. Estudios sobre la esclavitud antigua. Madrid: Gráf. Cóndor, 1971.

3444. Nehlson, Hermann. Sklavenrecht zwischen Antike und Mittelalter: Germanisches und römisches Recht in den germanischen Rechtaufzeichnungen. Vol. 1. Göttingen: Musterschmidt, 1972. (Göttinger Studien zur Rechtsgeschichte, 7)

3445. Oliva, Pavel. "Die Bedeutung der antiken Sklaverei," Acta antiqua (Academiae Scientiarum Hungaricae), 8, 3-4 (1960), pp. 309-19.

3446. _____. "The Significance of Ancient Slavery (Some Remarks to 'Brief Reply')," Acta antiqua (Academiae Scientiarum Hungaricae), 10 (1962), p. 417.

3447. Oppenheimer, Franz. "Sklaverei," Kölner vierteljahrshefte für soziologie, 5, 1-2 (1925), pp. 1-12.

3448. Parain, Charles. "Chronique d'histoire de l'antiquité: sur la révolution des esclaves," La Pensée, ser. 2, no. 46 (1953), pp. 103-10.

3449. Pavlovskaya, A. I. "On the Profitability of the Labour of Slaves and Coloni," Vestnik Drevnei Istorii, 139 (1977), pp. 161-71. (In Russian with English summary)

3450. Petit, P. "L'esclavage antique dans l'historiographie soviétique," Actes du Colloque d'histoire sociale, 1970 (Annales Littéraires de l'Université de Besançon, 128)(Paris, 1972), pp. 9-28. (Centre de Recherches d'Histoire Ancienne, vol. 4)

3451. Piacentini, Ugo, and Botho Wiele. "'Ohne antike Sklaverei kein moderner Sozialismus,' (Engels)," Altertum, 11, 4 (1965), pp. 235-38.

3452. Pippidi, D. M. "Problema sclavajului greco-roman la cel de-al XI-lea Congres Internationàl de Stiinte Istorice," Studii si cercetari de istorie veche, 12, 1 (1961), pp. 75-83. (In Rumanian with French and Russian summaries)

3453. Pleket, H. W. "Slavernij in de Oudheid: 'Voer' voor oudhistorici en comparatisten (review-essay on Finley, Ancient Slavery and Modern Ideology)," Tijdschrift voor Geschiedenis, 95, 1 (1982), pp. 1-30.

3454. Polay, Elemér. "Zeichen des Übergangs von der Sklavenhaltergesellschaft zum Feudalismus in den Schriften von Arcadius Charisius, dem nachklassischen Juristen der Digesten," Klio, 64, 1 (1982), pp. 161-70.

3455. Rädle, Herbert. "Freilassung von Sklaven im Theater (Inschriftliche Zeugnisse)," Revue internationale des droits de l'antiquité, 3e sér., 18 (1971), pp. 361-64.

3456. Raymer, A. J. "Slavery - The Graeco-Roman Defense," Greece and Rome, 10 (no. 28)(1940), pp. 17-21.

3457. Rubin, Simon. "Ein Kapitel aus der Sklaverei im talmudischen und römischen Rechte," in Samuel Krauss, ed., Festschrift Adolf Schwartz zum siebzigsten Geburtstag, 15 Juli 1916 (Berlin: R. Löwit, 1917), pp. 211-29.

3458. Russew, Pantscho. "Zur Widerspiegelung der Sklavenhaltergesellschaft in der antiken Philosophie," Altertum, 15, 3 (1969), pp. 142-46.

3459. Salvioli, G. "La dottrina dei Padri della Chiesa intorno alla schiavitù (review of Cicotti)," Rivista italiana per le scienze giuridiche, 29 (1900), pp. 214-33.

3460. Schiavitù, manomissione e classi dipendenti del mondo antico. Maria Capozza, et al. Rome: L'Erma di Bretschneider, 1979. (Colloquio, Bressanone-Brixen, 1976, Groupe Internationale de Recherches sur l'Esclavage Ancien)

3461. Schulz, Siegfried. Gott ist kein Sklavenhalter: die Geschichte einer verspäteten Revolution. Zürich, 1972.

3462. Sereni, E. "Recherche sur le vocabulaire des rapports de dépendance dans le monde antique," Actes du colloque sur l'esclavage (1973), pp. 11-48. With discussion "sur les formations économiques et sociales dans l'Antiquité," pp. 49-98.

3463. Shtaerman, Elena M. "La caida del régimen esclavista," in La transición del esclavismo al feudalismo (Madrid: Akal, 1976), pp. 59-107.

3464. _____, and Berta I. Sharevskaia. El régimen esclavista. Buenos Aires: Editorial Cartago, 1965.

3465. Sisova, Irina A. "Zum Übergang von der patriarchalischen zur entwickelten antiken Sklaverei," Klio, 62, 1 (1980), pp. 157-76.

3466. Snowden, Frank M., Jr. Blacks in Antiquity: Ethiopians in the Greco-Roman Experience. Cambridge, Mass.: Belknap Press, 1970.

3467. _____. "Ethiopians and the Graeco-Roman World," in Kilson and Rotberg, eds., African Diaspora, pp. 11-36.

3468. Starr, Chester G. "An Overdose of Slavery," Journal of Economic History, 18, 1 (1958), pp. 17-32.

3469. Steinmann, Alphons August. Sklavenlos und alte Kirche: eine historisch-exegetische Studie über die soziale Frage im Urchristentum. München-Gladbach: Volksvereins-verlag, 1910.

3470. Storia sociale ed economica dell'età classica negli studi polacchi contemporanei (a cura di Isabela Biezunska-Malowist). Milan: Cisalpino-Goliardica, 1975.

3471. Talamo, Salvatore. Il concetto della schiavitù da Aristotlo ai dottori scolastici. Rome: Tipografia dell'Unione cooperativa editrice, 1908.

3472. Thalheim. "Freigelassene," in Pauly-Wissowas Real-Encyclopädie der klassischen Altertumswissenschaften, Bd. 7, T. 1 (1910), Spalte 95-100.

3473. Tibiletti, G. "Marsyas, die Sklaven und die Marsen," in Studi in onore di Emilio Betti (Milan: A. Giuffrè, 1962), vol. 4, pp. 349-59. *Also in Rigobert Günther and Gerhard Schrot, eds., Sozialökonomische Verhältnisse im alten Orient und im klassischen Altertum (Deutsche Historiker-Gesellschaft, Sektion alte Geschichte)(Berlin: Akademie Verlag, 1961), pp. 291-96.

3474. Université de Besançon. See Actes du colloque sur l'esclavage.

3475. Utchenko, S. L., and I. M. Diakonoff. Social Stratification of Ancient Society. Moscow, 1970. (Proceedings, 13th International Congress of Historians (sic: for Historical Sciences))

3476. Velkov, Velizar. "Zur Frage der Sklaverei auf der Balkanhalbinsel während der Antike," Etudes balkaniques (Sofia), 1 (1964), pp. 125-38.

3477. Vidal-Naquet, P. "Les esclaves étaient-ils une classe?" in Ordres et classes (Colloque d'histoire sociale, Saint-Cloud, 1967)(Paris: Mouton, 1973), pp. 49-57.

3478. _____. "Esclavage et gynécocratie dans la tradition, le mythe, l'utopie," in Recherches sur les structures sociales dans l'antiquité classique (Colloque de Caen, 1969)(Paris: CNRS, 1970), pp. 63-80.

3479. Vierkandt, A. "Die Verbreitung der Sklaverei und ihre Ursachen," Zeitschrift für Sozialwissenschaft, 4 (1901), pp. 13-27.

3480. Vittinghoff, Friedrich. "Die Sklavenfrage in der Forschung der Sowjetunion," Gymnasium, 69 (1962), pp. 279-86.

3481. _____. "Die Theorie des historischen Materialismus über den antiken 'Sklavenhalterstaat': Probleme der Alten Geschichte bei den 'Klassikern' des Marxismus und in der modernen sowjetischen Forschung," Saeculum: Jahrbuch für Universalgeschichte, 11 (1960), pp. 89-131.

3482. Vogt, Joseph. "Alphabet für Freie und Sklaven," Rheinisches Museum für Philologie, 116, 2 (1973), pp. 129-42.

3483. _____. "Die antike Sklaverei als Forschungsproblem von Humboldt bis heute," Gymnasium, 69 (1962), pp. 264-78. Reprinted in idem, Sklaverei und Humanität, pp. 97-111. Translated as "Research on Ancient Slavery from Humboldt to the Present Day," in Ancient Slavery and the Ideal of Man (trans. Wiedemann), pp. 170-87.

3484. _____. Bibliographie zur antiken Sklaverei. See Brockmeyer.

3485. _____. "Die Humanisten und die Sklaverei," in idem, Sklaverei und Humanität, pp. 112-29. Translated as "Slavery and the Humanists," in Ancient Slavery and the Ideal of Man (trans. Wiedemann), pp. 188-210.

3486. _____. "La schiavitù antica nella storiografia moderna," Quaderni urbinati di cultura classica, 18 (1974), pp. 7-21.

3487. * _____. "Sklaventreue," in Mélanges d'archéologie et d'histoire offerts à André Piganiol (Paris, 1966), vol. 3, pp. 1499- . Reprinted in idem, Sklaverei und Humanität, pp. 83-96. Translated as "The Faithful Slave," in Ancient Slavery and the Ideal of Man (trans. Wiedemann), pp. 129-45.

3488. _____. Sklaverei und Humanität: Studien zur antiken Sklaverei und ihrer Erforschung. Wiesbaden: Steiner, 1965. (Historia: Zeitschrift für Alte Geschichte, Einzelschriften, Heft 4) 2nd expanded edition (Wiesbaden: Steiner, 1972), translated by Thomas Wiedemann as Ancient Slavery and the Ideal of Man (Oxford, 1974).

3489. _____. "Struktur der antiken Sklavenkriege," Abhandlungen der Akademie der Wissenschaften und der Literature (Mainz) (Geistes- und Sozialwissenschaftliche Klasse), 1 (1957), pp. 1-57. Revised version reprinted in idem, Sklaverei und Humanität, pp. 20-60. Translated as "The Structure of Ancient Slave Wars," in Ancient Slavery and the Ideal of Man (trans. Wiedemann), pp. 39-92.

3490. _____. "Wege zur Menschlichkeit in der antiken Sklaverei," Universität Tübingen Reden, 47 (1958), pp. 19-38. Reprinted in idem, Sklaverei und Humanität, pp. 69-82; in Finley, ed., Slavery in Classical Antiquity, pp. 33-52. Translated as "Human Relationships in Ancient Slavery," in Ancient Slavery and the Ideal of Man (trans. Wiedemann), pp. 103-21.

3491. Volkmann, Hans. "Die Massenversklavungen der Einwohner eroberter Städte in der hellenistich-römischen Zeit," Abhandlungen der Akademie der Wissenschaften und der Literatur (Mainz) (Geistes- und Sozialwissenschaftliche Klasse), 3 (1961), pp. 121-242.

3492. Walter, Johannes Wilhelm von. Die Sklaverei im Neuen Testament. Berlin-Lichterfelde: E. Runge, 1915.

3493. Welskopf, Elisabeth-Charlotte. "Bermerkungen zum Wesen and zum Begriff der Sklaverei," Zeitschrift für Geschichtswissenschaft, 5, 3 (1957), pp. 581-602.

3494. _____. "Einige Probleme der Sklaverei in der griechisch-römischen Welt," Acta antiqua (Academiae Scientiarum Hungaricae), 12 (1964), pp. 311-58. With reply by Lauffer, pp. 359-63.

3495. _____. "Über den Charakter der antiken Sklaverei als ökonomisches und als juristisches Verhältnis," Klio, 52 (1970), pp. 491-95.

3496. Westermann, William L. "Ancient Slavery," Scientific American (June 1949), pp. 40-43.

3497. _____. "Between Slavery and Freedom," American Historical Review, 50, 2 (1945), pp. 213-27.

3498. _____. "Enslaved Persons Who are Free," American Journal of Philology, 59, 1 (no. 233)(1938), pp. 1-30.

3499. _____. "Sklaverei," in G. Wissowa, W. Kroll, et al., eds., Paulys Real-Encyklopädie der classischen Altertumswissenschaft, suppl. 6 (Stuttgart, 1935), pp. 894-1068.

3500. _____. "Slave Maintenance and Slave Revolts," Classical Philology, 40, 1 (1945), pp. 1-10.

3501. _____. The Slave Systems of Greek and Roman Antiquity. Philadelphia: American Philosophical Society, 1955.

3502. _____. "Upon the Slave Systems of Greek and Roman Antiquity," Eos: Czasposimo filologiczne, 48, 1 (1956), pp. 19-25. ("Symbolae Raphaeli Taubenschlag Dedicati")

3503. Wiedemann, Thomas E. J. Greek and Roman Slavery: A Sourcebook. Baltimore: Johns Hopkins University Press, 1981.

3504. Zelin, K. "Principes de classification morphologique des formes de dépendance," Recherches internationales à la lumière du marxisme, no. 84, 3 (1975), pp. 45-77.

2. Ancient Near East

3505. Bicksler, William H. "Slavery Documents of Old Babylonia" (PhD diss., Brandeis University, 1973).

3506. Blawatsky, Tatiana. "Über den Sklavenmarkt am Aktion," Klio, 56, 2 (1974), pp. 497-500.

3507. Dandamayev, M. A. "The Condition of Slaves in Late Babylonia (Payan-bel-usur, a Slave in the House of Egibi)," Vestnik Drevnei Istorii, 110 (1969), pp. 3-17. (In Russian with English summary)

3508. David, M. "The Manumission of Slaves Under Zedekiah (A Contribution to the Laws about Hebrew Slaves)," Oudtestamentische Studien, 5 (1948), pp. 63-79.

3509. Durand, Jean-Marie. "Les slave-documents de Merodach-Baladan," Journal asiatique, 267, 3-4 (1979), pp. 245-60.

3510. Endesfelder, Erika. "Sklaven (hmw) in der Nekropole von Deir el Medine," Altorientalische Forschungen, 5 (1977), pp. 17-25.

3511. Giorgadze, G. "Die Begriffe 'Freie' und 'Unfreie' bei den Hethitern," Acta antiqua (Academiae Scientiarum Hungaricae), 22 (1974), pp. 299-308.

3512. Gulkowitsch, Lazar. "Der kleine Talmudtraktat über die Sklaven," (Angelos): Archiv für Neutestamentliche Zeitgeschichte und Kulturkunde, 1 (1925), pp. 87-95.

3513. Harmatta, Janos. "Das Problem der Sklaverei im altpersischen Reich," in E.-Ch. Welskopf, ed., Neue Beiträge zur Geschichte der alten Welt (Berlin: Akademie Verlag, 1964), vol. 1, pp. 3-11.

3514. Harris, Rivkah. "Notes on the Slaves' Names of Old Babylonian Sippar," Journal of Cuneiform Studies, 29, 1 (1977), pp. 46-51.

3515. *Häussler, E. "Sklaven und Personen minderen Rechts im Alten Testament" (Diss., Köln, 1956).

3516. Heltzer, M. L. "Slaves, Slaveowning and the Role of Slavery in Ugarit in the Fourteenth and Thirteenth Centuries B.C.," Vestnik Drevnei Istorii, 105 (1968), pp. 85-96. (In Russian with English summary)

3517. Jirku, Anton. "'Hebräische' und 'israelitische' Sklaven," Orientalistische Literaturzeitung, 21, 3-4 (1918), columns 81-83.

3518. Jusifov, Jusif B. "Das Problem der Freien und Sklaven nach den Schriftquellen Elams," Altorientalische Forschungen, 5 (1977), pp. 45-62.

3519. Khazanov, A. M. "The Character of Slavery among the Scythians," Vestnik Drevnei Istorii, 119 (1972), pp. 159-70. (In Russian with English summary) Translated as "Caractère de l'esclavage chez les Scythes," Recherches internationales à la lumière du marxisme, no. 84, 3 (1975), pp. 111-28.

3520. Klengel, Horst. "Sklaven aus Idamaraz," Altorientalische Forschungen, 5 (1977), pp. 63-70.

3521. _____. "Zur Sklaverei in Alalah," Acta antiqua (Academiae Scientiarum Hungaricae), 11 (1963), pp. 1-15.

3522. Klima, Josef. "Einige Bemerkungen zum Sklavenrecht nach den vorhammuropischen Gesetzesfragmenten," Archiv Orientální, 2 (1953), pp. 143-52.

3523. _____. "La posizione degli schiavi secondo le nuove leggi pre-hammurapiche," in Studi in onore di Vincenzo Arangio-Ruiz nel XLV anno del suo insegnamento (Naples: Jovene, 1953), vol. 4, pp. 225-40.

3524. _____. "Zur Stellung der mesopotamischen Sklaven," in E.-Ch. Welskopf, ed., Neue Beiträge zur Geschichte der alten Welt (Berlin: Akademie Verlag, 1964), vol. 1, pp. 19-29.

3525. Klima, Otakar. "Zur Problematik der Sklaverei im alten Iran," Altorientalische Forschungen, 5 (1977), pp. 91-96.

3526. Korosec, Viktor. "Einige Beiträge zum hethitischen Sklavenrecht," in Festschrift Paul Koschaker (Weimar: H. Böhlau, 1939), vol. 3, pp. 127-39.

3527. Lang, Bernhard. "Sklaven und Unfreie im Buch Amos (II 6, VIII 6)," Vetus testamentum, 31, 4 (1981), pp. 482-88.

3528. Lemche, N. P. "The Manumission of Slaves - The Fallow Year - The Sabbatical Year - The Jobel Year," Vetus Testamentum, 26, 1 (1976), pp. 38-59.

3529. Lewis, Naphtali. "P. Hibeh, 198 on Recapturing Fugitive Sailors," American Journal of Philology, 89, 4 (1968), pp. 465–69.

3530. Mendelsohn, Isaac. "Free Artisans and Slaves in Mesopotamia," Bulletin of the American Schools of Oriental Research, 89 (1943), pp. 25–29.

3531. _____. "On Slavery in Alalakh," Israel Exploration Journal, 5, 2 (1955), pp. 65–72.

3532. _____. "Slavery in the Ancient Near East," Biblical Archaeologist, 9, 4 (1946), pp. 74–88.

3533. _____. Slavery in the Ancient Near East: A Comparative Study of Slavery in Babylonia, Assyria, Syria, and Palestine, from the Middle of the Third Millennium to the End of the First Millennium. New York: Oxford University Press, 1949.

3534. _____. "State Slavery in Ancient Palestine," Bulletin of the American Schools of Oriental Research, 85 (1942), pp. 14–17.

3535. Nadel, B. "Slavery and Related Forms of Labor on the North Shore of the Euxine in Antiquity," Actes du colloque sur l'esclavage (1973), pp. 195–234.

3536. Nasgowitz, David W. "Prices of Commodities, Slaves, and Real Estate in Ugarit in the Fourteenth and Thirteenth Centuries B.C." (PhD diss., University of Chicago, 1976).

3537. Oelsner, Joachim. "Zur Sklaverei in Babylonien in der chaldäischen, achämenidischen und hellenistischen Zeit," Altorientalische Forschungen, 5 (1977), pp. 71–80.

3538. Orelli. "Sklaverei bei den Hebräern," in Johann Jakub Herzog, ed., Realencyklopädie für protestantische Theologie und Kirch (Leipzig: J. C. Hinrichs, 1896–1913), vol. 18, pp. 417–23.

3539. Petschow, Herbert P. H. "Die Sklavenkaufverträge des sandabakku Enlil-kidinni von Nippur (I) (mit Exkursen zu Gold als Wertmusser und Preisen)," Orientalia, 52, 1 (1983), pp. 143–55. ("Festschrift Annelies Kammenhuber")

3540. Popov, V. P. "The Status of Slaves in the Hittite Kingdom (based on §§ 93–99 of the Hittite Laws)," Vestnik Drevnei Istorii, 109 (1969), pp. 73–81. (In Russian with English summary)

3541. Roth, Martha T. "The Slave and the Scoundrel: CBS 10467, A Sumerian Morality Tale?" Journal of the American Oriental Society, 103, 1 (1983), pp. 275–82.

3542. Rubin, Simon. "Berichtigungen zum Sklavenrechte in der talmudischen Archäologie von S. Krauss," Monatsschrift für Geschichte und Wissenschaft des Judentums, 59 (1915), pp. 268–77.

3543. San Nicolo, Marian. "Ein babylonischer Sklavenkaufvertrag aus der Zeit Alexanders des Grossen," in Charisteria Alois Rzach zum achtzigsten geburtstag dargebracht (Reichenberg: Gebrüder Stiepel, 1930), pp. 163-65.

3544. Sarna, Nahum. "Zedekiah's Emancipation of Slaves and the Sabbatical Year," in Harry A. Hoffner, ed., Orient and Occident: Essays Presented to Cyrus H. Gordon on the Occasion of his Sixty-Fifth Birthday (Kevelaer: Butzon and Becker, 1973), pp. 143-49.

3545. Segrè, Angelo. "Liberi tenuti in schiavitù nella Siria, nella Fenicia e nell'Egitto tolemaico," Archivio giuridico, ser. 6, 1 (no. 132)(1945), pp. 161-82.

3546. Sharashenidze, D. M. "The Legal Status of the gemé and the Children of Slaves in the III Dynasty of Ur," Vestnik Drevnei Istorii, 133 (1975), pp. 96-101. (In Russian with English summary)

3547. Siegel, Bernard J. Slavery During the Third Dynasty of Ur. Menasha, Wisc.: American Anthropological Association, 1947. (AAA Memoir 66)

3548. Spicq, C. "Le vocabulaire de l'esclavage dans le Nouveau Testament," Revue biblique, 85, 2 (1978), pp. 201-26.

3549. Szlechter, Emile. "L'affranchissement en droit suméro-akkadien," Revue internationale des droits de l'antiquité, 2ème sér., 1 (1952), pp. 125-95.

3550. Urbach, Efraim E. "The Laws Regarding Slavery: As a Source for Social History of the Period of the Second Temple, the Mishnah and Talmud," in J. G. Weiss, ed., Papers of the Institute of Jewish Studies (London and Jerusalem), 1 (1964), pp. 1-94. Original version in Hebrew in Zion (Tsyion), 25, 3-4 (1960), pp. 141-89.

3551. _____. "Slavery in Palestine and Syria in the Hellenistic-Roman Period according to Contemporary Jewish Sources," summarized in Resumés des communications du XIe Congrès international des sciences historiques (Stockholm, 1960)(Uppsala, 1960), pp. 68-69.

3552. Vaiman, A. A. "Designations for Male and Female Slaves in Proto-Sumerian Writing," Vestnik Drevnei Istorii, 128 (1974), pp. 138-48. (In Russian with English summary)

3553. _____. "An Interpretation of Certain Signs in Proto-Sumerian Lists of Male and Female Slaves," Vestnik Drevnei Istorii, 158 (1981), pp. 81-87. In Russian with English summary.

3554. Yaron, Reuven. "Alienation and Manumission," Revue internationale des droits de l'antiquité, 3e sér., 2 (1955), pp. 381-87.

3555. _____. "Redemption of Persons in the Ancient Near East," Revue internationale des droits de l'antiquité, 3e sér., 6 (1959), pp. 155-76.

3556. Zeitlin, Solomon. "Mar Samuel and Manumission of Slaves," Jewish Quarterly Review, 55, 3 (1964-65), pp. 267-69.

3557. _____. "Slavery During the Second Commonwealth and the Tannaitic Period," Jewish Quarterly Review, 53, 3 (1962-63), pp. 185-218.

3558. Zieme, Peter. "Drei neue uigurische Sklavendokumente," Altorientalische Forschungen, 5 (1977), pp. 145-70.

3. Greece and dependencies

3559. Alfieri, T. "La position de M. Rostovzev à propos des laoi de l'Asie mineure hellénistique," Actes du colloque sur l'esclavage (1973), pp. 281-90.

3560. Amandry, Pierre. "Actes d'affranchissement delphiques," Bulletin de correspondance hellénique, 66-67 (1942-43), pp. 68-83.

3561. Annequin, Jacques. "Une étude sur l'esclavage," Revue des études grecques, 93 (nos. 442-444)(1980), pp. 493-97.

3562. Antalffy, Gy. "L'organisation de l'état d'Athènes sous le régime de l'esclavage," Acta juridica Academiae scientarium hungaricae, 4 (1962), pp. 225-29.

3563. Audring, Gert. "Herrschaftsmethoden und -erfahrungen athenischer Sklaveneigentümer," Altertum, 27, 2 (1981), pp. 77-83.

3564. _____. "Streitpunkt: Wie soll man über Sklaverei schreiben? (review of Lauffer, Bergwerkssklaven von Laureion)," Klio, 64, 2 (1982), pp. 565-69.

3565. Bennett, Emmett L. "Slavery," Nestor (1959), pp. 73-74.

3566. Beringer, Walter. "'Servile Status' in the Sources for Early Greek History," Historia, 31, 1 (1982), pp. 13-32.

3567. * _____. "Studien zum Bild vom unfreien Menschen in der griechischen Literatur von den Anfängen bis zum Ende des klassischen Dramas" (Diss., Tübingen, 1956).

3568. _____. "Zu den Begriffen für 'Sklaven' und 'Unfreie' bei Homer," Historia, 10, 3 (1961), pp. 259-91.

3569. Bicknell, P. J. "Demosthenes 24,197 and the Domestic Slaves of Athens," Mnemosyne, 21 (1968), p. 74.

3570. _____. "Some Missing Slaves," Mnemosyne, 18 (1965), pp. 187-88.

3571. Biezunska-Malowist, Iza. "Formen der Sklavenarbeit in der Krisenperiode Athens," in E.-Ch. Welskopf, ed., Hellenische Poleis: Krise, Wandlung, Wirkung (Berlin: Akademie-Verlag, 1974), vol. 1, pp. 27-45.

3572. Blavatskaja, Tatiana V., E. S. Golubcova, and A. I. Pavlovskaja. Die Sklaverei in hellenistischen Staaten im 3.-1. Jh. v. Chr. Translated by Maria Bräuer-Pospelova. Wiesbaden: Steiner, 1972. (Bd. 3, Übersetzungen ausländischer Arbeiten zur antiken Sklaverei)

3573. Bömer, Franz. Untersuchungen über die Religion der Sklaven in Griechenland und Rom, II: Die sogenannte sakrale Freilassung in Griechenland und die (. . .) (Abhandlungen der Akademie der Wissenschaften und der Literatur (Mainz) (Geistes- und Sozialwissenschaftliche Klasse), no. 1 (1960), pp. 1-207; III: Die wichtigsten Kulte der griechischen Welt, ibid., no. 4 (1961), pp. 243-510; IV: Epilegomena, ibid., no. 10 (1963), pp. 857-1144.

3574. Brandt, Herwig. Die Sklaven in den Rollen von Dienern und Vertrauten bei Euripides. Hildesheim, New York: Olms, 1973.

3575. Briant, Pierre. "Remarques sur les 'Laoi' et esclaves ruraux en Asie Mineure hellénistique," in Actes du colloque sur l'esclavage (1971), pp. 93-134.

3576. Bruni, Gian Bruno. "Mothakes, Neodamodeis, Brasideioi," in Schiavitù, manomissione e classi dipendenti, pp. 21-33. With intervention by T. Alfieri Tonini.

3577. Burian, J. "   a povstani spartakovo," Listy Filologické (Prague), 5 (80), 2 (1957), pp. 197-203. (In Czech with German summary)

3578. Cabanes, Pierre. "Les inscriptions du théâtre de Bouthrôtos," in Actes du colloque sur l'esclavage (1972), pp. 105-210.

3579. Calderini, Aristide. La manomissione e la condizione dei liberti in Grecia. Milan: U. Hoepli, 1908.

3580. Campbell, Mavis. "Aristotle and Black Slavery: A Study in Race Prejudice," Race, 15, 3 (1974), pp. 283-302.

3581. Camus, Pierre. "L'esclave en tant qu'organon chez Aritote," in Schiavitù, manomissione e classi dipendenti, pp. 99-113.

3582. Canfora, Luciano. "Lavoro libero e lavore servile nell'Atheneion Politeia anonima," Klio, 63, 1 (1981), pp. 141-48.

3583. Carrière-Hergavault, Marie-Paule. "Esclaves et affranchies de, (sic) chez les orateurs attiques," in Actes du colloque sur l'esclavage (1971), pp. 45-80.

3584. Cretia, P. "Dion de Pruse et l'esclavage," Studii clasice, 3 (1961), pp. 369-75.

3585. Cuffel, Victoria. "The Classical Greek Concept of Slavery," Journal of the History of Ideas, 27, 3 (1966), pp. 323-42.

3586. Daux, Georges. "Deux affranchissements delphiques," Bulletin de correspondance hellénique, 86, 1 (1962), pp. 314-18.

3587. _____. "Note sur l'intérêt historique des affranchissements de Delphes," in Proceedings of the IXth International Congress of Papyrology (Oslo, 19-22 August 1958) (Oslo: Norwegian Universities Press, 1961), pp. 286-92.

3588. Debord, P. "Esclavage mycénien, esclavage homerique," Revue des études anciennes, 75, 3-4 (1973), pp. 225-40.

3589. Demaret, Paul. "Contribution à l'étude du servage dans le monde grec antique: les origines du servage, l'hectémore pré-solonien et l'hilote spartiate" (Thèse de licence, Université de Liège, 1949).

3590. de Ste. Croix, Geoffrey E. M. The Class Struggle in the Ancient Greek World: From the Archaic Age to the Arab Conquests. Ithaca: Cornell University Press, 1981.

3591. Despotopoulos, Constantin. "La 'cité parfaite' de Platon et l'esclavage," Revue des études grecques, 83 (nos. 394-395)(1970), pp. 26-37.

3592. Diesner, Hans-Joachim. "Konservative Kolonen, Sklaven und Landarbeiter im Donatistenstreit," Forschungen und Fortschritte, 36, 7 (1962), pp. 214-19.

3593. _____. "Skythensklaven bei Herodot," Wissenschaftliche Zeitschrift der Martin-Luther Universität Halle, 8, 4-5 (1959), p. 687.

3594. _____. "Sparta und das Helotenproblem (bis zum Ausgang der klassischen Zeit)," Wissenschaftliche Zeitschrift der Universität Greifswald, 3 (1953-54), pp. 218-25.

3595. Dingel, Joachim. "Herren und Sklaven bei Plautus," Gymnasium, 88, 6 (1981), pp. 489-504.

3596. _____. "Die Magd Konigstochter: Sklaven bei Horaz," Gymnasium, 86, 2 (1979), pp. 121-20.

3597. Ducrey, Pierre. Le traitement des prisonniers de guerre dans la Grèce antique: des origines à la conquête romaine. Paris: E. de Boccard, 1968.

3598. Dunand, F. "L'esclavage dans Lysias," Actes du Colloque d'histoire sociale, 1970 (Annales Littéraires de l'Université de Besançon, 128)(Paris, 1972), pp. 117-24. (Centre de Recherches d'Histoire Ancienne, vol. 4)

3599. Feeley-Harnick, Gillian. "Is Historical Anthropology Possible? The Case of the Runaway Slave," in Gene M. Tucker and Douglas A. Knight, eds., Humanizing America's Iconic Book: Society of Biblical Literature Addresses 1980 (Chico, Cal.: Scholars Press, 1982), pp. 95-126.

3600. Finley, Moses I., ed., Westermann. "Between Slavery and Freedom," reprinted in idem, Economy and Society in Ancient Greece, pp. 116-32.

3601. _____. Economy and Society in Ancient Greece (Brent D. Shaw and Richard P. Saller, eds.). New York: Viking, 1982.

3602. _____. "The Servile Statuses of Ancient Greece," Revue internationale des droits d'antiquité, 3e sér., 7 (1960), pp. 165-89. Reprinted in idem, Economy and Society in Ancient Greece, pp. 133-49.

3603. _____. "La servitude pour dettes," Revue historique de droit français et étranger, 4th ser., 43 (1965), pp. 159-84. Translated and revised as "Debt-Bondage and the Problem of Slavery," in idem, Economy and Society in Ancient Greece, pp. 150-66. Also as "Die Schuldknechtschaft," in Hans G. Kippenberg, ed., Seminar: Die Entstehung der antiken Klassengesellschaft (Frankfurt am Main: Suhrkamp, 1977), pp. 173-204.

3604. _____. "Was Greek Civilization Based on Slave Labour?" Historia, 8, 2 (1959), pp. 145-64. Reprinted in Genovese, ed., Slave Economies, vol. 1, pp. 19-45; in Finley, ed., Slavery in Classical Antiquity, pp. 53-72; in idem, Economy and Society in Ancient Greece, pp. 97-115.

3605. Flacelière, Robert. "Comment vivaient les esclaves en Grèce?" Historia, no. 275 (1969), pp. 145-51.

3606. Foucault, J.-A. de. "Histiée de Milet et l'esclave tatoué," Revue des études grecques, 80 (nos. 379-383)(1967), pp. 182-86.

3607. Fuks, A. "Slave War and Slave Troubles in Chios in the Third Century B.C.," Athenaeum, n.s. 46, 1-2 (1968), pp. 102-11.

3608. Garlan, Yvon. Les esclaves en Grèce ancienne. Paris: Maspero, 1982.

3609. _____. "Les esclaves grecs en temps de guerre," in Actes du Colloque d'histoire sociale (Paris, 1972), pp. 29-62. (Annales littéraires de l'Université de Besançon, no. 128)

3610. _____. "Quelques travaux récents sur les esclaves grecs en temps de guerre," in Actes du colloque sur l'esclavage (1972), pp. 15-28.

3611. _____. "Les sociétés sans esclaves dans la pensée politique grecque," Klio, 63, 1 (1981), pp. 131-40.

3612. Gernet, Louis. "Sur le droit athénien de l'esclavage," Archives d'histoire du droit oriental, 5 (1950), pp. 159-87. Reprinted as "Aspects du droit athénien de l'esclavage," in idem, ed., Droit et société dans la Grèce ancienne (Paris: Accueil Sirey, 1955), pp. 151-72.

3613. Gigon, Olof. "Die Sklaverei bei Aristoteles," in La "Politique" d'Aristote (Geneva: Fondation Hardt, 1965), pp. 245-83. (Entretiens sur l'antiquité classique, no. 11)

3614. Gil, Luis. "Ärtzlicher Beistand und attische Komödie: Zur Frage der demosieuontes und Sklaven-Ärtze," Sudhoffs Archiv, 57, 3 (1973), pp. 255-74.

3615. Gilliam, J. F. "The Sale of a Slave Girl through a Greek diploma," Journal of Juristic Papyrology, 16-17 (1971), pp. 63-70.

3616. Glotz, Gustave. "Les esclaves et la peine du fouet en droit grec," Comptes rendus de l'Académie des Inscriptions et Belles-lettres, 37 (1908), pp. 571-87.

3617. Gomme, A. W. "The Population of Athens Again," Journal of Hellenic Studies, 79 (1959), pp. 61-68.

3618. _____. "The Slave Population of Athens," Journal of Hellenic Studies, 61 (1946), pp. 127-29.

3619. Grace, E. "Athenian Views on What is a Slave and How to Manage 'People'," Vestnik Drevnei Istorii, 111 (1970), pp. 49-66. (In Russian with English summary)

3620. Gschnitzer, Fritz. "Studien zur griechischen Terminologie der Sklaverei," Abhandlungen der Akademie der Wissenschaften und der Literatur (Mainz) (Geistes- und Sozialwissenschaftliche Klasse), 13 (1963), pp. 1281-1310.

3621. _____. Studien zur griechischen Terminologie der Sklaverei - 2 Teil: Untersuchungen zur älteren insbesondere homerischen Sklaventerminologie. Wiesbaden: Steiner, 1976. (Bd. 7, Forschungen zur antiken Sklaverei)

3622. _____. "Zur Sklaverei in der hellenistischen Welt," Ancient Society, 7 (1976), pp. 127-49.

3623. Hammond, N. G. L. "The Slave Population in Attica circa 350 B. C.," Proceedings of the Cambridge Philological Society, 1-2 (1935), pp. 160-61.

3624. Harsch, Philip Whaley. "The Intriguing Slave in Greek Comedy," Transactions and Proceedings of the American Philological Association, 86 (1955), pp. 135-42.

3625. Hatzfeld, Jean. "Esclaves italiens en Grèce," in Mélanges Holleaux; recueil de mémoires concernant l'antiquité grecque offert à Maurice Holleaux en souvenir de ses années de direction à l'Ecole française d'Athènes (1904-1912) (Paris: A. Picard, 1913), pp. 93-101.

3626. Heinen, Heinz. "Zur Sklaverei in der hellenistischen Welt," Ancient Society (Louvain), 7 (1976), pp. 127-49.

3627. Helly, Bruno. "Lois sur les affranchissements dans les inscriptions thessaliennes," Phoenix, 30, 2 (1976), pp. 143-58.

3628. Hermann, Johannes. "Personenrechtliche Elemente der Paramone," Revue internationale des droits de l'antiquité, 3e sér., 10 (1963), pp. 149-61.

3629. Hervagault, Marie-Paule, and Marie-Madeleine Mactoux. "Esclaves et société d'après Démosthène," in Actes du colloque sur l'esclavage (1972), pp. 57-104.

3630. Himmelmann-Wildschütz, Nikolaus. "Archäologisches zum Problem der griechischen Sklaverei," Abhandlungen der Akademie der Wissenschaften und der Literatur (Mainz) (Geistes- und Sozialwissenschaftliche Klasse), 13 (1971), pp. 615-59.

3631. Hirvonen, Kaarle. "Cledonomancy and the Grinding Slave Woman," Arctos, n.s. 6 (1970), pp. 5-21.

3632. Jacob, Oscar. "Les esclaves publics à Athènes," Le Musée belge, 30 (1926-27), pp. 57-106.

3633. _____. Les esclaves publics à Athènes. Liège: H. Vaillant-Carmanne, 1928.

3634. Jähne, Armin. "Sklaven, 'ein notwendiges, aber beschwerliches Eigentum': ökonomisches Denken im griechischen Altertum (review of Schinzinger, Ansätze ökonomischen Denkens von der Antike bis zur Reformationszeit; Klees, Herren und Sklaven; Heinen, Untersuchungen zur hellenistischen Geschichte)," Jahrbuch für Wirtschaftsgeschichte, 4 (1982), pp. 175-84.

3635. Jameson, Michael H. "Agriculture and Slavery in Classical Athens," Classical Journal, 73, 2 (1977-78), pp. 122-45.

3636. Joly, Robert. "Esclaves et médecins dans la Grèce antique," Sudhoffs Archiv, 53, 1 (1969-70), pp. 1-14.

3637. Klyachko, N. B. "The Hermokopid Stelae as Source Material on Slavery in the Fifth Century B.C.," Vestnik Drevnei Istorii, 97 (1966), pp. 114-27. (In Russian with English summary)

3638. Klees, Hans. "Beobachtungen zu den Sklaven Xenophons," Annali dell'Istituto italiano per gli studi storici (Naples), 1 (1967), pp. 89-112.

3639. _____. Herren und Sklaven: Die Sklaverei in oikonomischen und politischen Schrifttum der Griechen in klassischer Zeit. Wiesbaden: Steiner, 1975. (Bd. 6, Forschungen zur antiken Sklaverei)

3640. Koshelenko, G. A., and S. V. Novikov. "Manumissions from Seleucia on the Eulaeus," Vestnik Drevnei Istorii, 148 (1979), pp. 41-54. (In Russian with English summary)

3641. Kränzlein, Arnold. "Zu den Freilassungsinschriften aus Delphi," in Antonio Guarino and Luigi Labruna, eds., Synteleia Vincenzo Arangio Ruiz (Naples: Jovene, 1964), vol. 2, pp. 820-27.

3642. Kreissig, Heinz. "L'esclavage à l'époque hellénistique," Recherches internationales à la lumière du marxisme, no. 84, 3 (1975), pp. 99-110.

3643. _____. "L'esclavage dans les villes d'Orient pendant la période hellénistique," Actes du colloque sur l'esclavage (1973), pp. 235-56.

3644. Kuch, Heinrich. Kriegsgefangenschaft und Sklaverei bei Euripedes: Untersuchungen zur Andromache, zur Hekabe und zu den Troerinnen. Berlin: Akademie Verlag, 1974. (Schriften zur Geschichte und Kultur der Antike, vol. 9)

3645. _____. "Die 'Sklavin' Alkestis (Euripedes)," Klio, 48 (1967), pp. 93-95.

3646. Kudlein, Fridolf. Die Sklaven in der griechischen Medizin der klassischen und hellenistischen Zeit. Wiesbaden: Steiner, 1968. (Bd. 2, Forschungen zur antiken Sklaverei)

3647. Lambertz, Maximilian. Die griechischen Sklavennamen. Vienna: Selbstverlag des K. K. Staatsgymnasiums, 1907-08.

3648. Lauffer, Siegfried. Die Bergwerkssklaven von Laureion. Wiesbaden: Steiner, 1979. (Bd. 11, Forschungen zur antiken Sklaverei,)

3649. Lejeune, Michel. "Textes mycéniens relatifs aux esclaves," Historia, 8, 2 (1959), pp. 129-44.

3650. Lentsman, Iakov Abramovich. Die Sklaverei im mykenischen und homerischen Griechenland. Wiesbaden: F. Steiner, 1966. Translation by M. Bräuer-Pospelova of original Russian edition (Moscow, 1963).

3651. Levi, Mario Attilio. "Au sujet des laoi et des inscriptions de Mnesimachos," in Actes du colloque sur l'esclavage (1973), pp. 257-80.

3652. Lévy, Edmond. "Les esclaves chez Aristophane," in Actes du colloque sur l'esclavage (1972), pp. 29-46.

3653. Lopez, Enrique Martin. "El problema de la esclavitud en Aristoteles y sus implicaciones en la sociologia actual," Sociologia internationalis, 3, 2 (1965), pp. 169–88.

3654. Lotze, Detlef. "Der gentilizisch-personale Grundzug des frühen Gemeinwesen als eine Voraussetzung der griechischen Sklaverei," Eirene: Studia graeca et latina, 6 (1967), pp. 5–15.

3655. Lozano, Arminda. La esclavitud en Asia minor helenística. Oviedo: Asociación Trajano (1981?).

3656. _____. "La esclavitud en la isla de Rodas," Hispania antiqua, 6 (1976), pp. 97–123.

3657. Luria, S. "Frauenpatriotismus and Sklavenemanzipation in Argos," Klio, 26 (1933), pp. 211–28.

3658. McKinlay, A. P. "On the Road from Nysa, with the Attic Slaves," Transactions and Proceedings of the American Philological Association, 69 (1938), p. 45.

3659. Mactoux, Marie Madeleine. "Le champ sémantique de doulos chez les orateurs attiques," in Schiavitù, manomissione e classi dipendenti, pp. 35–97.

3660. _____. Douleia: esclavage et pratiques discursives dans l'Athènes classique. Paris: Belles lettres, 1980. (Annales littéraires de l'Université de Besançon, vol. 250; Centre de recherches spécialisées d'histoire ancienne, Equipe de recherche associée au CNRS, vol. 37)

3661. Masson, Olivier. "Les noms des esclaves dans la Grèce antique," in Actes du colloque sur l'esclavage (1971), pp. 9–24.

3662. Mele, A. "Esclavage et liberté dans la société mycénienne," in Actes du colloque sur l'esclavage (1973), pp. 115–58.

3663. Micknat, Gisela. Studien zur Kriegsgefangenschaft und zur Sklaverei in der griechischen Geschichte, I: Homer. Mainz: Akademie der Wissenschaften und der Literatur, 1955.

3664. *Modrzejewski, J. "Aspects de l'esclavage dans la Grèce ancienne et dans le monde hellénistique," Cours d'histoire des institutions hellénistiques (Paris II, 1972–73), typed.

3665. Morrow, Glenn R. "The Murder of Slaves in Attic Law," Classical Philology, 32, 3 (1937), pp. 210–27.

3666. _____. "Plato and Greek Slavery," Mind, 48 (no. 190)(1939), pp. 186–201.

3667. _____. Plato's Law of Slavery and Its Relation to Greek Law. Urbana, Ill.: University of Illinois Press, 1939. (Illinois Studies in Language and Literature, vol. 25, no. 3)

3668. Mossé, Cl. "Quelques problèmes du développement de l'esclavage à l'époque hellénistique," Actes du Colloque d'histoire sociale, 1970 (Annales Littéraires de l'Université de Besançon, 128)(Paris, 1972), pp. 75-82. (Centre de Recherches d'Histoire Ancienne, vol. 4)

3669. _____. "Le rôle des esclaves dans les troubles politiques du monde grec à la fin de l'époque classique," Cahiers d'histoire, 6 (1961), pp. 353-60.

3670. Nenci, G. "Il problema della concorrenza fra mandopera libera e servile nella Grecia classica," Annali della Scuola Normale Superiore di Pisa (Classe di Lettere e Filosofia), 3rd ser., 8, 1 (1978), pp. 1287-1300.

3671. Notopoulos, James A. "The Slaves at the Battle of Marathon," American Journal of Philology, 62, 3 (1941), pp. 352-54.

3672. Oates, John F. "A Rhodian Auction Sale of a Slave Girl," Journal of Egyptian Archeology, 55 (1969), pp. 191-210.

3673. Oliva, Pavel. "Die unentwickelte Form der Sklaverei im antiken Griechenland," in Acta antiqua philippopolitana, vol. 2, pp. 17-25.

3674. Olivier, Jean-Pierre. "Nouvelle mention d'esclaves dans les tablettes mycéniennes," L'antiquité classique (Louvain), 33 (1964), pp. 5-9.

3675. Perotti, Elena. "Esclaves [choris oikountes]," Actes du colloque sur l'esclavage (1972), pp. 47-56.

3676. _____, "Contribution à l'étude d'une autre catégorie d'esclaves attiques ... ," in Actes du colloque sur l'esclavage (1973), pp. 179-94.

3677. Petre, Zoe. "Les sophistes et la question de l'esclavage," in Acta antiqua philippopolitana, vol. 1, pp. 75-79.

3678. Protase, D. "Sclavii în opera lui Euripide si conceptia sa despre sclavaj," Studii clasice, 1 (1959), pp. 77-90. (In Rumanian with French and Russian summaries ["Les esclaves et l'esclavage dans l'oeuvre d'Euripide"])

3679. Rädle, Herbert. "Der Selbstfreikauf griechischen Sklaverei im Lichte der Luschrift SEG XII, 1955, 314 aus Berora," Zeitschrift der Savigny-Stiftung für vergleichende Rechtsgeschichte (Romanistische Abteilung), 89 (1972), pp. 324-33.

3680. _____. "Untersuchungen zum griechischen Freilassungswesen" (Thesis, Universität zu München, 1969).

3681. Raffeiner, Hermann. Sklaven und Freigelassene: Eine soziologische Studie auf der Grundlage des griechischen Grabepigramms. Innsbruck: Universitätsverlag Wagner, 1977.

3682. Reilly, Linda Collins. Slaves in Ancient Greece: Slaves from Greek Manumission Inscriptions. Chicago: Ares Publishers, 1977.

3683. Sargent, Rachel Louisa. The Size of the Slave Population at Athens during the Fifth and Fourth Centuries Before Christ. Urbana, Ill., 1924. (University of Illinois Studies in the Social Sciences, 12, 3)

3684. _____. "The Use of Slaves by the Athenians in Warfare: I. In Warfare by Land; II. In Warfare by Sea," Classical Philology, 22, 2 (1927), pp. 201-12; 22, 3 (1927), pp. 264-79.

3685. Schlaifer, Robert. "Greek Theories of Slavery from Homer to Aristotle," Harvard Studies in Classical Philology, 47 (1936), pp. 165-204. Reprinted in Finley, ed., Slavery in Classical Antiquity, pp. 93-132.

3686. Schönbauer, Ernst. "Paramone, Antichrese und Hypothek: Studien zu P. Dura 10," Zeitschrift der Savigny-Stiftung für vergleichende Rechtsgeschichte (Romanistische Abteilung), 53 (1933), pp. 422-50.

3687. Seymour, P. A. "The 'Servile Interregnum' at Argos," Journal of Hellenic Studies, 42 (1922), pp. 24-30.

3688. *Silverio, O. "Untersuchungen zur Geschichte des attischen Staatssklaven" (Diss. München, 1900).

3689. Stace, C. "The Slaves of Plautus," Greece and Rome, 2nd ser., 15, 1 (1968), pp. 64-77.

3690. Synodinou, Ekaterini. "On the Concept of Slavery in Euripides" (PhD diss., University of Cincinnati, 1974).

3691. _____. On the Concept of Slavery in Euripides. Ioannina: University of Ioannina, 1977. (Dodone, suppl. 7)

3692. Tovar, Antonio. "Talleres y oficios en el palacio de Pylos: teojo doero - ra, 'domestico - a del rey'," Minos: Revista de filologia egea (Salamanca), 7, 1 (1961), pp. 101-22.

3693. Vavrinek, Vladimir. "La révolte d'Aristonicos," Rozpravy Ceskoslovenské Akademie Ved, 67, 2 (1957), pp. 1-75. (In French with Russian and Czech summaries)

3694. Velkov, V. "The End of the Slave System in Ancient Thrace," Vestnik Drevnei Istorii, 141 (1977), pp. 64-68. (In Russian with English summary)

3695. _____. "Thracian Slaves in Ancient Greek Cities (Sixth-Second Centuries BC)," Vestnik Drevnei Istorii, 102 (1967), pp. 70-80. (In Russian with English summary)

3696. Vidal-Naquet, Pierre. "Les esclaves grecs étaient-ils une classe?" Raison présente, 6 (1968), pp. 103-12.

3697. _____. "Réflexions sur l'historiographie grecque de l'esclavage," in Actes du colloque sur l'esclavage (1971), pp. 25-44.

3698. Vigasin, A. A. "Precepts on Slaves in the 'Kautiliya arthacastra'," Vestnik Drevnei Istorii, 138 (1976), pp. 3-19. (In Russian with English summary)

3699. Vlastos, Gregory. "Does Slavery Exist in Plato's Republic?" Classical Philology, 63, 4 (1968), pp. 291-95.

3700. _____. "Slavery in Plato's Thought," Philosophical Review, 50, 3 (1941), pp. 289-304.

3701. Vogt, Joseph. "Die Sklaverei im utopischen Denken der Griechen," Revista storica dell'antichità, 1 (1971), pp. 19-32. Reprinted in idem, Sklaverei und Humanität (2nd ed.), pp. 131-40. Translated as "Slavery in Greek Utopias," in Ancient Slavery and the Ideal of Man (trans. Wiedemann), pp. 26-38.

3702. _____. "Sklaverei und Humanität in klassischen Griechentum," Abhandlungen der Akademie der Wissenschaften und der Literatur (Mainz) (Geistes- und Sozialwissenschaftliche Klasse), 4 (1953), pp. 161-83. Reprinted in idem, Sklaverei und Humanität, pp. 1-19. Translated as "Slavery and the Ideal of Man in Classical Greece," in Ancient Slavery and the Ideal of Man (trans. Wiedemann), pp. 1-25.

3703. _____. "Zum Experiment des Drimakos: Sklavenhaltung und Räuberstand," Saeculum, 24, 3 (1973), pp. 213-19.

3704. Welskopf, Elisabeth-Charlotte. "Einige Bemerkungen zur Lage der Sklaven und des Demos in Athen zur Zeit des dekeleisch-ionischen Krieges," Acta antiqua (Academiae Scientiarum Hungaricae), 8, 3-4 (1960), pp. 295-308.

3705. _____. "Gedanken und politische Entscheidung der Zeitgenossen der Krisenperiode Athens über Charakter und Entwicklung der Sklaverei," in idem, ed., Hellenische Poleis: Krise, Wandlung, Wirkung (Berlin: Akademie-Verlag, 1974), vol. 1, pp. 46-85.

3706. _____. "Loisir et esclavage dans la Grèce antique," in Actes du colloque sur l'esclavage (1973), pp. 159-78.

3707. _____. "Zusammenfassende Bemerkungen (summary and comments on Biezunska-Malowist, 'Formen der Sklavenrecht,' and Welskopf, 'Gedanken und politische Entscheidung')", in idem, ed., Hellenische Poleis: Krise, Wandlung, Wirkung (Berlin: Akademie-Verlag, 1974), vol. 1, pp. 86-91.

3708. Welwei, Karl-Wilhelm. Unfreie im antiken Kriegsdienst. Vol. 1: Athen und Sparta. Wiesbaden: Steiner, 1974. (Bd. 5, Forschungen zur antiken Sklaverei)

3709. _____. Unfreie im antiken Kriegsdienst. Vol. 2: Die kleineren und mittelerengriechischen Staaten und die hellenistischen Reiche. Wiesbaden: Steiner, 1977. (Bd. 8, Forschungen zur antiken Sklaverei)

3710. Westermann, William L. "Athenaeus and the Slaves of Athens," Harvard Studies in Classical Philology, suppl. vol. 1 (1940), pp. 451-70. Reprinted in Finley, ed., Slavery in Classical Antiquity, pp. 73-92.

3711. _____. "Extinction of Claims in Slave Sales at Delphi," Journal of Juristic Papyrology, 4 (1950), pp. 49-61.

3712. _____. "The Paramone as General Service Contract," Journal of Juristic Papyrology, 2 (1948), pp. 9-50.

3713. _____. "Slave Transfer: Deed of Sale with Affidavit of Vendor," Aegyptus, 13 (1933), pp. 229-37.

3714. _____. "Slavery and the Elements of Freedom in Ancient Greece," Quarterly Bulletin of the Polish Institute of Arts and Sciences in America, 1 (1943), pp. 332-47. Reprinted in Finley, ed., Slavery in Classical Antiquity, pp. 17-32.

3715. _____. "Two Studies in Athenian Manumission," Journal of Near Eastern Studies, 5, 1 (1946), pp. 92-104.

3716. Willetts, R. F. "The Servile System of Ancient Crete," in Geras: Studies Presented to George Thompson (Prague: Charles University, 1963), pp. 257-71.

3717. Wolski, Józef. "Les Ilotes et la question de Pausanias, régente de Sparte," in Schiavitù, manomissione e classi dipendenti, pp. 7-20. With intervention by M. M. Mactoux.

3718. Wood, Ellen. "Marxism and Ancient Greece," History Workshop, no. 11 (1981), pp. 3-23.

3719. Yelnitsky, L. A. "The Role of Slave and Freedmen in Certain Types of Greek State Administration in the V and IV Centuries BC," Vestnik Drevnei Istorii, 122 (1972), pp. 100-06. (In Russian with English summary)

3720. Zelin, K. K. "The Delphic Manumissions as a Source for the History of Slavery in Greece in the Hellenistic Period," Vestnik Drevnei Istorii, 93 (1965), pp. 35-53.

3721. Zimmern, Alfred E. "Was Greek Civilization Based on Slave Labor?" Sociological Review, 2, 1 (1909), pp. 1-19; 2, 2 (1909), pp. 159-76. Reprinted in idem, Solon and Croesus (London: H. Milford, 1928), pp. 105-63.

3722. Zlatkovskaya, T. D. "The Character of Slavery in Thrace in the Seventh and Fifth Centuries, BC," Vestnik Drevnei Istorii, 115 (1971), pp. 54-64. (In Russian with English summary)

3723. Zuretti, C. O. "Il servo nella comedia greca antica," Rivista di filologia e d'istruzione classica, 31 (1903), pp. 46-83.

4. Rome and provinces

3724. Affolter, Friedrich Xaver. Die Persönlichkeit des herrenlosen Sklaven: ein Stück aus dem römischen Sklavenrecht. Leipzig: Veit, 1913.

3725. Albanese, B. "La struttura della manumissio inter amicos," Annali del Seminario giuridico della Università di Palermo, 29 (1964), pp. 5-103.

3726. Albertario, Emilio. I problemi possessori relativi al servus fugitivus. Milan: Società editrice "Vita e pensiero", 1929. (Pubblicazioni della Università cattolica del Sacro Cuore, Serie 2, vol. 22)

3727. _____. "Schiavitù e favor libertatis," in idem, Studi di diritto romano (Milan: A. Giuffrè, 1933), vol. 1 (Persone e famiglia), pp. 61-74.

3728. Alföldy, Geza. "Die Freilassung von Sklaven und die Struktur der Sklaverei in der römischen Kaiserzeit," Rivista storica dell'antichità, 2 (1972), pp. 97-129.

3729. _____. "Die Sklaverei in Dalmatien zur Zeit des Prinzipats," Acta antiqua (Academiae Scientiarum Hungaricae), 9, 1-2 (1961), pp. 121-51.

3730. Amat di San Filippo, Pietro. "Della schiavitù e del servaggio in Sardegna," in Miscellanea di storia italiana, 33 (1895), pp. 33-74.

3731. Angelov, D. "Zur Frage des Zerfalls der Sklavenhalterischen Verhältnisse im Oströmischen Reich," in Studia in honorem Marin Stoianov Drinov (Sofia: Bulgarska Akademiiana Naukite, Institut za Istoriia, 1960), pp. 261-71. (In Bulgarian with German and Russian summaries)

3732. Annequin, Jacques. "Esclaves et affranchis dans la Conjuration de Catalina," in Actes du colloque sur l'esclavage (1971), pp. 193-238.

3733. _____, and Micheline Létroublon. "Une approche des discours de Cicéron: les niveaux d'intervention des esclaves dans la violence," in Actes du colloque sur l'esclavage (1972), pp. 211-48.

3734. Annibaldi, Giovanni. "Roma: piastra di collare di schiavo," Notizie degli scavi di antichità, sér. 7, 1 (no. 65)(1940), pp. 312-13.

3735. Appleton, Ch. "L'affranchissement par la vindicta ne s'appliquait anciennement qu'aux esclaves pour dettes," in Mélanges Paul Fournier (Paris: Recueil Sirey, 1929), pp. 1-16.

3736. Arangio-Ruiz, Vincenzo. "La cosiddetta tipicità delle servitù e i poteri della giurisprudenza romana," Foro italiano; Raccolta generale di giurisprudenza, 59 (parte IV) (1934), columns 49-64.

3737. Astin, A. E. "Leges aelia et fufia," Latomus, 23, 3 (1964), pp. 421-45.

3738. Atkinson, Kathleen M. T. "The Purpose of the Manumission Laws of Augustus," Irish Jurist, new ser., 1 (1966), pp. 356-74.

3739. Baldwin, Barry. "Two Aspects of the Spartacus Slave Revolt," Classical Journal, 62, 7 (1967), pp. 289-94.

3740. Bang, M. "Die Herkunft der römischen Sklaven," Mitteilungen des kaiserlichen deutschen archäologischen Instituts: Römische Abteilung, 25 (1910), pp. 223-51; 27 (1912), pp. 189-222.

3741. Barbu, N. I. "Les esclaves chez Martial et Juvenal," Acta antiqua philippopolitana, vol. 1, pp. 67-74.

3742. Barrow, Reginald H. Slavery in the Roman Empire. London: Methuen, 1928.

3743. Bartchy, Scott. [Mallon chresai]: First-Century Slavery and the Interpretation of 1 Corinthians 7:21. Cambridge, Mass.: Society of Biblical Literature, 1973. (Society of Biblical Literature Dissertation Series, no. 11)

3744. Baumgart, Julius. Die römischen Sklavennamen. Breslau, 1936.

3745. Beare, W. "Slave Costume in New Comedy," Classical Quarterly, 43, 1-2 (1949), pp. 30-31.

3746. Bellen, Heinz. Studien zur Sklavenflucht im römischen Kaiserreich. Wiesbaden: Steiner, 1971. (Bd. 4, Forschungen zur antiken Sklaverei)

3747. Benöhr, Hans-Peter. "Zur Haftung für Sklavendelikte," Zeitschrift der Savigny-Stiftung für vergleichende Rechtsgeschichte (Romanistische Abteilung), 97 (1980), pp. 273-87.

3748. Benveniste, E. "Le nom de l'esclave à Rome," Revue des études latines, 10, 2 (1932), pp. 429-40.

3749. *Benz, R. Unfreie Menschen als Musiker und Schauspieler in der römischen Welt. Diss., Tübingen, 1961.

3750. Berger, Adolf. "Streifzüge durch das römische Sklavenrecht," Zeitschrift der Savigny-Stiftung für vergleichende Rechtsgeschichte (Romanistische Abteilung), 43 (1922), pp. 398-415.

3751. _____. "Streifzüge durch das römische Sklavenrecht," Philologus, 73 (1914-1916), pp. 61-108.

3752. Berliri, Luigi Vittorio. "Sulla distinzione delle servitù in continue e discontinue," Archivo giuridico (Modena), ser. 4, 22 (no. 106)(1931), pp. 129-66.

3753. Biscardi, A. "La capacità processuale dello schiavo," Labeo: rassegna di diritto romano, 21 (1975), pp. 143-71.

3754. *Bitcker-Porteau, A. "Des unions inférieures contractées par les esclaves" (Thèse de droit, Paris, 1958).

3755. Blazquez, J. M. "L'esclavage dans les exploitations agricoles de l'Hispania romaine," in Mélanges de la Casa de Velazquez, 8 (1972), pp. 634-39.

3756. Bodor, A. "Contributii la istoria rascoalei sclavilor condusa de Spartacus," Studii clasice, 8 (1966), pp. 131-41.

3757. _____. "Dacian Slaves and Freedmen in the Roman Empire and the Fate of Dacien Prisoners of War," Acta antiqua philippopolitana, vol. 1, pp. 45-52.

3758. Bolz, B. Niewolnicy w pismach cicerona. Poznan: n.p., 1963. (In Polish with French summary ["Les esclaves dans les écrits de Cicéron"])

3759. Bömer, Franz. "Miszellen: Das Privateigentum eines Sklaven unde seine Freilassung," Historia, 12, 4 (1963), p. 510.

3760. _____. Untersuchungen über die Religion der Sklaven in Griechenland und Rom, I: Die wichtigsten Kulte und Religionen in Rom und im lateinischen Western. Wiesbaden: Steiner, 1958. (Abhandlungen der Akademie der Wissenschaften und der Literatur (Mainz) (Geistes- und Sozialwissenschaftliche Klasse), no. 7) 2nd ed., revised and expanded in collaboration with P. Herz: Wiesbaden: Steiner, 1981. (Bd. 14, Heft 1, Forschungen zur antiken Sklaverei)

3761. Bonfante, P. "Nota in tema di servitù," in Studi in onore di Salvatore Riccobono nel XL anno del suo insegnamento (Palermo: Arti grafiche G. Castiglia, 1936), vol. 4, pp. 147-59.

3762. Booth, Alan D. "The Schooling of Slaves in First-Century Rome," Transactions of the American Philological Association, 109 (1979), pp. 11-19.

3763. Boulvert, Gérard. Domestique et fonctionnaire sous le haut-empire romain: la condition de l'affranchi et de l'esclave du prince. Paris, 1974.

3764. _____. "Les esclaves et les affranchis impériaux sous le haut-empire romain" (PhD diss., Université d'Aix-en-Provence, Marseille, 1964). Published as Esclaves et affranchis impériaux sous le haut-empire romain: rôle politique et administratif. Naples: Editore Jovene, 1970.

3765. _____. "Nouvelles 'tabulae pompeianae': note sur un affranchi de Tibère et son esclave," Revue historique de droit français et étranger, 51, 1 (1973), pp. 54–61.

3766. _____, and M. Morabito. "Le droit de l'esclavage sous le Haut-Empire," in Hildegard Temporini and Wolfgang Haase, eds., Aufsteig und Niedergang der römischen Welt: Geschichte und Kultur Roms in Spiegel der neuern Forschung (Berlin: de Gruyter, 1982), Tome 2, Bd. 14, pp. 98–182.

3767. Bradley, Keith R. "The Age at Time of Sale of Female Slaves," Arethusa, 11, 1–2 (1978), pp. 243–52.

3768. _____. "Holidays for Slaves," Symbolae osloenses auspiciis societatis graeco-latinae, 54 (1959), pp. 111–18.

3769. _____. "Slaves and the Conspiracy of Cataline," Classical Philology, 73, 4 (1978), pp. 329–36.

3770. Bretone, Mario. Servus communis: contributo alla storia della comproprietà romana in età classica. Naples: E. Jovene, 1958.

3771. Brion, Marcel. La révolte des gladiateurs. Paris: Amiot-Dumont, 1952.

3772. Brisson, Jean Paul. Spartacus. Paris: Le Club français du livre, 1959.

3773. Brugi, Biago. "Un nuovo collare di servi romani: nota," Atti del Istituto veneto di scienze, lettere e arti (Classe di scienze morali e lettere), 76, 2 (1918), pp. 935–37.

3774. Brunt, P. A. "Work and Slavery," in John Percy Vyvian Dacre Balsdon, ed., The Romans (London: C. A. Watts, 1965), pp. 177–91.

3775. Buckland, William W. The Roman Law of Slavery: The Condition of the Slave in Private Law from Augustus to Justinian. Cambridge: The University Press, 1908.

3776. Buti, Ignazio. Studi sulla capacità patrimoniale dei servi. Naples: Jovene, 1976. (Pubblicazioni della Facoltà di giurisprudenza dell'Università di Camerino, 13)

3777. Calonge, Alfredo. "Problemas de la adopcion de un esclavo," Revue internationale des droits de l'antiquité, 3e sér., 14 (1967), pp. 245–62.

3778. Capogrossi, Luigi. "Il campo semantico della schiavitù nella cultura latina del terzo e del secondo secolo a.C.," Studi storici, 19, 4 (1978), pp. 716-33.

3779. Capozza, Maria. Movimenti servili nel mondo romani in età repubblicana. Rome: "L'Erma" di Bretschneider, 1966.

3780. _____. "Le rivolte servili di Sicilia nel quadro della politica agraria romana," Atti del Istituto veneto di scienze, lettere e arti (Classe di scienze morali e lettere), 115 (1956-57), pp. 79-98.

3781. Carandini, Andrea. Schiavi e padroni nell'Etruria romana: la villa di Settefinestre dallo scavo alla mostra. Bari: de Donato, 1979.

3782. Carcaterra, Antonio. Della estensione del pegno sulla cosa madre ai frutti e ai parti della schiava. Napoli: E. Jovene, 1938.

3783. _____. "Il servus fugitivus e il possesso," Archivio giuridico, ser. 4, 36 (no. 120)(1938), pp. 158-86.

3784. *Castello, Carlo. "La condizione del concepito da libero e schiava e da libera e sciava in diritto romano," Studi in onore di Siro Solazzi (Naples: E. Jovene, 1948).

3785. _____. "(Review of Boulvert, Esclaves et affranchis impériaux)", Studia et documenta historiae et iuris, 38 (1972), pp. 400-08.

3786. _____. "(Review of Robleda, Diritto degli schiavi nell'antica Roma)," Studia et documenta historiae et iuris, 42 (1976), pp. 576-90.

3787. _____. "Sui liberti e sugli schiavi imperiali (a proposito del volume di Gérard Boulvert [Domestique et fonctionnaire sous le Haut-Empire Romain])," Studia et documenta historiae et iuris, 44 (1978), pp. 488-509.

3788. Cavaignac, E. "A propos de Végoia: note sur le servage étrusque," Revue des études latines, 37 (1959), pp. 104-07.

3789. Cels, Dénis. "Les esclaves dans les 'Verrines'," in Actes du colloque sur l'esclavage (1971), pp. 175-92.

3790. Ceska, Josef. "Brachte der Dominat das Ende der sklavischen Unfreiheit?" Sborník prací filosofické fakulty Brnenské University (Rada archeologicko-klasiká), 13 (E. 9) (1964), pp. 113-17.

3791. _____. "Das Christentum und die Sklavenhalterordnung im IV. Jh. u.Z.," Sborník prací filosofické fakulty Brnenské University (Rada archeologicko-klasiká), 15 (E. 11)(1966), pp. 103-14.

3792. _____. "Die öffentliche Meinung und die Sklaven zu Zeiten des Prinzipats," Sborník prací filosofické fakulty Brnenské University (Rada archeologicko-klasiká), 7 (E. 3)(1958), pp. 140-42.

3793. _____. "Zu den Verboten der Sklavenkastration," Sborník prací filosofické fakulty Brnenské University (Rada archeologicko-klasiká), 6 (1957), pp. 125-28. (In Czech with German and Russian summaries)

3794. Chantraine, Heinrich. "Ausserdienststellung und Alterversorgung kaiserlicher Sklaven und Freigelassener," Chiron, 3 (1973), pp. 307-29.

3795. _____. Freigelassene und Sklaven im Dienst der römischen Kaiser: Studien zu ihrer Nomenklatur. Wiesbaden: Steiner, 1967. (Bd. 1, Forschungen zur antiken Sklaverei)

3796. _____. "Freigelassene und Sklaven kaiserliches Frauen," in Werner Eck, Hartmut Galsterer, and Hartmut Wolff, eds., Studien zur antiken Sozialgeschichte: Festschrift Friedrich Vittinghoff (Cologne: Böhlau, 1980), pp. 389-416. (Kölner historischen Abhandlungen, Bd. 28)

3797. _____. "Kaiserliche Sklaven in römischen Flottendienst," Chiron, 1 (1971), pp. 253-65.

3798. _____. "Zur Entstehung der Freilassung mit Bürgerrechtserweb in Rom," in Hildegard Temponini and Wolfgang Haase, eds., Aufsteig und Niedergang der römischen Welt: Geschichte und Kultur Roms in Spiegel der neuern Forschung (Berlin: de Gruyter, 1982), Tome 1, Bd. 2, pp. 59-67.

3799. Christ, Karl. "Spartaco e i suoi miti (review of Guarino, Spartaco: Analisi di un mito)," Labeo: rassegna di diritto romano, 25, 2 (1979), pp. 193-202.

3800. Christes, Johannes. Sklaven und Freigelassene als Grammatiker und Philologen im antiken Rom. Wiesbaden: Steiner, 1979. (Bd. 10, Forschungen zur antiken Sklaverei)

3801. Churruca, Juan de. "L'anathème du Concile de Gangres (340-341) contre ceux qui sous prétexte du christianisme incitent les esclaves à quitter leur maîtres," Revue historique de droit français et étranger, 60, 2 (1982), pp. 261-78.

3802. Claval-Lévêque, M. "Les rapports esclavagistes dans l'idéologie et la pratique politique de Cicéron: leurs représentations et leur fonctionnement d'après la correspondance des années 50-49 av. J.-C.," in Texte, politique, idéologie, pp. 235-302.

3803. Coleman-Norton, Paul Robinson. "The Apostle Paul and the Roman Law of Slavery," in idem, ed., Studies in Roman Economic and Social History in Honor of Allan Chester Johnson (Princeton: Princeton University Press, 1951), pp. 155-77.

3804. Cosentini, Cristoforo. Studi sui liberti: contributo allo studio della condizione giuridica dei liberti cittadini. Catania: Presso la Facultà giuridica, 1948-50.

3805. Crum, Richard Henry. "Slaves and Freedmen as Teachers in Rome," Classical Weekly, 25, 13 (1932), p. 104.

3806. Daube, David. "Slave-Catching," Juridical Review, 64 (1952), pp. 12-28.

3807. Daubigney, A. "Contribution à l'étude de l'esclavagisme: la propriété chez Cicéron," in Texte, politique, idéologie, pp. 13-71.

3808. Delcourt, Marie. "Le prix des esclaves dans les comédies latines," L'antiquité classique (Louvain), 17 (1948), pp. 123-32.

3809. Delplace, Christiane. "Le contenu social et économique du soulèvement d'Aristonicos: opposition entre riches et pauvres?" Athenaeum, 56, 1-2 (1978), pp. 20-53.

3810. de Ste. Croix, Geoffrey E. M. "Early Christian Attitudes to Property and Slavery," Studies in Church History, 12 (1975), pp. 1-38.

3811. Devilla, Vittorio. La liberatio legata nel diritto classico e giustinianeo. Milan: A. Giuffré, 1939. (Pubblicazione della Fondazione Guglielmo Castelli, no. 16)

3812. Dieter, Horst. "Zur Rolle der Sklaverei bei den Römern im 5. und 4. Jh. v. u. Z.," Altertum, 27, 2 (1981), pp. 84-87.

3813. Doer, Bruno. "Publilius Syrus - Volksdichter und Sklave," in Antichnoye obshchestvo (Moscow: Nauka, 1967), pp. 359-67.

3814. _____. "Spartacus," Altertum, 6 (1960), pp. 217-33.

3815. Donatuti, Guido. "La schiavitù per condanna," Bulletino dell'Istituto di diritto romano (Rome), 42 (1934), pp. 219-37. ("Studi alla memoria de V. Scialoja")

3816. Duff, Arnold Mackay. Freedmen in the Early Roman Empire. Oxford: Clarendon, 1928. Reprinted with additions, New York: Barnes & Noble, 1958.

3817. Dumont, François. "La responsabilité personnelle du maître du fait de l'esclave, en droit romain," Revue historique de droit français et étranger, 40 (1962), pp. 117-18.

3818. Dumont, Jean-Christian. "Cicéron, esclavage et analyse de contenu," Revue des études latines, 54 (1976), pp. 48-54.

3819. _____. "Guerre, paix et servitude dans les Captifs," Latomus, 33, 3 (1974), pp. 506-22.

3820. _____. "La stratégie de l'esclave plautinien," Revue des études latines, 44 (1967), pp. 182-203.

3821. Eder, Walter. Servitus publica: Untersuchungen zur Entstehung, Entwicklung und Funktion der öffentlichen Sklaverei in Rom. Wiesbaden: Steiner, 1981. (Bd. 13, Forschungen zur antiken Sklaverei)

3822. Ehrhardt, Arnold. "Rechtsvergleichende Studien zum antiken Sklavenrecht. I., Wehrgeld und Schadensersatz," Zeitschrift der Savigny-Stiftung für vergleichende Rechtsgeschichte (Romanistische Abteilung), 68 (1951), pp. 74-130.

3823. Eisele. "Zum römischen Sklavenrecht," Zeitschrift der Savigny-Stiftung für vergleichende Rechtsgeschichte (Romanistische Abteilung), 26 (1905), pp. 66-83.

3824. Eitrem, Samson. Ein Sklavenkauf aus der Zeit des Antoninus Pius. Kristiania: J. Dybwad, 1916. (Videnskopsselskapets Forhandlinger, no. 2).

3825. Emerit, Marcel. "Sur la condition des esclaves dans l'ancienne Roumanie," Revue historique du Sud-Est Européen, 7, 7-9 (1930), pp. 129-33.

3826. Etienne, Robert. "Cicéron et l'esclavage," Actes du Colloque d'histoire sociale, 1970 (Annales Littéraires de l'Université de Besançon, 128)(Paris, 1972), pp. 83-100. (Centre de Recherches d'Histoire Ancienne, vol. 4)

3827. _____. "Recherches sur l'ergastule," in Actes du colloque sur l'esclavage (1972), pp. 249-66.

3828. Fabbrini, Fabrizio. La manumissio in ecclesia. Milan: A. Giuffrè, 1964. (Pubblicazioni dell'Istituto di diritto romano e dei diritti dell'oriente mediterraneo, Università di Roma, no. 40)

3829. _____. "Un nuovo documento relativo alla Manumissio in ecclesia," Rendiconti Accademia Nazionale dei Lincei (Classi di scienze morali, storiche, e filologiche), ser. 8, 16 (1961), pp. 211-22.

3830. Fabre, Georges. "Les affranchis et la vie municipale dans la péninsule iberique sous le Haut-Empire romain: quelques remarques," in Actes du colloque sur l'esclavage (1973), pp. 417-62.

3831. _____. "Remarques sur la vie familiale des affranchis privés aux deux derniers siècles de la République: problèmes juridiques et sociologiques," in Actes du colloque sur l'esclavage (1971), pp. 239-54.

3832. Falchi, Gian Luigi. Richerche sulla legittimazione passiva alle azioni nossali: il possessore di buona fede del servo. Milan: A. Giuffrè, 1976. (Collana della Fondazione G. Castelli, 44)

Ancient

3833. _____. "Sulla posizione del 'servus obligatus'," Studia et documenta historiae et iuris, 46 (1980), pp. 490–506.

3834. Famiglietti, Gino. "Gli schiavi nell'esercito romano: principî e realtà (review of Rouland, Esclaves romains en temps de guerre)," Labeo: rassegna di diritto romano, 25, 3 (1979), pp. 298–309.

3835. Favory, François. "Classes dangereuses et crise de l'état dans le discours cicéronien (d'après les écrits de Cicéron de 57 à 52)," in Texte, politique, idéologie, pp. 109–233.

3836. * _____. 'L'esclavage d'après les écrits de Cicéron: bilan et perspectives," Revue de l'Université de Varsovie, (1977), pp. ?

3837. _____. "Présentation de l''Index thématique' de Besançon consacré à l'esclavage et aux formes de dépendance," in Schiavitù, manomissione e classi dipendenti, pp. 143–59.

3838. "Forma di produzione schiavistica e tendenze della società romane: II a.C. – II d.C. Un caso di sviluppo precapitalistico" (International seminar, Pisa, January 1979).

3839. Forrest, W. G. G., and T. C. W. Stinton. "The First Sicilian Slave War," Past and Present, 22 (1962), pp. 87–91. With reply by Peter Green, pp. 92–93.

3840. Franciosi, Gennaro. Il processo di libertà in diritto romano. Naples: E. Jovene, 1961. (Pubblicazioni della Facoltà giuridica dell'Università di Napoli, 51)

3841. Francisci, P. de. "La revocatio in servitutem del liberto ingrato," in Mélanges de droit romain dédiés à Georges Cornil (Gand: Vanderpoorten, 1926), vol. 1, pp. 297–323.

3842. Frankfort, Thérèse. "Les classes serviles en Etrurie," Latomus, 18 (1959), pp. 3–22.

3843. Freyburger, Gérard. "La morale et la fides chez l'esclave de la comédie," Revue des études latines, 55 (1977), pp. 113–27.

3844. Garnsey, Peter. "Independent Freedmen and the Economy of Roman Italy under the Principate," Klio, 63, 2 (1981), pp. 359–71.

3845. Garrido-Hory, M. Martial et l'esclavage. Paris: Centre de recherches d'histoire ancienne, vol. 40, 1981. (Annales littéraires de l'Université de Besançon, no. 255)

3846. Gayer, Roland. Die Stellung der Sklaven in den paulinischen Gemeinden und bei Paulus: zugleich ein sozialgeschichtlich vergleichender Beitrag zur Wertung der Sklaven in der Antike. Bern: Herbert Lang, 1976.

3847. Georgescu, Valentin-Al. "La 'manus iniectio' en matière de vente d'esclaves," Zeitschrift der Savigny-Stiftung für vergleichende Rechtsgeschichte (Romanistische Abteilung), 64 (1944), pp. 376-88.

3848. Giliberti, Giuseppe. "La crisi della società schiavistica (review of Shtaerman and Trofimova, Schiavitù nell'Italia imperiale)," Labeo: rassegna di diritto romano, 23, 2 (1977), pp. 225-31.

3849. _____. Servus quasi colonus: forme no tradizionali di organizzazione del lavoro nella società romana. Naples: Jovene, 1981.

3850. Giuffrè, Vicenzo. "Sui 'servi' e la 'militia' secondo il Codice Teodosiano," Labeo: rassegna di diritto romano, 24, 2 (1978), pp. 191-97.

3851. Gonfroy, Françoise. "Homosexualité et typologie esclavagiste chez Cicéron," Dialogues d'histoire ancienne, 4 (1978), pp. 219-64. With "dialogue" by J. Annequin, pp. 263-65.

3852. Gordon, Mary L. "The Nationality of Slaves under the Early Roman Empire," Journal of Roman Studies, 14 (1924), pp. 93-111. Reprinted in Finley, ed., Slavery in Classical Antiquity, pp. 171-90.

3853. Gozalbes Cravioto, Enrique. "Consideraciones sobre la esclavitud en las provincias romanas de Mauretania," Les Cahiers de Tunisie, 27 (1979), pp. 35-67.

3854. Gradenwitz, Otto. "Natur und Sklave bei der naturelis obligatio," in Festgabe der Juristischen Fakultät zu Konigsberg für ihren Senior Johann Theodor Schirmer zum 1. August 1900 (Königsberg: Hartungsche Verlags-druckerei, 1900), pp. 134-79.

3855. Green, Peter. "The First Sicilian Slave War," Past and Present, 20 (1961), pp. 10-29.

3856. Gsell, S. "Esclaves ruraux dans l'Afrique romaine," in Mélanges Gustave Glotz (Paris: Presses Universitaires de France, 1932), vol. 1, pp. 397-415.

3857. Guarino, Antonio. Spartaco: analisi di un mito. Naples: Liguori, 1979.

3858. _____. "Spartaco professore?" Labeo: rassegna di diritto romano, 26, 3 (1980), pp. 325-27.

3859. Gülzow, Henneke. Christentum und Sklaverei in den ersten drei Jahrhunderten. Bonn: R. Habelt, 1969.

3860. Gummerus, H. "Darstellung eines Sklavenverkaufs auf einem Grabstein in Capua," Klio, 12 (1912), pp. 500-03.

Ancient

3861. Günther, Rigobert. Der Aufstand des Spartacus: die grossen
sozialen Bewegungen der Sklaven und Freien am Ende der römischen
Republik. Berlin: Dietz, 1979.

3862. _____. "Die Entstehung der Schuldsklaverei im alten
Rom," Acta antiqua (Academiae Scientiarum Hungaricae), 7, 1-3
(1959), pp. 231-49. Reprinted in Hans G. Klippenberg, ed.,
Seminar: Die Entstehung der antiken Klassengesellschaft
(Frankfurt-am-Main: Suhrkamp, 1977), pp. 158-73.

3863. * _____. "Sklaverei, Wirtschaft und Ständekampf im
ältesten Rom" (Diss., Leipzig, 1957).

3864. Hadas, Moses. "Vestal Virgins and Runaway Slaves," Classical
Weekly, 24, 14 (1931), p. 108.

3865. Halkin, Léon. Les esclaves publics chez les romains. Brussels:
Société Belge de Librairie, 1897.

3866. Hanson, Craig Laverne. "From Roman Slave to Christian Saint: The
Life and Hagiographical Traditions of Onesimus of Colossae" (PhD
diss., University of Washington, 1980).

3867. Harmatta, Janos. "'Posei donios' Geschichtsphilosophie und die
Krise der römischen Sklavenhaltergesellschaft," in Antichnoye
obshchestvo (Moscow: Nauka, 1967), pp. 367-71.

3868. Harper, James. "Slaves and Freedmen in Imperial Rome," American
Journal of Philology, 93, 2 (1972), pp. 341-42.

3869. Härtel, Gottfried. "Einige Bemerkungen zur rechtlichen Stellung
der Sklaven und zur Beschränkung der Willkür bei der Bestrafung im
2./3. Jahrhundert u. Z. anhand der Digesten," Klio, 59, 2 (1977),
pp. 337-47.

3870. * _____. "Soziale Entwicklungstendenzen der Sklaverei
und des Kolonats im 2. Jr. und zu Beginn des 3. Jh. u.Z. im
Western des Römischen Reiches. Unter besonderer Berücksichtigung
der Rechtsquellen" (Phil. Habil., Leipzig, 1966).

3871. Hartwig, Wilhelm, and Karl Stelzer. Spartakus und der
Gladiatorenkrieg 73-71 vor Chr. Leipzig: R. Voigtländer, 1919.

3872. Havas, L. "Le mouvement de Catilina et les esclaves," Acta
classica Universitatis Scientiarum Debreceniensis, 10-11
(1974-75), pp. 21-29.

3873. Heinen, Heinz. "Aspekte der Sklaverei in der römischen Welt,"
Geschichte in Wissenschaft und Unterricht, 28, 6 (1977), pp.
321-26.

3874. Henrion, Roger. "'Satyricon' et 'manumission per mensam'," Revue
belge de philologie et d'histoire, 22, 1-2 (1943), pp. 198-204.

- 286 -

3875. Herrmann, Léon. "La genèse du senatus consultam silanien," Archives de droit oriental et revue internationale des droits de l'antiquité, 2e sér., 1 (1952), pp. 495-506.

3876. Hoben, Wolfgang. Terminologische Studien zu den Sklavenerhebungen der römischen Republik. Wiesbaden: Steiner, 1978. (Bd. 9, Forschungen zur antiken Sklaverei)

3877. Hofmann, Walter. "Plautinische Sklaven," in Rigobert Günther and Gerhard Schrot, eds., Sozialökonomische Verhältnisse im alten Orient und im klassischen Altertum (Deutsche Historiker-Gesellschaft, Sektion alte Geschichte)(Berlin: Akademie Verlag, 1961), pp. 140-47.

3878. Hopkins, Keith. Conquerers and Slaves. New York: Cambridge Unversity Press, 1978. (Sociological Studies in Roman History, no. 1)

3879. Imbert, J. "Réflexions sur le christianisme et l'esclavage en droit romain," Revue internationale des droits de l'antiquité, 2, 2 (1949), pp. 445-76. ("Mélanges Fernand De Visscher I")

3880. Impallomeni, Giovanni Battista. Le manomissioni mortis causa: studi sulle fonti autoritative romane. Padua: CEDAM, 1963.

3881. Jacota, Mihai. "Les pactes de l'esclave en son nom propre," Revue internationale des droits de l'antiquité, 3e sér., 13 (1966), pp. 205-30.

3882. Jeanselme, Edouard. Quelle était la ration alimentaire du citoyen, du soldat et de l'esclave romains?. Vannes: Imp. Lafolye frères, 1918. Extract from Bulletin de la société scientifique d'hygiène alimentaire.

3883. Jonkers, E. J. "De l'influence du christianisme sur la législation relative à l'esclavage dans l'antiquité," Mnemosyne, 1 (1933-34), pp. 241-80.

3884. _____. "Das Verhalten der alten Kirche hinsichtlich der Ernennung von Sklaven, Freigelassenen und Curiales," Mnemosyne, 3rd ser., 10 (1942), pp. 286-302.

3885. Kac, A. L. "The Problem of Slavery in Plautus and Terence," Vestnik Drevnei Istorii, 89 (1964), pp. 81-90.

3886. Kajanto, Iiro. "Tacitus on the Slaves: An Interpretation of the Annales XIV, 42-45," Arctos, n.s. 6 (1970), pp. 43-60.

3887. Kamienik, Roman. "Spartacus und die Seeräuber," Altertum, 27, 2 (1981), pp. 119-21.

3888. _____. "La ritirata di Spartaco e il mancato passaggio in Sicilia (Contributo allo studio della rivolta degli schiavi del 73-71 a.C.)," in Storia sociale ed economica, pp. 143-64.

3889. _____. "Die Zahlenangabe über den Spartakus-Aufstand und ihre Glaubwürdigkeit," Altertum, 16, 2 (1970), pp. 96-105.

3890. Kaser, Max. "Die Anfänge der Manumissio und das fiduziarisch-gebundene Eigentum," Zeitschrift der Savigny-Stiftung für vergleichende Rechtsgeschichte (Romanistische Abteilung), 61 (1941), pp. 153-86.

3891. _____. "Die Geschichte der Patronatsgewalt über Freigelassene," Zeitschrift der Savigny-Stiftung für vergleichende Rechtsgeschichte (Romanistische Abteilung), 58 (1938), pp. 88-135.

3892. _____. "'Partis ancilla'," Zeitschrift der Savigny-Stiftung für vergleichende Rechtsgeschichte (Romanistische Abteilung), 75 (1958), pp. 156-200.

3893. Kiechle, Franz. Sklavenarbeit und technischer Fortschritt im römischen Reich. Wiesbaden: Steiner, 1969. (Bd. 3, Forschungen zur antiken Sklaverei)

3894. Kolendo, Jerzy. "Les esclaves employés dans les vignobles de l'Italie antique," in "Eirene" - Komite zur Förderung der klassischen Studien in den sozialistischen Ländern (21-25 October, 1968)(Kazimierz Feliks Kumaniecki, ed.), Acta conventus XI (Bratislava: Ossolineum, 1971), pp. 33-40.

3895. _____. "Les femmes esclaves de l'empereur," in Actes du colloque sur l'esclavage (1973), pp. 399-416.

3896. _____. "Il lavoro servile e i mutamenti delle tecniche agrarie nell' Italia antica dal I secolo a.C. al I secolo d.C.," in Storia sociale ed economica, pp. 9-53.

3897. _____. "Les possibilités des études sur la productivité du travail des esclaves dans l'agriculture de l'Italie antique," Papers of the Fifth International Congress of Economic History (Leningrad, 1970) (Moscow, 1976), vol. 5, pp. 280-91.

3898. Konstan, David. "Marxism and Roman Slavery," Arethusa, 8, 1 (1975), pp. 145-71.

3899. Körner, Eberhard. "Warum scheiterte der Sklavenaufstand unter Spartacus?" Geschichte in der Schule, 9, 6 (1956), pp. 392-93.

3900. Korsunskij, Alexander R. "Zur Entstehung von Elementen feudaler Beziehungen im weströmischen Reich," Klio, 60, 2 (1978), pp. 247-58.

3901. Kotula, Tadeusz. "La poco nota rivolta degli Afri e degli schiavi contro Cartagine (Diod. sic. XIV 77)," in Storia sociale ed economica, pp. 131-42. Reprinted from Meander, 9 (1966), pp. 362-71.

3902. Kovelman, A. G. "Philo Judaeus of the Labor Freemen and Slaves in Roman Egypt," Vestnik Drevnei Istorii, 145 (1978), pp. 150–57. (In Russian with English summary)

3903. Krawczuk, Aleksander. "Gli agrarii come partito politico nella Roma antica," in Storia sociale ed economica, pp. 189–97. Translated from Zesguty Naukowe Uniwersytetu Jagiellonskiego, Prace Historyczne, 6 (1961), pp. 33–43.

3904. Krummrey, Hans. "Zwei Sklavinnen in einer samnitischen Ziegelei?" Altertum, 27, 2 (1981), pp. 69–76.

3905. Kügler, U.-R. "Die Paränese an die Sklaven als Modell urchristlicher Sozialethik" (Diss., Universität zu Erlangen-Nürnberg, 1976).

3906. Kuhn, G. B. "De opificum romanorum condicione privata quaestiones" (PhD diss., Halle, 1910).

3907. Kühne, Heinz. "Die stadtrömischen Sklaven in den collegia des Clodius," Helikon, 6, 1–2 (1966), pp. 95–113.

3908. _____. "Zur Teilnahme von Sklaven und Freigelassenen an den Bürgerkriegen der Freien im 1. Jahrhundert v. u. Z. in Rom," Studii clasice, 4 (1962), pp. 189–209.

3909. *Kuziscin, V. I. "The Evolution of Italian Agriculture and the Violence of Slaves," Vestnik Moskovskij Gosudarstvennyi Universitet, 5 (1966), pp. 77–95. (In Russian with English summary?)

3910. Langenfeld, H. Christianisierungspolitik und Sklavengesetzgebung der römischen Kaiser von Konstantin bis Theodosius II. Bonn: Habelt, 1977. (Antiquitas: Reihe 1, Abhandlungen zur alten Geschichte, Bd. 26)

3911. Lapicki, B. "Les esclaves et les prolétaires romains et leurs conceptions juridiques," in Studi Arangio-Ruiz (Naples, 1953), vol. 1, pp. 245–71.

3912. *Lappas, J. "Paulus und die Sklavenfrage" (Diss. Wien, 1954).

3913. Lauffer, S. "Ein Sklavenkapitel in Diokletians Preisedikt," Chiron, 1 (1971), pp. 377–80.

3914. Laum, Bernhard. "Sklavenversteigerung auf einem römischen Relief von Arlon," Germania: Korrespondenzblatt der Römisch-germanischen Kommission des Deutschen archäologischen Instituts, 2, 5–6 (1918), pp. 108–12.

3915. *Laurent, P. "Les guerres serviles en Sicile" (Diss. Louvain, 1931–32).

3916. Leicht, Pier Silverio. "Il matrimonio del servo," in Scritti in onore di Contardo Ferrini publicatti in occasione della sua beatificazione (Milan: Società editrice "Vita e Pensiero", 1947), vol. 1, pp. 305-16.

3917. Lemosse, Maxime. "Affranchissement, clientèle, droit de cité," Revue internationale des droits de l'antiquité, 2, 3 (1949), pp. 37-68. ("Mélanges Fernand De Visscher II")

3918. Levi, Marie Attillia. "La tradizione sul Bellum servile di Spartaco," in Actes du colloque sur l'esclavage (1971), pp. 171-74.

3919. Lévy-Bruhl, Henri. "Esquisse d'une théorie sociologique de l'esclavage à Rome," Revue générale du droit international publique, 55 (1931), pp. 1-17. Reprinted as "Théorie de l'esclavage," in Quelques problèmes du trés ancien droit romain (essai de solutions sociologiques) (Paris: Domat-Montchrestien, 1934), pp. 15-33; also in Finley, ed., Slavery in Classical Antiquity, pp. 151-69.

3920. _____. "Le maître instigateur ou complice du délit de son esclave," L'antiquité classique (Louvain), 114 (1945), pp. 141-42. (Première session de la Société d'histoire des droits de l'antiquité)

3921. _____. "La nature de la mancipatio familiae," in Festschrift Fritz Schulz (Weimar: H. Böhlaus Nachfolger, 1951), vol. 1, pp. 253-62.

3922. _____. "Il processo di libertà in Roma," Labeo: rassegna di diritto romano, 8, 3 (1962), pp. 404-07.

3923. Liast, P. E. "Manumission of Slave Craftsmen in the First Century B. C.," Vestnik Drevnei Istorii, 104 (1968), pp. 107-20. (In Russian with English summary)

3924. Libourel, Jan M. "Galley Slaves in the Second Punic War," Classical Philology, 68, 2 (1973), pp. 116-19.

3925. Luebtow, U. v. "Die bei Befreiung eines gefesselten Sklaven eingreifende actio," in Mélanges Philippe Meylan: recueil de travaux publiés à l'occasion de son soixante dixième anniversaire (Lausanne: Impr. Central de Lausanne, 1963), vol. 1, pp. 211-23.

3926. MacCormack, Geoffrey. "Nomination: Slaves and Procurators," Revue internationale des droits de l'antiquité, 3e sér., 23 (1976), pp. 191-202.

3927. _____. "The Thievish Slave," Revue internationale des droits de l'antiquité, 3e sér., 19 (1972), pp. 345-66.

3928. Manaricua y Nuere, Andrés E. de. El matrimonio de los esclavos: estudio historico juridico hasta la fijacion de la disciplina en el derecho canonico. Rome: Pontificia Universitas Gregoriana, 1940. (Analecta Gregoriana, no. 23)

3929. Manganaro, Giacomo. "Monete e ghiande inscritte degli schiavi ribelli in Sicilia," Chiron, 12 (1982), pp. 237-44.

3930. Mangas Manjarrés, Julio. Esclavos y libertos en la España roma. Salamanca, 1971.

3931. Manni-Piraino, M.-T. "Contribution épigraphique à l'étude de l'esclavage en Sicilie," in Actes du colloque sur l'esclavage (1973), pp. 385-98.

3932. Mantello, Antonio. Beneficium servile, debitum naturale: Sen, de ben. 3.18.1 ss., D. 35.1.40.3 (Iva., 2 ex post lab.). Milan: A. Giuffrè, 1979. (Pubblicazioni dell'Istituto di diritto romano e dei diritti dell'oriente mediterraneo, Università di Roma, 55)

3933. Manthe, Ulrich. "Zur Wandlung des servus fugitivus," Tijdschrift voor Rechtsgeschiedenis, 44 (1976), pp. 133-46.

3934. Marinovich, L. P. "(Paramone) in Delphic Manumissions of the Roman Period," Vestnik Drevnei Istorii, 118 (1971), pp. 27-46. (In Russian with English summary)

3935. Maróti, E. "De suppliciis: Zur Frage der sizilianischen Zusammenhänge des Spartacus-Aufstandes," Acta antiqua (Academiae Scientiarum Hungaricae), 9, 1-2 (1961), pp. 41-70.

3936. _____. "Sklavenbewegungen zur Zeit des zweiten Triumvirats," in Antichnoye obshchestvo (Moscow: Nauka, 1967), pp. 109-18.

3937. Martin, René. "Familia rustica: les esclaves chez les agronomes latins," in Actes du colloque sur l'esclavage (1972), pp. 267-98.

3938. Martini, Remo. "Autonomia negoziale dei servi e 'obligationes naturales' (review of Buti, Studi sulla capacità patrimoniale dei servi)," Labeo: rassegna di diritto romano, 26, 1 (1980), pp. 104-09.

3939. Marucchi, O. "Iscrizione del collare di un servo fuggitivo," Nuovo bulletino di archeologia cristiana (Rome), 8 (1902), pp. 126-27.

3940. Matilla Vicente, Eduardo. "Esclavitud en la Mauritania Cesariense," Revista internacional de sociologia, 13-14 (1975), pp. 109-36.

3941. _____. "Surgimiento y desarrollo de la esclavitud cartaginesa y su continuacion en época romana," Hispania antiqua, 7 (1977), pp. 99-123.

3942. Menaut, Geraldo Pereira. "La esclavitud y el mundo libre en las principales ciudades de Hispania romana. analisis estadistico según las inscripciones," Papeles del Laboratorio de arqueologia de Valencia, 10 (1970), pp. 159-88.

3943. _____. "El numero de esclavos en las provincias romanas del Mediterraneo occidental, en el Imperio," Klio, 63, 2 (1981), pp. 373-99.

3944. Michelini, F. Schiavitù, religioni antiche e cristianesimo primitivo. Manduria: Lacaita, 1963.

3945. Michelsen Délano, Juan. La esclavitud en el derecho romano. Santiago: Universidad de Chile (thesis), 1952.

3946. Misera, Karlheinz. "Die Drittwirkung des Schenkungsverbots unter Ehegatten (Erstreckung auf Hausverbände und Sklaven)," Zeitschrift der Savigny-Stiftung für vergleichende Rechtsgeschichte (Romanistische Abteilung), 93 (1976), pp. 33-59.

3947. Misulin, Aleksandr V. Spartacus: Abriss der Geschichte des grossen Sklavenaufstandes. (S. L. Uttschenko, ed.) Berlin: Volk und Wissen, Volkseigner Verlag, 1952.

3948. Mócsy, A. "Die Entwicklung der Sklavenwirtschaft in Pannonien zur Zeit des Prinzipates," Acta antiqua (Academiae Scientiarum Hungaricae), 4 (1956), pp. 221-50.

3949. Modrzejewski, Joseph. "Aut nascuntur aut fiunt! Les schémas antiques des sources de l'esclavage," Bulletino dell'Istituto di diritto romano (Vittorio Scialoja - Milan), 3rd series, 18 (no. 79)(1976), pp. 1-25.

3950. Mohler, S. L. "Slave Education in the Roman Empire," Transactions and Proceedings of the American Philological Association, 71 (1940), pp. 262-80.

3951. Montel, Alberto. "La condizione giuridica dei figli di schiava onorata di fedecommesso di liberta nati in periodo di mora o ritardo nella manomissione della madre," in Studi in onore di Pietro Bonfante nel XL anno d'insegnamento (Milan: Fratelli Treves Editori, 1930), vol. 3, pp. 631-48.

3952. Morabito, Marcel. Les réalités de l'esclavage d'après le Digeste. Paris: Les Belles Lettres, 1981. (Annales littéraires de l'Université de Besançon, vol. 254; Centre de recherches spécialisées d'histoire ancienne, Equipe de recherche associée au CNRS, vol. 39)

3953. Mrozek, Stanislaw. "Über die Arbeitsbedingungen in römischen Bergwerken des 2. Jahrhunderts u.Z.," Altertum, 14, 3 (1968), pp. 162-70.

3954. *Muszkat-Muszeowski, J. "Spartacus: eine Stoffgeschichte" (Diss., Leipzig, 1909).

3955. Noailles, Pierre. "Le procès de Virginie," Revue des études latines, 20 (1942), pp. 106-38.

3956. Oliva, Pavel. "Die charakteristischen Züge der grossen Sklavenaufstände zur Zeit der römischen Republik," in E.-Ch. Welskopf, ed., Neue Beiträge zur Geschichte der alten Welt (Berlin: Akademie Verlag, 1965), vol. 2, pp. 75-88.

3957. Ollivier, Marcel. Spartacus. Paris: Editions de l'Epi, 1929.

3958. Ors, Xavier d'. "La ley 'Aelia Sentia' y las manumisiones testamentarias (una exégisis de D. 40.9.5.2 y D. 40.1.21)," Studia et documenta historiae et iuris, 40 (1974), pp. 425-34.

3959. _____. "La manumisión del esclavo hipotecado en derecho romano," Anuario de historia del derecho español, 46 (1976), pp. 347-91.

3960. _____. "La manumisión del esclavo hipotecado en derecho romano. II - manumisión del esclavo bajo otras formas de garantia," Anuario de historia del derecho español, 47 (1977), pp. 69-98.

3961. Oxé, A. "Zur älteren Nomenklatur der römischen Sklaven," Rheinisches Museum für Philologie, 3rd ser., 59 (1904), pp. 108-40.

3962. Pack, E. "Manumissio in Circo: zum sog. Freilassungsrelief in Mariemont," in Werner Eck, Hartmut Galsterer, and Hartmut Wolff, eds., Studien zur antiken Sozialgeschichte: Festschrift Friedrich Vittinghoff (Cologne: Böhlau, 1980), pp. 179-95. (Kölner historischen Abhandlungen, Bd. 28)

3963. Palazzo, Alfredo. "Servitù personale sulle cose deteriorabili," Archivio giuridico, 4th ser., 20 (no. 104)(1930), pp. 32-42.

3964. Pandolfi-Marchetti, Anna. "Le cause generali e specifiche che prepararono le guerre servili in Sicilia nel II secolo a.C.," Atene e Roma (Florence), 2nd ser., 13 (1932), pp. 212-33.

3965. Pareti, Luigi. "I supposti 'sdoppiamenti' delle guerre servili di Sicilia," Rivista di filologia e di istruzione classica, n.s. 5 (no. 55)(1927), pp. 44-67.

3966. Paula, Euripedes Simoõs de. "Algumas considerações em tôrno da escravidão em Roma. o problema dos libertos," Anais do VI Simpósio nacional dos professores universitários de história (Goiâna, 1971)(São Paulo, 1973), vol. 1, pp. 95-156.

3967. Pavis d'Escurac, Henriette. "Le personnel d'origine servile dans l'administration de l'annone," in Actes du colloque sur l'esclavage (1972), pp. 299-314.

3968. Pfiffig, Ambros Josef. "Die Namen ehemals unfreier Personen bei den Römern und in Etrurien," Beiträge zur Namenforschung, 11, 3 (1960), pp. 256-59.

3969. Pflaum, H. G. "Sur les noms grecs portés par les romains et leurs esclaves," Revue des études latines, 51 (1973), pp. 48-54.

Ancient

3970. Piganiol, André. "Les empereurs parlent aux esclaves," Romanitas: Revista de cultura romana, 1 (1958), pp. 7-18.

3971. Poinssot, L. "Collier d'esclave trouvé à Thelepte," Revue africaine, 87, 3-4 (nos. 396-397)(1943), pp. 149-65.

3972. Pólay, Elemér."Sklaven-Kaufverträge auf Wachstafeln aus Herculanum und Dakien," Acta antiqua (Academiae Scientiarum Hungaricae), 10, 4 (1962), pp. 385-97.

3973. _____. "Die Sklavenehe im antiken Rom," Altertum, 15, 2 (1969), pp. 83-91.

3974. _____. Die Sklavenehe und das römische Recht. Szeged, 1967. (Acta Universitatis Szegediensis de Attila József nominatae. Acta iuridica et politica, t. 14, fasc. 7)

3975. Portal, Maria da Gloria Alves. "A escravidao na Dácia Romana (análise de três documentos de compra e venda de escravos)," Anais do VI Simpósio nacional dos professores universitários de história (Goiâna, 1971)(São Paulo, 1973), vol. 1, pp. 157-82.

3976. Prachner, Gottfried. Alte Geschichte: Untersuchungen zu Überlieferungsproblemen der frührömischen Sklaverei und Schuldknechtschaft. Münster, 1967.

3977. _____. Die Sklaven und Freigelassenen im arretinischen Sigillatagewerbe. Wiesbaden: Steiner, 1980. (Bd. 12, Forschungen zur antiken Sklaverei)

3978. _____. "Zur Bedeutung der antiken Sklaven- und Kolonenwirtschaft für den Niedergang des römischen Reiches," Historia, 22, 4 (1973), pp. 732-56.

3979. Prescott, H. W. "The Name of the Slave in Plautus' Aulularia," Transactions and Proceedings of the American Philological Association, 35 (1904), p. xcvii.

3980. Prete, Pasquale del. La responsibilità dello schiavo nel diritto penale romano. Bari: Istituto di diritto romano, 1937. (Università di Bari, Pubblicazione no. 3)

3981. Pringsheim, Fritz. "Acquisition of Ownership Through servus fugitivus," in Studi in onore di Siro Solazzi nel cinquantesimo anniversario del suo insegnamento universitario, 1899-1948 (Naples: E. Jovene, 1948), pp. 603-30.

3982. _____. "Servus fugitivus sui furtum facil," in Festschrift Fritz Schulz (Weimar: H. Böhlaus Nachfolger, 1951), vol. 1, pp. 279-301.

3983. Puglisi, Angelo. "Servi, coloni, veterani e la terra in alcuni testi di Costantino," Labeo: rassegna di diritto romano, 23, 3 (1977), pp. 305-17.

3984. Ramin, Jacques, and Paul Veyne. "Droit romain et société: les hommes libres qui passent pour esclaves et l'esclavage volontaire," Historia, 30, 4 (1981), pp. 472-97.

3985. Rascón, César. "Manumisiones modales multiples?" Revue internationale des droits de l'antiquité, 3ᵉ sér., 26 (1979), pp. 336-62.

3986. *Rawson, E. "Quand les Romains cessèrent-ils de réduire les Italiens en esclavage?" (Lecture given under auspices of the Institut de droit romain, Paris, 1983).

3987. Reggi, Roberto. Liber homo bona fide serviens. Milan: Giuffrè, 1958. (Università di Parma, Pubblicazioni della Facoltà di giurisprudenza, 9)

3988. Richter, Will. "Seneca und die Sklaven," Gymnasium, 65 (1958), pp. 196-218.

3989. Ridley, Francis A. Spartacus: The Leader of the Roman Slaves. Kenardington, Ashford, Kent: F. Maitland, 1963.

3990. Roberti, Melchiorre. La lettera di S. Paolo a Filemone e la condizione giuridica dello schiavo fuggitivo. Milan: Società editrice "Vita e Pensiero", 1933. (Pubblicazioni della Università Cattolica del Sacro Cuore, ser. 2, Scienze giuridiche, vol. 40)

3991. Robinson, Olivia. "Slaves and the Criminal Law," Zeitschrift der Savigny-Stiftung für vergleichende Rechtsgeschichte (Romanistiche Abteilung), 98 (1981), pp. 213-54.

3992. Robleda, Olis. Il diritto degli schiavi nell'antica Roma. Rome: Pontificia Università Gregoriana, 1976.

3993. Rodríguez Alvarez, Luis. Las leyes limitadores de las manumisiones en época augustea. Oviedo. Universidad, Servicio de Publicaciones, 1978.

3994. Rothenhöfer, Dieter. "Untersuchungen zur Sklaverei in den ostgermanischen Nachfolgestaaten des römischen Reiches" (PhD diss., Tübingen, 1967).

3995. _____. Untersuchungen zur Sklaverei in den ostgermanischen Nachfolgestaaten des romischen Reiches. Tübingen, 1967.

3996. Rouland, Norbert. Les esclaves romains en temps de guerre. Bruxelles: Latomus, 1977.

3997. _____. "A propos des servi publici populi romani," Chiron, 7 (1977), pp. 261-78.

3998. Rupprecht, Arthur A. "A Study of Slavery in the Late Roman Republic from the Works of Cicero" (PhD diss., University of Pennsylvania, 1960).

3999. Russell, Kenneth C. "Slavery as Reality and Metaphor in the Non-Pauline New Testament Books," Revue de l'Université d'Ottawa, 42, 3 (1972), pp. 439-69.

4000. Russu, I. I. "Epitaful sclavului scaurianus," Studii si cercetari de istorie veche, 6, 3-4 (1955), pp. 883-88. (In Rumanian with French summary)

4001. _____. "A Slave in the Service of the Custom House in Dacia," Studii si cercetari de istorie veche, 4 (1953), pp. 784-95. (In Rumanian)

4002. Sartori, Franco, "Cinna e gli schiavi," in Actes du colloque sur l'esclavage (1971), pp. 151-70.

4003. Sasel, J. "Contributo alla conoscenze del commercio con gli schiavi norici ed illirici al fine del periodo repubblicano," in Atti del Terzo congresso internazionale di epigrafia greca e latina (Rome, 4-8 September 1957) (Rome: "L'Erma" di Bretschneider, 1959), pp. 143-47.

4004. Schiller, A. Arthur. "Trade Secrets and the Roman Law: the 'actio servi corrupti'," Columbia Law Review, 30 (1930), pp. 837-45. Reprinted in idem, An American Experience in Roman Law: Writings from Publications in the United States (Göttingen: Vandenhoeck and Ruprecht, 1971), pp. 1-9.

4005. Schmidt, Joël. Vie et mort des esclaves dans la Rome antique. Paris: A. Michel, 1973.

4006. Schneider, W. "Gefesselte Menschen? Geschmiedete eiserne Fesseln - Für Sklaven gedacht?" Das neue Bild der alten Welt, Kölner Römer Illustrierte (Köln, Römisch-Germanisches Museum), 2 (1975), p. 161.

4007. Schuller, Wolfgang. "Sklavenarbeit und technischer Fortschritt im römischen Reich: Franz Keichles Buch in der Diskussion mit Studenten," Abhandlungen aus der Paedagogische Hochschule "Karl Marx" (Berlin), Bd. 1 (Aus Erziehungs-, Sozial-, und Geisteswissenshaften)(1974), pp. 121-36.

4008. Schulz, Fr. "Die fraudatorische Freilassung im klassischen und justinianischen römischen Recht," Zeitschrift der Savigny-Stiftung für vergleichende Rechtsgeschichte (Romanistische Abteilung), 48 (1928), pp. 197-284.

4009. *Sciascia, G. "Schiavi soldati dell'antica Roma," Rassegna dell'Arma di Carabinieri,   (1970), pp. 11-   .

4010. Seyfarth, Wolfgang. "Die Rechstheorie und die Entwicklung der Sklavenklasse an der Basis in der späten römischen Kaiserzeit," in Acta antiqua philippopolitana, vol. 2, pp. 59-66.

4011. Sherwin-White, Adrian N. Racial Prejudice in Imperial Rome. Cambridge: Cambridge University Press, 1967.

4012. Shtaerman, Elena M. Die Blütezeit der Sklavenwirtschaft in der römischen Republik. Translated by Maria Bräuer-Pospelova. Wiesbaden: Steiner, 1969.

4013. _____. "L'esclavage dans l'artisanat: les familiae urbaines," Dialogues d'histoire ancienne, 2 (1976), pp. 103-27.

4014. _____. Die Krise der Sklavenhalterordnung im Westen des römischen Reiches. Translated by Wolfgang Seyfarth. Berlin: Akademie Verlag, 1964.

4015. _____, and M. K. Trofimova. La schiavitù nell'Italia imperiale, I-III secolo. Rome: Editori Riuniti, 1975. (Trans. from 1971 Russian edition)

4016. Sicard, G. "Caton et les fonctions des esclaves," Revue historique de droit française et étranger, 35, 2 (1957), pp. 177-95.

4017. Sirks, A. J. B. "A Favour to Rich Freed Women (libertinae) in 51 A.D. on Sue. Cl. 19 and the Lex Papia", Revue internationale des droits de l'antiquité, 3e sér., 27 (1980), pp. 283-94.

4018. _____. "Informal Manumission and the Lex Junia," Revue internationale des droits de l'antiquité, 3e sér., 28 (1981), pp. 247-76.

4019. Smadja, E. "Esclaves et affranchis dans la correspondance de Cicéron: les relations esclavagistes," in Texte, politique, idéologie, pp. 73-108.

4020. Sokolowski, F. "The Real Meaning of Sacral Manumission," Harvard Theological Review, 47 (1954), pp. 173-81.

4021. Solidoro, Laura. "Produzione schiavistica e società romana," Labeo: rassegna di diritto romano, 25, 3 (1979), pp. 351-56.

4022. _____. "Produzione schiavistica nell'Etruria romana (review of Carandini, Schiavi e padroni nell'Etruria romana)," Labeo: rassegna di diritto romano, 27, 1 (1981), pp. 99-107.

4023. Solin, Heikki. "Die Namen der orientalischen Sklaven in Rom," L'onomastique latine (Actes du Colloque internationale sur l'onomastique latine, Paris, 1975) (Paris: Centre nationale de la recherche scientifique, 1977), pp. 205-20. (With French and English summaries)

4024. Soltau, Wilhelm. "Humanität und Christentum in ihren Beziehungen zur Sklaverei," Neue Jahrbücher für das klassische Altertum, Geschichte und deutsche Literatur und für Pädagogik, 11 Jahrgang, Bd. 21 (1908), pp. 335-50.

4025. Sotgiu, Giovanna. "Un collare di schiavo rinvenuto in Sardegna," Archeologia classica, 25-26 (1973-74), pp. 688-97.

4026. Spranger, Peter R. Historische Untersuchungen zu den
Sklavenfiguren des Plautus und Terenz. Wiesbaden: Steiner, 1960.
(Abhandlungen der Akademie der Wissenschaften und der Literatur
(Mainz) (Geistes- und Sozialwissenschaftliche Klasse), no. 8)

4027. Steinmann, Alphons August. Paulus und die Sklaven zu Korinth: 1
Kor. 7, 21 aufs neue Untersucht. Braunsberg: H. Grimme, 1911.

4028. Stojcevic, Dragomir. "De l'esclave au colon," summarized in
Resumés des communications du XIe Congrès international des
sciences historiques (Stockholm, 1960)(Uppsala, 1960), pp. 70-71.

4029. Szanto, Emil. "Freilassungstermine," Wiener Studien, 24 (1902),
pp. 582-85.

4030. Taylor, Lily Ross. "Freedmen and Freeborn in the Epitaphs of
Imperial Rome," American Journal of Philology, 82, 2 (1961), pp.
113-32.

4031. Texier, Jean Georges. "Les esclaves et l'esclavage dans l'oeuvre
de Polybe," in Schiavitù, manomissione e classi dipendenti, pp.
115-42. With intervention from M. M. Mactoux.

4032. Texte, politique, idéologie: Cicéron. Pour une analyse du système
esclavagiste: le fonctionnement du texte cicéronien (Actes de la
Table Ronde, 1975). Paris: Annales littéraires de l'Université de
Besançon, 1976. (Centre de Recherches d'Histoire Ancienne, vol. 20)

4033. Thompson, E. A. "Slavery in Early Germany," Hermathena, 89 (1957),
pp. 17-29. Reprinted in Finley, ed., Slavery in Classical
Antiquity, pp. 191-203.

4034. Tondo, Salvatore. Aspetti simbolici e magici nella struttura
giuridica della manumissio vindicta. Milan: A. Giuffrè, 1967.

4035. Torelli, M. "Pour une histoire de l'esclavage en Etrurie," in
Actes du colloque sur l'esclavage (1973), pp. 99-114.

4036. Treggiari, Susan. "Family Life among the Staff of the Volusii,"
Transactions of the American Philological Association, 105 (1975),
pp. 393-401.

4037. _____. "Questions on Women Domestics in the Roman
West," in Schiavitù, manomissione e classi dipendenti, pp.
185-201. With intervention from I. Biezunska-Malowist.

4038. _____. Roman Freedmen in the Late Republic. Oxford:
Oxford University Press, 1969.

4039. Tudor, D. "Despre sclavaj in Dacie inferioara," Studii si
cercetari de istorie veche, 1, 1 (1950), pp. 205-12. (In Rumanian
with French and Russian summaries)

4040. _____. Istoria sclavajului in Dacia Romana. Bucharest: Editura
Academiei Republicii Populare Romîne, 1957.

4041. _____. "O noua inscriptie privitoare la sclavii din Dacia," in
Analele Universitatea Seria: Stiinte Sociale (Universitatea din
Bucuresti), 10 (no. 20)(1961), pp. 7-11. (Summaries in French and
Russian)

4042. Vallejo, J. "Tacito 'Historiae' I, 7: Seruorum manus," Emerita:
Boletin de linguistica y filologia clasica (Madrid), 12, 2 (1944),
pp. 354-58.

4043. Velkov, Velizar. "Die Sklaverei in Nordbulgarien in der römischen
Kaiserzeit," in Acta antiqua philippopolitana, vol. 1, pp. 33-44.

4044. Verbrugghe, Gerald P. "The Elogium from Polla and the First Slave
War," Classical Philology, 68, 1 (1973), pp. 25-35.

4045. _____. "The Sicilian Economy and the Slave Wars c.
210-70 B. C.: Problems and Sources" (PhD diss., Princeton
University, 1971).

4046. Verdam, P. J. "Saint Paul et un serf fugitif," in M. David, B. A.
van Groningen, and E. M. Meijers, eds., Symbolae ad jus et
historiam antiquitatis pertinentes Julio Christiano van Oven
dedicatae (Leiden: E. J. Brill, 1946), pp. 211-30.

4047. Verstraete, Beert C. "Slavery and the Social Dynamics of
Homosexual Relations in Ancient Rome," Journal of Homosexuality,
5, 3 (1980), pp. 227-36.

4048. Veyne, Paul. "Le dossier des esclaves-colons romains," Revue
historique, 265 (1981), pp. 3-25.

4049. _____. "Suicide, fisc, esclavage, capital et droit romain,"
Latomus, 40, 2 (1981), pp. 217-68.

4050. Vidman, Ladislav. "Die Sklaven und Freigelassen der einheimischen
Bevölkerung in Noricum," Acta antiqua (Academiae Scientiarum
Hungaricae), 9, 1-2 (1961), pp. 153-57.

4051. Visky, Karoly. "Esclavage et artes liberales à Rome," Revue
internationale des droits de l'antiquité, 3e sér., 15 (1968),
pp. 473-85.

4052. _____. "Quelques remarques sur la question des
mancipations dans les triptyques de Transylvanie," Revue
internationale des droits de l'antiquité, 3e sér., 11 (1964),
pp. 267-79.

4053. Vogt, Heinrich. "Zur Gefahrtragung beim Sklavenkauf," in
Festschrift Paul Koschaker (Weimar: H. Böhlau, 1939), vol. 2, pp.
162-68.

4054. Vogt, Joseph. "De fide servorum," in Raymond Chevallier, ed.,
Mélanges d'archéologie et d'histoire offerts à André Piganiol
(Paris: Ecole Pratique des Hautes Etudes, S.E.V.P.E.N., 1966),
vol. 3, pp. 1499-1514.

4055. _____. "Ecce Ancilla Domini: Eine Untersuchung zum sozialen Motiv des antiken Marionbildes," Vigiliae Christianae, 23 (1969), pp. 241-63. Reprinted in idem, Sklaverei und Humanität (2nd ed.), pp. 147-64. Translated as "Ecce Ancilla Domini: the Social Aspects of the Portrayal of the Virgin Mary in Antiquity," in Ancient Slavery and the Ideal of Man (trans. Wiedemann), pp. 146-69.

4056. _____. "Free Arts and Unfree People in Ancient Rome," Vestnik Drevnei Istorii, 100 (1967), pp. 98-103. In Russian with English summary. Translated as "Freie Künste und unfreie Menschen im alten Rom," in idem, Sklaverei und Humanität (2nd ed.), pp. 141-46. Translated as "Slaves and the Liberal Arts in Ancient Rome," in Ancient Slavery and the Ideal of Man (trans. Wiedemann), pp. 122-28.

4057. _____. "Pergamon und Aristonikos," in Atti del Terzo congresso internazionale di epigrafia greca e romana (Rome, 1957) (Rome: "L'Erma" di Bretschneider, 1959), pp. 45-54. Revised version reprinted in idem, Sklaverei und Humanität, pp. 61-68. Translated as "Pergamum and Aristonicus," in Ancient Slavery and the Ideal of Man (trans. Wiedemann), pp. 93-102.

4058. _____. "Lo schiavo morente: Immagine di compiuta umanità," Studi romani, 20, 3 (1972), pp. 317-28.

4059. _____. "Die Sklaven und die unteren Schichten im frühen Christentum: Stand der Forschung," Gymnasium, 87 (1980), pp. 436-46.

4060. _____. "Die Sklaverei in antiken Rom," Antike Welt, 9, 3 (1978), pp. 37-44.

4061. Volterra, Edoardo. "Intorno a un editto dell'imperatore Claudio," Rendiconti Accademia Nazionale dei Lincei (Classe di scienze morali, storiche e filologiche), ser. 8, 11 (1956), pp. 205-19.

4062. _____. "Manomissione e cittadinanza," in Studi in onore di Ugo Enrico Paoli (Florence: F. Le Monnier, 1956), pp. 695-716.

4063. _____. "Manomissioni di schiavi compiute da peregrini," in Studi in onore di Pietro de Francisci (Milan: A. Giuffré, 1956), vol. 4, pp. 73-105.

4064. Wachtel, Klaus. Freigelassene und Sklaven in der staatlichen Finanzverwaltung der römischen Kaiserzeit von Augustus bis Diokletian. Berlin: Deutsche Akademie der Wissenschaften, Institut für griechisch-römische Altertumskunde, 1966.

4065. _____. "Sklaven und Freigelassene in der staatlichen Finanzverwaltung des römischen Kaiserreiches," Acta antiqua (Academiae Scientiarum Hungaricae), 15 (1967), pp. 341-46.

4066. Watson, Alan. "Morality, Slavery and the Jurists in the Later Roman Republic," Tulane Law Review, 42 (1967-68), pp. 289-303.

4067. _____. "Roman Slave Law and Romanist Ideology," Phoenix, 37, 1 (1983), pp. 53-65.

4068. Weaver, P. R. C. Familia Caesaris: A Social Study of the Emperor's Freedmen and Slaves. Cambridge: University Press, 1972.

4069. _____. "The Slave and Freedman 'Cursus' in the Imperial Administration," Proceedings of the Cambridge Philological Society, 10 (1964), pp. 74-92.

4070. _____. "Social Mobility in the Early Roman Empire: The Evidence of the Imperial Freedmen and Slaves," Past and Present, no. 37 (1967), pp. 3-20.

4071. _____. "The Status Nomenclature of the Imperial Slaves," Classical Quarterly, 14, 1 (no. 58)(1964), pp. 134-39.

4072. _____. "Vicarius and Vicarianus in the Familia Caesaris," Journal of Roman Studies, 54, 1-2 (1964), pp. 117-28.

4073. Webster, T. B. L. "Leading Slaves in New Comedy 300 B. C. - 300 A. D.," Jahrbuch des Deutschen archäologischen Instituts, 76 (1961), pp. 100-10.

4074. Welles, C. Bradford. "Manumission and Adoption," Revue internationale des droits de l'antiquité, 2, 3 (1949), pp. 507-20. ("Mélanges Fernand De Visscher II")

4075. Westermann, William L. "Industrial Slavery in Roman Italy," Journal of Economic History, 2, 2 (1942), pp. 149-63.

4076. Westrup, Carl Wium. Some Notes on the Roman Slave in Early Times: A Comparative Sociological Study. Copenhagen: Munksgaard, 1956. (Det Kongelige Danske videnskabernes selskab, Historisk-filologiske meddelelser, bd. 36, no. 3)

4077. Wetter, E. "Seneca über Sklavenbehandlung," Wiener Blätter für die Freunde der Antike, 1, 8 (1922), pp. 112-17.

4078. Wilinski, Adam. "Zur Frage von Latinern ex lege Aelia Sentia," Zeitschrift der Savigny-Stiftung für vergleichende Rechtsgeschichte (Romanistische Abteilung), 80 (1963), pp. 378-92.

4079. Wilkinson, Beryl Marie. "The Names of Children in Roman Imperial Epitaphs: A Study of Social Conditions in the Lower Classes" (PhD diss., Bryn Mawr, 1961).

4080. Wlassak, M. "Die prätorische Freilassungen," Zeitschrift der Savigny-Stiftung für vergleichende Rechtsgeschichte (Romanistische Abteilung), 26 (1905), pp. 367-431.

4081. Wolski, Józef. "Le classi inferiori della popolazione nel regno dei parti," in Storia sociale ed economica, pp. 55-61.

4082. Yeo, Cedric A. "The Development of the Roman Plantation and the Marketing of Farm Products," Finanz-Archiv, 13 (1952), pp. 321-42.

4083. Yuge, Toru. "Die Gesetze im Codex Theodosianus über die eheliche Bindung von freien Frauen mit Sklaven: zur rechtlichen und gesellschaftlichen Stellung der Sklaven," Klio, 64, 1 (1982), pp. 145-50.

4084. Zanker, Paul. "Grabreliefs römischer Freigelassener," Jahrbuch des Deutschen archäologischen Instituts, 90 (1975), pp. 267-315.

4085. Zeller, Martin. "Die Rolle der unfreien Bevölkerung Roms in den politischen Kämpfen der Bürgerkriege" (PhD diss., Tübingen, 1962).

4086. Zlatuska, Zdenek. "Namen der Sklaven und Freigelassenen in Moesia Inferior," Sborník prací filosofické fakulty Brnenské University (Rada archeologicko-klasiká), 16 (E. 12)(1967), pp. 173-83.

4087. _____. "Die Religion der Sklaven und Freigelassenen im Lichte der Inschriften aus Moesia Inferior," Sbornik praci filosofické fakulty Brnenské University (Rada archeologicko-klasika), 14 (E. 10)(1965), pp. 201-07.

4088. Zoz, Maria Gabriella. "'Restitutio in integrum' e manomissioni coatte," Studia et documenta historiae et iuris, 39 (1973), pp. 115-28.

4089. _____. "Sulla capacità a ricevere fedecommessi alimentari," Studia et documenta historiae et iuris, 40 (1974), pp. 303-28.

5. Egypt

4090. Albright, W. F. "Northwest-Semitic Names in a List of Egyptian Slaves from the Eighteenth Century B. C.," Journal of the American Oriental Society, 74, 4 (1954), pp. 222-33.

4091. Bakir, Abd al-Muhsin. Slavery in Pharaonic Egypt. Cairo: Impr. de l'Institut français d'archéologie orientale, 1952.

4092. Biezunska-Malowist, Iza. "Les affranchis dans les papyrus de l'époque ptolémaique et romaine," in Atti dell'XI Congresso internazionale di papirologia (Milan, 2-8 September 1965) (Milan: Istituto Lombardo di scienze e lettere, 1966), pp. 433-43.

4093. _____. "Les enfants-esclaves à la lumière des papyrus," in Jacqueline Bibauw, ed., Hommages à Marcel Renard (Brussels, 1969), vol. 2, pp. 91-96. (Collection Latomus, no. 102)

4094. _____. "L'esclavage à Alexandrie dans la période gréco-romaine," in Actes du colloque sur l'esclavage (1973), pp. 291-312.

4095. _____. L'esclavage dans l'Egypte gréco-romaine. Première partie. période ptolémaîque. Wroclaw-Warzawa-Kraków-Gdansk, 1974.

4096. _____. L'esclavage dans l'Egypte gréco-romaine: II: la période romaine. Wroclaw-Warzawa, 1977.

4097. _____. "L'esclavage en l'Egypte gréco-romaine," in Actes du colloque sur l'esclavage (1971), pp. 81-92.

4098. _____. "Les esclaves en co-propriété dans l'Egypte gréco-romaine," Aegyptus, 48 (1968), pp. 116-29.

4099. _____. "Les esclaves fugitifs dans l'Egypte gréco-romaine," in Studi in honore di Edoardo Volterra (Milan: A. Guiffré, 1971), vol. 6, pp. 75-90.

4100. _____. "Les esclaves impériaux dans l'Egypte romaine," in Schiavitù, manomissione e classi dipendenti, pp. 175-83.

4101. _____. "Les esclaves nés dans la maison du maître et le travail des esclaves en Egypte romaine," Studii clasice, 3 (1961), pp. 147-62.

4102. _____. "Les esclaves payant l'[apophora] dans l'Egypte gréco-romaine," Journal of Juristic Papyrology, 15 (1965), pp. 65-72.

4103. _____. "Le fonti di afflusso degli schiavi nell'Egitto dei Tolomei," in idem, ed., Storia sociale ed economica, pp. 63-109.

4104. _____. "Introduzione," to idem, ed., Storia sociale ed economica, pp. vii-xiii.

4105. _____. "Il lavoro 'salariato' degli schiavi nell'Egitto greco-romano," in idem, ed., Storia sociale ed economica, pp. 1 8.

4106. _____. "Niewolnicy urodzeni w domu i charakter pracy niewolniczej w Egypcie rzymskim," Przeglad historyczny, 50 (1959), pp. 433-47. (French summary, p. 655)

4107. _____. "Quelques problèmes de l'esclavage dans la période hellénistique," Eos, 20 (1949), pp. 1-70. (In Polish with summary in French)

4108. _____. "Recherches sur l'esclavage dans l'Egypte romaine," Comptes rendus de l'Académie des Inscriptions et Belles-Lettres (Paris), 102 (1959), pp. 203-10.

4109. _____. "Le rôle économique et social de l'esclavage en Egypte au Ier et IIe siècles de notre ère," summarized in Résumés des communications du XIe Congrès international des sciences historiques (Stockholm, 1960)(Uppsala, 1960), pp. 69-70.

4110. _____. "Gli schiavi nati in casa (...) e il carattere del lavoro servile nell'Egitto romano," in idem, ed., Storia sociale ed economica, pp. 111-29. Reprinted from Prezeglad Historyczny, 50 (1959), pp. 433-47.

4111. _____. "Le travail servile dans l'agriculture de l'Egypte romaine," Ve Congrès international d'histoire économique (Leningrad, 1974), vol. 5, pp. 292-93.

4112. Bonneau, D. "Esclavage et irrigation d'après la documentation papyrologique," in Actes du colloque sur l'esclavage (1973), pp. 313-32.

4113. Calderini, Aristide. Liberi e schiavi nel mondo dei papiri grecoegizii. Milan: Scuola tipolitografica "Figli della provvidenza", 1918.

4114. Dalby, Andrew. "On Female Slaves in Roman Egypt," Arethusa, 12, 2 (1979), pp. 255-63. With response by K. R. Bradley.

4115. Davis, Simon. Race-relations in ancient Egypt: Greek, Egyptian, Hebrew, Roman. New York: Philosophical Library, 1952.

4116. Eitrem, Samson. "A Greek Papyrus Concerning the Sale of a Slave," Journal of Egyptian Archaeology, 17 (1931), pp. 44-47.

4117. Gardiner, Alan H. "A Lawsuit Arising from the Purchase of Two Slaves," Journal of Egyptian Archaeology, 21 (1935), pp. 140-46.

4118. Holthöfer, E. "Ein Beitrag zur Auslegung und Interpretationsgeschichte des Fragments D. 18.7.7. (Papinianus über Sklavenverkauf)," Ius commune, 1 (1967), pp. 150-80.

4119. Janssen, Jac. J. "Eine Beuteliste von Amenophis II. und das Problem der Sklaverei im alten Ägypten," Jaarbericht van het Voorazlatisch-Egyptisch Genootschap "ex Oriente Lux" (Leiden), no. 17 (1963), pp. 141-47.

4120. *Kalex, H. "Zu einigen Problemen der Sklaverei im ptolemäisch-römischen Ägypten" (Diss., Leipzig, 1960).

4121. Lévêque, Pierre. "Esclavage et exploitation du travail dans l'Egypte hellénistique et romaine," Revue des études grecques, 92, 436-37 (1979), pp. 231-38.

4122. Liebesny, Herbert. "Ein Erlass des Königs Ptolemaios II: Philadelphos über die Deklaration von Vieh und Sklaven in Syrien und Phönikien," Aegyptus, 16 (1936), pp. 257-91.

4123. Muller, Wolfgang. "Sklaven in der Textilindustrie des ptolemäischen Agypten," in Acta antiqua philippopolitana, vol. 1, pp. 27-32.

4124. Pavlovskaya, A. I. "The Profitableness of Slave Labour in Hellenistic Egypt," Vestnik Drevnei Istorii, 126 (1973), pp. 136-44. (In Russian with English summary)

4125. _____. "Slaves in Agriculture in Roman Egypt," Vestnik Drevnei Istorii, 136 (1976), pp. 73-84. (In Russian with English summary)

4126. Preisigke, Friedrich. "Ein Sklavenkauf des 6. Jahrhunderts," Archiv für Papyrusforschung und verwandte Gebiete, 3 (1906), pp. 415-24.

4127. Steindorff, Georg. "Eine ägyptische Liste syrischer Sklaven," Zeitschrift für ägyptische Sprache und Altertumskunde, 38 (1900), pp. 15-18.

4128. Steinmann, Frank. "Gab es im alten Ägypten Sklavenarbeit in der Sphäre der handwirklich-künstlerischen Produktion?" Altorientalische Forschungen, 5 (1977), pp. 25-33.

4129. Straus, Jean A. "Courte note sur les 'dekania-lists'," Zeitschrift für Papyrologie und Epigraphik, 41 (1981), pp. 257-59.

4130. * _____. "L'esclavage dans l'Egypte romaine," in Hildegard Temporini and Wolfgang Haase, eds., Aufsteig und Niedergang der römischen Welt: Geschichte und Kultur Roms im Spiegel der neuern Forschung (Berlin: de Gruyter, 1982), Tome 2, vol. 10.1, forthcoming.

4131. _____. "Quelques activités exercées par les esclaves d'après les papyrus de l'Egypte romaine," Historia, 26, 1 (1977), pp. 74-88.

4132. _____. "Le statut fiscal des esclaves dans l'Egypte romaine," Chronique d'Egypte, 48 (no. 96)(1973), pp. 364-69.

4133. _____. "La terminologie de l'esclavage dans les papyrus grecs d'époque trouvés en Egypte," in Actes du colloque sur l'esclavage (1973), pp. 333-50.

4134. Swevers, Denise. "Essai sur les origines du servage d'après quelques papyrus grecs d'Egypte" (Thèse de licence, Université de Bruxelles, 1949).

4135. Taubenschlag, R. "Das Sklavenrecht im Rechte der Papyri," Zeitschrift der Savigny-Stiftung für vergleichende Rechtsgeschichte (Romanistische Abteilung), 50 (1930), pp. 140-69.

4136. Vandekerckhove, Willy. "De slavernij in Ptolemaeïsch Egypte" (Thèse de licence, Université de Louvain, 1946-47).

4137. Westermann, William L. Upon Slavery in Ptolemaic Egypt. New York: Columbia University Press, 1929.

4138. Wolff, Hans Julius. "Neue juristische Urkinder. III. Beaufsichtigung des Sklavenhandels im römischen Ägypten: Die Anakrisis," Zeitschrift der Savigny-Stiftung für vergleichende Rechtsgeschichte (Romanistische Abteilung), 83 (1966), pp. 340-49.

IX. Medieval and early modern Europe

1. General and comparative

4139. Agnel, Arnaud d'. "Rôle de soixante-quatorze esclaves provençaux échangés ou rachetés à Alger par le sieur de Trubert," Bulletin historique et philologique (jusqu'à 1715) (France. Comité des travaux historiques et philologiques) (1905), pp. 215-24.

4140. Andreev, Mihail. "Zur Frage des Übergangs von der Sklaverei zum Feudalismus und zur Entstehung frühester feudaler Verhältnisse," Klio, 49 (1967), pp. 305-12.

4141. Bloch, Marc. Slavery and Serfdom in the Middle Ages: Selected Essays. Berkeley: University of California Press, 1975. Translated by William R. Beer.

4142. Bosl, Karl. "Die Unfreiheit im Übergang von der archaischen Epoche zur Aufbruchsperiode der mittelalterlichen Gesellschaft," in Bayerische Akademie der Wissenschaften (Philologisch-historische Klasse, Sitzungsberichte 1973), 1 (1973), pp. 1-39.

4143. Büttner, Theodore, and Ernst Werner. Circumcellionen und Adamiten. Berlin. Akademie-Verlag, 1959. (Forschungen zur mittelalterlichen Geschichte, Bd. 2, 9)

4144. Dockès, Pierre. La libération médiévale. Paris. Flammarion, 1979. Translated as Medieval Slavery and Liberation (trans. Arthur Goldhammer). Chicago. University of Chicago Press, 1982.

4145. Falbel, Nachman. "A legislação cristã em relação ao emprêgo do trabalho escravo por parte dos judéus na Europa Ocidental durante a Alta Idade Média," Anais do VI Simpósio nacional dos professores universitários de história (Goiâna, 1971)(São Paulo, 1973), vol. 1, pp. 183-204.

4146. Hancock, Ian. Land of Pain: Five Centuries of Gypsy Slavery.
Austin, Tex.: Department of English, University of Texas, 1982.

4147. Heers, Jacques. Esclaves et domestiques au moyen âge dans le monde
mediterranéen. Paris: Fayard, 1981.

4148. Horsley-Meecham, Gloria. "The Monastic Slaver: Images and Meaning
in 'Benito Cereno'," New England Quarterly, 56, 2 (1983), pp.
261-66.

4149. Livi, Ridolfo. La schiavitù domestica nei tempi di mezzo e nei
moderni: richerche storiche di un antropologo. Padua: A. Milani,
1928.

4150. Logan, Rayford W. "The Attitude of the Church Toward Slavery Prior
to 1500," Journal of Negro History, 17, 4 (1932), pp. 466-80.

4151. Milani, Piero A. La schiavitù nel pensiero politico: dai Greci al
basso Medio Evo. Milan: A. Giuffré, 1972.

4152. Pijper, Frederick. "The Christian and Church Slavery in the Middle
Ages," American Historical Review, 14, 4 (1909), pp. 675-95.

4153. Riggio, A. "Schiavi calabresi nell'ospedale trinitano di Tunisi,"
Archivio storico per la Calabria e la Lucania, 8 (1938), pp. 31-46.

4154. Roleine, Roberte. "Esclaves, les Tsiganes," Historia, 397 (1979),
pp. 108-14.

4155. Schaub, Friedrich. Studien zur Geschichte der Sklaverei im
Frühmittelalter. Berlin-Leipzig: W. Rothschild, 1913.
(Abhandlungen zur Mittleren und Neueren Geschichte, vol. 44)

4156. Seyfarth, Wolfgang. "Die Spätantike als Übergangszeit zwischen
zwei Gesellschaftssystemen: Eigenständigkeit und Besonderheiten
der Jahrhunderte zwischen Sklavenhalterordnung und Feudalsystem,"
Zeitschrift für Geschichtswissenschaft, 15, 2 (1967), pp. 281-90.

4157. Tenenti, A. "Schiavi e corsari nel Mediterraneo orientale intorno
al 1585," in Miscellanea in onore di Roberto Cessi (Rome: Edizione
di Storia e Letteratura, 1938), vol. 2, pp. 173-85.

4158. Verlinden, Charles. L'esclavage dans l'Europe médiévale. Vol. 1:
Péninsule ibérique. France. Brugge: De Tempel, 1955.

4159. _____. L'esclavage dans l'Europe médiévale. Vol. 2:
Italie - Colonies italiennes du Levant - Levant latin - Empire
byzantin. Ghent: Rijksuniversiteit te Gent, 1977.

4160. _____. "Ist mittelalterliche Sklaverei ein
bedeutsamer demographischer Faktor gewesen?" Vierteljahrschrift
für Sozial- und Wirtschaftsgeschichte, 66, 2 (1979), pp. 153-73.

4161. _____. "L'origine de 'sclavus' - esclave," Archivum
latinitatis medii aevi, 17 (1943), pp. 97-128.

4162. _____. "Orthodoxie et esclavage au bas moyen âge," in
Mélanges Eugen Tisserant. studi e testi (Vatican City. Biblioteca
Apostolica Vaticana, 1964), vol. 5, pp. 427-56.

4163. Vittinghoff, Friedrich. "Die Bedeutung der Sklaven für den
Übergang von der Antike ins abendländische Mittelalter,"
Historische Zeitschrift, 192, 2 (1961), pp. 265-72. Summarized as
"Die Bedeutung der Sklaven für den Übergang von der Antike in das
abendländische Mittelalter," in Résumés des communications du XIe
Congrès international des sciences historiques (Stockholm,
1960)(Uppsala, 1960), pp. 71-73.

2. Byzantine

4164. Bees, Nikos A. "Byzantinisches über Spartakus,"
Byzantinisch-neugriechische Jahrbücher, 2 (1921), p. 158.

4165. Bell, H. Idris. "The Byzantine Servile State in Egypt," Journal of
Egyptian Archaeology, 4 (1917), pp. 86-106.

4166. Hadjinicolaou-Marava, Anne. Recherches sur la vie des esclaves
dans le monde byzantin. Athens. Institut Français d'Athènes, 1950.

4167. Köpstein, Helga. "Die byzantinische Sklaverei in der
Historiographie der letzten 125 Jahre," Klio, 43-45 (1965), pp.
560-76.

4168. _____. "Sklaverei in Byzanz," Altertum, 27, 2 (1981),
pp. 94-101.

4169. _____. "Zum Bedeutungswandel von 'sklavos/sclavus',"
Byzantinishe Forschungen, 7 (1979), pp. 67-88.

4170. _____. "Zum byzantinischen Sklavenhandel,"
Wissenschaftliche Zeitschrift der Karl-Marx-Universitat
(Gesellschaft- und Sprachwissenschaftliche Reihe)(Leipzig), 15, 3
(1966), pp. 487-93.

4171. _____. Zur Sklaverei im ausgehenden Byzanz.
Philologisch-historische Untersuchung. Berlin. Akademie Verlag,
1966.

4172. _____. "Zur Sklaverei in byzantinischer Zeit," Acta
antiqua, 15 (1967), pp. 359-68.

4173. Nadal, B. "Actes d'affranchissement des esclaves du Royaume de
Bosphore et les origines de la manumissio in ecclesia," in Hans
Julius Wolff, ed. (with Josef Modrzejewski and Dieter Nörr),
Symposion 1971: Vorträge zur griechischen und hellenistischen
Rechtsgeschichte (Cologne: Böhlau, 1975), pp. 265-91. (Akten der
Gesellschaft für griechische und hellenistische Rechtsgeschichte,
Bd. 1)

4174. Perentidis, Stavros. "L'ordination de l'esclave à Byzance. droit officiel et conceptions populaires," Revue historique de droit français et étranger, 59, 2 (1981), pp. 231-48.

4175. Seyfarth, Wolfgang. "Ehen zwischen freien Frauen und Sklaven. Ein Beitrag zur Frage der Entwicklung der Beziehungen zwischen den Freien und der Sklavenklasse in den ersten sechs Jahrhunderten u. Z.," in Johannes Irmscher, ed., Byzantinistische Beiträge. Gründungstagung der Arbeitsgemeinschaft Byzantinistik in der Sektion Mittelalter der Deutschen Historiker-Gesellschaft vom 18. bis 21.4.1961 in Weimar (Berlin. Akademie-Verlag, 1964), pp. 41-54.

4176. Verlinden, Charles. "Esclavage et ethnographie sur les bords de la Mer Noire (XIIIe et XIVe siècles)," in Miscellanea historica in honorem Leonis van der Essen (Brussels and Paris, 1947), vol. 1, pp. 287-98.

4177. _____. "Patarins ou Bogomiles réduits en esclavage," Studi e materiali di storia delle religioni (1967), pp. 683-700.

4178. _____. "Slavenhandel en slavenjacht in de Byzantijnse ruimte," in Anamnhcic: Gedenkboek Prof. E. A. Leemans (Brugge: De Tempel, 1970), pp. 413-36.

4179. Zepos, Panagiotis J. "Servi e paroeci nel diritto bizantino e postbizantino," Rendiconti Accademia Nazionale dei Lincei (Classe di Scienze morali, storiche e filologiche), ser. 8, 35, 5-6 (1980), pp. 419-35.

3. Italy and colonies

4180. Arenaprimo, Giuseppe. "Gli schiavi del conte di Condojanni," Archivio storico messinese, 3 (1903), pp. 199-200.

4181. Argentina, Nicola. "Turchi e schiavi in Francavilla d'Otranto," Rivista storica salentina, 5 (1908), pp. 19-25.

4182. Balard, Michel. "Remarques sur les esclaves à Gênes dans la seconde moitié du XIIIe siècle," Mélanges d'archéologie et d'histoire (Ecole française de Rome), 80, 2 (1968), pp. 627-80.

4183. _____. La Romanie Génoise (XIIe - début du XVe siècle). Rome: Ecole française de Rome, 1978. 2 vols. (See vol. 1, pp. 289-310, and vol. 2, pp. 785-833, for related bibliography on Black Sea slave trade.)

4184. Balbi, Giovanna. "La schiavitù a Genova tra i secoli XII e XIII," in Mélanges offerts à René Crozet (Poitiers: Société d'études médiévales, 1966), vol. 2, pp. 1025-29.

4185. Foscarini, Amilcare. "Schiavi e turchi in Lecce (secc. XVI-XVII)," Rivista storica salentina, 5 (1908), pp. 305-16.

4186. Franchina, A. "Un censimento di schiavi nel 1565," Archivio storico siciliano, 32 (1908), pp. 374-420.

4187. Gaudioso, M. La schiavitù domestica in Sicilia dopo i Normanni. Catania: Galàtola, 1926.

4188. Gioffré, Domenico. Il mercato degli schiavi a Genova nel secolo XV. Genoa: Fratelli Bozzi, 1971.

4189. Gür, André. "Les Génevois et le problème de l'esclavage au XVIIIe siècle," Musées de Génève, 11 (no. 101)(1970), pp. 5-7.

4190. Haverkamp, Alfred. "Zur Sklaverei in Genue während des 12. Jahrhunderts," in Geschichte in der Gesellschaft: Festschrift für Karl Bosl (Stuttgart: A. Hiersemann, 1974), pp. 160-215.

4191. Kuehn, Thomas James. "Emancipation in Late Medieval Florence" (PhD diss., University of Chicago, 1977).

4192. *Lopez, R. S. "La vendita d'una schiava di Malta a Genova nel 1248," Archivio storico di Malta, 7 (1936), pp.   .

4193. Luzio, Alessandro, and Rodolfo Renier. "Buffoni, nani e schiavi dei Gonzaga ai tempi d'Isabella d'Este," Nuova antologia, 3rd ser., 35 (1891), pp. 118-19.

4194. Luzzatto, Gino. I servi nelle grandi proprietà ecclesiastiche italiane nei secoli IX e X. Pisa, 1910. Reprinted in idem, Dai servi della gleba agli albori del capitalismo (Bari: Laterza, 1966), pp. 1-177.

4195. Marrone, Giovanni. La schiavitù nella società siciliana dell'età moderna. Rome: Edizioni Salvatore Sciascia, 1972.

4196. Massa, C. "La schiavitù in terra di Bari (dal XV al XVIII secolo)," Rassegna pugliese, 23 (1907), pp. 265-70.

4197. *Messina, S. "La schiavitù in Sicilia dal secolo XVI al XVII," Sabato sera (Giornale di Alcamo, 22 Oct. 1949).

4198. Monti, G. M. "Sulla schiavitù domestica nel regno di Napoli dagli Aragonesi agli Austriaci," Archivio scientifico del Regio Istituto Superiore di Scienze Economiche e Commerciale (Bari), 6 (1931-32), pp. 127-53.

4199. Mueller, Reinhold C. "Venezia e i primi schiavi neri," Archivio veneto, 113 (no. 148)(1979), pp. 139-42.

4200. Origo, Iris. "The Domestic Enemy: The Eastern Slaves in Tuscany in the Fourteenth and Fifteenth Centuries," Speculum, 30, 3 (1955), pp. 321-66.

4201. Pistarino, G. "Sul tema degli schiavi nel Quattrocento a Genova," in Miscellanea di storia ligure in memoria di Giorgio Falco (Genoa: Università di Genova, Istituto di paleografia e storia medievale, 1966), vol. 4, pp. 85-94. (Fonti e studi, no. 12)

4202. _____. "Tra liberi e schiave a Genova nel Quattrocento," Anuario de estudios medievales, 1 (1964), pp. 353-74.

4203. Prunaj, G. "Notizie e documenti sulla servitù domestica nel territorio senese (sec. XIII-XIV)," Bollettino senese di storia patria, n.s. 7, 3 (vol. 43) (1936), pp. 245-98; 7, 4 (1936), pp. 398-438.

4204. Rodocanachi, E. "Les esclaves en Italie du XIIIe au XVIe siècle," Revue des questions historiques, n.s. 25 (1906), pp. 383-407.

4205. *Teja, Antonio. "La schiavitù domestica ed il traffico degli schiavi," La rivista dalmatica, 22 (1941), pp.   .

4206. Tenenti, Alberto. "Gli schiavi di Venezia alla fine del cinquecento," Rivista storia italiana, 67, 1 (1955), pp. 52-69.

4207. Tria, Luigi, ed. La schiavitù in Liguria (richerche e documenti). Genoa, 1947. (Atti della Società ligure di storia patria, vol. 70)

4208. Verga, Ettore. "Per la storia degli schiavi orientali in Milano," Archivio storico lombardo, ser. 4, 4 (no. 32)(1905), pp. 188-95.

4209. Verlinden, Charles. "Aspects de l'esclavage dans les colonies médiévales italiennes," in Eventail de l'histoire vivant: hommage à Lucien Febvre (Paris, 1954), vol. 2, pp. 91-103.

4210. _____. "L'esclavage dans le Centre et le Nord de l'Italie continentale au bas moyen âge," Bulletin de l'Institut historique belge de Rome, 40 (1969), pp. 93-155.

4211. _____. "L'esclavage dans le royaume de Naples à la fin du moyen âge et la participation des marchands espagnols à la traite," Anuario de historia económica y social, 1 (1968), pp. 345-401.

4212. _____. "L'esclavage dans un quartier de Palerme: aspects quantitatifs," in Studi in memoria di Federigo Melis (Naples, 1978), vol. 3, pp. 505-26.

4213. _____. "L'esclavage en Sicile au bas moyen âge," Bulletin de l'Institut historique belge de Rome, 35 (1963), pp. 13-113.

4214. _____. "L'esclavage en Sicilie sous Frédéric II d'Aragon (1296-1337)," in Homenaje à Jaime Vicens Vives (Barcelona, 1965), vol. 1, pp. 675-90.

4215. _____. "L'esclavage sur la côte dalmate au bas moyen âge," Bulletin de l'Institut historique belge de Rome, 41 (1970), pp. 57-140.

4216. _____. "Esclaves alains en Italie et dans les colonies italiennes au XIVe siècle," Revue belge de philologie et d'histoire, 36, 2 (1958), pp. 451-57.

4217. _____. "La législation vénitienne du Bas Moyen âge en matière d'esclavage (XIIIe-XVe siècle)," in Richerche storiche ed economiche in memoria di Corrado Barbagallo (Napoli, 1969), vol. 2, pp. 147-72.

4218. _____. "Schiavitù ed economia nel Mezzogiorno agli inizi dell'età moderna," Annali del Mezzogiorno, 3 (1963), pp. 11-38.

4219. Vista, F. S. "Compra-vendita di schiavi in Barletta (1600-1661)," Rassegna pugliesi di scienze, lettere ed arti, 21 (1904), pp. 301-03.

4220. Vitale, Vito. "La schiavitù in Liguria (review of Tria, La schiavitù in Liguria)," Bollettino ligustico per la storia e la cultura regionale, 1, 2 (1949), pp. 43-47.

4221. Zamboni, Filippo. Gli Ezzelini: Dante e gli schiavi (Roma e la schiavitù personale domestica). Rome-Turin, 1906.

4. Iberia

4222. Aguiló, Estanislau K. "Indicent surgit ab motiu del canvi d'esclaus cristians i moros, pactat despres de la pau," Bolétin de la Sociedad arqueologica luliana, 15 (anos 30-31)(1914-15), pp. 226-33.

4223. al-Abbadi, Ahmad Mukhtar 'Abd al Fattach. Los esclavos in España: ojeada sobre su origin, desarrollo, y relación con el movimiento de la Su'ubiyya. Madrid: Ministerio de Educación Nacional de Egypto, 1953.

4224. Azevedo, Pedro A. d'. "Os escravos," Arquivo histórico português, 1 (1903), pp. 289-307.

4225. Brooks, John. "Slavery and the Slave in the Works of Lope de Vega," Romanic Review, 19, 3 (1928), pp. 232-43.

4226. Cabrillana, N. "Esclavos moriscos en la Almería del siglo XVI," Al-Andalus (Madrid), 40, 1 (1975), pp. 53-128.

4227. Camos Cabruja, L. "Nota relativa a esclavos orientales en Barcelona en el siglo XIV," Sefarad, 6, 1 (1946), pp. 128-29.

4228. Carreras y Candi, Francesch. "Esclaves negres en la cort reyal," Catalana (Barcelona), 2 (no. 57)(1919), p. 439.

4229. Carriazo, Juan de Mata. "Negros, esclavos, y extranjeros en el barrio sevillano de San Bernardo," Archivo hispalense, 20 (no. 63)(1954), pp. 121-33.

4230. Colom, Francisco Sevillano. "Cautivos sardos en Mallorca (siglo XIV)," Studi sardi, 21 (1968), pp. 147-74.

4231. Cortés Alonso, Vicenta. "La conquista de las Islas Canarias a través de las ventas de esclavos en Valencia," Anuario de estudios atlanticos, 1 (1955), pp. 479-547.

4232. _____. La esclavitud en Valencia durante el reinado de los Reyes Católicos (1479-1516). Valencia: Excmo. Ayuntamiento, 1964.

4233. _____. "La población negra de Palo de la Frontera (1568-1579)," Actas y memorias del XXXVI Congreso internacional de americanistas (Seville, 1964) (Seville, 1966), vol. 3, pp. 609-18.

4234. _____. "Procedencia de los esclavos negros en Valencia (1482-1516)," Revista española de antropologia americana, 7, 1 (1972), pp. 123-51.

4235. Doerig, J. A. "La situación de los esclavos a partir de las Siete Partidas de Alfonso El Sabio," Folia humanistica, 4 (no. 40)(1966), pp. 337-61.

4236. Domínguez Ortiz, Antonio. "La esclavitud en Castilla durante la edad moderna," Estudios de historia social de España, 2 (1952), pp. 367-428.

4237. Franco Silva, Alfonso. La esclavitud en Sevilla y su tierra a fines de la Edad Media. Seville: Deputación Provincial de Sevilla, 1979.

4238. _____. Registo documental sobre la esclavitud sevillana (1453-1513). Seville: Universidad de Sevilla, 1979. (Anales de la Universidad Hispalense, no. 46)

4239. Gonzalez Palencia, A. "Carta de esclavitud voluntaria de una Mora de Gaibel," Revista de archivos, bibliotecas y museos, 31, 9-12 (1917), pp. 347-56.

4240. Grau, M. "La esclavitud en 'els termes generals del castell de Morella' (Castellon de la Plana)," in Homenaje a Jaime Vicens Vives (Barcelona, 1965), vol. 1, pp. 445-82.

4241. Graullera Sanz, Vicente. La esclavitud en Valencia en los siglos XVI y XVII. Valencia: Instituto Valenciano de Estudios Históricos, 1978.

4242. *_____. "Los negros en Valencia en el siglo XVI," in Estudios juridicos en homenaje al Profesor Santa Cruz Teijeiro (Valencia, 1974), vol. 1, pp. 391-   .

4243. Gual Camarena, Miguel. "Una cofradía de negros libertos en el siglo XV," Estudios de edad media de la Corona de Aragón, 5 (1952), pp. 457-66.

4244. _____. "Un seguro contra crimenes de esclavos en el siglo XV," Anuario de historia del derecho español, 23 (1953), pp. 247-58.

4245. Hair, P. E. H. "Black African Slaves at Valencia, 1482-1516: An Onomastic Inquiry," History in Africa, 7 (1980), pp. 119-39.

4246. Heleno, Manuel. Os escravos em Portugal. Lisbon: Tip. de Emprêsa do Anuário Comercial, 1933.

4247. Johnson, Harold B. (review of Saunders, Social History of Black Slaves and Freedmen in Portugal), Canadian Journal of History/Annales canadiennes d'histoire, 18, 1 (1983), pp. 129-31.

4248. Ladero Quesada, Miguel Angel. "La esclavitud por guerra a fines del siglo XV: el caso de Málaga," Hispania, 27, (no. 105)(1967), pp. 63-88.

4249. Larquie, Cl. "Les esclaves de Madrid à l'époque de la décadence (1650-1700)," Revue historique, 244 (1970), pp. 41-74.

4250. Lluch, A. Rubio i. "Mitteilungen zur Geschichte der Griechischen Sklaven in Katalonien im XIV. Jahrhundert," Byzantinische Zeitschrift, 30 (1929-30), pp. 462-68.

4251. López de Coca Castañer, José-Enrique. "Esclavos, alfaqueques y mercadenes en la frontera del Mar de Alboran (1490-1516)," Hispania, 38, 139 (1978), pp. 275-300.

4252. Madurell Marimon, José M. "Los seguros de vida de esclavos en Barcelona (1453-1523): Documentos para su estudio," Anuario de historia del derecho español, 25 (1955), pp. 123-88.

4253. _____. "Vendes d'esclaus sards de guerra de Barcelona en 1374," Documentos y trabajos cientificos del VI Congrès d'historia de la Corona d'Aragó (Sardinia, 1957) (Madrid, 1959), pp. 285-89.

4254. Malagón Barceló, Javier. Código negro carolino. Santo Domingo: Edit. Museo del Hombre Dominicano, 1974.

4255. Mans Puigarnau, Jaime M. Las clases serviles bajo la monarquia visigoda y en los estados cristianos de la reconquista española. Barcelona: J. Bosch, 1928.

4256. Marrero Rodríguez, Manuela. La esclavitud en Tenerife a raíz de la conquista. La Laguna en Tenerife: Instituto de Estudios Canarios, 1966. (Monografías, sección I: Ciencias historicas y geográficas, no. 10)

4257. Miret y Sans, Joaquín. "La esclavitud en Cataluña en los ultimos tiempos de la Edad Media," Revue hispanique, 41 (1917), pp. 1-109.

4258. Nodal, Roberto. "Black Presence in the Canary Islands (Spain)," Journal of Black Studies, 12, 1 (1981), pp. 83-90.

4259. Pike, Ruth. "Penal Labor in Sixteenth-Century Spain: The Mines of Almadén," Societas - A Review of Social History, 3, 3 (1973), pp. 193-206.

4260. _____. "Penal Servitude in Early Modern Spain: The Galleys," Journal of European Economic History (Rome), 11, 1 (1982), pp. 197-217.

4261. _____. "Sevillian Society in the Sixteenth Century: Slaves and Freedmen," Hispanic American Historical Review, 47, 3 (1967), pp. 344-59.

4262. Putzulu, Evandro. "Schiavi sardi a Maiorca nella seconda metà del secolo XIV," Documentos y trabajos cientificos del VI Congrès d'historia de la Corona d'Aragó (Sardinia, 1957) (Madrid, 1959), pp. 365-78.

4263. Ramos y Loscertales, José Maria. El cautiverio en la Corona de Aragon durante los siglos XIII, XIV y XV. Zaragoza: Publicaciones del estudio de filología de Aragón, 1915.

4264. Sancho, Pedro Antonio. "Prohibición de traer esclavos moros à Mallorca si no han sido apresados por buques armados en corso en el Reino (1397)," Boletin de la Sociedad arqueologica luliana, 9 (1902), p. 42.

4265. Sancho y Vicens, Pedro A. "Documentos sobre cautivos," Boletin de la Sociedad arqueologica luliana, ano 58-59, 28 (nos. 695-703)(1942-43), pp. 547-50.

4266. Saunders, A. C. de C. M. A Social History of Black Slaves and Freedmen in Portugal, 1441-1555. New York: Cambridge University Press, 1982.

4267. Terán Sanchez, Antonio Collantes de. "Contribución al estudio de los esclavos en la Sevilla medieval," in Homenaje al Professor Carriazo (Seville, 1972), vol. 2, pp. 109-21.

4268. Verlinden, Charles. "L'esclavage dans le monde ibérique médiéval jusqu'au XIIIe siècle," Anuario de historia del derecho español, 11 (1934), pp. 283-448.

4269. _____. "L'esclavage dans la péninsule ibérique au XIVe siécle," Anuario de estudios medievales, 7 (1970-71), pp. 577-91.

4270. _____. "L'esclavage en Espagne au XIVe siécle," (Travaux du Congrès sur le XIVe siècle espagnole). Forthcoming.

4271. _____. "Esclaves du Sud-est et de l'Est européen en Espagne orientale à la fin du moyen âge," Revue historique du sud-est européen, 19, 2 (1942), pp. 371-406.

4272. _____. "Esclaves fugitifs et assurances en Catalogne (XIVe - XVe siècles)," Annales du Midi (1950), pp. 301-28.

4273. *Wettinger, G. "Coron captives in Malta," Melita historica, 2, 4 (1959), pp.   .

4274. Wilson, William E. "Some Notes on Slavery During the Golden Age," Hispanic Review, 7, 2 (1939), pp. 171-74.

5. France

4275. Bamford, Paul W. "Slaves for the Galleys of France, 1665 to 1700," in John Parker, ed., Merchants and Scholars: Essays in the History of Exploration and Trade (Minneapolis: University of Minnesota Press, 1965), pp. 171-91.

4276. Bernard, Pierre. Etude sur les esclaves et les serfs d'église en France du VIe au XIIIe siècle. Paris: Société du Recueil Sirey, 1919.

4277. Biondi, Carminella. Mon frère, tu es mon esclave!; teorie schiaviste e dibattitti antropologico-razziali nel Settecento francese. Pisa: Libraria Goliardica, 1973.

4278. Bloch, Marc. "Les 'colliberti': étude sur la formation de la classe servile," Revue historique, 157 (1928), pp. 1-48, 225-63. Reprinted in idem, Mélanges historiques (Paris: S.E.V.P.E.N., 1963), vol. 1, pp. 385-451. Translated by William R. Beer as "The 'Colliberti': A Study on the Formation of the Servile Class," in Bloch, Slavery and Serfdom in the Middle Ages (Berkeley: University of California Press, 1975), pp. 93-150.

4279. _____. "Liberté et servitude personnelles au moyen âge, particulièrement en France: contribution à une étude des classes," Anuario de historia del derecho español, 10 (1933), pp. 19-115. Reprinted in idem, Mélanges historiques (Paris: S.E.V.P.E.N., 1963), vol. 1, pp. 286-355. Translated by William R. Beer as "Personal Liberty and Servitude in the Middle Ages, Particularly in France: Contribution to a Class Study," in Bloch, Slavery and Serfdom in the Middle Ages (Berkeley: University of California Press, 1975), pp. 33-92.

4280. Corvisier, André. "Les soldats noirs du maréchal de Saxe, le problème des Antillais et Africains sous les armes en France au XVIIIe siècle," Revue française d'histoire d'outre-mer, 55, 4 (no. 201)(1968), pp. 367-413.

4281. Daubigney, Alain, and François Favory. "L'esclavage en Narbonnaise et Lyonnaise," in Actes du colloque sur l'esclavage (1972), pp. 315-88.

4282. Despien, Jean-Pierre. "Montesquieu était-il esclavagiste?" La pensée, 193 (1977), pp. 102-12.

4283. *Elisabeth, L. "Les problèmes des gens de couleur à Bordeaux sous l'Ancien Régime (1716-1787)" (Mémoire, dipl. d'études sup., Faculté des lettres, Bordeaux, 1955).

4284. Kieft, C. van de. "Les 'colliberti' et l'évolution du servage dans la France centrale et occidentale (X^e-XIIe siècle)," Tijdschrift voor rechtsgeschiedenis, 32 (1964), pp. 363-95.

4285. McCloy, Shelby T. "Further Notes on Negroes and Mulattoes in Eighteenth-Century France," Journal of Negro History, 39, 4 (1954), pp. 284-97.

4286. _____. "Negroes and Mulattoes in Eighteenth Century France," Journal of Negro History, 30, 3 (1945), pp. 276-92.

4287. _____. The Negro in France. Lexington: University of Kentucky Press, 1961.

4288. Malausséna, Paul-Louis. "Maîtres et esclaves en Provence au moyen âge," in Mélanges Roger Aubenas (Montpellier, 1974), pp. 527-44.

4289. Petot, Pierre. "L'évolution du servage dans la France coutumière du XIe au XIVe siècle," in Le servage: communications présentées à la Société Jean Bodin (Brussels: Libraire Falk, 1937), pp. 155-64.

4290. Verlinden, Charles. "Esclavage noir en France méridionale et courants de traite en Afrique," Annales du Midi (Mélanges Y. Renouard), 78 (1966), pp. 335-43.

4291. _____. "Note sur l'esclavage à Montpellier au bas moyen âge (XIIe -XIVe siècle)," Etudes d'histoire dédiées à la mémoire de H. Pirenne (Brussels: Nouvelle société d'éditions, 1937), pp. 451-69.

4292. _____. "Traite et esclavage dans la vallée de la Meuse," in Mélanges Félix Rousseau (Brussels, 1958), pp. 673-86.

6. England

4293. Bauer, Carol Phillips. "Law, Slavery, and Sommersett's Case in Eighteenth-Century England: A Study of the Legal Status of Freedom" (PhD diss., New York University, 1973).

4294. Blackett, R. J. M. "Fugitive Slaves in Britain: The Odyssey of William and Ellen Craft," Journal of American Studies, 12, 1 (1978), pp. 41-62.

4295. Dabyeen, David. "Blacks in Britain: Hogarth – the Savage and the Civilised," History Today, 31 (1981), pp. 48-51.

4296. Davies, C. S. L. "Slavery and Protector Somerset: The Vagrancy Act of 1547," Economic History Review, 19, 2 (1966), pp. 533-49.

4297. Edwards, Paul. "Blacks in Britain: Black Personalities in Georgian Britain," History Today, 31, 9 (1981), pp. 39-43.

4298. _____. "Blacks in Britain: Olaudah Equiano and Ignatius Sancho," History Today, 31, 9 (1981), pp. 44.

4299. _____, and James Walvin. "Africans in Britain, 1500-1800," in Kilson and Rotberg, eds., African Diaspora, pp. 172-204.

4300. Frey, Sylvia R. "The British and the Black: A New Perspective," Historian, 38, 2 (1976), pp. 225-38.

4301. Loewenson, Leo. "Escaped Russian Slaves in England in the 17th Century," Slavonic and East European Review, 42 (no. 99)(1963-64), pp. 427-29.

4302. Shyllon, Folarin O. Black Slaves in Britain. London: Oxford University Press, 1974.

4303. Walvin, James. Black and White: The Negro and English Society, 1555-1945. London: Allen Lane, 1973.

4304. _____. "Blacks in Britain: The 18th Century," History Today, 31, 9 (1981), pp. 37-38.

4305. _____, comp. The Black Presence: A Documentary History of the Negro in England, 1555-1860. New York: Schocken Books, 1972.

4306. Wilson, Nan. "Legal Attitudes to Slavery in Eighteenth-century Britain: English Myth: Scottish Social Realism and Their Wider Comparative Context," Race, 11, 4 (1970), pp. 463-75.

4307. Williams, Eric. "The Golden Age of the Slave System in Britain," Journal of Negro History, 25, 1 (1940), pp. 60-106.

7. Eastern Europe and Russia

4308. Blum, Jerome. Lord and Peasant in Russia from the Ninth to the Nineteenth Century. Princeton: Princeton University Press, 1961.

4309. Gaster, M. "Bill of Sale of Gypsy Slaves in Moldavia, 1851," Journal of the Gypsy Lore Society, 3rd series, 2 (1923), pp. 68-81.

4310. Hellie, Richard. "Recent Soviet Historiography on Medieval and Early Modern Russian Slavery," Russian Review, 35, 1 (1976), pp. 1-32.

4311. _____. Slavery in Russia, 1450-1725. Chicago: University of Chicago Press, 1982.

4312. Sakasov, Iv. "Documents récemment découverts datant de la fin du XIVe siècle, et concernant les Bulgares de la Macédoine vendus comme esclaves," Makedonski pregled, 7, 2-3 (1932), pp. 1-62. (In Russian with French summary, pp. 235-39.)

4313. Shakespear, J. "How Sir Richmond Shakespear Set Free the Russian Slaves at Kniva," Journal of the Central Asian Society, 8, 2 (1921), pp. 121-24.

4314. Vaux de Foletier, François. "L'esclavage des Tsiganes dans les principautés roumaines," Etudes Tsiganes, 16, 2-3 (1970), pp. 24-29.

4315. Zuzek, Niko. "Sacerdócio servil na Rússia medieval," Anais do VI Simpósio nacional dos professores universitários de história (Goiâna, 1971)(São Paulo, 1973), vol. 1, pp. 225-30.

8. Scandinavia

4316. Foote, Peter G. "Thraelahald a Islandi," Saga (Reykjavik), 15 (1977), pp. 41-74. (With summary in English)

4317. Hasselberg, Gösta. "Den s.k. Skarastadgan och träldomens upphörende i Sverige," Västergötlands fornminnesförenings tidskrift (Skara), 5, 3 (1944), pp. 51-90.

4318. Henning, Sam. "Träldomens försvinnande och de svenska landskapslagarna," Historisk Tidskrift (Stockholm), 50 (1930), pp. 86-95.

4319. Herdal, Harald. Traellene i norden. Kobenhavn: Hasselbach, 1967.

4320. Neveus, Clara. Trälarna i landskapslagarnas samhälle: Danmark och Sverige. Stockholm: Almquist and Wiksele, 1974.

4321. Pálsson, Arna. "Um lok thraeldóms a Islandi," Skírnir, 106 (1932), pp. 191-203.

4322. Skyum-Nielsen, Niels. Kvinde og Slave. Copenhagen: Munksgaard, 1971.

4323. _____. "Slaveriet i norden set mod international baggrund, Vortrag 1971," Beretning, foredrag og forhandlinger ved det Nordiske Historikermode i Kobenhavn (1971) (n.d.), pp. 301-23.

4324. *Sommarin, Emil. "Träldomen i Norden," Verdandis smaskrifter, 104 (1917), pp. .

4325. Wilde-Stockmeyer, Marlis. Sklaverei auf Island: Untersuchungen zur rechtlichsozialen Situation und literarischen Darstellung der Sklaven im skandinavischen Mittelalter. Heidelberg: Winter, 1978. (Skandinavistische Arbeiten, Bd. 5)

4326. Williams, Carl O. <u>Thraldom in Ancient Iceland</u>. Chicago. University of Chicago Press, 1937.

9. Other

4327. Buve, R. "Surinaamse slaven en vrije negers in Amsterdam gedurende de achttiende eeuw," <u>Bijdragen tot de Taal-, Land- en Volkenkunde van Nederlandsch Indiö</u>, 119, 1 (1963), pp. 8-17.

4328. Koch, Rainer. "Liberalismus, Konservativismus und das Problem der Negersklaverei: Ein Beitrag zur Geschichte des politischen Denkens in Deutschland in der ersten Hälfte des 19. Jahrhunderts," <u>Historische Zeitschrift</u>, 222, 3 (1976), pp. 529-77.

4329. Pankhurst, Richard. "Ethiopian and other African Slaves in Greece during the Ottoman Occupation," <u>Slavery and Abolition</u>, 1, 3 (1980), pp. 339-44.

4330. Rivers, Theodore John. "Symbola, manumissio et libertas Langobardorum. An Interpretation of gaida and gisil in Edictus Rothari 224 and its Relationship to the Concept of Freedom," <u>Zeitschrift der Savigny Stiftung für vergleichende Rechtsgeschichte (germanistische Abteilung)</u>, 95 (1978), pp. 57-78.

4331. Wergeland, Agnes Mathilde. <u>Slavery in Germanic Society During the Middle Ages</u>. Chicago. University of Chicago Press, 1916.

X. Other

1. Asia - General and comparative

4332. Harris, Joseph E. The African Presence in Asia: Consequences of the East African Slave Trade. Evanston, Ill.: Northwestern University Press, 1971.

4333. Melekechvili, G. A. "Esclavage, féodalisme et mode de production asiatique dans l'Orient ancien," in Centre d'études et de recherches marxistes, Sur le mode de production asiatique (Paris, 1974, 2nd ed.), pp. 257-77.

2. East Asia

4334. Chen, Nicholas Mu Yu. "Trabalho livre e trabalho escravo na historia da China," Anais do VI Simposio nacional dos professores universitarios de historia (Goiâna, 1971)(Sao Paulo, 1973), vol. 1, pp. 205-14.

4335. Erkes, Eduard. Das Problem der Sklaverei in China. Berlin: Akademie-Verlag, 1954.

4336. Felber, Roland. "Die Reformen des Shang Yang und das Problem der Sklaverei in China," in E.-Ch. Welskopf, ed., Neue Beiträge zur Geschichte der alten Welt (Berlin: Akademie-Verlag, 1964), vol. 1, pp. 111-21.

4337. Jaschok, Maria. "Mui Jai Slavery and Upper Class Women in Hong Kong" (Unpublished manuscript, School of Oriental and African Studies, n.d.).

4338. Kuo Mo-Jo. "La société esclavagiste chinoise," Recherches internationales à la lumière du marxisme, 2 (1957), pp. 153-64.

4339. McDermott, Joseph P. "Bondservants in the T'ai-hu Basin During the Late Ming: A Case of Mistaken Identities," Journal of Asian Studies, 40, 4 (1981), pp. 675-701.

4340. Meijer, Marinus J. "Slavery at the End of the Ch'ing Dynasty," in Jerome A. Cohen, Fu-Mei Chang, and Randle Edwards, eds., Essays on China's Legal Tradition (Princeton: Princeton University Press, 1980), pp. 327-38.

4341. Pippon, Toni. "Beitrag zum chinesischen Sklavensystem nebst einer Übersetzung des 'Chung-kuo nu pei chih tu' (das Sklavensystem Chinas) von Wang Shih Chieh," Mitteilungen der Deutschen Gesellschaft für Natur- und Völkerkunde Ostasiens, 29, Teil B (1936), pp. 1-140.

4342. Pokora, Timoteus. "Existierte in China eine Sklavenhalter-gesellschaft?" Archiv Orientální, 31, 3 (1963), pp. 353-63.

4343. _____. "Gab es in der Geschichte Chinas eine durch Sklaverei bestimmte Produktionsweise und Gesellschaftsformation?" in E.-Ch. Welskopf, ed., Neue Beiträge zur Geschichte der alten Welt (Berlin: Akademie Verlag, 1964), vol. 1, pp. 123-35.

4344. Pulleybank, E. G. "The Origins and Nature of Chattel Slavery in China," Journal of the Economic and Social History of the Orient, 1, 2 (1958), pp. 185-220.

4345. Salem, Ellen. "Slavery in Medieval Korea" (PhD diss., Columbia University, 1978).

4346. "Slavery in Korea," Korea Review, 2 (1902), pp. 149-55.

4347. Tökei, F. "Die Formen der chinesischen patriarchalischen Sklaverei in der Chou-Zeit," in Opuscula Ethnologica Memoriae Ludovici Bíró Sacra (Budapest, 1959), pp. 291-318.

4348. Unruh, Ellen S. "The Landowning Slave: A Korean Phenomenon," Korea Journal, 16, 4 (1976), pp. 27-34.

4349. Wang Ti-t'ung. "Slaves and Other Comparable Social Groups during the Northern Dynasties (368-618)," Harvard Journal of Asiatic Studies, 16 (1953), pp. 293-364.

4350. Watson, James L. "Chattel Slavery in Chinese Peasant Society: A Comparative Analysis," Ethnology, 15, 4 (1976), pp. 361-75.

4351. _____. "Transactions in People: The Chinese Market in Slaves, Servants, and Heirs," in Watson, ed., Asian and African Systems of Slavery, pp. 223-50.

4352. Wilbur, C. Martin. Slavery in China during the Former Han Dynasty, 206 B.C. - A.D. 25. Chicago: Field Museum, 1943. (Field Museum of Natural History Publication no. 525)

3. Southeast Asia

4353. Arcilla, José S. "Slavery, Flogging and Other Moral Cases in 17th Century Philippines," Philippine Studies, 20, 3 (1972), pp. 399-416.

4354. Arensmeyer, Elliott C. "The Chinese Coolie Labor Trade and the Philippines: An Inquiry," Philippine Studies, 28, 2 (1980), pp. 187-98.

4355. Bongert, Yvonne. "Note sur l'esclavage en droit Khmer ancien," in Etudes de droit privé offertes à Pierre Petot (Paris: Librarie générale de droit et de jurisprudence, 1959), pp. 7-26.

4356. Caplan, Lionel. "Power and Status in South Asian Slavery," in Watson, ed., Asian and African Systems of Slavery, pp. 169-94.

4357. Cruikshank, R. Bruce. "Slavery in Nineteenth-Century Siam," Journal of the Siam Society, 63, 2 (1975), pp. 315-33.

4358. Dang Trinh Ky. L'engagement des personnes en droit annamite. Paris: Editions Domat-Montchrestien, 1933. (Etudes de sociologie et d'ethnologie juridiques, no. 17)

4359. Knaap, Gerrit. "Europeans, Mestizos and Slaves: The Population of Colombo at the End of the Seventeenth Century," Itinerario (Leiden), 5, 2 (1981), pp. 84-101.

4360. Lasker, Bruno. Human Bondage in Southeast Asia. Chapel Hill: University of North Carolina Press, 1950.

4361. Lingat, Robert. L'esclavage privé dans le vieux droit siamois (avec une traduction des anciennes lois siamoises sur l'esclavage). Paris: Editions Domat-Montchrestien, 1931.

4362. Morris, H. S. "Slaves, Aristocrats and Export of Sago in Sarawak," in Watson, ed., Asian and African Systems of Slavery, pp. 293-309.

4363. Panananon, Chatchai. "Siamese 'Slavery': The Institution and its Abolition" (PhD diss., University of Michigan, 1982).

4364. *Sutherland, H. "Slavery and the Slave Trade in Indonesia, with Special Reference to Sulawesi" (Unpublished paper, 1980).

4365. Turton, Andrew. "Thai Institutions of Slavery," in Watson, ed., Asian and African Systems of Slavery, pp. 251-92.

4366. Warren, James F. "Slave Markets and Exchange in the Malay World: The Sulu Sultanate, 1770-1878," Journal of Southeast Asian Studies, 8, 2 (1977), pp. 162-75.

4367. _____. The Sulu Zone 1768-1898: The Dynamics of External Trade, Slavery, and Ethnicity in the Transformation of a Southeast Asian Maritime State. Singapore: Singapore University Press, 1981.

4368. _____. "Who Were the Balangingi Samal? Slave Raiding and Ethnogenesis in Nineteenth-Century Sulu," Journal of Asian Studies, 37, 3 (1978), pp. 477-90.

4369. Wheatley, Paul. "(Nu Pi) Slaves : Geographical Notes on Some Commodities Involved in Sung Maritime Trade," Journal of the Malayan Branch of the Royal Asiatic Society, 32, 2 (no. 186)(1959), pp. 54-55.

4. Indian subcontinent

4370. Agrawala, Ratna Chandra. "Position of Slaves and Serfs as Depicted in the Kharosthi Documents from Chinese Turkestan," Indian Historical Quarterly, 29, 2 (1953), pp. 97-110.

4371. Banaji, Dady Rustomji. Slavery in British India. Bombay: D. B. Taraporevala Sons, 1933.

4372. Bose, Atindra Nath. "Origin of Slavery in Indo Aryan Economy," Journal of Indian History, 19, 2 (1940), pp. 145-57.

4373. Chanana, Dev Raj. Slavery in Ancient India, as Depicted in Pali and Sanskrit Texts. New Delhi: People's Publishing House, 1960.

4374. Chattopadhyay, Amal Kumar. Slavery in India. Calcutta: Nagarjun Press, 1959.

4375. _____. Slavery in the Bengal Presidency, 1772-1843. London: Golden Eagle, 1977. Foreword by J. B. Harrison.

4376. Dange, Shripad A. India From Primitive Communism to Slavery. Bombay: People's Publishing House, 1949.

4377. Fukazawa, Hiroshi. "Some Aspects of Slavery in the Eighteenth Century Maratha Kingdom," Journal of Intercultural Studies, 1 (1974), pp. 10-20.

4378. Hjejle, Benedicte. "Slavery and Agricultural Bondage in South India in the Nineteenth Century," Scandinavian Economic History Review, 15, 1-2 (1967), pp. 71-126.

4379. _____. "The Social Policy of the East India Company with Regard to Sati, Slavery, Thagi, and Infanticide" (PhD diss., Oxford University, 1958).

4380. Kennion, R. L. "Abolition of Slavery in Nepal," Nineteenth Century, 98 (1925), pp. 381-89.

4381. Kusuman, J. J. Slavery in Travancore. Trivandrum: Kerala Historical Society, 1973.

4382. Naidis, Mark. "The Abolitionists and Indian Slavery," Journal of Asian History, 15, 2 (1981), pp. 146-58.

4383. _____. "India and the Slavery Question," South Atlantic Quarterly, 69, 4 (1970), pp. 534-42.

4384. Pescatello, Ann M. "The African Presence in Portuguese India," Journal of Asian History, 11, 1 (1977), pp. 26-48.

4385. Rao, Vasant D. "The Habshis, India's Unknown Africans," Africa Report (Sept./Oct. 1973), pp. 35-38.

4386. Regmi, Mahesh Chandra. "Documents on Slavery," Regmi Research Series, 1, 2 (1969), pp. 44-45.

4387. Saradamoni, K. "Agrestic Slavery in Kerala in the Nineteenth Century," Indian Economic and Social History Review, 10, 4 (1973), pp. 371-85.

4388. _____. "How Agrestic Slavery was Abolished in Kerala," Indian Economic and Social History Review, 11, 2-3 (1974), pp. 291-308.

4389. Sarup, V. L. "Some Aspects of Slavery," Journal of the Punjab Historical Society, 8 (1921), pp. 174-84.

4390. Schetelich, Maria. "Asatantra in der altindischen Rechtliteratur," Altorientalische Forschungen, 5 (1977), pp. 113-22.

4391. Singh, K. B. "Slavery in Manipur," Folklore (Calcutta), 17 (16), 1 (1975), pp. 7-9.

5. Oceania

4392. Mahajani, Usha. "Slavery, Indian Labour, and British Colonialism," Pacific Affairs, 50, 2 (1977), pp. 263-71.

4393. Rowley, C. D. "The Papuan Slave: East Side, West Side," New Guinea, Australia, the Pacific and Southeast Asia, 1, 2 (1965), pp. 23-30.

4394. Tate, Merze, and Fidele Fox. "Slavery and Racism in South Pacific Annexations," Journal of Negro History, 50, 1 (1965), pp. 1-21.

6. Amerindian

4395. Anderson, Arthur J. O. "The Institution of Slave-Bathing," Indiana (Berlin), 7 (1982), pp. 81-92. ("Gedenkschrift Walter Lehman, Teil 2")

4396. Baglai, V. Ye. "Slavery Among the Aztecs," Vestnik Drevnei Istorii, 157 (1981), pp. 168-77. In Russian with English summary.

4397. Bailey, Lynn Robison. Indian Slave Trade in the Southwest: A Study of Slavetaking and the Traffic of Indian Captives. Los Angeles: Westernlore Press, 1966.

4398. Bosch Garcia, Carlos. La esclavitud prehispanica entre los aztecas. México: Colegio de Mexico, Centro de estudios histÝricos, 1944.

4399. Choy, Emilio. "Desarrollo del pensamiento especulativo en la sociedad esclavista de los Incas," in Actas y trabajos. Segundo congreso nacional de historia del Perú (1961)(Lima. Centro de Estudios Históricos Militares del Perú, 1962), vol. 2, pp. 87-101.

4400. _____. "Estructuras de amortiguación y lucha de clases en el sistema esclavista incaico," in Atti del XL Congresso Internazionale degli Americanisti (Roma-Genova, 1972)(Genoa. Tilgher, 1975), vol. 2, pp. 511-13.

4401. Doran, Michael F. "Negro Slaves of the Five Civilized Tribes," Annals of the Association of American Geographers, 68, 3 (1978), pp. 335-50.

4402. Gammon, Tim. "Black Freedmen and the Cherokee Nation," Journal of American Studies, 11, 3 (1977), pp. 357-64.

4403. Geist, Christopher D. "Slavery Among the Indians: An Overview," Negro History Bulletin, 38, 7 (1975), pp. 465-67.

4404. González Torres, Yolotl. "La esclavitud entre los Mexica," in Pedro Carrasco and Johanna Broda, eds., Estratificación social en la mesoamérica prehispánica (México. Centro de Investigaciones Superiores, Instituto Nacional de Antropología e Historia, 1976), pp. 78-87.

4405. Gough, Barry M. "Send a Gunboat! Checking Slavery and Controlling Liquor Traffic Among Coast Indians of British Columbia in the 1860s," Pacific Northwest Quarterly, 69, 4 (1978), pp. 159-68.

4406. Grinde, Donald, Jr. "Native American Slavery in the Southern Colonies," Indian Historian, 10, 2 (1977), pp. 38-42.

4407. Halliburton, Janet. "Black Slavery in the Creek Nation," Chronicles of Oklahoma, 56, 3 (1978), pp. 298-314.

4408. Halliburton, R., Jr. "Black Slave Control in the Cherokee Nation," Journal of Ethnic Studies, 3, 2 (1975), pp. 23-35.

4409. _____. "Origins of Black Slavery Among the Cherokees," Chronicles of Oklahoma, 52, 4 (1974-75), pp. 483-96.

4410. _____. Red Over Black: Black Slavery among the Cherokee Indians. Westport, Conn.: Greenwood Press, 1977.

4411. Henshaw, H. W. "Slavery," in United States Bureau of American Ethnology, Handbook of American Indians: Northern Mexico (Washington, 1907-1910), vol. 2, pp. 597-600.

4412. Hicks, Frederic. "Dependent Labor in Prehispanic Mexico," Estudios de cultura Náhuatl, 11 (1974), pp. 243-66.

4413. Hoetinck, E. "Early Slavery on the Pacific Coast," Journal of Interamerican Studies, 17, 3 (1975), pp. 345-49.

4414. Hunt, H. F. "Slavery Among the Indians of Northwestern America," Washington Historical Quarterly, 9, 4 (1918), pp. 277-83.

4415. Katz, William Loren. "Black and Indian Cooperation and Resistance to Slavery," Freedomways, 17, 3 (1977), pp. 164-74.

4416. Lauber, Almon W. Indian Slavery in Colonial Times within the Present Limits of the United States. New York: Columbia University Press, 1913.

4417. Littlefield, Daniel F., Jr. Africans and Creeks: From the Colonial Period to the Civil War. Westport, Conn.: Greenwood Press, 1979.

4418. _____. Africans and Seminoles: From Removal to Emancipation. Westport, Conn.: Greenwood Press, 1977.

4419. _____, and Lonnie E. Underhill. "Slave 'Revolt' in the Cherokee Nation, 1842," American Indian Quarterly, 3, 2 (1977), pp. 121-31.

4420. MacLeod, William C. "Debtor and Chattel Slavery in Aboriginal North America," American Anthropologist, 27, 3 (1925), pp. 370-80.

4421. _____. "Economic Aspects of Indigenous American Slavery," American Anthropologist, 30, 4 (1928), pp. 632-50.

4422. McLoughlin, William G. "Cherokee Slaveholders and Baptist Missionaries, 1845-1860," Historian, 45, 2 (1983), pp. 147-66.

4423. _____. "Indian Slaveholders and Presbyterian Missionaries, 1837-1861," Church History, 42, 4 (1973), pp. 535-51.

4424. _____. "Red Indians, Black Slavery and White Racism: America's Slaveholding Indians," American Quarterly, 26, 4 (1974), pp. 367-85.

4425. Magnaghi, Russell M. "The Indian Slave Trader: The Comanche, A Case Study" (PhD diss., St. Louis University, 1970).

4426. Naidis, Mark. "The Abolitionists and Indian Slavery" (Paper read to the Annual Meeting of the American Historical Association, Los Angeles, 1981).

4427. Perdue, Theda. "Cherokee Planters, Black Slaves, and African Colonization," Chronicles of Oklahoma, 60, 3 (1982), pp. 322-31.

4428. _____. "People Without a Place: Aboriginal Cherokee Bondage," Indian Historian, 9, 3 (1976), pp. 31-37.

4429. _____. "Slavery and the Evolution of Cherokee Society, 1540-1866" (PhD diss., University of Georgia, 1976).

4430. _____. Slavery and the Evolution of Cherokee Society, 1540–1866. Knoxville: University of Tennessee Press, 1979.

4431. Porter, Kenneth W. "Relations Between Negroes and Indians within the Present Limits of the United States," Journal of Negro History, 17, 3 (1932), pp. 287–367.

4432. Quintero, Rodolfo. "No era esclavista: la sociedad de Venezuela pre-hispanica," América indigena, 16, 4 (1956), pp. 347–51.

4433. Roethler, Michael Donald. "Negro Slavery Among the Cherokee Indians, 1540–1866" (PhD diss., Fordham University, 1964).

4434. Ruyle, Eugene E. "Slavery, Surplus, and Stratification on the Northwest Coast: The Ethnoenergetics of an Incipient Stratification System," Current Anthropology, 14, 5 (1973), pp. 603–31.

4435. Searcy, Martha Condrey. "The Introduction of African Slavery into the Creek Indian Nation," Georgia Historical Quarterly, 66, 1 (1982), pp. 21–32.

4436. Sefton, James E. "Black Slaves, Red Masters, White Middlemen: A Congressional Debate of 1852," Florida Historical Quarterly, 51, 2 (1972), pp. 113–28.

4437. Smith, C. Calvin. "The Oppressed Oppressors: Negro Slavery Among the Choctaw Indians of Oklahoma," Red River Valley Historical Review, 2, 2 (1975), pp. 240–53.

4438. Snell, William R. "Indian Slavery in Colonial South Carolina, 1671–1765" (PhD diss., University of Alabama, 1972).

4439. Winston, Sanford. "Indian Slavery in the Carolina Region," Journal of Negro History, 19, 4 (1934), pp. 431–40.

4440. Woodward, John A. "Salmon, Slaves, and Grizzly Bears: The Prehistoric Antecedents and Ethnohistory of Clackamas Indian Culture" (PhD diss., University of Oregon, 1974).

4441. Zwink, Timothy A. "Review of Slavery and the Evolution of Cherokee Society by Theda Perdue," Georgia Historical Quarterly, 64, 4 (1979), pp. 481–82.

7. Other

4442. Barassin, J. "La révolte des esclaves à l'île Bourbon (Réunion), au XVIIIe siècle," in Mouvements de populations dans l'Océan Indien (Actes du 4e Congrès de l'Association Historique Internationale de l'Océan Indien et du 14e Commission Internationale d'Histoire Maritime) (Saint-Denis de la Réunion, 4–9 August 1972) (Paris: Champion, 1979), pp. 357–91.

4443. Gerbeau, M. "Des minorités mal-connues, esclaves indiens et malais des Mascareignes au XIXe siècle," in Migrations, minorités et échanges en Océan Indien, XIXe-XXe siècles (Table Ronde, 1978) (Aix-en-Provence: Institut d'histoire des pays d'outre-mer, 1978), pp. 160-242. (Université de Provence, Institut d'histoire des pays d'outre-mer, Etudes et documents, no. 11)

4444. *Noel, K. "L'esclavage à l'Ile de France pendant l'occupation française (1715-1810)" (Thèse, Paris, 1953).

4445. Nwulia, Moses D. E. The History of Slavery in Mauritius and the Seychelles, 810-1875. East Brunswick, N.J.: Fairleigh-Dickenson University Press, 1981.

XI. Slave trade

1. Atlantic - General

4446. Abanime, Emeka. "Equiano, précurseur de la littérature nigériane anglophone," Ethiopiques, 19 (1979), pp. 80-84.

4447. Abramova, Svetlana IUrrevna. Afrika: Chetyre stoletiia rabotorgovli (Africa: Four Centuries of the Slave Trade). Moscow: Izdatel'stvo "Nauka", 1978.

4448. _____. L'histoire de la traite des esclaves sur le haut littoral de la Guiné. Moscow, 1966. (In Russian: Istoriia rabotorgovlina Verkhne-Guineiskom poberszh'e.)

4449. _____. "Ideological, Doctrinal, Philosophical, Religious, and Political Aspects of the African Slave Trade," in UNESCO, African Slave Trade, pp. 16-30.

4450. Aguet, Isabelle. A Pictorial History of the Slave Trade. Geneva, 1971.

4451. _____. La traite des nègres. Geneva: Editions Minerva, 1971.

4452. Ajayi, J. F. Ade, and J. E. Inikori. "An Account of Research on the Slave Trade in Nigeria," in UNESCO, African Slave Trade, pp. 247-49.

4453. Anstey, Roger T. "The Slave Trade of the Continental Powers 1760-1810," Economic History Review, 30, 2 (1977), pp. 259-68.

4454. _____. "Travaux publiés, en anglais surtout, sur le commerce des esclaves dans l'Atlantique, son abolition et sa suppression," Etudes d'histoire africaine, 5 (1973), pp. 5-23.

4455. Armstrong, James C. "Madagascar and the Slave Trade in the Seventeenth Century" (forthcoming).

4456. Austen, Ralph A. "The Abolition of the Overseas Slave Trade: A Distorted Theme in West African History," Journal of the Historical Society of Nigeria, 5, 2 (1970), pp. 257-74.

4457. _____. "From the Atlantic to the Indian Ocean: European Abolition, African Slave Trade, and Asian Economic Structures," in Walvin and Eltis, eds., Abolition of the Atlantic Slave Trade, pp. 117-40.

4458. "Los barcos que transportaban los esclavos de Africa durante el siglo XVIII," Revista del Instituto de cultura puertorriqueña, 16 (no. 61)(1973), pp. 19-20.

4459. Bean Richard. "A Note on the Relative Importance of Slaves and Gold in West African Exports," Journal of African History, 15, 3 (1974), pp. 351-56.

4460. Berding, Helmut. "Die Achtung des Sklavenhandels auf dem Wiener Kongress 1814/1815," Historische Zeitschrift, 219, 2 (1974), pp. 265-89.

4461. Bethell, Leslie. "The Mixed Commissions for the Suppression of the Trans-atlantic Slave Trade in the Nineteenth Century," Journal of African History, 7, 1 (1966), pp. 79-93.

4462. Castelot, André. "Un cauchemar, la traite des noirs," Historia, no. 268 (1969), pp. 33-40.

4463. Chee-Mooke, Robert A. "White Indentured Servitude and the Atlantic Slave Trade," Negro History Bulletin, 43, 1 (1980), pp. 20-22.

4464. Chilver, E. M., P. M. Kaberry, and R. Cornevin. "Sources of the Nineteenth Century Slave Trade: Two Comments," Journal of African History, 6, 1 (1965), pp. 117-20.

4465. Clarke, John Henrik. "The Slave Community and the World Community: Some Notes Toward a New Inquiry into the Historiography of the Atlantic Slave Trade," in Gilmore, ed., Revisiting Blassingame's The Slave Community, pp. 111-22.

4466. Cohn, Raymond L., and Richard A. Jensen. "(Comment and Controversy) Mortality in the Atlantic Slave Trade," Journal of Interdisciplinary History, 13, 2 (1982), pp. 317-30. With a reply by Joseph C. Miller, pp. 331-36.

4467. _____. "The Determinants of Slave Mortality Rates on the Middle Passage," Explorations in Economic History, 19, 3 (1982), pp. 269-82.

4468. Conti, Luigi. "The Catholic Church and the Slave Trade," in UNESCO, African Slave Trade, pp. 265-68.

4469. Cook, Fred J. "The Slave Ship Rebellion," American Heritage, ser. 2, 2 (1957), pp. 61-64, 104-06.

4470. Cooper, Guy E. "Side Lights on the Slave Trade," Mariner's Mirror, 6, 2 (1921), pp. 34-37.

4471. Cornevin, Robert. "Oameni schimbati pe fier sau dantela," Magazin istoric, 11, 1 (1977), pp. 48-50.

4472. Curtin, Philip D. "The Abolition of the Slave Trade from Senegambia," in Walvin and Eltis, eds., Abolition of the Atlantic Slave Trade, pp. 83-98.

4473. _____. The Atlantic Slave Trade: A Census. Madison: University of Wisconsin Press, 1969.

4474. _____. "The Atlantic Slave Trade, 1600-1800," in J. F. A. Ajayi and Michael Crowder, eds., History of West Africa (New York: Columbia University Press, 1972), vol. 1, pp. 240-68. Second edition (New York, 1976), vol. 1, pp. 302-30.

4475. _____. "Epidemiology and the Slave Trade," Political Science Quarterly, 83, 2 (1968), pp. 190-216.

4476. _____. "Measuring the Atlantic Slave Trade," in Engerman and Genovese, eds., Race and Slavery, pp. 107-28.

4477. _____. "The Slave Trade and the Atlantic Basin: Intercontinental Perspectives," in Huggins, Kilson, and Fox, eds., Key Issues in the Afro-American Experience. vol. 1, pp. 74-93.

4478. _____. "Supplementary Report on Slave-Trade Studies in the United States," in UNESCO, African Slave Trade, p. 269.

4479. _____. "The Trade in Slaves," in idem, Economic Change in Precolonial Africa: Senegambia in the Era of the Slave Trade (Madison: University of Wisconsin Press, 1975), pp. 153-96.

4480. _____, ed. Africa Remembered: Narratives by West Africans from the Era of the Slave Trade. Madison: University of Wisconsin Press, 1967.

4481. _____, Roger T. Anstey, and J. E. Inikori. "Discussion: Measuring the Atlantic Slave Trade," Journal of African History, 17, 4 (1976), pp. 595-627.

4482. _____, and Jan Vansina. "Sources of the Nineteenth Century Atlantic Slave Trade," Journal of African History, 5, 2 (1964), pp. 185-208.

4483. Daaku, K. Y. "The Slave Trade and African Society," in T. O. Ranger, ed., Emerging Themes of African History (Nairobi: East African Publishing House, 1968), pp. 134-40.

4484. Daget, Serge. "A propos d'un instrument indispensable: la bibliographie de Peter C. Hogg sur la traite," Revue française d'histoire d'outre-mer, 62, 1-2 (nos. 226-27)(1975), pp. 343-49.

4485. Dantzig, Albert van. "Effects of the Atlantic Slave Trade on Some West African Societies," Revue française d'histoire d'outre-mer, 62, 1-2 (nos. 226-27)(1975), pp. 252-69. Reprinted in Inikori, ed., Forced Migration, pp. 187-201.

4486. Davidson, Basil. Black Mother: The Years of the African Slave Trade. Boston: Little, Brown, 1961. Revised and expanded edition: London: Penguin Books, 1980.

4487. Davies, K. G. "The Living and the Dead: White Mortality in West Africa, 1684-1732," in Engerman and Genovese, eds., Race and Slavery, pp. 83-98. With commentary by George Shepperson, pp. 99-106.

4488. Degn, Christian. Die Schimmelmanns im atlantischen Dreieckshandel: Gewinn und Gewissen. Neumünster: K. Wachholtz, 1974.

4489. Dehérain, Henri. "La traite des esclaves à Madagascar aux XVIIe siècle et XVIIIe siècle," La nature (Paris), no. 1618 (18 Mai 1904), pp. 401-03.

4490. Deschamps, Hubert J. Histoire de la traite des noirs de l'antiquité à nos jours. Paris: Fayard, 1972.

4491. _____. "La traite des noirs: vue d'ensemble et perspectives," Comptes-rendues mensuels des séances (Académie des sciences d'outre-mer), 39, 8 (1969), pp. 384-98.

4492. Diop, Louise-Marie. "Méthode et calcule approximatifs pour la construction d'une courbe représentative de l'évolution de la population de l'Afrique Noire, du milieu du XVIème siècle au milieu du XXème," African Historical Demography - II (Edinburgh: University of Edinburgh, Centre of African Studies, 1981), pp. 139-50.

4493. Donnan, Elizabeth, ed. Documents Illustrative of the History of the Slave Trade to America. 4 vols. Washington: Carnegie Institution of Washington, 1930-35. Republished New York: Octagon Books, 1969.

4494. Dow, George F. Slave Ships and Slaving. Salem, Mass.: Marine Research Society, 1927.

4495. Dubois, W. E. B. The Suppression of the African Slave Trade, 1638-1870 (forward by John Hope Franklin). Baton Rouge: Louisiana State University Press, 1969. Original edition New York, London: Longmans, Green, 1896.

4496. Ducasse, André. "Les négriers, 'bières flottantes'," Historia, no. 374 (1978), pp. 78-85.

4497. _____. Les négriers; ou le trafic des esclaves. Paris: Hachette, 1948.

4498. Duchet, Michèle. "Reactions to the Problem of the Slave Trade: An Historical and Ideological Study," in UNESCO, African Slave Trade, pp. 31-54.

4499. Dumbell, Stanley. "The Profits of the Guinea Trade," Economic History (supplement to Economic Journal), 2, 6 (1931), pp. 254-57.

4500. Edinburgh, University of. Centre of African Studies. The Trans-Atlantic Slave Trade from West Africa. Edinburgh, 1965.

4501. Eltis, David. "The Direction and Fluctuation of the Transatlantic Slave Trade, 1821-1843: A Revision of the 1845 Parliamentary Paper," in Gemery and Hogendorn, eds., Uncommon Market, pp. 273-301.

4502. _____. "The Export of Slaves from Africa: 1820-43," Journal of Economic History, 37, 2 (1977), pp. 409-33.

4503. _____. "The Export of Slaves from Africa, 1845-1865" (Unpublished paper read to the Annual Meeting of the African Studies Association, Bloomington, Indiana, October 1981).

4504. _____. "Free and Coerced Transatlantic Migrations: Some Comparisons," American Historical Review, 88, 2 (1983), pp. 251-80.

4505. _____. "The Impact of Abolition on the Atlantic Slave Trade," in Walvin and Eltis, eds., Abolition of the Atlantic Slave Trade, pp. 155-76.

4506. _____. "The Transatlantic Slave Trade, 1821-43" (PhD diss., University of Rochester, 1978).

4507. Emmer, Pieter C. "Engeland, Nederland, Afrika en de Slavenhandel in de negentiende eeuw," Economisch- en Sociaal-Historisch Jaarboek, 36 (1973), pp. 146-215; 37 (1974), pp. 44-144.

4508. _____, Jean Mettas, and Jean-Claude Nardin, eds. La traite des noirs par l'Atlantique: nouvelles approches. Paris: Société française d'histoire d'outre-mer, 1975. (Special issue of the Revue française d'histoire d'outre-mer, 62, 1-2 (nos. 226-27).)

4509. Engerman, Stanley L. "Comments on Richardson and Boulle and the 'Williams Thesis'," Revue française d'histoire d'outre-mer, 62, 1-2 (nos. 226-27), pp. 331-36.

4510. _____. "Some Implications of the Abolition of the Slave Trade," in Walvin and Eltis, eds., Abolition of the Atlantic Slave Trade, pp. 3-20.

4511. "Final Report" (Paper presented to UNESCO, Meeting of Experts on the Slave Trade, Port-au-Prince, 1978). (Not published in UNESCO, Meeting of Experts, see no. 4611 below.)

4512. Foster, Herbert J. "Partners or Captives in Commerce? The Role of Africans in the Slave Trade," Journal of Black Studies, 6, 4 (1976), pp. 421-34.

4513. Franco, José Luciano. "The Slave Trade in the Caribbean and Latin America," in UNESCO, African Slave Trade, pp. 88-100.

4514. Fugelstad, Finn. "Slaveriet i Afrika og den eksterne slavehandelen: en oversikt over nyere forskiningsresultater-forste del," Historisk tidskrift (Oslo), 62, 1 (1983), pp. 60-78.

4515. Fyfe, Christopher. "The Dynamics of African Dispersal: The Trans-atlantic Slave Trade," in Kilson and Rotberg, eds., African Diaspora, pp. 57-74.

4516. _____. "Four Sierra Leone Recaptives," Journal of African History, 2, 1 (1961), pp. 77-85.

4517. _____. "A Historiographical Survey of the Transatlantic Slave Trade from West Africa," in The Transatlantic Slave Trade from West Africa (Centre of African Studies, University of Edinburgh, 1965), pp. 1-12. With discussion.

4518. _____. "The Impact of the Slave Trade on West Africa," in The Transatlantic Slave Trade from West Africa (Centre of African Studies, University of Edinburgh, 1965), pp. 81-92. With discussion.

4519. Garçon, Maurice. "Le commerce du bois d'ébène," Revue de Paris, 70, 5 (1963), pp. 1-12.

4520. Gemery, Henry A., and Jan S. Hogendorn. "The Atlantic Slave Trade: A Tentative Economic Model," Journal of African History, 15, 2 (1974), pp. 223-46.

4521. _____. "Introduction," in idem, Uncommon Market, pp. 1-19.

4522. _____, eds. The Uncommon Market: Essays in the Economic History of the Atlantic Slave Trade. New York: Academic Press, 1979.

4523. Gray, Richard. "The Vatican and the Atlantic Slave Trade," History Today, 31, 9 (1981), pp. 37-39.

4524. Greene, Lorenzo J. "Mutiny on the Slave Ships," Phylon, 5, 4 (1944), pp. 346-54. Also Bobbs-Merrill Reprint no. BC-113.

4525. Guez, Nicole. "La traite des noirs: 1 - L'esclavage; 2 - La libération," Jeune Afrique, no. 583 (1972), pp 56-60; no. 584 (1972), pp. 54-57.

4526. Hair, P. E. H. The Atlantic Slave Trade and Black Africa. London: The Historical Association, 1978. (Pamphlet no. 93, General Series)

4527. Hansen, Thorkild. Slavernes oer: tegninger af birtelund. Copenhagen: Gyldendal, 1970.

4528. Hardyman, J. T. "The Madagascar Slave-Trade to the Americas (1632-1830)," Océan indien et Méditerranée (Travaux du 6e Colloque International d'Histoire Maritime et du 2e Congrès de l'Association Historique Internationale de l'Océan Indien)(Lourenço Marques, 1962) (Paris: S.E.V.P.E.N., 1964), pp. 501-21. Reprinted in Studia, no. 11 (1963), pp. 501-21.

4529. Hargreaves, John. "Synopsis of a Critique of Eric Williams' Capitalism and Slavery," in The Transatlantic Slave Trade from West Africa (Centre of African Studies, University of Edinburgh, 1965), pp. 30-32. With discussion, pp. 33-43.

4530. Harris, Joseph E. "A Commentary on the Slave Trade," in UNESCO, African Slave Trade, pp. 289-95.

4531. Heffernan, William. "The Slave Trade and Abolition in Travel Literature," Journal of the History of Ideas, 34, 2 (1973), pp. 185-208.

4532. Herskovits, Melville J., and Frances S. Herskovits. "A Footnote to the History of Negro Slaving," Opportunity, 11, 3 (1933), pp. 178-81.

4533. Hellmer-Wullen, Hilda von. "Der Sklavenhandel - die historische Grundlage der Negerfrage in Amerika: statistische Aufzeichnungen von 1492-1807," Zeitschrift für Rassenkunde, 9, 2 (1939), pp. 97-103.

4534. Hoeppli, R. Parasitic Diseases in Africa and the Western Hemisphere: Early Documentation and Transmission by the Slave Trade. Basel: Verlag für Recht- und Gesellschaft, 1969. (Acta Tropica: Zeitschrift für Tropenwissenschaft und Tropenmedizin, Supplementum 10)

4535. Hogendorn, Jan S. "A Supply-side Aspect of the African Slave Trade: The Cowrie Production and Exports of the Maldives," Slavery and Abolition, 2, 1 (1981), pp. 31-52.

4536. Hogg, Peter C. The African Slave Trade and its Suppression: A Classified and Annotated Bibliography of Books, Pamphlets and Periodical Articles. London: Frank Cass, 1973.

4537. Hollis, D. "In the Track of the Slave Ships," Chambers's Journal, 7th ser., 17 (1927), pp. 721-23.

4538. Houdaille, Jacques (J. Ho.). "Nombre d'africains introduits à Cuba," Population, 26, 4 (1971), pp. 761-62.

4539. _____. "Le nombre d'esclaves africains importés en Europe et en Amérique," Population, 26, 5 (1971), pp. 958-60.

4540. Hudson, E. H. "Treponematosis and African Slavery," British Journal of Venereal Disease, 40, 1 (1964), pp. 43-52.

4541. (International Conference for Economic History, 6th, Copenhagen, Denmark, 1974). La traite des noirs par l'Atlantique: nouvelles approches/The Atlantic Slave Trade: New Approaches. Paris: Société française d'histoire d'outre-mer, 1976. (Bibliothèque d'histoire d'outre-mer, nouvelle série, Etudes, vol. 4)

4542. Inikori, Joseph E. "Measuring the Atlantic Slave Trade: An Assessment of Curtin and Anstey," Journal of African History, 17, 2 (1976), pp. 197-223.

4543. _____. "The Origin of the Diaspora: The Slave Trade from Africa," Tarikh, 5, 4 (1978), pp. 1-19.

4544. _____. "The Slave Trade and the Atlantic Economies, 1451-1870," in UNESCO, African Slave Trade, pp. 56-87.

4545. _____. "Under-Population in 19th Century West Africa: The Role of the Export Slave Trade," in African Historical Demography: Volume II (Edinburgh: Centre of African Studies, University of Edinburgh, 1981), pp. 283-313.

4546. _____. "West African Import and Export Trade 1750-1807: Volume and Structure," in Obaro Ikime, ed., Essays in Honor of Professor K. O. Dike (Ibadan: Ibadan University Press, forthcoming).

4547. Jackson, Shirley. "Review Essay: The Middle Passage," Plantation Society in the Americas, 2, 1 (1983), pp. 111-15.

4548. Jeffreys, M. D. W. "Alt-Kalabar und der Sklavenhandel," Paideuma, 6, 1 (1954), pp. 14-24.

4549. Jervey, Theodore Dehon. The Slave Trade: Slavery and Color. Columbia, S. C.: The State Company, 1925.

4550. Kake, I. B. "The Slave Trade and the Population Drain from Black Africa to North Africa and the Middle East (From the Fifteenth Century to the Present Day)" (Paper presented to UNESCO, Meeting of Experts on the Slave Trade).

4551. Kay, F. George. The Shameful Trade. London, 1967.

4552. Kaysel, Paul. Die Gesetzgebung der Kulturstaaten zur Unterdrückung des afrikanischen Sklavenhandels. Breslau: Schletter, 1905.

4553. King, James F. "The Latin American Republics and the Suppression of the Slave Trade," Hispanic American Historical Review, 24, 3 (1944), pp. 387-411.

4554. Klein, Herbert S. The Middle Passage: Comparative Studies in the Atlantic Slave Trade. Princeton: Princeton University Press, 1978.

4555. _____. "Women in the Atlantic Slave Trade," in Robertson and Klein, eds., Women and Slavery in Africa, pp. 29-38.

4556. Knight, Franklin W. "The Atlantic Slave Trade and the Development of an Afro-American Culture," in Walvin and Eltis, eds., Abolition of the Atlantic Slave Trade, pp. 287-302.

4557. Kolchin, Peter. "The Slaving Business (review-essay on Rawley, Translatlantic Slave Trade)," Reviews in American History, 10, 2 (1982), pp. 173-76.

4558. Lara, Oruno D. "Traite négrière et résistance africaine," Présence africaine, no. 94 (1975), pp. 140-70.

4559. LeVeen, E. Phillip. "The African Slave Supply Response," African Studies Review, 18, 1 (1975), pp. 9-28.

4560. _____. "British Slave Trade Suppression Policies, 1821-1865" (PhD diss., University of Chicago, 1972). Published as British Slave Trade Suppression Policies, 1821-1825: Impact and Implications. (New York: Arno Press, 1977). (Dissertations in American Economic History)

4561. _____. "A Quantitative Analysis of the Impact of British Suppression Policies on the Volume of the Nineteenth Century Atlantic Slave Trade," in Engerman and Genovese, eds., Race and Slavery, pp. 51-81.

4562. Lima, Mesquitela. "L'anthropologie africaniste et la traite négrière," Revista de história econômica e social, no. 3 (1979), pp. 77-84.

4563. Lloyd, Christopher. The Navy and the Slave Trade: The Suppression of the African Slave Trade in the Nineteenth Century. London: Cass, 1968.

4564. Lovejoy, Paul. "The Volume of the Atlantic Slave Trade: A Synthesis," Journal of African History, 23, 4 (1982), pp. 473-502.

4565. MacInnes, C. M. "The Slave Trade," in C. Northcote Parkinson, ed., The Trade Winds (London: G. Allen and Unwin, 1948), pp. 251-72.

4566. Manning, Patrick. "The Slave Trade in the Bight of Biafra 1640-1890," in Gemery and Hogendorn, eds., Uncommon Market, pp. 107-41.

4567. Mannix, Daniel P., and Malcolm Cowley. Black Cargoes: A History of the Atlantic Slave Trade, 1518-1865. New York: Viking Press, 1962.

4568. Martin, Phyllis. "The Trade of Loango in the Seventeenth and Eighteenth Centuries," in Inikori, ed., Forced Migration, pp. 202-20. Reprinted from The External Trade of the Loango Coast (Oxford, 1972).

4569. Mathieson, William Law. Great Britain and the Slave Trade, 1839-1865. London: Longmans, Green, 1929.

4570. Miers, Suzanne. Britain and the Ending of the Slave Trade. New York: Africana, 1975.

4571. Miller, Joseph C. "Mortality in the Atlantic Slave Trade: Statistical Evidence on Causality," Journal of Interdisciplinary History, 11, 3 (1980), pp. 385-423.

4572. Minchinton, Walter E., and Pieter C. Emmer. "The Atlantic Slave Trade: New Approaches, An Introduction," Revue française d'histoire d'outre-mer, 62, 1-2 (nos. 226-27)(1975), pp. 11-18.

4573. *Monheim, Chr. "Etude sur la traite des nègres aux XVIe et XVIIe siècles d'après des documents contemporains," Les Brochures de l'AUCAM (Association universitaire catholique pour l'aide aux missions), 4 (1927), pp.

4574. Miramón, Alberto. "Los negreros del Caribe," Boletín de historia e antigüedades (Bogotá), 31 (nos. 351-52)(1944), pp. 168-87.

4575. Mouser, Bruce L. "Iles de Los as Bulking Centre in the Slave Trade, 1750-1880" (Unpublished paper read to the Annual Meeting of the African Studies Association, Bloomington, Indiana, October 1981).

4576. _____. "Trade, Coasters, and Conflict in the Rio Pongo from 1790-1808," Journal of African History, 14, 1 (1973), pp. 45-64.

4577. _____. "Women Slavers of Guinea-Conakry," in Robertson and Klein, eds., Women and Slavery in Africa, pp. 320-39.

4578. Nixon, J. A. "Health and Sickness in the Slave Trade," in C. Northcote Parkinson, ed., The Trade Winds (London: G. Allen and Unwin, 1948), pp. 273-77.

4579. Northrup, David. "African Mortality in the Suppression of the Slave Trade: The Case of the Bight of Benin," Journal of Interdisciplinary History, 9, 1 (1978), pp. 47-64.

4580. Parker, R. H. "Book-Keeping and the African Slave Trade," Accountant's Magazine, 62 (no. 620)(1958), pp. 116-19.

4581. Parkinson, Bradbury B. "A Slaver's Accounts," Accounting Research, 2, 2 (1951), pp. 144-50.

4582. Patterson, K. David. "A Note on Slave Exports from the Costa da Mina, 1760-1770," Bulletin de l'Institut fondamental d'Afrique noire, sér. B, 33, 2 (1971), pp. 249-56.

4583. *Peralta Rivera, Ernesto Germán. "Les mécanismes du commerce esclavagiste (XVIIe siècle)" (Thése de troisième cycle, EHESS, 1978).

4584. * _____ . "Les mécanismes du commerce esclavagiste (1595-1640)" (Diss., Paris: Ecole Pratique des Hautes Etudes, 1979).

4585. Pierce, Milfred C. "The Atlantic Slave Trade: A Case for Reparation," Negro History Bulletin, 35, 2 (1972), pp. 44-47.

4586. Putney, Martha. "The Slave Trade in French Diplomacy from 1814 to 1815," Journal of Negro History, 60, 3 (1975), pp. 411-27.

4587. Ransford, Oliver. The Slave Trade: The Story of Transatlantic Slavery. London: J. Murray, 1971.

4588. Rawley, James A. The Transatlantic Slave Trade: A History. New York: Norton, 1981.

4589. Reynolds, Edward. Stand the Storm: A History of the Atlantic Slave Trade. New York: Allison and Busby, 1985.

4590. Riley, James C. "Mortality on Long-Distance Voyages in the Eighteenth Century," Journal of Economic History, 16, 3 (1981), pp. 651-56.

4591. Rinchon, P. Dieudonné. La traite et l'esclavage des Congolais par les Europeéns: histoire de la déportation de 13 millions 250.000 noirs en Amérique. Brussels: Presses de L. de Meester et Fils, 1929.

4592. Rodney, Walter. "Gold and Slaves on the Gold Coast," Transactions of the Historical Society of Ghana, 10 (1969), pp. 13-28.

4593. _____ . "The State of Research (on the Slave Trade) in Guyana," in UNESCO, African Slave Trade, p. 298.

4594. Roncière, Charles de la. Négres et négriers. Paris, 1933.

4595. Rottenberg, Simon. "The Business of Slave Trading," South Atlantic Quarterly, 66, 3 (1967), pp. 409-33. Also Bobbs-Merrill Reprint no. BC-252.

4596. Ryan, T. C. I. "The Economics of Trading in Slaves" (PhD diss., Massachusetts Institute of Technology, 1975).

4597. Saint-Moulin, L. de, and J. L. Vellut. "Note critique: le commerce des esclaves à travers l'Océan Atlantique," Etudes d'histoire africaine, 3 (1972), pp. 313-16.

4598. Scott, Sir Henry Harold. "The Influence of the Slave-Trade in the Spread of Tropical Disease," Transactions of the Royal Society of Tropical Medicine and Hygiene (London), 37, 2 (1943-44), pp. 169-88.

4599. Sheridan, Richard B. "Africa and the Caribbean in the Atlantic Slave Trade," American Historical Review, 77, 1 (1972), pp. 15-35.

4600. Shick, Tom W. "A Quantitative Analysis of Liberian Colonization from 1820 to 1843 with Special Reference to Mortality," Journal of African History, 12, 1 (1971), pp. 45-59.

4601. "Summary Report of the Meeting of Experts on the African Slave Trade," in UNESCO, African Slave Trade, pp. 211-29. With 3 appendixes, pp. 233-44.

4602. Suret-Canale, J. "Réflexions sur quelques problèmes d'histoire de l'Afrique," La pensée, no. 212 (1980), pp. 92-112.

4603. _____. "Le Sénégambie à l'ère de la traite," Canadian Journal of African Studies, 11, 1 (1977), pp. 125-34.

4604. Takaki, Ronald T. A Pro-Slavery Crusade: The Agitation to Reopen the African Slave Trade. New York: Free Press, 1971.

4605. Talib, Y. "The Slave Trade from the Fifteenth to the Nineteenth Century," in UNESCO, African Slave Trade, pp. 299-305.

4606. Thomas, Robert P., and Richard N. Bean. "The Fishers of Men: The Profits of the Slave Trade," Journal of Economic History, 34, 4 (1974), pp. 885-914.

4607. Thompson, Alvin O. "Race and Colour Prejudices and the Origin of the Trans-Atlantic Slave Trade," Caribbean Studies, 16, 3-4 (1976-77), pp. 29-59.

4608. Thompson, V. B. Africa, The Atlantic Slave Trade and the West Indies: African Background to West Indian History. New York: Longmans, 1979.

4609. Thornton, John K. "The Demographic Effect of the Slave Trade on Western Africa, 1500-1850," in African Historical Demography: Volume II (Edinburgh: Centre of African Studies, University of Edinburgh, 1981), pp. 691-720.

4610. La traite des noirs par l'Atlantique: nouvelles approches. See (International Conference for Economic History, 6th).

4611. UNESCO. The African Slave Trade from the Fifteenth to the Nineteenth Century. (Reports and Papers of the Meeting of Experts Organized by UNESCO at Port-au-Prince, Haiti, 31 January to 4 February 1978). Paris: UNESCO, 1979. (The General History of Africa: Sources and Documents, no. 2)

4612. Uya, Edet Olon. "Slave Revolts of the Middle Passage: A Neglected Theme," Calabar Historical Journal, 1 (1976), pp. 65-88.

4613. Vissière, Isabelle, and Jean-Louis Vissière, eds. La traite des noirs au siècle des lumières: témoignages de négriers. Paris: A. M. Métailié, 1982.

4614. Walvin, James, and David Eltis, eds. The Abolition of the Atlantic Slave Trade. Madison: University of Wisconsin Press, 1981.

4615. Ward, E. W. F. The Royal Navy and the Slaves: The Suppression of the Atlantic Slave Trade. New York, 1969.

4616. Wätjen, Hermann. "Der Negerhandel in Westindien und Südamerika bis zur Sklavenemanzipation," Hansische Geschichtsblatter, 19 (1913), pp. 417-43.

4617. Wax, Darold D. "Negro Resistance to the Early American Slave Trade," Journal of Negro History, 51, 1 (1966), pp. 1-15.

4618. _____. "'A People of Beastly Living': Europe, Africa and the Atlantic Slave Trade," Phylon, 41, 1 (1980), pp. 12-24.

4619. Weyl, Nathaniel. "Natural Selection through Slavery and the African Slave Trade," Mankind Quarterly, 15, 1 (1974), pp. 3-17.

4620. Williams, David M. "The Shipping and Organization of the Atlantic Slave Trade (A Review Article)," Journal of Transport History, 4, 3 (1977-78), pp. 179-84.

4621. Wilson, Howard Hazen. "Devices Employed by Great Britain to Suppress the African Slave Trade" (PhD diss., University of Chicago, 1941).

4622. _____. "Some Principal Aspects of British Efforts to Crush the African Slave Trade, 1807-1929," American Journal of International Law, 44, 3 (1950), pp. 505-26.

4623. Wirz, Albert. "Transatlantischer Sklavenhandel, industrielle Revolution und die Unterentwicklung Afrikas: zur Diskussion um den Aufsteig des kapitalistischen Weltsystems," Geschichte und Gesellschaft, 8, 4 (1982), pp. 518-37.

4624. Wyndham, H. A. The Atlantic and Slavery. London: Oxford, 1935. (Series: Royal Institute of International Affairs, Problems of Imperial Trusteeship, no. 2)

2. Atlantic - Individual voyages and captains

4625. Akinjogbin, I. A. "Archibald Dalzel: Slave Trader and Historian of Dahomey," Journal of African History, 7, 1 (1966), pp. 67-78.

4626. Anderson, B. L. "The Lancashire Bill System and Its Liverpool Practitioners: The Case of a Slave Merchant," in W. H. Chaloner and Barrie Ratcliffe, eds., Trade and Transport: Essays in Economic History in Honour of T. S. Willan (Totowa, N.J.: Rowman and Littlefield, 1977). pp. 59-97.

4627. Antoine, Régis. "Aventure d'un jeune négrier français d'après un manuscrit inédit du XVIIIe siècle," Notes africaines, 142 (1974), pp. 51-58.

4628. "Aventuras de un negrero en Cuba," Revista bimestre cubana, 34 (1934), pp. 275-89; 35 (1935), pp. 64-100.

4629. Barber, John W. A History of the Amistad Captives. New York: Arno Press, 1969.

4630. Bellarosa, James M. "James Smith and the Rainbow: America's First African Slavers," New-England Galaxy, 19, 1 (1977), pp. 32-37.

4631. _____. "The Tragic Slaving Voyage of the St. John," American Neptune, 40, 4 (1980), pp. 293-97.

4632. Boucher, M. "The Voyage of a Cape Slaver in 1742," Historia (Pretoria), 24, 1 (1979), pp. 50-58.

4633. Bouge, L. J. "Théophile Conneau alias Théodore Canot: négrier en Afrique, fon- ctionnaire en Nouvelle-Calédonie, 1804-1860," Revue de l'histoire des colonies françaises, 40, no. 38 (1953), pp. 249-63.

4634. Bradley, Ian. "James Ramsey and the Slave Trade," History Today, 22, 12 (1972), pp. 866-72.

4635. Brásio, R. P. António. "Um extraordinário documento quinhentista," Studia, 15 (1965), pp. 155-74.

4636. Busson, Jean-Pierre. "La correspondance du négociant malouin Luc Magon de La Balue: Trois négriers en traite (1741-1743)," in Actes du 91e Congrès national des sociétés savantes (Rennes, 1966) (Paris: Bibliothèque nationale, 1969), vol. 1, pp. 155-67.

4637. Cable, Mary. Black Odyssey: The Case of the Slave Ship Amistad. Baltimore: Penguin Books, 1977.

4638. Cobb, R. C. "Réclamations d'un négrier d'Honfleur (1794) (Lacoudrais Père et Fils ainé et Cie)," Annales de Normandie, 4, 1 (1954), pp. 76-78.

4639. Collister, Peter. The Sullivans and the Slave Trade. London: Rex Collings, 1980.

4640. Conneau, Théophile. A Slaver's Log Book, or 20 Years' Residence in Africa. Englewood Cliffs, N.J.: Prentice-Hall, 1976.

4641. Crane, Verner W., ed. A Rhode Island Slaver: Trade Book of the Sloop Adventure, 1773-1774. Providence, 1922.

4642. Daget, Serge. "A Vieux-Calabar, en 1825: l'expédition du Charles (ou de l'Eugène) comme élément du modèle de la traite négrière illégale," in Etudes africaines offertes à Henri Brunschwig (Paris: Editions de l'Ecole des hautes études en sciences sociales, 1982), pp. 117-33.

4643. _____. "Encore Théodore Canot: quelques années de la vie d'un négrier et quelques questions," Annales de l'Université d'Abidjan (Histoire, série I), 5 (1977), pp. 39-53.

4644. _____. "An Exceptional Document: Legitimate Trade of the Ship 'Africain' on the West Coast of Africa in 1827," Journal of African Studies, 2, 2 (1975), pp. 177-200.

4645. Dart, Henry P., ed. "The First Cargo of African Slaves for Louisiana, 1718," Louisiana Historical Quarterly, 14, 2 (1931), pp. 163-77.

4646. Debien, Gabriel. "Le journal de traite de la Licorne au Mozambique, 1787-1788," in Etudes africaines offertes à Henri Brunschwig (Paris: Editions de l'Ecole des hautes études en sciences sociales, 1982), pp. 91-116.

4647. _____. "Théodore Canot condamné comme négrier en 1834," Revue française d'histoire d'outre-mer, 57, 2 (no. 207)(1970), pp. 214-24.

4648. _____, Marcel Delafosse, and Guy Thilmans. "Journal d'un voyage de traite en Guinée, à Cayenne et aux Antilles fait par Jean Barbot en 1678-79," Bulletin de l'Institut fondamental d'Afrique noire, sér. B, 40, 2 (1978), pp. 235-395.

4649. Dodd, Dorothy. "The Schooner Emperor: An Incident of the Illegal Slave Trade in Florida," Florida Historical Quarterly, 13, 3 (1935). pp. 117-28.

4650. Emeth, Omer (Emilio Vaisse). "El libro de cuentas de un negrero en 1621," Revista chilena de historia y geografía, 6 (1913), pp. 274-86.

4651. Emmer, Pieter C. "De laatste slavenreis van de Middelburgsche Commercie Compagnie," Economisch- en Sociaal-Historisch Jaarboek, 34 (1971), pp. 72-123.

4652. Ferrez, Gilberto. "Diário anônimo de uma viagem às costas d'Africa e às Indias Espanholas: o tráfico de escravos (1702-1703)," Revista do Instituto histórico e geográfico brasileiro, 267 (1965), pp. 3-42.

4653. Halgan, G. "A bord du 'Grillon' vers l'Afrique et Saint-Domingue," Bulletin de la Société archéologique et historique de Nantes et de la Loire-Inférieure, 66 (1926), pp. 89-96.

4654. _____. "A bord du navire négrier le 'Mars' vers l'Afrique et la Guyane," Bulletin de la Société archéologique et historique de Nantes et de la Loire-Inférieure, 80 (1938), pp. 52-65.

4655. Hand, Charles R. "The Kitty's Amelia, The Last Liverpool Slaver," Transactions of the Historic Society of Lancashire and Cheshire, 82 (1930), pp. 69-80.

4656. Henry, Armand. "Au temps du commerce du bois d'ébène: le périple tragique d'un négrier," Revue du Bas-Poitou et des provinces de l'Ouest, 76, 3-4 (1965), pp. 202-13.

4657. Hodson, J. H. "The Letter Book of Robert Bostock, a Merchant in the Liverpool Slave Trade, 1789-1792," Liverpool Bulletin, 3 (1953), pp. 37-59.

4658. Holsoe, Svend. "Theodore Canot at Cape Mount, 1841-1847," Liberian Studies Journal, 4, 2 (1972), pp. 163-81.

4659. Hurston, Zora Neale. "Cudjoe's Own Story of the Last African Slaver," Journal of Negro History, 12, 4 (1927), pp. 648-63.

4660. _____. "The Last Slave Ship," American Mercury, 58 (no. 243)(1944), pp. 351-58.

4661. Jones, Adam. "Théophile Conneau at Galinhas and New Sestos, 1836-1841: A Com- parison of Sources," History in Africa, 8 (1981), pp. 89-106.

4662. Kaplan, Sidney, ed. "Black Mutiny on the Amistad," Massachusetts Review, 10 (1969), pp. 493-532.

4663. Kromer, Helen. The Amistad Affair, 1839: The Slave Uprising Aboard the Spanish Schooner. New York: Franklin Watts, 1973.

4664. Ly, Abdoulaye. Un navire de commerce sur la côte sénégambienne en 1685. Dakar: Institut français d'Afrique noire, 1964. (Catalogues et Documents, no. XVII)

4665. Mackenzie-Grieve, Averil. "The Last of the Brazilian Slavers, 1851," Mariner's Mirror, 31, 1 (1945), pp. 2-7.

4666. McLendon, R. Earl. "The Amistad Claims, Inconsistencies of Policy," Political Science Quarterly, 48 (1933), pp. 386-412.

4667. Martin, Bernard. John Newton and the Slave Trade. London: Longmans, 1961.

4668. _____, and Mark Spurrell, eds. The Journal of a Slave Trader (John Newton) 1750-1754. London: Epworth Press, 1962.

4669. Martin, Christopher (Edwin Palmer Hoyt). The Amistad Affair. London: Abelard-Schuman, 1970.

4670. Mauny, Raymond. "Le livre de bord du navire Santa Maria da Comçeiça (1522)," Bulletin de l'Institut fondamental d'Afrique noire, sér. B, 29, 3-4 (1967), pp. 512-35.

4671. _____, and N. I. de Moraes. "Règlement du Sam Christovã allant de São Tomé à la Mine (1535)," Bulletin de l'Institut fondamental d'Afrique noire, sér. B, 37, 4 (1975), pp. 779-83.

4672. Mayer, Brantz. Captain Canot; or, Twenty Years of an African Slaver. New York: Arno Press, 1968.

4673. Minchinton, Walter E. "The Voyage of the Snow Africa," Mariner's Mirror, 37, 3 (1951), pp. 187-96.

4674. Montgomery, Charles J. "Survivors from the Cargo of the Negro Slave Yacht 'Wanderer'," American Anthropologist, 10, 4 (1908), pp. 611-23.

4675. Moraes, Nize Izabel de. "La campagne négrière du Sam-António-e-as-almas (1670)," Bulletin de l'Institut fondamental d'Afrique noire, sér. B, 40, 4 (1978), pp. 708-17.

4676. Mouser, Bruce L. "Théophilus Conneau: The Saga of a Tale," History in Africa, 6 (1979), pp. 97-107.

4677. _____. "The Voyage of the Good Sloop Dolphin to Africa 1795-96," American Neptune, 37, 4 (1978), pp. 249-61.

4678. Mousnier, Jehan, ed. Journal de la traite des noirs: Dam Joulin, Charles le Breton la Vallée, Garneray, Merimée . . . . Paris: Editions de Paris, 1957.

4679. Naish, F. D. Prideaux. "Extracts from a Slaver's Log," Mariner's Mirror, 6, 1 (1920), pp. 3-10.

4680. Owens, William A. Black Mutiny: The Revolt on the Schooner Amistad. New York: John Day, 1953; reprint ed., Philadelphia: Pilgrim Press, 1968.

4681. Pasquier, R. "A propos de Théodore Canot, négrier en Afrique," Revue française d'histoire d'outre-mer, 55, 3 (no. 200)(1968), pp. 352-54.

4682. Pernoud, Régine. L'Amérique du Sud au XVIIIe siècle ("Les tribulations d'un négrier"). Mantes. Imprimerie du "Petit Mantais", 1942. (Cahiers d'histoire et de bibliographie, no. 3)

4683. Perret, A. "René Montadoin, armateur et négrier nantais (1673-1731)," Bulletin de la Société archéologique et historique de Nantes et de la Loire-Inférieure, 88 (1949), pp. 78-94.

4684. Platt, Virginia Bever. "'And Don't Forget the Guinea Voyage': The Slave Trade of Aaron Lopez of Newport," William and Mary Quarterly, 3rd ser., 32, 4 (1975), pp. 601-18.

4685. Rinchon, Dieudonné. Pierre-Ignace-Liévin van Alstein, capitaine négrier, Gand 1733 - Nantes 1793. Dakar: IFAN, 1964. (Série Mémoires, no. 71)

4686. Ross, David A. "The Career of Domingo Martinez in the Bight of Benin 1833-64," Journal of African History, 6, 1 (1965), pp. 79-90.

4687. Ryder, A. F. C. "An Early Portuguese Trading Voyage to the Forcados River," Journal of the Historical Society of Nigeria, 1, 4 (1959), pp. 294-321.

4688. Saint-Mleux (sic), Georges. "Les armements de M. de Chateaubriand," Annales de Bretagne, 34 (1919-1920), pp. 1-14.

4689. Scisco, L. D. "Rolfe's Story of the First Slave Cargo," Magazine of History, 13, 3 (1911), pp. 123-25.

4690. Scott, Kenneth. "George Scott, Slave Trader of Newport," American Neptune, 12, 3 (1952), pp. 222-28.

4691. Sterne, Emma Gelders. The Long Black Schooner: The Voyage of the Amistad. New York: Aladdin Books, 1953.

4692. "Una expedición negrera salida de la Habana en 1815," Revista bimestre cubana, 71, 2 (1956), pp. 181-84.

4693. Vignols, Léon. "La campagne négrière de la Perle (1755-1757)," Revue historique, 163, 1 (1930), pp. 51-78.

4694. Wax, Darold D. "The Browns of Providence and the Slaving Voyage of the Brig Sally, 1764-65," American Neptune, 32, 3 (1972), pp. 171-79.

4695. _____. "A Philadelphia Surgeon on a Slaving Voyage to Africa," Pennsylvania Magazine of History and Biography, 92, 4 (1968), pp. 465-93.

4696. Watkin, Roland. "Captain Hugh Crow: A Liverpool Guineaman," Mariner's Mirror, 63, 2 (1977), pp. 177-85.

4697. Weisbord, Robert. "The Case of the Slave-Ship 'Zong'," History Today, 19, 8 (1969), pp. 561-67.

4698. Well, Tom Henderson. The Slave Ship Wanderer. Athens, Ga., 1968.

3. Atlantic - Portuguese and Brazilian

4699. Adams, Jane E. "The Abolition of the Brazilian Slave Trade," Journal of Negro History, 10, 4 (1925), pp. 607-37.

4700. Alencastro, Luiz-Felipe de. "La traite négrière et l'organisation de l'Etat brésilien" (Thèse de troisième cycle, Université de Paris X, forthcoming).

4701. _____. "La traite négrière et l'unité nationale brésilienne," Revue française d'histoire d'outre-mer, 66, 3-4 (nos. 244-45)(1979), pp. 395-419.

4702. _____. "La traite négrière et les avatars de la colonisation portugaise au Brésil et en Angola (1550-1825)," Cahiers du C.R.I.A.R. (Publication de l'Université de Rouen, P.U.B. Paris), no. 1 (1981), pp. 9-76.

4703. Almeida Prado, J. F. de. "A Bahia e as suas relações com o Daomé," in Anais do 4 Congresso de História Nacional (Rio de Janeiro, 1950), vol. 5, pp. 377-439.

4704. Beiguelman, Paula. "A extinção do tráfico negreiro no Brasil como problema político," Revista de ciência política, 1, 2 (1967), pp. 14-34.

4705. Bethell, Leslie. The Abolition of the Brazilian Slave Trade: Britain, Brazil, and the Slave Trade Question, 1807-1869. Cambridge: Cambridge University Press, 1970. Translated as A abolição do tráfico de escravos no Brasil (Rio de Janeiro, 1976).

4706. _____. "Britain, Portugal and the Suppression of the Brazilian Slave Trade: The Origins of Lord Palmerston's Act of 1839," English Historical Review, 80 (no. 357)(1965), pp. 761-84.

4707. _____. "The Independence of Brazil and the Abolition of the Brazilian Slave Trade: Anglo-Brazilian Relations, 1822-1826," Journal of Latin American Studies, 1, 2 (1969), pp. 115-47.

4708. Bourne, H. R. Fox. Slave Traffic in Portuguese Africa: An Account of Slave-Raiding and Slave-Trading in Angola and of Slavery in the Islands of San Tome and Principe. London: P. S. King & Son, 1908.

4709. Cabat, Geoffrey A. "O comércio de escravos no Brasil visto por functionários diplomáticos americanos, 1845-1857," Revista de história, 36 (no. 74)(1968), pp. 329-48.

4710. Camargo, Jovelino M. de, Jr. "A Inglaterra e o tráfico," in Freyre et al., Novos estudos afro-brasileiros, pp. 171-86.

4711. Capela, José. As burguesias portuguesas e a abolição da escravatura, 1810-1842. Porto: Afrontamento, 1979.

4712. _____. Escravatura: a empresa de saque, o abolicionismo (1810-1875). Porto: Afrontamento, 1974. Second edition, revised: Escravatura: a empresa do saque (Porto, 1978).

4713. Carreira, António. "As companhias pombalinas de navegação, comércio e tráfico de escravos entre a costa africana e o nordeste brasileiro," Boletim cultural da Guiné portuguesa, 23, 1-2 (nos. 89-90)(1968), pp. 5-88; 23, 3-4 (nos. 91-92)(1968), pp. 301-454; 24, 1 (no. 93)(1969), pp. 59-188; 24, 2 (no. 94)(1969), pp. 285-474. Republished as As companhias pombalinas de navegação . . . . (Porto, 1969).

4714. _____. Notas sôbre o tráfico português de escravos. Lisboa: Universidade Nova de Lisboa, 1978. (Ciências humanas e sociais, 6, Série investigação)

4715. _____. "Portuguese Research on the Slave Trade," in UNESCO, African Slave Trade, pp. 250-64.

4716. _____. "O tráfico clandestino de escravos na Guiné e em Cabo Verde no século XIX," Raizes, 2, 5-6 (1978), pp. 3-34.

4717. _____. O tráfico de escravos nos rios de Guiné e ilhas de Cabo Verde (1810-1850) (subsídios para o seu estudo). Lisbon: Junta de Investigações Científicas do Ultramar, Centro de Estudos de Antropología Cultural, 1981. (Estudos de antropología cultural, no. 14)

4718. Cesarino Júnior, António Ferreira. "A intervenção da Inglaterra na suppressão do tráfico de escravos africanos para o Brasil," Revista do Instituto histórico e geográfico de São Paulo, 34 (1938), pp. 145-66.

4719. Conrad, Robert. "The Contraband Slave Trade to Brazil, 1831-1845," Hispanic American Historical Review, 49, 4 (1969), pp. 617-38.

4720. _____. "The Struggle for the Abolition of the Brazilian Slave Trade, 1808-1853" (PhD diss., Columbia University, 1967).

4721. *Cruz, C. Coelho da. "O tráfico negreiro da 'Costa de Angola'" (Dissertação de licenciatura, Lisbon, 1966).

4722. Dias, Manuel Nunes. "Fomento ultramarino e mercantilismo: A Companhia Geral de Grão-Pará e Maranhão (1775-1778)," Revista de história, 36 (no. 73)(1968), pp. 71-113.

4723. Dietmann, Alfonso. "Los Brasileños en la trata de esclavos negro-africanos," Cuadernos afro-americanos, 1, 1 (1975), pp. 31-47.

4724. Faro, Jorge. "O movimento comercial do porto de Bissau de 1788 a 1794," Boletim cultural da Guiné portuguesa, 14, 2 (no. 54)(1959), pp. 231-58.

4725. Greenfield, Sidney M. "Entrepreneurship and Dynasty Building in the Portuguese Empire in the Seventeenth Century: The Career of Salvador Correia de Sá e Benevides," in idem et al., eds., Entrepreneurs in Cultural Context (Albuquerque, N.M.: University of New Mexico Press, 1979), pp. 21-63.

4726. Hill, Lawrence F. "The Abolition of the African Slave Trade to Brazil," Hispanic American Historical Review, 11, 2 (1931), pp. 169-97.

4727. Karasch, Mary C. "The Brazilian Slavers and the Illegal Slave Trade, 1836-1851" (MA thesis, University of Wisconsin - Madison, 1967).

4728. Klein, Herbert S. "The Internal Slave Trade in Nineteenth-Century Brazil: A Study of Slave Importations into Rio de Janeiro in 1852," Hispanic American Historical Review, 51, 4 (1971), pp. 567-85.

4729. _____. "The Portuguese Slave Trade from Angola in the Eighteenth Century," Journal of Economic History, 32, 4 (1972), pp. 894-918. Reprinted in Inikori, ed., Forced Migration, pp. 221-41.

4730. _____. "The Trade in African Slaves to Rio de Janeiro," Journal of African History, 10, 4 (1969), pp. 533-49.

4731. _____. "O tráfico de escravos africanos para o porto do Rio de Janeiro, 1825-1830," Anais de história, 5 (1973), pp. 85-101.

4732. _____, and Stanley L. Engerman. "Shipping Patterns and Mortality in the African Slave Trade to Rio de Janeiro, 1825-1830," Cahiers d'études africaines, 15, 3 (no. 59)(1975), pp. 381-98. Translated as "Padrões de embarque e mortalidade no tráfico de escravos africanos ao Rio de Janeiro, 1825-1830," in Carlos Manuel Peláez and Mircea Buescu, eds., Moderna história econômica (Rio de Janeiro: APEC, 1976), pp. 96-113.

4733. Lisanti, Luis. "Della importazione degli schiavi nel Brasile coloniale (1715)," Atti del XL Congresso Internazionale degli Americanisti (Rome-Genoa, 1972)(Genoa: Tilgher, 1975), vol. 4, pp. 305-07.

4734. Luttrell, Anthony. "Slavery and Slaving in the Portuguese Atlantic (to about 1500)," in The Transatlantic Slave Trade from West Africa (Centre of African Studies, University of Edinburgh, 1965), pp. 60-80. With discussion.

4735. Macedo, Sergio D. Teixeira de. Apontamentos para a história do tráfico negreiro no Brasil. Rio de Janeiro: L. D. Fernandes, 1942.

4736. Mauny, Raymond. "Livres de bord de navires portugais faisant la traite sur les côtes d'Afrique occidentale au XVIᵉ siècle," Provence historique, 25, 1 (nos. 99-102)(1975), pp. 79-85. ("Mélanges André Villard")

4737. Mauro, Frédéric. "L'Atlantique portugais et les esclaves (1570-1670)," Revista da Faculdade de Letras (Universidade de Lisboa), 22, 2 (1956), pp. 5-55. Separata as L'Atlantique portugais et les esclaves, 1570-1760. Lisbon: Faculdade de Letras, Universidade de Lisboa, 1956.

4738. _____. Le Portugal et l'Atlantique au XVIIe siècle (1570-1670): étude économique. Paris: S.E.V.P.E.N., 1960.

4739. Medeiros dos Santos, Corcino. "Relações de Angola com o Rio de Janeiro (1736-1808)," Estudos históricos (Marília), 12 (1973), pp. 7-68.

4740. Mello, Miguel António de. "Carta do governador para a Real Junta do Commercio, Agricultura, e Navegação e Fabricas do Reyno de Portugal e Seus Dominios, propondo medidas mais humanas no tráfico da escravatura, 12 de março de 1799," Arquivos de Angola, 2 (1936), pp. 593-602.

4741. Mettas, Jean. "La traite portugaise en Haute Guinée, 1758-1797: problèmes et méthodes," Journal of African History, 16, 3 (1975), pp. 343-63.

4742. Miller, Joseph C. "Legal Portuguese Slaving from Angola: Some Preliminary Indications of Volume and Direction, 1760-1830," Revue française d'histoire d'outre-mer, 62, 1-2 (nos. 226-27)(1975), pp. 135-76.

4743. _____. "The Slave Trade in Congo and Angola," in Kilson and Rotberg, eds., The African Diaspora, pp. 75-113.

4744. _____. "Some Aspects of the Commercial Organization of Slaving at Luanda, Angola - 1760-1830," in Gemery and Hogendorn, eds., Uncommon Market, pp. 77-106.

4745. Moraes, Evaristo de. Extincção do tráfico de escravos no Brasil (Ensaio histórico). Rio de Janeiro: Martins de Araujo, 1916.

4746. Múrias, Manuel. Portugal e o tráfico de escravatura. Lisbon: Agência Geral das Colonias, 1938.

4747. Neiva, Artur Heil. "Proveniência das primeiras levas de escravos africanos," in Anais do 4 Congresso de História Nacional (Rio de Janeiro, 1949) (Rio de Janeiro: Imprense Nacional, 1950), vol. 4, pp. 487-523.

4748. Otte, Enrique, and Conchita Ruiz-Burruecos. "Los portugueses en la trata de esclavos negros de la postrimerías del siglo XVI," Moneda y crédito: Revista de economia, 85, 2 (1963), pp. 3-40.

4749. Pinto, Françoise Latour da Veiga, assisted by A. Carreira. "Portuguese Participation in the Slave Trade: Opposing Forces, Trends of Opinion within Portuguese Society, Effects on Portugal's Socio-Economic Development," in UNESCO, African Slave Trade, pp. 119-47.

4750. Rebelo, Manuel dos Anjos da Silva. Relações entre Angola e Brasil (1808-1830). Lisbon: Agência Geral do Ultramar, 1970.

4751. Rego, Waldeloir. "The Present State of Research in Brazil (on the Slave Trade)," in UNESCO, African Slave Trade, pp. 296-97.

4752. Ribeiro Junior, José. "Alguns aspectos do tráfico escravo para o Nordeste Brasileiro no século XVIII," Anais do VI Simpósio nacional dos professores universitários de história (Goiâna, 1971)(São Paulo, 1973), vol. 1, pp. 385-404.

4753. Rinchon, Dieudonné. "Les capucins au Congo: l'esclavage et la traite des noirs au Congo (1482-1878)," Etudes franciscaines, 35 (no. 201)(1923), pp. 615-31.

4754. Rodney, Walter. "Portuguese Attempts at Monopoly on the Upper Guinea Coast, 1580-1650," Journal of African History, 6, 3 (1965), pp. 307-22.

4755. Ryder, A. F. C. "The Re-establishment of Portuguese Factories on the Costa da Mina to the Mid-eighteenth Century," Journal of the Historical Society of Nigeria, 1, 3 (1958), pp. 137-83.

4756. Salvador, José Gonçalves. Os judeus e o suprimento de escravos à América Latina. Forthcoming.

4757. Souza, José António Soares de. "O final do tráfico de escravos," Revista do Instituto histórico e geográfico brasileiro, 323 (1979), pp. 5-23.

4758. Taunay, Affonso de Escragnolle. "Subsídios para a história do tráfico africano no Brasil colonial," Anais do Museu Paulista, 10, 2 (1941), pp. 1-311. Preliminary version published in Anais do 3 Congresso de História Nacional (Rio de Janeiro, 1938), vol. 3, pp. 519-676.

4759. Tavares, Luis Henrique Dias. "O processo das soluções brasileiras no exemplo da extinção do tráfico negreiro," Revista de história, 35 (1967), pp. 523-37.

4760. _____. "As soluções brasileiras na extinção do tráfico negreiro," Journal of Interamerican Studies, 9, 3 (1967), pp. 367-82.

4761. Teixeira da Mota, Avelino. "Entrée d'esclaves noirs à Valence (1445-1482): le remplacement de la voie saharienne par la voie atlantique, " Revue française d'histoire d'outre-mer, 66, 1-2 (nos. 242-43)(1979), pp. 195-210.

4762. _____. "A viagem do navio Santiago à Sierra Leoa e Rio de S. Domingos em 1526 (Livro de armação)," Boletim cultural da Guiné Portuguesa, 24 (no. 95)(1969), pp. 529-79. Published separately, Lisbon: Agrupamento de Estudos de Cartografia Antiga, 1969, no. 53. Translated (with Raymond Mauny) as "Le voyage du navire Santiago à la Sierra Leone et à la Rivière de S. Domingos (1526)," Bulletin de l'Institut fondamental d'Afrique noire, sér. B, 37, 3 (1975), pp. 589-603.

4763. _____, and Raymond Mauny. "Livre de l'armement du navire São Miguel de l'île de São Tomé au Bénin (1522)," Bulletin de l'Institut fondamental d'Afrique noire, sér. B, 40, 1 (1978), pp. 66-86.

4764. Turner, J. Michael. "Brazilian and African Sources for the Study of Cultural Transferences from Brazil to Africa during the Nineteenth and Twentieth Centuries," in UNESCO, African Slave Trade, pp. 311-30. (Including "Appendix: Partial List of Researchers Working on Slavery in Brazil")

4765. Verger, Pierre. Bahia and the West African Trade, 1549-1851. Ibadan: Ibadan University Press, 1964.

4766. * _____. Bahia and the West Coast Trade (1549-1851). Ibadan, 1964.

4767. _____. Flux et reflux de la traite des nègres entre le
Golfe de Bénin et Bahia de Todos os Santos, du XVIIIe au XIXe
siècle. Paris, La Haye: Mouton, 1968. Translated as Trade
Relations Between the Bight of Benin and Bahia from the 17th to
the 19th Century (trans. Evelyn Crawford)(Ibadan: Ibadan
University Press, 1976).

4768. _____. O fumo da Bahia e o tráfico dos escravos do Gôlfo
de Benim. Salvador, Bahia: Universidade Federal da Bahia - Centro
de Estudos Afro-Orientais, 1966. (Série estudos, no. 6)

4769. _____. "Influence du Brésil au Golfe du Bénin," in Les
Afro-américaines (Paris, 1953), pp. 11-101. (Mémoires de
l'Institut français d'Afrique noire, no. 27)

4770. _____. "Mouvement de navires entre Bahia et le Golfe du
Bénin (xviie-xixe siècles)," Revue française d'histoire
d'outre-mer, 55, 1 (no. 198)(1968), pp. 5-36.

4771. _____. "Rôle joué par le tabac de Bahia dans la traite
des esclaves au Golfe du Bénin," Cahiers d'études africaines, 4, 3
(no. 15)(1964), pp. 349-69.

4772. Verlinden, Charles. "Les débuts de la traite portugaise en Afrique
(1433-1448)," Miscellanea mediaevalia in memoriam Jan Frederik
Niermeyer (Groningen: J. B. Wolters, 1967), pp. 365-77.

4773. Viana, Manoel Alvaro de Sousa Sá. "O tráfico e a diplomacia
brasileira," Revista do Instituto histórico e geográfico
brasileiro (Tomo especial: 1º Congresso de História Nacional,
parte 5, Rio de Janeiro, 1914), pp. 537-64.

4774. Vianna, Hélio. "Um humanitário alvará de 1813, sobre o tráfico de
africanos em navios portuguêses," Revista do Instituto histórico e
geográfico brasileiro, 256 (1962), pp. 79-88.

4775. Vianna Filho, Luiz. "Rumos e cifras do tráfico bahiano," Estudos
brasileiros, ano 3, 5 (no. 15)(1940), pp. 356-80.

4776. Vila Vilar, Enriqueta. "La sublevación de Portugal y la trata de
negros," Ibero-Amerikanisches Archiv, 2, 3 (1976), pp. 171-92.

4777. Vogt, John L. "The Early São Tomé-Príncipe Trade with Mina,
1500-1540," International Journal of African Historical Studies,
6, 3 (1973), pp. 453-67.

4778. _____. "The Lisbon Slave House and the African Trade,
1486-1521," Proceedings of the American Philosophical Society,
117, 1 (1973), pp. 1-16.

4779. _____. "Private Trade and Slave Sales at São Jorge da Mina:
A Fifteenth Century Document," Transactions of the Historical
Society of Ghana, 15 (1974), pp. 103-10.

4780. Wehling, Arno. "Aspectos do tráfico negreiro do Rio de Janeiro (1823-1830)," Anais do VI Simpósio nacional dos professores universitários de história (Goiâna, 1971)(São Paulo, 1973), vol. 1, pp. 521-32.

4781. Westphalen, Cecília Maria. "A introdução de escravos novos no litoral paranaense," Revista de história, 44 (no. 89)(1972), pp. 139-54.

4782. Wright, Antônia Fernanda de Almeida. "A posição norte-americana no problema do tráfico de escravos no Brasil (Contribuição ao estudo do trabalho escravo)," Anais do VI Simpósio nacional dos professores universitários de história (Goiâna, 1971)(São Paulo, 1973), vol. 1, pp. 565-98.

4. Atlantic - Spanish

4783. Acosta Saignes, Miguel. La trata de esclavos en Venezuela. Caracas: Revista de historia, 1961.

4784. Aguirre Beltrán, Gonzalo. "Comercio de esclavos en México por 1542," Afroamérica, 1, 1-2 (1945), pp. 25-40.

4785. _____. "The Slave Trade in Mexico," Hispanic American Historical Review, 24, 3 (1944), pp. 412-31.

4786. Amunátegui y Solar, Domingo. "La trata de negros en Chile," Revista chilena de historia y geografía, 44 (no. 48)(1922), pp. 25-40. Reprinted as "La trata de negros," in Historia social de Chile (Santiago de Chile: Editorial Nascimento, 1932), pp. 173-91.

4787. Assadourian, Carlos Sempat. El tráfico de esclavos en Córdoba de Angola a Potosí, siglos XVI-XVII. Córdoba: Dirección General de Publicaciones, 1966.

4788. _____. El tráfico de esclavos en Córdoba, 1588-1610, según las actas de protocolos del Archivo Histórico de Córdoba. Córdoba: Dirección General de Publicaciones, 1965. (Universidad Nacional de Córdoba, Instituto de estudios americanistas, Cuadernos de historia no. 32)

4789. Chandler, David L. "Health Conditions in the Slave Trade of Colonial New Granada," in Toplin, ed., Slavery and Race Relations in Latin America, pp. 51-88.

4790. Cleven, N. Andrew N. "Ministerial Order of José de Gálvez Establishing a Uniform Duty on the Importation of Negro Slaves into the Indies and Convention between Spain and the United Provinces Regulating the Return of Deserters and Fugitives in their American Colonies," Hispanic American Historical Review, 4, 2 (1921), pp. 266-76.

4791. Cortés Alonso, Vicenta. "La trata de esclavos durante los primeros descubrimientos (1489-1516)," Anuario de estudios atlánticos (Madrid), 9 (1963), pp. 23-50.

4792. Creer, Leland Hargrave. "Spanish-American Slave Trade in the Great Basin, 1800-1853," New Mexico Historical Review, 24, 3 (1949), pp. 171-83.

4793. Drake, Frederick C. "Secret History of the Slave Trade to Cuba Written by an American Naval Officer, 1861," Journal of Negro History, 55, 3 (1970), pp. 218-35.

4794. Fouchard, Jean. "The Slave Trade and the Peopling of Santo Domingo," in UNESCO, African Slave Trade, pp. 270-88.

4795. Franco, José Luciano. Comercio clandestino de esclavos negros en el siglo XIX. Havana: Academy of Sciences, 1971. (Historical Series, no. 21) Also "Comercio clandestino de esclavos en el siglo XIX," in idem, Ensayos históricos (Havana: Editorial de Ciencias Sociales, 1974), pp. 101-23.

4796. _____. Contrabando y trata negrera en el Caribe. Havana: Oficina Regional de Cultura para América Latina y el Caribe, 1973. (Centro de Documentación, La cultura en América Latina, Monografías, no. 1) *2nd ed. in Economia y desarollo (Havana), no. 25 (1974), pp.   , reprinted Havana: Editorial de Ciencias Sociales, 1976.

4797. *Gavira, J. "Negreros," Revista general de marina (Madrid), 121 (1941), pp.   .

4798. Gorbán, Samuel. "El tráfico negrero en el Río de la Plata," Estudos históricos (Marília), 10 (1971), pp. 117-39.

4799. Granda Gutierrez, Germán de. "Uma ruta maritima de contrabando de esclavos negros entre Panamá y Barbacoas durante el asiento inglés," Revista de Indias, 36, 143-44 (1976), pp. 123-42.

4800. Holsoe, Svend. "The Cuban Tie to the Grain Coast, 1820's and 1830's" (Unpub- lished paper read to the Annual Meeting of the African Studies Association, Bloomington, Indiana, October 1981).

4801. King, James F. "Evolution of the Free Slave Trade Principle in Spanish Colonial Administration," Hispanic American Historical Review, 22, 1 (1942), pp. 34-56.

4802. Kiple, Kenneth F. "The Cuban Slave Trade, 1820-1862: The Demographic Implications for Comparative Studies" (PhD diss., University of Florida, 1970).

4803. Kitchens, John W. "The New Granadan-Peruvian Slave Trade," Journal of Negro History, 65, 3 (1979), pp. 205-14.

4804. _____, and Lynne B. Kitchens. "La exportación de esclavos neogranadinos en 1846 y las reclamaciones británicas," Boletín de historia y antigüedades (Bogotá), 63, 2 (no. 713)(1976), pp. 239-93.

4805. Klein, Herbert S. "The Cuban Slave Trade in a Period of Transition, 1790-1843," Revue française d'histoire d'outre-mer, 62, 1-2 (nos. 226-27)(1975), pp. 67-89.

4806. Kordon, Bernardo. "La trata de negros en el Río de la Plata," Argumentos (Revista mensual de estudios sociales) (Buenos Aires), 1, 2 (1938), pp. 178-82.

4807. Lapeyre, Henry. "Le trafic négrier avec l'Amérique Espagnole," Homenaje a Jaime Vicéns Vives (Barcelona: Universidad, Facultad de Filosofía y Letras, 1965-67), pp. 285-306.

4808. _____. "La trata de negros con destino a la América española durante los últimos años del reinado de Carlos V, 1544-1555," Cuadernos de investigación histórica, 2 (1978), pp. 335-39.

4809. Love, Robert William, Jr. "The End of the Atlantic Slave Trade to Cuba," Caribbean Quarterly, 22, 2-3 (1976), pp. 51-58.

4810. Lunn, Arnold Henry Moore. A Saint in the Slave Trade: Peter Claver (1581-1654). London: Sheed and Ward, 1935.

4811. Marquez de la Plata, Fernando. "Documentos relativos a la introducción de esclavos negros en América," Revista chilena de historia y geografía, 57 (no. 61)(1928), pp. 226-49; 58 (no. 62)(1928), pp. 286-304; 59 (no. 63)(1928), pp. 204-14.

4812. Molinari, Diego Luis. La trata de negros: datos para su estudio en el Río de la Plata. Buenos Aires: Universidad de Buenos Aires, 1944.

4813. Morales Carrión, Arturo. Auge y decadencia de la trata negrera en Puerto Rico (1820-1860). San Juan: Instituto de cultura puertorriqueña, 1978.

4814. _____. "Recent Research on the Puerto Rican Slave Trade," Revista/Review Interamericana, 9, 4 (1979-80), pp. 593-97.

4815. *Moreira, E. D. Macarthy. "O caso das presas espanholas," Revista do Instituto de filosofia e ciências humanas da Universidade Federal do Rio Grande do Sul, (1974), pp. 185-205.

4816. Murray, David R. Odious Commerce: Britain, Spain and the Abolition of the Cuban Slave Trade. New York: Cambridge University Press, 1980.

4817. _____. "Statistics of the Slave Trade to Cuba, 1790-1867," Journal of Latin American Studies, 3, 2 (1971), pp. 131-49.

4818. Otte, Enrique. "Los Jerónimos y el tráfico humano en el Caribe: una rectificación," Anuario de estudios americanos, 32 (1975), pp. 187-204.

4819. _____. "Die Negersklavenlizenz des Laurent von Gorrevod: Kastilisch-genuesische Wirtschafts- und Finanzinteressen bei der Einfürhung der Negersklaverei in America," Gesammelte Aufsatze zur Kulturgeschichte Spaniens, 22 (1965), pp. 283-320.

4820. Palacios Preciado, Jorge. La trata de negros por Cartagena de Indias 1650-1750. Tunja, Colombia: Universidad Pedagógica y Tecnológica de Colombia, 1973.

4821. Palmer, Colin A. Human Cargoes: The British Slave Trade to Spanish America, 1700-1739. Urbana, Ill.: University of Illinois Press, 1981.

4822. *Paster y Fernández, Checa M. "Esclavos y negreros," Revista general de marina (Madrid), 155 (1968), pp.   .

4823. Pérez de la Riva, Juan. "Cuando llegaron a Cuba los últimos bozales?" Revista de la Biblioteca Nacional José Martí, 16, 2 (1974), pp. 176-79.

4824. _____. "Un diplomático ingles informa sobre la trata clandestina en Cuba," in idem and Pedro Deschamps-Chapeaux, Contribución a la historia de la gente sin historia (Havana: Editorial de Ciencias Sociales, 1974), pp. 251-82.

4825. _____. "El monto de la inmigración forzada en el siglo XIX," Revista de la Biblioteca Nacional José Martí, 16, 1 (1974), pp. 77-110.

4826. Ramos Pérez, Demetrio. "El negocio negrero de los Welser y sus habilidades monopolistas," Revista de história de America, 81, 1 (1976), pp. 7-81.

4827. Roig de Leuchsenring, Emilio. "De como y por quiénes se hacia en Cuba la trata de negros el ano de 1778," Revista bimestre cubana, 24 (1929), pp. 418-31.

4828. _____. "De cómo y por quiénes se realizaba en Cuba la trata de esclavos africanos durante los siglos XVIII y XIX," Estudios afrocubanos, 1, 1 (1937), pp. 122-38.

4829. Romero, Fernando. "La corriente de la trata negrera en Chile," Sphinx (Lima), 3, 4-5 (1939), pp. 87-93.

4830. Sampaio Garcia, Rosendo. "O Português Duarte Lopes e o comércio espanhol de escravos negros," Revista de história, 31 (1957), pp. 375-85.

4831. Scelle, Georges. "The Slave Trade in the Spanish Colonies of America: the Assiento," American Journal of International Law, 4, 3 (1910), pp. 612-61.

4832. _____. La traite négrière aux Indes de Castille, contrats et traités d'assiento: étude de droit public et d'histoire diplomatique puisée aux sources originales et accompagnée de plusieurs documents inédits. Paris: L. Larose et L. Tenin, 1906.

4833. Scheuss de Studer, Elena F. La trata de negros en el Río de la Plata durante el siglo xviii. Buenos Aires: Universidad de Buenos Aires, 1958.

4834. Silié, Rubén. "La trata de negros en Santo Domingo; siglo XVIII," Ciencia (Organo de la Dirección de Investigaciones Científicos de la Universidad Autonoma de Santo Domingo), 2, 3 (1975), pp. 97-109.

4835. Snow, William J. "Utah Indians and Spanish Slave Trade," Utah Historical Quarterly, 2, 3 (1929), pp. 68-75.

4836. Sousa, José António Soares de. "O tráfico de negros no Rio da Prata," Revista do Instituto histórico e geográfico brasileiro, 244 (1959), pp. 446-54.

4837. Tardieu, Jean-Pierre. "Les principales structures administratives espagnolles de la Traite des Noirs vers les Indes occidentales," Cahiers du monde hispanique et luso-brésilien, 37 (1981), pp. 51-84.

4838. Thornton, Anthony P. "Spanish Slave-Ships in the English West Indies, 1660-1685," Hispanic American Historical Review, 35, 3 (1955), pp. 374-85.

4839. Tollis-Guicharnaud, Michèle. "Le trafic négrier à Cuba de 1818 à travers les récits des voyageurs français," Cahiers des Amériques Latines, no. 20 (1979), pp. 183-96.

4840. Torres Ramírez, Bibiano. 'La Compañia gaditana de negros," in Atti del XL Congresso Internazionale degli Americanisti (Roma-Genova, 1972)(Genova: Tilgher, 1975), vol. 3, pp. 439-44.

4841. _____. La Compañia gaditana de negros. Seville: Publicaciones de la Escuela de Estudios Hispano-Americanos de Sevilla, 1973.

4842. Universidad de Buenos Aires. Facultad de Filosofia y Letras. Documentos para la historia argentina, vol. 7: Comercio de Indias, Consulado, Comercio de Negros y de Extranjeros (1791-1809). Buenos Aires, 1916.

4843. Vignols, Léon. "L'asiento français (1701-1713) et anglais (1713-1750) et le commerce franco-espagnole vers 1700-1730," Revue d'histoire économique et sociale, 17 (1929), pp. 403-36.

4844. Vila Vilar, Enriqueta. "Algunos datos sobre la navegación y los navios negreros en el siglo XVII," Historiografía y bibliografía americanistas, 17, 3 (1974), pp. 219-32.

4845. _____. "Los asientos portugueses y el contrabando de negros," Anuario de estudios americanos, 30 (1973), pp. 557-609.

4846. _____. Hispanoamérica y el comercio de esclavos: los asientos portugueses. Seville: Escuela de Estudios Hispano-Americanos, 1977.

4847. _____. "The Large-Scale Introduction of Africans into Veracruz and Cartagena," in Rubin and Tuden, eds., Comparative Perspectives, pp. 267-80.

4848. Williams, Eric. "The Negro Slave Trade in Anglo-Spanish Relations," Caribbean Historical Review, 1 (1950), pp. 22-45.

5. Atlantic - English

4849. Anstey, Roger T. The Atlantic Slave Trade and British Abolition, 1760-1810. London: Macmillan 1975.

4850. _____. "The Historical Debate on the Abolition of the British Slave Trade," in Anstey and Hair, eds., Liverpool, pp. 157-66.

4851. _____. "The Profitability of the Slave Trade in the 1840s," in Rubin and Tuden, eds., Comparative Perspectives, pp. 84-93.

4852. _____. "A Re-interpretation of the Abolition of the British Slave Trade, 1806-1807," English Historical Review, 87 (no. 343), pp. 304-32.

4853. _____. "The Volume and Profitability of the British Slave Trade, 1761-1807," in Engerman and Genovese, eds., Race and Slavery, pp. 3-31.

4854. _____, and P. E. H. Hair, eds. Liverpool, the African Slave Trade and Abolition. Liverpool: Historic Society of Lancashire and Cheshire, 1977. (Occasional Series, no. 2)

4855. Bean, Richard N. "The British Trans-Atlantic Slave Trade, 1650-1775" (PhD diss., University of Washington, 1971). Published as The British Transatlantic Slave Trade, 1650-1775 (New York: Arno Press, 1975). (Dissertations in American Economic History)

4856. Chamberlain, E. Noble. "The Influence of the Slave Trade on Liverpool Medicine," in Atti: Fourteenth International Congress of the History of Medicine (Rome and Salerno, 1954), vol. 2, pp. 768-73.

4857. Clemens, Paul G. E. "The Rise of Liverpool, 1665-1750," Economic History Review, 29, 2 (1976), pp. 211-25.

4858. Dart, Henry P. "The Slave Depot of the Company of the Indies at New Orleans," Louisiana Historical Quarterly, 9, 2 (1926), pp. 286-87.

4859. Davies, K. G. The Royal African Company. London: Longmans Green, 1957.

4860. Drake, B. K. "Continuity and Flexibility in Liverpool's Trade with Africa and the Caribbean," Business History, 18, 1 (1976), pp. 85-97.

4861. _____. "The Liverpool-African Voyage c. 1790-1807: Commercial Problems," in Anstey and Hair, eds., Liverpool, pp. 126-56.

4862. Drescher, Seymour. "Capitalism and Abolition: Values and Forces in Britain, 1783-1814," in Anstey and Hair, eds., Liverpool, pp. 167-95.

4863. _____. "Le 'déclin' du système esclavagiste britannique et l'abolition de la traite," Annales: économies, sociétés, civilisations, 31, 2 (1976), pp. 414-35.

4864. Eltis, David. "The British Contribution to the Nineteenth-Century Trans-atlantic Slave Trade," Economic History Review, 32, 2 (1979), pp. 211-27.

4865. _____. "The British Trans-Atlantic Slave Trade after 1807," Maritime History, 4, 1 (1974), pp. 1-11.

4866. _____. "The Traffic in Slaves Between the British West Indian Colonies, 1807-1833," Economic History Review, 25, 1 (1972), pp. 55-64.

4867. Engerman, Stanley L. "The Slave Trade and British Capital Formation in the Eighteenth Century: A Comment on the Williams Thesis," Business History Review, 46, 4 (1972), pp. 430-43.

4868. Galenson, David W. "The Atlantic Slave Trade and the Barbados Market, 1673-1723," Journal of Economic History, 42, 3 (1982), pp. 491-511.

4869. _____. "The Slave Trade to the English West Indies, 1673-1724," Economic History Review, 32, 2 (1979), pp. 241-49.

4870. Hargreaves, John D. "The Slave Traffic," in Alex Natan, ed., Silver Renaissance: Essays in Eighteenth Century English History (London: Macmillan, 1961), pp. 81-101.

4871. Hochstetter, Franz. Die wirtschaftlichen und politischen Motive für die Abschaffung des britischen Sklavenhandels im Jahre 1806/07. Leipzig, 1905. (Gustav Schmoller and Max Sering, eds., Staats- und Sozialwissenschaftliche Forschungen, no. 25, part 1)

4872. Hyde, F. E., B. B. Parkinson, and S. Marriner. "The Nature and Profitability of the Liverpool Slave Trade," Economic History Review, 5, 3 (1953), pp. 368-77.

4873. Inikori, Joseph E. "Market Structure and the Profits of the British African Trade in the Late Eighteenth Century," Journal of Economic History, 41, 4 (1981), pp. 745-76.

4874. Jackson, Luther P. "Elizabethan Seamen and the African Slave Trade," Journal of Negro History, 9, 1 (1924), pp. 1-17.

4875. Johnson, Vera M. "Sidelights on the Liverpool Slave Trade, 1789-1807," Mariner's Mirror, 38, 4 (1952), pp. 276-93.

4876. Killinger, Charles L. "The Royal African Company Slave Trade to Virginia, 1687-1713" (MA thesis, College of William and Mary, 1969).

4877. Klein, Herbert S. "The English Slave Trade to Jamaica, 1782-1808," Economic History Review, 31, 1 (1978), pp. 25-45.

4878. _____, and Stanley L. Engerman. "Slave Mortality on British Ships 1791-1797," in Anstey and Hair, eds., Liverpool, pp. 113-25.

4879. *Lamb, D. P. "The English Atlantic Slave Trade in its Final Phase from the Early 1770s to 1807" (MA thesis, University of Exeter, 1974).

4880. _____. "Re-landing and Trans-shipping of Slaves by British Vessels in the 1790s: A Note," Business History, 20, 1 (1978), pp. 100-04.

4881. _____. "Volume and Tonnage of the Liverpool Slave Trade 1772-1807," in Anstey and Hair, eds., Liverpool, pp. 91-112.

4882. LoGerfo, James W. "Sir William Dolben and 'The Cause of Humanity': The Passage of the Slave Trade Regulation Act of 1788," Eighteenth-Century Studies, 6, 4 (1973), pp. 431-51.

4883. Lowery, Ralph J. "The English Asiento and the Slave Trade," Negro History Bulletin, 24, 3 (1960), pp. 128-30.

4884. McDonald, Roderick A. "Measuring the British Slave Trade to Jamaica, 1789-1808: A Comment," Economic History Review, 33, 2 (1980), pp. 253-58.

4885. MacInnes, Charles M. Bristol and the Slave Trade. Bristol: University of Bristol, Branch of the Historical Association, 1963. (Local History Pamphlets, no. 7)

4886. Mackenzie-Grieve, Averil. The Last Years of the English Slave Trade, Liverpool, 1750-1807. London: Putnam, 1941.

4887. *Merritt, J. E. "The Liverpool Slave Trade from 1789 to 1791" (MA thesis, University of Nottingham, 1959).

4888. _____. "The Triangular Trade," Business History, 3, 1 (1960), pp. 1-7.

4889. Minchinton, Walter E. "The Slave Trade of Bristol with the British Mainland Colonies in North America 1699-1770," in Anstey and Hair, eds., Liverpool, pp. 39-59.

4890. _____. "The Triangular Trade Revisited," in Gemery and Hogendorn, eds., Uncommon Market, pp. 331-52.

4891. Oehlrich, Conrad. England als sklavenhandler und sklavenhalter. Berlin: E. Zander, 1940. (Pseud.: Ernst A. Olbert)

4892. Ostrander, Gilman M. "The Making of the Triangular Trade Myth," William and Mary Quarterly, 3rd ser., 30, 4 (1973), pp. 635-44.

4893. Pollitt, Ronald. "John Hawkins's Troublesome Voyages: Merchants, Bureaucrats, and the Origins of the Slave Trade," Journal of British Studies, 12, 2 (1973), pp. 26-40.

4894. Porter, Dale H. The Abolition of the Slave Trade in England, 1784-1807. Hamden, Conn.: Archon Books, 1970.

4895. Rawley, James A. "The Port of London and the Eighteenth Century Slave Trade: Historians, Sources, and a Reappraisal," African Economic History, 9 (1980), pp. 85-100.

4896. Richards, W. A. "Black Country Guns and the Slave Trade," Black Country Man, 8, 1 (1975), pp. 7-13.

4897. *Richardson, David. "The Bristol Slave Trade in the Eighteenth Century" (MA thesis, University of Manchester, 1969).

4898. _____. "The Efficiency of English Slave Trading in West Africa in the Eighteenth Century: Estimates and Implications" (Paper read to the Annual Meeting of the American Historical Association, Los Angeles, 1981).

4899. _____. "Profitability in the Bristol-Liverpool Slave Trade," Revue française d'histoire d'outre-mer, 62, 1-2 (nos. 226-27)(1975), pp. 301-08.

4900. _____. "Profits in the Liverpool Slave Trade: The Accounts of William Davenport, 1757-1784," in Anstey and Hair, eds., Liverpool, pp. 60-90.

4901. _____. "West African Consumption Patterns and Their Influence on the Eighteenth-Century English Slave Trade," in Gemery and Hogendorn, eds., Uncommon Market, pp. 303-30.

4902. Rudnyanszky, Leslie Imre. "The Caribbean Slave Trade: Jamaica and Barbados, 1680-1770" (PhD diss., Notre Dame, 1973).

4903. Sanderson, F. E. "The Liverpool Abolitionists," in Anstey and Hair, eds., Liverpool, pp. 196-238.

4904. _____. "Liverpool and the Slave Trade: A Guide to Sources," Transactions of the Historic Society of Lancashire and Cheshire, 124 (1972), pp. 154-76.

4905. _____. "The Liverpool Delegates and Sir William Dolben's Bill," Transactions of the Historic Society of Lancashire and Cheshire, 124 (1972), pp. 57-84.

4906. Schofield, M. M. "The Slave Trade from Lancashire and Cheshire Ports Outside Liverpool, c. 1750 - c. 1790," Transactions of the Historic Society of Lancashire and Cheshire, 126 (1976), pp. 30-72.

4907. Sheridan, Richard B. "The Commercial and Financial Organization of the British Slave Trade, 1750-1807," Economic History Review, 11, 2 (1958), pp. 249-63.

4908. Stetson, Kenneth Winslow. "A Quantitative Approach to Britain's American Slave Trade, 1700-1773" (MA thesis, University of Wisconsin - Madison, 1973).

4909. Suttell, Elizabeth Louise. "The British Slave Trade to Virginia, 1698-1728" (MA thesis, College of William and Mary, 1965).

4910. Tenkorang, Sammy. "British Slave Trading Activities on the Gold and Slave Coasts in the Eighteenth Century" (MA thesis, University of London, 1964).

4911. Thornton, Anthony P. "The Organization of the Slave Trade in the English West Indies, 1660-1685," William and Mary Quarterly, 3rd ser., 12, 3 (1955), pp. 399-409.

4912. Trench, Charles Chevenix. "Gordon and the Slave Trade," History Today, 25, 11 (1975), pp. 731-40.

4913. Waddell, D. A. G. "Queen Anne's Government and the Slave Trade," Caribbean Quarterly, 6 (1960), pp. 7-10.

4914. Walvin, James. "Slavery and the Slave Trade," Journal of Imperial and Commonwealth History, 5, 2 (1977), pp. 227-31.

4915. Williams, David M. "Abolition and the Re-Deployment of the Slave Fleet, 1807-11," Journal of Transport History, 2, 2 (1973), pp. 103-15.

4916. Williams, Eric. "The British West Indian Slave Trade after its Abolition in 1807," Journal of Negro History, 27, 2 (1942), pp. 175-91.

6. Atlantic - Dutch

4917. Andel, M. A. van. "Geneeskunde en hygiëne op de slavenschepen in den compagnietijd," Nederlands Tijdschrift voor Geneeskunde, 75, 1 (no. 6)(1931), pp. 614-37.

4918. Austen, Ralph, and K. Jacob. "Dutch Trading Voyages to Cameroun: 1721-1759: European Documents and African History," Annales de la Faculté des lettres et sciences humaines (Université fédérale du Cameroun/de Yaounde), 11, 6 (1974), pp. 1-27.

4919. Brakel, S. van. "Bescheiden over den slavenhandel WIC," Economisch- en Sociaal-Historisch Jaarboek, 4 (1918), pp. 47-83.

4920. _____. "Slavenhandel," in H. D. Benjamins and Joh. F. Snelleman, eds., Encyclopaedie van Nederlandsch West-Indie (The Hague: Nijhoff, 1914-17), pp. 634-37.

4921. Boogaart, Ernst van den, and Pieter C. Emmer. "The Dutch Participation in the Atlantic Slave Trade, 1595-1650," in Gemery and Hogendorn, eds., Uncommon Market, pp. 353-75.

4922. Buenaventura de Carrocera, Fr. "Los caribales, canibales y traficantes de indios esclavos por instigación de los holandeses, y unos y otros enemigos de las misiones capuchinas de la Guyana," Missionalia hispánica (Madrid), 20 (no. 59)(1963), pp. 249-52.

4923. Dantzig, Albert van. "Les Hollandais sur la Côte des Esclaves: parties gagnées et parties perdues," in Etudes africaines offertes à Henri Brunschwig (Paris: Editions de l'Ecole des hautes études en sciences sociales, 1982), pp. 79-89.

4924. _____. Het Nederlanse Aandeel in de Slavenhandel. Bussum: Fibula-Van Dishoeck, 1968.

4925. Eekhof, A. "Twee documenten betreffende den slavenhandel in de 17e eeuw," Nederlandsch archief voor kerkgeschiedenis, 11 (1914), pp. 271-98.

4926. Emmer, Pieter. "Abolition of the Abolished: The Illegal Dutch Slave Trade and the Mixed Courts," in Walvin and Eltis, eds., Abolition of the Atlantic Slave Trade, pp. 177-92.

4927. _____. "The History of the Dutch Slave Trade, a Bibliographical Survey," Journal of Economic History, 32, 3 (1972), pp. 728-47.

4928. _____. "Slavenhandel," in C. F. A. Bruijning, J. Voorhoeve, and W. Gordijn, eds., Encyclopedie van Suriname (Amsterdam: Elsevier, 1977), pp. 558-61.

4929. _____. "De slavenhandel van en naar Nieuw-Nederland," Economisch- en Sociaal-Historisch Jaarboek, 35 (1972), pp. 94-147.

4930. _____. "Surinam and the Decline of the Dutch Slave Trade," Revue française d'histoire d'outre-mer, 62, 1-2 (nos. 226-27)(1975), pp. 245-51.

4931. Goslinga, Cornelis Ch. "Curaçao as a Slave-trading Center During the War of the Spanish Succession," Nieuwe West-Indische Gids, 52, 1-2 (1977), pp. 1-50.

4932. *Groenhuis, G. "De zonen van Cham: gereformeerde predikanten over de slavernij, van Udemans Coopmansschip (1640) tot Capiteins Godgeleerd Onderzoekschrift (1742)," Kleio (The Hague), 21, 7 (1980), pp. 221-25.

4933. Kernkamp, G. W. "Een contract tot slavenhandel van 1657," Bijdragen en Medeleelingen van het Historisch Genootschap (Utrecht), 22 (1901), pp. 444-59.

4934. Kesler, C. K. "Uit de eerste dagen van den West-Indischen slavenhandel," West-Indische Gids, 22 (1940), pp. 175-85.

4935. Linde, Jan Marinus van der. Ballade van de slavenhaler, met historische toelichtingen. Nijkerk, the Netherlands: G. F. Callenbach, 1963.

4936. Menkman, W. R. "Nederlandsche en vreemde slavenaart," West-Indische Gids, 26 (1944-45), pp. 97-110.

4937. _____. "Slavenhandel en rechtsbedeeling op Curaçao op het einde der 17e eeuw," West-Indische Gids, 17 (1935-36), pp. 11-26.

4938. Postma, Johannes. "The Dimension of the Dutch Slave Trade from Western Africa," Journal of African History, 13, 2 (1972), pp. 237-48.

4939. _____. "The Dutch Participation in the African Slave Trade: Slaving on the Guinea Coast, 1675-1795" (PhD diss., Michigan State University, 1970).

4940. _____. "The Dutch Slave Trade: A Quantitative Assessment," Revue française d'histoire d'outre-mer, 62, 1-2 (nos. 226-27)(1975), pp. 232-44.

4941 _____. "Dutch Slave Trade Practices on the West African Coast during the Eighteenth Century" (Paper read to the Annual Meeting of the American Historical Association, Los Angeles, 1981).

4942. _____. "Mortality in the Dutch Slave Trade, 1675-1795," in Gemery and Hogendorn, eds., Uncommon Market, pp. 239-60.

4943. _____. "The Origin of African Slaves: The Dutch Activities on the Guinea Coast, 1675-1795," in Engerman and Genovese, eds., Race and Slavery, pp. 33-49.

4944. Ryder, A. F. C. "Dutch Trade on the Nigerian Coast during the Seventeenth Century," Journal of the Historical Society of Nigeria, 3, 2 (1965), pp. 195-210.

4945. Schoute, Dirk. "Scheepschirurijns-journaal van een slavenschip der Middelburgsche Commercie Compagnie," Nederlands Tijdschrift voor Geneeskunde, 92, 4 (no. 45)(1948), pp. 3645-62.

4946. Unger, W. S. "Bijdragen tot de geschiedenis van de Nederlandse slavenhandel," Economisch- en Sociaal-Historisch Jaarboek, 26 (1956), pp. 133-74; 28 (1958-60), pp. 3-148. Translated as "Essay on the History of the Dutch Slave Trade," in M. A. P. Meilink-Roelofsz, ed., Dutch Authors on West Indian History (trans. Maria J. L. van Yperen) (The Hague: Martinus Nijhoff, 1982), pp. 46-98.

4947. Vrijman, L.-C. Slavenhalers en slavenhandel. Amsterdam: P. N. van Kampen, 1937; enlarged, 1943.

4948. Wright, I. A. "The Coymans Asiento (1685-1689)," Bijdragen voor vaderlandse geschiedenis en oudheidkunde, 6, 1 (1924), pp. 23-62.

7. Atlantic - French

4949. Abénon, Lucien René. "Le problème des esclaves de contrebande à la Guadeloupe pendant la première moitié du XVIIIe siècle," Bulletin de la société d'histoire de la Guadeloupe, 4 (no. 38)(1978), pp. 49-58.

4950. *Bastard, Hubert le. "Les considérations économiques et juridiques sur le commerce négrier et l'esclavage au XVIIIe siècle" (Thèse?, Nantes, 1969).

4951. Bénard, J.-Cl. "L'armement honfleurais et le commerce des esclaves à la fin du XVIIIe siècle," Annales de Normandie, 10, 3 (1960), pp. 249-64.

4952. Berbain, Simone. Etudes sur la traite des noirs au Golfe de Guinée: le comptoir français de Juda (Ouidah) au XVIIIe siècle. Paris, 1942. (Mémoires de l'Institut français d'Afrique noire, no. 3) Republished Amsterdam: Swets and Seitlinger, 1968.

4953. *Blanche, Jean-Claude. "Guadeloupe et Afrique au XIXe siècle, un exemple de relation: l'apport de la main-d'oeuvre, 1848-1862" (Thèse de 3ème cycle, Paris VIII, n.d.)

4954. *Boulanger, Alain. "Deux négriers nantais de la première moitié du XVIIIe siècle d'après leur journaux (1741-1742 et 1743-1744)" (Mémoire de maîtrise, Université de Nantes, 1970).

4955. Boulle, Pierre H. "Marchandises de traite et développement industriel dans la France et l'Angleterre du XVIIIe siècle," Revue française d'histoire d'outre-mer, 62, 1-2 (nos. 226-27)(1975), pp. 309-30.

4956. _____. "Slave Trade, Commercial Organization and Industrial Growth in Eighteenth-Century Nantes," Revue française d'histoire d'outre-mer, 59, 1 (no. 214)(1972), pp. 70-112.

4957. *Brotovici, Livin Sorel. "L'hygiène et l'état sanitaire au temps de la navigation à voiles: navires négriers et galères" (Thèse en médecine, Paris, 1969).

4958. Buckley, Roger N. "Business as Usual: A Review Essay of Robert Louis Stein's The French Slave Trade in the Eighteenth Century: An Old Regime Business," Umoja: A Scholarly Journal of Black Studies, 4, 3 (1980), pp. 43-48.

4959. Buffet, H. E. "La traite des noirs et le commerce de l'argent au Port-Louis et à Lorient sous Louis XIV," Revue des études historiques, 102 (1935), pp. 433-50.

4960. Chiché, Marie-Claire. Hygiène et santé à bord des navires négriers au XVIIIe siècle. Paris: Foulon, 1957.

4961. Cohn, Raymond L. "Discussion: Mortality in the French Slave Trade," Journal of African History, 23, 2 (1982), pp. 225-26. With a reply by Robert Stein.

4962. Coolen, Georges. "Négriers dunkerquois," Bulletin de la Société des antiquaires de la Morinie, 19 (no. 362)(1960), pp. 289-320; 19 (no. 363)(1960), pp. 311-23.

4963. Czyka, Lucette. "Traite et esclavage dans Tamango," Europe, revue littéraire nouvelle, 53 (no. 557)(1975), pp. 30-38.

4964. Daget, Serge. "L'abolition de la traite des noirs en France de 1814 à 1831," Cahiers d'études africaines, 11, 1 (no. 41)(1971), pp. 14-58.

4965. _____. "Les archives de Sierra Leone et la traite illégale française du XIXe siècle," Annales de l'Université d'Abidjan (Série D, Lettres), 8 (1975), pp. 279-97.

4966. _____. "British Repression of the Illegal French Slave Trade: Some Considerations (trans. Charles Ferguson)," in Gemery and Hogendorn, eds., Uncommon Market, pp. 419-42.

4967. _____. Catalogue analytique des armements français soupçonnables de participation au trafic négrier illégal 1814-1861. Paris, 1977.

4968. _____. "La France et l'abolition de la traite des Noirs de 1814 à 1831: introduction à l'étude de la répression française de la traite des Noirs au XIXe siècle" (Thèse du 3ème cycle, Lettres, Paris, 1969).

4969. _____. "France, Suppression of the Illegal Trade, and England, 1817-1850," in Walvin and Eltis, eds., Abolition of the Atlantic Slave Trade, pp. 193-220.

4970. _____. "Long cours et négriers nantais du trafic illégal (1814-1833)," Revue française d'histoire d'outre-mer, 62, 1-2 (nos. 226-27)(1975), pp. 90-134.

4971. _____. "Les mots esclave, nègre, noir et les jugements de valeur sur la traite négrière dans la littérature abolitionniste française de 1770 à 1845," Revue française d'histoire d'outre-mer, 60, 4 (no. 221)(1973), pp. 511-48.

4972. _____. "La navigation nantaise pour le 'commerce légitime' à la côte occidentale d'Afrique (1833-1872)," Enquêtes et documents (Nantes: Centre de recherches sur l'histoire de la France atlantique), vol. 6 (1981), pp. 85-113.

4973. _____. "Le trafic négrier illégal français de 1814 à 1860: historiographie et sources," Annales de l'Université d'Abidjan (Histoire, série 1), 3 (1975), pp. 23-54.

4974. _____, ed. Répertoire des expéditions négrières françaises au XVIIIe siècle. By Jean Mettas. Paris: Société française d'histoire d'outre-mer, 1978.

4975. Debbasch, Yvan. "Poesie et traite: l'opinion française sur le commerce négrier au début du XIXe siècle," Revue française d'histoire d'outre-mer, 48, 3-4 (nos. 172-73)(1961), pp. 311-52.

4976. Debien, Gabriel. "Documents sur la traite (XVIIe-XIXe siècles)," Enquêtes et documents (Nantes: Centre de Recherches sur l'Histoire de la France Atlantique), vol. 2 (1972), pp. 185-226.

4977. _____. "Quelques précisions sur la traite nantaise entre les deux guerres de sept ans (1749-1756)," Revue française d'histoire d'outre-mer, 64, 4 (no. 237)(1977), pp. 521-28.

4978. _____. "Le R. P. Dieudonné Rinchon, historien de la traite française: vie et oeuvres," Revue française d'histoire d'outre-mer, 59, 4 (no. 217)(1972), pp. 701-04. (Notes d'histoire coloniale, no. 154)

4979. Delafosse, Marcel. "Les rochelais au Maroc au XVIIIe siècle: commerce et rachat des captifs," Revue d'histoire des colonies, 35, 1 (no. 122)(1948), pp. 70-83.

4980. *Derou, Jean. "L'émigration africaine aux Antilles au XIXe siècle (1848- 1862)" (Thèse de maîtrise, Paris VII, 1974).

4981. *Desclos le Peley, Bertrand. "Jacques-Joseph Muller, chirurgien nantais (1738-1811)" (Thèse de doctorat en médecine, Nantes, 1975-76).

4982. Everaert, John G. "Les fluctuations du trafic négrier nantais (1763-1792)," Cahiers de Tunisie, 11, 3 (no. 43)(1963), pp. 37-62.

4983. _____. De Franse Slavenhandel: Organisatie, Conjunctuur, en sociaal milieu van de driehoekshandel. Brussels: Swets, n.d.

4984. Fouchard, Jean. "La traite négrière et le peuplement de Saint Domingue" (Paper presented to UNESCO, Meeting of Experts on the Slave Trade).

4985. Gaulme, François. "Un document sur le Ngoyo et ses voisins en 1784: l''observation sur la navigation et le commerce de la côte d'Angole' du comte de Cappelis," Revue française d'histoire d'outre-mer, 64, 3 (no. 236)(1977), pp. 350-75.

4986. Halgouet, Hervé du. Au temps de Saint-Domingue et de la Martinique d'après la correspondance des trafiquants maritimes. Rennes: Imprimerie Oberthur, 1941.

4987. Jennings, Lawrence C. "France, Great Britain, and the Repression of the Slave Trade, 1841-45," French Historical Studies, 10, 1 (1977), pp. 101-25.

4988. _____. "French Policy Towards Trading with African and Brazilian Slave Merchants, 1840-1853," Journal of African History, 17, 4 (1976), pp. 515-28.

4989. _____. "The French Press and Great Britain's Campaign Against the Slave Trade, 1830-1848," Revue française d'histoire d'outre-mer, 67, 1-2 (nos. 246-47)(1980), pp. 5-24.

4990. _____. "French Reaction to the 'Disguised British Slave Trade': France and British African Emigration Projects, 1840-1864," Cahiers d'études africaines, 18, 1-2 (nos. 69-70)(1978), pp. 201-13.

4991. Kellenbenz, Hermann. "La place de l'Elbe inférieure dans le commerce triangulaire au milieu du XVIIe siècle," Revue française d'histoire d'outre-mer, 62, 1-2 (nos. 226-27)(1975), pp. 186-95.

4992. Kennedy, Melvin Dow. "The Suppression of the African Slave Trade to the French Colonies and its Aftermath (1814-1848)" (PhD diss., University of Chicago, 1947).

4993. Klein, Herbert S., and Stanley L. Engerman. "Facteurs de mortalité dans le trafic français d'esclaves au XVIIIe siècle," Annales: économies, sociétés, civilisations, 31, 6 (1976), pp. 1213-24.

4994. _____. "A Note on Mortality in the French Slave Trade in the Eighteenth Century," in Gemery and Hogendorn, eds., Uncommon Market, pp. 261-72.

4995. Lachance, Paul F. "The Politics of Fear: French Louisianians and the Slave Trade, 1786-1809," Plantation Society in the Americas, 1, 2 (1979), pp. 62-97.

4996. Martin, Gaston. Nantes au XVIIIe siècle: l'ère des négriers (1714-1774), d'après des documents inédits. Paris: F. Alcan, 1931.

4997. _____. Négriers et bois d'ébène. Grenoble: B. Arthaud, 1934.

4998. Maugat, Emile. "La traite clandestine à Nantes au XIXe siècle," Bulletin de la Société archéologique et historique de Nantes et de la Loire-Inférieure, 93 (1954), pp. 162-69.

4999. Mettas, Jean. "Honfleur et la traite des noirs au XVIIIe siècle," Revue française d'histoire d'outre-mer, 60, 1 (no. 218)(1973), pp. 5-26.

5000. _____. "Pour une histoire de la traite des noirs française: sources et problèmes," Revue française d'histoire d'outre-mer, 62, 1-2 (nos. 226-27)(1975), pp. 19-46.

5001. _____. Répertoire des expéditions négrières françaises au XVIIIe siècle (édité par Serge Daget). Paris: Société française d'histoire d'outre-mer, 1978. Tôme 1: Nantes.

5002. Meyer, Jean. L'armement nantais dans la deuxième moitié du XVIIIe siècle. Paris: S.E.V.P.E.N., 1969.

5003. _____. "Le commerce négrier nantais (1774-1792)," Annales: économies, sociétés, civilisations, 15, 1 (1960), pp. 120-29.

5004. _____. "Du nouveau sur le commerce négrier nantais du XVIIIe siècle," Annales de Bretagne, 73, 2 (1966), pp. 229-39.

5005. Nardin, Jean-Claude. "Encore des chiffres: la traite négrière française pendant la première moitié du XVIIIe siècle," Revue française d'histoire d'outre-mer, 57, 4 (no. 209)(1970), pp. 421-46.

5006. *Novas Calvo, Pedro. "El negrero: Nantes durante la trata de esclavos," Revista de Occidente,

5007. *Pilade, Roland. "La colonisation de la Guadeloupe et la traite des nègres de 1492 à 1848" (Thèse de 3ème cycle, Paris VIII, 1973).

5008. Pluchon, Pierre. La route des esclaves: négriers et bois d'ébène au XVIIIe siècle. Paris: Hachette, 1980.

5009. Putney, Martha Settle. "The Slave Trade in French Diplomacy 1815-1865" (PhD diss., University of Pennsylvania, 1955).

5010. Raut, Etienne, and Léon Lallement. "Vannes autrefois: la traite des nègres," Bulletin de la société polymathique du Morbihan, 1er partie (1933), pp. 53-74.

5011. Rinchon, Dieudonné. Les armements négriers au XVIIIe siécle. Brussels: Académie royale de sciences d'outre-mer, 1956. (Mémoires, nouv. série, tôme 1)

5012. _____. Le trafic négrier, d'après les livres de commerce du capitaine gantois Pierre Ignace Liévin van Alstein. Brussels: Editions Atlas, 1938.

5013. Stein, Robert. The French Slave Trade in the Eighteenth Century: An Old Regime Business. Madison: University of Wisconsin Press, 1979.

5014. _____. "Measuring the French Slave Trade, 1713-1792/3," Journal of African History, 19, 4 (1978), pp. 515-21.

5015. _____. "Mortality in the Eighteenth Century French Slave Trade," Journal of African History, 21, 1 (1980), pp. 35-43.

5016. _____. "The Nantes Slave Traders, 1783-1815" (PhD diss., York University (Canada), 1975).

5017. _____. "The Profitability of the Nantes Slave Trade, 1783-1792," Journal of Economic History, 35, 4 (1975), pp. 779-93.

5018. Vidalenc, Jean. "La traite des nègres en France au début de la Révolution (1789-1793)," Annales historiques de la révolution française, 29 (1957), pp. 56-69.

5019. _____. "La traite négriére en France sous la Restauration (1814-1830)," in Actes du 9le Congrès National des Sociétés Savantes (Rennes, 1966) (Paris: Bibliothèque Nationale, 1969), vol. 1, pp. 197-229.

5020. Viles, Perry. "The Slaving Interest in the Atlantic Ports, 1763-1792," French Historical Studies, 7, 4 (1972), pp. 529-43.

8. Atlantic - English North American colonies, United States

5021. Alderman, Clifford Lindsey. Rum, Slaves and Molasses: The Story of New England's Triangular Trade. New York: Crowell-Collier Press, 1972.

5022. Anstey, Roger T. "The Volume of the North American Slave-Carrying Trade from Africa, 1761-1810," Revue française d'histoire d'outre-mer, 62, 1-2 (nos. 226-27)(1975), pp. 47-66.

5023. Bailey, Ronald William. "The Slave Trade and the Development of Capitalism in the United States: A Critical Reappraisal of Theory and Method in Afro-American Studies" (PhD diss., Stanford University, 1980).

5024. Berlin, Ira. "The Slave Trade and the Development of Afro-American Society in English Mainland North America, 1619-1775," Southern Studies, 20, 2 (1981), pp. 122-36.

5025. Brady, Patrick S. "The Slave Trade and Sectionalism in South Carolina, 1787-1808," Journal of Southern History, 38, 4 (1972), pp. 601-20.

5026. Corbitt, D. C. "Shipments of Slaves from the United States to Cuba, 1789-1807," Journal of Southern History, 7, 4 (1941), pp. 540-49.

5027. Coughtry, Jay Alan. "The Notorious Triangle: Rhode Island and the African Slave Trade, 1700-1807" (PhD diss., University of Wisconsin - Madison, 1978).

5028. _____. The Notorious Triangle: Rhode Island and the African Slave Trade, 1700-1807. Philadelphia: Temple University Press, 1981.

5029. Crane, Elaine F. "'The First Wheel of Commerce': Newport, Rhode Island and the Slave Trade, 1760-1776," Slavery and Abolition, 1, 2 (1980), pp. 178-98.

5030. Deutsch, Sarah. "The Elusive Guineamen: Newport Slavers, 1735-1774," New England Quarterly, 55, 2 (1982), pp. 229-53.

5031. Donnan, Elizabeth. "Agitation Against the Slave Trade in Rhode Island, 1784- 1790," in Persecution and Liberty: Essays in Honor of George Lincoln Burr (New York: The Century Co., 1931), pp. 473-82.

5032. _____. "The New England Slave Trade after the Revolution," New England Quarterly, 3, 2 (1930), pp. 251-78.

5033. _____. "The Slave Trade into South Carolina before the Revolution," American Historical Review, 33, 4 (1928), pp. 804-28.

5034. Duignan, Peter, and Clarence Clendenen. The United States and the African Slave Trade, 1619-1862. Stanford: Hoover Institution, 1963.

5035. Duram, James C. "A Study in Frustration: Britain, the USA and the African Slave Trade, 1815-1870," Social Science, 40, 4 (1965), pp. 220-25.

5036. Finley, H. R. "The American Slave Trade," Americana, 18, 3 (1924), pp. 252-57.

5037. Hamm, Tommy T. "The American Slave Trade with Africa, 1620-1807" (PhD diss., Indiana University, 1975).

5038. Harmon, Judd Scott. "Suppress and Protest: The United States Navy, the African Slave Trade, and Maritime Commerce, 1794-1862" (PhD diss., The College of William and Mary, 1977).

5039. Higgins, W. Robert. "Charles Town Merchants and Factors dealing in the External Negro Trade, 1735-1775," South Carolina Historical Magazine, 65, 4 (1964), pp. 205-17.

5040. High, James. "The African Gentleman, a Chapter in the Slave Trade," Journal of Negro History, 44, 4 (1959), pp. 185-307.

5041. Howard, Warren S. American Slavers and the Federal Law, 1837-1862. Berkeley: University of California Press, 1963.

5042. James, Sydney V. "Of Slaves and Rum (review-essay on Coughtry, Notorious Triangle)," Reviews in American History, 10, 2 (1982), pp. 168-72.

5043. Jennings, Judith. "The American Revolution and the Testimony of British Quakers against the Slave Trade," Quaker History, 70, 2 (1981), pp. 99-103.

5044. Jillson, Calvin, and Thornton Anderson. "Realignment in the Convention of 1787: The Slave Trade Compromise," Journal of Politics, 39 (1977), pp. 712-29.

5045. Jones, Alison. "The Rhode Island Slave Trade: A Trading Advantage in Africa," Slavery and Abolition, 2, 3 (1981), pp. 227-44.

5046. Judd, Jacob. "Frederick Philipse and the Madagascar Trade," New York Historical Society Quarterly Bulletin, 55, 4 (1971), pp. 354-74.

5047. Kiple, Kenneth F. "The Case Against a Nineteenth Century Cuba-Florida Slave Trade," Florida Historical Quarterly, 49, 4 (1971), pp. 346-55.

5048. Klein, Herbert S. "North American Competition and the Characteristics of the African Slave Trade to Cuba, 1790 to 1794," William and Mary Quarterly, 3rd ser., 38, 1 (1971), pp. 86-102.

5049. _____. "Slaves and Shipping in Eighteenth-Century Virginia," Journal of Interdisciplinary History, 5, 3 (1975), pp. 383-412.

5050. Lydon, James G. "New York and the Slave Trade, 1700 to 1774," William and Mary Quarterly, 3rd ser., 35, 2 (1978), pp. 375-94.

5051. McNeilly, Earl E. "The United States Navy and the Suppression of the West African Slave Trade, 1819-1862" (PhD diss., Case-Western Reserve University, 1973).

5052. Marable, Manning. "Death of the Quaker Slave Trade," Quaker History, 63, 1 (1974), pp. 17-33.

5053. Ramos, Demetrio. "Indios y negros de los territorios españoles del Caribe llevados como esclavos a Norteamérica en el siglo XVIII," Revista española de antropología americana, 6 (1971), pp. 329-79.

5054. Ray, John Michael. "Newport's Golden Age: A Study of the Newport Slave Trade," Negro History Bulletin, 25, 3 (1961), pp. 51-57.

5055. Riddell, William Renwick. "Encouragement of the Slave Trade," Journal of Negro History, 12, 1 (1927), pp. 22-32.

5056. _____. "Pre-Revolutionary Pennsylvania and the Slave Trade," Pennsylvania Magazine of History and Biography, 52, 1 (1928), pp. 1-28.

5057. Satz, Ronald. "The African Slave Trade and Lincoln's Campaign of 1858," Journal of the Illinois State Historical Society, 65, 3 (1972), pp. 269-79.

5058. Spears, John R. The American Slave Trade: An Account of its Origin, Growth, and Suppression. London: Beckers and Son, 1901. Reprinted Detroit: Negro History Press, 1969.

5059. Terry, Roderick. "Some Old Papers Relating to the Newport Slave Trade," Bulletin of the Newport Historical Society, no. 62 (1927), pp. 10-35.

5060. Walton, Gary M. "New Evidence on Colonial Commerce," Journal of Economic History, 28, 3 (1968), pp. 363-89.

5061. Wax, Darold D. "Africans on the Delaware: The Pennsylvania Slave Trade, 1759-1765," Pennsylvania History, 50, 1 (1983), pp. 38-49.

5062. _____. "Negro Imports into Pennsylvania 1720-1766," Pennsylvania History, 32, 3 (1965), pp. 254-87.

5063. _____. "The Negro Slave Trade in Colonial Pennsylvania" (PhD diss., University of Washington, 1962).

5064. _____. "Quaker Merchants and the Slave Trade in Colonial Pennsylvania," Pennsylvania Magazine of History and Biography, 86, 2 (1962), pp. 143-59.

5065. _____. "Thomas Rogers and the Rhode Island Slave Trade," American Neptune, 35, 4 (1975), pp. 289-301.

5066. Wayne, James M. "Georgia and the African Slave Trade: Charge to Grand Jury at Savannah," Georgia Historical Quarterly, 2, 2 (1918), pp. 87-113.

5067. Westbury, Susan Alice. "Colonial Virginia and the Atlantic Slave Trade" (PhD diss., University of Illinois at Urbana-Champaign, 1981).

5068. Whitridge, Arnold. "The American Slave-Trade," History Today, 8, 7 (1958), pp. 462-72.

5069. Wish, Harvey. "The Revival of the African Slave Trade in the United States, 1856-1860," Mississippi Valley Historical Review, 27, 4 (1941), pp. 569-88. Also Bobbs-Merrill Reprint no. 325.

9. Atlantic - other

5070. Ekman, Ernst. "Sweden, the Slave Trade and Slavery, 1784-1847," Revue française d'histoire d'outre-mer, 62, 1-2 (nos. 226-27)(1975), pp. 221-31.

5071. Elkjaer, Bendt. Slavernes vej: danskere som slavhandlere og slaveejere i 1700-tallet. Copenhagen: Gyldendal, 1977.

5072. Everaert, John G. "Commerce d'Afrique et traite négrière dans les Pays-Bas autrichiens," Revue française d'histoire d'outre-mer, 62, 1-2 (nos. 226-27)(1975), pp. 177-85.

5073. Green-Pedersen, Svend E. "Colonial Trade Under the Danish Flag: A Case Study of the Danish Slave Trade to Cuba, 1790-1807," Scandinavian Journal of History, 5, 2 (1980), pp. 93-120.

5074. _____. "Danmarks ophaevelse af. negerslavehandelen: Omkring tilblivelsen af forordningen af 16. marts 1792," Arkiv, 3, 1 (1969), pp. 19-37.

5075. _____. "The Economic Considerations Behind the Danish Abolition of the Negro Slave Trade," in Gemery and Hogendorn, eds., Uncommon Market, pp. 399-418.

5076. _____. "The History of the Danish Negro Slave Trade, 1733-1807: An Interim Survey Relating in Particular to its Volume, Structure, Profitability and Abolition," Revue française d'histoire d'outre-mer, 62, 1-2 (nos. 226-27)(1975), pp. 196-220.

5077. _____. "The Scope and Structure of the Danish Negro Slave Trade," Scandinavian Economic History Review, 19, 2 (1971), pp. 149-97.

5078. *_____. "Om forholdene pa danske slaveskibe med saerligt henblik pa dodeligheden, 1777-89," Handles- og sofartsmuseets arbog (Elsinore, 1973), pp. 27-76.

5079. _____. "Teologi og negerslaveri," in Festskrift til Pove Bagge (Copenhagen, 1972), pp. 71-87. Translated as "Negro Slavery and Christianity," Transactions of the Historical Society of Ghana, 15, 1 (1974), pp. 85-102.

5080. Hansen, Thorkild. Slavernes skibe: Tegninger af Birte Lund. Copenhagen: Gyldendal: Gyldendal, 1968.

5081. Johansen, Hans Christian. "The Reality Behind the Demographic Arguments to Abolish the Danish Slave Trade," in Walvin and Eltis, eds., Abolition of the Atlantic Slave Trade, pp. 221-30.

5082. Knap, Henning Jojlund. "Negerslavedebatten i Danmark til 1807 belyst gennem de i tidsskriftartikler of boger udtrykte holdninger" (MA thesis, University of Aarhus, 1975).

5083. Koch, Rainer. "Liberalismus, Konservativismus und das Problem der Negersklaverei: Ein Beitrag zur Geschichte des politischen Denkens in Deutschland in der ersten Hälfte des 19. Jahrhunderts," Historische Zeitschrift, 222, 3 (1976), pp. 529-77.

5084. Lofton, Joseph Evans, Jr. "The Abolition of the Danish Atlantic Slave Trade" (PhD diss., Louisiana State University and Agricultural and Mechanical College, 1977).

5085. Rinchon, Dieudonné. "Les négriers belges au XVIIIe siècle," Revue de l'Academia unio catholicas adjuvans missiones, 9, 1 (1934), pp. 15-20.

5086. Waaben, Knud. "A. S. Orsted og negerslaverne i Kobenhavn," Juristen, 46 (1964), pp. 321-43.

10. Indian Ocean

5087. Alpers, Edward A. The East African Slave Trade. Nairobi: East African Publishing House, 1967.

5088. _____. "The French Slave Trade in East Africa (1721-1810)," Cahiers d'études africaines, 10, 1 (no. 37)(1970), pp. 80-124.

5089. _____. "The Impact of the Slave Trade on East Central Africa in the Nineteenth Century," in Inikori, ed., Forced Migration, pp. 242-73. Reprinted from Alpers, Ivory and Slaves . . . in East Central Africa (London, 1975).

5090. _____. Ivory and Slaves: Changing Pattern of International Trade in East Central Africa to the Later Nineteenth Century. Berkeley: University of California Press, 1975.

5091. *Armstrong, J. C. "Madagascar and the Slave Trade in the Seventeenth Century" (Paper delivered at a colloquium on "L'histoire et la civilisation du nord-ouest Malgache," Mahajanga, April 1981).

5092. Beachey, R. W. A Collection of Documents on the Slave Trade of Eastern Africa. New York: Barnes and Noble, 1976.

5093. _____. The Slave Trade of Eastern Africa. New York: Barnes and Noble, 1976.

5094. _____. "Some Observations on the Volume of the Slave Trade of Eastern Africa in the Nineteenth Century," in African Historical Demography (Centre of African Studies, University of Edinburgh)(Edinburgh, 1978), pp. 365-72.

5095. Campbell, Gwyn. "Madagascar and the Slave Trade, 1810-1895," Journal of African History, 22, 2 (1981), pp. 203-27.

5096. Carreira, António. O tráfico português de escravos na costa
oriental africana nos começos do século XIX (estudo de um caso).
Lisbon: Junta de Investigações do Ultramar, 1979. (Centro de
Estudos de Antropologia Cultural, Estudos de Antropologia
Cultural, no. 12)

5097. Collister, Peter. The Last Days of Slavery: England and the East
African Slave Trade 1870-1900. Dar-es-Salaam: East African
Literature Bureau, 1961.

5098. Filliot, Jean-Michel. "La traite africaine vers les Mascareignes,"
in Mouvements de populations dans l'Océan Indien (Actes du 4e
Congrès de l'Association Historique Internationale de l'Océan
Indien et du 14e Colloque de la Commission Internationale
d'Histoire Maritime) (Saint-Denis-de-la-Réunion, 4-9 September
1972) (Paris: Champion, 1979), pp. 235-44.

5099. _____. La traite des esclaves vers les Mascareignes
au XVIIIe siècle. Paris: ORSTOM, 1974.

5100. Gerbeau, Hubert. "Quelques aspects de la traite illégale des
esclaves à l'Ile Bourbon au XIXe siècle," in Mouvements de
populations dan l'Océan Indien (Actes du 4e Congrès de
l'Association Historique Internationale de l'Océan Indien et du
14e Commission Internationale d'Histoire Maritime) (Saint-Denis
de la Réunion, 4-9 August 1972) (Paris: Champion, 1979), pp.
273-308.

5101. _____. "The Slave Trade in the Indian Ocean: Problems
Facing the Historian and Research to be Undertaken," in UNESCO,
African Slave Trade, pp. 184-207.

5102. Kelly, John B. "The Arab Slave Trade, 1800-1842," in Britain and
the Persian Gulf, 1795-1880 (London: Oxford University Press,
1968), pp. 411-51.

5103. _____. "The Attack on the Slave Trade, 1842-1873," in
Britain and the Persian Gulf, 1795-1880 (London: Oxford University
Press, 1968), pp. 576-637.

5104. Martin, Esmond B., and T. C. I. Ryan. "A Quantitative Assessment
of the Arab Slave Trade of East Africa, 1770-1896," Kenya
Historical Review, 5, 1 (1977), pp. 71-91.

5105. _____. "The Slave Trade of the
Bajun and Benadir Coasts," Transafrican Journal of History, 9, 1-2
(1980), pp. 103-32.

5106. Newitt, M. D. D. "Angoche, the Slave Trade and the Portuguese c.
1844-1910," Journal of African History, 13, 4 (1972), pp. 659-72.

5107. Ogot, Bethwell A. "Population Movements Between East Africa, the
Horn of Africa and the Neighbouring Countries," in UNESCO, African
Slave Trade, pp. 175-82.

5108. Platt, Virginia. "The East India Company and the Madagascar Slave Trade," William and Mary Quarterly, 3rd ser., 26, 4 (1969), pp. 548-77.

5109. Sakarai, Lawrence J. "Indian Merchants in East Africa, Part I: The Triangular Trade and the Slave Economy," Slavery and Abolition, 1, 3 (1980), pp. 292-338.

5110. * _____. "Indian Merchants in East Africa," in Willis, ed., Servile Estate, forthcoming.

5111. Saldana, Jerome A., ed. Précis on Slave Trade in the Gulf of Oman and the Persian Gulf - 1873-1905, with a Retrospect into Previous History from 1882. Calcutta, 1906. (Part 5 of Persian Gulf Gazeteer)

5112. Sheperd, Gill. "The Comorians and the East African Slave Trade," in Watson, ed., Asian and African Systems of Slavery, pp. 73-99.

5113. Valette, J. "Considérations sur les exportations d'esclaves malgaches vers les Mascareignes au XVIIIe siècle," in Michel Mollat, ed., Sociétés et compagnies de commerce en Orient et dans l'Océan indien (Actes du Huitième Colloque international d'histoire maritime) (Beirut, 1966) (Paris: S.E.V.P.E.N., 1970), pp. 531-40.

5114. Verguin, J. "La politique de la Compagnie des Indes dans la traite des noirs à l'Ile Bourbon (1662-1762)," Revue historique, 216 (1956), pp. 45-58.

5115. Wolff, Richard D. "British Imperialism and the East African Slave Trade," Science and Society, 36, 4 (1972), pp. 443-62.

5116. Zimmermann, Matilde. "The French Slave Trade at Moçambique, 1770-1784" (MA thesis, University of Wisconsin - Madison, 1967).

11. Trans-Saharan and Red Sea

5117. *Abir, Mordechai. "The Ethiopian Slave Trade and its Relation to the Islamic World," in Willis, ed., Servile Estate, forthcoming.

5118. Adamu, Mahdi. "The Delivery of Slaves from the Central Sudan to the Bight of Benin in the Eighteenth and Nineteenth Centuries," in Gemery and Hogendorn, eds., Uncommon Market, pp. 163-80.

5119. Austen, Ralph A. "The Islamic Red Sea Slave Trade: An Effort at Quantification," Proceedings of the Fifth International Conference on Ethiopian Studies (Chicago, 1979), pp. 443-67.

5120. * _____. "The Islamic Slave Trade out of Africa (Red Sea and Indian Ocean): An Effort at Quantification," in Willis, ed., Servile Estate, forthcoming.

5121. _____. "The Trans-Saharan Slave Trade: A Tentative Census," in Gemery and Hogendorn, eds., Uncommon Market, pp. 23-76.

5122. Ayalon, David. "The European-Asiatic Steppe: A Major Reservoir of Power for the Islamic World," in Trud, XXV, Mezkunarod Kong. Vostokovedov (Moscow, 1960), vol. 2, pp. 47-52. (Proceedings of the 25th International Congress of Orientalists, Moscow, 1963)

5123. Azevedo, Mario J. "Precolonial Sara Society in Chad and the Threat of Extinction Due to the Arab and Muslim Slave Trade 1870-1917," Journal of African Studies, 7, 2 (1980), pp. 99-108.

5124. Bedis, Yunes. "Tales of the Wadai Slave Trade in the Nineties," Sudan Notes and Records, 23, 1 (1940), pp. 169-83. As told to W. E. Jennings Bramley.

5125. Kake, I. B. "The Slave Trade and the Population Drain from Black Africa to North Africa and the Middle East," in UNESCO, African Slave Trade, pp. 164-74.

5126. Labib, S. "Islamic Expansion and Slave Trade in Medieval Africa," in Mouvements de populations dans l'Océan Indien (Actes du 4e Congrès de l'Association Historique Internationale de l'Océan Indien et du 14e Commission Internationale d'Histoire Maritime) (Saint-Denis de la Réunion, 4-9 August 1972) (Paris: Champion, 1979), p. 33.

5127. Lewicki, Tadeusz. "Arab Trade in Negro Slaves up to the End of the XVIth Century," Africana Bulletin, 6 (1967), pp. 109-11. (Summary of unpublished paper by Alicja Melecka)

5128. Martin, B. G. "Ahmad Rasim Pasha and the Suppression of the Fazzan Slave Trade, 1881-1896," Africa (Rome), 38, 4 (1983), pp. 545-79.

5129. *Mire, Lawrence. "Al-Zubayr Pasha and the Zariba-based Slave Trade in the Bahr al-Ghazal," in Willis, ed., Servile Estate, forthcoming.

5130. Ochsenwald, William. "Muslim-European Conflict in the Hijaz: The Slave Trade Controversy, 1840-1895," Middle Eastern Studies, 16, 1 (1980), pp. 114-26.

5131. O'Fahey, R. S. "Slavery and the Slave Trade in Dar Fur," Journal of African History, 14, 1 (1973), pp. 29-43.

5132. Pankhurst, Richard. "The Ethiopian Slave Trade in the Nineteenth and Early Twentieth Centuries: A Statistical Inquiry," Journal of Semitic Studies, 9, 1 (1964), pp. 220-28.

5133. Renault, François. "La traite des esclaves noirs en Libye au XVIIIe siècle," Journal of African History, 23, 2 (1982), pp. 163-81.

5134. Stack, (Sir) Lee. "Slave Trade Between the Sudan and Arabia," Journal of the Central Asian Society, 8, 3 (1921), pp. 163-64.

5135. Tambo, David C. "The Sokoto Caliphate Slave Trade in the
Nineteenth Century" (MA thesis, University of Wisconsin - Madison,
1974).

5136. _____. "The Sokoto Caliphate Slave Trade in the
Nineteenth Century," International Journal of African Historical
Studies, 9, 2 (1976), pp. 187-217.

5137. Toledano, Ehud Rafael. The Ottoman Slave Trade and Its
Suppression, 1840-1890. Princeton: Princeton University Press,
1982.

12. Medieval

5138. Aymard, Maurice. "De la traite aux chiourmes: la fin de
l'esclavage dans la Sicile moderne," Bulletin de l'Institut
historique belge de Rome, 44 (1974), pp. 1-22. Republished in
Miscellanea offerts à Charles Verlinden (Ghent, 1975), pp. 1-22.

5139. Bromberg, Erik I. "Wales and the Mediaeval Slave Trade," Speculum,
17, 2 (1942), pp. 263-69.

5140. Delort, R. "Quelques précisions sur le commerce des esclaves à
Gênes vers la fin du XIVe siècle," Mélanges d'archéologie et
d'histoire (Ecole française de Rome), 78, 1 (1966), pp. 215-50.

5141. Ehrenkreutz, Andrew. "Strategic Implications of the Slave Trade
Between Genoa and Mamluk Egypt in the Second Half of the
Thirteenth Century," in A. L. Udovitch, ed., The Islamic Middle
East, 700-1900: Studies in Economic and Social History (Princeton:
Darwin Press, 1981), pp. 335-45.

5142. Fastidio, Don. "Commercio di schiavi a Napoli," Napoli
nobilissima, 15, 5 (1906), p. 79.

5143. Fisher, Alan W. "Muscovy and the Black Sea Slave Trade,"
Canadian-American Slavic Studies, 6, 4 (1972), pp. 575-94.

5144. Hansen, Thorkild. Slavernes kyst. Tegninger af Birte Lund.
Copenhagen: Gyldendal, 1967.

5145. _____. Slavernes oer. Tegninger af Birte Lund.
Copenhagen: Glydendal, 1970.

5146. Hoffmann, Johannes. "Die östliche Adriaküste als
Hauptnachschubbasis für den venezianischen Sklavenhandel bis zum
Ausgang des elften Jahrhunderts," Vierteljahrschrift für Sozial-
und Wirtschaftsgeschichte, 55, 2 (1968), pp. 165-81.

5147. Manca, C. "Problemi aperti sul commercio e sul riscatto degli
schiavi cristiani nel Mediterraneo dopo Lepanto," Africa (Rome),
29, 4 (1974), pp. 549-72.

5148. Mathiex, J. "Trafic et prix de l'homme en Méditerranée aux XVIIe et XVIIIe siècles," Annales: économies, sociétés, civilisations, 9, 2 (1954), pp. 157-64.

5149. Sakasov, Iv. "Documents récemment découverts datant de la fin du XIVe siècle, et concernant les Bulgares de la Macédoine vendus comme esclaves," Makedonski pregled, 7, 2-3 (1932), pp. 1-62. (In Russian with French summary, pp. 235-39)

5150. Schneider, Karl. "Der Sklavenhandel im mittelalterichen Italien," Zeitschrift für Sozialwissenschaft, 10 (1907), pp. 235-41.

5151. Seeley, Frank F. "Russia and the Slave Trade," Slavonic and East European Review, 23 (no. 62)(1945), pp. 126-36.

5152. Smythe, Alfred P. "Scandinavian Dublin and the Slave Trade with Islam," in idem, Scandinavian Kings in the British Isles, 850-880 (New York: Oxford University Press, 1977), pp. 154-68.

5153. Verlinden, Charles. "La colonie vénitienne de Tana, centre de la traite des esclaves au XIVe et au début du XVe siècle," in Studi in onore di Gino Luzzatto (Milan: A. Giuffrè, 1950), vol. 2, pp. 1-25.

5154. _____. "Le Crète, débouché et plaque tournante de la traite des esclaves au XIVe et XVe siècles," in Studi in onore di Amintore Fanfani (Milan: A. Giuffrè, 1962), vol. 3, pp. 593-669.

5155. _____. "Encore sur les origines de sclavus = esclave et à propos de la chronologie des débuts de la traite italienne en Mer Noire," in Cultus et cognitio: Studia z dziejow sredniowiecznej Kultury (Festschrift A. Gieysztor) (Warsaw, 1976), pp. 599-609.

5156. _____. "Medieval 'Slavers'," Explorations in Economic History, 7 (1969-70), pp. 1-14. Republished in David Herlihy, et al., eds., Economy, Society, and Government in Medieval Italy (Kent, Ohio: Kent State University Press, 1969), pp. 1-14.

5157. _____. "Le recrutement des esclaves à Gênes du milieu du XIIe siècle jusque vers 1275," in Fatti e idee di storia economica nei secoli XII XX: Studi dedicati a Franco Borlandi (Bologne: Il Mulino, 1976), pp. 37-57.

5158. _____. "Le recrutement des esclaves à Venise aux XIVe et XVe siècles," Bulletin de l'Institut historique belge de Rome, 39 (1968), pp. 83-202.

5159. _____. "Le relazioni economiche fra le due sponde adriatiche nel basso medioevo alla luce della tratta delgi schiavi," Recenti e antichi rapporti fra le due sponde dell'Adriatico (Brindisi, 1972), pp. 23-55.

5160. _____. "Une taxation d'esclaves à Majorque en 1428 et la traite italienne," Bulletin de l'Institut historique belge de Rome, 42 (1972), pp. 141-87.

5161. _____. "Traite des esclaves et cols alpins au haut moyen âge," in Erzeugung, Verkehr und Handel in der Geschichte der Älpenlander: Herbert-Hassinger-Festschrift (Innsbruck: Univ. Verlag Wagner, 1977), pp. 377-89.

5162. _____. "Traite des esclaves et traitants italiens à Constantinople (XIIIe-XVe siècles)," Le Moyen âge, 69 (1963), pp. 791-804.

5163. _____. "La traite des esclaves: un grand commerce international au Xe siècle," in Etudes de civilisation médiévale, IXe-XIIe siècles: mélanges offerts à Edmonde-René Labande à l'occasion de son départ à la retraite (Poitiers: C.E.S.C.M., 1974), pp. 721-30.

5164. * _____. "Verdun, centre de la traite des esclaves slaves aux IXe et Xe siècles".

5165. _____. Wo, wann und warum gab es einen Grosshandel mit Sklaven während des Mittelalters?. Köln, 1970. (Kölner Vorträge zur Sozial- und Wirtschaftsgeschichte, Heft 11)

13. Ancient

5166. Biezunska Malowist, Iza. "La traite d'esclaves en Egypte," Proceedings of the XIV International Congress of Papyrologists (London, 1975), pp. 11-18.

5167. Boese, Wayne Edward. "A Study of the Slave Trade and the Sources of Slaves in the Roman Republic and the Early Roman Empire" (PhD diss., University of Washington, 1973).

5168. Finley, Moses I. "The Black Sea and Danubian Regions and the Slave Trade in Antiquity," Klio, 40 (1962), pp. 51-59. Summarized in Resumés des communications du XIe Congrès international des sciences historiques (Stockholm, 1960)(Uppsala, 1960).

5169. _____. "The Slave Trade in Antiquity: The Danube and Black Sea Regions," in idem, Economy and Society in Ancient Greece, pp. 167-75.

5170. Harris, William V. "Towards A Study of the Roman Slave Trade," in J. H. D'Arms and E. C. Kopff, eds., The Seaborne Commerce of Ancient Rome: Studies in Archaeology and History (Rome: American Academy in Rome, 1980), pp. 117-40. (Memoirs of the American Academy in Rome, 36)

5171. Musti, Domenico. "Il commercio degli schiavi e del grano: il caso di Puteoli: sui rapporti tra l'economia italiana della tarda repubblica e le economie ellenistiche," in J. H. D'Arms and E. C. Kopff, eds., The Seaborne Commerce of Ancient Rome: Studies in Archaeology and History (Rome: American Academy in Rome, 1980), pp. 197-215. (Memoirs of the American Academy in Rome, 36)

14. Other

5172. Arensmeyer, Elliott C. "The Chinese Coolie Labor Trade and the Philippines: An Inquiry," Philippine Studies, 28, 2 (1980), pp. 187-98.

5173. Bailey, Lynn Robison. Indian Slave Trade in the Southwest: A Study of Slavetaking and the Traffic of Indian Captives. Los Angeles: Westernlore Press, 1966.

5174. Lacroix, Louis. Les derniers négriers: derniers voyages de bois d'ébène, de coolies et de merles du Pacifique. Paris: Amiot-Dumont, 1952.

5175. Maude, H. E. Slavers in Paradise: The Peruvian Slave Trade in Polynesia, 1862-1864. Palo Alto: Stanford University Press, 1982.

5176. O'Callaghan, Sean. Yellow Slave Trade: A Survey of the Traffic in Women and Children in the East. London: Blond, 1968.

5177. Phayre, Ignatius. "The Slave Trade Today," English Review, 60 (1935), pp. 55-65.

INDEXES

Author Index

Abanime, Emeka, 4446
Abbas, Mohammed Galal, 1
Abbenhuis, fr. M. F., 2796
Abd al-Wahid, Ali, 2
Abd-ar-Raziq, Ahmed, 3263
Abdul Jabbar Beg, Muhammad, 3229
Abénon, Lucien René, 4949
Abir, Mordechai, 5117
Abraham, Arthur, 2859
Abrahams, Roger D., 2349
Abramova, Svetlana IUrrevna, 4447-49
Abranches, Dunshee de, 1977
Abud, Katia, (2316)
Acosta Saignes, Miguel, 1685, 1760-61, 1888-90, 4783
Adams, Jane E., 4699
Adamu, Mahdi, 2861, 5118
Addington, Wendell G., 1580
Adefila, Johnson Ajibade, 1318
Adelaide, Jacques, 2653-54
Affolter, Friedrich Xaver, 3724
Afigbo, A. E., 2862
Africa, Philip, 1319
Agiri, Babatunde, 2864
Agnel, Arnaud d', 4139
Agonito, Joseph, 1125
Agrawala, Ratna Chandra, 4370
Aguessy, Honorat, 2865
Aguet, Isabelle, 4450-51
Aguilar Bulgarelli, Oscar R., 1812
Aguilo, E., 4222
Aguirre Beltrán, Gonzalo, 1762-68, 4784-85
Ahmad, Shafiq, 3188
Aimes, Hubert H. S., 1686, 2522
Aitken, Hugh G. J., ed. 442

Aizy, Christian, 2523
Ajayi, J. F. Ade, 2866, 4452
Akinjogbin, I. A., 4625
Akinola, G. A., 3332
Akiwowo, Akinsola, 3
al-Abbadi, Ahmad Mukhtar 'Abd al
    Fattach, 4223
Alagoa, E. J., (2866)
Albanese, Anthony, 1320-21
Albanese, B., 3725
Alberro, Solange B. de, 1687-88, 1769
Albert, Peter Joseph, 1126
Albertario, Emilio, 3726-27
Albright, W. F., 4090
Alcalá y Henke, Agustín, 1689
Alcina Franch, José, 1913
Alden, John, 2319
Alderman, Clifford Lindsey, 5021
Aldrich, Orlando, 1613
Alegría, Ricardo E., 2524-25
Alencastro, Luiz-Felipe de, 4700-02
Alexander, Herbert B., 4
Alexandre, Mireille, 2320
Alfieri, T., 3559
Alföldy, Geza, 3728-29
Alford, Terry, 1642
Alho, Olli, 5, 1322
Ali, Abbas Ibrahim Muhammad, 3299
Alilunas, Leo, 1614
Allain, Mathé, 1542
Allen, Cuthbert Edward, 443
Allen, Jeffrey Brooke, 1323
Allen, Theodore W., 6-7
Allison, Rebecca P., 1324
Almeida, Pedro Ramos de, 2867

Brown, Larissa V., (279)
Brown, Richard D., ed. 486
Brown, Soi-Daniel W., 2849
Brown, Steven E., 43
Browning, James, 1698
Bruce, Dickson D., Jr., 487
Bruce, Kathleen, 1146-47
Brugi, Biago, 3773
Bruni, Gian Bruno, 3576
Brunschvig, R., 3193
Brunt, P. A., 3774
Bryce-Laporte, Roy Simon, 488-89, 1337
Buckland, William W., 3775
Buckley, Roger Norman, 2361-62, 4958
Buehler, Richard D., 1148
Buenaventura de Carrocera, Fr, 4922
Buescu, Mircea, 1999-2003
Buffet, H. E., 4959
Buhler, Richard O., 2363
Buisseret, David J., 2364
Bulkley, Robert D., Jr., 1646
Bullock, Henry Allen, 490
Burian, J., 3577
Burnham, Dorothy, 491
Burnham, Philip, 3312
Burrows, Edward F., 1338
Burton-Page, J., 3194
Burtt, Joseph, 44
Bush, Barbara, 2365
Busson, Jean-Pierre, 4636
Buti, Ignazio, 3776
Butler, Alfloyd, 1257
Butlin, Noel G., 1339
Büttner, Thea, 3313
Büttner, Theodore, 4143
Butts, Donald Cleveland, 1340-41
Buve, R., 4327
Buxton, Travers, 2902
Byrne, William Andrew, 1258

Cabanes, Pierre, 3578
Cabat, Geoffrey A., 4709
Cable, Mary, 4637
Cabrera, Christian, 2663
Cabrillana, N., 4226
Cadbury, William A., 2903-04
Cade, John B., 492
Cahen, Claude, 3251
Cairns, Margaret, 2905
Caldas Britto, Eduardo A., 2179
Calderhead, William, 1499, 1647
Calderini, Aristide, 3579, 4113
Caldwell, John C., 2906

Calhoun, Daniel, 493
Calligaro, Lee, 1063
Calmon, Pedro, 2004
Calonge, Alfredo, 3777
Camargo, Jovelino M. de, Jr., 4710
Camos Cabruja, L., 4227
Campbell, Gwyn, 2907, 5095
Campbell, Mavis C., 45, 2366-68, 3580
Campbell, Penelope, 494
Campbell, Randolph B., (ed. 1408), 1584-87, (1595)
Camus, Pierre, 3581
Canabrava, A. P., 2269
Canarella, Giorgio, 46
Candler, Mark Allen, 1259
Canfora, Luciano, 3582
Cantú Corro, José, 1777
Cantos, Angel López, 2532
Capela, José, 4711-12
Caplan, Lionel, 4356
Capogrossi, Luigi, 3778
Capozza, Maria, 3779-80
Capozza, Maria, et al., 3374
Cappelle, H. van, 2798
Carandini, Andrea, 3781
Carcaterra, Antonio, 3782-83
Cardell, Nicholas Scott, 495
Cardoso, Ciro Flamarion S., 47-49, 2322-23, 2664
Cardoso, Fernando Henrique, 2270
Cardoso, Geraldo da Silva, 50-51
Cardoso, Jayme Antônio, 2271
Cardoso, José Fábio Barreto P., 2180
Cardoso, Onelio Jorge, 2533
Cardozo, Manoel, 2005
Carlsson, Robert J., (212), (1398)
Carneiro, Edison, 2006, 2181
Caro Costas, Cirda R., 2534
Carpentier, Alejo, 2535
Carper, N. Gordon, 496
Carrancá y Trujillo, Raúl, 1699
Carreira, António, 2908, 4713-17, (4749), 5096
Carrera Damas, Germán, 1700
Carreras y Candi, Francesch, 4228
Carriazo, Juan de Mata, 4229
Carrière-Hergavault, Marie-Paule, 3583
Carroll, Joseph C., 497
Carroll, Kenneth L., 1149-50
Carroll, Patrick J., 1778
Carroll, William Edward, 2369
Carstensen, Fred V., 498
Carter, Ralph D., 499

- 395 -

Coles, Harry L., Jr., 1588
Collins, Bruce, 509
Collins, Winfield H., 1345
Collister, Peter, 4639, 5097
Colom, Francisco Sevillano, 4230
Colp, Ralph, Jr., 511
Comas, Juan, 1704
Comitas, Lambros, ed. 2375
Congresso Afro-brasileiro do
    Recife, (1934), 2018
Conneau, Théophile, 4640
Conrad, Alfred H., (571), 1346-47
Conrad, David C., 2918
Conrad, Robert, 2019-23, 4719-20
Conti, Luigi, 4468
Conway, Alan, 512
Cook, Charles Orson, ed. 1545
Cook, Fred J., 4469
Cookey, S. J. S., 2919
Coolen, Georges, 4962
Cooney, Jerry W., 1970
Cooper, 3336
Cooper, Frederick, 2920, (3034),
    3337-40
Cooper, Guy E., 4470
Cooper, William J., 513
Cope, Robert S., 1154-55
Corbitt, Duvon C., 61, 5026
Cordell, Dennis Dale, 2921
Corlew, Robert E., 1503
Cornelius, Janet Duitsman, 1348-49
Cornevin, Robert, 2668, (4464),
    4471
Corrigan, Philip, 62
Corruccini, Robert S., (2424)
Cortés Alonso, Vicenta, 63, 1705,
    2539, 4231-34, 4791
Corvisier, André, 4280
Corwin, Arthur F., 2538
Corwin, Charles E., 2799
Cosculluela, Juan Antonio, 2540
Cosentini, Cristoforo, 3804
Costa, Emília Viotti da, (12),
    64, 2024-26
Costa, Iraci del Nero da, (2084),
    2234, (2250-52)
Cottrol, Robert J., 514-15, 1065
Couceiro, Solange Martins, 2027
Coughtry, Jay Alan, 5027-28
Coulter, E. Merton, 1350
Cousins, Winifred M., 2376
Coutinho, Ruy, 2028
Cowdrey, Albert E., 516
Cowley, Malcolm, (4567)
Cox, Edward Locksley, 2377-78
Coyner, Martin Boyd, Jr., 1351

Craddock, Emmie, 65
Crahan, Margaret E., (232)
Crane, Elaine F., 5029
Crane, Verner W., 517, ed. 4641
Craton, Michael M., 66, ed.
    67-68, 2379-92
Craven, Wesley Frank, 1156
Crawford, Stephen Cooban, 518
Creel, Margaret Washington,
    1352-53
Creer, Leland Hargrave, 4792
Crespo R., Alberto, 1925
Cresto, Kathleen M., 1354-55
Cretia, P., 3584
Crew, Spencer, 1066
Croiset, Alfred, 3380
Crone, Patricia, 3233
Crouchett, Lawrence, 2669
Crow, Jeffrey J., 1267
Crowe, Charles, 519-21
Cruikshank, R. Bruce, 4357
Crum, Richard Henry, 3805
Cruz, C. Coelho da, 4721
Cruz, Pedro Tobar, 1814
Cuchi-Coll, Isabel, 2541
Cuffel, Victoria, 3585
Cunha, Ciro Vieira da, 2029
Cunliffe, Marcus, 69
Curet, José, 2542
Curlee, Abigail, 1589-90
Curran, R. Emmet, 1157
Currier, James T., 1356
Curtin, Philip D., 70-74, 4472,
    4473-79, 4481-82, ed. 4480
Curtis, James C., ed. 522
Cushner, Nicholas P., 1917
Cuthbertson, G. C., 2922
Czyka, Lucette, 4963

D'Auvergne, Edmond B., 76
Daaku, K. Y., 4483
Dabney, Virginius, 1158
Dabyeen, David, 4295
Daeleman, Jan, 75
Daget, Serge, 2923, 4484,
    4642-44, 4964-73, ed. 4974,
    (5001)
Daglione, Vivaldo W. F., 2030
Dalby, Andrew, 4114
Dalton, Margarita, 2543
Dandamayev, M. A., 3507
Dang Trinh Ky, 4358
Dange, Shripad A., 4376
Daniel, Pete, 523
Daniel, W. Harrison, 524, 1159
Daniels, Winthrop More, 525

Izard, Michel, 3000

Jabbour, Micheline, 2735
Jackson, Bruce, ed. 708
Jackson, Harvey H., 1389
Jackson, James Conroy, 1390
Jackson, Luther P., 1184, 4874
Jackson, Shirley M., 1391, 4547
Jacob, K., (4918)
Jacob, Oscar, 3632-33
Jacobs, Donald M., 709
Jacobs, Michelle, (3190)
Jacota, Mihai, 3881
Jaffa, Harry V., 710
Jahn, Karl, 3258
Jähne, Armin, 3634
James, C. L. R., 209, 2736-38
James, Sydney V., 5042
Jameson, Michael H., 3635
Janssen, Jac. J., 4119
January, Alan F., 1392
Jany, Laura Beatriz, (1939)
Jara, Alvaro, 1930-31
Jaramillo Uribe, Jaime, 1845, 1867
Jaschok, Maria, 4337
Jeanselme, Edouard, 3882
Jeffreys, M. D. W., 3001, 4548
Jenkins, H. J. K., 2739
Jenkins, William Sumner, 711
Jennings, Judith, 5043
Jennings, Lawrence Charles, 3002,
    4987-90
Jennings, Stephen, 1185
Jensen, Richard A., (4466-67)
Jentz, John, 712
Jernegan, Marcus W., 713-14
Jerovsek, A., 3415
Jervey, Edward D., 1393
Jervey, Theodore Dehon, 4549
Jesse, Rev. Charles, 2441, 2740
Jewsiewicki, Bogumil, 3003
Jillson, Calvin, 5044
Jirku, Anton, 3517
Johansen, Hans Christian, 2853,
    5081
Johnson, Frank Roy, 1186
Johnson, Harold B., 4247
Johnson, Harry G., 210
Johnson, James Hugo, 1187
Johnson, Kenneth R., 1394
Johnson, Lyman L., 1944-46
Johnson, Marion, (2987), 3004
Johnson, Michael P., 715, 1395-96
Johnson, Vera M., 4875
Johnson, Whittington B., 1188,
    1397

Johnston, Harry H., 211
Johnston, James H., 716-17
Joly, Robert, 3636
Jones, A. H. M., 3416
Jones, Adam, 4661
Jones, Alison, 5045
Jones, Archer, 212, 1398
Jones, Bobby Frank, 1399
Jones, Everett L., (1591)
Jones, Howard, 1400
Jones, Norrece Thomas, 1401
Jones, Rhett S., 213
Jones, Robert R., (548)
Jong, Gerald Francis de, 2817
Jonkers, E. J., 3883-84
Jordan, Weymouth T., 718
Jordan, Winthrop D., 214-15,
    719-21, 1082
Joseph, L. C., 2741
Joubert, D. C., 3005
Joukovsky, F., 3417
Journal of Social History, 216
Joyner, Charles W., 722, 1402-03
Judd, Jacob, 5046
Jurema, Aderbal, 2075
Jusifov, Jusif B., 3518

Kaberry, P. M., (4464)
Kac, A. L., 3885
Kahane, Henry, 3418
Kahane, Renée, (3418)
Kahn, Morton Charles, 2818
Kajanto, Iiro, 3886
Kake, I. B., 4550, 5125
Kalex, H., 4120
Kamen, Henry, 1714
Kamienik, Roman, 3887-89
Kaplan, Sidney, ed. 4662
Kapsoli E., Wilfredo, 1922
Kapteijns, Lidwien, 3301
Karasch, Mary C., (286), (373),
    2239-42, 4727
Karcher, Carolyn L., 723
Kaser, Max, 3419, 3890-92
Kates, Don B., Jr., 724
Katz, Friedrich, 1784
Katz, Jonathan, 1083
Katz, Wallace, 2339
Katz, William Loren, 4415
Kaufman, Martin, 725
Kautsky, Karl, 217
Kay, F. George, 4551
Kay, Marvin L. Michael, 1284
Kaysel, Paul, 4552
Kehnscherper, Gerhard, 3420
Keim, Curtis A., 3006

McGettigan, James William, Jr., 1525
McGinty, Brian, 762
McGowan, James T., 1554-55
Machado (Filho), Aires da Mata, 2087, 2253
MacInnes, Charles M., 261, 4565, 4885
Mackenzie-Grieve, Averil, 4665, 4886
McKenzie, Edna Chappell, 763
McKinlay, A. P., 3658
McKitrick, Eric, 262
McKivigan, John R., 764-65
MacLachlan, Colin M., 2171-72
Maclear, J. F., 766
MacLeod, Duncan J., 767-69
MacLeod, William C., 4420-21
McLendon, R. Earl, 4666
McLoughlin, Peter F. M., 3302
McLoughlin, William G., 4422-24
McManus, Edgar J., 770, 1087-88
MacMunn, George, 263
McNeilly, Earl E., 5051
McSheffrey, G. M., 3044
Mactoux, Marie Madeleine, 264, (3629), 3659-60, (4031)
McWhiney, Grady, (760)
Maddex, Jack P., Jr., 1414
Madurell Marimon, José M., 4252-53
Maestri Filho, Mário José, 2294-96
Magnaghi, Russell M., 1526, 4425
Mahajani, Usha, 4392
Maianga, José, 3045
Malagon Barcelo, Javier, 2595, 4254
Malausséna, Paul-Louis, 4288
Malerbi, Eneida Maria, (2268)
Malowist, Marian, (33), 265, 3046
Maluquer de Motes Bernet, Jordi, 2596-97
Manaricua y Nuere, Andrés E. de, 3928
Manca, C., 5147
Mandle, Jay R., 266
Manganaro, Giacomo, 3929
Mangas Manjarrés, Julio, 3930
Manigat, Leslie F., 2753-54
Manni-Piraino, M.-T., 3931
Manning, Patrick, (2906), 3047-52, 4566
Mannix, Daniel P., 4567
Mans Puigarnau, Jaime M., 4255
Mantello, Antonio, 3932
Mantero, Francisco, 3053
Manthe, Ulrich, 3933

Manzano, Juan Francisco, 2598
Marable, Manning, 771, 5052
Marcílio, Maria Luiza, 2089, 2200
Marchand-Thébault, M., 2755
Marchant, Alexander, 2088
Margo, Robert A., 772
Marina, William, (1025)
Marinovich, L. P., 3934
Marketti, Jim, 773
Markoe, William M., 267
Marks, Bayly Ellen, 1208
Maroti, E., 3437, 3935-36
Marques, Rubens Murillo, (2089)
Marquez de la Plata, Fernando, 4811
Marrero Rodríguez, Manuela, 4256
Marriner, S., (4872)
Marrone, Giovanni, 4195
Marsh, Henry (Saklatvala, Beram), 268
Marshall, Bernard A., 2461-64
Marshall, Mary Louise, 774-75
Marshall, Woodville K., (286)
Martínez-Alier, Verena, 2599
Martínez Montiel, Luz María, 1790
Martin, B. G., 5128
Martin, Bernard, 4667, ed. 4668
Martin, Christopher (Edwin Palmer Hoyt), 4669
Martin, Esmond B., 5104-05
Martin, Gaston, 2756, 4996-97
Martin, James Kirby, ed. 776
Martin, Jean, 3343-44
Martin, Norman F., 1789
Martin, Percy Alvin, 2090-91
Martin, Phyllis, 4568
Martin, René, 3937
Martin, Victor, (2886)
Martinez Montero, Homero, 1960
Martini, Remo, 3938
Martins, Roberto Borges, 2254-55, (2256)
Martins Filho, Amilcar, 2256
Marucchi, O., 3939
Masini Calderón, José Luís, 1948-49
Mason, Michael, (2954), 3054, 3323
Massa, C., 4196
Massicote, E. Z., 1669
Massini Ezcurra, José M., 1950
Massio, Roger, (2729), 2757
Masson, Olivier, 3661
Mathieson, William Law, 2465, 4569
Mathiex, J., 5148
Mathurin, Lucille, 2466
Matilla Vicente, Eduardo, 3940-41

Savage, William Sherman, 1637
Savannah Unit, Georgia Writers
    Project, Work Projects
    Administration, 1448
Savitt, Todd L., 901, 1231-32
Scarano, Francisco, 2633-34
Scarano, Júlia Maria Leonor,
    (2272)
Scarano, Julita, 2263
Scarborough, William K., 902-03
Scelle, Georges, 4831-32
Schaefer, Donald F., (370), 904,
    (909)
Schafer, Daniel L., 2498
Schafer, Judith Kelleher, 1569-70
Schapiro, Herbert, 368
Schaub, Friedrich, 4155
Scheiber, Harry N., (571),, 905,
    (1347)
Scherer, Lester B., 906-07
Schetelich, Maria, 4390
Scheuss de Studer, Elena F., 4833
Schiller, A. Arthur, 4004
Schlaifer, Robert, 3685
Schlotterbeck, John Thomas, 1233
Schlüter, Herman, 908
Schmidt, Gerhard, 369
Schmidt, Joël, 4005
Schmitz, Mark D., 370, (904),
    909, 1571
Schnakenbourg, Christian, 2772
Schneider, Karl, 5150
Schneider, Tracy Whittaker, 1449
Schneider, W., 4006
Schoelcher, Victor, 371
Schoenwald, Richard L., (455)
Schofield, M. M., 4906
Schönbauer, Ernst, 3686
Schooler, Carmi, 372
Schoonover, Thomas, 1638
Schoute, Dirk, 4945
Schrot, Gerhard, (3405-06)
Schuler, Monica, 373-74, 2347,
    2499-2500
Schuller, W., 4007
Schulman, Ivan A., 2635
Schulz, Fr., 4008
Schulz, Siegfried, 3461
Schwartz, Karen Jean, 1104
Schwartz, Rosalie, 1639
Schwartz, Stuart B., 2148-50,
    2220-24
Schwarz, Philip J., 1234
Schweninger, Loren, 1572, 1655-57
Sciascia, G., 4009
Scisco, L. D., 4689

Scott, John Anthony, 910
Scott, Kenneth, 1105, 4690
Scott, Nolvert P., Jr., 1679
Scott, Rebecca J., 2636-38
Scott, Sir Henry Harold, 4598
Scruggs, Otey M., 911
Searcy, Martha Condrey, 4435
Seeley, Frank F., 5151
Sefton, James E., 4436
Segall, Marcelo, 1934
Segrè, Angelo, 3545
Seip, Terry L., 1235
Sellers, Charles G., Jr., 912
Sellers, James B., 1450
Sellin, Johan Thorsten, 913
Sellnow, Irmgard, 3330
Senior, Carl H., 2501
Sereni, E., 3462
Serfass, Charles, 3294
Serjeant, R. B., 3249
Sernett, Milton C., 914-15
Serson, William John, 3216
Settle, E. Ophelia, 916
Sewell, Richard H., 375
Seyfarth, Wolfgang, 4010, 4156,
    4175
Seymour, P. A., 3687
Shaked, Haim, 3304
Shakespear, J., 4313
Sharashenidze, D. M., 3546
Sharevskaia, Berta I., (3464)
Sharp, William F., 1878-83
Sharpe, Esther E., 1640
Sheldon, Randall G., 1534
Shell, R. C.-H., 3143
Shell, Robert, (2939)
Sheperd, Gill, 5112
Sheppard, Jill, 2502
Shepperson, George, (4487)
Sheridan, Richard B., 376,
    2503-09, 4599, 4907
Sheriff, A. M. H., 3350
Sherman, William L., 1834-36
Sherrard, Owen Aubrey, 377, 917
Sherwin-White, Adrian N., 4011
Shick, Tom W., 4600
Shingleton, Royce G., 1451-52
Shore, Laurence, 1453
Short, Kenneth R. M., 918, 2510
Shown, Elizabeth, (798)
Shtaerman, Elena M., 378,
    3463-64, 4012-15
Shukry, M. R., 3305
Shyllon, Folarin O., 4302
Sicard, G., 4016
Sides, Sudie Duncan, 919-22

Subject / Keyword Index

2394, 2613
Culture (African) in the New
World, 24, 28, 56, 152, 191,
199, 232, 410, 814, 1318,
1793, 1888, 1900, 2007, 2348,
4556, 4764, see also Culture,
Afro-American
Culture (African) in the New
World, Religion, 973
Culture, Afro-American, 285, 290,
295, 373, 391, 444, 467, 502,
745, 805, 841, 996, 1099,
1293, 1295, 1402, 1403, 1548;
see also Culture (African) in
the New World
Curaçao, 200, 203, 1710, 2805,
2816, 2836, 2837, 4931, 4937
Curtin, Philip D., 2885, 4542,
4603

D
Día de Reyes, 2613
Dacia, 3757, 3972, 3975, 4001,
4039, 4040, 4041
Dahomey, 1996, 2865, 2881, 2940,
2987, 2989, 3004, 3010, 3015,
3029, 3048, 3051, 3079, 3082,
3092, 3112, 3115, 3136, 3164,
3165, 4625, 4703
Dallas County, Ala., 1493
Dalmatia, 3729
Dalmatian Coast, 4215
Dalzel, Archibald, 4625
Damagaram (Zinder, Niger), 3314
Danish West Indies, 2850, 2853,
2854, 2855, 2856, 2857, 2858
Dante, 4221
Dar al-Kuti, 2921
Dar Fur, 3301, 3303, 5131
Dar Masali, 3301
Darwin, Charles, 107, 511
Davenport, William, 4900
Davis, David Brion, 41, 138, 1015
Davis, Jefferson, 575
Death penalty, 2158
Deaths, 886
Debbash, M. Y., 35
Debien, Gabriel, 35, 2722
Debt enslavement, 3735
Debt servitude, 2603
Defense of slavery – see
Pro-slavery
Definitions, 236, 245, 249, 264,
291, 294, 324, 325, 422
Degler, Carl, 6
Deir el Medine, 3510

Delaware Valley, 1107
Delaware, 1072, 1084, 1091, 1109
Delphi, 3560, 3586, 3587, 3641,
3711, 3720, 3934
Demography, 73, 126, 142, 196,
226, 253, 385, 554, 555, 582,
799, 894, 960, 992, 1006,
1166, 1180, 1194, 1210, 1265,
1315, 1317, 1415, 1443, 1468,
1487, 1528, 1764, 1829, 1830,
1831, 1917, 1941, 2080, 2155,
2249, 2337, 2399, 2434, 2437,
2438, 2468, 2492, 2507, 2555,
2577, 2606, 2649, 2654, 2719,
2727, 2824, 2825, 2850, 2853,
2906, 2942, 2954, 2958, 3047,
3049, 3054, 3143, 3156, 3157,
4492, 4545, 4609, 4802, 5081,
5125; see also Volume of the
slave trade
Demosthenes, 24, 197, 3569, 3629
Denmark, 5071, 5073, 5074, 5075,
5076, 5077, 5078, 5080, 5081,
5082, 5084, 5086, 5144, 5145
Deportation – see Colonization
Depression, 853
Descent rule, 187
Dessalines, 2761
de Ste. Croix, Geoffrey E. M.,
3366, 3400
Destrehan's slave roll, 1546
Devshirme, 3251
Dickson County, Tenn., 1503
Dion de Pruse, 3584
Discipline, 1358, 1458
Disciples of Christ, 1629
Discontent, 895
Diseases, 220, 221, 223, 224,
348, 456, 591, 731, 732, 966,
1232, 2052, 2340, 2382, 2553,
4534, 4578, 4598, 4789, 4917,
4957, 4960
Distribution of slave wealth, 1429
District of Columbia, 1089, 1196,
1226
Dolben, Sir William, 4882, 4905
Dolphin (ship), 4677
Domar, Evsey D., 327
Domestic life, 2422, 2616, 3348
Domestics, 1705, 2784; see also
House servants
Dominica, 2463
Dominican Republic – see Santo
Domingo
Donatists, 3592
Dorchester County, Md., 1150

2378, 2423, 2457, 2542, 2558,
2816, 3407, 3472, 3545, 3583,
3681, 3732, 3765, 3798, 3804,
3805, 3816, 3830, 3831, 3844,
3868, 3891, 3966, 3977, 4017,
4019, 4030, 4038, 4050, 4064,
4065, 4080, 4084, 4087, 4092,
4113; see also Free coloureds
Freedom, 517, 621, 804, 1276, 1389
French, 4843
French, in Mexico, 1770
French attitudes, 60
French diplomacy, 4586
French Guyana – see Guyane
française
French Revolution, 157, 350, 464,
726, 2663
Freud, Sigmund, 986
Freyre, Gilberto, 2160
Frontiers, 208, 468, 1299, 1310
Fugitive Slave Law of 1850, 581,
765, 819, 929, 950
Fugitive slaves, 484, 504,, 925,
1077, 1059, 1083, 1216, 1255,
1291, 1396, 1489, 1614, 1672,
1680, 1681, 1808, 2043, 2052,
2060, 2406, 2516, 3072, 3529,
3599, 3726, 3746, 3783, 3864,
3933, 3939, 3981, 3990, 4046,
4099
Funerals, 886
Futa Jallon, 3149

G
Gabriel, 1158, 1167, 1217, 1219,
1234
Galinhas, 4661
Galley slaves, 2153, 3375, 3924,
4260, 4275
Galt, William, Jr., 1179
Gálvez, José de, 4790
Garnet, Henry Highland, 876
Gauchos – see Cowboys
Gemé, 3546
Gender, 2365
Geniza records (Cairo), 3270
Genoa, 4182, 4183, 4184, 4188,
4189, 4190, 4201, 4202, 5140,
5141, 5157
Genovese, Eugene D., 41, 166,
218, 368, 444, 472, 493, 544,
547, 557, 604, 668, 712, 730,
787, 848, 864, 2863, 990,
1007, 1008, 1039
Geography, 1126
Georgetown County, S.C., 1443

Georgia, 580, 1259, 1263, 1275,
1280, 1300, 1302, 1308, 1312,
1313, 1320, 1327, 1336, 1338,
1349, 1360, 1361, 1364, 1424,
1442, 1448, 5066
German immigrants (U.S.), 1274
Germany, 3444, 3994, 3995, 4033,
4328, 4331, 5083
Gerontology, 342
Ghaznevids, 3231
Glynn County, Ga., 1434
Goiás, 2316, 2317, 2318
Gold Coast, 3044, 3126, 3170,
2935, 4592, 4910; see also
Costa da Mina
Gold exports from Africa, 4459,
4592
Good Hope plantation, 1277, 1482
Gordon, Charles George, 3304
Gordon, George, 765
Gorée, 2963, 3055
Gorrevod, Laurent von, 4819
Gracias al sacar, 1715
Gradual emancipation, 598
Graham, James D., 35
Graham, William, 1229
Gran Colombia – in general, see
Section III. 4. (Spanish
Mainland – New Granada and
Gran Colombia)
Granada, 2378
Gray, Simon, 1653
Great Revival, 1464
Greece, 3424, 4329, 5168; in
general, see Section VIII. 3.
(Ancient – Greece and
Dependencies)
Greeley, Horace, 398
Greene County, Va., 1233
Grillon (ship), 4653
Gruber, Reverend Jacob, 1644
Guadeloupe, 2656, 2666, 2670,
2709, 2739, 2741, 2746, 2747,
2772, 2790, 4949, 4953, 5007
Guarda Nacional Brasileira, 2013
Guarino, Antonio, 3799
Guatemala, 1814, 1817, 1823,
1836, 1837
Guerrilla warfare, 2447
Guinea (Bissau), 4717, 4718,
4724, 4741
Guinea (Conakry), 4577
Gullahs, 1352
Gumbu, 3058, 3059
Guns, 4896
Gutman, Herbert G., 510, 617,

Ideology of slavery, 1126, 3035,
3038, 3069, 3085, 3095, 3129,
3224, 3225, 3307, 3337, 3390,
4067
Igbo, 2919, 2972, 2993, 3031,
3084, 3085, 3086, 3089, 3090,
3097, 3166, 3167
Ih'ya de Ghazali, 3192
Ikom, 2979
Ila, 3161, 3162, 3163
Ile de France - see Mauritius
Iles de Los, 4575
Ilha Grande de Marajó, 2174
Illegal slave trade, 4642, 4649,
4716, 4719, 4727, 4793, 4795,
4809, 4824, 4916, 4926, 4965,
4966, 4967, 4972, 2973, 4970,
4980, 4997, 5019, 5069, 5174;
see also Suppression of the
(maritime) slave trade,
Abolition of the slave trade
Illinois, 1613, 1619, 1627, 1628,
1641
Illiricum, 4003
Imbangala, 3068, 3070
Immigration, 4504
Imperialism, 71, 75, 250
Import statistics, 1120, 1249,
1156, 1716, 1751, 2000, 2001,
2003, 2058, 2314, 2364, 4876,
5061, 5062, 5063; see also
Volume of the slave trade,
Smuggling
Imuhag, 297
Incas, 4399, 4400
Incomplete polities, 2450
Indentured labor, 25, 459, 626,
627, 699, 1209, 1275, 2794,
2795, 3044, 4463
Independence (Brazil), 2188
Independent Negro Church, 915
India - in general, see Sections
VII. 9. (Muslim India) and X.
4. (Other - Indian
subcontinent)
Indians (American), enslaved or
as slave owners - see
Amerindians
Indigo, 2774, 2781
Indonesia, 4364
Industrial growth (Europe), 4955,
4956
Industrial slavery, 1161, 1198,
1409, 1419, 1439, 1458, 1459,
1460, 1461, 1536, 3435, 4075,
4123

Industrialization, 457, 594, 714,
1025
Innes, Stephen, 1221
Input substitutability, 1058
Inquisition, 1688, 1769
Insurance costs, 643
Insurrection panics - see Fears
of slave revolts
Integration, 724, 1790
Inter-regional slave trade
(U.S.), 976, 1345, 1406,
1420, 1499, 1470, 1480, 1573,
1582
Intiguing slave, 3624
Involuntary labour, 230
Iowa, 1633
Iraq, 3230, 3248
Irish "slaves", 2502
Iron workers, 1127, 1138, 1146,
1147, 1198, 1200, 1201, 1202,
1203, 1204, 1227, 1358, 1504,
1510
Islam, 1, 2159; in general, see
Section VII. (Muslim)
Ismail, Khedive, 3305
Italian slavery, 4159; in
general, see Section IX. 3.
(Medieval and Early Modern
Europe - Italy and Colonies)
Ivory trade, 2884
Ivory, 5090

J
Jabaquara, 2208
Jackson County, Mo., 1505
Jacksonian politics, 761
Jacquezy estates, 2782
Jakhanke, 3329
Jamaica, 104, 260, 282, 388,
2355, 2356, 2357, 2358, 2359,
2360, 2364, 2366, 2367, 2368,
2382, 2384, 2385, 2389, 2392,
2397, 2404, 2408, 2416, 2417,
2419, 2429, 2431, 2434, 2435,
2437, 2439, 2440, 2442, 2444,
2445, 2446, 2447, 2448, 2450,
2451, 2458, 2460, 2478, 2479,
2480, 2482, 2484, 2488, 2489,
2493, 2498, 2501, 2490, 2504,
2512, 2514, 2515, 2511, 2520,
4877, 4884, 4902
James, C. L. R., 2761, 2777
Jamestown, Va. 1215
Jefferson, Lydia, 1545
Jefferson, Thomas, 1033, 1206,
1207, 1211

Newport, R.I., Providence, R.I.; in general, see Section XI. 8. (Slave Trade – Atlantic – North American, etc.)

Slave trade, Atlantic (Portuguese), 2233, 5096, 5106; in general, see Section XI. 3. (Slave Trade – Atlantic, Portuguese and Brazilian)

Slave Trade, Atlantic (Spanish), 1745, 1762, 1766, 1797, 1798, 1809, 1839, 1893, 2561; in general, see Section XI. 4. (Slave Trade – Atlantic – Spanish)

Slave trade, Black Sea, 5143, 5155, 5168, 5169

Slave trade, Brazil, 2094

Slave trade, Byzantine, 4170, 4178

Slave trade, Chile, 1932

Slave trade, Danubian, 5168, 5169

Slave trade, at Fernando Po, 3147

Slave trade, Impact on Africa, 2885, 2886, 2924, 2942, 2943, 2944, 2952, 2958, 2987, 2996, 2997, 2998, 3011, 3013, 3017, 3018, 3073, 3112, 3134, 3148, 3156, 3157, 3168, 4483, 4485, 4492, 4518, 4526, 4545, 4546, 4550, 4602, 4603, 4609, 5089

Slave trade, Indian Ocean, 3186, 4332; in general, see Section XI. 10. (Slave Trade – Indian Ocean)

Slave trade, Internal African, 2861, 2869, 2870, 2921, 2946, 2951, 2954, 2964, 2968, 3018, 3037, 3054, 3066, 3082, 3083, 3105, 3106, 3151, 3153, 3331

Slave trade, Internal U.S. – see Inter-regional slave trade (U.S.)

Slave trade, Medieval – in general, see Section XI. 12. (Slave Trade – Medieval)

Slave trade, Mexican, 1775

Slave trade, Mughul Bengal, 3353

Slave trade, Muslim, 5152; in general, see Sections XI. 10. – 12. (Slave Trade – Indian Ocean, Medieval, Red Sea, Trans-Saharan, etc.)

Slave trade, Peru, 1919

Slave trade, Red Sea – in

general, see Section XI. 11. (Slave Trade – Trans-Saharan and Red Sea)

Slave trade, Roman Egypt, 4138

Slave trade, Trans-Saharan, 2921, 3196, 3295, 3299, 4761; in general, see Section XI. 11. (Slave Trade – Trans-Saharan and Red Sea)

Slave trade and the Atlantic economies, 4544

Slave Trade Regulation Act of 1788, 4882

Slave wars, 3489

Slavery – see Elkins, Stanley M.

Smart, Gumbu, 2995

Smith, James, 4630

Smith of Demerara, 2372

Smothering, 715, 1231

Smuggling, 2268, 2269, 4796, 4799, 4949

Socialist thought, 753

Society for the Propagation of the Gospel in Foreign Lands, 2485

Sociological views on slavery, 324

Soil exhaustion, 1372

Sokoto Caliphate, 3317, 3322, 3323, 3325, 3327, 3331, 5135, 5136

Soldiers (non-Islamic), 516, 694, 800, 867, 1481, 1488, 2015, 2361, 2362, 3684, 3708, 3709, 3834, 4009, 4085, 4280; see also Military slaves (Islamic)

Somali, 2909, 3341

Somerset, 4296

Sommersett's Case, 4293

Songrai, 3023, 3093, 3095, 3319

Songs, 746

Sonthonax, 2655

Sophists, 3677

Soul food, 722

Sources, 42, 87, 453

Sources, Advertisements, 756, 1077, 1570

Sources, Arabic, 3209

Sources, Archaeological, 580, 3630

Sources, Archives, 316, 2137, 2233, 2271, 2720, 2819, 4904, 4965, 4973

Sources, Bills of sale, 1716, 1926

Sources, Biographies, 681

Sources, Church archives, 2087

Sources, Court records, 895

Sources, Diplomatic, 4709

Suppression of the (maritime) slave trade, 4461, 4495, 4506, 4516, 4553, 4562, 4570, 4579, 4615, 4621, 4622, 4706, 4709, 4710, 4718, 4773, 4926, 4965, 4969, 4987, 4988, 4989, 4992, 5035, 5038, 5041, 5051, 5097, 5103, 5128, 5130, 5137; see also Abolition of the slave trade; see also Illegal slave trade

Supreme Court, 980, 1029

Suriname, 75, 200, 203, 2333, 2700, 2797, 2801, 2802, 2803, 2807, 2810, 2811, 2813, 2814, 2816, 2822, 2825, 2826, 2827, 2828, 2829, 2835, 2838, 2840, 2844, 2848, 4930

Sweden, 4317, 4318, 5070

Swema, 2868

Syria, 3545, 3551

T

Ta'rikh al-Turubbe, 3300

Tacitus, 3886, 4042

Tacky, 2490

Talbot County, Md., 1150

Talmudic Law, 3457, 3512, 3542, 3550

Tamango, 4963

Tana, 5153

Tannenbaum, Frank, 108, 109, 1562

Task system, 1295

Tawana, 3159

Teachers (slave), 3800, 3805

Technology, 14, 49, 155, 169, 2116, 2185, 2261, 2323, 3893, 3896, 4007

Temne, 3185

Tenerife, 4256

Tennessee, 1500, 1501, 1508, 1512, 1513, 1514, 1520, 1523, 1527

Terence, 3885, 4026

Territorial expansion – see Expansionism (U.S.)

Testamentary manumission, 1519

Tevegó, 1976

Texas, 1597; in general, see Section II. 8. (North America – Texas)

Textile mills, 1409, 1419, 1439

Thagi, 4379

Thailand, 4365

Tharp Estate, 2384

Thorpe, Earl E., 455

Thomas, James P., 1656, 1657

Thrace, 3694, 3695, 3722

Thraldom – in general, see Section IX. 8. (Medieval and Early Modern Europe – Scandinavia)

Timbuktu, 3324

Time on the Cross, 452, 478, 519, 521, 526, 527, 528, 530, 531, 532, 547, 556, 557, 559, 603, 611, 624, 637, 673, 674, 675, 685, 686, 696, 738, 767, 786, 811, 860, 869, 870, 900, 971, 988, 1014, 1017, 1045, 1053

Tippu Tip, 2946, 3105, 3106, 3151

Tobacco factories, 881, 1144, 1227

Tobacco (traded for slaves), 4765, 4767, 4768, 4771

Tocqueville, 244

Tooke plantation, 1364

Tortue, 2658

Total institutions, 1337

Toussaint l'Ouverture, 2669, 2702, 2723, 2736, 2761, 2762

Traders (of slaves), 1602, 1611, 1647, 1651, 1659, 2788

Travancore, 4381

Treatment of slaves, 161, 431, 971, 1992, 2121, 2383, 2534, 2627, 2629, 2645, 3181, 3340

Tria, Luigi, 4220

Triangular trade, 4888, 4900, 4892, 4984, 4991, 5021, 5027, 5028

Trinidad, 2399, 2400, 2433, 2454, 2475, 2513

Trouwborst, A., 2730

Tsangui, 3124

Tswana, 3141

Tuareg, 2897, 3276, 3279, 3280, 3286, 3290, 3291, 3295

Tucumán, 1956

Tumbuka, 2948

Tunisia, 3292, 3293, 3296, 3297, 4153

Turkey – in general, see Section VII. 3. (Muslim – Ottoman Empire – Muslim Turkey)

Turnbull, David, 2575

Turner, Frederick Jackson, 758

Turner, Nat, 544, 1128, 1134, 1153, 1163, 1173, 1182, 1186, 1212, 1222, 1238, 1239, 1242, 1243, 1245, 1246, 1251, 1569

Tuscany, 4200

Tyler, Julia Gardiner, 862